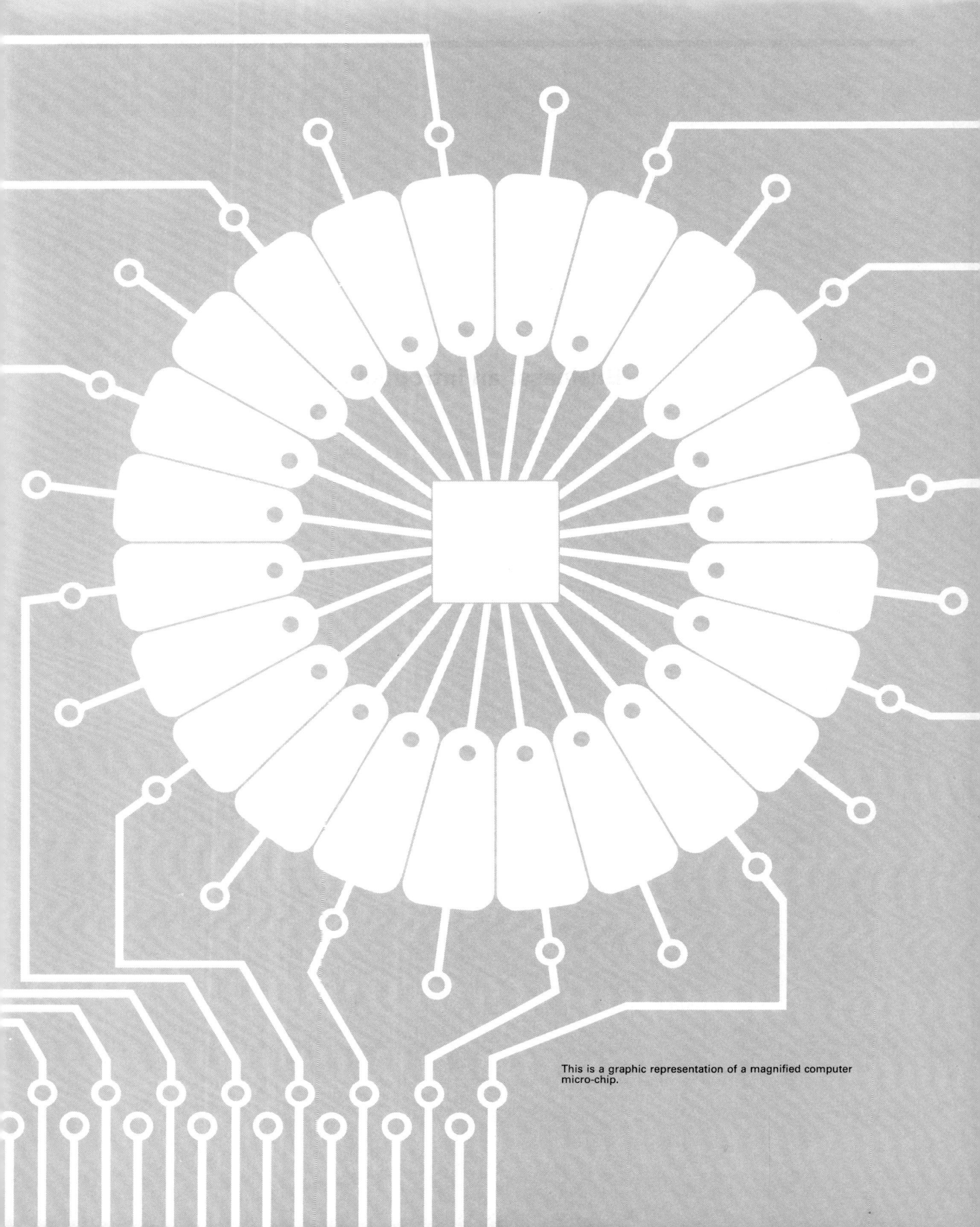
This is a graphic representation of a magnified computer micro-chip.

Business:
an introduction

Benjamin M. Compaine
Center for Information Policy Research

Robert F. Litro
Mattatuck Community College

The Dryden Press
Chicago New York Philadelphia San Francisco Montreal Toronto
London Sydney Tokyo Mexico City Rio de Janeiro Madrid

Acquisitions Editor: Anne Elizabeth Smith
Developmental Editor: Paul Psilos
Project Editors: Nancy Shanahan/Julia Ehresmann
Managing Editor: Jane Perkins
Design Director: Alan Wendt
Production Manager: Mary Jarvis

Text designer: Bernard Arendt
Cover designer: Alan Wendt
Copyeditors: Cynthia Fostle, Kathryn Jandeska
Indexer: Lois Oster
Compositor: Waldman Graphics
Text type: 10/12 Univers 55

Library of Congress Cataloging in Publication Data
Compaine, Benjamin M.
   Business: an introduction.

   Includes bibliographical references and index.
   1. Business. 2. Industrial management. 3. Commerce.
I. Litro, Robert F. II. Title.
HF5351.C575 1983   650   83-14025
ISBN 0-03-059902-4

Printed in the United States of America
456-032-987654321

Copyright 1984 CBS College Publishing
All rights reserved

Address orders to:
383 Madison Avenue
New York, New York 10017

Address editorial correspondence to:
One Salt Creek Lane
Hinsdale, IL 60521

CBS College Publishing
The Dryden Press
Holt, Rinehart and Winston
Saunders College Publishing

Photographs for Parts 1, 2, and 7 courtesy of H. Armstrong Roberts, Inc.;
Parts 3, 4, 5, 6, and 8 courtesy of Stock Boston, Inc.

To
Florence and Mark
and
Albert, Louise, and Jane

Preface

We have been teaching introductory business courses for many years. Our experience has shown us that students need a textbook that uses clear language to explain the basic concepts and functions of U.S. business. This is true both for students whose introductory course will be their only one, and for those planning further study in the field of business. *Business: an introduction* is our response to this need. The emphasis is on current and future conditions, using situations relevant to today's students.

Major objectives

Before starting to write the text, we established five major objectives which are reflected throughout the text.

The text must be exciting and easy to read, yet full of substance. This in itself is a challenge. Many students think the study of business will be dull or uninteresting. We show that it isn't: whenever possible, we write in the same conversational style used in the classroom. In addition, illustrations and examples, often drawn from real-world experiences, are used liberally. Stressing the values of entrepreneurship, ingenuity, and hard work, we try to make business success (and failure) real to students through examples drawn from smaller businesses. This focus makes the workings of business seem more concrete, less in the abstract world of huge sums and convoluted financial dealings.

The text must present a comprehensive overview of the essential business functions while still retaining the richness of the subject matter. To meet this objective, we cover the basics of the principal business functions but do not neglect the variety and vitality of business today. For example, a unique separate chapter on "Service Industries" treats the fastest-growing sector of the economy as an important aspect of the current business environment. Moreover, the way in which entrepreneurship continually changes the face of business through innovation and creativity is considered a significant aspect of business. Many of the vignettes, cases, and examples focus on the ideas, mainly of individual entrepreneurs, which have created the foundations of successful enterprises.

The text must be written with the student's perspective in mind. Currently, a decreasing number of undergraduate students go directly from high school to college. Many students have had work experience and tend to be older than the traditional college age. The text reflects this changing profile of the undergraduate. We refuse to "write down" to our readers, because we believe that students today know much more about the world than did their counterparts a generation ago.

The text must reflect rapid developments in technology and their impact on business operations and opportunities. The old manufacturing base of the U.S. economy is giving way to a service- and information-based economy. Microprocessors, the key element in the computerization of our economy, affect both how we live and how we conduct business. Throughout the text, we treat technology as *already* a pivotal influence—an influence that will continue to grow. We show what the implications of modern technology are for workers and labor unions, its effects on the way management organizes itself, and—most of all—the threats and opportunities it creates for both older and emerging businesses.

The book must be honest about business. Young people in the 1970s expressed widespread skepticism about the integrity of U.S. business and the entire capitalist system. Many textbooks written during that time held an almost antibusiness stance while claiming to teach its basics. This book's purpose is to present the American business system objectively—to explain how and why it works—not to present a critique of capitalism or to whitewash areas which could bear improvement. The profit motive is not treated as a secret agenda of U.S. business. Rather, it is presented as the force which drives the entrepreneurial impulse to identify demand and take risks to meet it. We do not feel that taken as a whole our economic system needs an apology. Honest and unbiased presentation makes its own case for private enterprise.

Preface

The instructional package

As an instructor in the current higher education environment, you may find yourself in the position of having more students, more sections, and less time to tailor instruction individually to student needs. We help meet today's instructional challenges by providing a totally integrated ancillary package.

Integrated instructional support materials

This includes (in one binding for easy reference) an explanation of the total package, course organization suggestions, term project suggestions, grading guidelines, key terms *defined*, chapter coverage, supplemental lecture topics, answers to end-of-chapter questions and cases, and a film guide with comprehensive resource listings. In addition, slightly reduced facsimiles of transparency acetates appear at relevant points in the chapter coverage, making it unnecessary to file through the entire package to make your selection.

Color transparency acetates

Approximately 140 color acetates, the majority of which are original rather than taken from the text, enable you to support concepts in class with graphic aids.

Study guide

Written by C. G. Petrides, Borough of Manhattan Community College, it includes a chapter review, learning goals, key term drill, programmed review, self-quiz and experiential exercises made up of hands-on projects for conceptual and empirical learning, all requiring action on the part of the student. Answer keys are at the end of each chapter.

Test bank

An all new 2000-item file of objective questions carefully coordinated with the level of the text.

Computerized test bank

Easy-to-use floppy disk program for use on personal computers.

Computer simulations for business

A user-friendly personal computer program on floppy disks designed to give students experience using business programs for decision making. The *Student Workbook* provides appropriate forms for calculating and recording input/output and results. An *Instructor's Manual* provides clear start-up instructions and concise objectives, as well as hints for getting students to use and enjoy computer-assisted learning.

Portfolio of business papers

Sample documents from all phases of business illustrating in sequence from start up through growth stages, the basic paperwork aspects of forming and operating a business.

Acknowledgments

Producing a textbook is a complex task requiring the commitment of many—people who advised, reviewed, and translated ideas into the final product.

Appreciation is expressed to Jack Neifert and Wayne Koch for their initial mandate to launch the project; to Anne Smith, Senior Acquisitions Editor at The Dryden Press, for her overall support and guidance; to Paul Psilos, Senior Developmental Editor, whose advice, literary sense, discipline, and good humor helped shape the book; to Nancy Shanahan and Julia Ehresmann, Project Editors whose creative organizational talents were critical in the production process.

Moreover, we would like to thank Alan Wendt of The Dryden Press, and Kathy Richmond, Cynthia Fostle, Kathryn Jandeska, and Bernard Arendt for their contributions to the book.

We also thank typist Elise Renoni and research and editorial assistants Karen Horowitz, Alison Kothe, Laurie Matthews, and librarian Jennie Jevutis-O'Neill.

Acknowledged below are the many business professors who reviewed and commented on drafts at various stages of the project. Their invaluable help and many suggestions are evident throughout the book. We are indebted to them.

Sidney M. Bernstein, *Chicago City College*
Stephen C. Branz, *Triton College*
John A. Cooney, *Wilkes College*
Vicky Davis, *Mississippi College for Women*
Andrea W. Freling, *Ferris State College*
Robert L. Goldberg, *Northeastern University*
Tom Grissom, *Mesa Community College*
Jack Heinsius, *Modesto Junior College*
Nathan Himelstein, *Essex County College*
Andrew R. Joppa, *Mercy College*
George Katz, *San Antonio Community College*
Jerome M. Kinskey, *Sinclair Community College*
Bill Lacewell, *Westark Community College*
Joseph G. Mattingly, *University of Maryland–College Park*
Judy Mier, *McNeese State University*
Dennis D. Pappas, *Columbus Technical Institute*
Barbara Piasta, *Somerset Community College*
Donald T. Sedik, *Harper College*
Jack E. Seitz, *Oakton Community College*
D. A. Stonebarger, *Indiana University–Purdue University*
Marguerite Will, *Foothill College*

Without the continued support of those closest to us, we could not have persevered. Our sincerest thanks to Martha and Jane.

Preface

In the last analysis, of course, we are responsible for the content of this book. We hope you will find *Business: an introduction* readable, informative, and, ultimately, a valuable part of your academic experience.

Benjamin M. Compaine
Cambridge, Mass.

Robert F. Litro
Watertown, Conn.

September 1983

Comments and suggestions

Please give us your feedback. We seriously seek the comments of instructors *and* students. Send suggestions to:
   Compaine and Litro
   The Dryden Press
   One Salt Creek Lane
   Hinsdale, IL 60521.

The Dryden Press series in management

Arthur G. Bedeian, Consulting editor

Albanese and Van Fleet
Organizational Behavior: A Managerial Viewpoint

Bedeian
Organizations: Theory and Analysis, Text and Cases, Second Edition

Bedeian and Glueck
Management, Third Edition

Boone and Kurtz
Contemporary Business, Third Edition

Bowman and Branchaw
Business Report Writing

Chen and McGarrah
Productivity Management: Text and Cases

Compaine and Litro
Business: An Introduction

Gaither
Production and Operations Management: A Problem-Solving and Decision-Making Approach, Second Edition

Higgins
Organizational Policy and Strategic Management: Text and Cases, Second Edition

Hodgetts
Management: Theory, Process and Practice, Third Edition

Hodgetts
Modern Human Relations at Work, Second Edition

Holley and Jennings
Personnel Management: Functions and Issues

Holley and Jennings
The Labor Relations Process, Second Edition

Huseman, Lahiff, and Hatfield
Business Communication: Strategies and Skills

Huseman, Lahiff, and Hatfield
Readings in Business Communication

Jauch, Coltrin, Bedeian, and Glueck
The Managerial Experience: Cases, Exercises, and Readings, Third Edition

Lee
Introduction to Management Science

Miner
Theories of Organizational Behavior

Miner
Theories of Organizational Structure and Process

Paine and Anderson
Strategic Management

Paine and Naumes
Organizational Strategy and Policy:
Text and Cases, Third Edition

Penrose
Applications in Business Communication

Ray and Eison
Supervision

Robinson
The Internationalization of Business:
An Introduction

Robinson
International Business Management,
Second Edition

Smith
Management System: Analysis and
Applications

Stone
Understanding Personnel Management

Tombari
Business and Society: Strategies for the
Environment and Public Policy

Trueman
Quantitative Methods in Decision Making
in Business

Zikmund
Business Research Methods

1 The foundations of business

2 The human side of business

3 Tools for decision making

4 Producing goods and services

5 Marketing

6 Financial concerns of business

7 From mom-and-pop stores to multinationals

8 ... And toward the 21st century

The foundations of business   1

Chapter 1 **The American business system** *3*
Overview *4*   Basic definitions *5*   The roles of consumers, producers, and governments *5*   Consumers *6*   Producers *7*   Governments *12*   How the economy works *13*   Forms of competition *15*   The factors of production *17*   Alternative economic systems *20*   The need for choices *22*   Summary *23*
Chapter 1 case: Comparative standards of living: United States and Soviet Union *24*

Chapter 2 **Forms of business organization** *26*
Overview *28*   Factors that affect the choice of business organization *28*   Sole proprietorship *29*   Partnership *31*   The corporation *33*   Other forms of business organization *39*   Summary *41*
Chapter 2 case: "We can manage anything" *43*

Chapter 3 **Business and the law** *47*
Overview *48*   Legal foundations *48*   The court system *49*   Business contract *50*   Agency law *53*   The law of tort *54*   Property law *54*   Commercial paper *55*   Bankruptcy law *56*   Business ethics *57*   Federal regulation of business *50*   Summary *63*
Chapter 3 case: The artificial sweeteners case *65*
Careers in business *67*

The human side of business

2

Chapter 4 **Essentials of management** *75*
Overview *76*   The nature of management *76*   The elements of management *77*   Levels of management *85*   Managers are problem solvers and decision makers *87*   Managerial skills *91*   Is management for you? *92*   Summary *93*
Chapter 4 case: Carlisle Corporation *95*

Chapter 5 **Organizing the firm's resources** *97*
Overview *98*   The nature of organizing *98*   Organizational elements *99*   The organization chart *100*   Authority-responsibility relationships *103*   Span of control *104*   Authority relationships *105*   Trends in organizational strategy: quality circles *110*   The informal organization *111*   Summary *113*
Chapter 5 case: "Sometimes I feel like crying" *114*

Chapter 6 **Developing human resources** *117*
Overview *118*   Do managers understand employees? *119*   What motivates employees? *119*   The history of motivation theory *121*   Morale *126*   Methods of motivating employees *127*   The communication process *129*   Summary *133*
Chapter 6 case: A supervisor's dilemma *135*

Chapter 7 **Organized labor and business** *137*
Overview *138*   History of the labor movement *139*   Labor legislation *142*   Union organizing *144*   The union contract *146*   Collective bargaining *147*   The settlement of union-management conflicts *150*   Issues facing organized labor *152*   Summary *156*
Chapter 7 case: Tough decisions for Local 555 UAW *158*
Careers in management *160*

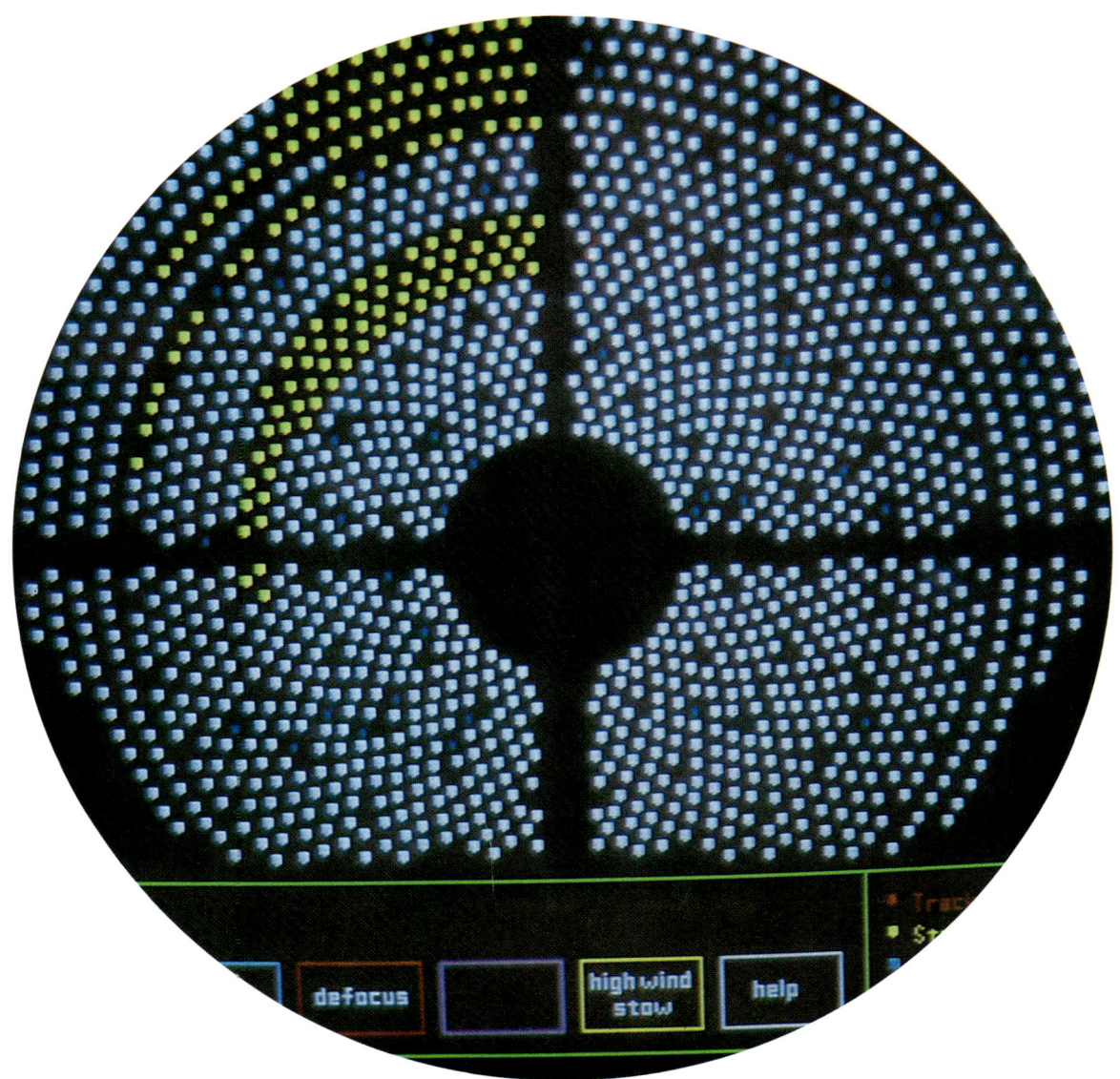

Tools for decision making   3

Chapter 8

Understanding computers *167*
Overview *168*   What is a computer? *168*   The components of a computer *169*   Programming and software *175*   How a computer works *176*   Computers in the future *179*   Summary *183*
Chapter 8 case: Mary Tyler Catalog Company 184

Chapter 9

Management information systems *187*
Overview *188*   The purpose of a management information system *188*   The need for a management information system *189*   Sources of information *191*   The use of statistics *194*   Presentation of data *197*   Computer applications in business *197*   Computer-aided design and computer-aided manufacturing *198*   Summary *200*
Chapter 9 case: The gasket formula 202
Careers in computers and information systems management *204*

Producing goods and services

4

Chapter 10

Production and operations management *209*
Overview *210* Characteristics of manufacturing *210*
Manufacturing processes *214* Managing manufacturing processes *215* Coordinating manufacturing operations *217*
Inventory and inventory control *219* Plant location *221*
Quality control *221* Plant design *223* Trends in manufacturing *224* Materials purchasing *226* Summary *228*
Chapter 10 case: Sonoma Manufacturing Company, Inc. *230*

Chapter 11

Service industries *233*
Overview *234* Services *234* The development of service industries *239* Improving service productivity *243* Regulation of service businesses *244* Summary *246*
Chapter 11 case: The disbelieving president *247*
Careers in manufacturing and service industries *249*

Marketing 5

Chapter 12

Marketing functions *255*
Overview *256*   Evolution of the marketing concept *256*   Creating utility through marketing *257*   The relationship of markets and products *259*   Defining a target market *261*   The marketing mix *262*   Marketing research *263*   Summary *269*
Chapter 12 case: Bud goes for the Lite drinker *271*

Chapter 13

Product and pricing decisions *273*
Overview *274*   The product *274*   Pricing *280*   Summary *287*
Chapter 13 case: North Central Tire Company *289*

Chapter 14

Promotional decisions *291*
Overview *292*   The objectives of promotion *292*   Advertising *294*   Choosing advertising media *298*   Publicity *306*   Personal selling *306*   Sales promotion techniques *309*   Summary *310*
Chapter 14 case: The Green Grass Seed Company *312*

Chapter 15

Channels of distribution *315*
Overview *316*   Participants in the channels of distribution *316*   The role of wholesalers *318*   The role of retailers *322*   Transportation and physical distribution *325*   Summary *331*
Chapter 15 case: The Learned Publishing Company *333*
Careers in marketing *334*

Financial concerns of business

6

Chapter 16

Financial institutions and business *341*
Overview *342*   Defining money *342*   The Fed—more than the bankers' bank *343*   How the Fed tries to control the economy *343*   The commercial banking system *349*   Life insurance companies *349*   Savings and loan associations and mutual savings banks *349*   Credit unions *350*   Commercial finance companies *351*   Investment banks *351*   Money market funds *351*   Recent developments affecting financial institutions *354*   Summary *356*   *Chapter 16 case: Starting an IRA*   *358*

Chapter 17

Raising and managing capital *361*
Overview *362*   What is finance? *362*   The financial-management process *362*   Short-term financing *363*   Long-term financing *367*   Summary *377*
Chapter 17 case: Oakland A's: financial forecast   *379*

Chapter 18

Securities markets *383*
Overview *384*   The importance of investment *384*   The securities exchanges *384*   Regulating the securities exchanges *387*   Buying and selling securities *388*   Understanding the financial news *392*   Reading the ticker *397*   Placing a securities order *398*   Summary *403*
Chapter 18 case: Which way to invest   *405*

Chapter 19

Accounting: understanding financial statements *407*
Overview *408*   The need for accounting *408*   Fundamentals of accounting *408*   Interpreting financial statements *415*   Summary *425*
Chapter 19 case: Southwest Fast Foods, Inc.   *426*

Chapter 20

Risk management and insurance *431*
Overview *432*   Kinds of risk *432*   Managing risk *432*   Requirements for an insurable risk *433*   The rules of risk management *437*   Risks and insurance *438*   Life insurance *442*   Kinds of insurance companies *447*   Summary *449*
Chapter 20 case: Frank Brothers Telecom, Inc.   *451*
Careers in banking, finance, investments, accounting, and insurance   *453*

From mom-and-pop stores to multinationals

7

Chapter 21

Small business management *459*
Overview *460* The nature of small business *460* Special problems of small business *462* The entrepreneurial role *465* The entrepreneurial personality *469* Starting a business *469* Choosing a location *471* Franchising *473* A few words of advice *476* Summary *477*
Chapter 21 case: Cynthia Creations 479

Chapter 22

International trade *481*
Overview *482* Why is foreign trade important? *482* Balance of trade and balance of payments *483* Government involvement in foreign trade *485* Trends in world trade *487* Other forms of international trade *490* Foreign exchange *492* Managing international business *493* Summary *494*
Chapter 22 case: U. S. mushroom capital battered by China imports 496
Careers in small business and international trade *497*

... And toward the 21st century

8

Chapter 23

Business and the future *503*
Overview *504*   Identifying forces and trends *504*
Developments in technology and their outcomes *504*   Increasing foreign competition *507*   Changing population characteristics *508*
Trends in government *509*   The future of the corporation *511*
The role of workers *512*   The role of the individual *513*   The Third Wave *514*   Summary *516*
Chapter 23 case: All the news that's fit to . . . ? *518*
Careers with new opportunities *519*

Glossary *525*

Index *535*

The foundations of business

1
2
3
4
5
6
7
8

Business in perspective

Greeting cards that germinate

The stodgy market for greeting cards is a pretty tough nut to crack, unless you come up with a "germ" of an idea and a little "seed" capital. That's the down-to-earth discovery of Scott Alyn, founder and president of the Great Northwestern Greeting Seed Co., Oregon City, Oregon. Alyn, a former promotional development director for Seven-Up in St. Louis, combined his marketing experience with a bent for gardening and came up with Greeting Seeds, cards that contain packets of seeds and herbs. The cards have messages too: "I'd like to hug you till your squashed," or "If we cantaloupe, let's just fool around." That may sound corny, but the two-and-a-half-year-old company will sell a million cards this year, Alyn says.

Getting a financial backer to start the business wasn't as easy as enlisting the help of Mother Nature. "I was turned down by a lot of financial people," Alyn says. "The venture capitalists want people with business backgrounds, and for a creative person, the answer was always 'no.'" Forsaking venture capitalists, he finally got a silent partner to put up $25,000 and to lend him $50,000 more.

When the cards, which retail for $1.50 each, first appeared in a Portland shop in April 1980, they sold out within two days. They are now distributed in 3000 gift, gourmet, and stationery stores across the United States and in Australia, New Zealand, Canada, and England, Alyn says. Dealer markup is 50 percent, and with the company expecting to sell over one million cards this year, sales should top $750,000, a 40 percent increase over 1981. Alyn adds that 1981 sales were 60 percent greater than 1980 sales. The company is profitable, he says, adding that, in keeping with its naturalist image, 2 percent of profits are channeled into an account used for community environmental projects.

Cards are designed by Alyn and his staff, but printed and manufactured by outside contractors. He says the company has about 60 suppliers, and buys the seeds from local growers.

In addition to Greeting Seeds, the company also sells Seasoned Greetings, cards containing spices, recipes, and messages like "Happy Birthday from one of your seedy little friends (poppy seeds)," and "Curry up and get well!" In the works are more seasoned cards to supplement the present line of eight, plus additions to the line of 40 Greeting Seeds. Even Alyn's business card contains pepper seeds.

Alyn insists that his rewards are more than financial. While he estimates that only one person in 10 who receives a card actually plants the seeds, he's proud of helping cultivate their interest in gardening.

Reprinted from the September 1982 issue of VENTURE, The Magazine for Entrepreneurs, by special permission. © 1982. Venture Magazine, Inc., 35 West 45th St., New York, NY, 10036.

Chapter 1

The American business system

Key terms

business
goods
services
consumers
demand
profit
loss
producers
entrepreneurs
capitalism
marketplace
prices
supply
pure competition
monopolistic competition
oligopolistic competition
monopoly
land
rent
labor
wages
capital
capital goods
interest
socialism
communism

Chapter objectives

In Chapter 1, you will learn:

What business is

The roles that consumers, producers, and governments play in our business system

The roles that the marketplace, prices, and competition play in our business system

The different forms of competition and their characteristics

The nature and importance of the four factors of production

The meaning of entrepreneurship and why it is so vital in our economic system

The characteristics of the major economic systems in the world

Part 1　The foundations of business

Overview

Business is an important part of American society. We hear about business every day on television and radio. We read about business in newspapers and magazines. We talk about business with other people. "How's business?" is a common question.

Despite all the talk about business, some people find the subject puzzling and forbidding. In fact, we are engaged in business activities every time we exchange our labor for wages and every time we use our wages to purchase goods and services. Every time we buy something—whether a car or a record album—we make decisions that help determine the kinds of goods and services business will provide. Although the subject of business may sound complicated, it is really an everyday part of our lives.

This chapter explains what businesses are and what they do. It shows how business is involved in our daily lives and discusses how basic business and economic concepts affect decisions made by consumers, producers, and governments. Understanding how these vital decisions are made is crucial in determining how well the American economy can meet our needs, now and in the future.

Figure 1.1 How the United States has changed in four decades

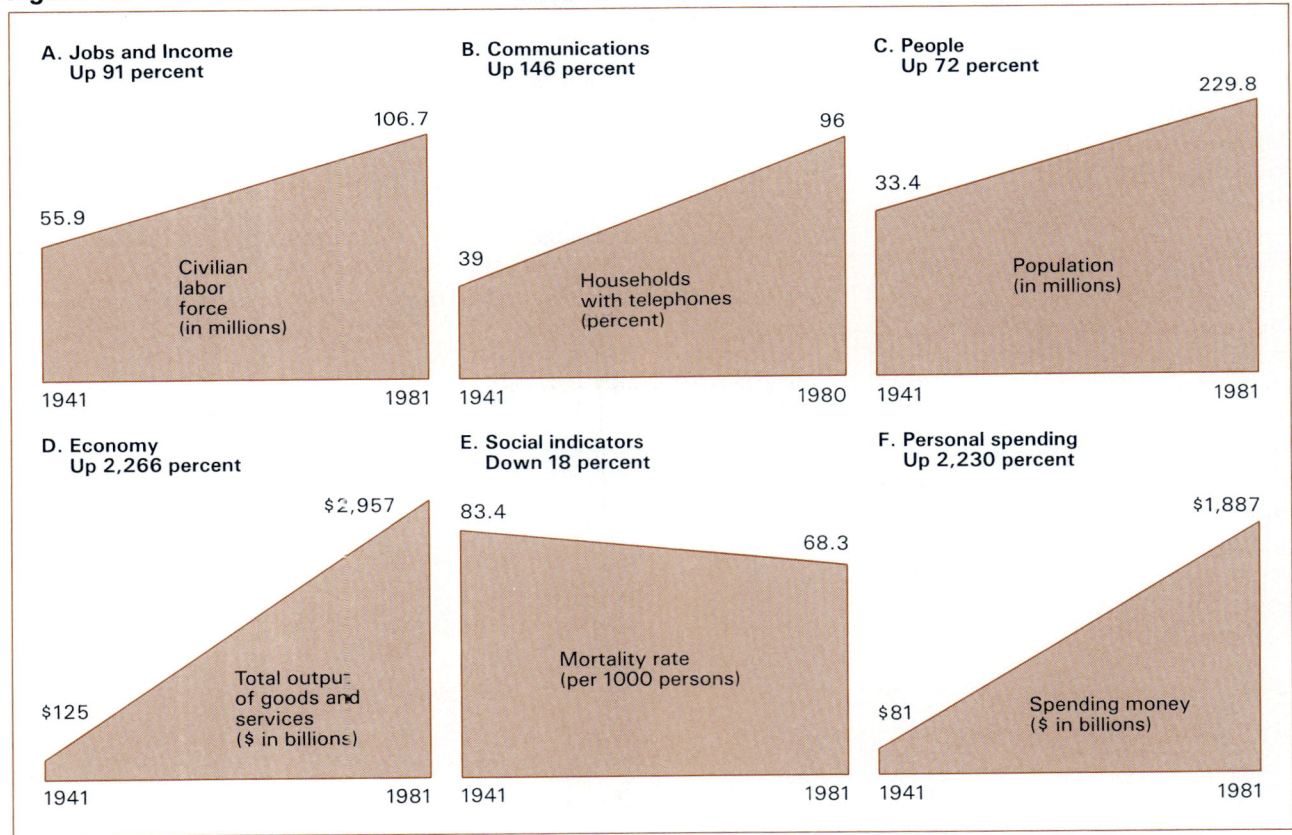

Reprinted from *U.S. News & World Report*, Dec. 7, 1981, p. 52. Copyright 1981, U.S. News & World Report, Inc.

Figure 1.2 The flow of consumer demand

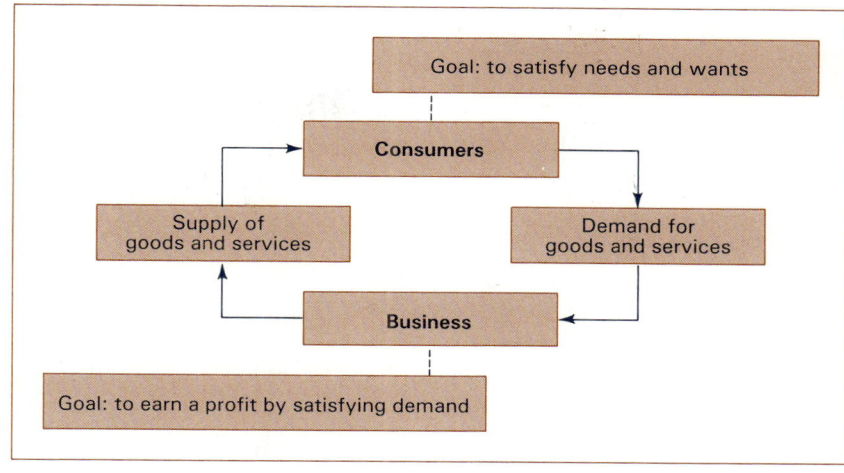

Basic definitions

A business is an organization that attempts to earn a profit by providing goods and/or services that society needs and wants.

Goods are tangible items that can be seen, touched, and or held, such as food, clothing, and books. **Services** on the other hand, **are useful activities that others provide for us,** such as haircuts, legal and medical advice, and car repairs.

Consumers are individuals or businesses who buy goods and services, usually paying for them with something of value (money).

In trying to satisfy their needs and wants through the purchase of goods and services, consumers create demand for these items. **Demand refers to a situation in which consumers have both the desire for a certain good or service and the ability to pay for it.**

By producing goods and services that are in demand, businesses hope to earn a profit. **A profit occurs when a business's income is greater than its expenses. A loss occurs when expenses are greater than income.** Businesses succeed and are profitable when they efficiently meet and satisfy consumer demand. Figure 1.2 shows the flow of consumer demand.

The roles of consumers, producers, and governments

The business system in the United States has three essential components: consumers, producers, and governments. Compared to economic systems elsewhere in the world, the interaction between U.S. consumers, producers, and governments is unique. But all economic systems have the same three components.

Supply and demand

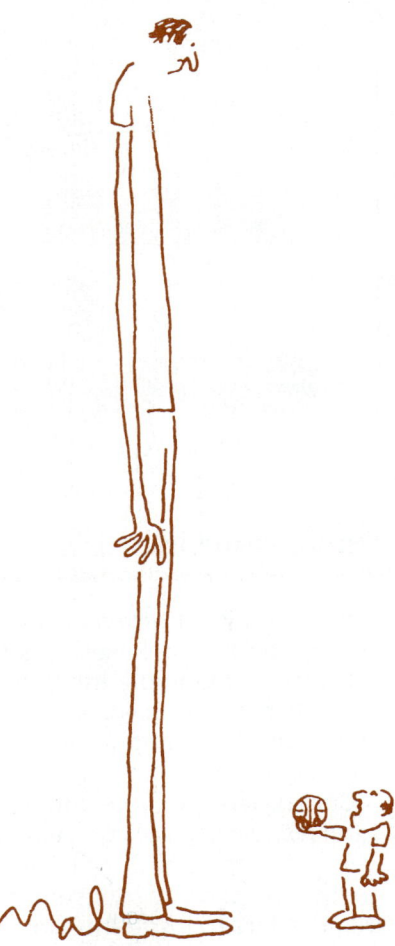

"Listen, son, with the average salary in the NBA being $120,000 a year, you are going to play basketball whether you like it or not!"

From the *Wall Street Journal,* Permission—Cartoon Features Syndicate

Consumers

Consumers play a major decision-making role in our economic system. They look for the best value when buying goods and services.

Individuals purchase over two-thirds of our nation's total output of goods and services. Businesses, institutions, and governments buy the remaining one-third.

Creating demand

Price and quality With each purchase we make—or decide not to make—we send signals that directly affect the economy. Consumers' willingness and ability to spend money for certain goods and services is influenced by price and quality. When the price of an item rises faster than the prices of other items, demand tends to decrease. Consumers often search for less-expensive substitutes. For example, the rapid increase in the price of gasoline in 1979 and 1980 helped cut consumption by almost 8 percent. On the other hand, decreasing prices stimulate demand. Hand-held calculators became common as prices dropped from $300 to as little as $10.

Income Demand is also affected by changes in income. If incomes drop, demand decreases and consumers shift to less-expensive items. As incomes increase, consumers tend to select more-expensive items or buy more of the items they have always purchased. These trends can be seen, for example, in the number and kinds of automobiles people purchase and in how often they dine in restaurants.

Satisfaction Once their basic needs are met, consumers buy the goods and services that provide the most satisfaction. They tend to look for value—the best quality at a given price. This process rewards efficient producers and penalizes inefficient ones. To stay successful, producers must continue to offer goods and services consumers want.

Producers

Until the nineteenth century, Americans were very self-sufficient. People produced goods and services primarily for their own consumption or for barter. Today, the economy has become more complex and production has become more specialized. We now depend on others to produce the goods and services that we need. And we expect to pay for their production.

Producers work to provide goods and services. They base their output on their estimate of the demand for their products or services. From this process, producers expect to earn an acceptable income.

Types of producers

Four groups of people contribute to the production process: workers, managers, investors, and entrepreneurs.

Workers as producers Workers apply their skills and energies to convert resources into desired goods and services.

In early U.S. history, most American workers were farmers. As the country became more industrialized, more and more workers moved

A pioneer on the housing frontier

If the price of real estate has you wondering whether you'll ever be able to afford a home, Richard Considine may have just the thing for you: a log house.

Considine is pushing such dwellings with a pioneer's zeal, but that's understandable. He is president of Lincoln Logs, Ltd., which sells a variety of stack-and-build log homes that he says can be erected in a matter of days by do-it-yourselfers with little or no building experience.

And he is succeeding—to the tune of about $5.5 million in sales in 1981. That compares with $3.5 million in 1980 and $600,000 in 1978.

For many people, the dream of homeownership is fading because of inflated prices. Companies like Lincoln Logs, which can provide an inexpensive alternative, are likely to do very well in the future.

Indeed, log home sales have soared 50 percent a year for the past two years while the conventional housing industry has become nothing short of a disaster. This year, more than 100,000 Americans will spend in excess of $1.5 billion on log homes. Lincoln Logs is considered a leader among the hundreds of firms that compete in this field.

Considine, who is 46, got the idea for Lincoln Logs in 1975. At the time, he was operating a hardware store in Chestertown, a small community in northern New York's Adirondack Mountains. Business was declining, and the outlook was not encouraging. Considine saw greener pastures elsewhere.

"Analyzing the economy, I figured that severe problems would continue to plague conventional housing and make homes even less affordable," he says. Surrounded by white pine, Considine saw log homes as a realistic alternative.

Throughout 1976 he developed the concept, drawing on past job experience and knowledge he acquired from extensive reading. Considine is the epitome of a jack-of-all trades, having worked as an electrician, oil wildcatter, truck driver, insurance salesman, real estate broker and retail merchant.

He persuaded a local lumberyard owner, Thomas Vesce, to join him as a business partner in devising a packaging and marketing system for the concept. In 1977, with an investment of $2500 each, they launched Lincoln Logs. Today, Vesce is executive vice president and is responsible primarily for the financial end of the business.

With his working knowledge of law, accounting and drafting, Considine formed the Lincoln Logs corporation and developed the floor plans for several home models. "If we had hired specialists to perform all the services needed to get started, we would never have made it," he says.

Ironically, an early crisis spurred Lincoln Logs' growth. Sales hit rock bottom in the autumn of 1978. To stave off bankruptcy, Considine and Vesce launched a desperation advertising campaign. Prospective home buyers were told they could put down minimal deposits on log homes and wait until the following spring to take delivery and pay the balance.

"It worked beyond our wildest expectations," recalls Considine. "We not only generated cash to meet emergencies but also set the stage for expanded sales the following year."

Chapter 1 The American business system

Unlike other companies that market standard precut parts, Lincoln Logs sells packages that can be adapted to any type of floor plan. This enables buyers to use one of Considine's designs in assembling the shell or to design their own home.

"I devised the system after researching the whole industry," he says. "We were the new kids on the block, so we needed something unique."

The prices of Lincoln Logs home packages range from just under $9000 for a small, single-level, two-bedroom unit to around $30,000 for a two-story, four-bedroom home with a two-car garage. Interior fixtures are not included. The do-it-yourselfer can move in for roughly 2½ times the price of the basic package. Local distributors sell 22 Lincoln Logs home packages in 23 states and in Canada and West Germany.

Considine, who is married and has three daughters, used to devote 90 hours a week to the business but now puts in only 50 hours. His favorite escape is reading, preferablly about motivation and psychology. "I owe a lot to book learning," says Considine, a high school dropout who earned his diploma while in the Navy.

He defines an entrepreneur as someone who can't work for others. Considine considered offering stock in Lincoln Logs but decided against it: "Too many regulations. Besides, I've been doing my own thing too long to have to answer to stockholders."

Those who choose to go it alone "quickly develop a cast-iron stomach or flunk." But, he adds, the rewards are worth the risk and sacrifice. "Knowing that you've created something out of nothing is one of the most exhilarating feelings you can experience."

Reprinted by permission from NATION'S BUSINESS, November 1981. Copyright 1981 by NATION'S BUSINESS, Chamber of Commerce of The United States.

into manufacturing. Due to advanced farming techniques and machinery, food for the entire nation is currently supplied by less than 4 percent of the total U.S. working population.

Meanwhile, the demand for services—such as education, transportation, medical care, and recreation—has outpaced the demand for goods. Today, a majority of the U.S. work force is involved in producing services.

Managers as producers Managers are producers when they organize, plan, and coordinate the actual production of goods and services. Managers, supervisors, and administrators make up about one-third of all employees.

Investors as producers Investors supply the money needed to acquire raw materials, facilities, and equipment for production. The money comes from savings accounts, pension funds, stock ownership, and life insurance premiums. Banks and other financial institutions use this money to finance business investments. Investors' money allows business to expand and create additional jobs.

Do you have what it takes to be an entrepreneur?

Under each question, check the answer that says what you feel or comes closest to it. Be honest with yourself.

Are you a self-starter?
- ☐ I do things on my own. Nobody has to tell me to get going.
- ☐ If someone gets me started, I keep going all right.
- ☐ Easy does it. I don't put myself out until I have to.

How do you feel about other people?
- ☐ I like people. I can get along with just about anybody.
- ☐ I have plenty of friends—I don't need anyone else.
- ☐ Most people irritate me.

Can you lead others?
- ☐ I can get most people to go along when I start something.
- ☐ I can give the orders if someone tells me what we should do.
- ☐ I let someone else get things moving. Then I go along if I feel like it.

Can you take responsibility?
- ☐ I like to take charge of things and see them through.
- ☐ I'll take over if I have to, but I'd rather let someone else be responsible.
- ☐ There's always some eager beaver around wanting to show how smart he is. I say let him.

How good an organizer are you?
- ☐ I like to have a plan before I start. I'm usually the one to get things lined up when the group wants to do something.
- ☐ I do all right unless things get too confused. Then I quit.
- ☐ You get all set and then something comes along and presents too many problems. So I just take things as they come.

How good a worker are you?
- ☐ I can keep going as long as I need to. I don't mind working hard for something I want.
- ☐ I'll work hard for a while, but when I've had enough, that's it.
- ☐ I can't see that hard work gets you anywhere.

Can you make decisions?
- ☐ I can make up my mind in a hurry if I have to. It usually turns out O.K., too.

☐ I can if I have plenty of time. If I have to make up my mind fast, I think later I should have decided the other way.

☐ I don't like to be the one who has to decide things.

Can people trust what you say?
☐ You bet they can. I don't say things I don't mean.

☐ I try to be on the level most of the time, but sometimes I just say what's easiest.

☐ Why bother if the other fellow doesn't know the difference?

Can you stick with it?
☐ If I make up my mind to do something, I don't let *anything* stop me.

☐ I usually finish when I start—if it goes well.

☐ If it doesn't go right away, I quit. Why beat your brains out?

How good is your health?
☐ I *never* run down!

☐ I have enough energy for most things I want to do.

☐ I run out of energy sooner than most of my friends seem to.

Now count the checks you made.
☐ How many checks are there beside the *first* answer to each question?

☐ How many checks are there beside the *second* answer to each question?

☐ How many checks are there beside the *third* answer to each question?

If most of your checks are beside the first answers, you probably have what it takes to run a business. If not, you're likely to have more trouble than you can handle by yourself. Better find a partner who is strong on the points you're weak on. If many checks are beside the third answer, not even a good partner will be able to shore you up.

Small Business Administration, "Checklist for Small Businesses."

Entrepreneurs as producers Entrepreneurs are people who take the risk of starting a new business or owning an ongoing business. They play a vital role in the economy by providing new goods, services, and jobs.

The private, or nongovernment, sector of the economy combines the efforts of workers, managers, investors, and entrepreneurs in the production process.

Governments

When the United States declared its independence from Britain, the U.S. government took relatively little control in business matters. Individuals and businesses in the private sector made almost all their own decisions. However, even at that time, there was much discussion about the extent to which government should involve itself in the economy.

Since that time, society has become more complex. The United States has grown and prospered. Likewise, government's role and involvement in the economy has expanded.

Areas of government involvement in the economy

There are five major ways in which federal, state, and local governments are involved in the economy.

1. Protection of the rights and freedoms of individuals Government protects economic, political, and religious freedoms through the legal system.

2. Provision of goods and services in the public interest The government is involved in providing national defense, education, highways, postal service, and many other goods and services to the public.

3. Regulation of economic activities The government maintains competition in the marketplace through such actions as antitrust and banking regulations. It also protects public health and safety, as typified by minimum wage laws and food and drug standards.

4. Promotion of economic growth and stabilization The federal government works through many agencies to promote economic policies and programs that support the economy.

5. Direct assistance to individuals Numerous government programs help individuals who need assistance due to poor health, age, unemployment, and similar problems.

The cost of government involvement

As the United States has grown and prospered, Americans have come to expect more and more goods and services from every level of government. Increased government goods and services cost money. They must be paid for with money raised in two basic ways: either by taxing individuals and businesses or by borrowing.

There is much debate about the amount of goods and services government should provide. Among the often-asked questions are: What programs are proper for the government to sponsor? What activities can be better accomplished by the private sector? Who benefits from government programs? How much do government programs cost? Do the benefits outweigh the costs? What sector of the economy will pay the cost? How can we be sure that funds aren't wasted?

The answers to these questions are not simple. But they must be faced to ensure that government programs best serve the needs of our society and its economy.

How the economy works

The American economic system is based on the principles of capitalism. Capitalism is also called the private-enterprise system. **Capitalism is based on the notion that the needs of society are best served when there is free competition among individual business firms.** This underlying principle is expressed in the following concepts.
1. Individuals should have the right to purchase, own, and sell private property—including the means of production.
2. Individuals should be free to choose their occupations and how they will spend their earnings.
3. In selling goods and services, individuals should be free to seek a profit by competing freely with others who sell similar goods or services.
4. Buyers and sellers should be able to meet for the purpose of transferring goods and services in the marketplace, with price a vital means of such transfer.

The concept of the marketplace

Markets are essential in a capitalist economy. **The marketplace is where buyers and sellers come together to exchange goods and services, usually for money.** In theory, it offers a place where consumers are free to purchase available goods and services from whomever they choose at whatever price they can negotiate. The buyers and sellers may be individual consumers, other businesses, government units, or foreign buyers or sellers.

Anywhere that transactions occur between buyers and sellers is the marketplace. It includes such familiar locations as grocery stores, automobile dealerships, bookstores, movie theaters, and laundries. But it also can include stock exchanges and corporate boardrooms.

The role of prices

In the market system, **prices are the means by which value is placed on goods and services.** For the most part, supply and demand affect the prices set for goods and services.

A business tends to offer a product or service only if consumers will pay more for the product than it costs to produce it. If demand is high and sales are profitable, other businesses may enter the marketplace with similar products. The entry of competition tends to increase the product's supply. **Supply is the amount of a good or service that is available in the marketplace.**

Clearance sale advertisements

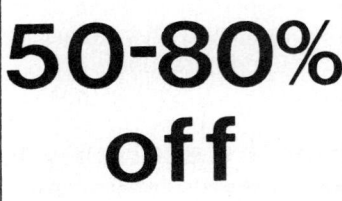

Heritage Villager (Southbury, Connecticut), 4 Feb. 1983.

On the other hand, consumers may decide to stop buying a particular product. When demand is low or declining, individual sellers may decide the product is not worth the cost of production. Competitors abandon the marketplace, reducing or eliminating supply.

What occurs in the marketplace is a delicate balancing of supply and demand. Prices play a key role in this process.

For example, when the automobile model year is over, last year's models are usually sold at reduced prices in an attempt to stimulate sales. Likewise, department stores often hold clearance sales to reduce their inventories of such seasonal items as clothing, lawn mowers, and furniture.

On the other hand, sellers often raise prices to decrease demand. This can be seen in the prices of perishable crops. In the summer, when many fruits and vegetables are plentiful, prices decrease so consumers will purchase more. But in the winter, supplies are reduced. Prices rise, so people buy less.

Competition

Through competition, businesses are forced to use the most efficient ways to produce goods and services. If a business isn't efficient, other businesses that provide similar goods or services can gain an advantage and be more profitable. Businesses that supply the best products at a given price generally prosper in the long run.

Forms of competition

Four forms of competition exist in a private-enterprise economic system: **pure competition, monopolistic competition, oligopoly, and monopoly.** Industries may be placed in one of these four categories depending on their degree of competitiveness.

The factors that affect competitiveness include the number of competing firms, type of product, amount of control an individual firm has over pricing, and ease of entering or leaving the market.

Pure competition

Pure competition exists when the businesses in an industry are so small that none can individually influence the price charged in the market. Also, it is difficult, if not impossible, to tell one producer's products from those of another. Pure competition is common in agricultural products. For example, all wheat is similar regardless of who produces it. In addition, the small size of each producer compared to total market size makes it relatively easy for a new producer to start selling wheat.

Monopolistic competition

Monopolistic competition exists in industries that have a large number of firms whose products differ from those of their competitors. **Because the products differ, each firm has some control over the price it charges.** Monopolistic competition is common in retailing, where manufacturers of brand-name products can vary their prices. For example, many firms manufacture blue jeans, and consumers show definite preferences for specific brands. Since consumers tend to be loyal to their favorite brands, producers have some choice about the prices they charge. The relatively small size of each firm makes it easy for a producer to enter or leave the industry.

Even monopolistic competition can be fierce.

"I swear that wasn't flat when we parked here!"

Cartoon by Dave Gerard; copyright © 1971 *Saturday Evening Post.* Reprinted by permission.

Oligopolistic competition

Oligopolistic competition exists when an industry has few sellers and each is large enough to influence the market price. It is very difficult for new competitors to enter the market because huge investments are required. Some oligopolies, such as the steel and aluminum industries, have similar products. Others, such as the automobile industry, have different products. Even in oligopolies, the competition for sales acts as a strong stimulus for developing new products and improving current ones. If one firm raises or lowers its prices, its competitors will usually follow suit.

Monopoly

A monopoly exists in a market where there is only one seller. That single seller can set prices and control supply without regard to competition. Unregulated monopolies are not acceptable in a capitalist system. But the U.S. government does permit a few regulated monopolies to exist, such as public utilities that provide electricity, water, and gas. In such cases, the government has determined that competition would not be in the public interest. Table 1.1 summarizes the forms of competition.

Government regulation of competition

Consumers benefit from competition. Without competition, prices of goods and services tend to be higher, and output may be lower. Producers have less incentive to improve efficiency when there is little competition. This results in wasted resources.

So the government tries to maintain a competitive environment for business. Over the years, the U.S. government has used antitrust laws and other regulations to encourage competition in the marketplace.

Table 1.1 Forms of competition

Type of competition	Characteristics			
	Number of firms	Product	Price control	Ease of entry/exit
Pure competition	Many	Similar	None	Easy
Monopolistic competition	Many	Different	Some	Relatively easy
Oligopolistic competition	Few	Similar or different	Substantial	Highly difficult
Monopoly	One	No readily available substitute	Usually government regulated	Virtually impossible

Chapter 1 The American business system

The factors of production

All goods and services result from some combination of the four factors of production: land, labor, capital, and entrepreneur. These basic inputs are crucial to the capitalist system.

Land

Land includes all resources provided by nature—such as oil, coal, and minerals—as well as the land itself. The payment for the use of land is rent.

Some natural resources are limited in quantity. Once they are used up, they will be gone forever. The fossil fuels—crude oil, natural gas, and coal—are examples of nonrenewable natural resources.

Some natural resources are renewable with careful planning. For example, timberland, with proper management, can be replenished to assure adequate wood for the future.

Labor

Labor is the physical and/or mental efforts that people contribute to production. People's skills, efforts, and motivation ultimately affect how productive any enterprise will be. **The payment for the use of labor is wages.**

Natural resources: critical commodities

Our nation depends primarily on oil and natural gas for energy. But our domestic supplies of these resources can't support higher energy demand for much longer. Half of our oil is imported—at great cost. We therefore face several critical decisions about energy. How can we conserve energy? How can we encourage exploration for new energy reserves? Should the government undertake the search, or should private industry?

We also depend more and more on foreign sources for other important raw materials, such as tin, chromium, and aluminum.

Some of our resources are almost unlimited. Energy from the sun is one example. Energy from nuclear fusion could be another. But safety and environmental concerns about nuclear energy must be resolved before its use can be widespread.

Figure 1.3 From concept to reality: How entrepreneurship works

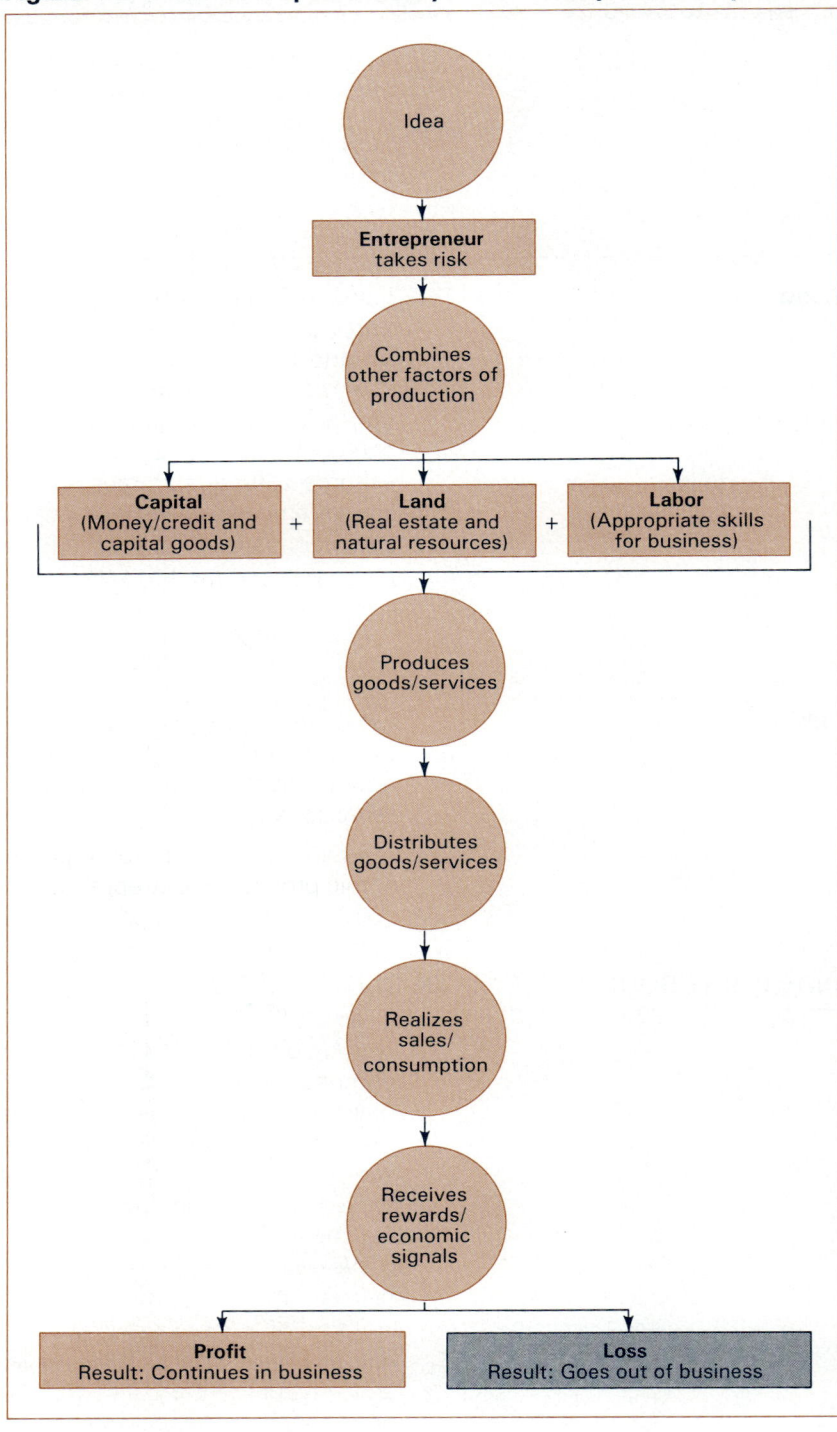

Capital and capital goods

Capital is the funding—usually money or credit—that enables a business to operate. Capital by itself does not actually produce anything. It allows a firm to purchase capital goods and other factors of production.

Capital goods actually produce goods and services. Examples of capital goods include office and factory buildings, machinery, and typewriters. Without a continuing supply of new capital goods, an economy cannot produce increased quantities of goods and services. Nor can it provide the associated jobs.

The payment for the use of capital is interest.

Entrepreneurs

Entrepreneurs perform two essential functions. First, based on the belief that there is consumer demand for certain goods and services, they bring together the other three factors of production. Second, they arrange and organize the factors of production into an operating unit that produces the desired goods or services. **Profit is the payment made to enterpreneurs.** Figure 1.3 summarizes how entrepreneurship works.

The role of profit

Why do people willingly face the risks and uncertainty of the entrepreneurial life? There are two fundamental reasons. One is the profit motive—the desire for a profitable return on one's time, effort, and capital. The second is the challenge of meeting consumer demand for a product or service.

As we can see, the entrepreneur is the driving force behind the economic process. If entrepreneurs can provide the right product or service at the right time and price, they will make a profit.

Figure 1.4 The four factors of production

Factor	Name of resource payment
Land	Rent
Labor	Wages
Capital	Interest
Entrepreneur	Profit

Snow job by Zamboni makes for nicer ice

Although he doesn't participate in the sports himself, Frank Zamboni, 81, may have done more than anybody else to make ice hockey, figure skating, and speed skating popular. He is the inventor of the Zamboni Ice Resurfacing Machine.

A native of Eureka, Utah, Zamboni had been operating the Iceland Skating Rink in Paramount, Calif., for three years before he began experimenting with different ways to clean off the rink's snow and slush. At that time, ice clearing was done manually—a process that took three men up to an hour and half.

In 1942 he rigged up a tractor and sled to clean his rink and then spent the next seven years refining his invention. "If an idea doesn't work out the first time," says Zamboni, a self-proclaimed perfectionist, "you just keep on trying."

Perseverance paid off; in the early 1950s, figure-skating star Sonja Henie saw a prototype of the machine and requested one of her own to take on a world tour. Since then the Zamboni has gone on to achieve worldwide popularity in 33 countries.

Zamboni's ice resurfacer has been used in the Olympics since 1960, preparing the ice on which 106 speed-skating records were set in the 1980 Winter Olympics. "Ice skating could never have gotten to where it is now unless a machine of this kind had been developed," he says.

Zamboni, who has 3 children, 14 grandchildren, and 7 great-grandchildren, may be the only nonskater named to the Ice Skating Hall of Fame. "I tried skating," he states. "It wasn't fun. You can't play when you have to work."

The manufacturing plant in Paramount sells between 70 and 90 Zambonis a year at prices ranging from $5000 to $40,000. Annual sales are over $1 million. Zamboni, chairman of the board, isn't placing all his faith in winter sports, though; the company also makes machines that roll down and dry Astro-Turf.

Reprinted with permission, INC., March 1982. Copyright © 1982 by INC. Publishing Company, 38 Commercial Wharf, Boston, MA 02110.

Alternative economic systems

All economic systems must deal with the same economic problem: how to allocate scarce resources when society may have almost unlimited wants and needs. The allocation of resources is a matter of weighing the *costs versus the benefits* of each possible resource use.

An economic system is the way in which a society's labor, natural resources, and human skills combine to produce and distribute the things people need and want. All economic systems must answer these three basic questions:

1. **What** goods and services should be produced from limited resources?

2. **How** and in what combinations will resources be used to produce the desired goods and services?

3. **Who** will get the goods and services and under what criteria?

Comparing economic systems

Different societies have different economic systems. In the United States, we have a system of modified capitalism. Other important economic systems include socialism and communism.

Capitalism

As mentioned earlier, capitalism is based on the notion that the needs of society are best served when there is free competition in the marketplace. Thus, in a capitalist economic system, most factors of production are privately owned. Capitalists believe that when buyers and sellers operate freely, they will automatically allocate resources in the best possible way.

Early capitalists thought that business should operate with a minimum of interference from government. This "hands-off" approach to business enterprises was first described by Adam Smith. In *Wealth of Nations,* published in 1776, Smith called it "laissez faire capitalism."

Modified capitalism

Modified capitalism reflects the changes that have occurred in capitalism over the past century. Most economic decisions remain in the marketplace between buyers and sellers. But the government can directly affect the operation of the market system. Laws concerning pollution, occupational safety, minimum wages, organized labor, banking, and the like all affect the marketplace.

Socialism

Socialism is an economic system in which the government controls the major industries. Among the industries the government might control are mining, transportation (such as railroads and airlines), steel, health care, and communications (including telephones and broadcasting). Such industries, it is felt, are too important to society to leave their ownership in the hands of the private sector of the economy. The private sector can own smaller and less essential businesses, however. Most of the industrialized nations of Western Europe, including France and Great Britain, practice some degree of socialism.

Table 1.2 Comparing the major economic systems

	Modified capitalism	Socialism	Communism
Resource ownership	Private ownership	State ownership	State ownership
Economic philosophy	Individual self-determination with some government intervention	State involvement necessary in major industries	State best qualified to make economic decisions
Resource organization	System of competitive markets with government intervention	Public ownership of major industries, some markets for smaller industries	Central government ownership and planning

Communism

Communism is an economic system in which almost all factors of production are owned by the government. Communist theory holds that the government is the most important force in society and, therefore, should control the economy.

Under communism, resources are allocated through government planning. China, the Soviet Union, and many Eastern European countries practice a form of communism.

Table 1.2 summarizes the key differences of the three major economic systems.

The need for choices

In comparing the three major economic systems, it becomes apparent that each has flaws. In a world of limited resources, no society can satisfy all its members' needs and wants.

Economic freedom and personal freedom are intertwined. Some societies attempt to control both individual needs and wants and how these needs and wants are met.

In our private-enterprise economy, decision making is a shared process. It includes consumers, producers, and government. It is our responsibility, as participants in a private-enterprise system, to be wise users and producers.

1 The American business system

Summary

Business is an important part of American society. It affects our daily lives and provides us with the goods and services we demand.

Businesses expect to make a *profit* by providing *goods* and *services*.

As individuals, we are often both *consumers* and *producers* of goods and services.

In our American economic system, three groups play major decision-making roles: consumers, producers, and governments.

Local, state, and federal governments participate in our economy in five ways: protecting individual rights and freedoms, providing goods and services in the public interest, regulating economic activities, promoting economic growth and stabilization, and giving assistance to needy individuals.

The American economy is a private-enterprise, or capitalist, system. According to capitalist philosophy, the needs of society are best served when there is free competition among business firms.

The *marketplace* is a key concept in *capitalism*. In the marketplace, buyers and sellers come together to exchange goods and services. *Prices* and competition also are important because they reward production efficiency. An important government function is to promote and maintain competition.

The four major types of competition are *pure competition, monopolistic competition, oligopolistic competition,* and *monopoly*.

The four factors of production are *land, labor, capital,* and *entrepreneurs*. They are the resources required to produce goods and services. Each resource receives a payment: *rent, wages, interest,* and *profits*.

The three major economic systems are *capitalism, socialism,* and *communism*. Any economic system must choose how to allocate its resources. No society can satisfy all the wants and needs of its members.

Review questions

1. What is the difference between goods and services? Give some familiar examples of each.
2. What are profits? What role do they play in the business world? How do profits differ from losses?
3. What are the two major elements of demand?

4. What roles do each of the following play in our business system?
   a. consumers
   b. producers
   c. governments
5. What are the basic principles of capitalism as an economic system?
6. Explain the functions of the following terms in relation to capitalism.
   a. markets
   b. competition
   c. prices
7. What are the characteristics of each of the following forms of competition?
   a. pure competition
   b. monopolistic competition
   c. oligopolistic competition
   d. monopoly
8. Identify the four factors of production and explain the importance of each.
9. Describe the three major economic systems. How are they similar? How are they different?

Discussion questions

1. Identify six goods and services you use personally.
2. Explain how this statement relates to the meaning of demand: "If you have to ask the price of this Rolls-Royce, you probably can't afford it."
3. What other factors besides price and quality may affect consumer demand for goods or services?
4. Explain this statement: "During our lifetime, we are always consumers, but not always producers."
5. Government involvement in our economic system may have both beneficial and harmful effects. Give examples of each case.
6. What are some possible reasons why some individuals are paid more for their work than others?

Chapter 1 The American business system 25

Chapter 1 case

Comparative standards of living: United States and Soviet Union

These pie charts show comparative standards of living based on approximate worktime required for a "typical" manufacturing employee to buy selected commodities in retail stores in Washington, D.C., and at state-fixed prices in Moscow during March 1982.

Case Figure 1.1 Comparative standards of living: United States and Soviet Union

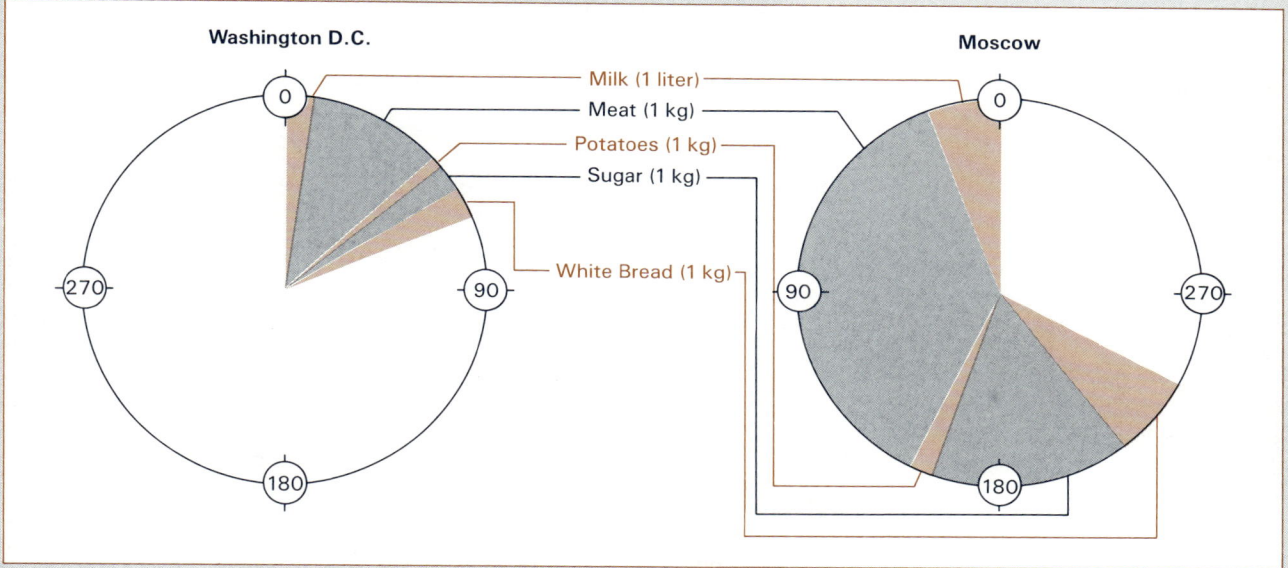

National Federation of Independent Business Research and Education Foundation, 1982

1. What general conclusion can be seen in comparing Moscow and Washington, D.C., worktime needed to purchase commodities?
2. For which kinds of commodities are there the most similar time periods? For which kinds of commodities does scarcity seem greatest in Moscow?
3. What are some reasons for the apparent relative scarcity of consumer goods in Moscow?

Business in perspective

Employees make dough while the moon shines

The "company man" who dedicates his time and energy to a corporation 40 hours a week is likely to have an extracurricular activity his employer doesn't know about. After hours, he may be a "moonlighting entrepreneur."

Just how many corporate employees own and run businesses on the side is hard to pin down. Often, says Stuart L. Meyer, a professor of management at Northwestern University, "an employee in a large company doesn't want to risk his job until his business is off the ground, so the exact numbers remain hidden."

But the incidence of such moonlit businesses is on the rise, reports Meyer, because the economy is not. "When times are bad," he says, "people are wary of leaving their fate in the hands of some corporation that isn't the safe haven it used to be. Layoffs are common, giants like Lockheed and Chrysler have nearly gone under. People start up their own enterprises to put their security back into their own hands."

In addition, Meyer says, many people realize that working for another company while starting their own is a logical way to proceed. "You can fail 99 times while you still have an income and keep on trying until you've got it right," he points out. "It's really a very common way to go into business for yourself."

William Whiston, the director of economic research at the U.S. Small Business Administration's Office at Advocacy, agrees. "Doing business on evenings and weekends is really an old American tradition," he says. "I'd say it's still the most common way businesses in this country get their start."

"Ever since I was a young man I wanted to start my own company," says a 51-year-old corporate employee from a northern Chicago suburb, who plans to leave his job at a metalworking company soon to run a similar business of his own full-time. "But I wasn't the kind of entrepreneur who wanted to start out with only two pennies to rub together. Working for someone else has given me the money and time I needed to get my company to where it'll work."

Reprinted with permission, INC., December 1981. Copyright © 1981 by INC. Publishing Company, 38 Commercial Wharf, Boston, MA 02110.

Chapter 2

Forms of business organization

Key terms

sole proprietorship
unlimited liability
partnership
general partner
limited partner
silent partner
secret partner
corporation
stockholders
limited liability
board of directors
Subchapter S corporation
cooperative
franchise operation

Chapter objectives

In Chapter 2, you will learn:

The factors to consider in choosing a form of business organization

The three major forms of business organizations and the advantages and disadvantages of each

Why a corporation is considered an artificial being and how the law interprets this

The benefits of a Subchapter S corporation

The nature and functions of the three major elements of a corporation: stockholders, board of directors, and officers

The key elements of cooperatives and franchises as business organizations

Overview

This chapter looks at how a business develops the organizational structure that best serves its needs. Choosing the appropriate form of business organization requires intelligent thought and planning.

We will first discuss the forms of business organization: the sole proprietorship, the partnership, and the corporation. Each has distinct characteristics and important advantages and disadvantages. We will then examine three other forms of business: the Subchapter S corporation, the cooperative, and the franchise.

The most desirable form for an individual business depends on the current situation. Over the years, circumstances may change and another form may become more appropriate.

Factors that affect the choice of business organization

Several factors influence the choice of a particular form of business organization:

1. How difficult is the business to start, organize, and operate?
2. How much capital will be needed?
3. How much personal wealth is the entrepreneur willing and able to risk? How much personal liability can the entrepreneur accept for the business's success or failure?
4. How much control does the owner wish to have in the operation of the business?
5. How much control does the owner wish to have over transferring or selling ownership rights in the business?
6. What kinds of tax liability is the owner willing to assume?

Figure 2.1 shows the progress of sole proprietorships, partnerships, and corporations in the United States from 1960 to 1980.

Business and other group efforts require careful organizational planning.

© King Features Syndicate, Inc., 1978. Reprinted by permission.

Figure 2.1 Proprietorships, partnerships, and corporations, 1960–1980

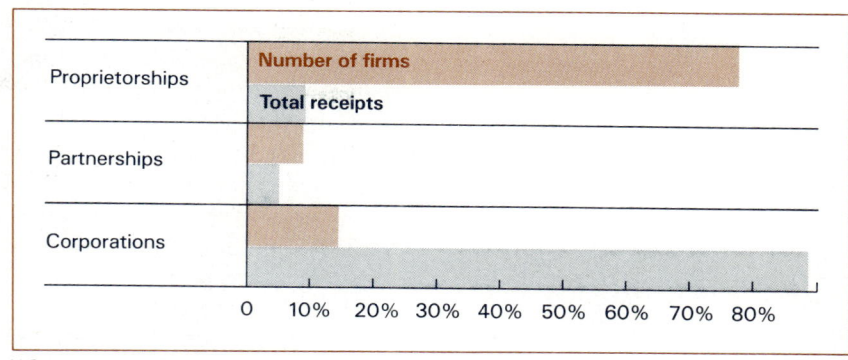

U.S. Internal Revenue Service

Sole proprietorship

A sole proprietorship is a business that is owned and operated by a single individual. It is the most common form of business organization in the United States. The number of sole proprietorships is almost four times greater than the combined total of partnerships and corporations.

Advantages of sole proprietorship

1. Ease of formation A sole proprietorship can be started with very little money or equipment.

2. Profits not shared A sole proprietor can keep all profits from business operations.

3. Owner makes all decisions A sole proprietor is the only boss and is free to make all decisions.

4. Personal motivation and interest A sole proprietor can get great satisfaction from meeting the personal challenges involved in operating a business.

5. Tax advantages Since the sole proprietor *is* the business, he or she pays only personal income taxes on the firm's profits.

6. Direct contact with customers A sole proprietorship is usually small enough that the owner can have direct contact with customers. The owner's personality is an important factor in the business operation.

The fifty-million-dollar diet

A successful franchisor enriches himself, but a good one, someone like Harold Katz, enriches others as well. The Nutri/System formula perfected by Katz has provided dozens of franchisees with a business opportunity that seems hard to beat; a number have won millionaire status via the weight-loss route.

Ed Richey and Barry Goodman, both 30, were college classmates who had gone into the insurance and concrete businesses, respectively, in Nashville. In 1980, after hearing about Nutri/System from a mutual friend, they and a third party raised $63,000—$43,000 for the franchise fee and $20,000 for start-up expenses—to open a center in Evansville, Ind. It paid off more richly than anyone had expected. They recovered their initial investment in four months, grossed $800,000 during the first year, and enjoyed earnings of 25 percent.

Realizing that they were onto a good thing, Richey and Goodman began securing other locations. They had trained local people to manage the first weight-loss center, so they could simply oversee the operation from their headquarters in Tennessee. That made it relatively simple for them to become, in effect, subfranchisers. In July, less than four months after they had opened their first center, they opened a second, in Topeka, Kansas. The following month, they added two others, in Wichita, Kansas, and Des Moines, Iowa; in September, a fifth began providing Nutri/System service to the overweight residents of Omaha, Nebraska. Since then, the growth has continued unabated. The young entrepreneurs are now principal stockholders in six companies that own or manage 27 centers in 12 states and that last year had revenues of more than $11 million. According to the partners, all but the first four centers were financed by Nutri/System profits.

Richey and Goodman term their experience with Katz a "very rewarding" one. "It's considerably better than the concrete business," attests Goodman.

The Nutri/System money machine

Fiscal year (ends 7/1)	1977 (10 mos.)	1978	1979	1980	1981
Revenues ($ in millions)	2.4	6.1	15.0	23.2	49.2
Net earnings ($ in millions)	.4	.6	2.9	3.8	9.2
Net earnings (% revenues)	18	10	19	16	19
Current assets ($ in millions)	2.0	2.6	7.6	10.6	24.4
Current liabilities ($ in millions)	1.2	1.5	3.9	5.7	12.3
Working capital ($ in millions)	8	1.1	3.7	4.9	12.1
Return on equity (%)	484	110	268	97	131
Company-owned centers	4	11	16	38	58
Franchised centers	51	100	151	210	350

Reprinted with permission, INC., May 1982. Copyright © 1982 by INC. Publishing Company, 38 Commercial Wharf, Boston, MA 02110.

Disadvantages of sole proprietorship

1. **Unlimited liability** Unlimited liability means that all business debts are the owner's personal responsibility. In the eyes of the law, the owner and the business are one and the same. As a result, creditors can make claims on the owner's personal assets in order to satisfy business debts. Personal assets may include automobiles, real estate, and savings accounts.

2. **Decision-making responsibilities** As the boss, the owner must take responsibility for all decisions. But some decisions may require knowledge the owner lacks. Also, the owner may be so busy that decision making becomes a hurried, haphazard process.

3. **Limited capital resources** Business expansion may be severely limited because the only money available is the amount the owner can personally invest or borrow.

4. **Limited duration of business** The stability and continuity of a sole proprietorship is directly tied to the personal life and health of its owner. If the owner becomes sick, retires, or dies, the business may be forced to close.

5. **Losses are not shared** Any losses suffered by the sole proprietorship must be absorbed by the sole proprietor alone.

Partnership

A partnership is a form of business in which two or more persons share ownership. Although it is not required, a written legal contract is the best way to form a partnership. This written agreement is called the articles of co-partnership. It sets out such important information as the names of the partners, the purpose of the business, the responsibility of each partner, and how profits (and losses) will be shared between the partners.

The articles would also define procedures for ending the partnership, including what will happen if a partner decides to sell his or her interest in the business, retires, or dies.

It may not be possible to cover all potential problems in a partnership agreement. But the partners should work out as many details as possible in advance. Partnerships require mutual trust and cooperation. Many partnerships fail for personal reasons rather than business reasons.

Forms of partnership

By law, at least one member of a partnership must be a general partner. **A general partner actively runs the firm and takes responsibility for the firm's actions and potential losses.** A general partner assumes unlimited liability for the firm's debts.

Besides one or more general partners, a partnership agreement may include limited partners, silent partners, and secret partners.

A limited partner is one whose contribution and liability are limited. For example, someone who invests in a firm may be made a limited partner. That partner's liability would then be limited to the amount he or she invested. A limited partner's share of the profits may be less than that of a general partner with a similar-sized investment.

A silent partner is not actively involved in a business's operation. Sometimes such partners provide services and may even have their names associated with a firm. Other times they merely provide financial backing and have no direct interest in management.

A secret partner prefers to keep his or her participation in a business from becoming public knowledge. A secret partner may nonetheless provide a firm with specialized services, such as legal, accounting, or financial help. Secret partners are also silent partners.

Partnerships are most common in small retail businesses and among providers of professional services, such as doctors, lawyers, and accountants. Such businesses do not require large investments in fixed assets.

Advantages of partnership

The advantages of partnership are similar to those of sole proprietorship. But partnerships also have some unique characteristics.

1. Increased capital capacity Partners can combine their individual assets and credit capacity to raise more money than a sole proprietor.

2. Distribution of decision making and specialization Partnerships make use of each partner's unique talents and expertise. Decision making is thus distributed among the partners.

3. Tax advantages A partnership is the sum total of the individual partners. As a result, each partner's share of the profits is taxed as individual personal income.

4. Minimal government regulation A partnership is a private agreement among partners. It is therefore exempt from certain state and federal laws that apply to corporations.

Disadvantages of partnership

1. Unlimited liability General partners have unlimited liability for all business debts. Their personal assets may be subject to claims from business creditors.

2. Agency power All partners may be liable for the actions of one general partner. If one partner incurs debts or is found guilty of malpractice, the other partners can be held liable even if they weren't directly involved.

3. Limited business life If one partner leaves, the partnership ends. With every change in partners, a new partnership must be established.

4. Possible interpersonal conflicts A partnership requires the cooperation of all partners. As in all personal relationships, disagreements and misunderstandings may arise. Such conflicts can damage the business and even cause it to dissolve.

5. Difficulty of ending A partnership is more complex to dissolve than is a sole proprietorship. Partnership agreements often include agreements that give other partners the first bid on a departing partner's share. Or they may specify the requirements of a suitable replacement.

Both sole proprietorships and partnerships have distinct advantages and disadvantages. Major difficulties common to both include limited capital capacity, unlimited liability, and limited duration of business.

The corporation

The third major form of business organization is the corporation. **A corporation is a business form created by law in which a business's identity and liability are separate from those of its individual owners.** U.S. Supreme Court Justice John Marshall explained the corporation's legal basis in *Dartmouth College* v. *Woodward* (1819). Marshall wrote:

> A corporation is an artificial being, invisible, intangible, and existing only in contemplation of the law. Being the mere creature of law, it possesses only those properties which the charter of its creation confers upon it, either expressly or as incidental to its very existence. . . . Among the most important are immortality, and, if the expression may be allowed, individuality; properties by which a perpetual succession of many persons are considered as the same, and may act as a single individual. They enable a corporation to manage its own affairs, and to hold property without the perplexing intricacies, the hazardous and endless necessity, of perpetual conveyance for the purpose of transmitting it from hand to hand. . . .

Justice Marshall's interpretation is the key to the corporate form of business organization: its identity and liability are separate from those of its individual owners. **Stockholders are investors who become part-owners of a corporation by buying shares of its stock.**

Forming a corporation

The individual states grant permission for a private business corporation to be formed based on the corporation's charter and bylaws. A corporate charter includes such information as:

1. Name and address of the corporation
2. Purpose(s) of the corporation
3. Nature of business
4. Names and addresses of founders (incorporators)
5. Number of ownership shares to be issued

Corporate bylaws state rules for the election of officers and directors and the date and location of the annual corporate meeting.

A new corporation submits its charter and bylaws for state approval and pays state incorporation fees. The state may then grant approval for creation of the corporation. Note that the federal government does not confer corporate status.

State-approved charters become a contract between the state and the corporation. The corporation, under the limits imposed by its charter and bylaws, is allowed to operate in the state.

All states do not have the same incorporation regulations. Some are less strict than others. Delaware, for example, has relatively lenient incorporation requirements. As a result, it has become the home state for many corporations. While a company must have an address in its state of incorporation, it can do business and have major offices anywhere.

The board of directors

A board of directors is elected by stockholders. **It develops broad company policies and goals and has overall legal responsibility for the corporation's affairs.** The board of directors also chooses company officers to implement corporate goals and policies. Company officers typically include the president, vice-president(s), treasurer, and secretary. Company officers may also own some stock in the corporation and be members of the board of directors.

Because of its nature and characteristics, the corporate form of organization occupies a dominant position in American business activity.

Table 2.1 lists the fifteen largest corporations in the United States. Seven of the top ten are oil companies.

Advantages of the corporation

1. **Separate legal identity.** A corporation is given a legal status separate from its owners. As explained by Justice Marshall, a corporation is considered an artificial person, with the legal ability to enter into contracts, buy and sell goods and services, sue and be sued, own property, and the like.

2. **Limited liability** Limited liability means that the owners' liability is no greater than the amount of their financial investment in the business. If a corporation runs into debt, its owners' personal assets are safe from creditors.

Table 2.1 The fifteen largest U.S. industrial corporations

Company	Rank	Sales ($ in thousands)	Rank	Assets ($ in thousands)
Exxon	1	$108,107,688	1	$62,931,055
Mobil	2	64,488,000	3	34,776,000
General Motors	3	62,698,500	2	38,991,200
Texaco	4	57,628,000	5	27,489,000
Standard Oil of California	5	44,224,000	7	23,680,000
Ford	6	38,247,100	8	23,021,400
Standard Oil of Indiana	7	29,947,000	9	22,916,000
International Business Machines	8	29,070,000	4	29,586,000
Gulf Oil	9	28,252,000	11	20,429,000
Atlantic Richfield	10	27,797,436	13	19,732,539
General Electric	11	27,240,000	10	20,942,000
E.I. du Pont de Nemours	12	22,810,000	6	23,829,000
Shell Oil	13	21,629,000	12	20,118,000
International Telephone & Telegraph	14	17,306,189	16	15,052,377
Phillips Petroleum	15	15,966,000	20	11,264,000

Source: "The 500 Largest U.S. Industrial Corporations," FORTUNE, May 3, 1982, p. 260. Reprinted from the FORTUNE Directory; © 1982, Time Inc.

3. Potential for capital expansion Because individual owners are not responsible for a corporation's debts, investment in ownership units (shares) is financially attractive. This gives a corporation great potential for raising capital. Shares of ownership may be purchased by many different investors.

4. Unlimited life Unlike a sole proprietorship or a partnership, a corporation does not end when its owners change. The stability of a corporation is less dependent on its owners. Many corporations are old enough to have long outlived their original investor-owners.

5. Ease in transferring ownership Corporate stock is usually easy to transfer from one person to another. Special markets, such as the New York Stock Exchange and the American Stock Exchange, provide a place to buy and sell corporate stocks.

6. Credit potential Due to their legal status and stability, corporations are usually good credit risks. As a result, financial institutions are often willing to lend them large amounts of money.

7. Separation between owners and managers Two distinct and important groups often exist in a corporation: owners (or stockholders), who invest their money; and managers, who are employees with specialized skills to operate the business. Owners are primarily interested in earning a return on their investment and quite often are not actively involved in day-to-day business operations. This separation of owners and managers also has distinct disadvantages.

Disadvantages of the corporate form

1. Legally complex to organize and dissolve The corporate form of organization is the most complex to create and dissolve. It requires legal approval from the state in which it is to be incorporated. When starting a corporation, a charter, bylaws, and incorporation fees must be submitted to the state. The assistance of a lawyer is useful, though not mandatory.

2. Legal restrictions on business activity A corporation may legally engage only in those activities specified in its charter. To make any changes, a corporation must submit a charter amendment for state approval. To avoid complications, most corporate charters are broadly written to cover numerous possible business activities.

3. Double taxation A major disadvantage of the corporate form is its special tax position. As an entity separate from its owners, a corporation pays federal and state taxes on its net profits. If the corporation then uses its after-tax profits to pay dividends, stockholders must pay personal income tax on the dividends. So the corporation and its stockholders pay taxes on the same money. This does not happen in sole proprietorships and partnerships. Sole proprietors and partners pay only personal income taxes on their profits.

4. Separation between owners and managers Stockholders and managers often have different interests. Owners seek reasonable dividends and growth of their investment. Managers are often most interested in maintaining their own jobs.

5. Limited ownership control Stockholders, especially in large corporations, have little real influence over business operations. Their main power is in their ability to elect members to the corporation's board of directors. Individual owners also "vote" when they decide either to buy or sell shares of the company stock.

Chapter 2 Forms of business organization

6. Government reporting requirements Because corporations are given their legal status by the state, they are subject to state reporting requirements. Among the many forms that must be filed are financial ownership statements, public disclosure statements of financial information, and statements about raising capital through the sale of additional shares of stock. At the federal level, corporations whose stock is available to the general public must comply with the many reporting requirements of the Securities and Exchange Commission.

The board of directors must report to the owners about company progress. Usually, reports are given periodically in written form and at the corporation's annual stockholders' meeting.

Figure 2.2 shows the flow of authority delegation and reporting responsibilities within a corporation. Although owners often are far removed from company operation, in theory they exercise final control.

Subchapter S corporations: a special arrangement

As previously mentioned, double taxation is a distinct disadvantage of the corporate form of business operation. Subchapter S corporations, however, are taxed as partnerships. No corporate income tax is paid. The owners pay only personal income taxes on their business profits. Subchapter S is a section of the tax code.

The Subchapter S option is available to corporations that have no more than 25 stockholders. By electing this option, corporations can have lower tax liabilities.

Conflict between management and stockholders often surrounds a corporation's attempt to acquire a new business.

"High fives! Something big must be happening over in Corporate Acquisitions."

Drawing by Lorenz; © 1981 The New Yorker Magazine Inc.

Figure 2.2 Corporate delegation of authority and reporting

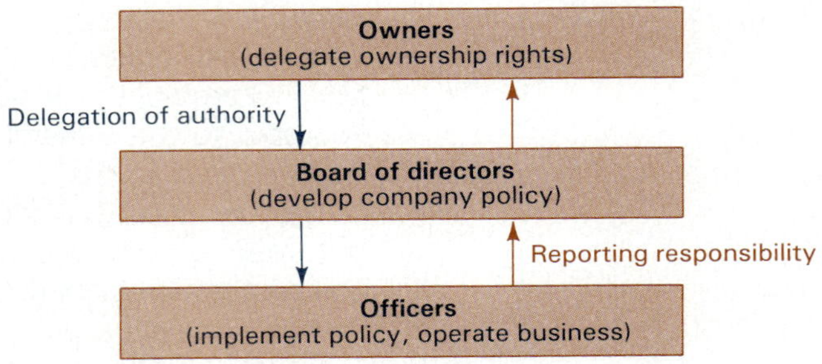

```
                    Owners
                    (delegate ownership rights)
Delegation of authority ↓                    ↑
                    Board of directors
                    (develop company policy)
                                              ↑ Reporting responsibility
                    ↓
                    Officers
                    (implement policy, operate business)
```

Table 2.2 Advantages and disadvantages of the three major business forms

Form	Advantages	Disadvantages
Sole proprietorship	1. Ease of formation 2. Profits not shared 3. Owner makes all decisions 4. Personal motivation and interest 5. Tax advantages 6. Direct customer contact	1. Unlimited financial liability 2. Decision-making responsibilities 3. Limited capital resources 4. Limited business life 5. Losses not shared
Partnership	1. Increased capital capacity 2. Distribution of decision making and specialization 3. Tax advantages 4. Minimal government intervention	1. Unlimited financial liability 2. Agency power 3. Limited business life 4. Possible interpersonal conflicts 5. Termination difficulties
Corporation	1. Separate legal identity 2. Limited financial liability 3. Potential for capital expansion 4. Unlimited business life 5. Ease in transferring ownership 6. Credit potential 7. Separation between owners and managers	1. Legally complex to organize and dissolve 2. Legal restrictions on business activity 3. Double taxation of income 4. Separation between owners and managers 5. Limited ownership control 6. Government reporting requirements

Some exceptions

The size of a business organization does not necessarily dictate its form. While most big businesses tend to be corporations, not all corporations are large. In fact, almost 80 percent of all corporations had total receipts of under $500,000 in 1974. Only 12 percent had receipts of more than $1 million. At the same time, a small number of sole proprietorships and partnerships had sales of more than $1 million.

Moreover, a sole proprietorship or partnership that incorporates does not automatically gain all the advantages of an established corporation. For example, before a bank extends a loan, it may require the owners of a small, closely held corporation to sign personal guarantees. Because the corporation has limited liability, the bank wants to make sure it can get its money back from the owners if the corporation is unable to repay the debt.

A corporation's owners are not always separate from its management. In smaller corporations, the stockholders are often the managers and the board of directors as well. It is not required that owners and managers be separate. Naturally, as a firm grows and sells stock to more and more people, ownership and management tend to become separate. But exceptions are numerous. The Ford Motor Company, for example, was still run by Henry Ford II until 1980. The Ford family continues to hold a substantial portion of the corporation's stock, and many family members are active in its management.

Other forms of business organization

Most of the businesses in the United States are sole proprietorships, partnerships, and corporations. Two other important forms of business ownership, however, are the cooperative and the franchise.

Cooperatives

A cooperative is a group of persons who pool resources to carry out specific business activities. A cooperative has several unique characteristics:
1. Each cooperative is owned by its user-members.
2. Capital is raised through members' investments, usually with limits placed on the maximum possible investment.
3. Each member has one vote, regardless of the amount invested.
4. Members are paid interest on their investments.
5. After investment interest is paid, members share in the profits based on the amount of business each transacts with the cooperative.

Cooperatives exist in many kinds of businesses. Consumer cooperatives are formed to gain increased purchasing power in such areas as food products, fuel, and farm machinery.

Producer cooperatives also exist, especially in agriculture. Examples include milk producers, grain producers, and fruit growers.

Just don't ask them to send Mary Poppins

Denver might become the babysitting capital of the United States, thanks to Jim Kone.

Kone, the co-owner of a steel service center, sold his interest in the $14-million business to found Rent-A-Mom, a company that provides professional child care to Denver residents and visitors.

After a Denver bank "quit laughing at the name of the company, it told me to come back in two years," says Kone. Instead of waiting, he invested $10,000 of his own money and opened shop in August 1981. Sales for 1982 are projected at $250,000.

Kone originally planned to provide qualified, insured child-care workers to major hotels in Denver, but he soon expanded his service to offer live-in nannies, traveling nannies, tutors, pet and house sitters, and city tours for children. He has sent one nanny to Switzerland, and filled another family's request for a French-speaking woman over 50.

The hardest part of the business, says Kone, is coordinating personalities—he usually sends three nannies to a home before one works out. Kone, who is just as choosy as his customers, interviews between 15 and 20 people a day and rejects 60 percent of them.

Kone's staff includes five office workers, a manager, and more than 200 nannies who range in age from 22 to 75. The majority of Rent-A-Mom's customers are middle- to high-income working couples who pay between $5 and $6 an hour for residential and hotel sitting. "Our business serves as an extension of the working family," says Kone, whose biggest demand is for sitters to "greet the kids home from school, entertain them, cook them dinner, and then go home."

These days, Kone has no problems finding a sitter for his two children, and he thinks the service is "great." His opinion is biased, however: "I always get the cream of the crop," the 40-year-old entrepreneur admits.

Reprinted with permission, INC., June 1982. Copyright © 1982 by INC. Publishing Company, 38 Commercial Wharf, Boston, MA 02110.

Franchises

A franchise operation sells the exclusive right to use its idea and name to individuals (franchisees) who want to start their own businesses. The franchising company is thus able to expand without investing its own capital.

The franchisee gains the right to sell the franchised product. The franchisor may provide financial aid, management advice, and training, and may help establish and operate the business. In return for use of the franchisor's name, image, and support system, the franchisee pays an initial fee plus a monthly fee, usually based on a percentage of profits. The franchisor is often a corporation, and each franchisee may be a separate corporation.

Chapter 21, "Small Business Management," discusses franchises in greater detail.

2 Forms of business organization

Summary

Forms of business organization have evolved to meet changing economic and business needs. The three major forms of organization are sole proprietorships, partnerships, and corporations. Several factors influence the choice of form, and this form may change during the course of a business's life.

The advantages of a *sole proprietorship* are ease of formation, owner retention of profits, owner control of decision making, personal motivation and interest, tax benefits, and direct customer contact. Disadvantages include *unlimited liability,* decision-making responsibilities, limited capital resources, limited business life, and owner assumption of all losses.

The advantages of a *partnership* include increased capital capacity, the distribution of decision making and specialization, tax benefits, and minimal government intervention. Disadvantages include unlimited financial liability, agency power, limited business life, possible interpersonal conflicts, and difficulties in terminating the partnership.

Partnerships can have a variety of partners. Every partnership must have at least one *general partner,* who actively runs the firm and takes responsibility for the firm's actions and potential losses. A *limited partner* takes a limited role in company affairs. A *silent partner* is not actively involved in the operation of the business. Often the silent partner provides financial backing for a business. A *secret partner* may provide some services to a business, but prefers to keep that information from becoming public knowledge. A formal written contract between partners is highly desirable.

The *corporation* greatly contributed to American industrialization. The primary advantage of this form of business organization is that its legal identity is separate from that of its individual owners, or *stockholders.* Stockholders elect a *board of directors* to develop company goals and policies and to assume legal responsibility for the corporation.

Corporations also offer *limited liability* to owners, increased capital potential through the sale of stock, unlimited business life, ease in transferring ownership, credit potential, and separation between owners and managers. Disadvantages of the corporate form include the legal complexities of formation and dissolution, legal restrictions on business activity, double taxation of income, separation between owners and managers, limited owner control, and substantial government reporting requirements.

A small business may find tax relief by becoming a *Subchapter S corporation*. Such a corporation is treated as a partnership for tax purposes, and double taxation of profits is avoided.

The members of a *cooperative* benefit from group ownership of resources. A cooperative may be either consumer- or producer-oriented.

Franchises have become popular since the 1950s. A *franchise operation* sells others the right to use its idea and name. It can thus expand without investing its own capital.

Review questions

1. Why are sole proprietorships the most popular form of business organization?
2. Give four examples of sole proprietorships you know. What kinds of businesses seen most suitable for sole proprietorship?
3. What are the major advantages of a partnership? What kinds of businesses do you know that are partnerships?
4. How do corporations differ from sole proprietorships and partnerships?
5. What are the main advantages of a Subchapter S corporation?
6. How does a cooperative differ from a franchise?
7. Why is it necessary for every partnership to have at least one general partner?
8. What form of business organization would be most likely for each of the following?
    a. shoe repair shop
    b. antique shop
    c. oil-drilling venture
    d. commuter airline
9. What is the difference between unlimited and limited financial liability? Why is liability an important business consideration?
10. In a corporation, what is the role and function of the following groups?
    a. board of directors
    b. officers
    c. stockholders

Discussion questions

1. Select a business in your area that is either a sole proprietorship or a partnership. Arrange to meet with the owner or owners to find out how and why they started that particular business. What do they see as the major advantages and disadvantages?
2. What factors might cause a business originally formed as a originally formed as a sole proprietorship to evolve into a partnership and then into a corporation?
3. If you were planning to form a partnership with two other people, what understandings would you want to have clear from the very beginning?
4. Why might having too many partners affect the management of a partnership?

Chapter 2 Forms of business organization   43

5. What is meant by double taxation of corporate profits?
6. Why is a corporation considered an artificial being?
7. What benefits can a small sole proprietorship provide its customers that a large corporation cannot?
8. What benefits can a large corporation provide its customers that a small sole proprietorship cannot?

Chapter 2 case

"We can manage anything"

Business organization requires efficient management to achieve production of goods and services at competitive prices.

The president of a very successful conglomerate commented recently on the secret of his firm's success. "In the not-too-recent past, it was taken for granted that a successful manager or management team had to be technically proficient in the business they were managing in order to succeed. Thus, there were steel managers, railroad managers, food products managers, and so on. The idea that a good man could start, say, in a paper company, learn to manage well, and then move on to an airline and be successful was considered absurd.

"However, in our business, we can manage anything. One of our major divisions is in aerospace—they're now making space capsules for the Mars shot. Another division is selling soft drinks in the consumer market, while a third is in the machine tool business. We take bright young managers and teach them how to manage, not how to be a soft-drink man or a machine tool man. Of course, we need very good technical people, and we pay well for such skills. But our managers can run any division of the company. We know how to plan and control our divisions in all their critical dimensions. Our managers know what questions to ask the technicians, and they know how to evaluate the answers they get.

"We have expanded very rapidly (and have made fortunes for our shareholders) by taking advantage of this technique. We look for companies who feel that they have only one business to be in, and we look where that business has a slow rate of growth. Then we buy the company, get rid of the old product-oriented man, and put in our own top general managers. We can use funds that the sluggish company generates to invest in fast-growing, highly profitable divisions.

"Our machine tool division is a case in point. It was an old, single-line, profitable company with very few prospects for long-term growth. The old managers really didn't know what to do with their cash flow. They invested in a new tool plant that returned only 5 percent on the investment, simply because it never occurred to them that these funds could be used more profitably elsewhere. When we took over, we used this cash to invest in our soft-drink line, where we were making 27 percent on investment.

"Incidentally, we also found that we could earn over 20 percent on machine tools once we began to utilize proper management planning and controls. A real weakness of single product managers is narrow management skills. They are so used to talking to one kind of guy that they often don't really know what is going on in terms of new developments in management."

1. Do you think it is possible to manage anything? Why?

2. Give examples of situations where managers have to know a great deal about the technology, markets, finance, etc., of the firm they are managing.

3. Do you think a manager of a conglomerate is likely to be more exposed to general management philosophies, problems, and techniques than a manager of an equally large, single-product firm? Why?

Richard N. Farmer, *Incidents for Introduction to Business* (Belmont, CA: Wadsworth Publishing Co., Inc., 1969), pp. 42–43.

Business in perspective

Jeep will inform customers, owners that its CJ models handle differently from ordinary cars, FTC announces

Jeep Corporation has agreed to attach stickers to its new Jeep CJ models warning prospective buyers that the vehicles handle differently from ordinary passenger cars, and that sudden, sharp turns may cause the driver to lose control, the Federal Trade Commission has announced. This is the first time an American car manufacturer has agreed to place warning stickers on its products as a result of FTC action.

The company will attach the stickers to the instrument panel or windshield frame of each new Jeep CJ, and will also send stickers to current owners. The agreement covers Jeep CJ-5, CJ-6, and CJ-7 models manufactured since 1972.

The sticker will read:

"This multipurpose vehicle handles and maneuvers differently from an ordinary passenger car. As with other vehicles of this type, sudden sharp turns and abrupt maneuvers may result in loss of control. Read driving guidelines in Owner's Manual and Supplement.

WEAR SEATBELTS AT ALL TIMES."

Source: *FTC News Summary,* vol. 10-82, December 4, 1981.

Chapter 3   Business and the law

Key terms

law
common law
statutory law
contract
injunction
recission
agency
tort
property
real property
deed
personal property
title
commercial paper
endorsement
bankruptcy
ethics

Chapter objectives

In Chapter 3, you will learn:

The meaning of law and why it is important for businesses

The two major sources of U.S. law

How the U.S. court system is organized

The elements of a contract and the remedies for a broken contract

The characteristics of agency law and tort law

How real property differs from personal property

The importance of commercial paper to business activities

The four types of check endorsements and their characteristics

What bankruptcy is and how a bankruptcy is settled

What ethics are and how they apply to business

Why government has become involved in business activities

Overview

In our society, political, social, and economic forces continually interact. To avoid chaos, we developed a legal system. Laws may be thought of as legal "rules of the game." They apply to both businesses and individual citizens. Knowledge of the legal system and how it operates can help managers in making decisions.

It would be difficult, if not impossible, for businesses to function in a society where contracts were not honored or where ownership of private property was not respected. Widespread bribery, fraud, cheating, and lying would all undermine business operations.

In this chapter, we consider the legal foundations of business in the United States. This includes the laws and the structure of the U.S. judicial system. We look at the elements of a contract and the remedies available when a contract is broken. Specific laws relating to business are presented, including those that apply to agency, tort, property, and bankruptcy. Finally, we focus on business ethics and their role in forming corporate policies and government regulations.

Legal foundations

Law is the enforceable set of rules that governs the relationship of individuals and institutions to each other and to an organized society.

There are two major approaches to the law. The *traditional approach* views the law as all rules that are in effect within a state or nation at a given time. The *environmental approach* focuses on the processes by which rules are formulated rather than on the rules themselves.

For a legal system to function properly, it must command the respect of most of the people it governs. To do so, its laws must possess certain characteristics. They must be (1) relatively certain, (2) relatively flexible, (3) known or knowable, and (4) apparently reasonable.

As society changes, laws also change. Laws are constantly being added, repealed, or amended. Such changes can be seen, for example, in laws that define obscenity, civil rights, and the responsibilities of businesses to society.

Sources of law

There are two primary sources of law. **Common law is based on previous decisions made by judges.** It is often called the unwritten law because it stems from custom and past court rulings. American common law can be traced to England. It was brought to this country by the early settlers.

Statutory law, on the other hand, is all written laws passed by local, state, or federal legislative bodies. Statutory law includes state and federal constitutions and even treaties.

Chapter 3 Business and the law

Figure 3.1 Requisites of a properly functioning legal system

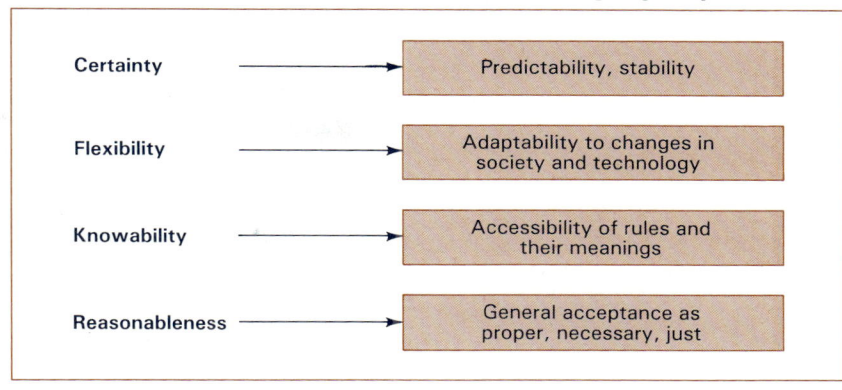

An example of important statutory law that affects business is the *Uniform Commercial Code* (UCC). The UCC was developed to ease interstate trade by ensuring that trade laws would be the same from state to state. The UCC consists of ten articles, or chapters, that relate to bank deposits and collections, letters of credit, sales, commercial paper, and secured transactions.

The court system

Because laws apply to human conduct and human conduct can vary greatly, legal controversies may arise. In such cases, people turn to the court system to settle their disagreements.

Figure 3.2 illustrates the state and federal court systems. Not all states have state courts of appeal. In addition, cities or counties usually have courts that are below the state general trial courts.

Figure 3.2 Court system structure

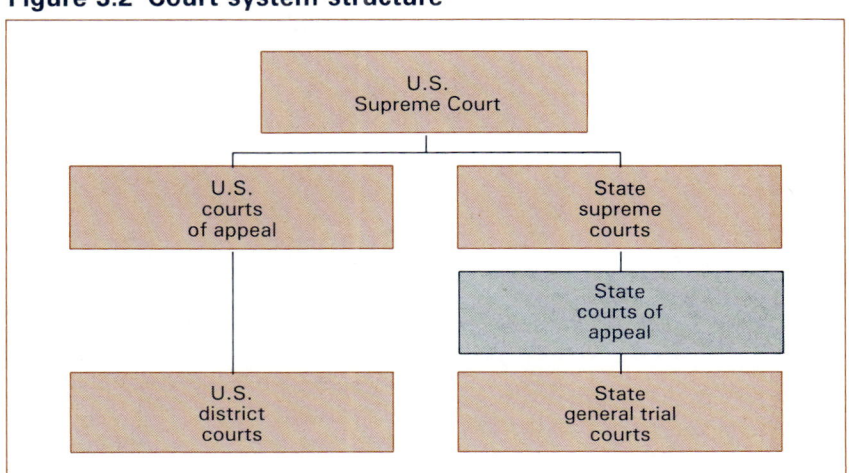

Justice is not well served by simple conformity.

"Well, heck! If all you smart cookies agree, who am I to dissent?"

Drawing by Handelsman; © 1972 The New Yorker Magazine, Inc.

Trial courts, shown in the lowest box in each system, are where most business-related cases are handled. In some states, these courts are called district courts or common pleas courts. Trial courts also handle criminal cases, but most trials involve civil disputes such as disagreements over contracts.

Appellate courts exist in both federal and state court systems. An appellate court may review a decision made by a lower court when a party to the case believes that the decision was incorrect. If the appellate court finds that the lower court (trial court) made an incorrect decision, the decision of the appellate court holds.

At the state level, a further appeal may be made to the state supreme court, whose decision is final in matters relating to *state law.* At the federal level, a further appeal may be made to the U.S. Supreme Court. The U.S. Supreme Court, however, decides which cases it feels are important to consider. It typically selects only about 5 percent of all appeals it receives.

Business contract

A contract is an agreement between two or more parties regarding specific activities that a court will enforce. Many important personal business activities involve contracts. These include rental leases, installment loans, and insurance policies. Many business executives and all professional athletes and entertainers have contracts that describe their terms of employment. Labor unions have contracts with employers.

Choosing an attorney; How small business selects a law firm

Top 10 factors	Percent of respondents
1. Personal contact with members of firm	54%
2. Reputation	40
3. Prior relationship with firm	26
4. Recommended by other clients	15
5. Recommended by banker or accountant	14
6. Location	13
7. Range of services	13
8. Industry expertise	12
9. Fee	3
10. Small business's parent company	2

Reprinted with permission, INC., June 1982. Copyright © 1982 by INC. Publishing Company, 38 Commercial Wharf, Boston, MA 02110.

Elements of a contract

Most business contracts are in writing and contain many pages of legal terms and conditions. However, a contract may also be made orally, or even without any words being spoken. Consider, for example, a coffee-vending machine. The machine offers users an implied contract. It says that if you put in the specified amount of money, you will get a cup of coffee.

There are four elements of a valid contract.

1. Agreement between the parties There must be a valid and voluntary offer and acceptance between the parties to a contract. If a buyer offers to pay $3000 for a car, the seller must accept the price of $3000 in order for them to have a valid contract. If the buyer and seller can't agree on price, they cannot make a contract.

2. Consideration exchanged between the parties Consideration is something of value that is exchanged between the parties to a contract. Consideration may take many forms. It may be money, goods, or services. To have a valid contract, each party must receive something of value. There can be no real contract if one person gives up something without getting anything in return.

3. Capacity of the parties Capacity refers to a person's legal ability, or competence, to enter into a contract. A contract is not valid unless all parties are legally able to make contracts. Among those not competent to make contracts are minors and people who are legally insane.

4. Legality of purpose To be enforceable, a contract must not involve an illegal act. For example, an agreement to loan money at rates higher than permitted by law would be an illegal and unenforceable contract. A contract for delivery of illegal drugs would be similarly invalid.

In addition, most business contracts are in writing. The greater the value of a transaction, the more likely it is to be contained in a written contract. Oral contracts are more difficult to enforce in court.

Remedies for a broken contract

A contract is broken, or *breached,* when one of the parties fails to fulfill the contract's terms. In that case, the wronged party has four possible remedies.

1. Damages If a contract is broken, the wronged party may ask the court to force the other party to pay for damages. For example, suppose that Breachco made a contract to deliver $50,000 worth of wire to Springco by June 1. But Breachco failed to deliver the wire. As a result, Springco had to buy the wire elsewhere for $72,000. Springco might sue Breachco in court for breach of contract. Springco would ask for $22,000 (the additional cost of the wire) plus any other damages that resulted from the broken contract.

2. Specific performance The wronged party might also seek to have the contract carried out as originally agreed. This remedy is usually used when special or unique goods are involved. For example, if an individual contracted to sell a piece of land and later refused to sell it, a court may order that the contract be fulfilled as originally agreed. The purchaser may argue that no other piece of land can replace the land mentioned in the contract.

3. Injunction An injunction is a court order that prohibits a certain activity from taking place. For example, in 1979, the coach of the New England Patriots football team was contacted by the University of Colorado. The university wanted to hire the coach, even though his Patriots contract had four more years to run. In response, the Patriots organization got a court injunction that prohibited the university from further efforts to hire the coach. (Eventually, all parties reached an agreement and the coach was released from his contract.)

4. Recission Recission results when a court rules to cancel, or rescind, a contract. While recission may be agreed on by both parties to a contract, it typically occurs when one party has been wronged. A common cause for recission is the discovery that one party misled the other or misrepresented the facts at the time the contact was made.

A crackerjack kid

The clerk in the Noblesville, Indiana, small claims court was rather startled when Wendy Potasnik, 9, stood on tiptoe before his desk to file suit against Borden, Inc., the huge food and chemical-products company based in Columbus, Ohio. It seems that Wendy got to the bottom of a box of Cracker Jack one day and found no free toy, as advertised. Recalls her mother: "She was so sad-faced." Wendy wrote to Borden to complain, but received no response. So she and her father composed a complaint asking the court for a replacement box of Cracker Jack and $19 to cover court costs. Says Wendy in her suit: "I feel since I bought their product because of their claim, they broke a contract with me." Borden officials pleaded for a little understanding, pointing out that since 1912 they have packed some 16 billion little prizes in those boxes; they sent Wendy a letter of apology and a coupon good for one free box of Cracker Jack. But Wendy was unmoved. Says she: "I hope next time they'll have toys in the Cracker Jack." Says her father: "It was just meant to be a nice, educational experience for her." Not to mention for Borden.

Time, August 23, 1982, p. 15. Copyright 1982 Time Inc. All rights reserved. Reprinted by permission from TIME.

Agency law

Agency relationships are very common. When you buy something in a store or wait on tables in a restaurant, you participate in an agency relationship.

Agency exists when one party—the principal—authorizes another person—the agent—to represent the principal in business transactions. Agency is important in the business world because most transactions are handled by agents. The principal gives the agent the authority to enter into contractual relationships. From then on, the agent's actions bind the principal. Among the most commonly encountered agents are bank tellers (agents of the bank in dealing with customers), stockbrokers (agents of the various companies whose stock is traded), and salesclerks (agents of the store that employs them).

A *power of attorney* is a formal written authorization given by a principal to an agent. In many agency relationships, however, there is no written agreement. For example, a salesperson usually does not have a written agreement with a retail store. Instead, it is implied that the salesperson has the authority to make sales.

Whether the principal and the agent have a written agreement or not, any contract made by the agent on behalf of the principal is binding on the principal. If an agent acts illegally or wrongfully outside of the principal's delegated authority, the agent is liable to the principal for any damages.

The law of tort

A tort is an act that injures another person or another person's property. An intentional tort may include fraud, slander, libel, trespass, assault and battery, and embezzlement. An unintentional tort may result from careless or negligent behavior.

If an employee acting within the terms of his employment is negligent, both the employee and his company may be sued. For instance, if the people delivering your new TV set scratch your floor while placing the set in your living room, the delivery people and their employer may be legally bound to repair the floor. Such small adjustments are usually handled informally. But sometimes the wronged party may bring the matter to court.

Product liability

Under tort law, increasing attention has been given to manufacturers' responsibilities to the users of their products. Traditionally, a manufacturer could be held responsible for any negligence related to manufacturing and product design. Recently, however, courts have begun to judge a manufacturer's responsibility based on the strict liability theory. Under this theory, a manufacturer may be held liable for product defects, even without proof of negligence. A person injured by a product need simply show that (1) the product was defective, (2) the defect was the cause of injury, and (3) the defect caused the product to be unreasonably dangerous.

Property law

Property is any item that can be owned. Property ownership, especially ownership of the factors of production, is an essential part of our American economic system. There are two types of property—real and personal. Real property is land, buildings, and other structures permanently attached to land. Ownership of real property is granted through a deed. A deed is a written document that represents ownership rights in real property.

Personal property is any item other than real property that can be owned. Goods and services are considered personal property. This includes such items as stocks, bonds, checks, promissory notes, television sets, automobiles, and jewelry.

Title is legal ownership of property and the right to use the property. Title can take the form of a document that serves as proof of ownership. The ownership of most real property is proven by a title document, as in the ownership of an automobile.

Commercial paper

Commercial paper is a form of personal property that is especially important in business. **Commercial paper is a written promise to pay a specified sum of money.** Commercial paper includes checks, money orders, drafts, and promissory notes. Commercial paper such as checks and drafts are substitutes for U.S. currency. Promissory notes are used for credit purposes.

In order for commercial paper to be negotiable, or transferable, to other people, it must satisfy certain requirements. According to Article 3 of the Uniform Commercial Code, it must (1) be signed by the maker or drawer, (2) contain an unconditional promise or order to pay a specific sum of money, (3) be payable on demand or at a definite time, and (4) be payable to order or to the bearer.

Endorsement

In order to be exchanged for cash, commercial paper must be endorsed. **An endorsement is the signature of the person to be paid, usually written on the back of a negotiable instrument.** An endorsement, as shown here, also sets the limits of liability for the endorser.

Blank endorsement. A blank endorsement is the most common form of endorsement. It makes no specific restrictions on the use of the check. The person to be paid merely signs his or her name on the back of the check. Then the check is payable to anyone who holds it. A blank endorsement should be made only at the time a check is cashed.

Blank endorsement

Restrictive endorsement. A restrictive endorsement limits the purpose for which a check can be used. A common restrictive endorsement is "For Deposit Only."

Restrictive endorsement

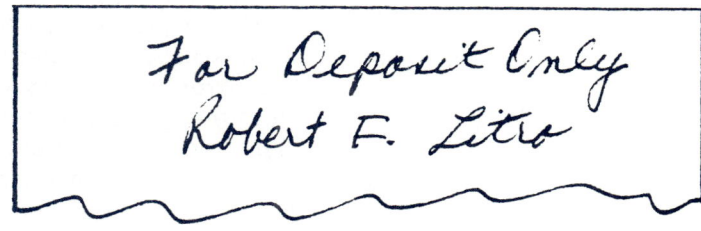

Special endorsement

Special endorsement. A special endorsement identifies a specific party to whom the instrument is payable. A typical special endorsement is "Pay to the Order of."

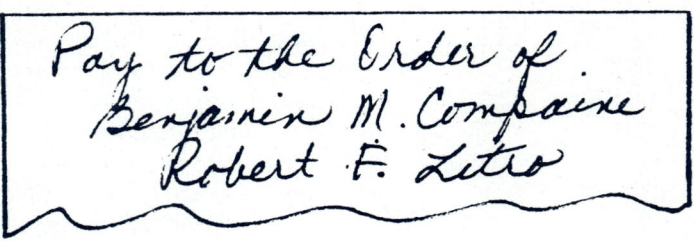

Qualified endorsement. A qualified endorsement indicates that the endorser does not guarantee payment of the check if the checking account of the original maker contains insufficient funds. The wording used in this case is "Without Recourse."

Qualified endorsement

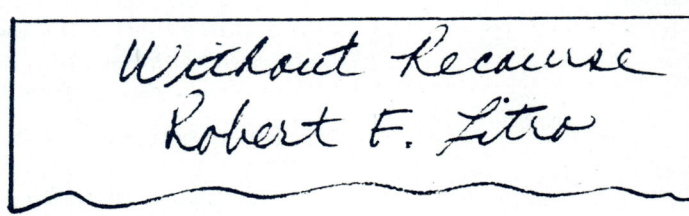

Bankruptcy law

Many business transactions are conducted on credit. The seller expects to be paid in the future. In such cases, the seller becomes the creditor, and the buyer is the debtor.

Secured credit arrangements require that the buyer transfer something of value to the seller before the transaction takes place. The creditor can then sell the buyer's property if the buyer becomes unable or unwilling to repay the debt. An automobile loan is secured credit: the automobile is security for the bank if the borrower fails to repay the loan.

Unsecured credit is credit based solely on the reputation of the buyer. The buyer provides no security for the debt, so the creditor may be unable to collect anything if the debtor fails to pay the money owed.

Bankruptcy is a legal process in which debtors who are unable to meet their financial obligations have their assets divided among their creditors. In return, the debtors are released from their financial responsibilities. Bankruptcy proceedings are usually a last resort for settling financial obligations between creditors and debtors.

Chapter 3 Business and the law

According to the U.S. Constitution, Congress has the power to establish uniform bankruptcy laws for the whole country. The most recent congressional revision of these laws is the Bankruptcy Reform Act of 1978. This legislation attempt to ensure that creditors will be fairly treated and that debtors will have the opportunity for a fresh start.

Bankruptcy can be either voluntary or involuntary. Voluntary bankruptcy proceedings are started by the debtor. This usually occurs when a debtor has more liabilities than assets. Involuntary bankruptcy proceedings are started by creditors in an attempt to receive payment from a debtor.

In a liquidation proceeding, a debtor's assets are sold and the proceeds divided among the creditors. If a bankruptcy court believes that a bankrupt party can eventually pay off all debts, the court can appoint a trustee to reorganize the firm's business to try to make it profitable again. In the meantime, the court protects the business from creditors' demands. The Penn Central railroad operated under such an arrangement during the 1970s.

Business ethics

Ethics are principles that state what people ought to do. Ethics deal with what is good and bad, with moral obligation and duty. Business ethics are standards of conduct for institutions and individuals in the business world.

Business ethics apply to traditional business goals such as profit making, economic growth, and technical advancement only in terms of how these goals relate to the good of society. For example, business ethics do not concern corporate profits as such. But ethics do apply to how profit-seeking behavior might result in increased investor satisfaction, higher levels of employment, and improved working conditions.

The scope of business ethics

Most criticism of business practices is based on the extent to which modern business benefits society. For example, people who criticize corporations for polluting the environment are evaluating business on ethical grounds. They believe that polluters neglect the public good.

On the other hand, businesses are praised for achieving high levels of efficiency and satisfying consumer needs. Efficiency and consumer satisfaction are positive contributions to society.

Business ethics cover any business issue that relates to human values. These include the following:
1. advertising practices
2. product safety
3. monopolistic price schemes
4. treatment of workers
5. effects of pollution

6. payments to foreign governments or agents in exchange for contracts
7. pursuit of profits
8. proper roles of shareholders, management, government, and the public in determining corporate policy
9. discriminatory hiring or promotion practices
10. limits of private ownership.

Questions of ethics

1. As an employee of a large corporation, you find that certain aircraft parts are defective but are being shipped anyway. Would you inform the local newspaper of the story even if it meant the probable loss of your job?
2. You are employed by an advertising agency and know that one of the ads you are working on contains misleading information. Would you request a change in the advertisement?
3. You are the purchasing agent for your firm. One of your suppliers sends a color television set to your home as a Christmas gift. Company policy prohibits the acceptance of gifts worth more than $25. Would you return the television?
4. A fire inspector finds some minor fire-code violations at your store. Fixing them would be costly. He offers to "forget" the violations in return for a cash "contribution" that he will give to the firemen's benevolent fund. Would you make the contribution?

Extremely unethical business practices are usually illegal.

"My client now realizes that crime doesn't pay, your honor, so he would like to file for bankruptcy. . . ."

From the *Wall Street Journal,* Permission—Cartoon Features Syndicate

Levels of unethical behavior

Boundaries between levels of ethical business practices often are not clear. Unethical behavior can be divided into four levels.

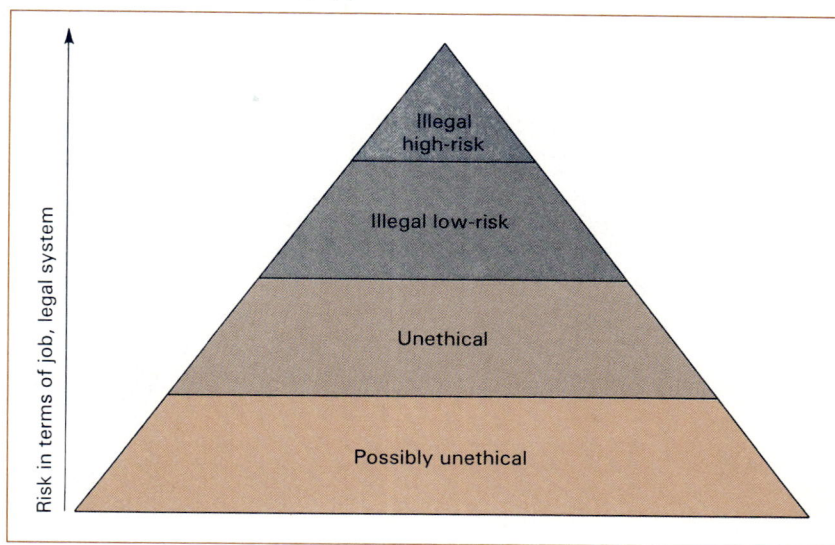

"A Model of Ethical Business Practices," *Collegiate News & Views,* Winter 1981–1982, pp. 11–13.

Possibly unethical behavior is certainly not illegal, and many would not even consider it unethical. Nonetheless, it should be approached with caution. Possibly unethical behavior includes using a fictitious company name in order to disguise the true identity of a research study's sponsor and promoting one's own brand as special because it contains super-ingredient X when in reality competing brands contain the same ingredient.

Unethical behavior includes acts that are clearly unacceptable but have not been declared illegal by the government. Deceptive research tactics and the use of two-way mirrors in fitting rooms to guard against shoplifting are unethical.

Illegal, low-risk activities include tax evasion, kickbacks, bribes, and applying for undeserved government support or subsidies. This type of behavior is often excused with such statements as, "Technically, it's illegal, but everybody does it."

Illegal, high-risk behavior is the lowest level. It is behavior that most businesspeople shun. Price fixing, embezzlement, and fraud are illegal, high-risk activities.

Federal regulation of business

In general, the federal government prefers not to interfere in the nation's business activities. Sometimes, however, it must take steps to ensure that business competition remains free and open. Federal regulations pertaining to mergers, monopolistic agreements, and price fixing attempt to encourage competition in the marketplace.

Important government regulations

The first important federal law regulating business practices was the Interstate Commerce Act, passed in 1887. This act established the Interstate Commerce Commission (ICC). It sought to regulate interstate shipping and transportation rates, primarily for railroads. Today, ICC jurisdiction includes truck and bus rates as well. In recent years, the ICC has been gradually reducing its regulatory role.

The Sherman Antitrust Act (1890) encourages competition by declaring illegal any contract or combination that tends to promote monopoly.

The Clayton Act (1914) expanded on the Sherman Act by declaring tying contracts and interlocking directorates illegal. Tying contracts force buyers to purchase goods they do not want as a condition for purchasing goods they do want. An interlocking directorate occurs when an individual serves on the board of directors of more than one company in the same industry.

The Robinson-Patman Act (1936) amended portions of the Clayton Act to prohibit price discrimination and price concessions. As a result, any discounts given to one purchaser must also be given to all other purchasers of a similar quantity of goods.

The Celler-Kefauver Antimerger Act (1950) further amended the Clayton Act. The Clayton act made anticompetitive mergers using purchase of stock illegal. The Celler-Kefauver Antimerger Act also made illegal any anticompetitive mergers using other means, especially purchase of the company's assets.

The Federal Trade Commission Act (1914) was passed to accompany the Clayton Act. It provided for the establishment of the Federal Trade Commission (FTC) to enforce statutes relating to business operations. The act gave broad authority to the FTC to deal with unfair methods of competition and unfair or deceptive business activities.

The Wheeler-Lea Act (1938) expanded the Clayton Act to include actions that adversely affect the public at large. This includes false or misleading advertising of drugs, cosmetics, and foods.

The need for consumer protection has also received substantial attention from lawmakers. Table 3.1 shows the variety of statutes that protect consumers today.

Table 3.1 Current consumer protection statutes

Popular name	Purpose
Child Protection Act	Requires special labeling and childproof devices
Public Health Cigarette Smoking Act	Warns of possible health hazard
Consumer Credit Protection Act	Provides comprehensive protection in all phases of credit transactions
Consumer Product Safety Act	Protects consumer against defective or dangerous products
Equal Credit Opportunity Act	Prohibits discrimination in extending credit
Fair Debt Collection Practices Act	Prohibits abuses by debt collectors
Fair Credit Reporting Act	Protects consumer's credit reputation
Fair Packaging and Labeling Act	Requires accurate name, weights, quantities
Federal Trade Commission Act	Prohibits unfair or deceptive trade practices
Flammable Fabrics Act	Eliminates or controls manufacture and marketing of dangerous fabrics
Food, Drug, and Cosmetic Act	Prohibits marketing of impure, adulterated products
Fur Products Labeling Act	Prohibits misbranding of fur products
Magnuson-Moss Warranty Act	Establishes rules governing content of warranties
National Traffic and Motor Vehicle Safety Act	Promotes traffic and auto safety
Real Estate Settlement Procedures Act	Requires disclosure of home-buying costs
Truth in Lending Laws	Requires complete disclosure of credit terms

Table 3.1 Current consumer protection statutes (*continued*)

Uniform Consumer Credit Code	Establishes rules similar to federal Truth in Lending Laws
Uniform Commercial Code	Establishes law of sales—unconscionable contracts
Wholesome Meat Act	Controls meat processing
Wholesome Poultry Products Act	Controls processing of poultry and poultry products
Wool Products Labeling Act	Requires accurate labeling of wool products

FTC approves Georgia-Pacific's purchase of corrugated-container plants from Johns-Manville Corporation

The Federal Trade Commission announced it has approved Georgia-Pacific Corporation's proposed acquisition of eight corrugated-container plants from Johns-Manville Corporation.

FTC approval of the acquisition was required under the terms of a consent order with Georgia-Pacific that was signed in 1972 and modified in 1978. That order followed the firm's purchase of 16 companies in the 1960s and required FTC approval before Georgia-Pacific could acquire assets of other firms making softwood plywood. Manville Forest (a wholly-owned subsidiary of Johns-Manville) has two such facilities.

Georgia-Pacific, with headquarters in Portland, Oregon, manufactures and distributes forest products and chemicals. It operates 11 corrugated-container facilities located throughout the country. Johns-Manville, based in Denver, has diversified manufacturing and mining operations, including production of fiberglass products, insulation, pipe, and roofing materials.

Source: *FTC News Summary,* vol. 9-82, November 27, 1981.

3 Business and the law

Summary

Laws are necessary in society to prevent chaos. It would be difficult, if not impossible, for businesses to operate if contracts were not honored or if bribery, fraud, and cheating were widespread.

Laws are directly related to human activity and reflect changing social and political attitudes. *Law* is the set of enforceable rules that governs the relationship of individuals and institutions to each other and to an organized society.

For a legal system to be respected by most of society, laws must be (1) relatively certain, (2) relatively flexible, (3) known or knowable, and (4) apparently reasonable.

The two major sources of the law are *common law,* which is based on previous judicial decisions, and *statutory law,* which is based on laws passed by local, state, or federal legislative bodies, state and federal constitutions, and treaties. An important statutory law for business is the Uniform Commercial Code (UCC). It ensures that trade laws are the same from state to state.

The court system provides a means for settling disputes about the law. There are state courts and federal courts, each with similar structures.

Contracts are essential for business. A *contract* is an agreement between two or more parties regarding specific activities that a court will enforce. It must include (1) an agreement between the parties, (2) an exchange of consideration, (3) legally competent parties, and (4) legality of purpose. If a contract is broken, the wronged party has four remedies: (1) damages, (2) specific performance, (3) *injunction* (a court order that prohibits a certain activity from taking place), and (4) *recission* (court action rescinding the contract).

Agency exists when one party—the *principal*—authorizes another person—the *agent*—to represent the principal in business transactions. Most business activities are handled by agents.

A *tort* is an act that injures another person or another person's property. An intentional tort may include fraud, slander, libel, trespass, assault and battery, or embezzlement. An unintentional tort results from negligent behavior.

Property is any item that can be owned. *Real property* is land, buildings, and other structures permanently attached to land. A *deed* is a document that represents ownership rights in real property. *Personal property* is any item other than real property that can be owned. *Title* is legal ownership of property and the right to use property.

Commercial paper is a written promise to pay a specified sum of money. Checks, money orders, drafts, and promissory notes are forms of commercial paper. An *endorsement* is the signature of the person to be paid, usually written on the back of negotiable documents. It is required for transferring commercial paper from one party to another. There are four types of check endorsements: (1) blank, (2) restrictive, (3) special, and (4) qualified.

Bankruptcy is a legal process in which a debtor's assets are divided among the debtor's creditors to release the debtor from his or her debts.

Ethics are principles that state what people ought to do. Ethics deal with good and bad, moral obligation and duty. Business ethics are standards of conduct for institutions and individuals in the business world.

Government regulation of business focuses on promoting and maintaining competition. Important federal legislation includes the Interstate Commerce Act (1887) and the Sherman Act (1890). The Clayton Act (1914) and its amendments promote competition and ban restraint of trade and unfair competition. Other legislation deals with specific aspects of business and economic life. The Federal Trade Commission (FTC) is charged with enforcing many of these laws.

Review questions

1. What is the difference between the traditional and environmental approaches to law?
2. Identify the two major sources of law.
3. Why is an understanding of law important for businesspeople?
4. Briefly describe the structure of the U.S. court system.
5. What is a contract? Explain the four elements of a valid contract.
6. What remedies are available to a wronged party in a broken contract?
7. Describe the law of agency.
8. What is a tort?
9. Explain the difference between real and personal property.
10. What is commercial paper? What elements make commercial paper a negotiable instrument?
11. Briefly explain the four kinds of check endorsements.
12. Why are bankruptcy laws important?
13. What are ethics? How do ethics apply to business activities?
14. How do government regulations affect business operations?

Discussion questions

1. Evaluate the degree of responsibility Jeep Corporation had to attach warning stickers to Jeep CJ models. Do you believe they would have done this without FTC action?
2. In what ways do government antitrust laws seek to promote competition among businesses? Do government regulations promote the public interest? Can government regulations have a negative effect?

3. If your competitors give money to suppliers in return for favors, should you follow suit to survive?
4. What place do ethics have in business decision making?
5. Why did the constitutional amendment outlawing alcoholic beverages eventually have to be repealed?

Chapter 3 case

The artificial sweeteners case

This case asks you to weigh uncertain evidence to arrive at an ethically correct decision.

The potential for cyclamates as artificial sweeteners was discovered in the 1940s. By the 1950s, cyclamates were commonly sold to diabetics who needed to limit their intake of sugar. Since cyclamates did not leave a bitter aftertaste, as did saccharin, they became the preferred sweetener. During the 1960s, producers capitalized on the public's calorie-consciousness to introduce many foods containing cyclamates for weight control. Moreover, since cyclamates were far less expensive than sugar, it was cheaper to substitute cyclamates for sugar. Nearly all Americans ate some foods with cyclamates.

Gradually, the safety of cyclamates came under question. The first doubts were raised as early as 1955. By 1962, the National Academy of Sciences–National Research Council (NAS–NRC) recommended that cyclamates be used only in special dietary food, and by 1968, NAS–NRC said that the unrestricted use of cyclamates was not warranted. By 1969, there was evidence that rats that ate large amounts of cyclamates developed bladder cancer. Under the terms of the Delaney Clause of the Food Additives Amendment to the Federal Food, Drug, and Cosmetic Act, cyclamates were banned from general use. The Delaney Clause stipulates that "no additive shall be deemed to be safe if it is found to induce cancer in man or animal." At first the ban was only partial, but legal proceedings forced a complete ban on August 14, 1970.

After cyclamates were banned, the only available artificial sweetener was saccharin. However, as the 1970s progressed, similar doubts were raised about its safety. A Canadian study tipped the scales, and in the summer of 1977, the FDA announced plans to ban saccharin. If the FDA program had gone into effect, almost all dietetic products would have been removed from the market.

The public strongly objected. Some people challenged the adequacy of the tests on which the FDA had relied. Others, including many physicians, argued that the health risks associated with obesity far outweighed the risk of contracting cancer. If these people were correct, on a cost/benefit basis it would be better to permit products containing artificial sweeteners on the market. As a result of the public outcry, products containing saccharin continue to be sold.

1. Is the public interest served by allowing cyclamates to be commonly used?

2. Should cyclamates be produced at all? Under what circumstances should they be made available to the public?

3. Are cyclamate manufacturers meeting their responsibility to the public? Are the standards of the Delaney Amendment too strict in this case?

4. Identify and compare the trade-offs between using artificial sweeteners and banning them completely.

5. Who is responsible for the safety of cyclamates?

Source: Tom L. Beauchamp and Norman E. Bowie, *Ethical Theory and Business* (Englewood Cliffs, N.J.: Prentice-Hall, 1979), pp. 375–376.

Careers in business

In today's complex and changing society, the number of available careers is rapidly increasing. As a result, making sound career decisions has become more challenging.

Business: An Introduction introduces its readers to a variety of business careers. Each part of the text is followed by a career exploration section that examines related career possibilities.

Steps in choosing a career

Developing career-exploration skills is a lifelong process that requires more than occupational training. Work is a means of self-expression and self-fulfillment.

Career exploration involves five steps:

1. Self-awareness Evaluate and become better acquainted with yourself—your interests, values, likes, dislikes, and abilities.

Careers Figure I.1 Career-exploration process

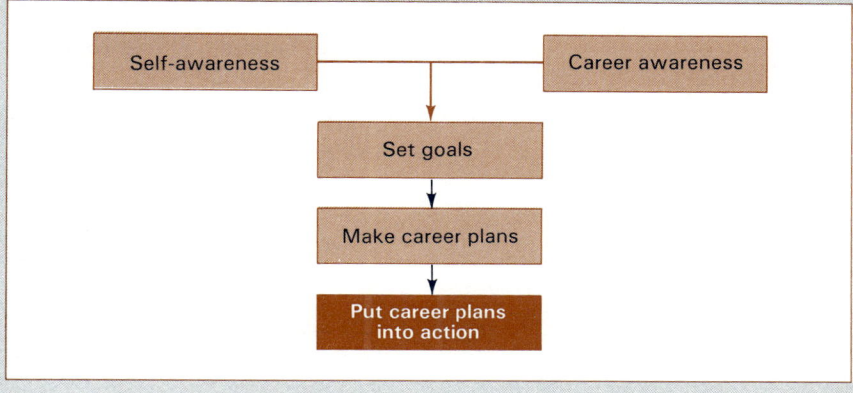

Careers Figure I.2 America's fading blue collar

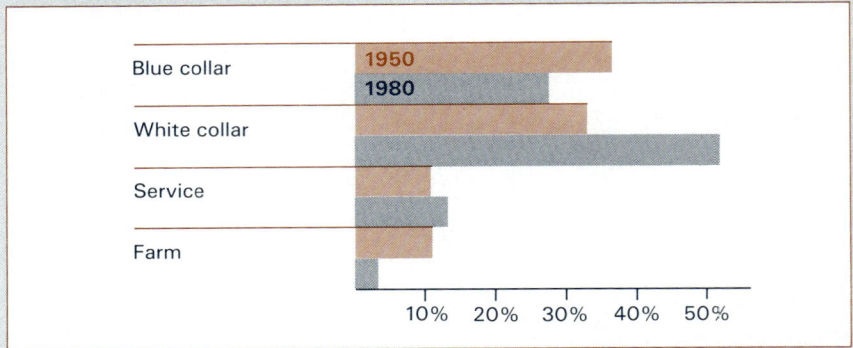

Adapted from *U.S. News & World Report,* Sept. 13, 1982, p. 54. Copyright 1982, U.S. News & World Report, Inc.

2. Career awareness Explore different occupations. Learn how to obtain accurate information about careers and evaluate how this information fits your personality and talents.

3. Goal-setting Based on increased knowledge of yourself and key occupational characteristics, choose the job areas you intend to pursue.

4. Career planning Having developed specific goals and directions, plan how you will progress from where you are now to where you want to be.

5. Career path decisions Put all four previous steps together to pursue a specific long-term goal. Self-awareness must remain first and foremost.

Work won't be the same again

The United States is well launched on the voyage from the industrial age into the information age. What happens in the next decade or two will perhaps change the way Americans work as much as the Industrial Revolution did in the last century.

Careers Figure I.3 The decline in blue-collar employment

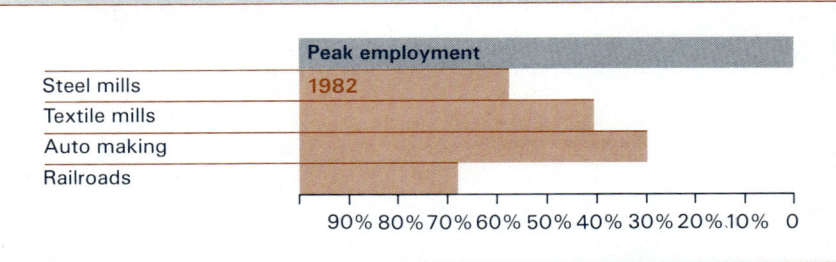

Adapted from *U.S. News & World Report,* Sept. 13, 1982, p. 55. Copyright 1982, U.S. News & World Report, Inc.

Millions of new jobs will be created, mostly in information systems, but they'll be so different that today's laid-off workers will be hard pressed to fill them. The net outcome will be more jobs, probably better jobs at better pay; but getting there is going to be painful for many Americans.

U.S. businesses have, of course, been working with computers and robots for years. Banks have long had automated check processing, for instance, and many plants use computer-controlled robot welders. But these are stand-alone systems that have taken over single functions, and their impact has been "very modest," according to Professor Wickham Skinner of the Harvard Business School.

Now companies are moving to integrated office and factory systems with hierarchies of computers and robots. The number of robots will grow from a few thousand today to an estimated 100,000 by 1990, and the number of electronic work stations from 4 million to as many as 30 million.

Jeremy Main, "Work Won't Be the Same Again," FORTUNE, June 28, 1982, pp. 58–61.

Women on the move

In one of the most significant trends of the 1980s, women are steadily toppling barriers and assuming leadership in fields that traditionally have been closed to them.

The process is slow, difficult, and often unnoticed. While the numbers are still small, the attitude changes they signal are enormous.

A decade ago, the nation's space program allowed no women as astronauts. Now it has eight.

Ten years ago, even the largest U.S. banks could count on one finger the number of female vice-presidents. Now some giant banks have more than 100 women as vice-presidents and one or two as senior vice-presidents.

In 1972, women in companies with 100 or more employees held only one of eight management jobs. Now they occupy one of five. Also, in 1972, just over 300 women sat in state legislatures. The current figure exceeds 900.

Statistics can deceive. A different set of figures, equally valid, shows that women—who comprise 51.3 percent of the U.S. population—still hold only 5 percent of the executive positions in the top 50 top corporations, 10 percent of astronauts, 12 percent of state legislators, and 2 percent of U.S. senators.

However, the momentum can be seen in the legal field. In 1960, only 3.3 percent of lawyers and judges were women. Since then, the figure has jumped four times. Women now make up a third to a half of today's law-school classes.

Numerically, women are still getting off the ground in positions of leadership. But, as the space program shows, they are finding that literally even the sky is no limit.

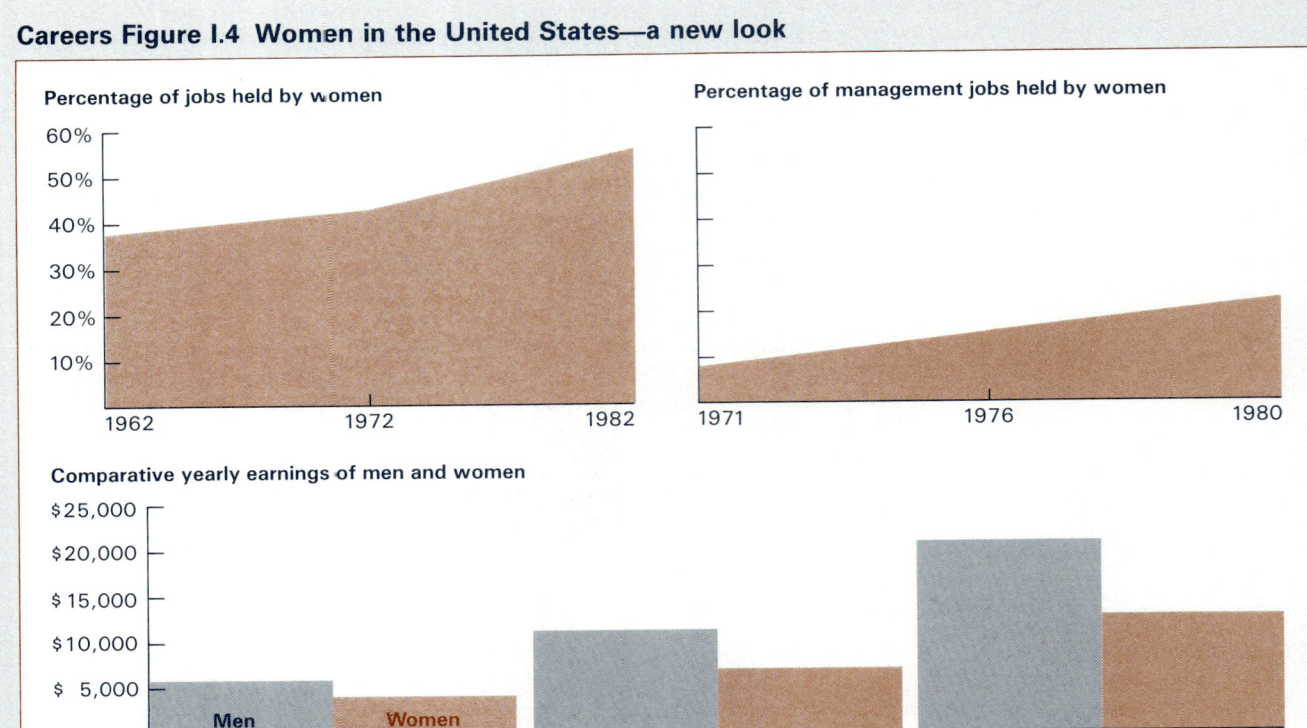

Careers Figure I.4 Women in the United States—a new look

Adapted from *U.S. News & World Report,* Nov. 29, 1982, p. 54. Copyright 1982, U.S. News & World Report, Inc.

Number: more than half of the population

The nation's 119.1 million females comprise 51.3 percent of the total population. Ten years from now, they will number 130.3 million, but their proportion of the total population will be about the same as today. Now, there are 88.4 million women age 18 and up.

Race: 6 of 7 are white

Of all females—
101.6 million, or 85 percent, are whites.
14.6 million, or 12 percent, are blacks.
2.9 million are of other races

Age: older than men on the average

The median age of females is 31.9 years, compared with 29.3 years for males. And females are getting older: in 10 years, their median age will be 34.5 years, and by the year 2000, 36.8 years.

Life span: women live longer than men

The average female lives to a little more than 78 years, or nearly eight years longer than the average male. The gap in life expectancy is widening—it was little more than seven years two decades ago.

Careers Figure I.5 Women in the United States—how their lives are changing.

Education: more likely to attend college

Among persons age 18 to 24, 35 percent of women are enrolled in college, compared with 34 percent of men. At last count, 23.4 percent of graduating medical doctors were women, as were 30.2 percent of lawyers.

Marriage: more women are putting it off

Just over half of the women age 20-24 have never been married, compared with 35.8 percent in 1970 and 28.4 percent in 1960. But 83 percent of women ultimately do marry.

Families: those headed by women rise sharply

More than 1 in 7 families—9.1 million—are headed by women. The number has risen by 65 percent since 1970, largely because of the climbing divorce rate.

Children: women want fewer offspring

Of childless married women age 18-24, 23 percent expect to have one child or none, while 72 percent expect to bear two or three children. Only 5 percent expect four or more. If fulfilled, these plans mean little population growth.

Political power: an edge in numbers at the polls

Women of voting age are 52.2 percent of all Americans age 18 and up. With women living longer than men, the proportion is growing.

Percentage of women employed in sterotyped female jobs	
Secretaries, typists	98.3%
Receptionists	97.3
Bank tellers	93.5
Telephone operators	92.9
Nurses, dietitians, therapists	92.6
Bookkeepers	91.1
Cashiers	86.2
Librarians, archivists, curators	82.8
Health technicians	72.3
Salesclerks	71.2
Teachers (noncollege)	70.6

"Women in the U.S.—A New Look," reprinted from *U.S. News & World Report,* copyright 1982, U.S. News & World Report, Inc. November 29, 1982, p. 50.

2
The human side of business

Business in perspective

Wheeler-dealer's rambling wrecks are good business

Why do stars like Paul Newman, Alan Alda, and Warren Beatty patronize a used-car rental business in West Los Angeles known as Rent-A-Wreck? "They know the cars are dependable," replies owner David Schwartz.

The car-rental business has traditionally been dominated by giants like Hertz and Avis, but Rent-A-Wreck's used cars rent for $19.95 a day in New York City, compared to Hertz's $55 to $60. In Los Angeles, they go for $14.95, compared to $35 to $47 for Hertz, and in other metropolitan areas they're as low as $11.95.

Rent-A-Wreck already has 150 franchises in the United States and abroad, and Schwartz expects that figure to more than triple by 1984. Annual revenues in Los Angeles alone are estimated at $3 million. Applicants for franchises include many new-car dealers "who know a serious business when they see one," Schwartz says. "We're not a mail-order franchise company. Each applicant is closely checked out."

Although the company does rent out new cars, Schwartz is proudest of his fleet of well-maintained Mustangs, VWs, Valiants, Darts, and other models, ranging in age from two to ten years. "Our old cars are very safe," Schwartz insists. "It's the new cars that have the most breakdowns."

Schwartz spent ten years selling used cars before he decided to rent them. He has spent the last several years promoting Rent-A-Wreck on talk shows and in the press. "I hate cars," admits Schwartz, who nevertheless owns several of them. "I just want one that starts and stops, and has clean insides and a good radio."

Reprinted with permission, INC., September 1981. Copyright © 1981 by INC. Publishing Company, 38 Commercial Wharf, Boston, MA 02110.

Chapter 4

Essentials of management

Key terms

management
planning
organizing
directing
leadership
controlling
top management
middle management
supervisory management
decision
problem
managerial skills

Chapter objectives

In Chapter 4, you will learn:

What management is and where it exists

The four functions of management and how they are related

The three basic leadership styles

The three management levels and how they are similar and different

The five steps in the decision-making process

The three kinds of managerial skills

The key personal characteristics of a successful manager

Overview

To produce goods or services, one must combine the four factors of production: land, labor, capital, and entrepreneurial ability. A key resource in this process is people. They are essential because they manage the other resources to accomplish agreed-upon goals and objectives.

This chapter looks at the management process and the role of managers. It briefly discusses the three levels and four major functions of management. The chapter also considers the personal skills managers should possess and presents examples of different management styles.

The nature of management

Managers may be found in any organization in which a group of people seek to accomplish common goals. This is true for professional sports teams, households, college administrations, profit-seeking businesses, and nonprofit organizations.

What is management?

Management is a process through which people seek to meet goals and objectives by efficiently coordinating available resources. A manager must use both human and physical resources. Managers work with and through other people in performing the tasks necessary to achieve common objectives.

Managers use available resources. A family allocates its income in the form of a budget. A baseball team manager decides on the best team batting order. A college president plans a new building program. And the president of General Motors decides whether the company should build its own diesel engines or buy them from a foreign manufacturer.

In smaller businesses, managers can be directly involved in producing goods and services. However, as a business becomes larger, managers often find themselves more and more removed from the actual production process. They begin to spend more time coordinating the use of resources.

And, as a business increases in size, the distance between its owners and the people who run it on a daily basis grows, too. In larger corporations, professional managers take over entrepreneurial activities, such as risk-taking. In smaller businesses, owner-managers retain control of such activities.

Figure 4.1 The four management functions

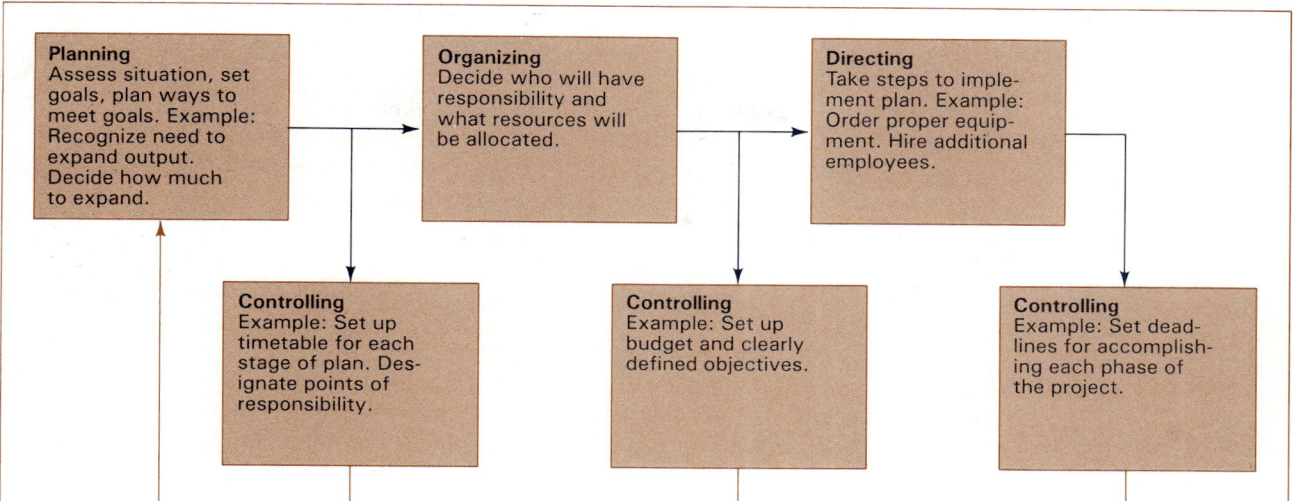

The elements of management

The process a manager uses in achieving goals involves the planning, organizing, directing and controlling of an organization's human and physical resources. Although we will discuss the four functions separately, it is important to view them as a continuous, interrelated process. Controls must be exercised at many points in the management process. Figure 4.1 illustrates the process.

Managers coordinate the four management functions, from the development of plans and organization of resources to the directing and controlling of overall operations. Not all managers are charged with all four functions. But management in general must see that all are ongoing.

The management process seeks answers to the following questions:
1. What will be the goals of the organization, department, or project? What future events might affect these goals? What programs and activities will be necessary? (Planning)
2. How will the organization's human and physical resources be arranged and structured to accomplish the goals? (Organizing)
3. What leadership activities will be necessary to guide the tasks involved in meeting the goals? (Directing)
4. What procedures are necessary to check actual output against the planning goals? Will these procedures lead to corrective action when needed? (Controlling)

Management is very important if an organization is to survive and prosper. Managers must make decisions at each stage of the process.

Planning

Planning seeks to prepare for the future by developing goals, objectives, and priorities in the present. Planning also sets priorities for the use of available resources.

Change is constant in the business world. New technologies may make existing processes obsolete. The government may impose new restrictions or remove old ones. The introduction of new products may threaten the market share of established ones.

Successful managers recognize that future profits and growth are not guaranteed, regardless of current or past performance. Planning helps a business to cope with change in such areas as consumer tastes and demand, increasing resource costs, new competitive products and markets, and government regulations.

Although planning is future-oriented, it must give careful attention to two vital activities. The first is analysis of past and present business activities. The planning process must examine the circumstances and events that brought the organization to its current position. The other activity is the development of clear, realistic goals and objectives.

Knowing the past and present Knowledge about the organization's past and current performance helps managers to plan for the future. Setting realistic goals—goals that are possible to achieve—is important. When goals are set too high, they become impossible to meet. This may result in resource shortages, employee frustration, and business losses. On the other hand, when goals are set too low, resources may be underutilized. This may cause the organization's output and competitive position to decline.

Goals and objectives Establishing organizational goals involves setting priorities for the use of resources. It may include a broad goal—such as increased market share—as well as several supporting objectives that will help accomplish the broad goal.

Examples of broad goals include the following:

- Reach sales of $10 million by 1984.
- Achieve a 3 percent increase in market share.
- Increase profit margins by one-third within two years.

Objectives for reaching some of these goals could be these:

- Look for appropriate companies to acquire.
- Expand product distribution nationwide.
- Replace older, inefficient machinery with new, more productive equipment.

Long-term planning involves goals that will take several years to accomplish. Building a new manufacturing plant, introducing a new product line, or seeking additional capital resources through a new common stock issue requires long-term planning. *Short-term planning* typically applies to a time period no longer than one year. It may involve developing an employee-safety program or devising a new advertising strategy.

Chapter 4 Essentials of management

Since plans are guides to future action, they must be clearly understood by all involved personnel. Ideally, organizational goals should be consistent with the personal goals of managers and other employees. Plans should be flexible enough to be changed, if necessary, and consistent with overall company activities.

Organizing

Organizing is the process of combining and arranging human and material resources in a system of activities that will attain established goals.

Warner-Lambert Company: Strategic planning for the 1980s

> "The successful companies of the 1980s will not necessarily be the biggest, but rather those which make the most effective use of their assets."
>
> Warner-Lambert Company *Annual Report 1980*

Warner-Lambert is a worldwide manufacturer and marketer of health-care and consumer products. Among their most familiar consumer products are Listerine, Efferdent, Rolaids, and Chiclets gum.

The company conducts its business in more than 140 countries, employs approximately 56,000 people, operates more than 140 manufacturing facilities, and maintains three major research centers.

During 1979 and 1980, management in every major unit of the company's worldwide business participated in the planning process. They reviewed all phases of business: marketing, production, distribution, research and development, and organizational structure.

Company goal

The firm established a long-term goal of significantly improving its earnings and financial strength by 1982 and the years beyond.

Master corporate growth plan

The master corporate growth plan has three major goals:
1. To significantly strengthen the company's existing basic business in pharmaceuticals and consumer products.
2. To identify and pursue emerging high-technology health-care markets.
3. To remove Warner-Lambert from those businesses that do not meet the company's criteria for profitability and growth, thus providing additional resources to achieve other objectives.

Figure 4.2 shows Warner-Lambert's summary of the objectives of its strategic plan, its recent strategic actions to achieve objectives, and the potential benefits of its actions.

Warner-Lambert Company, Inc., Morris Plains, New Jersey, *Annual Report 1980*.

Figure 4.2 Warner-Lambert's strategic plan

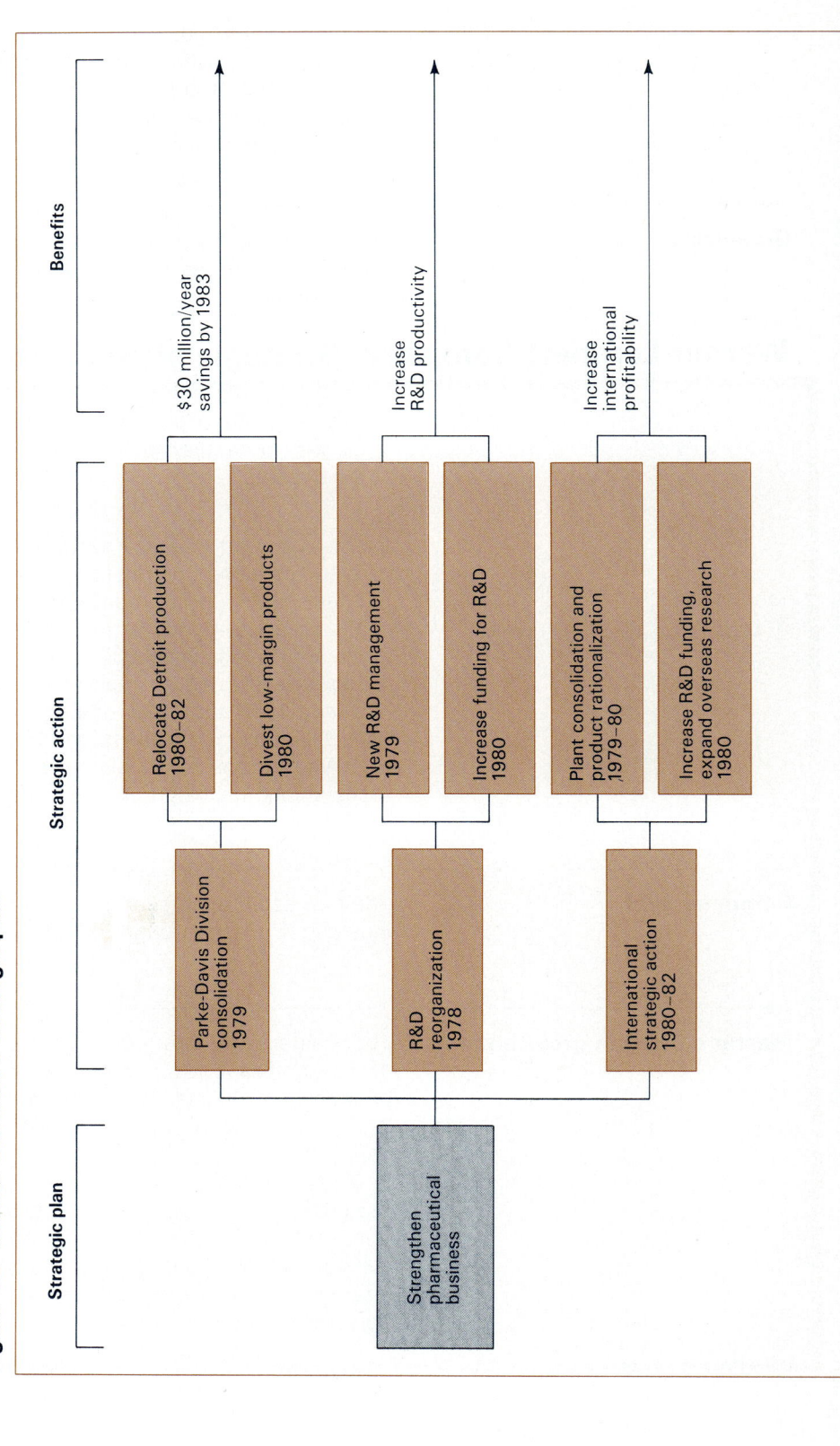

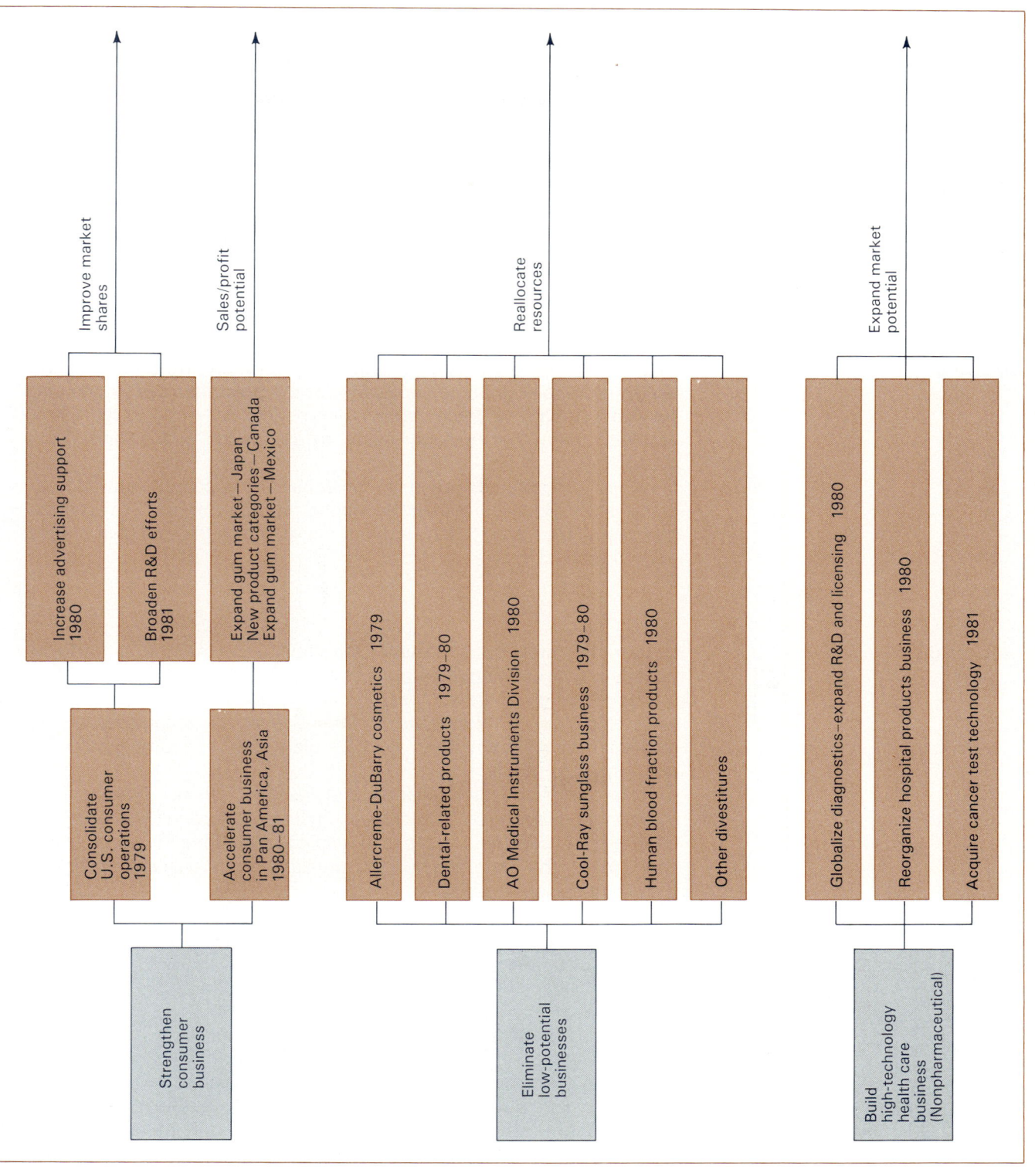

To convert goals into a workable system, managers must (1) determine the specialized tasks and functions necessary to meet their goals, (2) arrange the necessary tasks into a logical sequence of activities, and (3) assign authority to subordinates so that they can carry out their responsibilities.

If the planning process was not thorough, and if goals are not clear, it may be difficult to decide how to organize resources. (Chapter 5 discusses organizational aspects in greater detail.)

Once the planning process has provided organizational goals and objectives and company resources have been organized to achieve the plans, the directing function becomes critical.

Directing

Directing is the process of coordinating and guiding people in the tasks and responsibilities necessary for the production of goods and services. It requires direct contact with people, for it is through them, and with them, that managers seek to accomplish the organization's objectives.

Managers must understand human behavior and possess strong leadership skills. Because managers depend on others to perform specialized tasks, they must create a work environment that enables people to do their best work.

Leadership styles

Leadership refers to a manager's ability to get people to perform well by creating an environment that inspires them to achieve. Managers may be given the authority to manage people, but they also need leadership qualities to motivate workers. The leadership process occurs within an environment that has three elements: a leader, a follower, and a specific situation.

There are three broad leadership styles that reflect individual management personalities: (1) autocratic, (2) democratic, and (3) laissez-faire (free-rein). A manager's success in leading often depends on the manager's leadership style, the specific situation, and the characteristics of the group being managed.

Autocratic leaders make decisions and issue orders. They rely on the authority of their position. They give little, if any, consideration to the opinions of their subordinates.

Democratic leaders place emphasis on communication with subordinates. They seek their subordinates' input when they make decisions. As a result, they may take longer to make a decision than an autocratic manager would. But their decisions are more likely to reflect the feelings of the group. Because of this, their subordinates may be more able to work on their own, without close supervision and control.

Laissez-faire (free-rein) leaders permit the group to make most of its own decisions. Such leaders exercise little supervisory control. They may present a business problem and then give the group responsibility for making a decision. One difficulty with this style is that group agreement is often difficult to obtain.

Controlling

The fourth management function is controlling. **Controlling is the measurement of actual behavior or output against established goals and objectives.** It should be a continuously applied process. Three steps are important in the controlling process:

1. **Setting performance standards for the production process** What levels of output, quality, or behavior are necessary to attain the goals?

2. **Comparing actual performance with established standards** Measurements must be taken and compared to desired goals.

3. **Determining if corrective action is needed** If actual performance deviates from expected performance, are changes needed in the plan, in organization, in direction? When, where, and how should they be made?

Effective control requires a feedback system that provides accurate and current information. Such information may exist in the form of sales records, inventory figures, levels of output, production costs, levels of rejected output, or absenteeism.

The control function is an evaluation and review process that allows a company to see where it stands in relation to its projected goals. If changes are called for, revisions may be needed in one or more of the other management functions.

For example, production goals may become unreachable due to changes that were not foreseen during the planning phase. Unforeseen events, such as increased raw material costs, labor strikes, and lower demand for products, could all result in output that is lower than expected.

Or, assume that a company has a production goal of 10,000 units per month. But over a period of six months, it produces only 8,000 units per month. What should be done?

Management may decide that the original goal of 10,000 units was too high, given existing resources. Perhaps a lower production goal would be more realistic.

Testing original goals against the reality of the production process makes it possible to determine if the goals were based on sound assumptions.

Figure 4.3 What's happened to executive compensation and how it compares with some other occupations

	1971		1981		
Industry	Largest company	Chief executive's compensation	Largest company	Chief executive's compensation	Increase (decrease)
Aerospace	Boeing	$80,000	Boeing	$957,551	1,096.9%
Food	Swift	68,053	Dart & Kraft	748,647	1,000.1
Pharmaceuticals	American Home Products	240,000	Johnson & Johnson	968,542	303.6
Publishing	Time Inc.	203,025	Time Inc.	633,367	212.0
Metal manufacturing	U.S. Steel	300,000	U.S. Steel	821,322	173.8
Retailing	Sears Roebuck	386,800	Sears Roebuck	1,010,137	161.2
Utility	AT&T	360,500	AT&T	894,400	148.1
Office equipment	IBM	394,331	IBM	940,000	138.4
Commercial banking	Bankamerica	171,643	Bankamerica	390,325	127.5
Petroleum refining	Standard Oil (N.J.)	505,100	Exxon	1,105,412	118.9
Brokerage	Merrill Lynch	296,501	Merrill Lynch	642,524	116.7
Advertising	J. Walter Thompson	191,587	JWT Group	372,881	94.6
Mutual life insurance	Prudential	300,000	Prudential	582,744	94.2
Conglomerates	General Electric	500,000	General Electric	853,976	70.8
Automotive	General Motors	838,750	General Motors	489,250	(41.7)
Other occupations		**Compensation**		**Compensation**	**Increase**
Major-league baseball player (average)		$31,543		196,500	523.0
Starting lawyer in a Wall Street law firm		15,500		43,300	179.4
Harvard MBA graduate entering consulting (median)		18,000 (1972 data)		46,100	156.1
Auto worker (average hourly wage)		4.72		11.01	133.3

Other occupations	1971 Compensation	1981 Compensation	Increase
Airline pilot (average for union members)	28,390	60,280 (1980 data)	112.3
President of AFL-CIO	70,000	110,000	57.1
U.S. senator	42,500	60,663	42.7
President of the United States	200,000	200,000	0.0
Consumer Price Index (1967 = 100)	121.3	272.4	124.6
Minimum wage	1.60	3.35	109.4
Standard & Poor 500 stock index (year-end)	102.09	122.55	20.0

From: Carol J. Loomis, "The Madness of Executive Compensation," FORTUNE, July 12, 1982, p. 45. Courtesy of FORTUNE Magazine Art Department.

Levels of management

Managers receive their authority indirectly from their company's owners or shareholders. The owners delegate their authority to an elected board of directors. The board of directors, in turn, selects top-level managers to operate the business.

Specialized management activities are divided into three basic levels: top, middle, and supervisory. These three major management levels make up the management pyramid, or management hierarchy. These levels may be divided into many sublevels. The total number of management levels and sublevels depends on a company's size and the type of business.

Top management

Top management is the highest level of the management pyramid. **Top management includes the president and other high-level executives, who spend the largest portion of their time on the planning function.** These managers are hired by the board of directors and report directly to it. Managers at the top level have the most authority and also the most responsibility. Top-level managers spend much of their time on the planning function, making broad organizational decisions. Typical top-management decisions pertain to such issues as building a new manufacturing plant, developing a new product line, or expanding marketing operations overseas.

Top-level managers work directly with the board of directors and are responsible for carrying out policies and plans approved by the board.

Managers at all levels feel pressure to control expenditures.

"Oh, it's great here, all right, but I sort of feel uncomfortable in a place with no budget at *all*."

Drawing by D. Reilly; © 1976 The New Yorker Magazine, Inc.

Middle management

Middle management is the second management level and includes individuals who develop plans and procedures for carrying out top management's decisions.

Plant managers, department heads, and division managers are all members of middle management. Middle managers usually have responsibility for a broad task, such as operating a manufacturing plant. They must determine production schedules, plan resource needs, select raw materials, determine personnel needs, and develop evaluation systems to measure efficiency. In large measure, middle management organizes and directs the long-range plans established by top management.

Middle managers are often given much freedom to develop plans. But their plans always reflect the goals and objectives set by top management.

Supervisory management

Supervisory management is the lowest management level and includes individuals who are directly responsible for accomplishing specific, narrowly defined tasks performed by nonmanagement employees. The employees who report to supervisors are responsible for the actual physical production, sales, or supporting operations of the organization. People at this management level may also be called first-line managers or foremen. Supervisory managers are responsible for implementing plans established by middle managers.

Chapter 4 Essentials of management

Figure 4.4 Levels of management

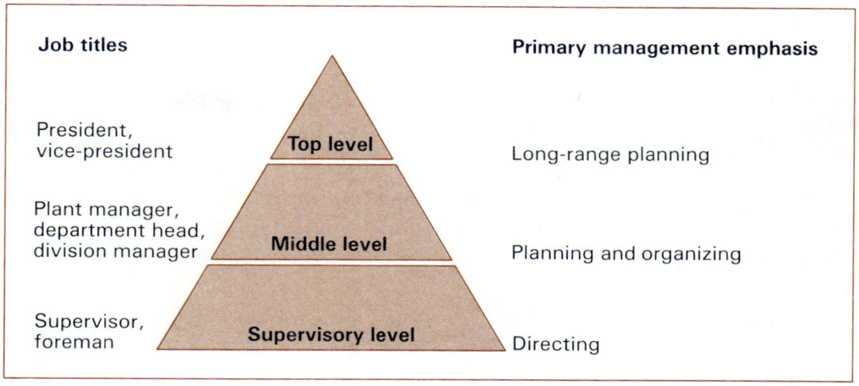

Job titles		Primary management emphasis
President, vice-president	Top level	Long-range planning
Plant manager, department head, division manager	Middle level	Planning and organizing
Supervisor, foreman	Supervisory level	Directing

Typical supervisory activities include assigning jobs, evaluating employee performance, directing a district sales force, and providing production reports.

Management levels differ in function

At each management level, activities are specialized and amounts of responsibility vary. In smaller companies, one person, or a small group of persons, may operate at all three management levels. If managers have too many different specialized functions to perform, however, their performance may suffer. Figure 4.4 shows the primary management functions found at each management level.

Managers are problem solvers and decision makers

The higher a manager rises in the organizational structure, the more he or she is called on to make decisions. These decisions often involve solving problems. The ability to identify, analyze, and solve problems is crucial to successful management.

A problem is a deviation or change from the routine. It is the difference between what should be happening and what is actually happening. **A decision is a choice made about what should or should not be done in a given situation.** Solving a problem may involve several decisions.

Managers are both decision makers and problem solvers. They are decision makers first. No problems are ever solved without a decision. But decisions are often made when there are no problems.

The decision-making and problem-solving processes seek to use an orderly system to get at the nature of a decision or the cause of a problem. The outcome is an action that resolves the problem.

The guru of gizmos

Wang corporate headquarters in Lowell, Massachusetts

Photo courtesy of Wang Laboratories, Inc.

The premier peddler of the new machines showing up in business offices is neither IBM nor Xerox, but An Wang, 61, a Chinese-born inventor who founded Wang Laboratories in 1951. The Lowell, Mass., company produces state-of-the-art equipment for the office of the future. Wang Laboratories dominates the market for so-called integrated information systems. These are elaborate combinations of computerized word and data processors, high-speed printers, telecommunications hook-ins and video display terminals used by secretaries and their bosses. And such office innovations are likely to continue. Says Wang: "The cost of parts keeps getting lower, and the applications are getting wider."

The son of a Shanghai English teacher, Wang came to the United States in 1945 to earn a Ph.D. in applied physics at Harvard. Three years later, at age 28, he invented the magnetic core, a tiny, doughnut-shaped data storage element that remained the key to computer memory technology for more than 20 years until it was replaced by sophisticated semiconductor equipment in the late 1960s. Wang started his company in a dingy room above an electrical fixtures store on Boston's Columbus Avenue. The firm engineered one-of-a-kind products to fill special customer needs. One result was the first digital scoreboard, built for the opening of New York's Shea Stadium in 1964.

In the same year the company's reputation began to grow when it introduced one of the first desk-top electronic calculators. But eight years later Texas Instruments began selling hand-held machines made with silicon chips and stole the market. Wang then quickly shifted his company's efforts into large-scale office electronics. In 1972 the company entered the word processor market, and soon introduced the television-like screen that nearly all electronic word processing equipment now uses for displaying text. The company at present has 35 percent of the world market.

Nonstop innovation and a sales force that is among the best in the industry have kept Wang Laboratories expanding rapidly. The company has averaged a 75 percent annual growth in profits over the past five years, including an 82 percent increase in the fiscal year that ended June 30. In the quarter that ended Sept. 30, earnings were up 84 percent over the same period last year.

Further growth, though, will be more difficult. The office-of-the-future market has become so attractive that the computer giants are now aggressively going after it. IBM, for example, last summer introduced its low-priced Displaywriter that will compete with certain Wang products.

Wang, who has been an American citizen since 1955, is now about to start operation in the land of his birth. He is currently completing negotiations with the People's Republic of China on a joint venture to produce small computers in Nanjing. Having heard of Wang's spectacular record, Chinese bureaucrats are already planning on $4 million to $5 million worth of production in the project's first year, and a 60 percent annual growth rate thereafter.

Source: Reprinted by permission from TIME, November 17, 1980, p. 81. Copyright 1980, Time Inc. All rights reserved. Reprinted by permission.

Figure 4.5 Steps in the decision-making process

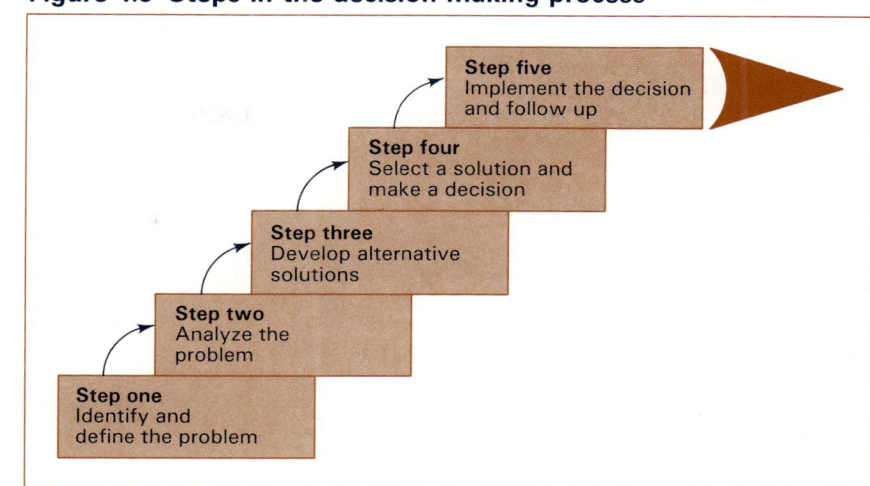

Steps in decision making and problem solving

All managers, from first-line supervisors to company president, constantly make decisions that affect an organization's progress.

The decision-making process consists of a systematic series of five steps. Using such a system does not guarantee a favorable solution to all problems. It does, however, increase the likelihood that better decisions will be made more often. Figure 4.5 illustrates the decision-making process.

Step one: identify and define the problem

This first step is critical to the success of the entire process. To decide on a course of action, a manager must recognize that a problem exists. The problem must be clearly identified and stated in simple, understandable terms.

It is important not to confuse a symptom with a problem. For example, when you get sick, you may complain of fever and chills. You may be tempted to call these symptoms your problem. But if you treat the symptoms, you may hide the actual cause of the fever and chills—an infection or pneumonia, for instance. Similarly, a firm may be tempted to identify as a problem the high rate of defective products made on its assembly line. In reality, the badly made products could be a symptom of something else—low employee morale or a misfunctioning machine, for example. Product quality won't improve until morale is raised or the machine is fixed.

A good problem solver is careful to identify the real problem.

Step two: analyze the problem

This step involves analyzing information to determine what is contributing to the problem. At this stage, managers must decide what information they need to best understand what is happening. They may gather information by interviewing employees, working through previous calculations, calling in experts, and many other methods. They must then distinguish between useful and useless information.

To obtain the best results, the information for decision making should be as accurate, complete, and up-to-date as possible. Often, however, needed information is not available. Or perhaps a decision must be made before all necessary information can be gathered. Then managers must make reasonable estimates based on existing information and previous experience. During the analysis stage, a manager breaks down a problem into its component parts.

Analytical skills form the foundation of a manager's value to an organization.

Step three: develop alternative solutions

After managers have analyzed a problem, they should develop a range of possible solutions. Each solution will have its own set of advantages and disadvantages. Developing alternative solutions allows managers to think through the situation and look at it from several angles.

Having many alternatives does not necessarily guarantee a perfect solution. But a greater range of choices tends to increase the likelihood of making a good decision.

Developing alternative solutions requires managers to use their intelligence, specialized knowledge, judgment, creativity, energy, and personality. Many elements enter into the problem-solving process.

Step four: select a solution and make a decision

At this point, a decision is made. The decision depends on all the earlier steps.

A problem often has several good solutions. But the final decision may depend on many "ifs." For example, a manager might prefer one of two alternatives: "if the company will let me spend X dollars." But if that much money isn't available, another alternative is more likely to be selected.

The focus in decision making is on finding a choice that will both adequately solve the problem and be acceptable to the people who are affected by it. The "best" decision usually offers the most satisfying solution that can be found, given the limitations and conditions of the specific situation.

Step five: implement the decision and follow up

The decision itself is only a portion of the decision-making process. Management must also make sure that action is taken and the decision is implemented.

Once action is taken, its results must be checked. Such follow-up is part of the control function.

Most decisions require only a short time to make. For effective decision makers, the five steps in the decision-making process become automatic.

Managerial skills

Nonmanagement workers often have strong specialized skills. For example, they may be excellent typists, expert gardeners, or crack electricians. However, people who have such special skills do not always make good managers. Good managers must possess a range of skills. **Managerial skills fall into three categories: (1) technical skills, (2) human skills, and (3) conceptual skills.** Each management level requires a different mix of skills.

Technical skills

Technical skills are necessary in using specialized tools, procedures, and techniques. They are especially important to a first-line supervisor because they are closely related to the actual production process. For example, the foreman in a tool and die shop must know how to operate the machinery in order to manage production.

As managers ascend the organizational ladder, they have less need for narrow technical skills. Managers may start in an organization with well-honed technical skills. But as they become more involved in policy making and overall operations, they usually do not use such specialized skills. Instead, they need broader, general management skills.

Human skills

A manager needs human skills to work with and motivate other people. Human skills are needed in all phases of management. But they probably are most important in the directing function.

An increasingly important human skill at all mangement levels is the ability to communicate—that is, the ability to exchange information. Communication is the means by which an organization maintains its information network.

Excellent communication skills are necessary to maintain high levels of productivity and good relationships with workers. Being a good communicator requires the development of both oral and written skills. Furthermore, managers must be sensitive to the way people react to information. And they must also listen carefully to what their subordinates have to say.

Conceptual skills

Conceptual skills enable a manager to see and understand how various pieces fit into a whole. Conceptual skills are invaluable at all managerial levels. But they become most important as a manager moves higher in the organization. Lower- or middle-level managers who lack conceptual skills may not be promoted. Such managers may be good at details, but they fail to understand how the details fit together to form a total operation.

Top-level managers must possess conceptual skills in order to do long-range planning. They must develop overall organizational goals and activities through integration of resources at all levels.

Is management for you?

With rare exception, a college education is the minimum requirement for entry into management. A well-rounded business background with some liberal arts courses is an advantage for general management. Specific technical skills are frequently taught on the job. Graduate business school training is considered an asset for those seeking a good start on a managerial career. Demand for managers is expected to increase during the 1980s.

Among the personal traits that contribute to success in management are above-average intelligence, ambition, good judgment, good communication skills, good health, emotional stability, and the ability to make logical decisions and to get along with others.

Other characteristics in highly rated managers include willingness to work hard, loyalty, integrity, ability to adapt to change, and creativity.

4 Essentials of management

Summary

All organizations need management. *Management* is a process through which people seek to meet goals and objectives by efficiently coordinating available resources. The management process includes four functions: (1) planning, (2) organizing, (3) directing, and (4) controlling. Each function is part of a continuous, interrelated process.

Planning is the function of preparing for the future by developing goals and objectives in the present. Good planning includes analysis of past and present business activities and development of clear, realistic goals and objectives.

Organizing is the function of arranging human and material resources to achieve established goals. It involves converting goals into a workable system of specialized tasks arranged in a logical sequence. Authority and responsibility are also assigned.

Directing is the process of coordinating and guiding people in the production of goods and services. Leadership styles fall into three basic categories: autocratic, democratic, and laissez-faire.

Controlling is the process of checking actual output against established goals and objectives. In the control process, three steps are important: setting performance standards for the production process, comparing actual performance with established standards, and determining if corrective action is necessary. Effective controls provide a feedback system that gives management accurate and up-to-date information.

The three major management levels are *top management, middle management,* and *supervisory management.* Top management spends most of its time on the planning function. Middle management develops plans and procedures for carrying out top management's decisions. And supervisory management is directly responsible for accomplishing specific tasks performed by nonmanagement personnel.

A *problem* is a deviation or change from the routine. A *decision* is a choice made about what should or should not be done in a given situation.

The decision-making and problem-solving process is an important part of management. It includes five steps: (1) identify and define the problem; (2) analyze the problem; (3) develop alternative solutions; (4) select a solution and make a decision; and (5) implement the decision and follow up.

Managerial skills are those qualities an individual needs to become an effective manager. These skills fall into three categories. Technical skills pertain to the use of specialized tools, procedures, and techniques. Human skills are needed to work with and motivate other people. Conceptual skills allow a manager to see the organization as a whole and to understand the relationship of the parts to the whole.

The demand for managers will continue to grow during the coming decade. Successful managers tend to show intelligence, ambition, good judgment, decision-making ability, ability to get along with people, good communication skills, flexibility, and creativity.

Review questions

1. Why is management called a process?
2. Figure 4.1 shows the flow of management functions. Explain how each function contributes to the management of an organization.
3. What factors should be considered in developing goals?
4. How does the organizing function relate to a firm's goals? In what ways does specialization of tasks contribute to the process?
5. Explain how the directing function uses human skills.
6. What are the advantages and disadvantages of the three leadership styles?
7. What three steps make up the control process? Why is feedback so important to an organization?
8. Identify the three levels of management. How do their activities and responsibilities differ?
9. Describe the five steps involved in the problem-solving process.
10. Why are communication skills important for managers at all levels?
11. What are conceptual skills? Why are they so important for top-level managers?
12. What background must a good manager have? What personal characteristics contribute to a manager's success?

Discussion questions

1. Why are managers important for each of the following organizations?
    a. a baseball team
    b. a restaurant
    c. a college
2. Explain this statement: "Top-level managers get paid mostly for thinking, not for doing."
3. Compare the planning function with the controlling function. How are they closely related?
4. In the Warner-Lambert case, how is the company trying to make the most effective use of its assets? Give examples.
5. Why do conceptual skills become increasingly important as a manager moves from supervisory management to middle- and top-level management?

Chapter 4 case

Carlisle Corporation

Sometimes a top executive has an opportunity to start fresh. Here is a business ripe for organizational change.

The Carlisle Corporation is an established company that produces a full line of men's clothing, including sports jackets, shirts, pajamas, and underwear. The company was founded in 1946 by James Carlisle. Carlisle and his son Peter own all but 3000 of the 100,000 shares of stock issued by the corporation.

Three years ago, James Carlisle promoted Peter to president and named himself chairman of the board of directors. James continued to make most of the major company decisions, however, often without consulting Peter or any of the other top executives.

The company markets its clothing line through several department stores, men's clothing stores, and discount stores. But other manufacturers are becoming more competitive as they try new ideas. James Carlisle has resisted changing the company structure to meet the competition and has even refused to advertise on television.

In addition, the Carlisle Corporation manufacturing facilities are 25 years old and need modernization, according to an outside consulting firm that Peter hired. James has objected to any modernization, claiming that the machinery is in good operating condition.

First-quarter profits for this year were lower than last year's, and production costs are increasing. Three major competitors recently announced price cuts that make their goods substantially cheaper than Carlisle's.

On a recent business trip to California, James Carlisle suffered a serious heart attack and died. Peter was appointed executive officer of Carlisle Corporation at an emergency meeting of the board of directors.

Advise Peter Carlisle.

1. What major problems does Peter face?
2. What should Peter do to meet these problems?

Business in perspective

A mill town is reborn

An old building on Canal Street in this historic city symbolizes the changing economy in Southern New Hampshire and in much of the United States.

Sheathed in gray concrete and dingy brick, the former textile warehouse is a monument to the first Industrial Revolution that provided the mill and factory jobs for New England for more than a century.

But the image is disturbed by the lighted blue emblem of the current owners, the Sanders Associates electronics firm—a sign of this area's second industrial revolution from mill/factory to high technology.

The turnabout is dramatic. Today, 65 percent of New Hampshire's work force labors in electronics, instrumentation, and metals. Ten years ago, 65 percent worked in shoes, textiles, and apparel. The state's five top employers now are high-tech in whole or in part: Digital Equipment, Sanders, General Electric, Kollsman Instrument and Nashua Corporation.

"We were hit by a catastrophe," explains James Chandler, chairman of the Indian Head Bank, "so we had to latch onto the postindustrial economy early."

That catastrophe was the decision by Textron, Inc., in 1948 to close its mills here. Though replacement industry began to arrive in the 1950s, it wasn't until the 1970s that high tech brought prosperity. Nashua's joblessness, about 4 percent last summer and 7.5 percent in July, hangs well below the national average.

The key to New Hampshire's success is its hospitality to business—in contrast to neighboring "Taxachusetts," as it's known here. "I'm pro-business," declares Democratic Governor Hugh Gallen. "I need the jobs."

New Hampshire has neither an income tax nor a sales tax. Paul Guilderson, state industrial-development director, says an easing of the business tax in 1971 started a "new ball game." New Hampshire also pioneered in the use of tax-exempt industrial bonds that allow corporations to borrow cheaply.

The state boasts of the reliability of its work force. Only 12.4 percent is unionized. "The work ethic is a heritage from those who worked in the mills," says Charles Clough, a Nashua Corporation executive.

Yet problems exist. In Nashua, for example, crime is up and the schools are losing teachers to the computer firms. "Look at Main Street—it's dying," says ex-Governor Hugh Gregg, a former mayor.

Sam Tamposi, the leading industrial builder, criticizes the high-tech executives for taking benefits but not contributing their "fair share" to the community.

Jack Mixon of Teradyne Connection Systems, Inc., says the new arrivals from Massachusetts "naïvely expected the same services they were used to."

New Hampshire provides little aid to higher education. Dean Dwight Ladd of the state-university Wittemore business school calls the tax system "idiotic."

Still, it's clear the second industrial revolution has improved life here. "My father worked in shoes, my mother in textiles," recalls Mayor Maurice Arel of Nashua. "From them, I knew what I didn't want to do."

Now, because of high-tech, New Hampshirites don't have to work in the factories or mills any more.

Reprinted from *U.S. News & World Report,* September 13, 1982, p. 56. Copyright 1982, U.S. News & World Report, Inc.

Chapter 5

Organizing the firm's resources

Key terms

organization
organization chart
departmentalization
functional (process)
   departmentalization
product departmentalization
geographic
   departmentalization
customer departmentalization
authority
power
responsibility
delegation
accountability
span of control
centralized authority
decentralized authority
line organization
unity of command
line-and-staff organization
functional organization
committee organization
quality circles
informal organization
grapevine

Chapter objectives

In Chapter 5, you will learn:

The meaning and nature of organizing

Three basic organizational elements and how they are related

Why businesses develop organization charts and how they use them

What is meant by departmentalization

The meaning of authority, responsibility, delegation, and accountability in an organization

What is meant by span of control

How the concept of delegation is related to centralized and decentralized organization structures

The ways in which line organization structures are similar to line-and-staff organization structures

The new concept of quality circles and what they can contribute to a business

The nature and impact of informal organization structures

Overview

Planning and developing goals are essential business activities. They are the cornerstones from which other business activities flow. As a business defines and refines its goals, it must consider how to organize its available resources.

This chapter considers the nature of the organizing process. It presents organizational guidelines and concepts and provides examples of common organizational structures. The chapter relates the planning function discussed in Chapter 4 to the development of an efficient organization that puts its plans into action. All organizations must allocate the same types of resources: time, human energy, and physical resources. An efficient organization seeks to use its resources as wisely as possible.

The nature of organizing

At one time or another, we have all probably heard someone say, "Let's get organized." All of us participate in many different kinds of organizations. Hardly a day goes by without our being involved in some form of organizational activity. We belong to political parties, social clubs, athletic teams, churches, and business organizations.

We usually join an organization because we believe that it can satisfy some of our personal goals and interests. Each individual, however, joins an organization with different personal goals that he or she hopes to have satisfied.

What is an organization?

Organizing is the process of combining and arranging human and material resources in a system of activities that achieves established goals. **An organization is the structure that results from combining human and material resources.** In both cases, the emphasis is on achieving established goals in a coordinated and efficient way.

Business and individual goals

The goals of a business may not always be the same as those of an individual. A business's major goal, for example, may be to meet demand for its goods and services. Its ultimate goal is probably to earn a profit. An individual's goals, on the other hand, may be to earn a reasonable wage and to feel satisfied and challenged in the use of his or her talents and abilities.

A business and its employees require a structure within which both can achieve their objectives. A firm can have highly talented personnel and an abundance of physical resources and still fail to be successful and profitable.

It has been said that without organization, an automobile is just a pile of parts. Only through an organized structure can those parts take the form of an automobile. The same is true of business firms.

Figure 5.1 Organizational elements

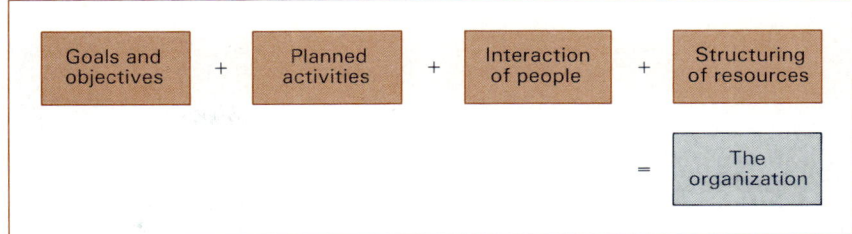

Organizational elements

Many of the resources that businesses need are scarce or limited. This requires a cohesive and coordinated plan for structuring the use of resources.

When developing a plan for the efficient use of resources, a firm must first establish its goals and objectives. Then it must incorporate three essential organizational elements: (1) planned activities to accomplish objectives, (2) interaction of people in both formal and informal work settings, and (3) an arrangement, or structuring, of physical resources. Figure 5.1 illustrates how these elements are related.

A case study: Barry's Sports Shop

Planned activities to accomplish objectives

Barry is the owner-manager of a small sporting-goods store. His overall objective, naturally, is to earn a profit. But he knows that to do this he must have a more specific goal. Therefore, Barry's more specific goal is to carry the goods he thinks customers will buy and to sell his goods at competitive prices. He believes that providing knowledgeable service is part of this goal. Thus, Barry plans the following specific activities in order to achieve his goal:

- careful selection and ordering of sports equipment
- attractive arrangement of merchandise
- informing potential customers of his business
- keeping track of his inventory
- maintaining financial records
- preparing advertisements for local newspaper and radio
- paying his business accounts when due
- directing the job activities of employees.

Interaction of people

As Barry's Sports Shop grows in size, Barry finds it necessary to employ a full-time salesperson to assist with the increased customer volume. He must also hire an additional employee to handle incoming merchandise and stock the display shelves.

Barry finds it increasingly difficult to remain directly involved in all aspects of his business. Thus, he must determine which tasks require his personal attention and which can be performed by others.

Figure 5.2 Organization chart for Barry's Sports Shop

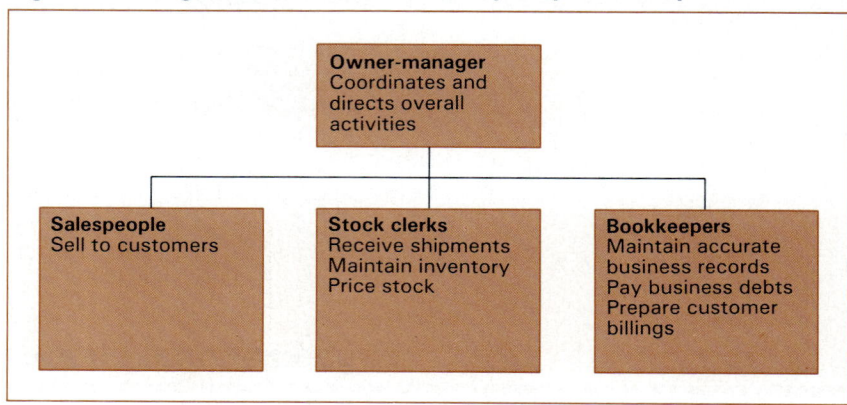

As the owner-manager, Barry must supervise other people. He must ensure that each employee knows exactly what is expected on the job and how his or her work fits into the overall store operation.

Structuring of resources

With continued growth, Barry finds that additional specialization of tasks is required. He must determine the formal relationship of each employee's task to himself and to the other employees. Because Barry's business is still small, its organization is rather simple. Each individual performs specialized functions that contribute to the overall operation of the business.

In Figure 5.2, the lines going from the owner-manager (Barry) show that he is responsible for the overall operation of the store. The other three boxes show the specialized functions that the salespeople, stock clerk, and bookkeeper perform. There are no lines connecting the three boxes because each group functions independently. One group is not responsible to another. Only Barry has authority over how the three areas operate.

As time passes, Barry finds that there is heavy demand for ski equipment. He therefore decides to establish a special ski department. One of the sales clerks is an avid skier and is very familiar with the latest ski equipment. So Barry makes her the supervisor of this new specialized department. Barry's Sports Shop has now specialized its sales force and products.

The organization chart

An *organization chart* is a visual or written description of how a firm is organized. It shows how work is divided and who has authority and accountability. Each box represents the division of job activities required to produce a good or render a service. In effect, an organization chart is like a map of an organization.

Fired corporate execs move to small firms

When executives of large companies get fired, they tend to look for jobs in smaller companies. So say a number of specialists in "outplacement," counseling for people whose employment has been terminated.

Robert Swain, president of Eaton-Swain Associates of New York, counsels from 200 to 300 fired executives a year, almost all from corporations with annual sales of more than $1 billion. Two-thirds of them, he says, find new jobs in companies with less than $100 million in sales; less than 10 percent return to companies over $1 billion. Many accept a cut in pay in their new positions in return for an ownership share in the company. Swain says their former salaries averaged $50,000 to $55,000.

Another New York outplacement specialist, James J. Gallagher of J.J. Gallagher Associates, says 40 percent to 50 percent of his clients from billion-dollar companies obtain new employment at companies of less than $100 million.

Why don't these big-business executives look for positions at similar size corporations? Gallagher cites current economic conditions, which include sweeping white-collar layoffs at large, established companies. "These businessmen become disillusioned about the myth of security in corporate life," he says. "If they've been fired once, they figure it can happen again."

Swain notes that it often makes sense for a small company to hire someone with big-business experience. "Small companies are growing more rapidly, and they usually don't have the ability to produce in-house the talent that they need," he says.

Reprinted with permission, INC., August 1982. Copyright © 1982 by INC. Publishing Company, 38 Commercial Wharf, Boston MA 02110.

The organization charts of larger businesses may have many boxes representing large numbers of people performing similar functions. Regardless of an organization's size, the chart's purpose remains the same. It is to structure resources to avoid waste and to accomplish established goals.

In the real world, organizations and their structures do not start out fully developed. As suggested in the Barry's Sports Shop example, organizations evolve. Therefore, what seems to be a question of organization is really more often a question of *re*organization. As a business grows, its goals change and its mission becomes more complex. Its organization must also change to reflect its new needs.

In setting up or revising an organization's structure, the first issue is how people can be most efficiently divided into separate groups. Each group and person must be assigned specific tasks that will contribute to the firm's goals. How well this issue is addressed has a direct bearing on the organization's ultimate success or failure. Determining the most appropriate division of labor is an essential step toward an efficient operation.

Departmentalization: dividing tasks into related areas

Departmentalization is the grouping of job activities and functions into specific, related areas. Grouping is most commonly based on function, product, and/or geography. There is no best method of departmentalization. What works best for a given firm depends on its size, the nature of its business, the geographic territory it covers, and the style of its managers. Over time, the most appropriate form of departmentalization for a company may change.

Functional (or process) departmentalization groups people according to job functions. Some common functional departments include production, marketing, finance, accounting, information processing, law, and purchasing. Each company must build its own functional structure to fit its own purposes and resources. **Product departmentalization is an organizational structure based on specific product lines.** In effect, each product line becomes a mini-company within the overall company structure. Each grouping is responsible for all aspects of manufacturing and marketing its particular product line. Within each product category are departments for marketing, manufacturing, accounting, and the like.

Geographic departmentalization is the grouping of a firm's resources and activities by location. This method may be desirable for a business whose sales efforts cover a wide territory. In such cases, geographic organization can make operations more manageable at the local level. Using this system, the production of goods and services uses resources closer at hand.

Although these three basic methods of departmentalization are most common, a fourth method, customer departmentalization, may also be used. **Customer departmentalization is based on special groups of customers who have unique requirements and characteristics.** This may include customers such as government agencies, wholesalers, retailers, schools and colleges, health-care providers, and the like.

Business uses a mixture of department types

Businesses constantly seek the most efficient uses of their resources. Thus, they usually employ several forms of departmentalization because no single form best satisfies all their needs. A firm's managers weigh the costs and benefits of adopting the various departmental formats in order to find the system that best fits their operational needs and objectives.

Often, the most appropriate system changes with a firm's growth or mix of operations. For example, a small firm may begin with a functional structure. As it grows, it will probably need to adjust its structure to include other department types. Eventually, the company may adopt geographic departmentalization, product departmentalization, or whatever combination suits its new needs.

Authority-responsibility relationships

In addition to adjusting an organization according to the tasks required to accomplish its goals, management must consider authority-responsibility relationships. In a corporation, management's authority comes from the board of directors, which represents the owners (or stockholders). The board of directors delegates authority to management for use in achieving the owners' goals of profits, increased investment value, social welfare, and the like.

Top management, in turn, delegates some of its authority to lower management levels. But along with authority must come responsibility for accomplishing goals. Similarly, those to whom authority has been delegated are held accountable for their actions. Therefore, four concepts are central to understanding the interactions within a management structure: authority, responsibility, delegation, and accountability.

Authority

Authority is the right to act and make decisions in carrying out assignments. It is a necessary ingredient for accomplishing goals through other people. In business, the nature and degree of an individual's authority depends upon his or her management level. For example, a company president has a broader range of authority than does a plant manager or a department supervisor.

While formal authority comes with managerial position, informal authority stems from a person's unique personality, social, and cultural characteristics.

Authority differs somewhat from power. **Authority is the right to do something while power is the ability to do something.** A mugger who points a gun at a victim at that moment has the power (ability) to take the victim's money. But the mugger takes the money without the authority (right) to do so.

Responsibility

Responsibility is an individual's duty or obligation to perform assigned tasks. When responsibility for certain tasks is assigned to subordinates, sufficient authority to accomplish the tasks must be included. For example, a department manager may be given responsibility for increasing production by 25 percent in the next six months. However, if the manager is not given the authority to hire more workers, control work schedules, and obtain additional machinery and raw materials, his success in meeting this responsibility is unlikely.

Responsibility without the means to accomplish assigned tasks creates frustration and leads to ineffective performance. It is therefore important to balance the levels of authority and responsibility assigned to individuals.

Delegation

Delegation is the assignment of a portion of authority to a subordinate along with the accompanying responsibility for performing assigned tasks. No manager, at any level, can do everything. Therefore, the essence of management is delegation. Departmentalization is an example of how this may be accomplished.

Managers must give careful consideration to the extent to which they delegate tasks to others. Some managers delegate too much responsibility to subordinates, while others may not delegate enough. In both cases, an imbalance exists between authority and responsibility.

When delegating, a manager must be sure to provide subordinates with clear instructions and sufficient authority to accomplish assigned tasks. As we shall see in Chapter 6, an important part of a manager's role is to develop worker's talents through effective delegating.

Accountability

Accountability is an individual's liability for performing assigned activities. Although a manager may delegate authority, he or she remains accountable for completion of the delegated task. If a baseball team loses games, its manager is more likely to be replaced than are the individual players.

A manager often is only as efficient as his or her subordinates. This applies to company presidents as well as to department supervisors. People are the critical element in an organization. And it is a manager's job to organize those people in the most productive manner possible.

Span of control

Span of control is the optimal number of persons a manager can effectively supervise. This number varies according to specific situations. In most circumstances, however, six to eight subordinates is believed to be the maximum for effective management.

A smaller span of control allows closer supervision. A manager who has too many people to supervise may be unable to give adequate individual attention and may have a hard time keeping track of what is going on.

Certain industries and situations may benefit from small spans of control. For example, in laboratories doing highly technical research, small spans of control may be desirable. In situations where work is very routine, however, larger spans of control may be equally effective.

Centralized versus decentralized authority

We have said that authority is the right to act and make decisions. Delegation is the assignment of a portion of that authority to others. Along with authority comes the responsibility for performing assigned tasks and accountability for this performance. Top management must make decisions about the amount of authority that can be most effec-

The span of control must be appropriate to the kind of tasks performed in the company

Drawing by Lorenz; © 1977 The New Yorker Magazine, Inc.

tively delegated to various levels of the organization. These decisions are often reflected in the organization's structure.

Centralized authority exists when most decision-making authority and responsibility are retained at upper-management levels. The U.S. Army is an example of an organizational structure with centralized authority.

Decentralized authority exists where substantial authority and responsibility are delegated to middle- and supervisory-management levels. General Motors, with its many automobile divisions, is highly decentralized. Sears, the giant retailer, is also largely decentralized.

A major influence on the extent of centralization in a firm is top management's philosophy of control. Another consideration may be the ability and desire of other management levels to assume more authority and responsibility in making important decisions.

Authority relationships

Thus far, we have looked at a firm's internal organizational structure in terms of departmentalization and location of authority. We will now consider internal organizations based on the nature of authority relationships.

Although all managers are delegated formal authority, it is not all the same type. The nature of a manager's authority depends upon the organization's structure of authority relationships. **Three basic types of authority exist: line, staff, and functional.** The two most common forms of authority structure are line organization and line-and-staff organization. We will also consider functional organization and committee organization.

Line authority: the line organization

A line organization is one in which direct authority flows from upper management levels to each lower management position. Line authority establishes a chain of command from the top of the organization to the bottom. The chief executive officer gives directions to the chief operating officer, who directs the vice-presidents, who in turn give orders to their subordinates. In this arrangement, each person knows who is responsible to whom. From top to bottom, everyone is accountable to someone.

Unity of command

Unity of command means that each person in a chain of command should have only one supervisor to whom he or she is accountable. Unity of command seeks to minimize the duplication and confusion that can arise when an individual is given conflicting orders from two supervisors. Clear authority relationships, understood by everyone, are necessary to develop a smooth flow of activities.

Figure 5.3 shows a simplified line organization structure for a manufacturing company. Authority and decision-making powers flow from the board of directors to the president, vice-presidents, managers, and supervisors.

Advantages of a line organization

Line organization is the simplest form of authority structure. It provides a clear, chain-of-command distribution of authority-responsibility relationships at all levels. Since the chain of command is easy to identify, decision making can be rapid once orders are given.

Disadvantages of a line organization

Line organization has three major disadvantages. First, top management may become the center of power and decision-making authority because it does not delegate sufficient authority. Second, managers may face increasingly complex duties for which they lack both the specific expertise and the time to perform. Third, as a company grows, its chain of command may become too long. Decision making and communication may become slow, disjointed, and confused.

Figure 5.3 Consolidated Electronics Company Line organization

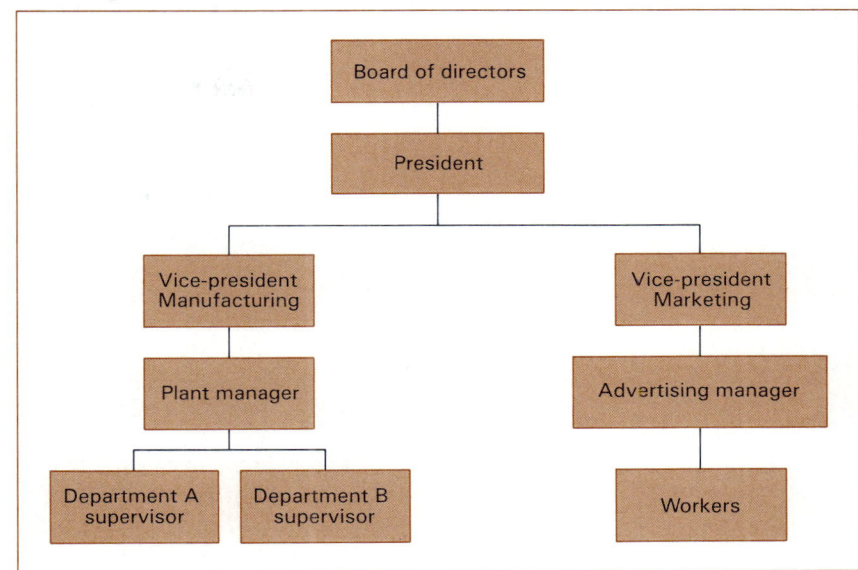

Line-and-staff organization

A line-and-staff structure combines the direct authority relationships found in a line organization with staff departments that provide advice, assistance, and support in specialized areas. Line managers depend on staff specialists to help in their decision-making processes. In general, line managers deal with the basic operations of the company—those tasks directly related to the production of goods or supply of services. Staff managers, on the other hand, provide specialized technical, legal, financial, administrative, and similar services. Staff functions may be quite important in accomplishing a business's goals. But it is the line functions that usually produce revenues and profits.

Let us assume that the company shown in Figure 5.3 grows to the point where it requires the skills of several specialists. Its president recognizes the need for a new department to specialize in personnel needs. She also decides that to maintain its competitive position, the company must add a separate research and development department.

Figure 5.4 shows the new relationships that emerge from the addition of these two new departments. Neither department would have direct line authority in its relationships with other departments. Each would be a staff department because it provides specific expertise—one in the area of manpower needs and the other in the area of product development. However, neither department is directly engaged in manufacturing and marketing operations.

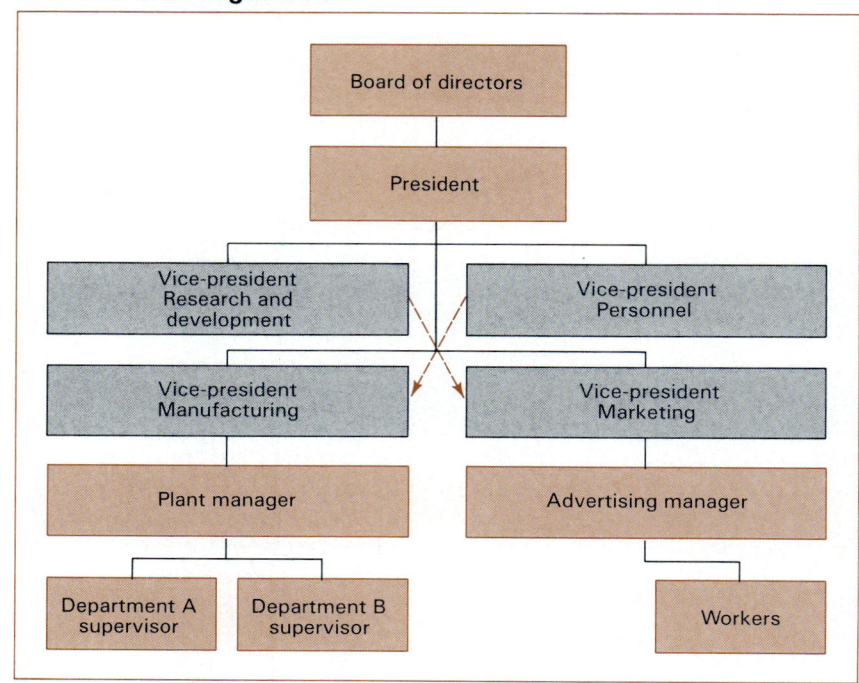

Figure 5.4 Consolidated Electronics Company Line and staff organization

The dotted lines in Figure 5.4 are important. They indicate that the staff departments have no direct authority over line executives. Nonetheless, staff departments have very real roles. In fact, company policy may require that line managers seek advice from staff personnel.

Advantages of line-and-staff organization

Line-and-staff organization provides line management with expertise that cuts across the chain of command. This expertise saves managers time and improves the quality of the information that goes into decision making. Through staff positions, it is possible to avoid adding levels to the chain of command.

Disadvantages of line-and-staff organization

Conflicts often arise between line and staff. Line managers are directly responsible for getting work done, while staff members are responsible for providing support serivces. Staff managers must convince line managers that their advice and recommendations are useful.

Serious conflicts may arise when staff managers attempt to give orders to line managers. Also, when line managers must wait for staff input before acting, they may feel that their productivity is slowed.

Another difficulty may arise because staff personnel add costs without making direct contributions to productive output. Some companies prefer to hire outside consultants for specialized services rather than maintain full-time staff departments.

Figure 5.5 Consolidated Electronics Company Functional authority relationships

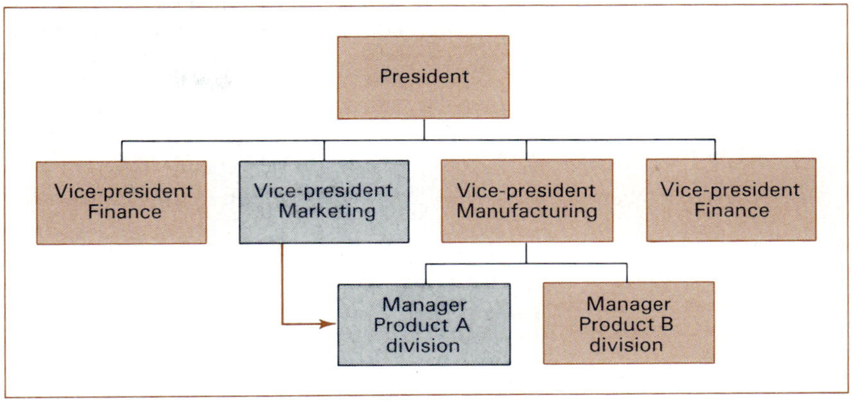

```
                          President
        ┌───────────────┬────┴─────┬───────────────┐
   Vice-president  Vice-president  Vice-president  Vice-president
      Finance        Marketing     Manufacturing      Finance
                         │              │
                         │         ┌────┴────┐
                         └──────▶ Manager    Manager
                                  Product A  Product B
                                  division   division
```

Functional authority: the functional organization

A functional organization gives authority to an individual or department based on a specific task or process. This authority then extends to other departments. For example, the marketing department may have functional authority to develop advertising material for a particular product division. Thus, the marketing department may have functional authority over the product division manager when it comes to making decisions about advertising. Figure 5.5 illustrates functional authority.

Use of functional authority may create several problems. First, it can undermine the authority of the manager in the product division. Second, it may lead to individuals in the product division receiving conflicting orders from two sources—the marketing department and the product division. This situation violates the unity of command principle, but it is often necessary for coordination purposes.

The committee organization

Businesses may use committees for specific purposes within their existing organizational structures. **A committee organization is composed of groups of individuals sharing authority and responsibility, usually for specific activities.** Committees are often formed to address such specific issues as research, new product development, budgeting, and the like. Committee members may represent broad areas of the firm: marketing, engineering, finance, and manufacturing.

Committees provide an opportunity for individuals with many different kinds of expertise to work together on a particular problem. The individuals' combined experience and talents can improve the quality of decisions.

On the other hand, there is always the possibility that one person will dominate the committee, causing it to reflect his or her position or beliefs. Also, a committee may reach a compromise decision that is agreeable to the group but is not necessarily best for the firm.

Trends in organizational strategy: quality circles

Quality circles are voluntary groups of employees who meet, with management support, to identify, analyze, and solve problems in the work place. Started in Japan in 1962, they are groups of from three to fifteen employees who do similar work and report to the same managers or supervisors. The members of each quality circle recommend solutions to management and, when possible, actually implement the changes themselves.

Quality circles do not change existing management structure or the ways managers relate to people in the work place. Rather, they seek to motivate employees to become more interested in the goods and services they produce.

The philosophy behind quality circles is that people will take more interest in their work if they are allowed to influence work-related decisions. The quality-control approach recognizes that workers have the ability and desire to participate in solving problems.

A quality-circle program can be successful only if:

1. Employee participation is voluntary.
2. Management is supportive of the program.
3. There is a "people-building" philosophy based on trust, respect, and caring.
4. Employee training is an integral part of the program.
5. Members work as a team.
6. Team members not only identify problems but also solve them.

In Japan, more than 7 million workers are currently involved in quality circles. This concept is also being tried in Brazil, Holland, Mexico, Sweden, and the United States. General Motors, Hughes Aircraft, Northrup Corporation, Sperry Corporation, and Westinghouse are among the U.S. companies experimenting with the quality circle approach. Figure 5.6 shows how quality circles fit into an existing formal organization.

The facilitator is a key person in any quality-circle program. He or she coordinates group activities and maintains open communication channels with all levels of management. One of the facilitator's most important functions is to promote the quality-circle concept.

Quality circles encourage participants to improve their performance and their work place and to be alert for ways to help their company succeed. Each individual's contribution is considered important.

Figure 5.6 Quality circles and the formal organization

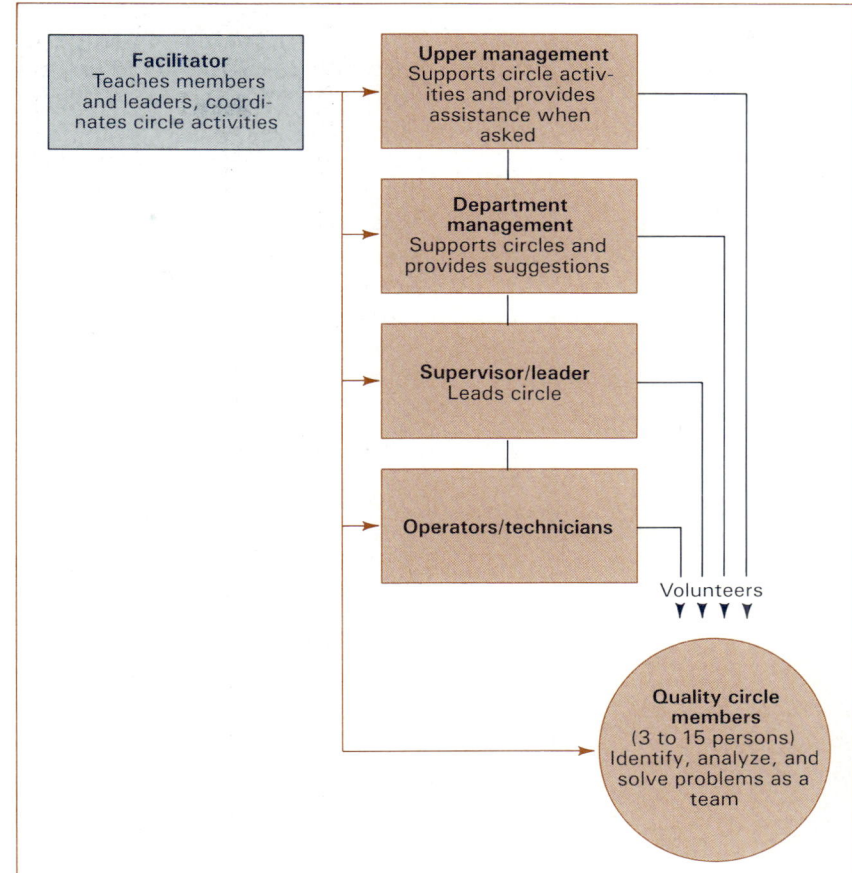

The informal organization

A firm's organization is the structure established by its managers. The organization chart shows the authority-responsibility relationships that ought to exist. **An informal organization is the network of interpersonal relationships that develops within the formal structure of a firm.** It is the way relationships *actually* work. As such, it may parallel the formal organization or it may be quite different.

Informal groups develop for many reasons. They may arise from the natural affiliation of individuals with similar interests and values. They may also reflect the different levels of recognition and status within the organization. Some informal groups provide relief from boredom, tension, and job pressures. Above all, informal groups are valuable communication links.

A grapevine is an informal communication system that transmits both personal and business-related news and information. Grapevine communications may take place during coffee breaks, in the cafeteria, on the golf course, or anywhere else that employees gather. Often the accuracy of such information is questionable, based on rumor without factual foundations.

Managers must recognize that informal groups exist within all formal structures. By reinforcing informal groups and creating a sense of togetherness, a manager can often increase his or her ability to achieve company objectives.

5 Organizing the firm's resources

Summary

Once an organization has defined and redefined its goals and objectives, it must organize its available resources. An *organization* is a structure that results from combining and arranging human and material resources in a system of activities designed to achieve established goals. During the organizing process, the goals of both the firm and its individual employees must be recognized.

The three essential organizational elements are: (1) planned activities to accomplish objectives, (2) interaction with people, and (3) structuring of resources.

A firm's organization chart illustrates how work should be divided and where authority lies. The chart may be used to examine how the company organizes its resources and to evaluate how effectively the planned structure actually works.

Departmentalization is the grouping of job activities and functions into specific, related areas. There are three commonly used departmentalization forms: (1) *functional (process),* (2) *product,* and (3) *geographic.* A less common form, *customer departmentalization,* is based on customers with similar characteristics.

Authority is the right to act and make decisions in carrying out assignments. *Responsibility* is the individual's duty or obligation to perform assigned tasks. *Delegation* is the assignment of authority and responsibility to a subordinate for the purpose of completing a designated task. *Accountability* is an individual's liability for performing a task. Authority-responsibility relationships are crucial to the organization of resources. To be effective, managers must have sufficient authority to fulfill their responsibilities.

A manager's *span of control* refers to the optimal number of people he or she can effectively supervise. Although the number of people may vary according to circumstances, one rule of thumb advises a limit of six to eight subordinates per supervisor.

Centralized organizations retain most decision-making power at upper-management levels. *Decentralized organizations* delegate substantial authority and responsibility to middle and supervisory managers.

There are three common types of organizational structures: (1) *line,* (2) *line-and-staff,* and (3) *functional.* Committee organizations may also be used for specific purposes.

Quality circles are voluntary groups of employees with similar job functions. They emphasize individual involvement in meeting company goals by encouraging workers to identify, analyze, and solve work-related problems. Quality circles began in Japan in 1962.

An *informal organization* is a network of interpersonal relationships that develops among employees within a formal organization. It satisfies employee needs to join others who have similar interests and values. The informal organization provides important communication links among employees. A *grapevine* is an informal communication system that employees use to exchange news and information. Managers must recognize the existence of informal structures and learn to use them so that informal group attitudes will support and contribute to company goals and objectives.

Review questions

1. How do organization and organizing pertain to all groups?
2. How do the three organizational elements combine to form an organizational structure?
3. In what ways does the need for specialization affect Barry's Sports Shop?
4. How does an organization chart contribute to a business operation?
5. What are the three common forms of departmentalization?
6. Explain the source of managerial authority and how it filters through the organization.
7. How are authority and responsibility related? Why should there be a balance between them?
8. Explain the process of delegation. How is it related to authority and responsibility?
9. Why is there no "right" span of control?
10. How does line organization differ from line-and-staff organization?
11. What are the major elements of quality circles? Why have they been successful?
12. What causes the formation of an informal organization? How can management work productively with a grapevine?

Discussion questions

1. Name five organizations you belong to. What is your role in each? Why did you join them?
2. Why is it important for an organization to fulfill the goals of its employees insofar as possible?
3. In Figure 5.2, what functions does Barry perform as owner-manager of Barry's Sports Shop?
4. Select four companies in your city or town. Which departmentalization types do they use? Why?
5. Draw an organization chart for the business you are most familiar with. Where are you located on the chart? How does your job contribute to the overall functioning of the business?
6. President Harry Truman had a sign on his desk reading "The buck stops here." What did it mean?

7. Briefly explain the meaning and importance of each of the following:
   a. span of control
   b. unity of command
   c. chain of command.
8. What positive influences can an informal organization have on a business? What negative influences can it have?

Chapter 5 case

"Sometimes I feel like crying"

The problem here, while more extreme than most cases, can be heard in many organizations.

Charlie Barnett, dock foreman for Speedy Motor Freight, sat on a large container near the loading area, his head buried in his hands. The traffic manager, who happened to walk by, asked what the trouble was.

"I can't figure it out," mumbled Charlie. "I've really tried to do a good job around here, but nothing I do seems to be good enough. Yesterday, the superintendent of operations climbed on my back because the average truck load has decreased. And then, just about an hour ago, the sales manager phoned and chewed me out because I didn't give priority treatment to one of his best customer's shipments.

"Honestly, there just doesn't seem to be any system around here. I don't know what to do or what to expect. On top of that, things keep changing all the time. I don't even know what the load average should be or who the top accounts are. And if I don't know, then how in blazes are the men working under me supposed to know? All of us here want to do a good job, but it sure is frustrating. Sometimes it gets so I just feel like crying."

Having heard Charlie Barnett's observations, what can you conclude about the organizational structure and practices of Speedy Motor Freight? In particular:

1. What is the major problem (or problems)?
2. What factors seem to be causing the problem(s)?
3. What are some possible solutions to consider? What consequences do you see for each?
4. Of the possible solutions, which would you use? Explain your choice(s).

Business in perspective

Mechanisms of reward

Christmas bonuses . . . Olympic-size pools . . . discounts on gas . . . Are these presents from some overly indulgent grandmother? Not really. These are just some of the features of worker incentive programs at two major industrial companies. While one company offers unusually lucrative pay rates, the other lures its workers with fringe benefits more typical of a country club. The goal, however, in both cases is to increase worker productivity, thereby decreasing the cost of the product and underselling the competition. And produce they do.

Lincoln Electric Company of Cleveland, Ohio, can boast sales of $456 million in 1980. It experienced a sales growth of 13.6 percent in 1979 and of 5.8 percent in 1980.

Just how has Lincoln managed to achieve this? How do 2600 workers make $456 million in product? Lincoln is a no-nonsense company. It rewards the workers handsomely, and it expects a lot in return. The company maintains the traditional time clocks, supervisors, and inspectors. It guarantees a 32-hour week but it usually expects at least 45, paying overtime for everything over 40. . . .

The heart, however, of Lincoln's system is piecework. The worker is paid exactly for what he produces. This enables an employee to work as hard, and to earn as much, as he wants. Notes George E. Willis, Lincoln's President, "Piecework makes a Lincoln worker outproduce his fellow industrial worker." Mr. Manross predicts the selling prices of Lincoln's products would increase by 30 percent if the policy were to be eliminated. . . .

Rewarding all this diligent work is the unusually high pay. In addition to the wage, the worker receives an annual performance-based bonus. Last year these bonuses amounted to $47 million. In all, the *average* Lincoln worker makes an enviable $38,000. It is the philosophy of the company to allow the worker to spend his money as he wishes. Thus, it doesn't offer many fringes.

Lincoln is able to pay high wages because of its high productivity. While its competition spends 35 to 38 percent of its revenues on wages, Lincoln only yields 25 percent.

Diametrically opposite to Lincoln but equally notable in its productivity is the Sullair Corp. of Michigan City, Indiana.

Unlike Lincoln, it has no foremen or time clocks. Instead of being paid by the piece, the Sullair worker is on salary, and he only works four days of the week, putting in 40 hours, however. David Swanson, vice-president of manufacturing, notes, "it would be easy for us to fall into the general pattern of industry, to hire supervision and have time clocks, but it would be a very boring thing. It takes away from the freedom which a person would like to have."

If the less pressured environment is not enough to lure the Sullair worker, there are plenty of fringes. An Olympic-size pool, saunas, baseball fields, and tennis and basketball courts all grace the plants. There is a 15 percent discount at all neighboring grocery stores and a 30 percent cut in the price of gas at the company pumps.

In addition, there is a profit-sharing plan scaled to the responsibility of the job. Indeed, the company feels that the worker may get less money than their counterparts at Lincoln do, but they enjoy the fringes.

With this lenient and, indeed, gracious working atmosphere, one might think that workers would work less instead of working more. However, the company has enjoyed a phenomenal growth in its productivity since initiating its various fringe programs. . . . Henry Meywes, vice-president of human resources, asserts that Sullair's productivity is 30 to 50 percent higher than that of most other companies.

Both Lincoln and Sullair are relatively small, highly technological, capital-intensive enterprises. They also both benefit from being nonunion. This affords a great deal of flexibility in job assignments. Observes Lincoln's Mr. Manross, "We don't have any opposition to labor unions; we just don't think we need them." Mr. Willis notes that the goals of unions are not necessarily the goals of the company. Whatever the case, the workers do not press for unions since they are so well paid. Many of them, in fact, feel that unions are counterproductive.

Adapted from "Mechanisms of Reward," *Business Today,* Fall 1981, p. 12 with permission of the publisher. © 1981.

Chapter 6

Developing human resources

Key terms

need
motivation
Hawthorne effect
physiological needs
safety needs
social needs
esteem needs
self-actualization needs
Theory X
Theory Y
morale
management by objectives (MBO)
flextime
job enrichment
communication

Chapter objectives

In Chapter 6, you will learn:

Why managers must understand their employees

What needs are and how they relate to motivation

How the motivation process works and why it is a continuous process

The meaning of Frederick W. Taylor's classical theory of motivation

What the Hawthorne studies were and what the Hawthorne effect shows

The characteristics of the five need levels in Abraham H. Maslow's hierarchy of needs

The major assumptions about human behavior presented in Douglas McGregor's Theory X and Theory Y

How certain management approaches seek to motivate employees, including management by objective (MBO), flextime, and job enrichment

What the quality of worklife concept is and why managers are giving it increased attention

How the communication process works and why two-way communication is vital in an organization

The guides to effective listening

Overview

Human intelligence, creativity, and judgment are valuable resources. Organization charts, computers, and business plans may all contribute to a firm's efficiency. But they cannot replace human beings. Just as natural resources like oil, coal, and timber are limited, so, too, are human resources. They, like natural resources, must be used carefully and not wasted.

This chapter looks at how human relations affect a business organization. It examines the basic motivations and needs employees bring to their jobs. The chapter also surveys some management theories about employee motivation and the current quality of worklife programs that promote employee involvement and job commitment. The concluding section discusses the communication process and its importance in an organization.

Figure 6.1 What do employees want from their jobs?

Job factor	Rankings by Employees	Rankings by Managers
Good wages	5	1
Job security	4	2
Promotion and growth with company	7	3
Good working conditions	9	4
Interesting work	6	5
Management loyalty to workers	8	6
Tactful disciplining	10	7
Full appreciation for work done	1	8
Sympathetic understanding of personal problems	3	9
Feeling "in" on things	2	10

Paul Hersey and Kenneth H. Blanchard, *Management of Organizational Behavior: Utilizing Human Resources,* 3d edition (Englewood Cliffs, NJ: Prentice-Hall, 1977), p. 47.

Do managers understand employees?

A company hires people for their physical and mental abilities. But how can management inspire and stimulate employees to do their best work?

Managers often are unable to explain their employees' behavior. Because they are unable to put themselves in their workers' places, they do not understand what employees consider important.

Figure 6.1 lists some job factors that a group of employees and managers were asked to rank in order to importance. Managers ranked the job factors according to the importance they thought employees gave them.

The differences between the managers' and employees' answers suggest that these managers, at least, were quite out of touch with the needs of their workers.

Managers are often in a difficult position. On one hand, managers are accountable to someone else for their performance. On the other hand, they must rely on subordinates to perform their work. Subordinates may claim that too much is expected of them. But the manager's boss may say that the subordinates are not doing enough and need to be more productive.

To succeed in such situations, managers must understand human motivation. Then they can help employees to satisfy their needs in the workplace. When an employee's needs are satisfied, the employee, the manager, and the company benefit.

What motivates employees?

A need is an individual's perceived lack of something seen as useful or desirable. Motivation is a response to a need that makes an individual work toward achieving a particular goal. A sense of need is the basis of motivation. A motivated person tries to act in ways that will fulfill a need.

For example, a person who has not eaten for two days is motivated by the need for food. The need to eat motivates the person to take action to satisfy the hunger. Satisfying the hunger becomes a goal. Figure 6.2 summarizes the motivational process followed in seeking goal satisfaction or need fulfillment.

There is a basic motivational sequence:
1. A felt need causes tension and unrest.
2. The tension triggers action to resolve the need.
3. The action achieves goal satisfaction.
4. The tension is reduced, the specific need goes away, and other goals and needs replace the original need.
5. The process begins again with another need.

Individuals almost never completely satisfy all their needs. Instead, they arrange their needs by order of importance. Then they concentrate on satisfying the most important needs first.

Figure 6.2 The motivation process

Goals may be seen as satisfiers. When goals are attained, needs are satisifed. Employees bring their own goals and needs to the work setting. At the same time, the organization also has its own goals and objectives. For an organization to function most effectively, company goals and employee goals must be as similar as possible. Coordinating employee goals and company goals is a major challenge for managers.

Motivation can be a response to unusual needs.

"The pay is immaterial. The real reward comes in saying 'strike three' to an $800,000-a-year man."

From the *Wall Street Journal,* Permission—Cartoon Features Syndicate

The history of motivation theory

Since the nineteenth century, managers have looked for ways to motivate employees to provide a fair day's work for a fair day's pay. As a result, various motivation theories were developed. These theories show how assumptions about employees' behavior and its causes have changed over the years.

The classical theory of motivation

Frederick W. Taylor has been called the father of scientific management. In the late nineteenth century, he developed what came to be called the classical theory of motivation. According to this theory, workers are motivated primarily by money.

Taylor believed that management should develop more efficient work processes. Then managers could show workers that using the improved methods would lead to increased wages. There was a double appeal: workers would earn more money and the company would benefit from increased output.

Taylor was among the first to use time-and-motion studies to determine the most efficient ways to perform specific tasks. Based on the studies, a standard could be set that would measure acceptable levels of output.

Taylor recommended the use of a piece-rate system. Employees would receive a certain price for each piece they produced. Workers who produced less than the established quota were paid the minimum rate for each piece produced. Workers who exceeded the quota were paid a higher price for each piece they produced.

A scientific analysis of job operations was combined with a wage incentive plan. Workers were guaranteed greater income if they increased their output. Taylor's scheme was innovative for its time. It had a profound effect on many manufacturing plants.

The Hawthorne studies

From 1927 to 1932, a group of researchers led by Elton Mayo conducted a series of studies at Western Electric's Hawthorne plant near Chicago. They wanted to find out if there was a relationship between employees' physical surroundings and their productivity.

The researchers made many changes in the workplace and measured their affects on output. At various times, they changed the level of lighting, regrouped workers into special units, interviewed employees about supervisory practices, and observed work behavior and output.

The researchers made several unexpected discoveries. In particular, they found that employee performance was affected by more than physical surroundings. Pressure from fellow workers was an especially strong influence. Employees seemed to show as much interest in being accepted as group members as in earning higher wages. Output standards set by the group were more important than those established by

Tapping the pool of student labor

When summer rolls around, many college students find themselves broke and unemployed, despite being eager to work. Aware of this waste of manpower, a young Canadian entrepreneur is making a successful business of setting up students in the house-painting business by offering interest-free loans.

Greig Clark started out painting houses on spring and summer breaks from the University of Western Ontario, and now, at the age of 28, has put together a $10-million empire of "franchised" student house painters in the United States as well as Canada. Using what Steven Vanstone, vice-president of College Pro U.S.A., a subsidiary in Rochester, N.Y., calls the "reverse franchise" method, College Pro Painters Ltd., Toronto, has set up 128 Canadian and 44 American outlets since its foundation in 1976.

"You have to make the assumption that all college students are broke," Vanstone says. Thus, the company advances capital to students who repay the loan later in the summer, when cash flow has been established.

Student managers are recruited on college campuses in October and November. The prospect of profits far surpassing most traditional summer jobs, combined with the chance to test fledgling entrepreneurial wings, helps to draw top business students from the universities. Managers are given a 600-page tome written by Clark which describes everything from how to paint to how keep accounts; hire, fire, and train personnel; and deal courteously with customers.

During February and March breaks, student managers attend a five-day training session in which they review painting techniques and business practices, Vanstone says. By April, the student manager has recruited between 10 and 20 other students who work as painters full- or part-time for $4 to $6 an hour. The training, along with the startup capital, up-front bills and salaries, T-shirts, uniforms, coverage under the company's $2-million liability insurance, telephone answering services, and marketing and advertising, is free. College Pro advances several thousand dollars in cash and equipment to the average franchisee, Vanstone says. "There is no exchange of money until well into the summer," he adds.

As he begins getting work, the student pays back the costs of startup interest-free, plus a percentage of sales, which Vanstone says varies depending on the size of the area, its location, and the amount of potential business. So far, Vanstone says, the average student manager pockets between $4000 and $5000 for three months of work. The company clears slightly less than that. College Pro hopes to up the managers' average earnings this year, he adds.

Reprinted from the September 1982 issue of VENTURE, The Magazine for Entrepreneurs, by special permission. © 1982 Venture Magazine, Inc. 35 West 45th Street, New York, N.Y. 10036.

Chapter 6 Developing human resources

management. Workers who differed too much from the average production rate of the group were pressured to conform.

This group pressure could be both good and bad. Some work groups valued high productivity. Members who were too slow were encouraged to speed up. On the other hand, some work groups developed lower standards. They discouraged members who worked too fast.

Mayo and his associates also discovered what they termed "the Hawthorne effect." **The Hawthorne effect is the positive influence a change in the work environment has on increasing employee output.** Output was especially high when employees felt that they were an important factor in the work process. Workers who felt that they could contribute to management's decisions developed an increased commitment to their work. They felt that their input was valuable. Their morale improved, which provided even greater incentive than money.

As a result of the Hawthorne studies, managers focused their attention on the things besides money that motivated employees. This included morale, social pressure, attitudes, and communication between workers and managers.

The hierarchy of needs

In the 1940s, psychologist Abraham H. Maslow developed a theory of motivation that classified human needs in order of importance.* His major assumptions were the following:

1. People are always trying to satisfy their needs. When one need is satisfied, others arise.

2. Only unsatisfied needs affect behavior. Satisfied needs are not motivators.

3. Needs can be classified by levels of importance. Lower-level needs must be at least partly satisfied before a person can move to other need levels.

Figure 6.3 illustrates the levels of human needs according to Maslow's theory.

Physiological needs are the basic needs for food, clothing, and shelter that are required to sustain life. A person who is hungry will be motivated to obtain food above all else. Once physiological needs are at least partly satisfied, those needs lose some of their power as motivators. Most workers earn enough money to satisfy their physiological needs.

Safety needs cause people to try to avoid threatening events such as physical or financial harm. Companies try to meet their employees' safety needs by offering work safety programs, health insurance, unemployment insurance, pension plans, and similar benefits.

Social needs are needs for friendship, belonging, and love. People want to give and receive affection and to feel needed. Group acceptance and membership is an important force in work settings.

---

*A. H. Maslow, "A Theory of Human Motivation," *Psychological Review,* July 1943, pp. 370–396.

Figure 6.3 Maslow's hierarchy of needs

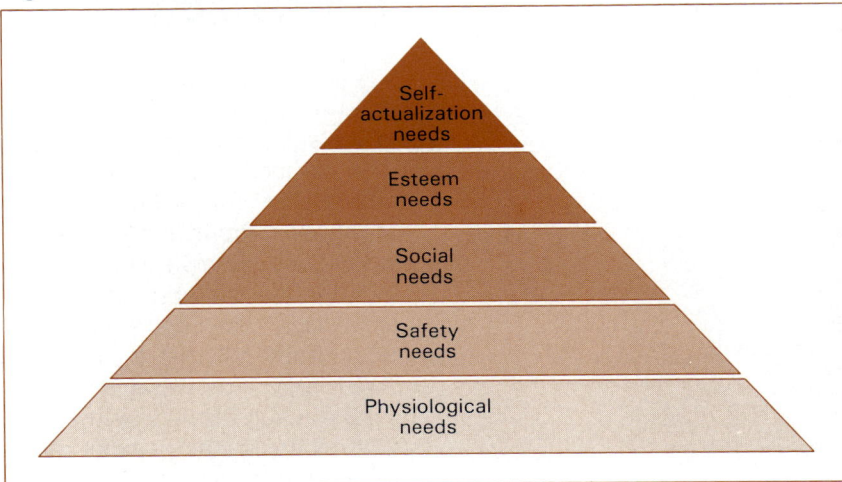

Esteem needs include the need for respect from others and the need to have respect for oneself. This respect must be based on accomplishments rather than friendship. Esteem needs lead people to compete for achievement, prestige, and power. Satisfaction of esteem is up to the individual.

Self-actualization needs lead to a desire to fulfill oneself through total use of one's talent and potential. At this level, working on a personally challenging and satisfying task is more rewarding than money or recognition from others.

How individuals fit into Maslow's theory

Maslow's theory contains valuable insights for managers. But, of course, it does not apply uniformly to all people. Most Americans have fairly well-satisfied physiological and safety needs. Therefore, they are more strongly motivated by social, esteem, and self-actualization needs.

Individual differences may be based on personal background, experience, and education. Managers must be sensitive to employees' individual needs and how the company can help satisfy them.

Theory X and Theory Y

Douglas McGregor believes that there are two basic management attitudes toward employee behavior. He calls them Theory X and Theory Y.*

---

*Douglas McGregor, *The Human Side of Enterprise* (New York: McGraw-Hill, 1960), pp. 33–34.

Theory X assumptions

Theory X holds that employees basically dislike work and must therefore be closely supervised and controlled. It assumes that employees seek to satisfy only physiological and safety needs. Its assumptions are the following:

1. Employees dislike work and will avoid it if possible.
2. Because employees dislike work, they must be controlled, pushed, and even threatened with punishment before they will put forth adequate effort.
3. Employees want security above all else. They lack ambition, prefer to be directed, and wish to avoid responsibility.

Managers who believe in Theory X tend to be very strict because they expect the worst from their employees. As a result, their employees may actually begin to act badly.

Theory Y assumptions

Theory Y assumes that employees are individuals who have ability and potential that should be encouraged in the workplace. It focuses on social, esteem, and self-actualization needs. Theory Y assumptions include:

1. Work is natural. If conditions are favorable, people will not only accept responsibility, they will seek it.
2. If people are committed to company goals, they will show self-direction and self-control.
3. Employees will be committed to company goals if they believe they will be rewarded.
4. Many people are capable of solving organizational problems, but most are not given the opportunity to try.

Believers in Theory Y try to promote employee growth and development and encourage creativity. In beliefs and actions, they are the exact opposites of Theory X managers.

Of course, Theory X and Theory Y describe two extreme styles of management. In practice, managers must consider their workers and the specific situation before they adopt a management style. No single approach will achieve the same results with all employees.

Morale

Morale is the attitude employees have toward their employer and their jobs. The morale level in a company will often be reflected in the quality and quantity of employee output.

Most theories of motivation deal with morale in terms of employee satisfaction and personal commitment to the company. Some factors that lead to high morale are the following:

Theory Z: a Japanese export

William Ouichi, a professor at the University of California at Los Angeles, has proposed Theory Z. He believes that the real secret to Japan's economic success is better management, especially in personnel policies. According to Ouichi, a Theory Z corporation emphasizes long-range planning, decision making by general agreement, and strong loyalty between workers and employers.

Japanese companies encourage workers' loyalty through
1. guaranteed lifetime employment
2. evaluation and promotion
3. nonspecialized careers
4. collective decision making.

- A feeling of individual importance within the organization
- Delegation of increasing responsibility to employees
- Employee involvement in decision making
- A sense of personal accomplishment through challenging work
- Recognition of employee achievement
- Opportunity for employee advancement and promotion.

For some employees, a job promotion is a morale-building event. If they also receive a salary increase, they may be able to satisfy higher-level physical needs. A promotion may also give employees greater social acceptance and status and help them to achieve self-realization goals.

Effects of low morale

Low morale affects job performance. Job dissatisfaction may result in lower profits and decreased productivity. It wastes employee talents and lowers the quality of goods and services.

Job dissatisfaction may take such forms as these:

- High employee turnover, which adds to the costs of replacing and training new employees.
- High employee absenteeism, which results in lost wages and lower productivity.
- Poor job performance, which wastes employee talents and affects company image.
- Employee theft or damage of company products and equipment.

If employers accept such behavior, job dissatisfaction may spread to other employees.

Methods of motivating employees

To maintain and improve employee morale, managers must find ways to meet employees' needs. Three approaches have been given considerable attention: (1) management by objectives, (2) flextime, and (3) job enrichment.

Management by objectives

Management by objectives (MBO) is a process by which managers and subordinates work together to set employee goals and to evaluate performance. It is based on a clear understanding of overall company goals and enables employees to better understand how their specific jobs fit into the total company structure. In an MBO program, each employee meets with his or her supervisor. During the meeting, the employee establishes personal work goals, usually for the next year. The goals must be in keeping with the organization's goals. The employee's performance will then be judged against the goals that were set during the meeting.

The employee and manager meet at regular intervals to evaluate the employee's progress toward the goals. When the specified time period is over, the employee and manager measure overall performance against the goals. New goals are then developed and the process is repeated.

Flextime

Flextime is a scheduling system that gives employees some control over the hours they work. Under flextime, employees are free to choose when they will begin and end their workday. They can usually begin work at any time within a two-hour period in the morning. Their lunch and departure times are then adjusted accordingly. For example, Employee A might arrive at work at 7 a.m., take lunch from 11 a.m. til noon, and leave work at 4 p.m. Employee B, on the other hand, might arrive at 8:30 a.m., lunch from 12:30 to 1:30, and leave work at 5:30 p.m.

The flextime approach offers employees the opportunity to avoid rush-hour traffic, schedule personal appointments, and fulfill such family responsibilities as seeing children off to school before coming to work. A typical flextime schedule is shown in Figure 6.4.

Although there may be similarities in flextime programs, no two companies use exactly the same system. However, all flextime programs have some characteristics in common:

All personnel must be present during a specified period of each day called *core time*.

At the beginning and end of each day are flexible time periods called *windows*.

All employees' work hours are accounted for either mechanically or on an honor system.

Figure 6.4 A typical flextime work schedule

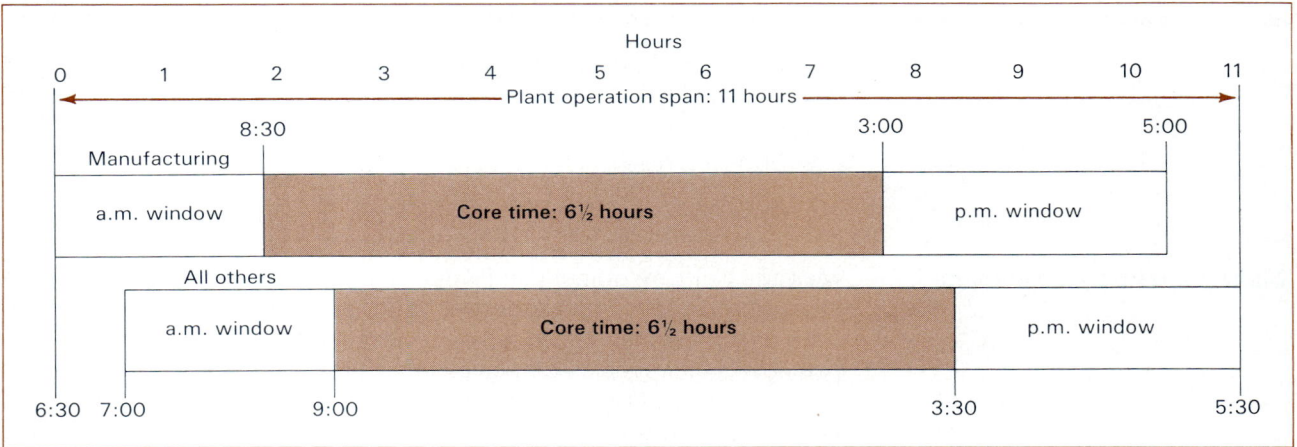

A limit is set on the amount of worktime that can be carried over from one period to another.

Everyone must work a given number of hours per week—usually from 35 to 40.

Job enrichment

Job enrichment gives employees increased authority and responsibility for their work. It encourages employees to use their intelligence and abilities to participate in solving work problems. Job enrichment helps to satisfy employees' needs for esteem and self-development.

Concern for quality of worklife grew out of interest in job enrichment. Believers in the quality of worklife concept think it is important to expand the responsibilites and influence of nonmanagement employees. They assume that people want to work together to achieve common purposes. They challenge the old-fashioned distinction between the physical work of producing goods or services and the planning and coordination of that work.

Quality of worklife systems are based on the belief that employees are willing and able to participate in management decisions at all levels. When all employees can share in decision making, authority can be delegated to the lowest possible level.

Quality of worklife principles can be applied to factory, office, and service workers alike. And they can help to offset the dissatisfaction that arises when employees feel that they aren't using their full talents.

Quality of worklife programs have been introduced in such large corporations as General Motors and Procter & Gamble. Many smaller firms have also adopted quality of worklife principles, often without recognizing that they were doing so. All hope to develop a sense of common purpose among their workers.

Figure 6.5 The communication process

Message → Sender → Encoding → Transmission means → Decoding → Receiver

The communication process

For managers to understand and motivate their employees, communication must take place. Without communication, management cannot give instructions or learn workers needs and suggestions. And employees cannot learn what is expected of them.

The nature of communication

Communication is a process by which information and understanding are transmitted from a sender to a receiver. Sometimes messages are sent but their intended meanings are not understood or received. This is *not* communication.

The communication process consists of six basic elements shown in Figure 6.5.

Communication begins with a message that a sender wishes to express. Effective communication depends on the sender having a clear idea or thought.

During encoding, the sender translates the message into suitable symbols. The symbols may be words, gestures, letters, numbers, drawings, or something else.

The sender next chooses a transmission mechanism. The transmission mechanism is the means by which a message is sent. Transmission means include face-to-face conversations, telephone conversations, written memos, tape recordings, and the like.

Once the message is transmitted, it leaves the sender's control. It is then decoded by the receiver. During decoding, the receiver translates or interprets the sender's message. At this point, communication often breaks down. The receiver may misunderstand the message for many possible reasons. Perhaps the sender did not begin with a clear thought. Or perhaps the sender used the wrong means of transmission.

For example, a complex message is more effectively transmitted in a written memo than in a telephone conversation. With a written memo, the sender can make sure that all important information is included. The receiver can then read the memo at his own pace and check his understanding. Both sender and receiver can refer to the memo whenever necessary.

Figure 6.6 The two-way communication process

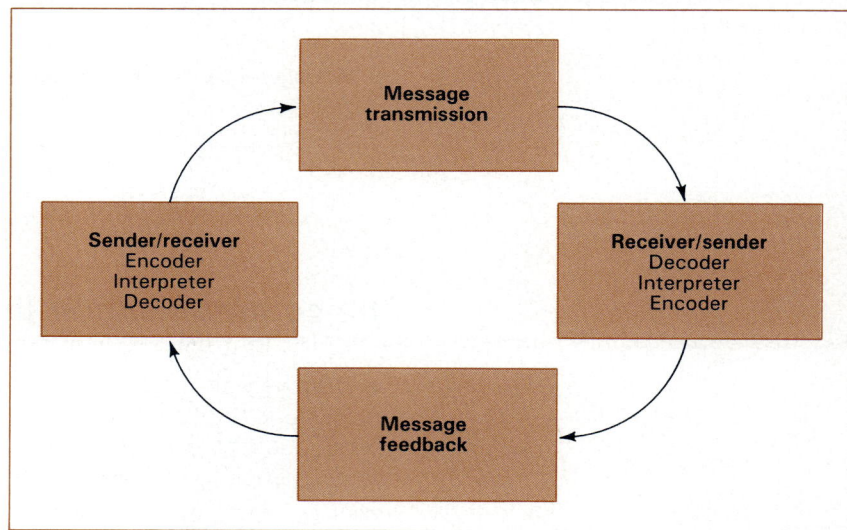

One way to check that a message was actually received and understood is through two-way communication. Figure 6.6 illustrates this process.

Two-way communication provides feedback between the sender and the receiver. Both parties act as encoders, decoders, and interpreters.

If managers are to be effective, they must recognize that communication involves more than just sending out information. Communication includes what the receiver understands as well as what the sender intended to say. In two-way communication, feedback enables the sender to make sure that the receiver actually understood the message.

Tell employees where they stand

Tom Gerrity is president of Index Systems, Inc., a company in Cambridge, Mass., specializing in consulting on and writing computer programs for clients in banking, insurance, and manufacturing. Gerrity formed a seven-member task force for a year-long analysis of the company's hierarchy, and developed a new structure reflecting four key management principles:

Make sure all employees have job titles that accurately reflect their roles and ranks in the company.

Define the logical career paths within your company.

Encourage employees to take responsibility for their own career development.

Develop consistent evaluation and promotion standards.

Since the restructuring plan has been put into effect, the turnover rate has dropped from 30 percent to about 15 percent. According to Gerrity, "It was costing us about $20,000 to replace one employee, and turnover alone was taking $500,000 a year from our bottom line."

Titles, ranks, and career paths at Index Systems

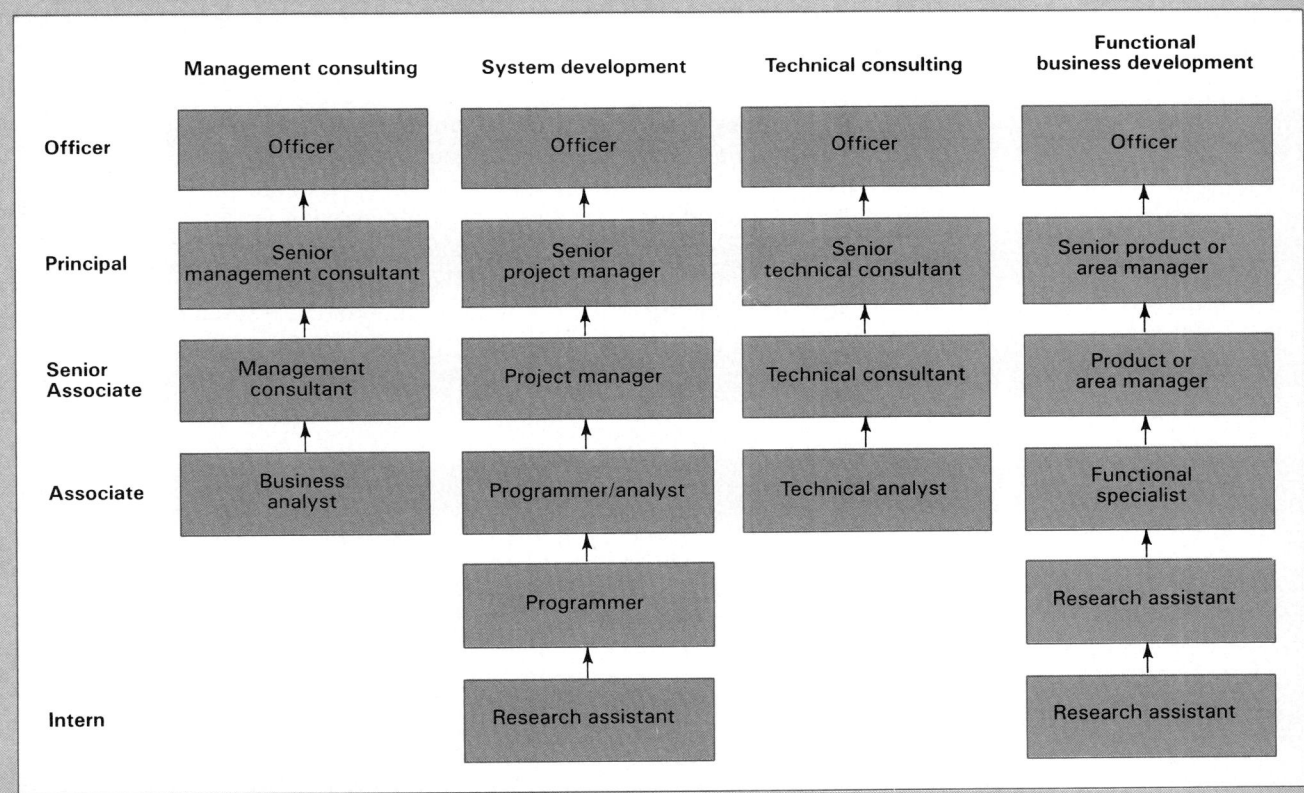

Source: David DeLong, "Tell Employees Where They Stand," *INC.*, April 1982, pp. 81–82. Reprinted by permission of the author.

Developing effective listening skills

Effective listening helps a receiver to understand a sender's messages. Better understanding leads in turn to better decision making. Effective listeners also save time because they require less explanation and repetition of information. Here are some guidelines for becoming an effective listener.*

1. **Stop talking!** If you are talking, you cannot be listening.

2. **Put the talker at ease** Let the other person know he or she is free to talk.

3. **Show the speaker you are interested** Listen to understand rather than to find fault with what is being said.

4. **Remove distractions** Avoid interruptions, screen out noise. Create an appropriate setting for listening.

5. **Empathize with the speaker.** Try to put yourself in the other person's shoes. Seek to understand his or her point of view.

6. **Be patient** Allow the speaker time to develop the point. Do not interrupt or walk away when the speaker is talking.

7. **Hold your temper** An angry person may take the wrong meaning from the message.

8. **Go easy on criticism and argument** This puts the speaker on the defensive and closes down communication.

9. **Ask questions** This encourages the speaker. It also helps to further develop the point and shows you are interested.

10. **Stop talking!** This is both the first and the last guideline. All other guidelines depend on it.

---

*Ralph G. Nichols, "Listening: What Price Inefficiency?" *Office Executive,* April 1959, pp. 15–22.

6 Developing human resources

Summary

People are the most important resource in an organization. Like any scarce resource, they must be used with maximum efficiency and minimum waste. This requires managers to be sensitive to employees' needs.

A *need* is an individual's perceived lack of something seen as useful or desirable. *Motivation* is a response to a need that makes an individual work toward a particular goal. A motivated person tries to act in ways that will fulfill a need.

The motivation process follows a specific sequence: (1) a felt need causes tension and unrest; (2) the tension triggers action to resolve the need; (3) the action achieves goal satisfaction; (4) the tension is reduced, the specific need subsides, and other goals and needs replace the original need; and (5) the process begins again with another need. People almost never completely satisfy all their needs. Instead, they arrange their needs by order of importance.

Since the nineteenth century, a number of researchers have tried to explain what motivates workers. According to Frederick W. Taylor's classical theory of motivation, workers are motivated primarily by money. Elton Mayo's studies in the 1920s and 1930s, however, showed that social pressure from coworkers has a strong influence on job performance. Mayo discovered what he called the *Hawthorne effect*—a change in the work environment bringing about an increase in productivity.

Maslow's hierarchy of needs stresses that unfilled needs are key motivational forces. He identified five need levels. *Physiological needs* are life-sustaining needs like food, clothing, and shelter. *Safety needs* are those that cause people to avoid threatening events. *Social needs* are those for friendship, belonging, and love. *Esteem needs* involve respect from others and from oneself. *Self-actualization needs* lead to the desire for self-fulfillment.

McGregor proposed that there are two basic management attitudes toward workers: Theory X and Theory Y. *Theory X* suggests that workers dislike work and need close control. *Theory Y* asserts that workers have abilities and potential that should be encouraged in the workplace. Japan's management system is based on Theory Z, which encourages strong worker-employer loyalty through consensus decision making.

Morale is the attitude employees have toward their employer and their jobs. The morale level in a company is often reflected in the quality and quantity of employee output. The factors that affect morale relate to Maslow's hierarchy of needs. Three management approaches to improved employee morale are management by objectives (MBO), flextime, and job enrichment. *Management by objectives (MBO)* is a process by which managers and subordinates work together to set employee goals and to evaluate performance. *Flextime* is a scheduling system that gives employees some control over the hours they work. *Job enrichment* gives employees increased authority and responsibility for their work. Quality of worklife programs expand employees' responsibilities and influence by having them share in the planning and coordination of their work.

Good management requires good *communication,* the process by which information and understanding are transmitted from a sender to a receiver. The six basic elements in the communication process are: (1) message, (2) sender, (3) encoding, (4) transmission means, (5) decoding, and (6) receiver. Two-way communication allows for feedback between sender and receiver. The sender can thus check that the message was correctly understood. Effective listening skills help a receiver to understand a sender's message.

Review questions

1. What are needs? How do they motivate people into taking action?
2. Describe the basic motivational sequence for satisfying needs.
3. Outline the major assumptions and beliefs about human behavior expressed by the following management theories:
    a. the classical theory
    b. the Hawthorne studies
    c. the hierarchy of needs
    d. Theory X and Theory Y
    e. Theory Z
4. What is morale? What factors promote morale? Provide common examples showing job dissatisfaction.
5. What are the pros and cons of flextime?
6. What is job enrichment? Why is it gaining in popularity?
7. What is communication? Describe how the communication process works. What is two-way communication?
8. List the guidelines for developing effective listening skills.

Discussion questions

1. In Figure 6.1, what need levels did managers focus on? What need levels did workers focus on? Why do you think there was a difference?
2. Maslow believed unfulfilled needs were basic motivational forces stimulating action. Comment on Maslow's theory.
3. Why did Taylor's emphasis on economic rewards not prove to be a strong, sustaining motivational force for workers?
4. What new information did the Hawthorne studies provide to improve everyone's understanding of employee behavior?

5. Explain how working for an "A" grade in this course represents fulfilling more than one need.
6. How may quality of worklife programs assist employees to work smarter?
7. Why do you think management approaches in the 1980s stress work involvement in basic management decisions?
8. Explain this statement: "Communication is what the receiver understands, not what the sender intended to say."

Chapter 6 case

A supervisor's dilemma

Supervisors must often make decisions that are difficult. In this case, a serious breach of company policy by the local union president presents a supervisor with a challenging situation.

An employee, highly regarded by all his fellow workers, has been caught stealing company equipment and selling it. The facts of the case are clear: the employee, a worker in the shipping department, admits taking goods and selling them. But, he explains, he had to "borrow" the goods in order to pay for an expensive operation for his child. He claims that he intended to repay the money after the operation was over.

The employee handbook states that company policy for theft of company property is job termination. However, if you fire this employee, almost all the workers will believe you have taken advantage of a technicality to get rid of the president of the local union. This could seriously lower morale and probably be quite expensive in reduced employee production.

The question of what action to take is up to you.

1. What is the major issue you as a supervisor face?
2. What action would you take as a supervisor in this situation?

Business in perspective

Raises by ballot

Romac Industries, Inc., of Seattle, Washington, has a wage-increase system intended to make a union unnecessary for its workers. It works like this:

Romac hires a worker at a specific wage and gives that worker an additional dollar an hour after six months. From then on, the employee receives raises only by vote of fellow workers. Each employee fills out a form stating his current wage, the amount he wants for a raise, and why he thinks he deserves more money. The worker's picture and request are posted on a bulletin board for at least five days. During that period, fellow workers observe the raise-seeker's work. On a designated day, the workers vote to either grant or deny the wage hike.

Management has veto power, but it rarely uses it. Manford R. MacNeil, the founder of the company, believes the system is fairer than a union pay scale. Each worker has a different level of productivity, he believes, and should be paid accordingly. Furthermore, the workers can make more informed judgments because they work together every day and have firsthand knowledge of each other's performance.

Some think the "ballot box raises" are merely popularity contests. But MacNeil is pleased with the system and says that it has increased productivity. He also holds biweekly meetings with a representative from each department and plantwide meetings every two months.

MacNeil hopes these programs will reduce the need for organized unions at Romac. He believes that unions are unnecessary if workers feel important to their company and are included in the decision-making process.

Chapter 7

Organized labor and business

Key terms

labor union
business unionism
craft union
industrial union
National Labor Relations Act
Taft-Hartley Act
Landrum-Griffin Act
organizing
bargaining unit
closed shop
union shop
open shop
agency shop
collective bargaining
strike
slowdown
picket
boycott
lockout
injunction
employer association
grievance
grievance procedure
arbitration
mediation

Chapter objectives

In Chapter 7, you will learn:

Why we have unions

The history of the labor movement in the United States

How federal legislation has helped unions—and limited them

The contents of a union contract

How collective bargaining works

The weapons unions and management can use against each other

How the grievance procedure works and the difference between arbitration and mediation

Why unions represent a declining portion of the work force and what organized labor is doing to turn the tide

How unions exercise their political power

Overview

People often decide to work together when their individual actions have failed to achieve satisfactory results. Labor unions, as formal organizations, grew out of workers' decisions to take joint action. **A labor union is a group of workers who have joined together to work toward common job-related goals such as improved wages, benefits, and working conditions.**

Labor unions were not very important in the United States until the late nineteenth century. At that time, mechanization and the growth of the factory system brought workers together in large numbers. This grouping of workers with common interests led to the growth of union organization and collective bargaining.

The growth of the labor movement resulted in many struggles. Business owners wanted to keep costs down and maintain as much control of the manufacturing process as they could. Thus, most businesses opposed the formation of unions, and some even resorted to violence to fight their growth.

This chapter takes a brief look at the development, goals, and current situation of labor unions in the United States. It also discusses the collective-bargaining process between labor and management.

Why unions?

At a college in Pennsylvania, a few students asked that the library be kept open later in the evening. Eventually, their request reached the president of the college, who said that there was no money in the budget to pay for extended hours.

The students, however, were not satisfied. So, with the support of the student government and the newspaper, they called for a sit-in. Hundreds of students showed up and refused to leave the library at closing time.

In response, the college president came to the library for a midnight negotiating session with a delegation of student leaders. A compromise was quickly reached. Library hours were lengthened four nights a week. And the president promised that the budget for the next year would include money for late hours every night. Having achieved their objective, the students quietly, but cheerfully, left the building.

Joint action by many students was successful in achieving what a few students were unable to accomplish. A display of solidarity from a group with common goals can be quite effective in many situations. Such is the philosophy behind the organized labor movement.

By historical standards, today's average industrial worker makes a comfortable wage. In 1980, the average weekly wage for a production worker was $235 a week. But in 1890, a typical worker in a textile mill had to work six ten-hour days and settle for $9 a week. Even though costs have increased since then, today's workers live much better than their nineteenth-century counterparts, in part thanks to the success of organized labor.

Figure 7.1 **Difference in structure of traditional craft and industrial unions. In craft unions, workers belong to a union that describes their trade, regardless of the industry they work in. In industrial unions, workers belong to a union that describes their industry, regardless of their actual job function.**

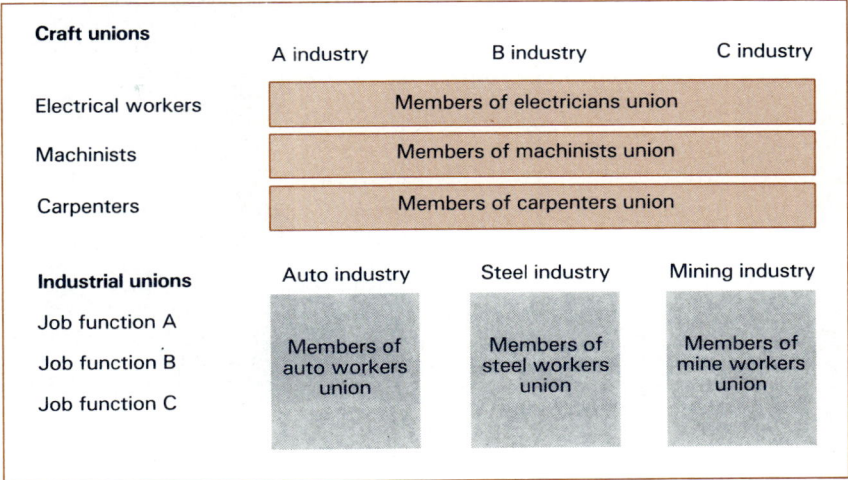

History of the labor movement

The first unions in the United States were formed in the early nineteenth century by craftsmen such as shoemakers, carpenters, and bricklayers. Craft unions are made up of skilled workers from a single trade. Early craft unions were small local organizations that dealt only with matters related to their members' trade.

The first national union was the Knights of Labor, which reached its peak of 700,000 members in 1886. The Knights of Labor included both skilled craftsmen and less-skilled industrial workers such as miners. Because its members lacked common goals, however, the Knights of Labor failed.

The American Federation of Labor

As the Knights of Labor began to decline, a cigar maker named Samuel Gompers brought together a number of skilled craftsmen's unions to form the American Federation of Labor (AFL). The AFL flourished for several reasons.

First, Gompers limited the AFL to business unionism. **Business unionism is the belief that a union should concentrate on matters of direct interest to workers—wages, working conditions, and hours.** Gompers promoted collective bargaining as the most effective tool for union success.

Samuel Gompers

Courtesy of the Library of Congress

Second, Gompers founded the AFL as a federation of independent craft unions. It included carpenters, electricians, plumbers, and the like. Gompers believed that these craft unions were in a better bargaining position than other workers because they had specialized skills. These skills served as a common bond among members and gave them greater power in contract negotiations with employers.

Union expansion	The AFL grew steadily in membership and influence. By 1920, most craftworkers had been organized and the AFL's growth slowed. To gain new members, some AFL unions began to recruit workers from mass-production industries such as the steel, mining, and automobile industries. They became industrial unions. **Industrial unions are groups of workers from the same industry.**
The Congress of Industrial Organizations	In 1935, the industrial unions broke away from the AFL to form the Congress of Industrial Organizations (CIO). Their leader was John L. Lewis, the mineworkers' president. The two groups remained rivals until 1955, when they merged into the AFL-CIO, led by George Meany. Of the 175 unions now in the United States, about 60 percent—including most of the largest—are affiliated with the AFL-CIO. An exception is the largest single union, the International Brotherhood of Teamsters, with nearly two million members. The Teamsters were expelled from the AFL-CIO in 1957 for alleged corruption.

Chapter 7 Organized labor and business

The 1892 clash between Pinkerton agents and employees of the Carnegie Steel Works in Homestead, Pennsylvania, damaged the cause of unionism.

Courtesy of the AFL-CIO

The struggle for acceptance

Organized labor's attempts to gain recognition resulted in bitter fights. Today, federal laws protect workers' rights to organize, but there was little protection in the early days. Business owners did not want to be bound by union demands, so they developed tactics to oppose the unions.

Firing union organizers Companies often fired employees who attempted to organize or join a union. The threat of being fired scared off potential members.

Blacklists Employers circulated the names of workers who were fired for union activities. Such workers then had difficulty finding another job in the same location.

Yellow-dog contracts Some employers forced new employees to sign special agreements before they would hire them. The employees had to promise not to engage in union activity at the risk of losing their jobs.

Use of strikebreakers If workers went on strike, the company often hired new workers to replace them. The replacements are known as strikebreakers, or scabs (an uncomplimentary term). This practice often led to violence.

Even today, employers sometimes replace striking workers. In 1981, the air traffic controllers, members of the Professional Air Traffic Controllers Union (PATCO), went on strike. As government employees, the strike was illegal. After a warning to return to work, President Ronald Reagan fired all striking controllers. Then, the government set about training new controllers as replacements.

Armed safety guards Some companies hired special security guards to deal with unions. The companies claimed that the guards were there to prevent violence during a strike or to protect nonunion workers from alleged threats by organizers. But the guards were known to use heavy-handed tactics to intimidate union organizers or sympathizers. Ford Motor Company gained a reputation for hiring tough security guards to discourage union organizing.

Labor legislation

By the time Franklin D. Roosevelt became president in 1933, labor was strong enough to demand help from his sympathetic administration.

National Labor Relations Act

The most far-reaching piece of labor legislation took effect in 1935. It was the National Labor Relations Act, also known as the Wagner Act after its author, Senator Robert Wagner of New York. **The National Labor Relations Act gave legal recognition to labor unions and has been called labor's Bill of Rights.**

The Wagner Act outlawed many of the coercive tactics that employers had used in fighting unions. Second, it legalized collective bargaining and required employers to bargain with a union representative once the union local was certified. Third, it set up the National Labor Relations Board (NLRB) to oversee the law's enforcement and to supervise union elections. Fourth, the Wagner Act made it illegal for an employer to fire or even threaten to fire an employee for any union activity. And, finally, it outlawed yellow-dog contracts and prohibited employers from interfering with a union's self-government.

The Wagner Act encouraged the growth of organized labor. In 1935, only 13.2 percent of the nonfarm work force was unionized. But by 1945, union membership had increased to 36 percent.

The Labor-Management Relations Act

The Labor-Management Relations Act, popularly known as the Taft-Hartley Act, which became law in 1947, **gives the president the power to ask the federal courts to order striking workers back to work for an 80-day cooling-off period.** This power can be used only after an investigation determines that the strike is harmful to the nation's health or safety. Negotiations are supposed to continue in the meantime. Presidents rarely use this power, and it is sometimes difficult to enforce. During the long coal miners' strike in the winter of 1978, the workers were ordered back to work under the Taft-Hartley Act, but they refused. Short of bringing in the National Guard, which would have been a very unpopular move, there was no way the president could force the miners to work.

One of the most controversial sections of the Taft-Hartley Act is Section 14-B, the right-to-work provision. It gives individual states the power to pass laws banning union shops, in which employees must join the union after a short trial period. This makes open shops, in which union membership is completely voluntary, the only alternative for union locals in those states. Although an individual's right to work is hard to oppose in principle, the repeal of such laws is a top priority in the labor movement. Nineteen states, mostly in the West and South, have passed right-to-work laws and use them to attract new businesses.

The Taft-Hartley Act also bans certain unfair union practices, such as refusing to bargain with management and refusing to work with materials that were supplied by another firm whose employees are on strike. The law also states that unions must give employers 60 days' notice of their intent to strike if no contract is negotiated.

The Landrum-Griffin Act

In 1959, Congress passed the Landrum-Griffin Act as an amendment to the Taft-Hartley Act. Its purpose was to force reforms in union management, which was often corrupt. An investigation had shown that some union officials took union funds for personal use and demanded payoffs from employers. **The Landrum-Griffin Act required that union officials who handle funds be bonded and established federal penalties for embezzlement of union funds. It also required unions to have regularly scheduled elections of officers, using secret ballots.**

Union organizing

Organizing is the process through which nonunion workers form a union. An organizing drive may be initiated by workers or by a union.

Sometimes workers feel the need to organize because they are not being paid or treated fairly by their employer. They may then ask a local union to represent them.

More frequently, however, unions seek out unrepresented workers, often in companies that once were small but have grown large enough for union attention. In an effort to enlarge their membership, unions have begun organizing workers who have not had much union representation in the past, such as teachers, salesclerks, stockbrokers, and doctors.

No matter who starts the organizing drive, a union official meets with the workers and explains how the union will benefit them. In some cases, more than one union tries to organize the same group.

The first step—a vote

Under National Labor Relations Board rules, if 30 percent of the workers in a company sign cards showing their interest in a union, the employer must allow an election. Sometimes the union election requires a simple yes (for the union) or no (against the union) vote. If several unions are competing, workers may select among them or vote against all of them.

If any union gets more than 50 percent of the vote, the employer must recognize its authority to represent the workers. If the majority of workers reject the union, another attempt to organize the group can be made after a year has passed.

Defining the bargaining unit

Only the members of the bargaining unit may vote in a union election. **The bargaining unit is the specific group that the union will represent.** Defining who belongs to the bargaining unit is very important and not always simple. For example, workers with management decision-making authority cannot be part of the bargaining unit. But there are often disputes over the definition of management decision-making authority.

Consider the case of a college faculty that is organizing. The administration may say that department heads are part of management because they make decisions about budgeting, scheduling, appointing part-time faculty, and the like. If they are management, they should be excluded from the bargaining unit.

The union could argue that department heads teach courses, have academic-year schedules, and cannot hire and fire full-time faculty. Therefore, they should be included in the bargaining unit.

Figure 7.2 Secret ballot for a union representation section

UNITED STATES OF AMERICA
National Labor Relations Board
OFFICIAL SECRET BALLOT
FOR CERTAIN EMPLOYEES OF

Do you wish to be represented for purposes of collective bargaining by

MARK AN "X" IN THE SQUARE OF YOUR CHOICE

YES ☐   NO ☐

DO NOT SIGN THIS BALLOT. Fold and drop in ballot box.
If you spoil this ballot return it to the Board Agent for a new one.

Courtesy of the National Labor Relations Board

In the end, a compromise might be reached: department heads would not be in the unit, but each department would have the power to select its own chairperson and set a limit on the chairperson's term of office. The contract could describe the responsibilities and teaching loads of department heads. And even their pay could be defined in the contract.

Union security

Once the bargaining unit is defined, union and management must decide which members of the bargaining unit will belong to the union and pay dues. The union wants a membership system that will give it maximum protection.

Closed shop

A closed shop is one in which every eligible worker must belong to the union and the employer can hire only people who are already union members. It is the surest way to preserve union strength.

Unions argue that because they bargain for everyone and everyone benefits from a union contract, everyone should belong to the union.

Employers, on the other hand, believe that this provision limits their hiring freedom and takes free choice away from workers who might not want to join the union. The Taft-Hartley Act banned the closed shop.

Union shop

A union shop is one in which the employer is free to hire anyone, but after a short trial period, new workers must join the union. This still limits employees' freedom of choice, but it gives management a freer hand in hiring. The union shop is the most common union arrangement in most industries.

Open shop

A third alternative is the open shop. **An open shop is one in which union membership is completely voluntary.** The union is recognized as the bargaining agent for all workers. Everyone, member or not, is covered by all provisions of the contract. But no employee is required to join the union or pay dues.

Agency shop

Most unionists think the open shop is a weak arrangement. A compromise between an open shop and a union shop is an agency shop. **An agency shop is one in which nonmembers must pay the union an amount equal to the dues paid by the members.** This system is based on the belief that nonmembers should help support the union because they benefit from its efforts.

The union contract

At the heart of the union-management relationship is the contract. A union contract describes the duties and responsibilities of both labor and management. Most contracts run for two or three years. But some contracts run for only one year while others run for ten. Long-term contracts often contain a provision to reopen negotiations on specific issues, usually wages.

The exact details of union contracts vary greatly, but all contracts tend to cover the same subjects. They usually address each of the following topics.
1. Definition of the bargaining unit
2. Union security: union shop, open shop, agency shop
3. Wages and hours: hourly wage rates for each category of job and length of employment, normal hours of work, conditions and rates of overtime pay
4. Fringe benefits: vacations, holidays, personal days, medical benefits, pension programs, etc.
5. Management and union rights and responsibilities: acknowledgment of the union's rights to conduct union business on company property and the workers' responsibility to help management operate profitably

6. Seniority: definitions and privileges of seniority
7. Working conditions: terms of employment, breaks, facilities (showers, lockers, lunchrooms), etc.
8. Grievance procedure and arbitration: steps to follow in settling disputes, extent to which there is binding arbitration
9. Strikes and lockouts: agreement that union members will not strike during the term of the contract and that management will not lock workers out.

Collective bargaining

A union contract is arrived at through collective bargaining. **Collective bargaining is a process in which an employer and union representatives meet as equals to agree on the provisions of an employment contract.** Collective bargaining is a careful and delicate process. It involves every possible method of persuasion—give-and-take compromise, bluffing, shouting, behind-the-scenes maneuvering, and more.

Negotiating strategy

The collective bargaining process usually begins with the union presenting a list of changes it wants in the existing contract. Management either accepts, modifies, or rejects each demand. Management may also present its own proposals for change. Both sides know that they cannot achieve all that they want. At the beginning of the process, good bargaining strategy requires that neither side disclose which items it is willing to discard or modify and which it is serious about keeping. Thus, the usual union strategy is to ask for far more than it can reasonably expect to gain. Then, the union agrees to give up certain items, one by one, if management will also make concessions.

Each side must convince its members that it is driving the best bargain possible. Once union and management representatives have reached an agreement, all union members vote on whether to accept the contract. If union members reject the contract, union representatives must go back to the bargaining table to find a more agreeable settlement. This can be difficult because management may not be willing to make any more concessions.

To supplement their collective bargaining tools, both unions and management have methods of putting pressure on the other party to adopt a settlement that favors their side.

Labor's weapons
Strike

The best-known union weapon is the strike, sometimes called a *walk-out.* **A strike occurs when members of a bargaining unit refuse to work, usually after a contract has expired.** Even the threat of a strike is a potent union weapon.

Unions in declining industries often face loss of jobs if they strike.

Reprinted by permission of Tribune Company Syndicate, Inc.

Nonetheless, a strike can cause hardships for workers as well as for management. Workers do not get paid by the company and usually lose their benefits, such as medical coverage, if a strike is long. Some large unions have strike funds that they use to pay striking members. But the payments are usually small. A long strike is expensive for both sides.

Although strikes are often in the news, most labor contracts are negotiated without strikes. According to estimates, only 2 percent of all labor contract negotiations result in strikes.

Slowdown

Rather than strike and lose work, a bargaining unit may institute a slowdown. **A slowdown is a job action in which union members come to work but stall production.** Often, workers perform their activities "by the book." Air traffic controllers, for example, are responsible for making sure that planes take off and land safely. Before their illegal strike in 1981, PATCO members sometimes delayed air traffic by insisting that every rule be applied in great detail.

Picket

A picket is a gathering of workers outside their workplace as a public protest against their employer's actions. Workers may picket as part of a strike or to protest unfair labor practices. The right to picket is guaranteed by the First Amendment as a form of free speech.

Chapter 7 Organized labor and business

Union give-backs at Chrysler

> By tradition, unions bargain fiercely for higher wages. But high labor costs are one reason U.S.-built cars cannot compete in price with many imported cars—especially those from Japan. So the United Auto Workers (UAW) is being forced to take a new approach to contract negotiations.
>
> In 1981, the UAW voted to grant Chrysler Corporation wage and benefit concessions that would save the company $622 million. The move was necessary because Chrysler was in serious financial trouble.
>
> As one of the most powerful unions in America, the UAW has managed to win very generous contracts. In 1981, the auto workers made 60 percent more per hour than the average worker in a manufacturing company. Nonetheless, the auto workers were faced with massive layoffs. The leaders as well as the workers came to realize that high pay rates were of no benefit if there were no jobs.
>
> Thus, in 1981, the union decided to work out compromises with management just so its members could continue to work. If prosperity returns to the U.S. auto industry, the UAW will no doubt expect the manufacturers to restore the pay cuts—with interest.

Boycott

A boycott is an attempt to discourage people from buying goods or services from a particular firm. A secondary boycott is an attempt to keep a firm from buying or selling goods and services to a firm that faces a primary boycott.

It is very difficult to mount an effective boycott, but there have been some successes. In the late 1960s, the United Farm Workers had trouble getting some farmers to negotiate contracts for their field laborers. The union asked the general public not to purchase grapes unless the fruit carried an emblem showing it came from a union-organized farm. It took years, but eventually most farmers agreed to recognize the United Farm Workers and bargain on contracts.

Management's weapons

Lockout

Employers have fewer weapons than unions have. In a lockout, an employer shuts down the firm until the union agrees to some management demands. A lockout is common when union picketing halts deliveries or prevents trucks from taking away finished goods. The company may then tell all employees, even those not on strike, to stay home from work. This puts pressure on the strikers to resolve the problem.

Injunction

In some cases, an employer can obtain an injunction. An injunction is a court order that prohibits picketing or some other labor practice. Injunctions were once a common management weapon. But in 1932, the Norris-LaGuardia Act decreed that the court could issue an injunction only when there is or may be violence, massive picketing, or possible damage to company property. Refusal to obey an injunction may result in fines and even jail.

Employer association

In some cases, employers have banded together. **An employer association is a group of employers that join together to deal with labor unions.** Its purpose is to present a unified front to organized labor. At times, a strike against one member of an association has resulted in the other members voluntarily shutting down, although such a tactic may not always be legal.

The settlement of union-management conflicts

Most union contracts contain a section that tells how disagreements between workers and management can be resolved. It enables individual workers and the union to appeal hiring and promotion decisions, awarding of business to nonunion contractors, and similar issues.

The grievance procedure

A grievance is an individual or union complaint that management has violated a provision of a union contract. A grievance procedure is a formal process set forth in a union contract that is used to settle disputes between union and management.

A grievance procedure is set in motion by a worker or union official. It can go through five possible steps. All parties hope to settle the dispute at the earliest possible step. Each step involves progressively higher levels of management and union officials.

Step 1 At the first step, the employee explains the grievance to the shop steward, who is a fellow worker in charge of union business for the employees' work group. In a few cases, the shop steward may tell the worker that management acted within its rights. But in most instances, the steward meets with the employee's supervisor—the lowest management level—and tries to work out a solution informally.

Step 2 If the union or the worker is unsatisfied with the supervisor's response, the business agent or chief shop steward files a second-level grievance with the next highest supervisor. Most grievances are settled at Steps 1 or 2.

Step 3 At this point, the local union president or a special union grievance committee meets with the plant manager or an industrial relations officer of the same status. Grievances that reach this level tend to be relatively important because union officers usually refuse to pursue minor matters this far.

Chapter 7 Organized labor and business

Unions and management often disagree on an acceptable starting point for negotiations.

"Sometimes ballpark figures aren't in the ballpark."

Drawing by Wm. Hamilton, © 1976 The New Yorker Magazine, Inc.

Step 4 At the fourth level of the grievance procedure, a national union officer may join the talks, as will the top corporate officer in charge of labor relations. This may happen with serious problems, such as what level employee may perform a given job or the dismissal of a worker.

Step 5 If all else fails and the grievance is very important, the employee may ask that a solution be reached through arbitration. **Arbitration is a process in which an impartial third party listens to the arguments of both labor and management and renders a final decision.** In many contracts, the arbitrator's decision is binding on both sides. There is no further appeal and both sides must respect the arbitrator's ruling.

Mediation

Like arbitration, mediation involves an impartial third party. But unlike an arbitrator, who renders a decision, a mediator acts as a go-between. **Mediation is an attempt to help the two sides in a dispute find areas of agreement.** Mediators are often useful in major contract negotiations. They listen to the issues and arguments of each side and try to find some common ground. A mediator's job is to get both sides to make necessary compromises.

Under certain circumstances, unions and employers who are negotiating a contract must notify the Federal Mediation and Conciliation Service. This is a government agency with several hundred mediators who participate in major negotiations that are in difficulty. Some states offer similar services.

Mediators perform a useful function, especially in bitter negotiations. In such cases, the mediator may meet separately with each side. He or she suggests proposals or carries ideas from one side to the other. In that way, personality clashes and face-to-face confrontations can be avoided.

Issues facing organized labor

Since 1945, the growth of labor unions has not kept pace with the growth of the work force as a whole. As a result, today fewer than 25 percent of all workers are unionized, down from a high of 36 percent. In all, about 22 million workers are organized.

There are several reasons for the decline in union membership. First, the U.S. economy is becoming increasingly service oriented. Service workers, from accountants, doctors, and teachers to retail clerks and stockbrokers, have traditionally been less interested in unionization than were blue-collar workers. Holders of service jobs have had more prestige and better working conditions than industrial or trade workers. By education, temperament, and tradition, white-collar workers are less prone to accept unionization. Yet they are the fastest-growing portion of the work force.

Second, manufacturers from the North have been relocating to new factories in the South. Because the South is largely agricultural, it has less of a history of unionization, and workers there have been less likely to organize. Companies can pay slightly lower wages and avoid many of the restrictions they face in union plants. Most southern states have taken advantage of the right-to-work provision of the Taft-Hartley Act.

Third, employers have learned more about unions and are better prepared to resist union-organizing drives. Nonunion companies often meet or even exceed pay scales for the same jobs. They offer high wages and good benefits so that employees are not receptive to union organizers.

Union responses

Organized labor has been slowly making progress, both in the South and among white-collar workers. For example, between 1964 and 1978, the number of union workers in the Deep South increased 178 percent, while union membership in the country as a whole grew only 19 percent. Similarly, union membership in white-collar occupations rose 86 percent between 1960 and 1978.

Efforts to organize teachers have been especially successful. The number of unionized teachers grew 402 percent from 1964 to 1980. State, county, and municipal workers, although generally prohibited from striking, have nonetheless begun to organize and engage in collective bargaining. They are represented mostly by the American Federation of State, County, and Municipal Employees (AFSCME). Figure 7.3 shows that this union's membership grew 367 percent in 16 years. The retail clerks union, one of the oldest white-collar unions, merged with the meat cutters and increased only 42 percent.

Figure 7.3 Percentage change in membership of selected unions 1964–1980

Union	Percentage change
Teachers	402%
State, county, and municipal workers	367
Service employees	103
Communications workers	87
Government workers	83
Firefighters	55
Food and commercial workers*	42
Plumbers	38
Operating engineers	36
Teamsters	25
Transit union	22
Auto workers	16
Steelworkers	(1)
Transportation workers	(4)
Oil and chemical workers	(5)
Machinists	(8)
Hotel and restaurant workers	(10)
Textile and clothing workers	(18)
Garment workers, ladies	(27)
Railway and steamship workers	(33)

*Formed from 1979 merger of retail clerks with meat cutters.
U.S. Department of Commerce, *Statistical Abstract of the United States,* 1976 and 1981 eds.

Clerks and secretaries start to organize

Until very recently, secretaries and clerical workers avoided unionization. Boston Local 925 of the Service Employees Union and an organization called Working Women, however, are working together to organize this group of workers.

Working Women is not a labor union, but it has brought about many successful discrimination suits and forced companies to make changes in the announcement of job vacancies. It even inspired the 1980 movie *9 to 5*, starring Jane Fonda, Dolly Parton, and Lily Tomlin.

Boston Local 925 is a trade union and will serve as the model for the organizing effort. It formed because secretaries and office workers—jobs in which women outnumbered men 3 to 1 in 1981—felt they were underpaid and underappreciated. In seven years, Local 925 gained 1000 members.

Once the Boston local was firmly established, it began a national effort. This drive coincided with a widespread shortage of qualified secretaries and clerks. If the organizing campaign is successful, the union's negotiating base will thus be very strong.

Logo courtesy of Local 925, Service Employees International Union, AFL-CIO.

The political power of unions

Samuel Gompers found that the key to creating a strong union movement was to give basic employment issues priority over political activity. Today, however, unions have a powerful voice within government circles. They actively support political candidates who vote on the side of organized labor.

But the power of large national unions, such as the Teamsters or United Auto Workers, goes beyond such direct activity. A long strike by the Teamsters, for example, could seriously hurt the economy by stopping the shipment of goods that other workers need. Thus, the top levels of government as well as the affected businesses are interested in settling such national contracts without a strike.

Moreover, certain large, highly visible unions set standards in their contracts that other unions try to imitate. For example, in 1978, President Jimmy Carter actively tried to control inflation by keeping wage increases to about 7 percent. The Teamsters' contract, which covered 500,000 workers, was up for renegotiation. The president believed that this contract was crucial because it would set an example for other unions. Unfortunately, the Teamsters announced that they wanted a wage increase of around 29 percent over three years.

The White House feared public reaction to such a settlement, so it tried hard to change the mind of the Teamsters' president. At last, the Teamsters took a more moderate position.

Of course, the Teamsters expected President Carter to return the favor. If a union does something for a politician, it expects favorable treatment in return. This may be support for a higher minimum wage or a law that makes it easier for unions to picket nonunion businesses.

Despite some setbacks, organized labor is expected to remain a powerful force for business to contend with and a strong influence on the economy.

7 Organized labor and business

Summary

A *labor union* is a group of workers who have joined together to work toward common job-related goals. The growth of unions was a direct response to increased industrialization in the United States. Samuel Gompers organized the first strong national union, the American Federation of Labor, by stressing *business unionism*—the belief that a union should concentrate on matters of direct interest to workers—and concentrating on craft workers.

Unions arose because people decided to work together when their individual actions failed. Largely as a result of labor struggles, workers today have better pay, shorter hours, and better working conditions than at any time in history.

Industrial unions are organized groups of workers within one industry.

Most large national unions are affiliated with the AFL-CIO, which resulted from the 1955 merger of the American Federation of Labor and the Congress of Industrial Organizations. The largest union, however, the Teamsters, is independent.

Employers did not accept unions willingly. They believed that organized labor limited their freedom to run their companies as they chose. They tried to discourage workers from joining unions by firing union activists and blacklisting them, requiring new workers to sign yellow-dog contracts, employing strikebreakers, and hiring safety guards to intimidate union organizers. Many of these tactics were banned by the National Labor Relations Act, passed by Congress in 1935.

The *National Labor Relations Act* gave legal recognition to labor unions, but it also led to union abuses. In 1947, Congress passed the Labor-Management Relations Act, or *Taft-Hartley Act,* which limited union power by restricting secondary boycotts, allowing states to pass right-to-work laws, and giving the president power to order striking workers back to work for a cooling-off period. The *Landrum-Griffin Act* tried to curtail the corrupt practices of union officials and provided for regularly scheduled, secret-ballot elections.

Organizing is the process by which nonunion workers form a union. The most basic component of a union is the *bargaining unit*—the group for which a contract is negotiated. Any business or plant may have several bargaining units represented by more than one union. At the heart of the union-management relationship is the contract, which is arrived at through a negotiating process called *collective bargaining*.

In a *closed shop,* every eligible worker must belong to the union and the employer may hire only people who are already union members. It was banned by the Taft-Hartley Act. A *union shop* permits an employer to hire a nonunion member, but that individual must join the union after a period of time. In an *open shop,* union membership is completely voluntary. Workers in an *agency shop* must pay an amount equal to union dues if they are not union members.

Among the weapons labor may use against management are a *strike,* a *slowdown,* a *picket,* and a *boycott.* Management may retaliate with a *lockout,* a court *injunction,* and membership in an *employer association.*

A *grievance* is an individual or union complaint that management has violated a provision of a union contract. Most contracts define a method for handling disputes, called a *grievance procedure.* A worker with a complaint can appeal to progressively higher levels of union and management officials until the dispute is settled or dropped. *Arbitration* is a process in which union and management submit their dispute to an unbiased third party, whose decision must be accepted. Another process, *mediation,* attempts to help two parties in a dispute reach agreement.

Although the actual number of union workers has continued to increase, the percentage of union workers in proportion to the total work force has declined since 1945. This is due in part to the increasing number of service workers in our economy and the movement of much industrial activity to the South, where there is little tradition of union membership. In response, unions have concentrated on organizing white-collar workers such as teachers, clerks, and government workers. Unions are also making some progress in the South.

Because of their size and financial strength, unions can use their power to help elect government officials who are sympathetic to union issues. Union leaders can also influence many events that affect the national economy.

The union movement has greatly improved the status of all American workers, both union and nonunion. The balance of power between management and labor is constantly being adjusted so that neither side can dominate.

Review questions

1. Why did unions come into existence?
2. Why did the AFL survive when the Knights of Labor did not?
3. What five actions did management take most frequently to thwart the rise of union power?
4. What three federal laws have most affected union activity since 1930? Which union activities have they affected?
5. Briefly describe the organizing process.
6. Explain the difference between a closed shop, a union shop, an agency shop, and an open shop.
7. What subjects are covered in a labor contract?

8. How does collective bargaining work? What are some common negotiating strategies?
9. What weapons can labor use against management?
10. What weapons can management use against labor?
11. Describe the five steps of a grievance procedure.
12. Why has union growth slowed? What are unions doing to counteract this problem?

Discussion questions

1. Firefighters, teachers, and police are considered public servants. Should their rights to form unions and go on strike be different from the rights of other workers? Why or why not?
2. Do you think that unions play a valuable role in our society? Or are they simply a weapon to keep management activity "honest"? Why?
3. In some cases, high school and college students working part-time for their schools have formed unions and bargained for higher wages. Why might this be against their best interests?
4. Some union organizers are bitter about declining union membership. They believe that workers who reject unions don't realize that their high standard of living stems from the union battles fought by their predecessors. Why do you think there is less interest in unions today?
5. Can you picture a situation in which violence might be an excusable response to a strike or a lockout?
6. Samuel Gompers believed that unions should be concerned only with improving economic conditions. Do you agree with Gompers? In order to improve economic conditions, must unions take political action?
7. Employers sometimes hire new workers to replace employees who go out on strike. Such practices are scorned by unions. If you were an employer faced with a strike, under what circumstances would you hire replacement employees? If you were a skilled unemployed worker, would you accept a job as a replacement for a striking worker?
8. Instead of strikes, should unresolved labor issues be settled by binding arbitration? Why or why not?

Chapter 7 case

Tough decisions for Local 555, UAW

When negotiating a new contract, a union usually tries to improve its position. In this case, we look at a need to consider "give-backs."

Frank Masters, the president of Local 555 of the United Automobile Workers (UAW), knew that the Zip Automobile Company was facing another rough year. Car sales were down industrywide. And American makes faced stiff competition from Japanese imports. Masters was also aware that over the years, the American auto worker had become one of the best-paid of all industrial workers in the United States, largely due to the tough negotiating of his union.

Now the Zip management was asking Masters and his membership to give up certain benefits that they had won over the years. Management wanted more flexibility in scheduling overtime at the plant. They wanted the right to use outside contractors to do certain maintenance work. And they asked for the right to assign freight handlers to drive forklifts instead of walking alongside as the lifts were operated by other workers.

Zip management was seeking these concessions as a way of making their plant more productive. "Right now, it's cheaper for us to import parts from Japan than it is to make them ourselves," complained Horace Ledbetter, the plant's general manager. "We'll just have to close down this plant if we can't become cost-competitive with outside suppliers."

This particular Zip plant employed 3500 men and women. Granted, the work-rule changes might cost a few jobs. But the plant had already laid off 600 workers due to decreased sales. And if the plant closed, all 3500 would be out of jobs, with little hope of finding new work soon.

Masters had scheduled a meeting with the union negotiating committee. They had to decide what position to take at the bargaining table. Frank Masters needed to think about what he should recommend.

Suppose you were Frank Masters. What would you recommend and what facts would you cite to support your recommendation? Among the questions you would want to consider are these:

1. Would agreeing to give-backs now set a precedent for the future? Is this just a "foot in the door" for management?
2. Are there some major concessions the union could get from management that would help make the give-backs more acceptable? What would these be?
3. Even if the negotiating committee saw the need to accept the company's position, could Masters sell the plan to his membership? How could he explain the give-backs to his fellow workers?

Careers in management

Management is the process of getting things done through people. In getting things done through people, managers need three kinds of skills: technical, human, and conceptual. A manager with technical skills knows how things work. A manager with human skills can work effectively with others in reaching goals. A manager with conceptual skills can view the total business operation and the relationships between its parts. Managers also need communication skills.

Between 1978 and 1990, the Bureau of Labor Statistics projects that occupations in human resource management will increase by 20.8 percent. Some careers in this area are discussed below.

Management trainees

Management trainees may be employed in almost every kind of business and industry. They work closely with experienced personnel to gain the knowledge and experience required for promotion to management positions. They study staff functions and operations, management viewpoints, and policies that affect the business. Trainees must have organizational, verbal, and mathematical abilities, as well as leadership qualities. Helpful college courses include business, English, math, and psychology.

Benefits managers

Benefits managers usually work in the personnel department. They specialize in programs to insure employees against loss of income due to illness, injury, layoff, and retirement. They analyze company benefits policies, laws concerning insurance coverage, and agreements with labor unions to be sure that company benefits meet legal requirements and are competitive with other firms. Benefits managers need organizational, mathematical, and verbal skills. They also must relate well to other people.

Careers in management

Someone who wants to be a benefits manager should take college courses that include business, economics, English, public speaking, social studies, and psychology. A bachelor's degree is usually the minimum educational requirement.

Personnel managers

Personnel managers work in almost every kind of private business and in federal, state, and local government. They plan and carry out human resource policies. They recruit, interview, and select workers for jobs and operate orientation and training programs. Personnel managers keep records of insurance coverage and pension plans and hires, promotions, transfers, and terminations. They also investigate accidents and prepare insurance company reports. A personnel manager needs organizational, analytical, verbal, and mathematical abilities and must relate well to people. Someone who wants to be a personnel manager should take college courses in business, economics, English, sociology, and psychology. Personnel management usually requires a bachelor's degree, with graduate degrees required for some jobs.

Retail store managers

Retail store managers operate stores that sell consumer goods. They hire and supervise store employees, plan work schedules, and coordinate employee activities. Retail store managers order merchandise, supervise inventory, set prices, and plan and prepare advertising. This position requires organization skills and the ability to maintain employer-employee-customer relations. Employers of retail store managers range from owners of single small stores to huge conglomerates that own chains of stores. A store manager's college courses should include business, English, and math.

Additional information about these careers can be obtained from the following organizations:

American Management Association
135 West 50th Street
New York, NY 10020

American Society for Personnel Administration
30 Park Drive
Berea, OH 44017

National Association of Retail Grocers
P.O. Box 17208
Washington, DC 20041

In a national study, top management listed the following as the ten biggest problems with middle managers of smaller businesses (average net sales of about $4 million).

Problem	Percent of respondents
1. Motivation, defining roles and goals	38%
2. Training	24
3. Recruitment	17
4. Turnover	9
5. Skills with subordinates	6
6. Communication with top management	5
7. Quality adherence and accountability	4
8. Creativity, generating innovative ideas	4
9. Too many the same age	2
10. Room for advancement	1

(Total exceeds 100 percent because of multiple responses.)
Bradford W. Ketchum, Jr., "What Managers Make," *INC.,* September 1982, p. 36. Copyright © 1982 by INC. Publishing Company, 38 Commercial Wharf, Boston, MA 02110

What's a middle manager?

In most smaller companies, middle management is the only line of management between top-level executives and all other employees. Typical middle-management positions include the following:

Major groups	Subgroups (positions included)
General management: General, division, department assistant manager; supervisor; foreman	
Finance: Controller; accounting, credit, finance, audit, business manager	Controller Accounting manager

Careers in management

Major groups	Subgroups (positions included)
Operations: Operations, office, store, branch, data processing, personnel, warehouse, plant, land manager	Data processing manager Personnel manager Service manager (national service, customer relations manager) Store/branch manager (station manager) Warehouse manager (distribution, transportation, fleet manager) Office manager
Manufacturing: Engineering, plant, maintenance, purchasing, production manager; research and development director	Engineering/research and development manager (chief engineer; technical director; development, design manager) Plant manager (plant foreman) Purchasing manager (purchasing director, agent; material manager) Production manager (shift, shop supervisor; quality assurance manager; shop, press foreman)
Marketing: Marketing, sales, merchandise, advertising, public relations manager	Sales manager (district, field, counter manager)
Other: Service, parts, bodyshop manager	

Adapted from: Bradford W. Ketchum, Jr., "What Managers Make," *INC.*, September 1982, p. 36. Copyright © 1982 by INC. Publishing Company, 38 Commercial Wharf, Boston, MA 02110

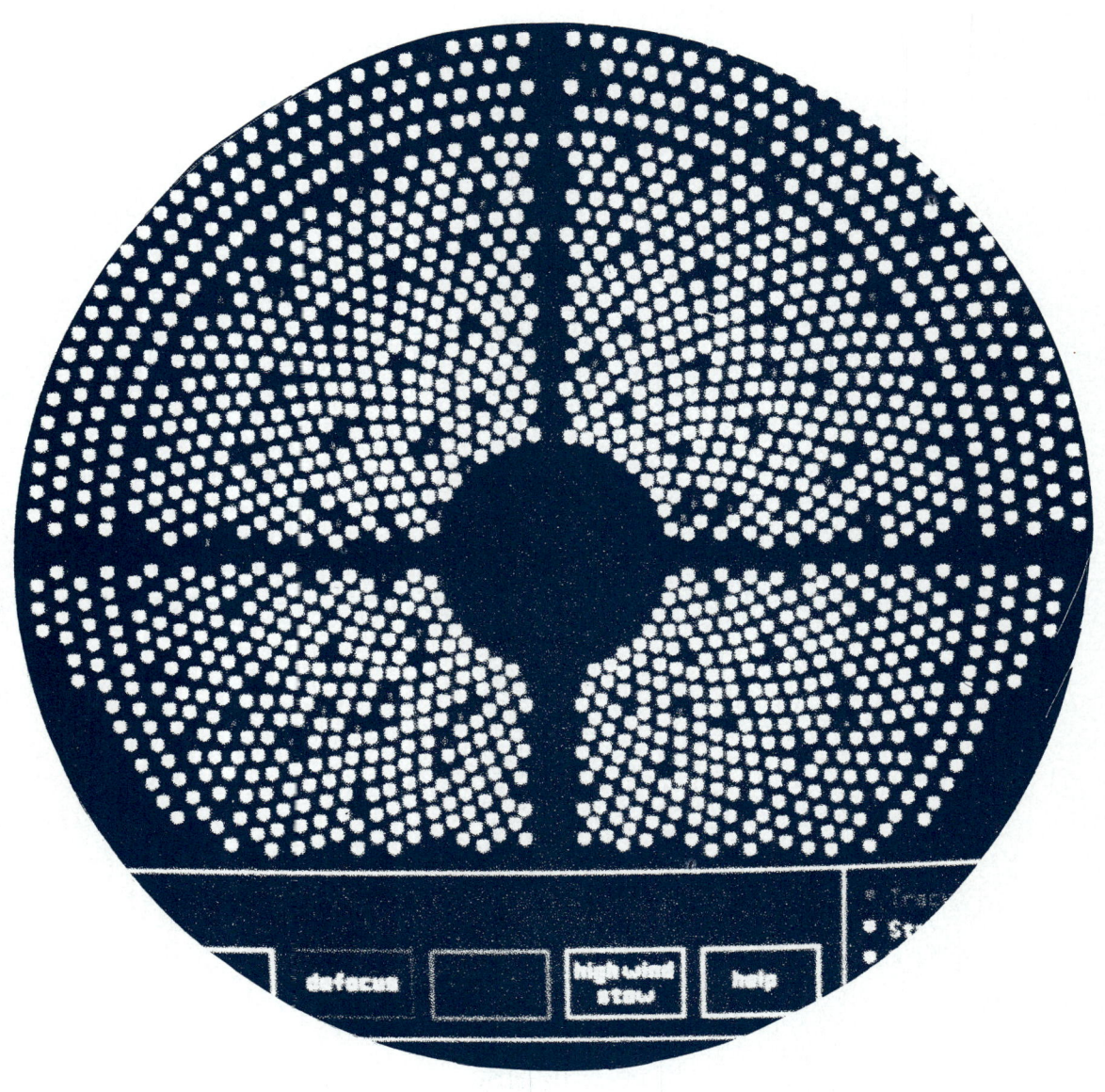

Tools for decision making

1
2
3
4
5
6
7
8

Business in perspective

Do computers lead to unemployment?

Workers have always worried about mechanization and automation. Without a doubt, some people may lose their jobs due to computerization. When retail businesses automated their credit card operations, their need for bookkeepers declined. Automobile manufacturers have been adding computer-controlled "robots" to assembly lines, which has reduced the need for auto workers. Computer-controlled typesetting has eliminated the market for highly skilled—and highly paid—typesetters.

But, in reality, very few workers have been fired as a direct result of computerization. By and large, automation has come gradually. While no new workers are hired for jobs being automated, existing employees are kept on. Labor savings come as workers retire or are retrained for other jobs.

Organized labor has worked hard to protect their members' jobs. They have negotiated contracts that eased the introduction of computers, but sometimes only after years of struggle and strikes.

Overall, however, computers have led to greater employment and a higher standard of living for our society. The computer industry itself, nonexistent in 1950, employed about 1 million workers in 1983. They design, engineer, build, sell, repair, maintain, operate, and program computers.

Even more significant are the side effects of the computer industry. Computer printouts use tons of paper, which creates more business for paper manufacturers. Personal computers are being sold in retail stores, which opens up a whole new line of business for entrepreneurs.

Despite the general rise in the cost of living, many services to which the computer contributes have become cheaper or increased very little in price. This benefits everyone's standard of living.

Bank checking accounts are one example. The handling of billions of checks would be impossible without computers that read, sort, and route checks and balance accounts. The widespread use of credit cards has also been the result of cheap computing. And, due to computers, telephone service not only keeps improving but cost less in 1982 in real dollars than it did in 1960.

Indeed, more people are employed in the United States (and in the rest of the industrialized world) than at any time in history. We are working shorter hours, yet producing as much or more than ever. Much of this stems from the electronic computer and the information it provides.

Chapter 8

Understanding computers

Key terms

computer
hardware
software
central processing unit (CPU)
memory
registers
input devices
output devices
hard copy
cathode ray tube (CRT)
program
BASIC, FORTRAN, PASCAL, COBOL
binary number system

Chapter objectives

In Chapter 8, you will learn:

Why computers and automation lead to more jobs and a higher standard of living

What a computer is—and is not

The components of a computer

The methods of communicating with computers

How a computer works

Four important trends for computing in the future

Overview

Computers are everywhere. They are at checkout counters in supermarkets. They are under the hoods of some automobiles. The telephone system today *is* a computer. Many people have computers on their desks.

Computers work fast. They do not go on strike or demand higher pay. They do exactly as they are told and don't talk back. Often computers do talk with other computers.

Computers cannot think. They must be told everything to do and can make no adjustments on their own. Occasionally, they break down at very inappropriate times.

Computers once were large. They understood only a strange language that few people had the desire or ability to master. There was a small world of people who loved computers and enjoyed speaking computer jargon, using such terms as "on line," "real time," "bits," "bytes," "nanoseconds," "binary," "input-output," "CRT," "crash," "loop," and "BASIC."

The objective of this chapter is to help explain the world of computers—to demystify it a bit. We will describe what a computer is and is not, what it can and cannot do, and why. Chapter 9 explains how computers are used by business and management.

What is a computer?

First, a computer is a machine. Unlike any other machine, however, it is capable of storing instructions that it can then follow on its own. In effect, it is a calculator that does not need humans to push the keys to tell it what to do. The essence of a computer is that it can manipulate data according to stored instructions.

A computer is a programmable machine that can store, retrieve, and process data with great speed and accuracy.

Hardware and software

Hardware refers to the physical components of a computer system. The units shown in Figure 8.1 are hardware. This includes the cabinets, electronic components, wires, and so forth. The computer itself is perhaps the least conspicuous piece of hardware. It is often housed in a small box. The rest of the computer system consists of storage, input, and output devices.

Software refers to the instructions that make a computer work. It is the code that tells the computer what to do. Software takes the form of programs that are written in a language the computer can understand. The real value of a computer is in its software. The software determines how valuable the computer is and to whom.

Chapter 8 Understanding computers 169

Figure 8.1 Computer hardware

Photo courtesy of IBM Corporation

The components of a computer

The computer itself is essentially a collection of circuits. Everything it does is through a series of "on" and "off" positions for each circuit. The term *binary* describes the two positions of a circuit. The magic of a computer is the speed at which it turns its circuits on and off and the large amount of information it can store in the form of unique words formed by this binary code.

At the heart of the computer

The computer itself has three distinct sectors, as illustrated in Figure 8.2. Each has its own function. The heart of the computer is the **central processing unit, or CPU, which is the part of a computer where all arithmetic and logic functions are performed.** It also controls all other pieces of hardware.

A second component is memory. **Memory is the part of a computer in which instructions and data are stored.**

The third component is the registers. **Registers transfer what is stored in memory to the CPU.**

Input and output devices

Input devices are the computer components that feed instructions and data into the memory for processing by the central processing unit. These devices include punched cards readers, magnetic tape, punch

Figure 8.2 Basic sectors of a computer

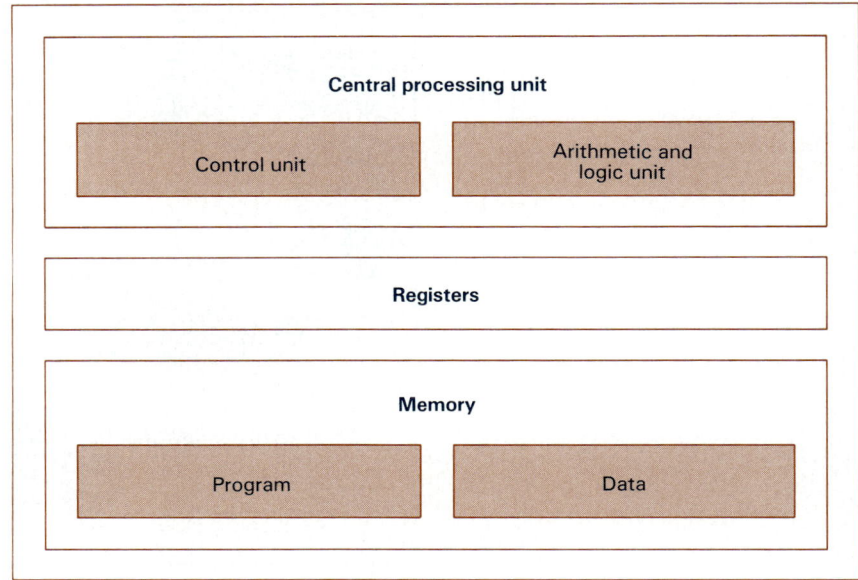

paper tape, keyboards, optical character readers (OCR), discs, and voice recognition devices.

Output devices are the components that enable a computer to report information to its users. Some are the same as input devices (such as punched cards, magnetic and paper tape, and discs). Line printers, teletype printers, cathode ray tubes (CRT), and voice synthesis may also be used.

Punched cards We all are familiar with those rectangular cards that have a punched pattern of oblong holes. For input, punched cards are created by typing on a keyboard. The holes correspond to the binary code that computers understand. Computers can also control machines that produce punched cards. The computer-produced cards are put through a reader that translates them into language that humans can understand.

For many years, punched cards were the primary method of input. Their drawback is that they are cumbersome and take up a great deal of space. A large program may require hundreds of cards, each containing a single instruction. Data may take up many more cards. Moreover, cards are expensive because they cannot be reused. If one card gets out of order, the entire program can be ruined.

Punched paper tape Punched tape works on the same principle as punched cards. It is read or punched out on long, continuous rolls. Although for many years it was used as input for typesetting machines, it is not commonly used anymore.

Optical character reader (OCR) The optical character reader reads typed material. Some can read actual typed letters. Other read a bar code that

Chapter 8 Understanding computers

Figure 8.3 How to read a Universal Product Code

is created as each letter is typed (see Figure 8.3). The bar codes on grocery products and magazines can be read through optical scanning.

Magnetic tape Magnetic tape is wound onto large reels and can store millions of pieces of information. "Mag" tape is the least expensive of all storage mechanisms for computer-readable information. It is therefore the most common output medium. It is best for creating and storing long sequences of information, such as the mailing lists used by magazine publishers.

Discs Discs may be either rigid or floppy. They are similar in concept to phonograph records in that they have grooves and spin very rapidly.

Figure 8.4 The Apple II Plus Personal Computer System equipped with a Monitor III and a Disk II Floppy Disc Drive

Courtesy of Apple Computer, Inc.

But because computer discs store data magnetically, they can be used, erased, and reused.

Keyboards Almost all input data and instructions for a computer must be entered using some form of keyboard. A computer keyboard resembles that of a typewriter. But instead of creating type on paper, a computer keyboard creates code—on tape, cards, or discs, or directly into the central processing unit's memory. Most keyboards use codes that can be understood by almost any computer in the world.

Line printers and teletype printers Line printers are the most rapid form of hard-copy output. **Hard copy is a computer-produced document that is printed in ordinary language.** A line printer prints line by line rather than letter by letter. Line printers commonly create 600 lines per minute and often move much faster. Teletypelike printers commonly

Chapter 8 Understanding computers

Inexpensive personal computers allow the smallest businesses to innovate.

Drawing by Lorenz; © 1980 The New Yorker Magazine, Inc.

print 80 characters per second but may also move much faster. Teletype printers may be bidirectional—printing one line left to right and the next line right to left—to save time.

Cathode ray tube (CRT) The cathode ray tube is an output device similar in appearance to a television screen. Computer-produced text appears on the tube. CRTs often come with keyboards so they can be used for both input and output. The keyboard enters data into the computer and the computer writes it out on the CRT.

Cathode ray tubes are becoming quite common. About 6 million were in use in 1983. They are used by airline ticket agents, stockbrokers, bank tellers, and others who do not always need a hard copy of output. Another term for a CRT display is VDT, for *video display terminal.*

Other input/output devices Several input and output devices are still in the developmental stage. But computer technology changes so quickly that we can assume that new devices will soon be common.

Perhaps the most exciting possible method of input is voice recognition. A computer capable of voice recognition can understand the spoken word. Special skills, such as learning how to operate a keyboard, would be unnecessary. In Stanley Kubrick's film *2001: A Space Odyssey,* the computer, nicknamed HAL, could converse with people because it could understand their spoken words.

Figure 8.5 Howard Aiken's huge MARK I calculator, completed in 1944, was 51 feet long and contained 500 miles of wiring. The tiny Hewlett-Packard 75 is far faster and more sophisticated.

Harvard University News Office, Cambridge, MA 02138

Many computer engineers dream of making voice recognition a reality. And they have already had some success. Some computers can understand a few words or numbers quite well. One problem with voice recognition, however, is the many pronunciations a computer would have to understand. Nonetheless, such problems will eventually be overcome and voice recognition will become common. Someday you will be able to pick up your telephone, dial a computer, and tell it to perform tasks, such as transferring $500 from your savings account to your checking account, or ask it for information, such as the latest headlines or the price of gold.

The output side of voice recognition is voice synthesis—the ability of a computer to speak. Progress in this area has been rapid. Computerized educational products ask the user to spell words or do arithmetic. Some automobile makers use tiny computers to create voices that warn drivers to buckle their seatbelts. Voice recognition and voice synthesis will make it easier for everyone—not just computer professionals—to use computers.

Chapter 8 Understanding computers

Courtesy of Hewlett-Packard

Programming and software

A program is the instructions that tell a computer what, when, and how to do something. These instructions are written by programmers. The term *software* refers to all programs. Software makes a computer versatile. Because it can store and execute numerous programs, a single computer can tackle many different tasks.

Programming language

Before a computer can understand an assignment, it must be given very basic operating instructions. Thus, a new computer is first loaded with an operating system. This is a very concise program written in the most basic computer codes, called machine language. Another special program, called the *compiler,* performs the translation that tells the computer how to understand the more high-level computer programming languages.

Figure 8.6 FORTRAN statement and machine equivalent

FORTRAN	Machine Code
C = A + B	0101100000110000
	1100000000000000
	0101110001000000
	1100000000000100
	0001101000110100
	0101000000110000
	1100000000001000

BASIC, FORTRAN, PASCAL, and COBOL are higher-level languages that make it easier for humans to communicate with computers. These languages are based on words and symbols used in English. The computer then translates these words and symbols into its own binary machine language. An example of computer machine language and the same statement in FORTRAN is shown in Figure 8.6.

In general, then, there are two kinds of computer language. A source code, such as FORTRAN, is the language used by a programmer to tell the computer what to do. An object code is the machine's language based on the binary system. Unless you plan to go into computer design and engineering, you probably will never use an object code.

Limitations of computers

By themselves, computers are not very smart. If they appear smart, it is because humans have programmed them. The important difference between a computer and a human brain is that the computer cannot reason. It can follow instructions. But it does this literally. It cannot compensate for errors. For example, suppose you saw this written:

COMPLTE

You might reasonably assume that it was a typographical error and that it really should be:

COMPLETE

A computer couldn't do that. It could not make the reasonable assumption that a letter was left out. As a result, programming a computer is a demanding task. Programmers must anticipate every possibility that may occur in the use of a program and prepare the computer for a response. If the programmers have not told a computer what to do with a certain kind of data, the computer may quit working.

How a computer works

Compared to human intelligence, then, computers have many deficiencies. But once provided with a good set of instructions, they can solve complex problems at lightning speed. To reduce a computer to its most basic elements, one could say it is simply a very fast adding machine.

Computers and automation change millions of jobs

Work is changing drastically as the drive towards workerless factories and automated offices continues.

Current work skills are losing value and new skills are being created. Workers will have to readjust, both psychologically and in terms of training. Company management will be challenged by the need for huge retraining programs.

According to experts, both factories and offices will be affected. In factories alone, 7 million existing jobs could be performed by robots. Nearly half of these jobs are covered by union contracts. As many as 38 million white-collar jobs will be affected out of the 50 million that now exist. A vice-president at Xerox anticipates that office productivity will increase by 20 percent due to these changes.

As production speeds up, excess workers can be reassigned to finding new business or doing tasks once neglected because of time shortages.

Automation affects workers both positively and negatively. On the positive side, some employees enjoy their new jobs more. An executive secretary now has more time to research and write reports, since her word processor speeds up the routine work.

Other individuals do not accept automation so easily or find themselves in dead-end jobs. This happened to a librarian who refused—or was unable—to computerize the library system for which she worked.

Some health problems have been related to automation. Some workers feel intense psychological and emotional pressure. Others feel tied to their machines. Still others have trouble adjusting to increased demands on their productivity.

Smart management can lessen the ill effects of automation. Many companies are already involved in such programs. For example, Lockheed has a retraining program for 3000 engineers in computer-aided design that is costing $30 million.

Another approach is to let workers help design their new jobs. Digital Equipment Corp. tried this with about 70 workers and supervisors. "Everyone ended up feeling a part of how the area was changed and improved," according to a Digital official.

A more fundamental solution involves educating more engineers. According to the National Science Foundation, in 1985 the supply of new engineers will be 15,000, but there will be a demand for 51,000. Related to this is the need to get computers into schools so that the next generation of workers can be properly trained.

While the productivity of American workers will increase and the quality of their products will improve, the transition to automation will require careful attention from both white-collar and blue-collar workers.

Figure 8.7 Converting decimal numbers to binary form

Decimal number	Binary equivalent
0	0000000
1	0000001
2	0000010
3	0000011
4	0000100
5	0000101
6	0000110
7	0000111
8	0001000
9	0001001
13	0001101
100	1100100

What a computer does

All instructions to a computer are turned into numerical codes, as shown in Figure 8.6. Using these codes, the computer adds or subtracts to solve problems. By adding and subtracting very rapidly, the computer can also multiply and divide.

These are very basic mathematical skills. But what makes computers so impressive is their speed, accuracy, and ability to repeat. Fast computers can perform billions of calculations per second. They can do it with an infinitesimal error rate. And they can keep calculating for long periods of time without getting tired or asking for more pay.

The computer process

All numbers and letters that enter the computer are converted by a program into binary form. **A binary number system is based on two digits—0 and 1.** The system we are used to is the decimal system, based on ten digits—0 through 9.

Any number expressed in decimal form can be represented in binary form using only a 0 and a 1. Figure 8.7 shows how to write the equivalent of 0 to 9 as well as some other numbers in binary. We will not actually teach the binary system here. If you are curious, you can spend some time analyzing the examples to see how it works.

The binary system is the key to how a computer works. A computer uses electrical currents to turn switches on and off to correspond to a binary code. A "1" means an "on" state. A "0" means an "off" state. By creating binary words (called *bytes*) out of binary digits (called *bits*), all instructions and data can be stored in memory in the form of "on" and "off" states.

Computers in the future

Four important trends will affect computer use and technology in the future. They are (1) declining computing costs; (2) greater use of smaller computers for distributed processing; (3) increased merging of telecommunications and computers; and (4) the shortage of applications programmers.

Declining costs

Computer costs are usually measured as cost per unit of storage. Cost may also be based on speed—or cost per computation. By either measure, computer costs have declined dramatically, even though the cost of so many other products has risen. The drop in costs is due to rapid improvements in computer technology. As computer performance improves, computer costs decline.

As costs drop, more individuals and businesses can afford to use computers. At first, computers were so expensive that only very large businesses and the government could cost-justify their use.

But today, minicomputers can perform sophisticated functions at a small fraction of the cost of the old, large computers. Whereas large IBM 370 series computers cost $500,000 or more (still inexpensive compared to early systems), many minicomputers cost well under $100,000. And the microcomputer systems sold by Apple, Radio Shack, IBM, and others cost well under $5000. Yet they can perform inventory, billing, accounting, word processing, and many other functions.

In fact, computer costs have fallen so low that many consumers are buying them for home use. Home computers are being used to keep family financial records, store recipes and Christmas card lists, and manage personal stock portfolios. The hand-held calculator has become a common instrument. Before long, the personal computer may be just as common.

Distributed processing

When computers were huge and expensive, users tended to come to the computer. Now that computers are smaller and cheaper, they can go to the user.

In the early days of computing, most jobs were batch processes. That is, a particular job would be loaded into the computer, often using punch cards. The computer would run the job and print out the results. Then the next job would be loaded and run, and so on. Projects would have to wait in line until it was their turn to be loaded and run.

Later computers were capable of multiprocessing. They were so large and powerful that they were most efficient when running several jobs at once. This led to time sharing.

The workerless computerized office is more of a dream than a reality.

"Just listen to all that whirring and buzzing and clicking, and not a single demand for a raise!"

Drawing by Whitney Darrow, Jr.; © 1971 The New Yorker Magazine, Inc.

In time sharing, many users share a single computer. They can use input and output terminals in many different locations, with data transmitted via telephone lines. Because the computer works so fast, each user can feel that he or she is the only one using the computer. Time sharing is a popular and useful technique.

However, lower-cost minicomputers allow more computing power to be located exactly where it is needed. Many offices today use word processors, for example. These are actually microcomputers used for creating text material such as business letters, memos, and reports.

In many large firms, secretaries work at word processors instead of at regular typewriters. Each word processor operates independently, and is not hooked up to a central computer. This is called *distributed processing*. With distributed processing, if one machine has a problem, the others aren't affected.

The "Golden Arches" of the home electronics industry

Radio Shack, a division of the Tandy Corporation, has more stores than McDonald's has restaurants. Its success is impressive. An investor who bought 1,000 shares of Tandy Corporation stock in 1967 at $15 each would have had an investment worth $2.35 million in 1981.

Through Radio Shack, Tandy sells more than 2500 electronics products. They range from batteries to home computers. The computer area is especially competitive.

John Roach, chief executive officer of Tandy, is the undisputed father of Tandy's personal computers. He was first intrigued by personal computers in the early 1970s. But he did not receive full support for marketing them until 1977, when Charles Tandy's interest was sparked by a demonstration.

By 1982, Radio Shack had more than 225 computer centers. Each computer center has a classroom where demonstrations are held for the public.

Tandy's personal computers retailed for between $299 and $2000 in 1983. Owners of the Tandy system can use the computer's video screen, keyboard, and telephone line to retrieve information from newspapers and several financial agencies. According to company officials, the computers' many uses are a strong selling point. Increasingly, the computers are being purchased by small businesses, which now can afford the advantages big business has enjoyed for years.

"Computers on a chip," the tiny microprocessors, allow "intelligence" to be placed almost anywhere. Video games use them. Educational toys, such as *Speak & Spell,* use them. And some automobile manufacturers are using computers in their engines to control fuel and air ratios during combustion. This helps to minimize pollution and maximize fuel economy.

In the coming years, we will see widespread use of such localized computer powers. Businesses will find that information, in the form of small, special-purpose computers, can replace other scarce resources, such as energy, labor, and even capital.

Merging computers and communications

"Compunications" is the merging of computers and communications. The result is a system that is more powerful than either component standing alone.

The telecommunications network in the United States makes it possible for any telephone anywhere to be connected to any other telephone. Adding computers to the telephone network has created an increasingly intelligent telephone system. For example, it allows us to have telephone calls meant for our home phone forwarded to another telephone away from home.

An intelligent telephone network also makes it easier for different brands of computers to "talk" with each other. For example, an IBM computer at one business can exchange data with a Burroughs computer at another location. This is not simple, since there are many different computer systems. Each has its own object codes that make communication difficult. The telephone system helps overcome these difficulties.

Computers are frequently interconnected into computer networks through the telephone system. With such a network, it's possible to search a particular computer's memory for certain information. If the local computer does not contain the data, it can be programmed to "ring up" another computer. The other computer may be located a mile—or a continent—away. The second computer transmits the desired information by telephone signals to the local computer and the result appears on the user's cathode ray tube or printer. The entire process may happen so rapidly that the user is never aware of its complexity.

In coming years, it is likely that cable systems—the ones that bring television signals to many homes—will also be used to connect television sets with computers. Users at home could get news, sports information, supermarket prices, airline schedules, and other information by connecting their television sets to computers. The TV set will then act as a computer output device.

Shortage of applications programmers

The development of computer technology has largely outpaced our ability to use the computer's capabilities. There are many things that computers *can* do that they are not doing. This is due to a shortage of programmers to write the codes that make computers perform. Many large firms have a shortage of programmers, and as a result companies compete for them by offering very high salaries.

At the same time, computer users are finding that hardware costs are declining. Buying or leasing a computer is relatively inexpensive. Instead, the salaries of the people who write the instructions and run and maintain the computers have become a major expense. This is a significant change from the first 25 or 30 years of computer history.

Clearly, there is great opportunity for programmers today. And the demand for programmers is likely to be greater than supply into the next decade.

8 Understanding computers

Summary

A *computer* is a programmable machine that can store, retrieve, and process data with great speed and accuracy.

The computer itself is a piece of *hardware*. Besides the *central processing unit (CPU),* the hardware includes input and output devices. *Input devices* include punched card readers, punched paper tape, keyboards, magnetic tape, discs, optical character recognition (OCR), and voice recognition. *Output devices* include *cathode ray tubes* (*CRT*s), also called video display terminals (VDTs), line printers, teletypelike printers, and voice synthesis. Magnetic tape, discs, punch cards, and punched paper tape may also be used for output.

Software contains the instructions that tell a computer what to do at every step along the way. Software is entered into a computer in the form of a program. A *program* is a series of very detailed instructions. It may be written in a source code, such as *FORTRAN, BASIC,* or *COBOL*. But ultimately all such programs must be translated (by another program stored in the computer) into object code—the only true language a computer understands. Object code is machine language based on the *binary number system.*

A computer works by interpreting two states: off and on. It forms binary words (called *bytes*) out of binary digits (called *bits*) in a series of on and off impulses. All computer functions can be reduced to the four basic arithmetic functions: addition, subtraction, multiplication, and division.

The key to the computer is its ability to store information. This is called *memory.* Both programs and data are stored in memory for use in controlling an operation or for actual processing. The fastest—and most expensive—form is core memory, which is inside the central processing unit. Cheaper forms of memory storage are magnetic tapes and discs.

Four important trends that will affect computer use and technology are (1) the declining costs of computers; (2) greater use of distributed processing; (3) the merging of computers and communications; and (4) the shortage of applications programmers.

Computers and automation may result in some individuals losing their jobs. But on the whole, computers have created more jobs than they have eliminated. Computers have also helped society by increasing productivity and simplifying many services, such as checking accounts, credit cards, and telephone service.

Review questions

1. What is a computer?
2. Describe three specific computer input devices.

3. Explain voice recognition and voice synthesis.
4. Why is programming a computer an exacting task?
5. What are the three sectors of the central processing unit and what function does each serve?
6. Describe briefly how a computer's memory works.
7. List and briefly explain each of the four current trends in computers.
8. What impact has the computer had on U.S. employment?

Discussion questions

1. Is the computer really only a very fast adding machine? In your opinion, are computers overrated or underrated?
2. Apple, IBM, and Xerox are among the many firms that sell low-cost personal computers. Do you think that the average American home will indeed have its own computer by 1990? What uses would you find for such a computer?
3. Of the four recent trends in computers discussed in this chapter, which do you think is the most significant? Defend your reasoning.
4. Should technology be restrained by society if it might cause unemployment or similar problems for some people? What are the trade-offs?
5. Take a routine job with which you are familiar (such as balancing your checkbook). How would you instruct a computer to perform the operations needed to perform that function?

Chapter 8 case

Mary Tyler Catalog Company

The decreasing cost of computer systems makes them more appropriate for smaller businesses. Here, a successful small business must first decide how a computer can help solve its problems. Only then can it choose the most appropriate hardware.

Herman Gonzalez, general manager of the Mary Tyler Catalog Company, was looking over a pile of information from a dozen computer manufacturers. Company president Mary Tyler had asked him to investigate the possibility of automating many of the manual procedures being used by the firm.

Mary Tyler had started her business out of her living room. Her friends had long complimented her on her knack for finding unique gifts. At first she helped them with their own gift purchases. Soon she started a gift-buying service. This led to her first catalog, with 24 pages of specialty items. Instead of going out to shop for each order, she started to keep an inventory of the items she selected for her catalog. When her basement and garage got full, she moved into larger offices and a warehouse.

Chapter 8 Understanding computers

At first, order processing was rather simple. When an order came in, it was entered in the order book. Then a copy was sent to the warehouse for shipping. Once shipped, the order slip was sent back to the office with a stamp showing it had been filled.

Problems arose when popular items went out of stock. Sometimes it took days for the office to find out that an order had not been shipped. With multiple-item orders, in-stock items were sent but out-of-stock items were not. Yet the order slip sometimes came back to the office marked "shipped." Customers complained that they did not receive their total orders when office records showed they had been shipped.

As the catalog became more popular, customers started calling in their orders. But the order-takers sometimes accepted orders for out-of-stock items because inventory reports were updated only weekly. Other customers called to ask the status of their orders. To find out if the orders had been shipped, the office staff had to put the callers on hold and leaf through stacks of records.

By this time, Mary Tyler could see that if she didn't improve her inventory and ordering procedures, her business could be in real trouble. Mr. Gonzalez had all this information on computer systems. But what he really had to know was what the computer should be able to do.

Acting as an adviser to Mr. Gonzalez, write up a report that answers the following questions:

1. What should the computer system do to help the inventory control problem? Describe in your own words how the system can keep track of and report on inventory status.

2. How can a computer system help the order-takers when they take telephone orders and questions from customers?

3. What type of input and output devices would be most appropriate for this type of system?

Business in perspective

There's gold in them there mailing lists

A name by itself ordinarily isn't worth much. But assemble a few thousand names into a mailing list and you've got a valuable commodity.

Valuable enough to make these lists worth stealing. "Security is a hot topic in the direct-mail industry, and the potential for theft is a major problem," says Kenneth Emens, a director of treasury operations at Franklin Mint Corporation, a unit of Warner Communications Inc., and a company that does much of its business by mail order.

The appeal of mailing lists is that they define a specific audience in terms of sex, age, and income. This information is worth a lot to advertisers, political candidates, and others who want their messages to reach the most susceptible or sympathetic audiences. A mailing list "is a priceless asset, accumulated over many years," says Kurt Burghardt, president of Neodata Services of Boulder, Colo. Neodata handles billing and renewals for 120 magazines including *The New Yorker, Playboy, Smithsonian,* and *Vogue.* Its mailing lists run to 39 million names.

Despite high-security measures at Neodata's headquarters, including employee badges, push-button combination locks, and shredding of computer printouts, *The New Yorker* magazine claims that some 30,000 names and addresses of the magazine's 460,000 subscribers fell into the hands of another company.

The magazine says it never sells its subscribers' names. "We believe that one of the most significant assets we have is our subscriber list and we will go to any lengths to protect it," says George Green, president of *The New Yorker.*

Adapted from Jeffrey H. Birnbaum, "Firms Try Shredders, Special Locks to Protect Valuable Mailing Lists," *Wall Street Journal,* April 27, 1981. Reprinted by permission of the *Wall Street Journal,* © Dow Jones & Company, Inc. All rights reserved.

Chapter 9

Management information systems

Key terms

management information system (MIS)
internal data
external data
primary data
secondary data
statistic
statistics
mean
median
mode
automated teller machine (ATM)
computer-aided design (CAD)
computer-aided manufacturing (CAM)

Chapter objectives

In Chapter 9, you will learn:

What a management information system (MIS) is and why a business needs one

The forms data take: internal versus external and primary versus secondary

How a statistic differs from the study of statistics

Three measures of central tendency—mean, median, and mode—and how each is calculated

Four ways in which data are often presented

Some common applications of computers in management information systems

How computer-assisted design and manufacturing may revolutionize production

Overview

Managers make decisions aimed at achieving their company's objectives and goals. To make effective decisions, managers must be able to analyze a situation, consider relevant data, identify alternatives, choose the best alternative, and obtain feedback about the decision.

To do this, managers need information. They need facts about their resources, people, materials, machines, and money. Most managers spend much of their workday handling information. Much of this information is constantly changing and being replaced by new information. This places additional burdens on managers.

Managers need information when it will be most useful. Information obtained *after* a decision is made is worth little.

In this chapter, we consider the major elements of management information systems. We look at important sources and types of information. We also discuss why managers must understand basic statistics to analyze and interpret data. The ability to discriminate between important and unimportant data is critical in decision making. We will also examine how computers can contribute to management information systems.

The purpose of a management information system

A management information system (MIS) is an organized method of providing past, present, and projected information about a business's internal operations and external environment. It supports a company's planning, control, and operating functions by furnishing information when it is needed to assist the decision-making process.[1]

Management information systems have one basic purpose: to provide managers at each level with the information they need to make sound decisions. To do this, the information must reflect these managers' needs.

Figure 9.1 shows the operation of a management information system. No matter what the value of the information entering the system, the decisions can be no better than the intelligence added by the human manager.

---

[1]Walter J. Kennavan, "MIS Universe," *Data Management,* September 1970, p. 63.

Figure 9.1 A management information system

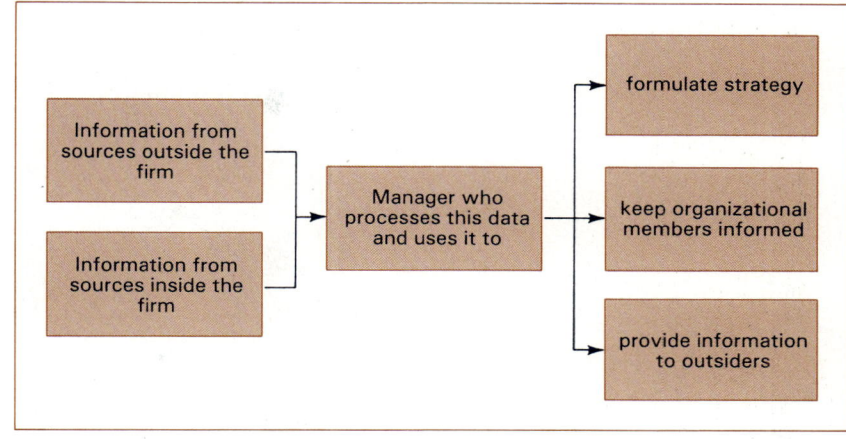

Adapted from Richard M. Hodgetts, *Management: Theory, Process and Practice* (Philadelphia: W. B. Saunders, 1979), p. 212.

The need for a management information system

Businesses, large and small, need useful information about many facets of the operation, including the following:
1. Their own factors of production, including machinery, people, money, and natural resources. Data is collected on costs, required quantities, and past, present, and future needs.
2. Their own business operations, including resource inputs, resource costs, and resource efficiency
3. Their own output, including quality and quantity, as well as expectations for future demand
4. Competitors' organizations, products, and business performance
5. Consumer characteristics and habits
6. Government regulations, laws, tax decisions, and the like

A successful business must be able to gather, store, combine, and use data at a reasonable cost. Information is most useful to managers when it is: (1) accurate, (2) available when needed, (3) concise and relevant, and (4) as complete as possible.

Dealing with uncertainty

Even when they have useful information, managers cannot be absolutely certain that their decisions are the right ones. Moreover, managers tend to work under cost and time pressures. Often they must make decisions before all desired information has been obtained. Or, the cost of obtaining certain information may be too great. Also, many events cannot be foreseen. This uncertainty makes it even more important for managers to have good data on which to base their decisions.

Management information systems should be able to pinpoint problems.

"Here's where we went wrong."

From the *Wall Street Journal,* Permission—Cartoon Features Syndicate

As a result, managers, often make decisions based on a combination of elements: information resources, their own experience and training, and their personal judgments and expectations about the future.

Finding the best information often requires sifting through huge masses of material. To save time and trouble, a manager must decide how much information is really necessary. Too much information can lead to confusion, indecision, and delay.

Common complaints about information processes

Here are some common complaints that managers make about the information they receive:

"When I ask for information, I get plenty of reports, but they aren't relevant to the questions I am asking."

"I need specific information. There is so much material here that even Sherlock Holmes couldn't find what I'm looking for."

"The information I want is always available. The only problem is that it arrives *after* I need it."

"I know some departments are not giving me accurate reports. They are covering up poor performance with distorted information."

"There is a lot of information here, but I have no way of knowing how accurate it is because I can't tell where it came from."

Thus, getting information is not a manager's only problem. A manager must have the *right* information, *when* it is needed, from *reliable* sources, in a *usable* form.

Chapter 9 Management information systems

Sources of information

As shown in Figure 9.1, data may come from inside the company (internal sources) or from outside the company (external sources). In addition, data may be classified as either primary or secondary.

Sources of internal data

Internal data are facts obtained directly from a firm's own records. This includes information from receipts, invoices, purchase orders, sales slips, personnel files, and other company records. It might also show labor, material, and rental costs of producing goods or services. Comparing these costs with selling prices will help reveal profits, as well as cost per unit sold.

Internal data may include financial information about accounts payable and accounts receivable, inventory levels, and the profitability of specific business units. Production data relating to material use, quality control, and rejection rates may be generated. Personnel information relating to employee turnover, safety records, absenteeism, and employee suggestions may also be obtained. Data on changes in these areas provide useful information for managers and cover all aspects of a firm's operation.

Through the management information system, internal data may be gathered as often as minute by minute or as infrequently as once a year. As the need arises, reports from these data can be generated and analyzed for comparison with company goals and objectives.

Figure 9.2 illustrates a comprehensive financial management system using a computer data bank. It includes information on the firm's

Questions managers ask

Typical questions managers ask include these:

What are our sales figures for this year? How do they compare with our figures for last year?

How does our inventory turnover for the past six months compare with our goal for the period?

How many work hours were lost due to accidents this year? Is there a trend for the past five years? What are the major causes of the accidents?

Does our market research support the extra expense needed to promote our new product?

How does our return on investment compare with the industry average for the past year?

Figure 9.2 Management information system

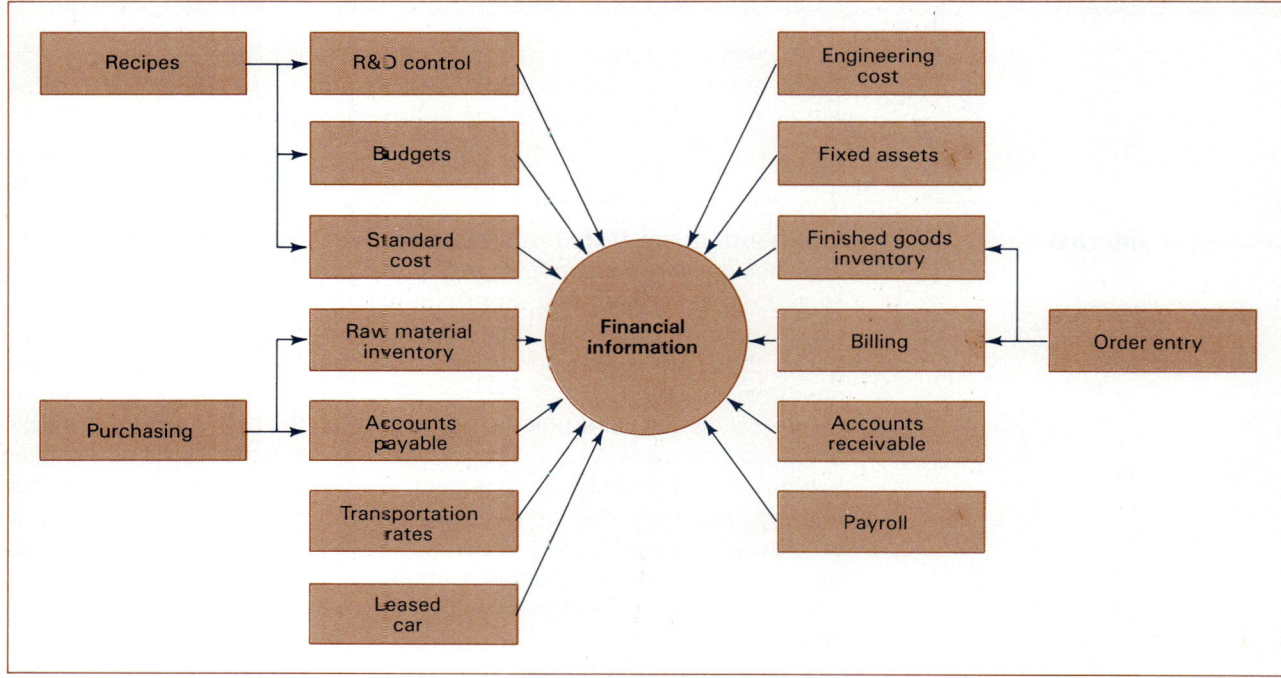

Reprinted with permission of DATAMATION® Magazine.

budgets, sales, engineering, billing, assets, payroll, transportation, and accounts receivable and payable. The system handles order processing, inventory, and accounting functions.

Order processing, for example, involves collecting data on customer orders. It combines that with information relating to routing, shipment, contract price, base price, credit, and raw materials and finished goods inventories.

Sources of external data

External data are facts obtained from sources outside the firm. Three important sources of external data are government sources, private sources, and competitors.

Government sources Government publications provide useful information about legislation, population characteristics, taxes, employment trends, production and manufacturing output, and sales figures for all kinds of industries.

The federal government's publications include the *U.S. Census of Population and Housing, Census of Business,* and *Census of Manufactures.* Most federal reports are available to the public for free or for a small charge. Valuable data are also published by state and local governments.

'Belle System

Instead of using six employees to take telephone orders, "Annabelle" is now handling all calls from Bishop Graphics Inc.'s 90 distributors across the country.

"Annabelle" is a tape recorder with her own direct telephone line and number. She works a 24-hour day and can be called when long distance rates are lowest, whether Bishop Graphics is open or not. Orders are transcribed during the next working day.

"Several interesting by-products have come from our order 'person,'" notes Jerrold Asher, former national sales manager for the manufacturer of engineering and drafting aids in Westlake Village, Calif., Telephone calls are shorter, dealers' orders are better organized, and there is less waiting around for missing data that dealers used to look for during the telephone conversation. (Annabelle automatically "hangs up" if she is kept waiting longer than 12 seconds.) And there is never any argument over what the dealer actually said and what the order desk person wrote on his or her order form.

Today, the order desk crew no longer has to serve as "human transcriber equipment," says Asher. "They work on sales and promotions directed at dealers and customers."

Reprinted with permission, *INC.,* April 1982. Copyright © 1982 by INC. Publishing Company, 38 Commercial Wharf, Boston, MA 02110.

Private sources Nongovernment sources also provide useful information. Trade associations, made up of firms in the same industry, often provide information to their members. One such group is the National Association of Manufacturers (NAM).

Other sources include trade magazines such as *Sales & Marketing Management.* Financial publications such as *Dun & Bradstreet, Moody's Reports,* and *Wall Street Journal,* and popular magazines such as *Fortune, Forbes, BusinessWeek,* and *U.S. News & World Report* can provide useful facts.

Finally, some companies specialize in selling information. For example, certain publishing firms conduct marketing research and sell their findings to customers. And credit bureaus provide important information about the credit ratings of potential customers.

Competitors A business is also interested in data on its competitors. This includes information about other firms' past, present, and future activities. Most useful is information about competitors' products and internal operating procedures, such as marketing techniques, pricing policies, engineering structure, and personnel practices. Obtaining such data is, of course, difficult. Some information may be found in annual reports and other financial statements that many larger corporations are required to file with public agencies such as the Securities and Exchange Commission.

Primary and secondary data

Primary data are facts gathered for the first time for use in solving a specific business problem. Primary data are usually collected in three ways: (1) observation, (2) survey, and (3) experimentation. Methods of collecting primary data are explained in Chapter 12.

Secondary data are previously gathered facts, often published for purposes other than the solution of a particular business problem. Secondary data are often more general than primary data. As a result, necessary information must be sifted from unnecessary information.

External sources are common providers of secondary data.

Advantages and disadvantages of secondary data Compared to primary data, secondary data are less expensive to collect and more easily available.

On the other hand, secondary data may be out of date or unsuitable for a manager's particular needs. Sometimes the data may be biased and misleading. Some secondary information may be too general or too specific. And some data cannot be verified.

The use of statistics

It is important to distinguish between a statistic and the study of statistics. **A statistic is a fact expressed as a number.** Three examples are "Annual sales were $4.1 million," "The cost of living for October increased by 0.6 percent," and "Auto sales in the United States declined by 1.1 million cars."

By contrast, **statistics is a field of mathematics that deals with the collection, analysis, interpretation, and presentation of numerical information.** Statistics can be applied to many business situations. Three statistics that managers often use are the measures of central tendency—mean, median, and mode.

Measures of central tendency

Measures of central tendency provide information about the midpoint of a group of numbers.

Mean A mean is the arithmetic average of a group of numbers. The mean is found by adding together all related numbers and dividing their sum by the number of items in the group. The owner of a restaurant, for example, may be interested in finding the average amount of money spent by her customers during lunch on a particular day. She would compute the mean expenditure as follows:

Customer	Purchase
1	$4.00
2	5.50
3	4.50
4	8.00
5	6.20
6	9.00
7	7.20
8	3.00
9	3.00
Total purchases:	$50.40

$$\frac{\$50.40}{9} = \$5.60 = \text{Mean}$$

The mean, or average, luncheon was $5.60 for that particular day.

Median A median is the middle number when data are ordered from highest to lowest. Half the data are higher than the median and half are lower. To find the median of a set of data, first arrange the numbers in ascending or descending order. Here is how the restaurant owner would find the median luncheon purchase:

Ranked order of purchases		Amount
1		$3.00
2		3.00
3		4.00
4		4.50
5	Median:	5.50
6		6.20
7		7.20
8		8.00
9		9.00

The median amount spent on lunch is $5.50. Half of the customers spent more than $5.50 and half spent less.

Mode A mode is the number that appears most often in the series of data. It is the most common point and can be useful when one value occurs frequently. In our restaurant example, the mode is $3.00. In this case, since it only occurs twice, its usefulness is limited. The mode could also be used to discover the most popular item on the menu.

Limitations of mean, median, and mode The mean, median, and mode are very common and useful measures of central tendency, but each has limitations. For example, the mean may be distorted if one or two numbers are much higher or lower than the others. In such cases, the median may be a more accurate indicator of the middle range.

The mode is usually quick and easy to compute, but it can present problems, too. Sometimes there is no mode because no number occurs more than once. Other times there may be more than one mode because two different numbers each occur the same number of times.

Whether the mean, median, or mode is the most useful statistic in a particular case depends on the nature of the problem and the data to be analyzed.

Figure 9.3 Four forms of data presentation

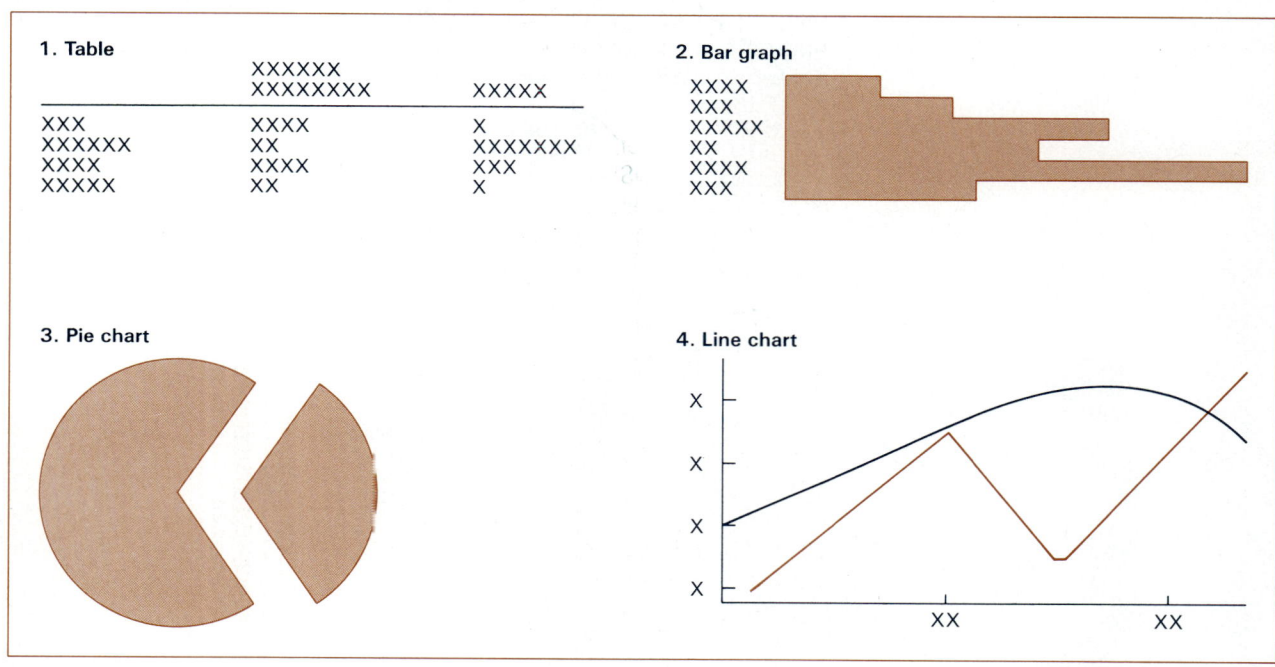

Presentation of data

Data are often presented in tables, graphs, and charts. These visual displays help to organize and present data in ways that are easy to understand. Figure 9.3 shows four ways in which data are commonly presented: tables, bar graphs, pie charts, and line charts.

Computer applications in business

Computers are an increasingly important part of management information systems. This is due to the computer's ability to provide information that is timely, accurate, and concise. Here are some common business uses of computers.

Maintenance of records

The speed and accuracy of the computer simplify such activities as payroll accounting, inventory, tracking, sales records, and billing. For example, when data on all sales transactions are stored by computer, management reports showing overall sales, individual products sales, and even consumer characteristics can be quickly generated.

Production automation

Computers now perform many tasks in producing goods. Among other things, they are used to test and monitor manufacturing processes and to provide instructions for operating machines.

Retailing

The cash register, a rather simple MIS device, has been replaced by point-of-sale (POS) computer terminals. POS terminals can store money, report the kind and quantity of merchandise sold, and check a customer's credit limit and payment status. As a result, retailers can know immediately which merchandise is selling and which remains in inventory. This information often influences marketing decisions. For example, a store manager can more easily spot slower-moving goods and put them on sale to help stimulate demand.

Supermarkets

The Universal Product Code (UPC) is part of a computerized checkout system. It consists of a coded series of bars that are printed on most supermarket items (see Figure 8.3). These bars can be "read" by optical scanning devices and interpreted by a computer. Cashiers pass each item over the electronic reader, and the computer displays and records the sale. It also gives the customer a detailed printed receipt. Computerized checkout systems provide supermarket managers with the same useful inventory information that POS terminals provide retailers.

Declining prices for small personal computers put them within reach of very small businesses.

"I never use my crystal ball anymore."

From the *Wall Street Journal,* Permission—Cartoon Features Syndicate

Banks

Bank tellers may also have computer terminals. Deposits and withdrawals are recorded immediately in the computer and the appropriate transfers of funds are made.

These terminals are so easy to operate that thousands of them are available for direct use by bank customers. **An automated teller machine (ATM) is a computer terminal that performs many banking transactions in place of human tellers.** Many banks locate ATMs in strategic public places. A customer inserts a plastic card in the terminal, gives a code number, and enters the transaction request. The terminal then checks the account status, provides an authorization, and carries out the requested transaction. This provides management with up-to-the-minute information about any customer's account and helps keep track of funds flowing in and out of the bank.

Computer-aided design and computer-aided manufacturing

Computer-aided design (CAD) and computer-aided manufacturing (CAM) will shape the future of manufacturing. **Computer-aided design is the process of designing, drafting, and analyzing with computer graphics displayed on a screen.** According to Ronald A. Cenowa, a computer engineer in General Motor's Fisher Body division, "Anything that a draftsman conventionally does using triangles, pencils, compasses . . . will be done mathematically within this system."

Computer-aided design speeds up the work of drafting. It also allows designers to study various aspects of a model by rotating its image on the computer screen, separating it into segments, or enlarging or shrinking details.

CAD communicates with a designer using computer-generated pictures on video display tubes. It allows a designer to analyze and test things by subjecting them to electronically simulated temperature changes, mechanical stresses, and other conditions that might occur in real life. This on-screen testing saves the time and expense of making prototypes, testing, modifying, and retesting.

Using CAD, for example, DuPont engineers can view a model of a chemical-processing plant in three dimensions. The views can easily be rotated on the screen for checking how well the parts fit together. DuPont expects the new system to cut design time to one-fifth of its former amount.

Computer-aided manufacturing is the use of computer-controlled machines in production processes. CAM is now quite common. It ranges from machine tools running on punched-tape instructions to programmed robots. CAM provides speed, accuracy, tirelessness, and dependability that human operators cannot match.

The joining of computer-aided design and computer-aided manufacturing introduces the potential for on-screen designing and testing of products. The final result can be immediately translated into computer instructions for manufacturing the product.

The CAD/CAM linkage shortens the time between design and production. It makes it less costly to change to new models. It reduces the likelihood and expense of making design changes after most of the work has already been done. And it makes customized products and short production runs easier and cheaper.

9 Management information systems

Summary

Managers need continuous information about the operation of their business. Much of their time is spent gathering, analyzing, and using data to make decisions. These tasks have become more important and complex with the rapid increase of information.

A *management information system (MIS)* is an organized method of providing past, present, and projected information about a business's internal and external environment. Its basic purpose is to provide managers with the decision-making information they need at the time they need it.

Businesses need information about (1) their factors of production, (2) their business operations, (3) the quality and quantity of their output, (4) competitors' performance, (5) consumers' characteristics and habits, and (6) government regulations and laws. To be useful, information should be accurate, available when needed, concise and relevant, and as complete as possible.

Uncertainty in decision making cannot be totally avoided. But good information can relieve much uncertainty. In the end, most managers make decisions based on their information resources, their own experience and training, and their personal judgments and expectations about the future.

Managers often must sift through large amounts of information to find answers to specific questions. Too much information can lead to confusion and indecision.

Information comes from both internal and external sources. *Internal data* are facts obtained directly from the firm's own records. They may include information about finances, production, and personnel. Using internal data, company operations can be compared with goals and objectives.

External data are facts obtained from sources outside the firm. Three important external sources are government sources, private sources, and competitors.

Primary data are facts gathered for the first time for use in solving a specific business problem. *Secondary data* are previously gathered facts, often published for purposes other than the solution of a particular business problem. Secondary data are often more general than primary data and often require careful sifting.

A *statistic* is a fact expressed as a number. *Statistics* is a field of mathematics that deals with the collection, analysis, interpretation, and presentation of numerical information.

Three statistics that managers often use are the measures of central tendency—mean, median, and mode. A *mean* is the arithmetic average of a group of numbers. A *median* is the middle one of a group of numbers in numerical order. A *mode* is the number that appears most often in a given set of numbers. Data are often presented in tables, graphs, and charts. Tables, bar graphs, pie charts, and line charts help to organize and present data in ways that are easy to understand.

Computers support a firm's planning, control, and operation. Computers are commonly used in maintaining records, production, retailing, supermarkets, and banking. An *automated teller machine (ATM)* is a computer terminal that handles a variety of banking transactions.

The linking of computer-aided design (CAD) with computer-aided manufacturing (CAM) is being called the new industrial revolution. *Computer-aided design* is the process of designing, drafting, and analyzing with computer graphics. *Computer-aided manufacturing* is the use of computer-controlled machines in production processes.

The joining of CAD and CAM introduces potential for designing and testing products on a video display tube. The final results can be translated immediately into computer instructions for manufacturing the product. The CAD/CAM linkage reduces the time between design and production. It promotes flexibility in design changes, new model development, and short production runs.

Review questions

1. What is a management information system (MIS)? How is an MIS related to the four management functions of planning, organizing, directing, and controlling?
2. What six subjects do businesses need information about?
3. What problems do managers often have with their information system?
4. Identify five sources of internal business data. What kinds of information can they provide?
5. Identify three sources of external data. What kinds of information can they provide?
6. What are the differences between primary and secondary data?
7. What is the difference between a statistic and the study of statistics?
8. What is a mean? A median? A mode? How is each computed?
9. Why are data often presented in tables, graphs, and charts?
10. Identify four common business uses of computers.
11. What are computer-aided design (CAD) and computer-aided manufacturing (CAM)? How can they affect present design and manufacturing practices?

Discussion questions

1. Explain this statement: "All successful managers learn how to cope with uncertainty."
2. At the opening of this chapter, mailing lists were discussed. Why are mailing lists valuable? How do you feel about having your name sold on a mailing list? Evaluate the pros and cons.
3. Comment on this statement: "The sign of intelligent people is *not* that they know everything, but that they know where to find the information they need."
4. A personnel manager studied the amount of time company employees spent on coffee breaks. She discovered that the mean was 15 minutes and the median was 10 minutes. How would you interpret these results?
5. Assume that your exam scores in this course were 88, 92, 78, 94, and 80. What would be your mean score? What would be your median score? What would be the mode?
6. Why is the linkage of CAD/CAM called the next industrial revolution? Do you agree? Why?

Chapter 9 case

The gasket formula

[*The competitive battle for information may result in questionable and ethical conflicts for any employee. This case shows how an employee is placed in the middle of the battle to gain a competitive edge.*]

Johns Company is a leading national manufacturer of industrial gaskets, enjoying approximately 60 percent of the gasket business in the United States. Bernard Hager was a sales engineer in the industrial products division of the Johns Company. Over a period of four years, Bernard had developed into the division's outstanding authority in the highly specialized and complicated field of metallic gaskets.

Metallic gaskets are used extensively in the oil refining industry and are generally manufactured to customer specifications. The gaskets have different configurations, sizes, and thicknesses. Designed to provide a leakproof seal between connecting pipe flanges, they are subjected to tremendous heat and pressure. Usually they are clad in stainless steel such as nickel, inconel, or monel. The formula for calculating an industrial sales price on these gaskets reflects the "formula" for highly complicated manufacturing processes. This pricing formula was known only to Hager and the company's district sales manager.

Chapter 9 Management information systems

Recently Hager was approached by the personnel director of the Roetzert Gasket Company, a leading competitor in the business. He offered Hager the position of district office manager, indicating that Roetzert's management was impressed with Hager's management potential. The new job paid $300 a month more plus some additional fringe benefits. Since Hager wanted to be a manager, he accepted the offer and turned in his resignation at Johns Company.

When he had been in his new position for only two weeks, Hager received a memo from George Davis, Roetzert's vice president of engineering in the home office. The memo read: "Please arrange to see me next Monday afternoon here in New York for the purpose of discussing stainless steel gasket pricing formulas and the manufacturing processes of metallic gaskets for the oil refining industry."

Hager was stunned. This was the first time anyone at Roetzert had asked him to divulge secret information from his former job at Johns Company. Hager realized he would have to decide immediately to what extent he would reveal data concerning the secret pricing formulas being used by his former employer.

1. What is the central ethical issue in this incident?
2. Is it unethical for Davis to attempt to learn from Hager the secret pricing formulas used at the Johns Company?
3. How would you respond to such a request from Davis?

Bernard A. Deitzer and Karl A. Shillif, *Incidents in Modern Business* (Columbus, Ohio: Charles E. Merrill, 1975), pp. 10–11.

3 Careers in computers and information systems management

Almost every study of employment opportunities points to the high demand for people with computer-related skills. These included computer programmers, systems analysts, computer service technicians, and data base managers. By one estimate, as many as 54,000 new jobs per year may be available in these fields, but colleges are graduating only about one-fifth that number of qualified students.[1]

The growth in these fields by 1990 will far exceed the growth in total employment. Here are some estimates of the number of computer specialists employed in 1980 and the number that will be needed in 1990:[2]

Job	1980 Employment	1990 Employment
Computer service technicians	83,000	168,000
Computer programmers	260,000	400,000
Systems analysts	190,000	324,000

Job descriptions

Computer programmer Programmers write the instructions that tell the computer what to do. They may write source programs or application programs (see Chapter 8 for the difference).

Systems analyst Analysts are highly trained computer experts who help an organization put together its information system. They determine what kinds of information the organization needs, how best to gather and process that information, and what equipment (computers and otherwise) are needed in the process.

---

[1] George Anders, "Colleges Faltering in Effort to Ease Critical Shortage of Programmers," *Wall Street Journal,* August 24, 1981.

[2] "Sharp Rise Predicted in Computer Jobs Is Forecast for Next 8 Years," *New York Times,* May 12, 1982. From *Occupational Outlook Handbook,* U.S. Bureau of Labor Statistics.

Computer service technician Technicians are trained to test and repair computers and related equipment. Often this is done at the site of the installation. Smaller computers may be brought to the technician.

Data base manager Because this is one of the newest computer-related occupations, there are many job openings. Data base managers keep huge banks of information—the inventory of a department store, for example—up to date and instantly available.

In general, the better educated a programmer is, the greater the demand for that person's services. According to one estimate, the demand for programmers with a two-year college degree is about equal to the supply of graduates. There is much greater demand for people with four-year college and graduate degrees. The National Center for Education Statistics, for example, found that 3597 persons earned master's degrees in computer science in 1981. Demand for people with this background was believed to be about ten times that figure.

Salaries reflect demand. Computer science graduates of four-year schools started at a minimum salary of $23,000 in 1981. Those with advanced degrees were commanding $50,000 and more as systems architects. Programmers with two-year degrees would start by assisting in the writing of payroll programs. Advanced-level programmers, who know computer structure as well as computer languages, might write more complex programs, such as an airline-ticketing program.

Additional information about some of these careers can be obtained from

American Federation of Information Processing Societies
1815 North Lynn Street
Arlington, VA 22209

Association for Systems Management
24587 Bagley Road
Cleveland, OH 44138

4
Producing goods and services

Business in perspective

The irony of our technology: It's harder today to keep a plant running

As steelmaker Jones & Laughlin Company will attest, a plant breakdown causes serious production problems. An electrical short-circuit hit its Cleveland plant in October 1979. The repair cost was about $500,000. But this was small compared to the loss of $30 million in orders that the break in production could have meant. This illustrates the significance of production breakdown for today's manufacturers.

Since 1945, the growth of new technology has complicated the struggle to keep factory production lines moving. Innovation and rapid growth have meant bigger, more complex machinery. In addition, the high cost of the machinery has made the problem worse. Plants used to have back-up machinery and an ample stock of spare parts. But today, the costs of such emergency measures are too high for most firms.

The cost of repairs is also astronomical. The electric utilities industry, which cannot tolerate frequent breakdowns, is a good example. It has been estimated that the accident at Three Mile Island nuclear power plant in 1979 cost more than $1 billion to fix. Final repairs will take about 8 years to complete.

Fortunately, obtaining replacement parts is not a problem today. Most firms trade spare parts as needed. On the other hand, the supply of repair technicians is severely limited. Some equipment specialists say that the shortage of service personnel is a national manufacturing crisis.

Many experts blame management for the entire maintenance problem. They say that managers are too interested in short-term profitability to recognize the importance of production. Such managers don't consider the long-term needs of plants and equipment. To counteract this, maintenance experts are calling for more operations people in top management.

Ultimately, the high costs of repairs and lost production due to breakdowns may lead to a change in managerial attitudes. A trend toward improved preventive measures in maintenance is seen by several experts in the field.

Chapter 10

Production and operations management

Key terms

manufacturing
mechanization
automation
mass production
standardization
specialization of labor
extractive process
analytic process
synthetic process
fabricating process
production planning
routing
scheduling
dispatching
PERT
critical path
inventory
inventory control
quality control
job shop
batch process
continuous process

Chapter objectives

In Chapter 10, you will learn:

The difference between mechanization and automation

The advantages of mass production

The four kinds of manufacturing processes

How PERT charts can help managers coordinate manufacturing processes

The importance of inventory control

The factors that affect the location of a manufacturing plant

How size, technology, and manufacturing process affect plant layout

Some significant trends in manufacturing

Part 4 Producing goods and services

Overview

The manufacture of goods occupies a central position in the U.S. economy, providing jobs for about one-fifth of the civilian labor force. Manufacturing industries provide us with the many goods that we consider important to our standard of living: automobiles, computers, houses, petroleum products, household appliances, and clothing.

Manufacturing (or production) is the process of coordinating material, people, machines, and money to create finished goods. In a private-enterprise economy, it is assumed that these goods will satisfy society's needs and wants.

Characteristics of manufacturing

The features that distinguish modern manufacturing processes are (1) mechanization and automation, (2) large-scale operation, (3) standardization, and (4) specialization of labor.

Mechanization and automation

Mechanization and automation enable workers to produce more than they could using only their own hands and strength.

Mechanization is the use of human-operated machines to do work that was previously performed by humans alone. Mechanized manufacturing is built around the machine, not around the people. For example, when the sewing machine was invented, it required human control. Skilled operators had to align the cloth, operate the pedal, and make other adjustments. Even so, the sewing machine was infinitely faster and produced a stronger garment than an individual could make by hand.

Similarly, an automobile assembly line is a mechanized process. But the requirements of the tools and the need to assemble the automobile in a certain order determine the organization of the assembly plant. The workplace is not designed around the needs of the workers.

Over the years, increased mechanization has led to increased worker productivity, higher-quality goods, and improved uniformity of goods.

Automation is the use of machines to perform production processes without direct help from humans. For example, if a sewing machine could automatically measure, feed, guide, and sew cloth without human help, the sewing process would be automated. Computers and microprocessors have helped to spread automation. By eliminating human control, an automated process is often even faster and more accurate than a mechanized one. Automation also helps reduce labor costs.

For example, automation has revolutionized the printing industry. From the time movable type was invented in the mid-fifteenth century until the late 1800s, printers had to set type one letter at a time. Working

Chapter 10 Production and operations management 211

this way, they could produce only one line per minute. Then a machine was invented that picked up the letters when an operator used a typewriterlike keyboard. That speeded up tyepsetting to about 4.9 lines per minute.

Today, computers can automatically set type at 80 lines per minute—and, in some cases, at thousands of lines per minute. In addition, a computer will make fewer mistakes than a human operator at a keyboard. This, of course, makes typesetting less expensive because the automated machinery is far less costly than the salaries of the many printers it replaces.

Large-scale operation

Mass production is the process of manufacturing an item in quantity. It results in lower costs per unit than small-scale production. Whether producing bolts or constructing houses, making many copies of one model can reduce costs.

For example, compare the cost of having a house built to your own specifications versus the cost of purchasing one in a builder's subdivision. For a custom-built house, you must pay for a single parcel of land. This may be more costly than the per-acre price a builder would pay for a large tract. Second, an architect must draw up plans to your exact specifications. Then a builder must familiarize himself with the plans. Wood must be cut and materials ordered that are unique to your needs. Finally, the construction workers must build a house that differs from others they have worked on. All this takes time—which costs money.

Survival requires expanded production at Freihofer Bakery

To increase productivity, the Charles Freihofer Baking Company launched a $10-million expansion program in the late 1970s. For the Albany, New York-based commercial bakery, such a production strategy was necessary to keep pace with its bigger competitors.

"We're at that uncomfortable stage where we're not small and we're not big. But we can't go backward. Survival is a significant part of the equation," said vice-president of operations Wayne Freihofer. By replacing outdated plants and adding new distribution outlets, the bakery (started in 1912 by Freihofer's great-grandfather) expected significant annual sales growth. Previously, annual sales growth was about 15 percent. By the final year of the program, Freihofer hoped to achieve a 30 percent sales increase.

In addition to modernizing its plants, the company has increased its automation. These strategies have helped Freihofer prosper through the years in which other independent bakeries have been bought out by conglomerates and suffered from a decline in the consumption of bakery products.

Contrast that to mass-produced houses in a subdivision. Suppose the builder constructs 90 houses in three different styles, each on one-quarter acre. The builder can save money by buying a single plot of 22.5 acres. The architect needs to draw up only three plans, the cost of which are shared by the 90 buyers. Specifications for lumber and other components are identical for each house. The construction workers can move speedily through the same assembly process for each house. As a result, the mass-produced houses can be sold for much less than a custom-designed house. The same principle holds true for mass-producing television sets, automobiles, can openers, overcoats, and just about every other common product.

Standardization

Of course, mass production is possible only when many identical products are made. **Standardization is the use of uniform methods to produce uniform goods.**

If you've ever assembled a jigsaw puzzle, hung wallpaper, or fixed a flat tire, you know that at first such tasks require a slow trial-and-error process. Usually, you have to refer to instructions. You make mistakes and must redo certain steps. After many tries, however, you learn the best approach, and from then on you can move along more quickly.

Similarly, by discovering the best way to handle a manufacturing process, industrial engineers can standardize the procedure. Then, no matter which worker performs the task or where the factory is set up, the manufacturing process can be done the same efficient way each time.

Standardized products are made with interchangeable parts of standard size. Thus, a 100-watt light bulb from any manufacturer will fit the socket of any lamp. More importantly, parts do not have to be individually machined to fit a specific unit.

With standardized parts, a worker on an assembly line who attaches the antennas to television sets can take any antenna and attach it to any television set moving down the assembly line. This is possible because each antenna is manufactured to line up the same way with every television set.

Today, we tend to take standardization for granted. But in the days of handcrafted, one-of-a-kind manufacturing, standardization did not exist. Today, if a car or appliance part wears out, we can usually buy a standard replacement part. Sometimes the replacement is made by someone other than the original manufacturer—but the part will still fit.

Specialization of labor

Mass production requires specialization of labor. To produce large quantities of identical products, one must establish a routine assembly process in which each item moves through the same series of steps. For custom-made goods, one or two craftsmen often make the entire product. But mass production is most efficient when each worker specializes in a single operation. **Specialization of labor is the breaking down of an**

Specialization requires workers to produce goods at uniform rates of speed to keep the production flow smooth.

Drawing by Lorenz; © 1976 The New Yorker Magazine, Inc.

assembly process into individual tasks, each of which is performed by a different worker.

The need for specialization exists in many areas. Physicians often become specialists in a particular field of medicine, such as ophthalmology (eyes) or cardiology (heart). Lawyers frequently specialize in corporate, criminal, or other areas of law. Any worker who thoroughly learns a well-defined job can perform more quickly and accurately.

In manufacturing, a common complaint is that specialization sometimes leads to boredom. As a result, some manufacturers give workers the opportunity to specialize in more than one area. Saab, the Swedish auto maker, is trying another way to reduce the boredom caused by specialization. On Saab assembly lines, workers belong to teams that are responsible for assembling almost the entire auto. Team members can trade jobs as they wish.

Mass production goes beyond specialization on the assembly line. Businesses themselves tend to specialize. To be able to perform certain kinds of large-scale production—and to be able to sell the output—businesses have become highly skilled in their specialties. For example, a soup manufacturer is unlikely to make insect sprays, and a coal mining company is unlikely to make refrigerators. (Often, of course, a company does diversify into other areas. But it does so by acquiring a going concern in another field and letting that firm's management continue to run the business.)

Manufacturing processes

Manufacturing processes can be classified according to the method used to change the form of raw materials. There are four such categories: (1) extractive, (2) analytic, (3) synthetic, and (4) fabrication.

Extractive process

An extractive manufacturing process withdraws, or separates, a substance from its natural form. This includes mining and drilling for coal, copper, oil, or other substances. In such cases, the product already exists in nature and the manufacturing process involves extracting it to a usable form.

Analytic process

An analytic process breaks down raw materials into their component parts. The transformation of crude oil into gasoline, aviation fuel, heating oil, and the other oil components is an analytic process. In analytic processes, the sum of the end products always equals the total that went into the process. Thus, a 44-gallon barrel of crude oil may become 10 gallons of gasoline, 15 gallons of heating oil, 13 gallons of aviation fuel, and 6 gallons of other oil products.

Synthetic process

A synthetic process combines two or more raw materials into a new and different finished product. Plastic, for example, does not exist in nature but must be created by combining several ingredients. Nylon and polyester fabrics are also synthetics. The manufacture of chemicals and metal alloys are other examples of synthetic processes.

Fabricating process

A fabricating process changes the shape or form of a material without changing its basic nature. Examples include sheet metal stamped into fenders and hoods for automobiles, lumber sawed and hammered into bookcases, and fabric stitched into overcoats. Most assembly is a fabricating process.

Managing manufacturing processes

A well-managed manufacturing operation ensures a smooth, constant work flow. The production process should take the shortest possible time from start to finish and have the lowest possible cost per unit. Because there are so many different kinds of manufacturing, no single standard for efficient production exists. A workshop that makes custom-designed furniture, for example, has far different needs from a factory that mass-produces one kind of chair. But within a given situation, procedures must be managed to accomplish efficient production.

For any manufacturing operation, effective management follows a similar series of steps.

Production planning

The manufacturing-control process begins with planning. Production planning analyzes the resources (raw materials, machinery, personnel, capital, and so forth) necessary to produce the desired amount and quality of goods.

Thus, the first step in manufacturing control is to map out the desired work flow before work starts. In an assembly line, this has to be done only once, but it must be done right. Because much money and machinery are involved, a mistake could be costly. During the planning phase, machines, time limits, and workers must be assigned to each step of the manufacturing process.

Routing

Routing spells out the order of each step in the production process. This is necessary to maintain an orderly work flow.

Scheduling

Scheduling is the development of timetables to keep machines and their operators busy and to avoid bottlenecks. A schedule indicates how long each step in the manufacturing process takes and when it should be performed.

For example, a book printer knows that the camera room, plate-making facility, press, and bindery each have a certain capacity. As each new printing job comes in, the scheduler must predict when each de-

The United States started it all—but Japan has pulled ahead

The preface for the proceedings of the Robots VI Conference, held in Detroit in March 1982, included this warning: "No war . . . no strike . . . no depression, can so completely destroy an established business, or its profits, as new and better methods . . . new and better equipment in the hands of our enlightened competitors."

The "new and better," in this case, referred to robots, and the "enlightened competitors," as far as most of the 2300 conferees were concerned, were the Japanese.

Robot technology is U.S. technology: the modern industrial robot is the brainchild of American inventors and engineers, and the first units went to work in Ford and General Motors plants in 1961. The United States enjoyed a 15-year lead in research time and an 8-year lead in production—Japan didn't get its hands on a robot until 1967. But, by the end of 1981, Japan had 14,246 robots, the vast majority produced by domestic manufacturers. The United States has only 4100. The United States still enjoys a technological advantage—it manufactures the "Cadillacs" of the robotics industry—but, in the marketing and implementation of the technology, the Japanese clearly dominate. There are now more than 150 Japanese robot manufacturers; last year, they did $246 million in business. About 30 U.S. makers had 1981 revenues of $155.5 million. Fourteen of the Japanese companies distribute their products in the United States, eight others are ready to move in, and a number have entered into licensing or manufacturing agreements with U.S. firms.

Japan has also concentrated on relatively simple and inexpensive robots—Hondas, rather than Cadillacs. "The Japanese just can't understand why, in America, we put six-axis $100,000 robots on three-axis $10,000 jobs," says Walt Weisel, vice-president of Prab Robots Inc. "There's an awful lot of overkill in the U.S. market today."

The upshot is that U.S. businesspeople now face the threat of "new and better" methods and equipment in the hands of "enlightened competitors." And who pointed it out to them? The warning contained in the preface of the Robots VI Conference proceedings first appeared on a bulletin board outside the plant of a Japanese robot manufacturer.

Craig R. Walters, "There's a Robot in Your Future," *INC.*, June 1982, p. 64. Reprinted with permission, *INC.* Copyright © 1982 by INC. Publishing Company, 38 Commercial Wharf, Boston, MA 02110.

Chapter 10 Production and operations management

partment will have time to perform each step. The scheduler must also accurately estimate how long each project will take so that the next project can be scheduled.

Dispatching

When a job is finished, it may be put into inventory or immediately sent to a customer. In most cases it must be held, if only for a short time. **Dispatching is the task of making sure that finished goods get delivered on time, to the right customer, and by the least expensive or most efficient means possible.**

Coordinating manufacturing operations

Most manufacturing processes are quite complex. They often involve many interdependent steps. Some steps must be completed before others can be started. Some steps can be carried out without regard for other steps in the process. And often, several steps can be performed all at the same time.

Production managers must analyze all steps in a manufacturing process and arrange them into the most logical and least costly sequence. Two systems can help production managers to analyze, plan, schedule, and control complex manufacturing processes: the Gantt chart and PERT.

Gantt chart

One simple and useful production-control device is the Gantt chart, shown in Figure 10.1. In this example, the available time for each operation is broken down by hours per day. Each job is then scheduled for each department. The chart also shows the amount of time it actually took to do the job. In this way, the scheduler can check the accuracy of the estimates and spot areas that may cause bottlenecks.

PERT and the critical path

On complex jobs, such as constructing an office building, the huge number of operations required can be very confusing. Even more important, in such a project, many operations depend on each other. A delay in one step may delay the entire project. To coordinate the overall process and minimize delays, a manager may use a PERT chart.

PERT (Project Evaluation and Review Technique) is a scheduling technique that uses network diagrams to coordinate complex production processes. A PERT chart can help a manager organize the production sequence, spot possible scheduling difficulties, estimate completion time, and control the entire production process.

To begin a PERT chart, a manager first lists each step in the production process and how long each step takes to complete. He or she then

Figure 10.1 Gantt chart

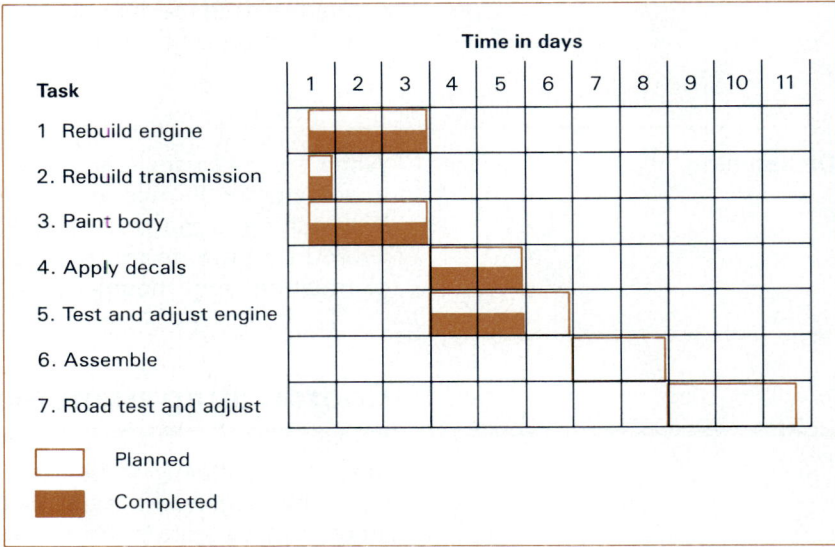

In this Gantt chart, the activities necessary to rebuild a racing car have been laid out. The blocks show what activities are scheduled to be done each day. The heavy line in the blocks show what activities have been accomplished. This chart shows that after 5 days of work, the job is on schedule. Day 6 requires completing task number 5, Test and adjust engine.

arranges the steps in the order in which they must be completed. Using this information, the manager draws a diagram that shows how each step relates to all the others (see Figure 10.2).

One series of steps in the chart becomes the critical path. **A critical path is the sequence of operations in a PERT chart that takes the**

Figure 10.2 Using the PERT critical path method: preparing for an auto race

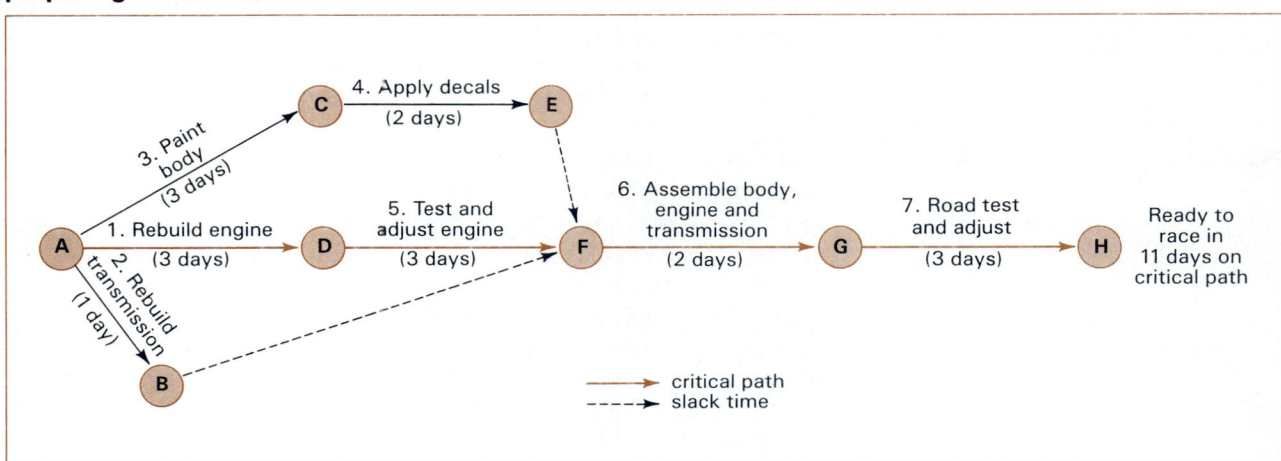

The activities to be most concerned with are those along the critical path. A delay there will delay final completion.

longest time to complete if no time is wasted. The operations along the critical path are the ones whose time limits are most important. A delay in any operation along the critical path will delay the whole production process.

PERT charts often contain thousands of steps that span many months of production. Such complex networks and their critical paths are usually generated by computers rather than by humans.

Inventory and inventory control

Inventory is the supply of goods not yet used or sold. Manufacturers have two basic kinds of inventory: raw materials and finished goods. For production management, raw materials inventory is the more important. The uninterrupted flow of the manufacturing process depends on having all the materials needed. This is especially true on an assembly line, when running out of a crucial part can stop the entire production process.

Inventory control

Inventory control is the balancing of the need to keep adequate supplies of raw materials with the cost of buying and storing raw materials.

Need for adequate inventory

There is an optimal level of inventory for each material used in a production process. This level allows an uninterrupted supply of the material to the production process, but it does not tie up too much money in inventory.

Purchasing materials for inventory is like putting savings into a bank account that doesn't pay interest. The manufacturer who purchases supplies must pay for them. Then the supplies sit idle. They make no money until they are used in the manufacturing process and the final product is sold.

Cost of inventory

In the meantime, holding inventory costs money. Inventory ties up cash, takes up warehouse space, and requires handling. It is subject to deterioration, damage, theft, and obsolescence.

A manager must balance the costs of carrying inventory against the cost of losing a sale or stopping production if supplies run out. Moreover, by purchasing in quantity, an inventory manager may obtain price discounts that compensate for all or part of the costs of carrying the inventory.

Many companies now rely on computers to weigh the trade-offs involved in inventory control and determine appropriate inventory levels.

Quality control

Quality control is a process that seeks to find defective products before they are shipped to customers. Quality control also attempts to find the cause of defects and adjust the production process to minimize or eliminate the problems. Although having no defective products shipped to customers is the ideal, it is not economically feasible to achieve this for most products. In the case of certain products, however, such as pacemakers for a human heart or parts for a spaceship, it is essential that there be no defects, regardless of the quality control costs.

There are several approaches to quality control. In a few instances, every finished product is examined, either visually or by testing. More often, only a sample of goods is tested. If a particular batch shows a high defect rate, more extensive testing may be done. Fixing defective products, either before they leave the factory or when returned by the customer, can be quite expensive. A bad reputation for quality can also damage a firm's long-term sales. One firm admitted it was spending 20 percent of sales to fix defects.

Improving quality control has become a major goal of American industry in the 1980s. In part, this is in response to the challenge from Japanese manufacturers, who have achieved a reputation for higher quality than their American counterparts. Electronics manufacturer Hewlett-Packard estimates that adopting a zero-defect program would result in the need for one-third fewer workers, 25 percent less floor space, and a 66 percent decrease in inventories.

Plant location

A manufacturing plant is very expensive to buy and equip. And it is not easy to move manufacturing operations from one facility to another. As a result, plant location is one of the most serious decisions a company makes.

When a company chooses a location for a manufacturing plant, it must consider many factors. These factors vary according to the firm's products and market. This section identifies the major considerations, but their order of importance will vary from industry to industry and from company to company.

Nearness to markets

Manufacturers of bulk goods, such as concrete, want to build plants close to their customers. This is logical because transportation costs rise as the distance from the plant increases. Beer breweries are located close to the regions they serve because the product is heavy to ship and because they want to ensure freshness. Industries that emphasize service, such as sawmills and commercial printers, also consider proximity to their customers a top priority.

American Airlines: quality control taken seriously

The next time you are in an American Airlines airport waiting room, a man with a stopwatch and clipboard may well be hanging around. He's there to see how long it takes you to get your ticket—the company standards say 85 percent of their passengers should not have to stand in line more than five minutes. When you land, you may find another such fellow checking to see how long it takes to get the bags off the plane.

American Airlines employees are held to dozens of standards—and checked constantly. Reservations phones must be answered within 20 seconds. Eighty-five percent of all flights must take off within five minutes of scheduled departure time and land within fifteen minutes of scheduled arrival time. Cabins must have the proper supply of magazines. Performance summaries drawn up every month tell management how the airline is doing and where the problems lie. Late arrivals may be caused by disgruntled air controllers. That can't be helped. But an outbreak of dirty ashtrays may be traced to a particular cleanup crew. The manager responsible for the crew will hear about it. His pay and promotion depend on meeting standards. If he fails to meet them three months running without unforeseen circumstances, he may have to look for a job.

Constant checking has helped make American Airlines the preferred domestic line in the latest Airline Passengers Association survey. American has a good on-time record, too. On major domestic routes monitored by the Civil Aeronautics Board, 92.7 percent of American flights were on time last November, compared with only 54.7 percent of Pan American/National flights.

To keep track of the competition, American inspectors clock the performance of United and TWA. American tries to keep slightly, but not too far, ahead of them. "We can't afford to be a whole lot better," says American vice-president Jerry R. Jacob.

Jeremy Main, "Toward Service Without a Snarl," FORTUNE, March 23, 1981, p. 61. Reprinted from FORTUNE Magazine by permission. © 1981 Time Inc. All rights reserved.

Access to raw materials

Some industries find it more important to be near a source of raw materials than to be near their customers. Finished steel girders are heavy and expensive to ship. But coal and iron ore are even greater shipping problems, so steel mills tend to be located close to coal- and iron-mining regions. Processors of perishable products, such as orange juice, prefer to operate near growing fields. It would be unnecessarily troublesome, for example, to ship raw oranges from California and Florida to North Dakota for processing. But frozen and canned juice can be shipped almost anywhere with ease.

Transportation

Good transportation plays an important role in determining plant location. The city of Chicago grew rapidly during the nineteenth century because it was a crossroad for trains from the East and West coasts. St. Louis, Kansas City, New York, Philadelphia, and Baltimore all developed because they served as transportation centers.

Today, manufacturing and transportation are still closely linked. Access to deep-water ports, interstate highway networks, railroad lines, canals, and major airports are of prime importance to manufacturers.

Availability and cost of labor

Most manufacturing companies need a mix of skilled and unskilled workers. Often, workers with specialized skills are concentrated in certain parts of the country. For example, certain parts of the South have skilled furniture makers. Therefore, a furniture manufacturer may find it easier to build or expand in Tennessee, North Carolina, and South Carolina. Similarly, computer engineers and designers are concentrated around Boston and San Francisco. A manufacturer who does not need skilled labor has more freedom when choosing a location.

Companies also look for areas where labor costs are relatively low. The highest wages must be paid in the Northeast and North Central states, such as Ohio, Pennsylvania, Illinois, and Michigan. The lowest wages can be paid in the South and Southwest, where living costs are less. Many manufacturers also prefer the Sunbelt states because labor unions are not yet strong there.

Cost of energy

The cost of energy is an important consideration for many manufacturers, such as those in the aluminum and chemical industries. The availability of cheap energy can help them keep production costs down. So, if possible, such plants will try to locate in areas served by cheaper forms of energy. The hydroelectric power produced by the great dams of the West costs far less than the oil-generated power of the Northeast. As a result, the West is a more attractive location for manufacturers who need large amounts of electricity.

Community and government support

Some communities and states try to attract manufacturers by offering incentives like low-cost loans and long-term tax benefits. They hope that new industry will produce more jobs, population growth, and additional tax revenues.

On the other hand, some areas try to discourage commercial growth through zoning and taxation. They believe that industrial growth places strains on school systems, hospitals, and police and fire departments; increases traffic problems; and pollutes the environment.

Chapter 10 Production and operations management

Table 10.1 Factors involved in plant location

Factors for location decision	Greatly affected manufacturers
Access to markets	Bakeries, breweries, commercial printers, cement producers
Access to raw materials	Food processors, steel fabricators, sawmills, paper mills
Transportation	Meat packers, oil refineries
Availability and cost of labor	Electronics firms, furniture makers, auto makers
Energy	Aluminum smelters, paper mills, chemical producers
Community and government support	All

Before they decide to locate a plant in a new area, management studies state and local tax laws, operation and pollution regulations, community and government attitudes toward industry, and availability of community services (roads, sanitation, schools, hospitals, recreation, and the like).

Other factors

Still other location factors may be important to certain industries. Climate may be important to some. The availability of inexpensive land or ready access to financial institutions may matter to others.

Because so many factors come into play, plant location is a very complex and difficult decision. Management must carefully weigh each factor against its company's individual needs before making a final choice. Table 10.1 summarizes the factors involved in site selection.

Plant design

A plant's layout depends on the size, technology, and kind of manufacturing operation it will house. Machines and work stations must be arranged to provide the most efficient work flow.

Job shop

When a manufacturer has small orders for many different products, a job-shop setup is most appropriate. **In a job shop, production is set up around individual customer orders.** Each order requires adjustments to machinery to meet custom specifications. Commercial printers, makers of custom-designed furniture, and photographic laboratories are job shops. For example, a printer has to change type, ink, and paper for each order and adjust the presses accordingly.

In a job shop, equipment must be placed so that individual orders can be processed from start to finish by one or several workers. Because job-shop manufacturing involves small quantities of custom-made products, it tends to be more expensive than mass production.

Batch process

Most manufactured goods are mass-produced in batches. **A batch process is used to make many identical products from a single machine setup.** Once one batch is completed, the same machinery is adjusted and used to produce a different batch of products. For example, a furniture maker may set up a saw to cut several thousand chair legs and then change the saw's setting to produce several thousand chair rungs. A soup maker will cook a large batch of chicken noodle soup and then a few months' supply of vegetable soup rather than make small quantities of each more often.

Continuous process

A continuous process is used to produce large quantities of products over long periods of time without adjusting machines. Steel production is a continuous process, with blast furnaces almost never shut down. Auto making is also a continuous process. Production runs are large and usually span an entire model year.

In a continuous-process plant, equipment is usually arranged to follow the flow of production. Raw materials enter in one place, flow through a logical series of manufacturing steps, and exit as finished goods. It is assumed that machinery will rarely need adjustment. Most assembly lines are continuous-process operations.

Materials purchasing

In most manufacturing firms, the cost of materials accounts for a substantially greater proportion of total expenses than does any other single item. A ratio of $5 in materials for each $1 in labor is common. Thus, there is considerable incentive for manufacturers to be as efficient as possible in buying raw materials and supplies. In all but the smallest companies, purchasing is so important that it is assigned to one person or an entire department of purchasing agents. They are skilled at shopping around for the supplies in which they are specialists. But getting the best price is only part of the purchasing decision.

Chapter 10 Production and operations management

Make or buy?

General Motors manufactures the engines it puts in its car. But it purchases from outside suppliers most of the parts that go into assembling those engines. On the other hand, Chrysler Corporation for many years purchased engines from Volkswagen to put into some of their subcompact automobiles.

One of the most basic yet frequent decisions a manufacturer must make is the extent to which it should purchase parts or finished components from outside suppliers, or make the components itself.

Many factors go into these classic "make or buy" decisions. Among them are the following:

1. Is the component available elsewhere? Sometimes, a product requires materials that are new or different from what already exists. The company may have to commission another firm to make the part—or make it itself.

2. Does the manufacturer have or understand the technology? An electronics manufacturer, for example, may be capable of making its own semiconductors. But a manufacturer of microwave ovens that needs a semiconductor for its product may have no expertise in that area. So it would be most likely to purchase that part.

3. Is it a short- or long-term need? When doing custom work or a limited production run, a manufacturer would probably want to purchase as many of its parts and components as possible. On the other hand, important materials that may be part of the manufacturing process for many years are more likely candidates for in-house production.

4. What is the capital investment required? Having the skills necessary to make components is only part of the picture. Some materials may require heavy investment in machinery, buildings, and other facilities. Chrysler Corporation, for example, could have made the small engines it purchased from Volkswagen. But at the time Chrysler was in a precarious financial position. Rather than tie up capital in a production line for engines, Chrysler decided to buy the engines from someone else who had already made the investment.

Policies and procedures

In larger firms, purchasing agents often specialize in buying particular kinds of goods. That way they can become very familiar with the products or services of a group of potential suppliers. In smaller firms, purchasing agents may be generalists. But in all cases, there are certain policies and procedures that are best followed for the most efficient purchasing.

1. Buy to meet engineered specifications. If a company simply surveys what materials are "out there" and purchases whatever is closest to the company's needs, it may not be getting the best buy for its money. Also, the materials may not be best for the company's needs.

2. Always be on the lookout for cheaper (but acceptable) substitutes. Over the years, manufacturers have found that in many cases plastic can be substituted for more expensive steel. Aluminum has also replaced some steel. Synthetic fabrics are often appropriate in place of more expensive or less durable natural fibers. Cheaper substitutes do not necessarily mean inferior quality. At the same time, purchasing agents must be careful that, in their desire to save money on materials, they do not lessen the quality that the original product sought to achieve.

3. Buy in large quantity when prices seem low. The converse of this, of course, is to buy smaller quantities when prices are high. Knowing when prices for commodities (such as cocoa, cotton, etc.) have peaked or troughed is not an exact science. A purchasing agent for a chocolate manufacturer, for example, has to know a great deal about the world market conditions for cocoa in trying to decide whether the supply will increase. If he or she thinks the current harvest will be poor, he or she may try to lock up some long-term contracts before prices soar. But if it seems there might be a generous supply, it would be wise to order just enough cocoa to keep the manufacturing process going. Perhaps the new harvest will bring lower prices. In volatile commodity markets, purchasing agents are often most interested in stability of prices. One technique they use to ensure stability is called "straddling" the market. Purchasing agents straddle the market by buying contracts to both purchase and sell a certain commodity in the future at a price set in the present.

4. Seek discounts for quantity buying. Smaller firms often do not have enough working capital to buy materials in quantities that permit sizable savings. One strategy is to borrow from the bank. This can be a profitable decision, as long as the interest on the borrowed funds is less than the money saved by buying in quantity. Another possibility is to arrange a line of credit with the supplier.

Trends in manufacturing

Manufacturing has traditionally been concentrated in the urban areas of New England, the Middle Atlantic and North Central states, and the West Coast. This was due to the large labor force, excellent transportation, substantial markets, and many raw materials located in these areas.

In the second half of the twentieth century, manufacturing operations have become increasingly decentralized. The South and Southwest have enjoyed the greatest growth. This growth has been aided by improved transportation and communication. Lower labor costs have also attracted manufacturers to the Sunbelt.

Many kinds of manufacturing have increased long-term productivity through mechanization and automation. This has put some individuals out of work, but it has also saved countless jobs. Automation enables U.S. manufacturers to stay competitive with producers overseas, where labor is often cheaper. Technology has also created new jobs in manufacturing and servicing the very devices that have reduced labor requirements.

Manufacturing operations are spreading worldwide. Many U.S. firms are moving their manufacturing operations to underdeveloped nations whose large, trainable work forces will accept lower pay than U.S. workers. Recently, textile and electronics companies have been relocating to South Korea, Taiwan, Singapore, and Mexico. In the future, China and perhaps Africa will become sources of manufactured products made by U.S.-owned firms.

Such movement can benefit both the U.S. standard of living and the newly employed workers abroad. When routine, labor-intensive operations are sent to other parts of the world, the United States can concentrate its resources on high-technology industries in which it has a clear advantage.

10 Production and operations management

Summary

Manufacturing is the process of coordinating material, people, machines, and money to create finished goods. The four features that distinguish modern business are mechanization and automation, large-scale operations, standardization, and specialization of labor. By increasing productivity, *mechanization* and *automation* have lowered the cost of goods and raised the standard of living for everyone. *Mass production,* the practice of manufacturing in great quantity, results in lower costs per unit than custom or small-scale operations. Mass production depends on *standardization,* the use of uniform methods to produce identical, interchangeable parts. Mass production also depends on *specialization of labor*. When workers perform only one step in the production process, their efficiency is increased.

There are four basic manufacturing processes. An *extractive process* withdraws or separates a substance from its natural form. Coal mining is an extractive process. An *analytic process* breaks down a raw material into its components. The refining of crude oil into gasoline, heating oil, lubricants, and so forth is an analytic process. A *synthetic process* combines two or more raw materials into a new and different finished product. Plastic and rayon manufacturing are synthetic processes. A *fabricating process* changes the shape or form of a material without changing its basic nature. Stamping a sheet of metal into an automobile fender is a fabricating process.

The efficiency of a manufacturing process depends on a smooth, constant work flow. *Production planning* analyzes the resources necessary to produce the desired amount and quality of goods. Routing spells out the order of each step in the process. *Scheduling* develops timetables to keep the work flow steady. *Dispatching* coordinates the role that each department plays in the production process. One technique for planning and controlling complex projects is PERT (Planning and Evaluation Review Technique). A *PERT* chart shows the network of steps that must be followed to complete a job. The *critical path* is the series of activities that takes the longest time to complete if no time is wasted. A delay in any operation along the critical path will delay the whole production process.

Inventory is the supply of goods not yet used or sold. It may be in the form of finished goods or raw materials. An adequate supply of raw materials is necessary to keep a production process running smoothly. *Inventory control* is the balancing of the need to keep adequate supplies of raw materials with the cost of buying and storing raw materials. *Quality control* is the process of monitoring the product to determine if it meets company standards.

The best location for a manufacturing plant depends on many factors, whose order of importance varies by industry and company. Among the considerations are (1) nearness of the facility to the markets in which the finished goods will be sold, (2) proximity of the plant to sources of raw materials, (3) adequacy of transportation facilities, (4) availability and cost of labor, (5) cost of energy, and (6) community and government support.

The actual design and layout of a manufacturing facility depends on the kind, size, and technology of the manufacturing process it will house. The goal is to provide the most efficient work flow. For custom and small-scale manufacturing, a *job shop* layout is probably best. For most large-scale production, a *batch process* layout is appropriate. For production processes that are repeated over a long period of time, a *continuous process* layout is usual.

In recent years, manufacturing companies have been moving from the industrialized Northeast to the Sunbelt states of the South and Southwest. In the long run, it is likely that many manufacturing operations will be moved to parts of the world that have lower labor costs than the United States. For example, Taiwan, South Korea, Singapore, and Mexico now manufacture many textiles and electronic components for sale in the United States. This allows the United States to concentrate its resources on high-technology industries in which it has a technological advantage.

Review questions

1. What is the difference between mechanization and automation?
2. What are the advantages of mass production over custom building?
3. What are the advantages and disadvantages of specialization of labor? What can be done to counteract the disadvantages?
4. Describe the four basic kinds of manufacturing processes. Give an example of each.
5. Explain the five steps of production management.
6. What is PERT? How can it help a production manager?
7. Why is inventory control important?
8. What factors should a company consider when choosing the location of a new plant?
9. What factors affect a plant's layout? What are the three basic layouts? How does each adapt to a different production process?
10. What are some significant trends in manufacturing?

Discussion questions

1. What are the advantages and disadvantages of automation for a society as a whole?
2. How do you assess the specialization of labor in most U.S. assembly lines? As a production manager, would you change the standard arrangement? How?
3. How has the computer modernized manufacturing processes? Discuss at least two examples.
4. Why are many U.S. manufacturers relocating to the Sunbelt?
5. Are there disadvantages to having U.S. manufacturers relocate to countries with cheaper labor forces? If so, do the advantages outweigh the disadvantages? Explain.

Chapter 10 case

Sonoma Manufacturing Company, Inc.

Manufacturing companies are sometimes tempted to make most or all of the pieces that go into their finished products instead of purchasing the pieces from an outside supplier. Yet to do so may not be as cost-effective as it may first appear. In this case, you are asked to help the Sonoma Company make a classic make-or-buy decision.

The computer printout of the most recent analysis of manufacturing costs had been sitting on Kurt Sterling's desk for two days now. He picked up the stack of accordion-folded pages and decided he had better study them. Kurt Sterling was vice president of manufacturing for Sonoma. The company produced many kinds of small home appliances, including a popular food processor.

Looking over the various costs associated with the production of their very popular food processor, Sterling was struck by the increased cost, compared with the last analysis 6 months earlier. Comparing the costs for labor, material, and overhead, Sterling found few differences that would account for the rise in total cost; that is, until he came to an entry labeled "blades." There he saw that the cutting blades that were included with the food processor had jumped from $5 each to $6 each.

These blades were not made by Sonoma. The company had been buying them, under contract, from another company that specialized in fabricated steel and aluminum products. Sterling called in LeRoy Thompson, the purchasing manager. "LeRoy, tell me about the blades we've been buying. They seem to have skyrocketed in price."

Thompson was prepared for the question. "I was just drafting you a memo on this, Kurt. The supplier just signed a new labor contract and also has had to pass on higher costs of raw materials.

And I checked around. No one else can offer us a better price on blades of this quality."

The increased cost of blades reduced the profit margin on Sonoma's best-selling product. But they couldn't raise their price, because the competition was holding the line on price. "Maybe we should consider making the blades ourselves," thought Sterling. That evening, after dinner, he took out his calculator and tried out some rough figures. The machinery needed would cost about $600,000. An addition to their building to house the new equipment would be about $400,000. And the cost of hiring and training workers to make blades would be about $200,000. That would be an investment of $1.2 million. As they hadn't planned on this expenditure. it would all have to come from a bank loan, which he figured would carry about 14 percent interest annually.

Sonoma had been buying 300,000 blades annually from its supplier, at a current cost of $6 each. Sterling figured that if they made this investment, the cost of materials and direct labor for Sonoma would average about $5 per blade. The question he had to answer was whether the company would be better off making the blades or continuing to buy them from the supplier.

Complete the analysis for Kurt Sterling:

1. How much, if anything, would Sonoma save by making its own blades?
2. How long would it take before this savings would add up to enough to pay back the investment in equipment, building, and training of the blade-making department? Include in your calculation the 14 percent interest Sonoma is paying on the loan.
3. What other factors should Sterling take into account before making the final make-or-buy decision?
4. What would be your decision? Why?

Business in perspective

Fantasy Land and the fantastic growth of service industries

They call themselves Orlandoans, but the 700,000 folks who live in the central Florida city sometimes feel like munchkins. There in the distance are castles and magic kingdoms, talking bears and dancing whales. To Orlando, fantasy is big business.

Walt Disney started it all in 1971 when he bought 28,000 acres outside of town and built Walt Disney World. Then came Sea World . . . then Circus World . . . Little England . . . and then EPCOT (Disney's Experimental Prototype Community Of Tommorow, which opened in 1982).

In a decade the city's population has doubled. Orlando had to build a new air terminal as its annual passenger flow soared from 1.3 million to 6.5 million.

The proliferation of theme parks has also made Orlando one of the nation's top convention cities, spawning a boom in hotel and motel construction. Today, Orlando lists itself as fifth in the world in the number of hotel and motel rooms (33,000), crowding behind only New York, London, Chicago, and Las Vegas. Another 22,000 rooms will be built by 1986.

It may not be enough—a California firm now is ogling Orlando for a $170 million theme park featuring Hollywood.

Del Marth, "Where Business Presents Tomorrow," *Nation's Business,* November 1981, p. 65. Reprinted by permission from *Nation's Business;* copyright 1981 by *Nation's Business,* Chamber of Commerce of the United States.

Chapter 11

Service industries

Key terms

service
distributive services
producer services
consumer services
nonprofit and government services
human capital

Chapter objectives

In Chapter 11, you will learn:

What a service is

The four service sectors of the U.S. economy

The four key features of services

How goods and services are interrelated

The increasing importance of service industries in the U.S. economy

The concept of human capital and its relationship to education

Which services are important foreign exports

How service productivity benefits from advancing technology

How some service industries are regulated

Overview

Two out of every three people working in the United States today are employed in service industries. Think of the people you saw working today. What kind of work were they doing? Chances are high that they were providing services rather than producing goods. Police officers, fire fighters, postal workers, waiters and waitresses, lawyers, physicians, salespeople, and college professors—all of these are service occupations.

Consider your college's business courses. They include subjects like marketing, management, accounting, finance and banking, data processing, and secretarial science. All provide information and skills related to service industries.

During the past 20 years, service industries have become an increasingly important part of the American economy. As business has become more complex and specialized, management has been forced to use services in areas such as advertising, labor relations, research, and taxation. And their importance is expected to grow throughout the twentieth century.

In this chapter, we discuss the nature and makeup of service industries. Service industries have always been important, but more emphasis was once placed on manufacturing. Today, the service sector must be given equal attention.

Services

A service is a useful activity that fulfills a need. Service industries do not usually produce products. People who provide services usually possess specialized skills and talents.

The four service sectors

According to the U.S. Government, a service is any output that does not come from such goods-producing sectors as agriculture, mining, manufacturing, and construction. There are four service sectors. **Distributive services involve activities bringing needed services to consumers.** They include industries such as wholesale and retail trade, communications, transportation, and public utilities. **Producer services are professional activities for consumers.** They include professions such as accounting, legal counseling, banking, architecture, engineering, and management counsulting. **Consumer services are activities providing consumers with personal need satisfaction.** They include industries such as restaurants, hotels, resorts, laundries, and dry-cleaning establishments. **Nonprofit and government services refer to activities providing for the broad needs of society.** They include areas such as education, health care, and the administration of justice and national defense.

Chapter 11 Service industries

Characteristics of services

Services have four main characteristics: (1) they are intangible; (2) they are perishable; (3) they are difficult to standardize; and (4) customers often take an active role in their development and distribution.

Intangibility

The essence of most services is intangible. It is difficult to promote a service business because it doesn't lend itself to description, display, or demonstration. A service is difficult to package. Trial samples and other such devices are an impossibility. How, for example, can an accountant or a private investigator give a sample of service? Because of this, consumers often cannot judge the quality of a service before they purchase it. The reputation of the service is a strong point in the buying decision, because word-of-mouth becomes a powerful influence.

Perishability

Services are perishable. That is, that which a service business sells cannot be produced ahead of time and stored in inventory. For example, the accountant must handle each client's income tax return on an individual basis. She cannot keep an inventory of completed tax returns on hand to sell as the need arises. The private investigator works on a case-by-case basis. He cannot gather facts in advance of clients' requests.

Difficulty of standardization

Two size 15½ men's shirts will fit about the same even if they are made by two different manufacturers. But such standardization is often impossible among sellers of the same service. In fact, it is even difficult to assure consistency in all the services provided by a single seller. For example, no two performances from the same rock group are identical. Standardization of services occurs only in special situations. Some examples include automatic banking services, a drive-through carwash, and certain fast-food restaurant chains. McDonald's has been especially successful in standardizing the services of its fast-food franchises.

Talk is expensive: approximate fees paid per lecture engagement, as reported by agents and speakers bureaus

$20,000	$15,000	$10,000
Alexander Haig	Kareem Abdul-Jabbar	David Brinkley
Paul Harvey	Dick Cavett	William F. Buckley, Jr.
Henry Kissinger	Milton Friedman	John Connally
Dan Rather	Walter Mondale	Betty Ford
	Carl Sagan	John Kenneth Galbraith
	Barbara Walters	Joe Granville
		Ann Landers
		Louis Rukeyser
		William Safire
		James Schlesinger
		Alvin Toffler
		George Will

Reprinted from *U.S. News & World Report,* August 23, 1982. Copyright 1982, U.S. News & World Report, Inc.

Because services are not standardized, a low price may not be a bargain.

Drawing by Ziegler; © 1978 The New Yorker Magazine, Inc.

Figure 11.1 A goods-services continuum

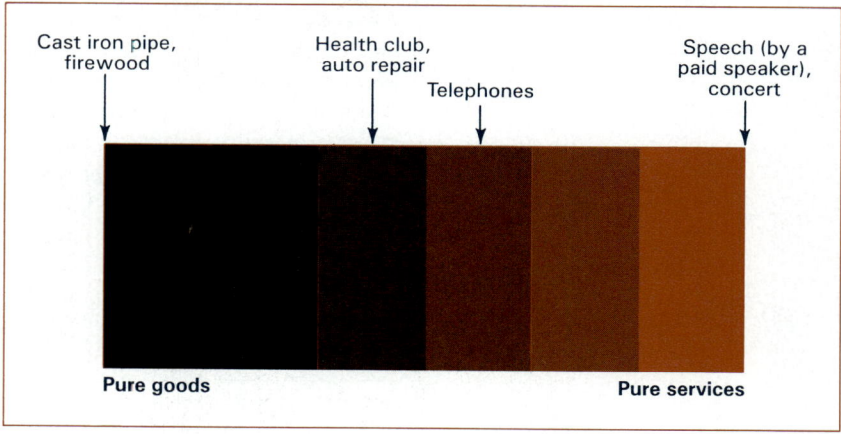

McDonald's: cooking by the same book

McDonald's may not be everyone's idea of the best place in town to dine, but at its level, McDonald's provides a quality of service that is the envy of the industry. Whether you go to the McDonald's on Queens Boulevard in New York or the one in Elk Grove Village near Chicago's O'Hare Airport, you know exactly what you will get. They all go by the same book.

Cooks must turn, never flip, hamburgers one, never two, at a time. If they haven't been purchased, Big Macs must be discarded ten minutes after being cooked and french fries in seven minutes. Cashiers must make eye contact with and smile at every customer.

Exact specifications alone aren't enough, however. The help, mostly eager youngsters, must also be motivated to perform a monotonous, low-paying job with sustained enthusiasm. Debbie Thompson, who started out at McDonald's as a cashier 8 years ago and now, at 24, manages the company-owned store at Elk Grove Village, sometimes livens up the lunchtime rush hour by offering $5 bonuses to the cashiers who take in the most dollars and handle the most customers. She gives a plaque to the crew member of the month. Ira Meyer, a onetime stockbroker who owns the Queens store, gives every employee a daily rating on a scale of one to five. Like Debbie Thompson, he sometimes puts the store on "60-second service": any customer not served within 60 seconds of placing an order gets free french fries. "You've got to create excitement and instant recognition," says Meyer.

Jeremy Main, "Toward Services Without a Snarl," FORTUNE, March 23, 1981, p. 66. Reprinted from FORTUNE Magazine by permission; © 1981 Time Inc. All rights reserved.

Customer involvement

Customers often play an important role in service businesses. A travel agent, for example, helps a customer plan a vacation trip. But the customer will suggest changes in itinerary or accommodations while the travel agent sets up the trip. Of course, buyers' wants and needs also affect the creation of some manufactured products, but the interaction of buyer and seller during both production and distribution is a common feature of service businesses.

Goods and services

The production of services and goods is often interrelated. For example, such services as planning, maintenance, delivery, collection, and bookkeeping are necessary to the success of manufacturing operations.

Sometimes it is difficult to distinguish goods from services. Such services as shoe repair and income-tax service are easy to distinguish. But services of this nature are just one small segment of the total industry.

Figure 11.2 Types of service businesses

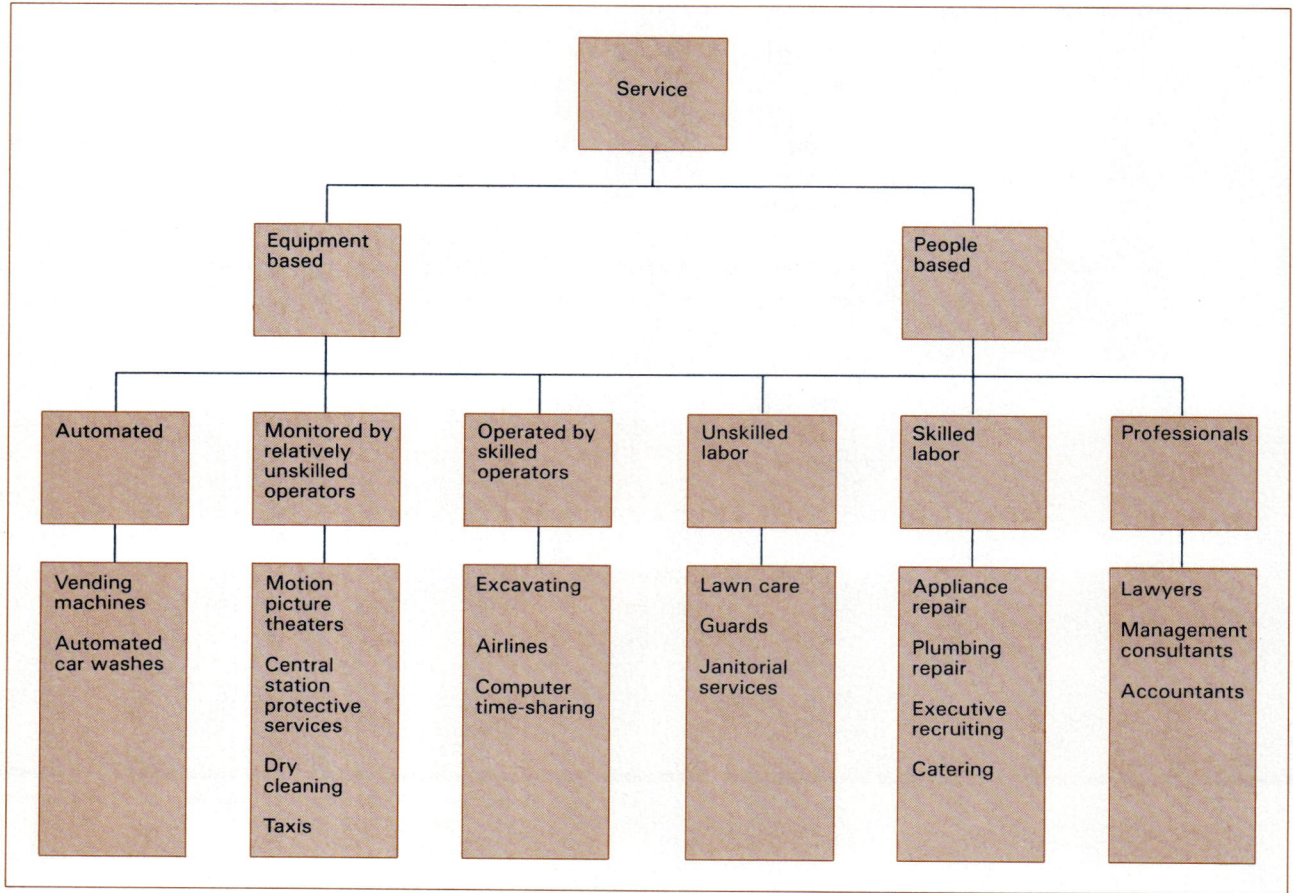

Dan R.E. Thomas, "Strategy Is Different in Service Businesses," *Harvard Business Review*, July–August 1978, p. 161. Copyright © 1978 by the President and Fellows of Harvard College, all rights reserved. Reprinted by permission of the *Harvard Business Review*.

Many businesses sell a combination of goods and services. A computer designer may sell goods like computer hardware and software and also provide a consulting service on the client's future electronic needs. An interior decorator may sell window coverings and furniture (goods) but also helps clients plan the furnishing of a room or an entire house (service).

Furthermore, the selling of some goods is closely related to providing good back-up services. For example, when selling a photocopy machine, a Xerox sales representative may emphasize the firm's maintenance and repair services.

Figure 11.2 provides a classification of services based on the following two factors: the degree of reliance on equipment in providing the service, and the degree of skill possessed by the people who provide the service.

Chapter 11 Service industries

Some goods are stocked by retailers as a service to customers.

"Where are the silicone chips?"

From the *Wall Street Journal*, Permission—Cartoon Features Syndicate.

The development of service industries

In the past, service industries were often considered unimportant and unproductive because no tangible products were visible. However, the importance of service industries has been steadily increasing since the 1930s.

Figure 11.3 shows how the working population changed between 1929 and 1979. In 1929, 45 percent of the working population was employed in the production of goods, while 55 percent was employed in the service sector. By 1979, the goods-producing sector employed only 34 percent of the working population, while the service sector

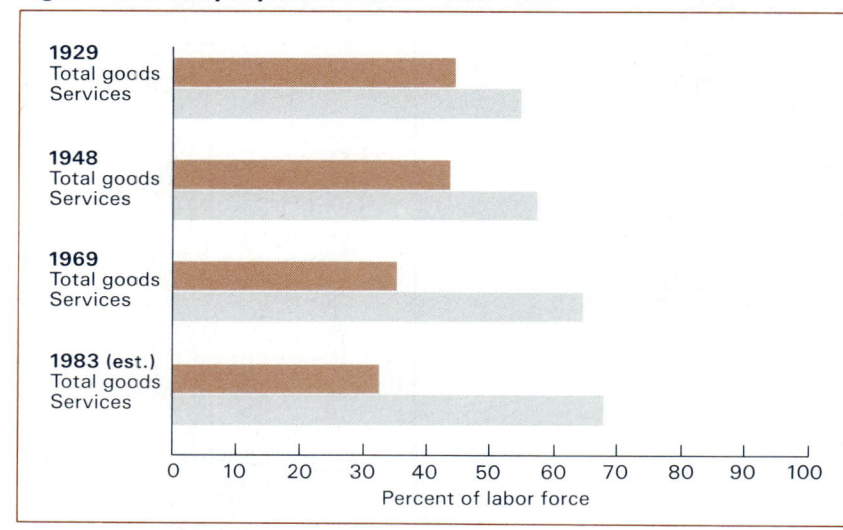

Figure 11.3 Employment shifts: 1929–1979

U.S. Bureau of Labor Statistics

House calls for sick chips

To distinguish itself in the increasingly competitive home computer market, Scientific Machines Corporation of Dallas has come up with a new idea—home repairs.

"The most frequent computer breakdown is a faulty chip," says H. Eugene Levine, SMC senior vice-president. "Our new suitcase-size tester [13 × 18 × 9 inches] can find the defective chip in a circuit board within a minute." Rival testers are too slow and too big for home repairs, he says. Neither operating the $19,000 tester nor replacing a defective chip requires a high-salary, trained engineer.

SMC has decided to go commercial with this idea. Levine hopes to build a national chain that corresponds to the rapid growth in the number of computer stores. SMC's first Test and Service Center opened in September 1981 in San Diego, and ten more opened by year-end.

Operating much like television repairers, SMC technicians drive to homes, identify the trouble, and replace chips, which generally cost under $20 each. Customers can bring in their computers and get same-day service. "Success at the retail level depends on good service," Levine says.

Howard Falk, "The Small Computer Stands Tall," *Nation's Business,* November 1981, p. 86. Reprinted by permission from *Nation's Business.* Copyright 1981 by *Nation's Business,* Chamber of Commerce of the United States.

Figure 11.4 What people spend for services

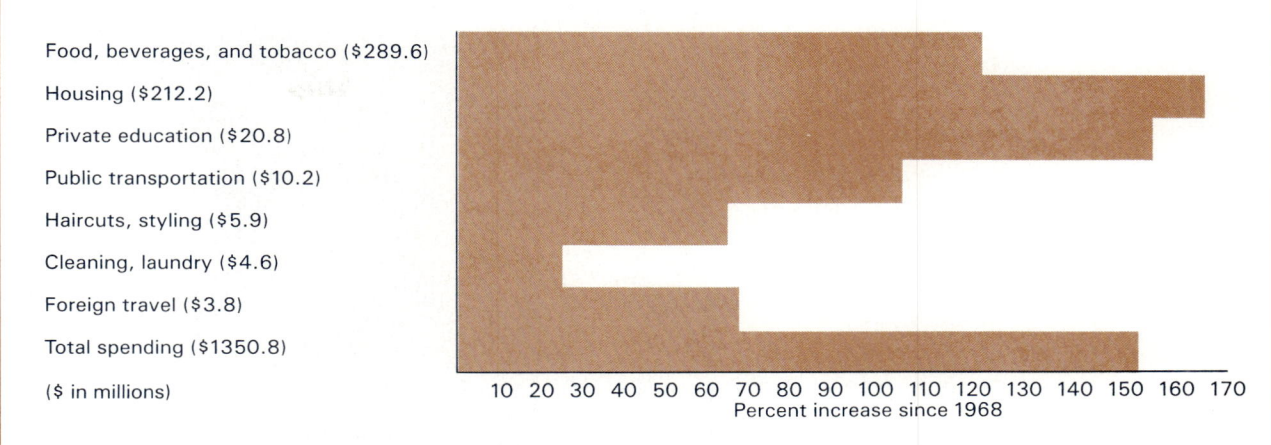

U.S. Bureau of Economic Analysis

employed 66 percent. Most of this shift occurred after the end of World War II.

Figure 11.4 shows how much money consumers spend on services and how rapidly their spending has increased.

Human capital

Service industries depend heavily on human capital. **Human capital is the skill and knowledge possessed by a population.** It is the personnel resources that can be combined with economic resources. Human capital enables a society to obtain and use other essential resources, such as physical capital, materials, and technology. Education enriches human capital. As a result, education has become a high priority for American society. About two-thirds of the growth in the U.S. economy since 1948 stems from the growth in the size and education of the work force.

Physical capital continues to be important to the economic growth of the United States. But human capital is now recognized as the dominant force. The expansion of knowledge, skills, and creativity in the work force produces economic resources that allow industry to grow. In the long run, this raises our standard of living.

The rising price of services

As our demand for services has grown, the costs of services have risen. Figure 11.5 shows how the average costs of services increased from 1970 to 1980.

Figure 11.5 Average increases in service costs, 1970–1980

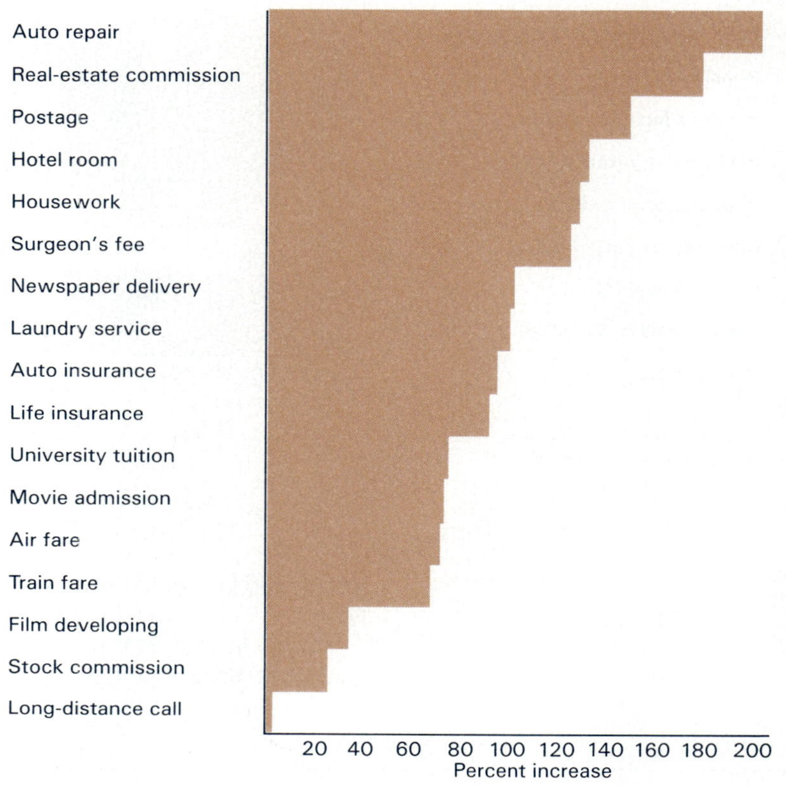

Auto repair	
Real-estate commission	
Postage	
Hotel room	
Housework	
Surgeon's fee	
Newspaper delivery	
Laundry service	
Auto insurance	
Life insurance	
University tuition	
Movie admission	
Air fare	
Train fare	
Film developing	
Stock commission	
Long-distance call	

Percent increase: 20 40 60 80 100 120 140 160 180 200

Adapted from "Services: Where Price Surge Really Hits Hard," *U.S. News & World Report,* November 24, 1980, p. 63. Copyright 1980, U.S. News & World Report, Inc.

Participation of women

From 1950 to 1980 the proportion of women in the labor force rose from about a third to slightly more than half. Three out of five additions to the work force were women. Most found their jobs in the expanding service sector.

Many women entered the work force because they wanted careers, not just jobs. They frequently worked for banks, real estate brokers, and other service businesses.

Exporting services

The export of services is the fastest growing segment of U.S. foreign trade. In 1979, exports of services such as insurance sales, engineering, communications systems, movies, banking, and accounting produced revenues of about $36 billion for U.S. corporations.

The world market for services grew at 15.7 percent a year during the 1970s while the world market for goods grew only 6.7 percent per year.

The stakes for the biggest service industries are huge. In 1979, foreign operations for CitiCorp, the second largest bank in the United States, brought in 65 percent of its total revenue. Foreign billings for the ten biggest U.S. advertising agencies in 1978 were 51.3 percent of their total billings.[1]

Law and accounting firms have expanded overseas by establishing branches, partnerships, and franchises. Legal services have recently become the largest export industry in New York City, outranking even the clothing industry.

Improving service productivity

In today's world, better service often seems to mean increased speed and efficiency with much less personal attention. Every consumer experiences service breakdowns.

Are increased services improving our lives or are the services we receive deteriorating? The question is difficult to answer because we tend to remember our frustrating experiences and forget the great majority of cases when services were rendered well. The U.S. Postal Service, for example, handles more than 100 billion pieces of mail annually. If only one-tenth of one percent of those pieces go astray, it still means that 100 million pieces of mail are delayed or destroyed.

Productivity is a serious problem for service industries. Productivity is expected to increase as advanced technology and improved management techniques are introduced. Many firms are hiring outside specialists to perform certain internal services more efficiently. For example, some firms hire outside companies to provide food services in their plant cafeterias or to process payrolls.

Some of the biggest gains in productivity in the service sector come from substituting capital for labor. The key to service productivity gains is the computer. With their enormous capacity to store and manipulate information, computers make it much easier to schedule and control both staff and equipment. They also provide easy access to information managers need to run their operations more efficiently.

For example, with computerization, modern hotels can use fewer employees to handle the same number of guests as in the past. Or, instead of reducing their staffs, hotels can offer their guests more and better services. Computers can take over many of the routine tasks of personnel management, reservations, checking in and out, billing, physical inventories, and day-to-day work assignments.

Quality control can reduce error rates in processing checks in banks or measuring medicine in hospitals. Like the average factory, an office spends perhaps 20 percent of its effort making and correcting errors. The modest cost of quality control is far less than the cost of mistakes.

---

[1]"The U.S. Lead in Service Exports Is Under Siege," *BusinessWeek,* September 15, 1980, pp. 70–73.

Packing in the popcorn eaters

It's the hottest summer in movie history, with fans paying an average of $3.5 million a day to view what well may turn out to be the biggest hit of all time, *E.T. The Extra-Terrestrial.*

Variety predicts that Americans will spend a record $3.2 billion going to the movies in 1982, 10 percent more than in 1981. One beneficiary of the boom is General Cinema Corporation of Chestnut Hill, Mass., the nation's largest theater chain, with nearly 1000 screens in 40 states.

General Cinema makes practically no money from ticket sales but plenty from dispensing popcorn, candy, and drinks. Explains Richard A. Smith, General Cinema's chief executive, "The theater is a money collector for the distributor. We couldn't live without the refreshments."

General Cinema lives well indeed. In the first six months of its 1982 fiscal year, earnings soared 49 percent to $21 million on revenue of $390 million. And the crowds lining up for *E.T., Rocky III,* and *Poltergeist* suggest the best is yet to be.

Smith scoffs at critics who view home video systems as a threat. "Consumers will continue to look forward to a night out and the experience of watching films on a large screen with a participating audience," he maintains.

Still, Smith has been diversifying General Cinema since he took over from his founder-father, who died in 1961. The company is the largest independent bottler in the United States, with Pepsi-Cola, Dr Pepper, and 7-Up in the corporate icebox. Four years ago the company concocted its own orange drink, Sunkist, now among the ten best-selling soft drinks.

"Packing in the Popcorn Eaters," FORTUNE, August 9, 1982, p. 7. Reprinted from FORTUNE Magazine by permission; © 1981 Time Inc. All rights reserved.

Regulation of service businesses

Services are more governed by regulation than most other business concerns. Many service industries are subject to special government regulations besides the usual taxes, antitrust legislation, and restrictions on promotion and price discrimination. A day-care center, for example, must comply with state licensing requirements. Restaurants must meet local health codes.

The U.S. government has established many federal agencies to regulate service industries at the national level. They include the Federal Communications Commission (radio, television, and interstate telephone), the Federal Power Commission (electric utilities), the Interstate Commerce Commission (interstate trucking), and the Securities and Exchange Commission (stock exchanges). State and local governments are responsible for regulating certain service industries, notably banking, insurance, and real estate. State and local governments also impose various limitations on services through certification, licensing, and taxes. Services affected by these kinds of controls include accountants, attorneys, elementary and high school teachers, funeral directors, physicians, some engineers, and other professionals.

11 Service industries

Summary

Service industries now employ two of every three people working in the United States. A *service* is a direct person-to-person activity that meets a human need. Service industries do not usually produce tangible products.

The federal government has identified four service sectors: (1) *distributive services,* (2) *producer services,* (3) *consumer services,* and (4) *nonprofit and government services.*

Services have four key features: (1) they are intangible; (2) they are perishable; (3) they are difficult to standardize; and (4) customers often take an active role in their development and distribution.

Goods and services are often interrelated, and it is sometimes difficult to distinguish between the two. Some firms provide a combination of goods and services to their customers. Examples include computer-design services and interior decorators.

Service industries have gained importance in the United States economy during the past 50 years. Consumers are demanding more services and the costs of services are rising. As a result, the service sector of the economy must be given as much attention as the manufacturing sector.

Service industries depend heavily on human capital. *Human capital* is the skill and knowledge possessed by a population. Education enriches human capital. As a result, American society places a high value on education. The expansion of human capital produces economic resources that allow industry to grow.

The export of services is becoming increasingly common and profitable. Among the services exported by U.S. firms are insurance, engineering, communications, movies, banking, accounting, and legal counseling.

Service productivity is increasing as advanced technology and improved management techniques are introduced. Computers are a key to gains in service productivity. Besides storing and manipulating information, computers provide easy access to information managers need to run their operations more efficiently.

Many service industries are highly regulated and are subject to government regulations at the federal, state, and local levels. Laws may require special fees or taxes, certification, and licensing.

Review questions

1. What is a service? How do services differ from goods?
2. List the four service sectors in our economy and give examples of each.
3. What are the four key features of services?
4. How is the production of goods and services often interrelated?
5. Briefly explain the nature and significance of employment shifts in the U.S. economy from the 1930s to the present.
6. What is human capital? How is education related to human resource development?
7. What services does the United States commonly export?
8. How can computers assist service businesses?
9. Describe how the following service businesses might be regulated:
    a. restaurants
    b. bus companies
    c. physicians
    d. accountants
    e. radio stations

Discussion questions

1. Evaluate this statement: "Because service businesses do not produce tangible products, they are less valuable than manufacturers of goods."
2. What are the pros and cons of standardizing a service business? (See "McDonald's: Cooking by the Same Book" in this chapter.)
3. Production of goods and services is often interrelated. Give three examples of combinations of goods and services that you have used recently.
4. How might quality control improve services provided by (a) restaurants, (b) hotels, and (c) banks?

Chapter 11 case

The disbelieving president

Key jobs in a company, especially those giving access to financial records, may offer tempting opportunities for personal gain.

"It's incredible, just absolutely incredible," mumbled J. Harrison Marshall, president of Fidelity National Bank, to the state examiner. "I just can't believe it happened—and here at Fidelity. You just don't know whom to trust anymore!"

The data processing department at Fidelity National Bank is responsible for processing checking accounts, savings accounts, and unpaid loans, and performing other daily transactions of the bank. There are about fifteen employees in the department, but only three of the employees have access to all the input and output data. The remaining employees have only limited access in order to ensure internal control over the data. The three employees who are allowed full access to data are the department's top management personnel. Paul Green is the operations manager of the department. He supervises the processing of the transactions. John Black is the manager of the entire department. His duties are the general supervision of the department. Alice White is in charge of the actual storage of the data used in the department.

To ensure security and control, it is the bank's policy to have the employees take their entire vacation over one uninterrupted period. The vacations are from two to four weeks in duration depending on length of employment and position in the department. This policy is rigidly adhered to for internal control purposes. While an employee is vacationing, another employee is assigned to take over his duties for the period. This period of new control permits the auditing of an employee's previous actions.

This policy is strictly followed except in the case of Paul Green. Green is known for his devotion and extreme loyalty to the bank. He is entitled to a month-long vacation, but, contrary to the bank's policy, he does not take all of his vacation at one time. Green's supervisor, John Black, feels that Green is much too important to the department's operation to allow him to be absent for longer than one week at a time.

The invaluable Mr. Green has been in his present position for 13 years. In fact, there is no one trained or equipped to handle his job. In many of the years, he has taken only one or two weeks' vacation, giving the other weeks to the job at the bank. His personnel file contains a letter from Black commending him on his sheer, selfless dedication to Fidelity Bank.

Just recently, Green was involved in an auto accident. It was a serious one which required his hospitalization for six weeks. During Green's absence, numerous fraudulent errors were found in both his checking account and mortgage loan account. It was found after extensive internal investigation that Green had been altering the input data to cover up his extremely overdrawn checking account and overdue mortgage loan. The checking account was overdrawn by $112,000 and the loan had been past-due for over a year. While he lay in traction, Green was immediately discharged and the bank brought suit against him to recover the funds.

I wonder what went wrong," mused the president. "You just can't trust anybody nowadays."

1. What did go wrong at Fidelity? Who or what is to blame for the loss?
2. What other actions or approaches might improve management control and prevent such incidents from occurring?

Bernard A. Dietzer and Karl A. Shilliff, *Incidents in Modern Business* (Columbus, Ohio: Charles E. Merrill, 1975), pp. 26–27.

4 Careers in manufacturing and service industries

Because of the wide variety of goods and services offered in our society, a wide choice of jobs is available in manufacturing and service industries.

White-collar workers (professional, managerial, clerical, and salesworkers) account for nearly one-third of the employment in manufacturing. Workers in many diverse manufacturing industries process foods and chemicals; print books and newspapers; spin fibers into thread and weave them into textiles; make clothing and shoes; and produce the thousands of other products needed for our personal and national needs.

Service industry workers also perform a wide variety of tasks ranging from providing automobile repair, food, and lodging to operating airlines, hospitals, and radio stations. Employment in service occupations is expected to grow faster than the average for all occupations through the 1980s. Some estimates of specific service industries are shown in the table.

Some manufacturing and service careers are discussed below.

Manufacturer's representatives

Manufacturer's representatives sell products to wholesalers and other customers on a commission basis. They may sell the products of one or several manufacturers. They demonstrate products and point out their special features, and they answer questions about price, credit terms, and durability.

Representatives who sell technical or scientific products must often complete specialized training programs given by the manufacturer. They may be employed by manufacturers of packaged foods, apparel, fabricated metal products, publications, and many other goods.

Manufacturer's representatives must have initiative, drive, and verbal, mathematical, and persuasive abilities. They must also relate well to people. Their college courses should include business, business math, English, and typing.

Projected growth areas for service jobs 1979 to 1990

	Jobs forecast in 1990	Percent increase from 1979
Water, sanitary services	163,000	123%
Automobile repair	1,137,000	100
Medical, dental offices	1,882,000	81
Hotels, lodging places	1,747,000	72
Nonprofit organizations	2,673,000	66
Hospitals	4,307,000	60
Credit, finance agencies	1,167,000	51
Advertising	219,000	45
Retail trade	21,482,000	43
Amusement, recreation services	1,010,000	42
Banking	2,054,000	36
Transportation services	252,000	31
Radio, TV broadcasting	252,000	27
Insurance	2,117,000	25
Real estate	1,358,000	19
Airlines	511,000	18
Motion pictures	239,000	14
Trucking	1,587,000	13
Wholesale trade	5,888,000	12
Communications, except radio and TV	1,221,000	8
Electric utilities	522,000	4

Source: "Service Industries: Growth Field of '80s," Reprinted from *U.S. News and World Report*, March 17, 1980, p. 81. Copyright 1980, U.S. News & World Report, Inc.

Careers in manufacturing and service industries

Hotel or motel managers

Hotel and motel managers ensure the efficient and profitable operation of their businesses. They establish standards for worker performance, service to patrons, room rates, advertising, credit, food selection, and the like. Managers plan dining room, bar, and banquet operations. They hire staff and assign duties and responsibilities to department heads. Managers also develop budgets and distribute funds.

Hotel and motel managers need organizational, mathematical, and verbal skills. They must be flexible and relate well to people. Their college courses should include business, English, public speaking, social studies, and psychology. A bachelor's degree in hotel administration is the best preparation.

Business managers (amusement and recreation)

Business managers oversee the financial affairs of entertainers and athletes and negotiate with agents and representatives for contracts and appearances. They promote their clients' interests and advise them on income, investments, taxes, laws, and other financial matters. Managers act as middlemen between their clients and people who have contracted for their clients' services. They periodically issue statements to their clients that summarize their investments, property, and financial status.

This job requires the ability to work closely with others under considerable pressure and stress. Helpful college subjects would include business, English, math, and social studies. Some jobs may require formal training or managerial experience, while others may require a bachelor's degree.

Additional information about some of these careers can be obtained from:

Sales & Marketing Executives International
Career Education Division
380 Lexington Avenue
New York, NY 10017

American Hotel & Motel Association
888 Seventh Avenue
New York, NY 10019

Marketing

5

Business in perspective

Inventing Pampers

Is there a real consumer need for an alternate form of diaper? Does Proctor & Gamble have the technological ability to develop the product? Is the potential market for such a product large enough to turn a profit?

These questions were posed during a meeting at Proctor & Gamble, the giant manufacturer of consumer products. A Proctor & Gamble engineer brought up the subject after babysitting with his grandchild for the first time. The discussion led to one of the greatest success stories in modern marketing.

Proctor & Gamble believed that the market for a good disposable diaper was huge. There were 15 billion diaper changes a year, it estimated. Its research showed that mothers of babies would be interested in buying a good disposable diaper. And the company could get the technology to produce the product at a profitable level.

Market research showed that cloth diapers bunched up, did not keep babies dry enough, and required plastic pants that could irritate a baby's skin. So P&G engineers were told to design a product that would be free of such problems.

When Proctor & Gamble had developed what they believed to be a good alternative diaper, they tested the product in Dallas, Texas. They gave a small number of free diapers to mothers for trial use. The tests found that the diaper was comfortable and absorbent, but it still required the use of plastic pants.

After about six months of intensive work, an entirely new design was created. It did not require plastic pants but still had the positive features of the first design. Preliminary tests showed very positive results.

Proctor & Gamble was now ready to put the diaper into a test market. They would select several cities and put the product on sale under actual market conditions.

While the product was being developed for test marketing, other experts worked on packaging, promoting, and naming it. The most difficult task was determining the price.

At last Pampers passed all tests. The entire process, from a grandfather's suggestion to the launching of the product across the United States, took 20 years.

Adapted from "P&G Uses Story to Teach the Consumer About Marketing," *Advertising Age*, April 4, 1977. Reprinted with permission from the April 4, 1977, issue of *Advertising Age*. Copyright 1977 by Crain Communications, Inc.

Chapter 12 Marketing functions

Key terms

marketing
marketing concept
utility
form utility
place utility
time utility
possession utility
social utility
market
consumer goods
convenience goods
shopping goods
specialty goods
industrial goods
market segment
target market
marketing mix
product
marketing research

Chapter objectives

In Chapter 12, you will learn:

What marketing is

How the marketing concept has evolved

The five forms of utility

The difference between consumer goods and industrial goods

How markets are segmented and targeted

The elements of the marketing mix and how they interact

What marketing research is and how it can help marketers

Overview

Marketing is a system of activities that businesses use to plan, price, promote, and distribute goods and services that consumers will want and need.

Marketing is a two-phase process. First, a company gathers and evaluates information about consumers' needs and wants. Then it translates the information into the goods and services it offers in the marketplace. Private companies, nonprofit organizations, and government institutions all use marketing techniques.

This chapter introduces the marketing concept and explains why it is important to business and society.

Evolution of the marketing concept

During the eighteenth and nineteenth centuries, most companies were production oriented. They only worried about obtaining raw materials, producing their products, and transporting finished goods to customers. There were few goods and little competition for consumer dollars. Selling was not a very important activity.

From the mid-nineteenth century until World War II, improved manufacturing processes made more and more products available to consumers. The supply of goods began to catch up with demand. As competition grew, companies began to focus on selling rather than production.

After World War II, another change took shape as many companies moved from simple selling to a **marketing concept—a total company-wide effort to find out what customers needed or wanted and to develop products that would fill those desires.** They used marketing research and feedback from customers to decide product or service design, price, and distribution. Figure 12.1 illustrates the shift from production to marketing orientation.

An example: raising more dough from wheat

The wheat-processing industry provides a good example of how companies adopted the marketing concept. Wheat processors had always concentrated simply on grinding wheat into flour and delivering it to market by whatever transportation was available. Primitive grinding processes limited their output and consumers would buy all the flour they could produce.

When transportation and manufacturing capacities improved at the end of the nineteenth century, the processors changed their approach. They tried to produce as much flour as possible and sent out salespeople to find customers for their expanding output.

After 1945, customers had more money to spend and a large choice of competing products. A wheat processor could no longer survive by making flour. Research into consumers' needs became necessary. The wheat processors needed to know the following:

Figure 12.1 Changing patterns of business orientation, 1700 to present

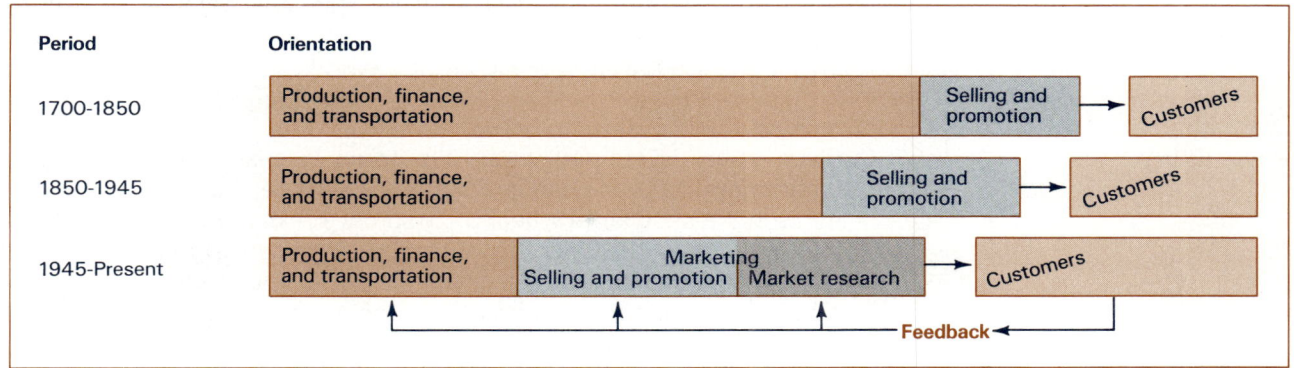

The marketing concept has gradually grown in importance. In the eighteenth century, businesses concentrated on producing goods. Since the end of World War II, production has been incorporated into the concept of what goods and services customers need or want.

What products made from wheat or flour did consumers want?

Which new products offered the most profitable opportunities?

Where were the markets for these new products?

How big were the markets?

Who bought the new products and why?

These questions reflect the marketing concept. A company that asks such questions can often learn much about itself and its present and potential customers. Companies that adopt the marketing concept try to find out what consumers want and need. They believe that the production of goods and services that satisfy consumer wants and needs will lead to long-term profits.

Creating utility through marketing

More than half the cost of consumer goods can be traced to marketing activities. The goal of marketing often seems to be to encourage consumers to buy goods and services. What are the economic and social costs and benefits of marketing?

Marketing creates utility

If we consider only the monetary cost of a product or service, we can easily overlook the value that marketing activities have added. In economic terms, something has value only when it satisfies a person's need or want—that is, when it has utility. **Utility is the satisfaction consumers gain from having goods and services.** There are five kinds of utility: form, place, time, possession, and social.

Form utility

Form utility is created when a product is extracted, grown, or manufactured. For example, coal is of little value until it is taken out of the earth. Flour has form utility to a baker, but most people find its value only in a finished loaf of bread or a cake.

Place utility

Place utility is created when a product is easily available where consumers want or need it. Thus, a pair of shoes has place utility only if it is in the shoe store where a consumer seeks it. A loaf of bread has little value to a consumer until it reaches a grocery store. A movie has place utility for some people when it is shown at a nearby theater. For others, it has place utility only when shown on television for viewing at home.

Time utility

Time utility is created if a product is available when consumers want or need it. If it is cold outside and a family needs heating oil, a promise to deliver oil the following week has little value. People are often willing to pay more for a good or service that is available immediately. In such cases, saving time adds value to the product.

Possession utility

Possession utility is created by transferring the ownership of a product from the seller to the buyer. Form, time, and place utilities are of little use if the seller cannot or will not allow potential consumers to take possession of a product.

Social utility

Social utility is the importance that society attaches to a good or service. It applies to the benefit society gains from the sale of a good or service. Does the product improve the quality of life? Will it lead to greater employment? Or is it a waste of resources?

Consumerism and social utility

Social utility became more important to marketers as the consumer movement gained strength in the 1970s. Companies responded to the rising interest in consumerism by establishing consumer-affairs departments.

Whirlpool, for example, set up a nationwide toll-free telephone complaint line. Shell Oil Company created a series of booklets about safe driving and car care. A 300-person consumer-affairs department at Polaroid Corporation reviewed company advertisements for accuracy and spot-checked Polaroid repair centers for quality.

Executives at these and other firms recognized that social utility had a direct and strong impact on profits. They felt a responsibility to treat customers fairly and provide safe, useful products.

Figure 12.2 Utility created when marketing a loaf of bread

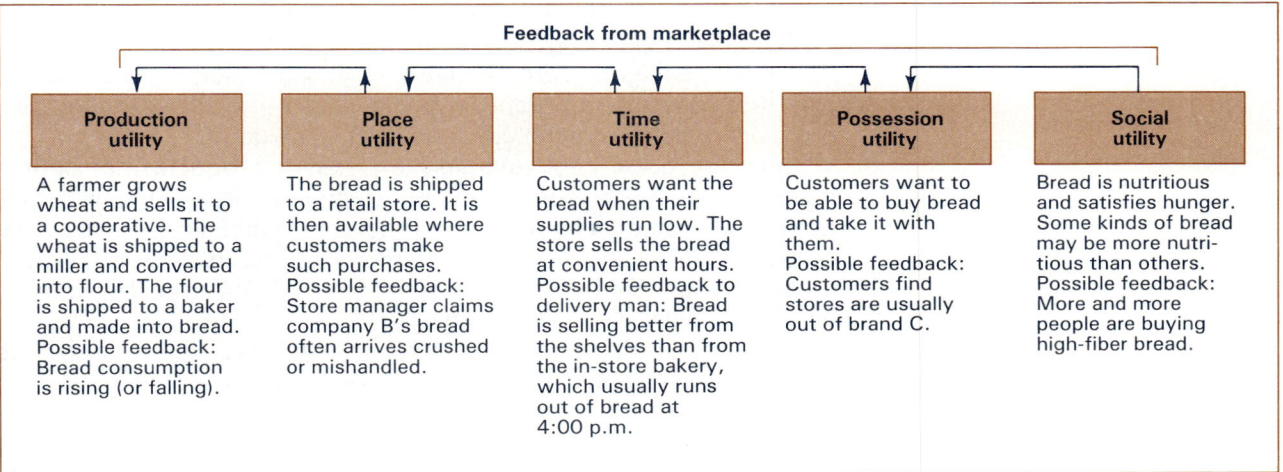

The public's concept of social utility may explain why certain products fail. The consumer movement is especially concerned about social utility. Whether such products as cigarettes and liquor should be advertised and sold is a question of social utility. Some people ask how these products' social benefits compare to their social costs.

Figure 12.2 illustrates how the five kinds of utility are created when a loaf of bread is marketed.

The relationship of markets and products

Markets have both buyers and sellers. **To a seller, however, a market is any group of potential buyers with the authority and the ability to make purchases.** Sometimes it is easy to define a market. The market for disposable diapers, for example, is families with infants and toddlers. The market for large printing presses is newspapers and commercial printers.

Many markets, however, are not so simple to pinpoint and understand. What is the market for sports cars? What is the market for fast food? For designer clothes? For ''introduction-to-business'' textbooks? For tours of Europe? The potential buyers of these and many other such products and services possess many different characteristics. As a result, professional marketers have developed techniques to define and identify potential customers.

Consumer goods versus industrial goods

Products and services can be classified as consumer goods or industrial goods, depending upon their probable users. Different marketing efforts are required to reach each group.

Kinds of consumer goods

Consumer goods are products and services purchased by individual consumers for their own use. Consumer goods may be classified as convenience goods, shopping goods, or specialty goods.

Convenience goods are relatively low-cost, widely available products that consumers purchase quickly and often. Newspapers, gasoline, and most food products are convenience goods.

Shopping goods are relatively expensive products that people purchase only after comparing price, quality, style, and other important characteristics. Before buying stereo components or a television set, for example, most consumers visit several stores, look at several brands, and evaluate competing models. Automobiles, clothing, and furniture are also shopping goods.

Speciality goods are products that consumers perceive as unique and will make a special effort to seek out. These products often have brand names. Limited production automobiles, designer clothing, and French perfume are all specialty goods. Someone who wants a certain brand of running shoes may be willing to spend considerable effort to find a store that carries them.

It is easy to identify the category of most goods. But some expectations occur due to differences in consumers' values. For example, although cigarettes are usually classified as convenience goods, the smoker of a rare imported brand would view that brand as a specialty good.

Industrial goods

Industrial goods are products and services purchased by businesses for use in producing other goods and services. They include such things as parts, raw materials, machinery, and office equipment. Computers, typewriters, iron ore, printing presses, rubber gaskets, and transistors, consequently, can all be classified as industrial goods.

Industrial goods tend to have much smaller and more easily identified markets than consumer goods. For example, there is a huge market for hair shampoo. But the number of potential buyers of bottling machines is quite limited.

Some goods may be sold to both consumer and industrial markets. Portable typewriters, for example, are sold as consumer items, while more expensive office typewriters are sold through industrial goods channels.

Industrial customers are easier to reach, but because of their limited number, they must be catered to. The purchasers of industrial products are usually specialists who understand the technicalities of the products they buy. As a result, buyers and sellers often exchange much technical information.

Industrial sales often involve huge amounts of money. A new computer may cost $1 million, so a company will think very seriously before buying one. Computer manufacturers' sales representatives may spend as much as a year trying to persuade the company to purchase a particular brand.

Industrial sales tend to be much more sensitive to economic climate and general business conditions than are consumer products. At the first sign of a downturn in the economy, many businesses put off major purchases, and industrial goods sales drop. At the beginning of a recovery, on the other hand, the opposite is true. Businesses rush to prepare for the expected sales boom.

Defining a target market

To market a product successfully, a company must know a great deal about its potential buyers. Such knowledge shapes the nature of the product and how it will be presented.

No product appeals to everyone. And no marketing plan can appeal to all potential buyers. In devising a marketing plan, a company must decide how its resources can best be spent. It must focus on reaching the consumers who offer the best opportunity for profit.

Market segments

Consumer markets and industrial markets are two broad categories of customers. To increase the effectiveness of marketing efforts, such broad categories usually must be broken down into smaller, more specialized groups. **A market segment is a subgroup of individuals with distinct characteristics within a total market.**

Bases of market segmentation Consumer markets are often segmented on the basis of demographic variables—age, sex, religion, race, occupation, income, family size, education, and similar basic information. These variables are good indicators of consumer wants and product usage. And they are quite easy to measure.

Markets may also be segmented by geography, buying behavior, lifestyle (called psychographic segmentation), and many other variables, depending on the product.

The importance of each variable differs according to the situation. But planners must examine the impact of each on the total marketing strategy.

Target market

All market segments are not equally attractive to all companies. A company must decide which market segments it can serve best. The decision should be based on the segments' preferences, patterns of competition, and the company's strengths and weaknesses.

The market segments a company chooses to serve become its target market. **A target market is the group of consumers at which a company aims its marketing efforts.** A company tailors its products and appeals to the wants and needs of its target market.

The members of a good target market have the following characteristics
1. They have similar needs and characteristics.
2. They are similarly motivated.
3. They have the money to buy the product.
4. They are numerous enough to justify the marketing effort.

The marketing mix

The marketing mix is the combination of product, price, promotion, and distribution strategies a company uses to reach a specific target market. Each element of the marketing mix can be considered separately. But for a marketing effort to be successful, product, price, promotion, and distribution must be coordinated into a logical system.

How the marketing mix works: the $190 pen versus the 29¢ pen

Marketing managers have many choices for each element of the marketing mix. For example, Cartier, the prestigious jeweler, has sold elegant gold ballpoint pens for $190. In complete contrast, Bic sold its plastic pens for $.29.

Product and price strategies were important. Bic could not expect to sell plastic pens for $190. On the other hand, Cartier had to offer a pen whose design and price would be consistent with the image of its other high-status products. Bic hoped to sell many of its low-priced pens to many different people. Cartier, on the other hand, designed its pen to appeal to an elite few.

The distribution of the two pens was also totally different. Cartier treated its pens as specialty goods and sold them only at the most exclusive stores. Bic pens, however, are seen as convenience goods and are widely available at dimestores, drugstores, and other mass-market retail outlets.

In addition the two companies' promotional strategies differed. Cartier chose a target market of wealthy individuals who valued style and image. The Cartier pens had snob appeal. They were more than a simple writing instrument. Cartier's advertising was low-key and tasteful. Ads for the pen would appear in such "classy" magazines as the *New York Times Sunday Magazine*.

Bic's basic pen called for a totally different approach. The company focused on mass-circulation publications. It also had advertisements and brochures aimed at businesses and institutions that might order hundreds of pens as office supplies.

Bic sold a basic pen—a plain piece of steak. Cartier marketed an image—the sizzle. The two companies combined the elements of the marketing mix in completely different ways. Between these two extremes are numerous other strategies designed to reach other target markets. The elements of the marketing mix are discussed in greater detail in Chapters 13, 14, and 15.

Marketing research

Marketing research is the systematic gathering and analysis of information about marketing problems. It helps management to decide what products or services to offer, what market segments to target, what prices to ask, what advertising message to stress, and what channels of distribution to use. Through marketing research, management can assess the size of a market it wishes to enter and estimate its chance of success. A good marketing research program can provide much useful information to marketing managers.

Questions for marketing researchers

Before a new product or service is introduced, management wants to know as much as possible about its potential market. New products are expensive to develop, so management wants to be sure that each product will be profitable.

For example, the decision to publish this textbook was based on the answers to many questions. How large was the potential market for an introductory business text? What similar books were already available? Was there a need in the marketplace that other textbooks did not fill? Could the book be produced cheaply enough to price it competitively with similar products? Could the publisher expect to sell enough copies of the book to justify investing in its development? How could the book be promoted to attract the attention of teachers who would use it in their classes?

If these questions had not been answered to the publisher's satisfaction, this book would not have been published. Nonetheless, many well-researched and expensive product failures are shown in Figure 12.3.

Figure 12.3 Notable product failures and estimated losses

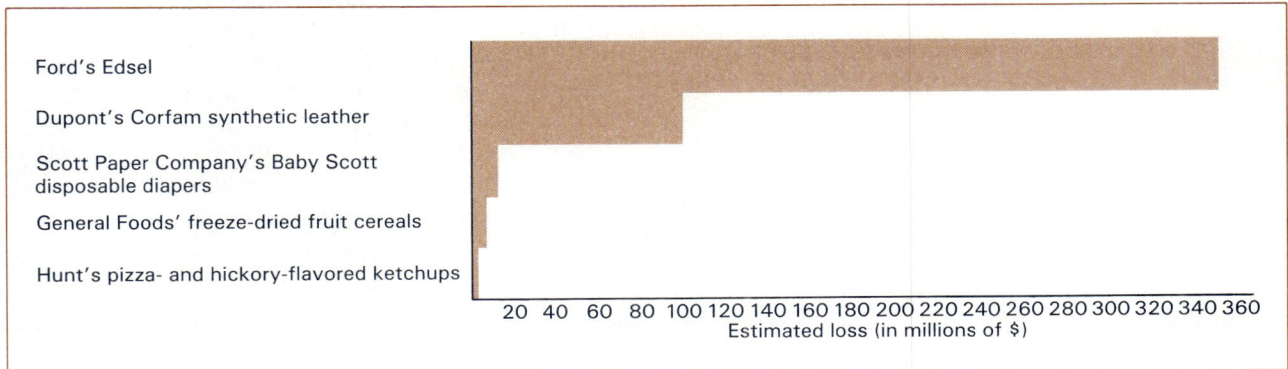

David W. Cravens et al, *Marketing Decision Making: Concepts and Strategy* (Homewood, Ill.: Richard D. Irwin, 1976), p. 459.

Pudding Pops versus ice cream

Jell-O brand gelatin and pudding have been highly successful products for the General Foods Company. However, due to changes in people's eating patterns and the maturity of the pudding market, General Foods decided to introduce a new frozen pudding product, Pudding Pops.

Research indicates that consumers now prefer afternoon dessert snacks that require no preparation, such as ice cream and prepackaged cakes. So General Foods developed frozen pudding on a stick with the hope of generating new pudding sales and directly challenging the ice cream market.

The introduction of such a new product involves high risks. General Foods takes more new-product gambles than most companies because so many of its products are in mature food categories (such as gelatin and coffee). The company outdistances its competitors on research and development expenditures, spending $96 million in 1981.

Because the content of Pudding Pops is so similar to pudding, the product's development was not a major project. The biggest financial investment went into marketing. During pre-test marketing, the company distributed pictures and descriptions of the product. The consumer response was enthusiastic, so General Foods decided to send out a limited number of samples door-to-door.

The company soon started test marketing Pudding Pops, but it was still hesitant. According to one General Foods executive, "However sophisticated the research, it's hard to rely on the information you get from consumers. People sometimes say things because they want to please you."

Nonetheless, the product was introduced into stores in four U.S. cities, and sales were extremely good. Soon General Foods' competitors began to imitate Pudding Pops. For instance, Popsicle Industries launched Good'n Puddin' nationwide.

Both the cost of test marketing and the pressure of potential rival products pushed General Foods to market Pudding Pops nationwide. The investment in a product like Pudding Pops runs into the tens of millions of dollars by the time it goes national, so it's important that Pudding Pops develop enduring consumer appeal. Because it takes from five to seven years to earn back the initial investment in a major new product, consumer product companies worry that a product may turn out to be a fad. In that case, they never earn their money back.

Pudding Pops, however, has been an outstanding success. Helped by a promotion budget of $25 million, Pudding Pops had sales of $65 million in its first eight months in national distribution in 1983. It is well on its way to being one of the most successful new food products in the past 15 years.

Steps for effective marketing research

To yield reliable results, marketing research must be carefully controlled. Effective marketing research consists of five steps: (1) problem definition, (2) research design, (3) data collection, (4) data analysis, and (5) final report preparation.

Problem definition

The first step in marketing research is to pinpoint and define the real problem. The more clearly a problem is defined, the more likely it is that useful information can be found.

For example, a department store manager may have noticed that sales are decreasing. He believes he could solve the problem if he knew more about consumers. So he asks a marketing research consultant to study consumer attitudes toward the store.

Such an assignment would be much too general. Before she can start her work, the researcher needs to know if the manager wants to attract new customers or get present customers to buy more. Does the manager want to know why some potential customers don't shop at the store at all? Should the study focus on how consumers view the store as compared to other department stores in the area? Or should it include attitudes toward discount stores, mail-order shopping, specialty stores, and other kinds of competitors? A more specific description of the problem and what the manager wants to know will help the researcher to design a study that will yield more useful information.

Research design

A research design is a plan that specifies how data will be collected and analyzed. The nature of the problem will suggest the most appropriate research design. An especially important decision is what data-collection methods to use. Researchers may decide to use data that have already been gathered by trade associations, marketing research firms, publishers of trade magazines and directories, or other reliable sources. Marketing researchers can save time and money by using such information. But they must carefully evaluate its probable accuracy because they have no way of knowing how it was collected.

In many cases, researchers need data that do not exist. In such cases, they must gather original information from customers, salespersons, competitors, and other knowledgeable individuals. Original data are gathered in three ways.

1. Observation. Researchers can simply watch how people behave. To determine the best location for a new store, a pharmacy chain could have researchers count the number of passersby at several possible sites. To learn if the purchase of a laundry detergent depends heavily on price, observers can go to a supermarket and watch as shoppers make their choices. How many just reach for their usual brands? How many look at the prices of one or more brands? How many choose without regard to brand?

2. Survey. Information can be gathered through interviews and questionnaires. An extremely wide variety of information can be collected

Misuse of statistical date is a hazard of marketing research.

"This survey indicates you can fool seventeen percent of the people a hundred percent of the time, thirty-four percent of the people fifty-one percent of the time, and a hundred percent of the people twelve percent of the time."

Drawing by Stevenson; © 1977 The New Yorker Magazine, Inc.

this way. Questions can explore attitudes, behavior, opinions, demographic characteristics, and many other topics. Surveys may be taken in person, by mail, or over the telephone. Two-way cable television is providing a hybrid system that combines some elements of personal and telephone surveying.

3. Experimentation. Certain kinds of information are best obtained under scientifically controlled circumstances. To determine which recipe of a new chocolate pudding to market, researchers might ask a selected group of people to taste several alternatives and indicate their preferences. By varying the recipe in specific ways and keeping all other circumstances constant, the researcher can determine which pudding formula appeals to different people's tastes.

A research design specifies how people will be chosen to participate in the research, how data will be recorded, how data will be analyzed, how long the study will take, and how much it will cost. A good research design tries to anticipate every detail of the research study and prescribe every action that will be taken. Such careful planning is necessary to ensure that the results will be accurate and logical.

Inconclusive results from marketing research are a major complaint.

"Well, among the names we researched, that was the most favored choice."

Reprinted with permission from the June 1978 issue of *Advertising Age,* copyright © 1978 by Crain Communications, Inc.

Data collection

Once the research design is completed, data collection can begin. Data collection can be fairly simple if published sources are used. In such cases, information can be gathered through visits to libraries and bookstores and by ordering reports.

When original information is needed, data collection can be expensive and time consuming. Errors may occur if some of the selected participants refuse to cooperate, answer dishonestly, or are unavailable. Interviewers may also cause problems if they do not follow instructions, ask leading questions, or falsify information.

Data analysis

Data are disjointed facts. Knowledge is the insight gained from data. Market research often results in a mass of responses, numbers, and observations. But these data mean nothing until they are analyzed into meaningful categories. This often requires sophisticated statistical techniques.

Then someone must interpret the statistics. Failure to notice significant trends or perform the right calculations can undo all previous work.

Final report preparation

Management is not usually interested in all the details of marketing research. They do not have time to worry about all the data that were collected or the methods that were used. Management is mainly interested in results.

Thus, a final report should clearly state the marketing problem and summarize the major findings of the research. The research design may be briefly stated. But all supporting technical data should be presented in an appendix.

Marketing researchers often include a single cover page with an executive summary of their reports. Because they want management to pay attention to their findings, they try to write the reports in simple, easy-to-understand language.

12 Marketing functions

Summary

Marketing is a system of activities that businesses use to plan, price, promote, and distribute goods and services that consumers will want and need. Companies once focused only on producing products. As the marketplace became more competitive, they switched their emphasis to selling. Now companies try to market what customers want. This new approach is called the *marketing concept.* Instead of producing goods and then trying to find buyers, companies try to produce goods that customers want and need.

Marketing creates *utility*—the satisfaction consumers gain from having goods and services. There are five kinds of utility: *form, place, time, possession,* and *social utility.* Marketing activities can create jobs and contribute to the quality of life.

A *market* is all people who are logical, potential buyers of a good or service. The nature of a marketing effort depends on whether the product is a *consumer good*—those purchased for individual use—or an *industrial good*—those purchased by businesses to produce other goods. Consumer goods can be further identified as *convenience, shopping,* or *specialty* goods.

No product can appeal to everyone. So a company must focus its marketing effort on the consumers who offer the best opportunity for profit. To determine who these consumers are, the marketer first divides the total market into *market segments*—groups of purchasers with similar needs and characteristics. Based on the segments' preferences, competition in the marketplace, and its own strengths and weaknesses, the company decides which market segments it can serve best. These segments become its *target market*—the group at which the marketer aims its marketing efforts.

The *marketing mix* is the combination of product, price, promotion, and distribution strategies a company uses to reaach a specific target market. Each element of the marketing mix can be considered separately. But for a marketing effort to be successful, product, price, promotion, and distribution must be coordinated into a logical system.

Marketing research is the systematic gathering and analysis of information about marketing problems. It helps management to decide what products or services to offer, what market segments to target, what prices to ask, and what channels of distribution to use.

A marketing research project consists of five steps: (1) problem definition, (2) research design, (3) data collection, (4) data analysis, and (5) final report preparation. To yield reliable information, every step of the research process must be carefully planned and controlled.

Review questions

1. What are the two phases of the marketing process?
2. Why has marketing become increasingly important to American business since 1946?
3. Name and briefly define the five forms of utility.
4. How do consumer goods differ from industrial goods? How do these differences affect marketers?
5. What are the three categories of consumer goods?
6. What bases might be used to segment a market?
7. What is the difference between a market segment and a target market?
8. Why is it important for a company to target its markets? What factors affect the choice of target markets?
9. What is the marketing mix?
10. How can marketing research be used?
11. What are the five steps of marketing research?

Discussion questions

1. Assume you're a manufacturer of computer games. How would you relate the five forms of utility to your product?
2. Compare and contrast the characteristics and needs of the buyers of industrial goods and consumer goods.
3. Assume you are ready to launch a new portable car that can be folded up and carried like a briefcase. How would you define the market for this product? How would you segment the market? Which segments would you target?

Chapter 12 case

Bud goes for the Lite drinker

A company may be the overall leader in its market but be weak in one or two segments of the market. This case looks at one firm's response and asks you to analyze the risks involved.

Anheuser-Busch Companies is the leading beer brewer in the United States, based on sales volume. In 1981, Anheuser-Busch's brands accounted for 30 percent of all beer sold. Its best-known brand is Budweiser, aimed at the popular-priced segment of the market. Michelob, its super-premium brand, accounts for 80 percent of all the higher-priced beer sold.

Its closest competitor is Miller Brewing Company. Miller is a subsidiary of Philip Morris, Inc. Its Miller and Lite brands account for 22 percent of the beer market. The third largest brewer, Joseph Schlitz Brewing Company, trails way behind the top two, with only 8 percent of U.S. beer sales.

Between 1976 and 1981, Anheuser-Busch increased its market share from 18 percent. But it was weakest where Miller was strongest—in the battle for drinkers of lower-calorie beers. Moreover, it was this segment of the market that was growing the fastest.

Miller Lite had 60 percent of the light beer market in 1981. In fact, this accounted for 8 percent of all beer sold. Anheuser-Busch had tried to sell light beers under the brand names of Natural Light and Michelob Light. But neither was very successful in cutting into Miller's share.

In an attempt to make some headway in the market, Anheuser-Busch adopted a new strategy; they decided to introduce a light beer with the Budweiser name. The test markets were tried out in 1981 and first results seemed positive.

Analyze this situation, addressing these questions in particular:
1. What marketing risks did Anheuser-Busch face in adopting this new strategy?
2. How could they measure the success of this strategy?
3. What would you name the new beer?

Logo courtesy of Needham, Harper, & Steers, Adv., Inc.

Business in perspective

Product proliferation

A relatively recent marketing strategy that major consumer goods producers have adopted is product proliferation. A company greatly increases its number of products and offers consumers a huge range of choices. For example, at one point, Campbell Soup Company offered 12 varieties of chicken soup alone. The manufacturer thus gains more shelf space in the stores at the expense of would-be competitors.

On the surface, it would seem that consumers benefit from a greater number of choices. But some critics say that this is not necessarily the case.

First, many producers vary their products so slightly that the differences are barely noticeable. Second, consumers must pay higher prices to cover the cost of developing, promoting, and distributing the many new products. Third, many of the products fail.

Brand proliferation also has serious effects on retailers. Supermarkets that used to carry 2500 different products in 1950 now carry nearly 10,000. Even so, a supermarket can stock only 10 percent of the new products that appear. By one count, 53,000 new or modified products and sizes were introduced between 1971 and 1979. Consumers expect to find a variety of choices, so supermarkets must stock more products or lose customers.

Product proliferation will probably be an important marketing strategy for years to come. Companies that have not diversified their product lines have suffered enormous losses. Liggett & Myers Tobacco Company, which had 30 percent of the cigarette market in 1950, held only 3 percent of the market by 1979. It had been slow in introducing new brands over the years.

In the absence of a "nonproliferation treaty," which many marketers might welcome, no company appears willing to be the first to cut back on new-product development.

Chapter 13   Product and pricing decisions

Key terms

product
product mix
product life cycle
brand
trademark
private brand
packaging
pricing
penetration pricing
market skimming
pricing with the market
markup
breakeven
price lining
psychological pricing
discount
nonprice competition

Chapter objectives

In Chapter 13, you will learn:

Why there is more to a product than meets the eye

The four stages in a product's life cycle

Why manufacturers use brand names

The factors that affect a firm's pricing decisions

How to calculate markup and breakeven

How marketers use prices to shape customers' perceptions and encourage buying

Some methods of nonprice competition

Overview

The long-term success of any marketing effort depends on a strong product. Good pricing, promotion, and distribution strategies cannot save a poorly conceived product from failing in the marketplace. No amount of advertising was able to sell gas-guzzling American automobiles in the late 1970s. And the distribution of a record album to all the best record stores will not ensure its sale if its music is not appealing.

This chapter discusses what makes a good product. It examines how marketers decide which products to introduce and keep in the marketplace. And it explains how the price of a product is determined.

The product

There is often more to a product than meets the eye. Actually, *a product is a bundle of attributes that consumers want or need.* Mercedes-Benz does not sell just a car. It sells image, status, quality, dependability, and good taste as well as transportation. Manufacturers of disposable diapers offer convenience to parents as well as the diapers themselves. A retailer may offer services such as gift wrapping and delivery, convenience in its large selection, and economy in its prices besides offering goods for sale. Some toothpastes imply that their use brings social and health benefits in addition to clean teeth.

Before a company decides to introduce a new product or boost the sales of an existing one, it must know exactly what the product is—and what they want it to be. Defining the product is the first step in product planning.

Most firms sell a number of products. **The product mix is all the similar products a company offers for sale.** By carrying many different products in a variety of sizes, colors, and models, a company can appeal to more than one target market.

For example, a clothing manufacturer may make a line of menswear and a line of women's wear. Within each line would be many different items of apparel (slacks, jackets, coats, etc.), each in a variety of styles, sizes, and colors. In addition, the manufacturer might divide each line into high-priced, medium-priced, and low-priced goods. With this strategy, the manufacturer can appeal to the taste of many different kinds of customers.

Sometimes we don't even know that apparently competing products are actually part of a single firm's product mix. Heublein, the company that makes high-priced Smirnoff vodka, also markets a much lower-priced brand aimed at a different market segment.

The product life cycle

A product life cycle is a series of stages a product passes through in the course of its sales history. A product's life cycle usually includes four phases, as summarized in Table 13.1.

Table 13.1 Marketing strategy: four phases

	Price	Promotion	Distribution	Product change
Introduction	High, to recover development costs	Heavy, emphasizing product benefits	Many outlets, to assure wide public access	None
Growth	High, because consumer demand is high	Heavy, emphasizing brand name to win consumer loyalty	Additional outlets	New sizes, packages, and styling features; service extras
Maturity	Lower, to draw in remaining potential customers	Heavy, emphasizing superiority over competition	Additional outlets, including discount retailers	New uses, new users, flanker products, major modifications
Decline	Low, to liquidate inventory quickly	Moderate, discouraging product use	Contracting number of outlets	Major modifications, if not already made

1. Introduction. When a product is first introduced, its sales are low. Its producer cannot be sure that the product will ever succeed in the marketplace. Promotional expenses are very high because customers must be informed of the product's existence and persuaded to try it. Because costs are high and sales are low, little or no profit is made.

2. Growth. A product's sales rise rapidly during the growth stage. Profits usually peak at this stage, so a producer tries to prolong rapid growth as much as possible. Competitors may try to copy a successful new product, so its originator must keep improving it to keep ahead of rivals.

3. Maturity. At some point, a product's sales will slow down. This signals its entry into the maturity stage. This can be a relatively long stage, but it poses many challenges to marketers.

When profits start to fall, some producers abandon the market. For example, when portable electronic calculators were first introduced in the early 1970s, dozens of companies offered models. Many were able to survive because of the rapidly expanding market. But many of the weaker firms dropped out once the market matured.

More aggressive marketers seek other solutions besides dropping out. Increased advertising, lower prices, product improvements, and targeting new markets can help a company defend its sales in a mature market.

4. Decline. Eventually, technical advances or changes in consumers' tastes spell the end of many products. The slide rule died suddenly after many years of maturity because it was replaced by the electronic calculator. Movie attendance fell sharply after the widespread adoption of television. In the case of fads, new interests quickly replace established ones. Products like pet rocks, yo-yos, and skateboards come and go.

Figure 13.1 Products in various stages of their life cycle in 1983

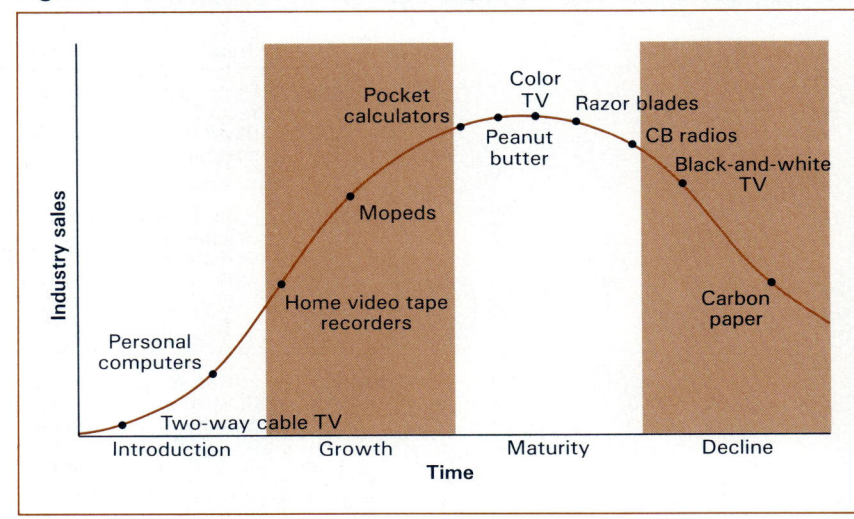

The costs of continuing to market a product in the stage of decline can be very high. In most cases, a company's human and financial resources can be better spent on new and growing products. As a result, unprofitable old products are usually dropped from the market.

Marketers must understand the product life cycle in order to plan marketing strategies and estimate a product's profit potential. Figure 13.1 shows the current life cycle stages of some products.

Brands

A brand is a name, symbol, design, or term used singly or in combination to identify the goods or services of a specific producer and to distinguish these products from those of competitors.

Brands help a customer to readily recognize a firm's products. This is necessary if a company wants to encourage repeat purchases and brand loyalty among its customers. Green Giant, Pepsi-Cola, Scott, Ivory, Honda, and Contac are examples of well-known national brands.

A company may use different brands to identify goods of different price and quality. This is one way of dividing a product line for promotion and distribution to specific target markets. For example, General Motors markets Chevrolets, Pontiacs, Oldsmobiles, Buicks, and Cadillacs to different target markets. In many ways, the cars are quite similar in construction. But each has its own brand identity.

Protecting brand names

Sometimes a brand name becomes so strongly identified with a product that people start using the brand name to refer to the product in general. For example, people often call all facial tissue *Kleenex,* even though Kleenex is a brand name that applies only to Kimberly-Clark's line of facial tissues. Similarly, people often say that they will "xerox" a docu-

Marketing a mature operation

Often, a fresh marketing strategy can restore growth to an otherwise mature product. This explains why marketers frequently attach a "new, improved" label to familiar soaps or toothpastes. A similar strategy can also work on a larger scale. A supermarket chain in New England serves as proof.

Star Market believed it could improve sales by changing its negative, high-priced image. One of its first steps was to introduce generic (unbranded) products as alternatives to high-priced, name-brand items like tuna fish and peanut butter. It also converted some of its less profitable stores into independently owned stores under the Star name. This lowered corporate overhead.

Star's high prices were the result of better quality and services. Its goal was to maintain its high-quality image while convincing its customers that its prices were not particularly high. It was a delicate task. Advertising themes through the years changed from "The Quality Leader" to "Food Values Daily" to "We'll Find a Way."

It is exceedingly difficult to alter the public image of a mature operation like Star. Consumers are very slow to change their perceptions. Star had an uphill struggle to identify and change the substance of its problem and then convince the public to see the change for themselves.

ment when they really mean that they will photocopy it. Xerox Company was such a strong leader in developing the photocopying process that its name is closely associated with all copying machines.

A brand name is often followed by the symbol ® or ™, as in Kodak®. This means it is a trademark. **A trademark is a brand and any art or symbol associated with it that is legally registered with the federal government.** Other companies and individuals are then restrained from using the trademark. Companies such as Coca-Cola, Xerox, IBM, and Kodak sometimes take ads in newspapers and magazines to remind people that their products are trademarked. The legal departments of such companies notify people who use those brand names that they are in violation of trademark laws.

In some cases, the courts have ruled that brand names left unprotected by their owners could become everyday words. A famous case concerned a popular toy. "Yo-yo" had been the brand name for Duncan Company's spinning top. But a court declared that Duncan could not stop other toy makers from calling their products yo-yos, too. Because the term *yo-yo* had become synonomous with the product and because Duncan had not gone out of its way to protect its claim to the brand name, yo-yo could not be considered a trademark. More recently, the courts have told Parker Brothers that its Monopoly game could not retain its trademark status.

Private brands

Although we are most familiar with brands that belong to manufacturers, some brands are created by retailers. **A private brand is a brand name associated with a single retailer.** Private-brand products are sometimes even made by name-brand manufacturers who put the retailer's own label on the finished goods. In many cases, the product may be identical to the manufacturer's own branded product. For example, Sears uses the private brand names Kenmore for appliances and Craftsman for tools. Kenmore and Craftsman products are made, however, by well-known national manufacturers. Whirlpool or Black & Decker, for example, may be among Sears' suppliers.

Barbara Isenberg is bullish in a bear market—and don't sell her short

Barbara Isenberg and friends

The idea had been hibernating in Barbara Isenberg's mind for years. Ever since her son, Christopher, now 7, was a tot, the 36-year-old New Yorker had stitched together toy bears for his amusement. But she noticed that the infant-size cubs invariably found their way into the arms of adults. "People would come into the house and keep them on their laps," marvels Isenberg. "They don't talk back and don't need to be fed. I realized by the adult reactions that the toys had real possibilities." Thus was born the North American Bear Company, Inc.

The forebear of North American, introduced in New York stores by Isenberg in 1979, is the pot-bellied, sweat-suited Running Bear, retailing for $30. After the first shipment sold out, she decided to expand the concept. Now her V.I.B.'s—Very Important Bears—line is turning out 10,000 animals annually and grossing $150,000. Among the best-sellers: Scarlett O'Beara and Chef Bearnaise ($37 each) and the stripped-down Bare Bear ($25). Even the toy's eponyms are ecstatic: Douglas Fairbanks Jr. ordered five of the pin-striped Douglas Bearbanks model ($37) last Christmas.

Initially Isenberg lost money, but then her businessman brother Paul Levy took over marketing (Isenberg's husband, Steven, is a lawyer). Also, some V.I.B.'s models that Barbara dreamed up weren't ready for Teddy; Cyrano de Beargerac, Shakesbear, and Charles Lindbeargh have not yet made it past the drawing board because they may be too esoteric.

Levy and Isenberg are now confident, however, that their V.I.B.'s will take the business by storm when nationwide distribution begins this spring. New models include Mikhail Bearyshnikov, Anna Bearvlova and a Hollywood bear whose name remains under wraps until copyright problems are cleared up. North American's next candidate will be Sen. Teddy Bear, with the first copy already earmarked for the Smithsonian Institution's Political History Division. Even in a Republican era, the North American Bear Co. is convinced he will top the polls. Proclaims Isenberg: "I'll have him running by 1983."

Republished from Victoria Everett, PEOPLE Weekly, January 26, © 1981, Time Inc.

Retailers use private brands in the same way that manufacturers use name brands. Private brands provide recognition and encourage repeat purchases. In addition, since the brands are not available elsewhere, customers must return to the store for repeat purchases.

Packaging

Packaging is the container, wrapper, or other means in which a product is presented to consumers. Cans, boxes, wrapping paper, bottles, tubes, and cards are all used as packaging. And packages come in many different sizes, shapes, colors, and materials.

Packaging serves several useful purposes. It helps to sell a product, display a brand or label, make a product more visible on the shelf, protect a product from breaking, and make a product easier to handle.

Packaging gives consumers clues about a product. The $190 Cartier pen comes individually boxed in a velvet-lined, hardboard container. This is appropriate for a luxury item that may be displayed with jewelry and bought as a gift. Bic pens are fastened on cards or sealed by the dozen in plastic bags. The package has eye-catching printing on it. Such packaging is appropriate for an inexpensive item that will be part of a mass display in a drugstore or variety store.

Pricing

Pricing is the process of deciding what to charge for a good or service. Setting an appropriate price for a good or service is a complex decision based on many factors in the company and in the marketplace. These include the following:

1. Market objectives
2. Costs and desired profit margin
3. Legal, social, and ethical restrictions
4. Projected company image
5. Pricing policies of the firm
6. Nonprice competition.

Market objectives

Three basic pricing strategies correspond to a company's market objectives.

Penetration pricing is the setting of low prices in order to capture a large share of the market. Many companies who use penetration pricing believe that long-term profitability is more important than short-term gains.

Market skimming is the setting of high prices in order to attract a small but highly profitable market share. With market skimming, a high profit is made on each item sold, but the number of buyers is limited. This strategy is often used by companies whose products are so unique that some consumers will buy them no matter what the price.

Pricing with the market is the setting of prices to match the prices of competitors. This strategy is especially common in very competitive industries where products are all similar. For example, most consumer products are priced with the market. By pricing with the market, a company avoids competing with fellow producers over price. Instead, competition often focuses on differences between brands.

Sometimes a firm combines all three strategies. For example, when the Polaroid Company first introduced the SX-70 camera, it brought out a luxury model priced at $200 to skim the market. A small number of people were willing to pay the high price in order to be the first to have the new camera. After a while, Polaroid introduced a slightly less expensive version. Two years later, they added two SX-70 models priced to sell for as little as $25 in discount stores. Polaroid's strategy was to begin by skimming the market and then gradually move toward penetration pricing. The company *could* have come out with the low-priced version in the first place, but that was not their objective.

Using the product life cycle

The decision to penetrate the market is based on analysis of the product life cycle. When a company decides to penetrate the market, it sets as low a price as possible with a view toward discouraging competition. In the meantime, many people buy the product. A company should use penetration pricing with a new product only if the product is expected to have a long enough life for the firm to recover its investment and make a profit.

A price that is set too high will encourage competitors to enter the market at a lower price. A price that is set too low may take too long to repay the firm's investment. A product like the Polaroid SX-70 is somewhat rare. The highly technological process was patented by Polaroid, so it did not have to worry much about immediate competition. Kodak did eventually come out with similar cameras.

Cost and desired profit

Some companies base their prices solely on the cost of producing their products. They may use one of several mathematical techniques for setting a product's price.

Markup pricing

Markup is the difference between the cost of producing a product and its selling price. If a product costs $2.00 to make and has a selling price of $3.20, its markup is $1.20, or 60 percent. When using markup pricing, the selling price of a product is determined by adding a fixed percentage to the cost of manufacturing or purchasing it. Table 13.2 shows how to calculate markup.

Table 13.2 Calculating markup

A shirt costs a retailer $8.00 to purchase and he or she uses a markup of 80 percent. What will be the selling price? What is its markup in dollars?
Selling price = cost + $ markup
where
$ markup = cost × percent markup:
If   C = $8.00
and   MU = 80 percent,
then   MU = $8.00 × .80 = $6.40.
Selling price:
SP = C + $ MU
= $8.00 + $6.40
= $14.40

Markup pricing is common in retailing, where a storeowner will add different markups to different goods. Retail clothing stores, for example, typically mark up their goods 100 percent over purchase price. Supermarkets use much lower markup, while fine-jewelry merchants may have higher markups.

Although markup pricing does not take into consideration all the factors that affect price, it has the advantage of being easy to calculate. When sellers use the same markups, price competition is minimized.

Breakeven analysis

Breakeven analysis can be useful for pricing new ventures or products that require prior investment. **Breakeven is the number of units that must be sold in order to earn back the money invested in developing, manufacturing, and marketing a product.** If a company sells fewer units than breakeven, it loses money. If it sells more units, it makes a profit.

To calculate breakeven for a given product, you need to know its selling price and its fixed and variable costs. Fixed costs are costs that remain the same regardless of the number of units produced and sold. They include such costs as machinery, rent, and insurance. Variable costs rise or fall in direct response to the number of units produced. Variable costs include some labor, raw materials, sales commissions, and the like. Fixed costs plus variable costs equal total costs, or the amount of revenue that must be raised before there is any profit.

A marketer can use breakeven information to choose an appropriate price for a product. Or breakeven analysis might show that, based on expected sales, a product will easily cover its fixed costs and earn a solid profit, as the example in Figure 13.2 shows.

Chapter 13 Product and pricing decisions

Figure 13.2 Breakeven analysis for automobile production with revenue of $6000 per car and fixed costs of $100 million

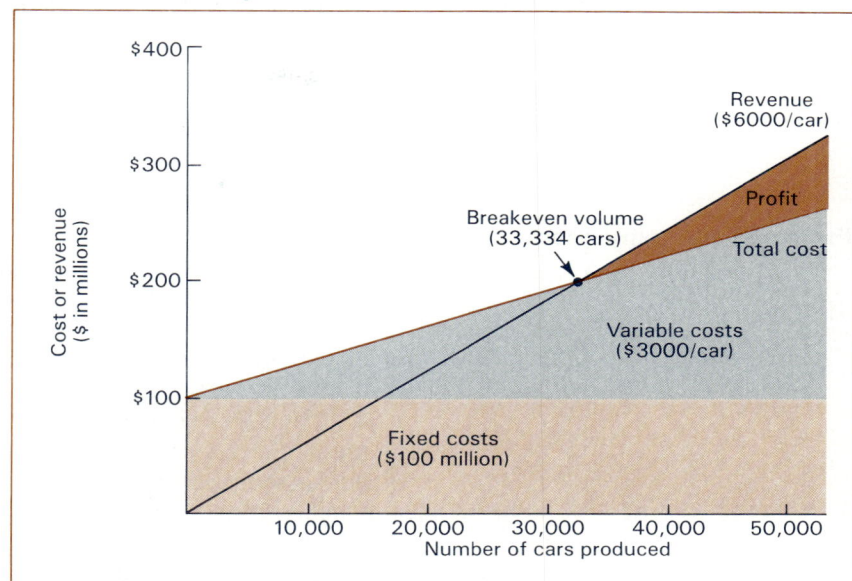

The fixed costs for producing an automobile are $100 million. Variable costs are $3000 per car, and the selling price is $6000 per car. How many cars must be sold to break even?

Basic formula:

$$\text{Breakeven in units} = \frac{\text{Fixed Cost}}{\text{Selling price per unit} - \text{Variable costs per unit}}$$

$$Q = \frac{FC}{(P - VC)}$$

$FC = \$100,000,000$

$P = \$6000$

$VC = \$3000$

$$Q = \frac{\$100,000,000}{\$6000 - \$3000}$$

$$Q = \frac{\$100,000,000}{\$3000} = \textbf{33,334 cars}$$

Legal, social, and ethical restrictions on pricing

There are many national, state, and local pricing laws in the United States. For example, the Robinson-Patman Act requires that manufacturers charge all customers the same price for the same item. Exceptions are allowed only for quantity purchases and delivery methods that save the seller money.

The Sherman Antitrust Act and the Clayton Act also regulate prices. Both try to prevent companies from working together to fix prices and thus restrict competition. Executives of several well-known national companies have been fined and imprisoned for price fixing.

A company also faces certain social and ethical restraints on its pricing policies. A company may hold back price increases if it believes that public opposition would be too great. This is frequently done when food staples such as sugar, beef, or coffee are in short supply. On the other hand, some companies will not cut their prices if the lower price would drive out other competition and create a monopoly.

Projected company image

Prices often reflect the image a firm is trying to create. Most consumers have a strong sense of price-quality relationships. They tend to believe that the more expensive something is, the better it will be. This is generally, although not always, the case. A firm that wants to project a bargain image will set its prices low. Conversely, a company that wants consumers to associate its products with high quality will set its prices high. Sony, the manufacturer of television and radio equipment, prices its products higher than most competitors, which is consistent with the quality image it has created.

Some companies are pricing leaders. Other companies base their prices on the leader's prices. When a well-respected firm with a large market share raises its prices, smaller companies may feel confident in raising their own.

Some companies are always followers. They wait to see what others do rather than initiate price changes themselves. Neither policy is necessarily better. But to be a price leader, a company usually must have a significant share of the market.

Pricing policies

Policies are general guides for specific actions. They enable a company to carry out its objectives. Price lining, psychological pricing, flexible prices, and discounts are common pricing policies that a company may adopt.

Price lining

Price lining is the practice of selling groups of products at a limited number of prices rather than pricing each product individually. Thus, a store may sell a number of products for $.98. Another group of products may be available at $1.69, another at $1.98, and so forth. A clothing store may have a selection of slacks for $17.95, and a higher-priced selection at $29.95. Within each price line or level, an assortment of items may be offered.

Psychological pricing

Buyers seem to find some prices more attractive than others. As a result, prices often are set at slightly less than a round number. For example, a skirt might be priced at $39.95 rather than $40.00. This is done because the buyer perceives the slightly lower price as a better bargain.

Chapter 13 Product and pricing decisions

Pricing decisions must acknowledge buyers' subjective perception of the product.

"It can't be much good."

Drawing by Dana Fradon; © 1971 The New Yorker Magazine, Inc.

Psychological pricing is the setting of prices to appeal to buyers' subjective perceptions. The use of price to project company image is another form of psychological pricing.

One price and flexible prices

Some sellers have one price for all buyers while others have flexible prices that vary with the buyer. Flexible pricing may violate the Robinson-Patman Act unless prices are based on real cost differences. A seller's prices may vary with the quantity purchased. Prices may also vary when a manufacturer sells to customers at different marketing levels, such as wholesalers, retailers, or consumers.

Discounts

A discount is a reduction in the price of a product. A manufacturer may offer four kinds of discounts to attract customers.

A trade discount is a price reduction given to a retailer or wholesaler. It is usually based on a product's suggested list price. For example, if a tennis racquet has a list price of $100, its manufacturer might sell it to a sporting goods store at a 40 percent trade discount, or for $60. The sporting goods store can then cover its other expenses and have some profit when it sells the racquet at the list price.

A cash discount is a price reduction offered for prompt payment of a bill. The terms of a cash discount usually are included on the bill of sale. For example, "2/10, net 30" means that the purchaser will receive a 2 percent discount if the bill is paid within ten days and that the full amount must be made within 30 days of the invoice date.

A quantity discount is a price reduction given to purchasers of large amounts of goods. A retailer who buys 100 typewriters will pay less per unit than a retailer who buys only 12. The purpose of a quantity discount is to encourage buying in volume.

A promotional discount is given to customers who agree to participate in special marketing activities. The customer might agree to give the product extra advertising, special displays, and/or lower prices. In return, the manufacturer may give the customer rebates, special allowances on purchases, promotional posters, advertising, and display materials.

Nonprice competition

When competition is based on price, a seller tries to attract more customers by offering lower prices. **Nonprice competition is the attempt to attract customers by offering other buying incentives besides low prices.** These may include attractive credit terms, sweepstakes and prizes, special packaging, personal selling, customized services, improved quality, advertising and sales promotions, convenient shopping locations, repair centers, special guarantees and warranties, and many other forms of encouragement tailored to the product and the customer.

13 Product and pricing decisions

Summary

The long-term success of any marketing effort depends on a strong product. In fact, there is often more to a product than meets the eye. A *product* is really a bundle of attributes that consumers want or need. The *product mix* consists of all the products a business sells.

A marketing campaign must be based on a product's stage in the *product life cycle*. The first stage is an introductory period that generates little revenue. Then comes a phase of rapid growth during which profits peak. In the third stage, maturity, the product's sales level off and slowly start to fall. In the final stage, sales fall sharply and the product is usually taken off the market.

A *brand* is a name, symbol, design, or term used singly or in combination to identify the goods or services of a specific producer. Companies build brand identification to distinguish their goods from those of their competitors. A *trademark* is a legally protected brand name and/or any associated art or symbol that cannot be used without permission from the company that owns it. A *private brand* is one sold under the retailer's own name, but manufactured by another company.

Packaging is the container, wrapper, or other means in which a product is presented. The package plays a useful function in marketing. It protects the contents, helps sell the item, facilitates handling, and can make the product more visible on the shelf.

Pricing—the process of setting a price for a product—is a second major element of the marketing mix. Many factors enter into a pricing decision. The costs of producing and marketing the product are important considerations. But so are the company's market objectives, image, desired profit, pricing policies, and certain legal and social factors.

There are several pricing strategies. *Penetration pricing* is the setting of low prices in order to capture a large market share. In *market skimming,* a business sets high prices to attract only the most profitable customers. *Pricing with the market* involves setting prices that match the competition's. *Markup* and *breakeven* are two mathematical calculations used in pricing decisions. *Price lining* involves offering products at different levels of price, rather than all at one price. *Psychological pricing* sets prices to appeal to buyers' subjective perceptions. A *discount* is a reduction in the price of a product.

A *trade discount* is a price reduction given to retailers and wholesalers. Based on the manufacturer's suggested list price, a trade discount enables a retailer or wholesaler to make a profit when the product is resold. A *cash discount* may be offered for prompt payment of a bill. A *quantity discount* may be given to a purchaser of large quantities of goods. A *promotional discount* is given to customers who agree to participate in special marketing activities.

Nonprice competition is a seller's attempt to attract customers by offering incentives besides low prices. This may include attractive credit terms, customized service, warranties, free repairs, and other forms of encouragement.

Review questions

1. What are the four phases in the product life cycle? Briefly describe the characteristics of each phase.
2. Why must marketers understand a product's life cycle?
3. What problems may arise during the maturity phase of a product? How might a seller solve these problems?
4. What purposes do brands serve?
5. What steps can a company take to guard its brand names?
6. What market objectives correspond to (a) penetration pricing, (b) skimming, and (c) pricing with the market?
7. What is markup pricing? In what industry is it most common? Why?
8. What is the purpose of breakeven analysis?
9. How can a company use prices to project an image?
10. Describe the four kinds of discounts that a manufacturer may offer.
11. What is nonprice competition? Cite five specific examples.

Discussion questions

1. According to the information presented in Figure 13.1 and Table 13.1, why might product managers for CB radios, color TVs, and razor blades design similar marketing strategies? What would be some characteristics of their strategies?
2. Pricing is one of the most complex and important features of the marketing mix. Briefly discuss the factors that influence a pricing decision and the implications of each.
3. You are the product manager in charge of marketing a miniature stereo cassette player that is in the growth phase of its product life cycle. Describe at least three possible marketing strategies. Choose one of these strategies and defend your choice.
4. What marketing strategy did the makers of designer jeans use? What roles did brand and price play in this strategy? Why would people be willing to pay $50 for one product when a comparable product could be bought for $20? What other products are marketed this way? What products could be marketed like this in the future?

Chapter 13 case

North Central Tire Company

Many manufacturers spend much money establishing a brand identity. Retailers, on the other hand, like to carry a line of goods with their own private brand. This case is about a conflict faced by one brand name manufacturer.

North Central Tire Company is a major tire manufacturer in the United States. It has always sold its tires under the North Central brand. A recent market research study found that the company held 17 percent of the U.S. tire market. However, this percentage had not increased for several years.

Recently, North Central was approached by a large national retailer and asked to supply tires under the retailer's own name. North Central had had many requests to make private-brand tires in the past, but it had always refused. Company management believed that such private-label tires would cut into the sales of their own brand tires. Moreover, the profit was lower on private-brand tires.

This time, management decided to rethink their policy. In recent years, several large retailers had sold large quantities of private-label tires. Sears had been particularly successful.

Suppose you were a consultant hired by North Central Tire Company to help make the decision.

1. What factors favor the supplying of private-brand tires to the retailer?
2. What factors favor staying with the company's current policy of selling only their own brand?
3. What would you advise North Central to do? Why?

Business in perspective

Mr. Whipple, Madge, and Old Lonely—winning personalities

In the world of TV commercials, "stars" such as Mr. Whipple, Madge, and the lonely Maytag repairman are the envy of their competition. Charmin toilet paper, Palmolive dishwashing liquid, and Maytag washers have succeeded in developing ad campaigns whose characters provide instant recognition. They've achieved that basic goal of advertising: to place the product in a class by itself, distinct from and above all others. In addition, the firms get more advertising value for their money.

When Mr. Whipple chides shoppers for squeezing the Charmin, the notion of Charmin's "squeezable softness" is implanted in the viewer's mind. This message, humorously expressed, presumably separates Charmin from the rest of the pack.

This advantage is translated into "more bang for the buck." Advertisers know it is easier and cheaper to maintain a successful campaign than to generate a new one.

On the other hand, Mr. Whipple and Madge run the risk of overexposure. The Whipple character was created in 1964 and Madge in 1963. Old Lonely celebrated his fourteenth anniversary in 1981. Advertisers fear overexposure. To safeguard a product's campaign, many firms test back-up commercials that revolve around other characters.

Despite the risks, Old Lonely, the repairman who has bemoaned Maytag dependability over the years, will probably not retire for quite some time. His complaints about underemployment may take place in new settings to keep him fresh in our minds. But Old Lonely will probably suffer a bit longer. Maytag has invested more than $20 million in Old Lonely advertising. The firm expects the character's symbolic message will continue to be useful in maintaining strong brand identity.

Adapted from Lawrence Ingrassia, "As Mr. Whipple Shows, Ad Stars Can Bring Long-Term Sales Gains," *Wall Street Journal,* February 12, 1981. Reprinted by permission of the *Wall Street Journal,* © Dow Jones & Company, Inc., 1981. All rights reserved.

Chapter 14

Promotional decisions

Key terms

promotion
promotional mix
brand recognition
advertising
print media
electronic media
publicity
personal selling
sales promotion

Chapter objectives

In Chapter 14, you will learn:

The four elements of the promotional mix

The objectives of a promotional campaign

The characteristics of the five most common advertising media

How publicity differs from advertising

The advantages of personal selling

Some sales promotion techniques that can supplement other promotional activities

Overview

Promotion plays an important role in the marketing mix. Every producer of goods or services, whether profit-oriented or nonprofit, uses some form of promotion to attract attention.

Promotion is an organization's communication about itself to potential users of its goods and services. Companies use promotion to increase their sales. Promotional messages try to inform consumers and influence their opinions, attitudes, and behavior.

Most companies spend more on promotion than on any other marketing activity. In fact, in many companies, promotion is the single largest expense—even greater than production.

There are four basic forms of promotion: advertising, publicity, personal selling, and sales promotion. Most companies' promotional strategies include a combination of these four activities.

The promotional mix is the blend of activities a company uses to persuade a target market to buy a product. This chapter examines the purposes of promotion and the four basic elements of the promotional mix.

The objectives of promotion

A promotional campaign must be based on a well-planned strategy. Advertising, publicity, personal selling, and sales promotion activities must be coordinated into a logical system. The promotional strategy, in turn, must fit into the overall marketing strategy. To ensure that all elements will work well together, marketers must establish specific objectives for their promotional campaigns. Here are some of the most common objectives.

To achieve brand recognition, or acceptance

Brand recognition is the consumer's awareness of a specific brand name. Many brands are well known because of strong promotional campaigns. But it is often difficult to establish a new brand. In the mid-1970s, many new brands of cigarettes were introduced. Real, Decade, and Merit were among them. Their manufacturers ran ambitious promotional campaigns that included repeated newspaper and magazine advertisements. Their objective was to establish their new brands alongside such familiar brands as Marlboro, Camel, and Winston. Few succeeded.

To gain a trial purchase

Many promotional efforts try to persuade consumers to try a product at least once. When a new product is introduced, marketers will try to prove that it is worth trying. They may give away free samples or cents-off coupons. They may also emphasize the product's uniqueness or its superiority to older brands. With a mature product, marketers may try to increase sales by wooing users of other brands. For example, the "Pepsi Challenge" ad campaign was designed to demonstrate to drinkers of Coke and other soft drinks that Pepsi has superior taste.

To reach the buyer at a time of decision	Most of us are familiar with billboards along the highway that announce, for example, "Holiday Inn, 45 miles, Exit 18." This advertisement is directed at travelers who may be considering where to spend the night. Posters in city buses and at railroad stations advertise, among other things, telephone numbers to call to enroll in community college courses, the benefits of reading the morning newspaper, and the refreshing effects of cold beer. All of these messages promote a specific action at or near a place where the reader could easily follow up. On the way home, for example, the reader may pick up the newspaper or a frosty six-pack. Once home, a traveler may call the local college to find out about evening course offerings.
To add value	A common promotional objective is to convince the audience that a product or service is worth its price. Promotion can enhance a product's image, raising its value and differentiating it from the competition. For example, if an automobile is merely a means of transportation, a Dodge or Ford should suffice. Why spend $30,000 for a Mercedes-Benz? To a large extent, people buy a Mercedes because its manufacturer, and others, have suggested that a car is more than basic transportation. A car may project image, status, wealth, and other glamorous characteristics. These projected characteristics make the car more valuable to certain people. Image also adds value to designer clothes, twelve-year-old Scotch, and limited-edition collectors' items.
To build distribution	A manufacturer may advertise in special publications that are directed only to retailers and wholesalers. Such advertising may cause these middlemen to be more receptive when the manufacturer's sales representative calls. For example, an advertiser may promote a new line of cake mixes or an existing brand of peanut butter in a publication for supermarket owners. Advertising to retailers and wholesalers is important because consumers cannot buy a product if stores do not stock it.
To aid personal selling	Automobile commercials often highlight a car's smooth ride. One manufacturer ran a series of ads with a noise meter to prove that its car was as quiet as a much more expensive one. Auto makers also often display

SAAB advertisement reflecting many promotional objectives

Prepared by Ally & Gargano, Inc.

their products at local auto shows and sponsor race cars. Such promotional activities simplify the salesperson's job by establishing the car's identity in the marketplace. When customers walk into the auto showroom, they already know something about the product and are interested in learning more. This saves the salesperson time and effort.

Marketers usually set one or two objectives for a specific promotional campaign. For example, when promoting a new product, marketers might start with a campaign to build distribution and establish brand recognition. In a later campaign, they may concentrate on gaining a trial purchase. At another time, their objective could be to add value to the now-established product.

Advertising

Advertising is any form of paid message presented through the media by an identifiable sponsor. It tries to create acceptance or awareness of a product, service, or idea.

Table 14.1 Advertising expenditures 1935–1981

	Total advertising expenditures ($ in millions)	Percent spent on					
		Newspapers	TV	Radio	Magazines	Direct mail	Other
1935	$ 1,690	45.1%	—	6.7	11.1%	16.7%	20.5%
1945	2,875	32.0	—	14.7	20.4	10.1	23.0
1950	5,710	36.4	3.0%	10.6	13.8	14.1	22.2
1955	9,194	33.6	11.1	5.9	13.2	14.1	22.0
1960	11,932	30.8	13.6	5.8	13.3	15.3	21.2
1965	15,255	29.0	16.5	6.0	12.5	15.2	20.6
1970	19,600	29.3	18.3	6.7	10.7	14.1	20.9
1975	28,230	29.9	18.6	7.0	8.8	14.8	20.8
1980	54,480	28.5	20.9	6.8	9.1	13.1	21.0
1981	61,230	28.4	20.6	6.9	9.0	14.3	20.8

Annual tables published in *Advertising Age* from figures tabulated by McCann-Erickson, Inc.

In 1981, more than $61.2 billion was spent on advertising in the United States. Of that total, about 28 percent was spent on newspaper ads, about 21 percent on television, 7 percent on radio, 9 percent on magazines, 14 percent on direct mail, and the remainder on various other media, such as billboards, posters, and the like. Table 14.1 shows how advertising expenditures have changed since 1935. Table 14.2 lists the 25 largest advertisers in 1981.

Table 14.2 Twenty-five largest advertisers, 1981

Rank	Advertiser	Expenditures ($ in millions)
1	Procter & Gamble	$671.8
2	Sears	544.1
3	General Foods	456.8
4	Philip Morris	433.0
5	General Motors	401.0

Table 14.2 Twenty-five largest advertisers, 1981 (continued)

Rank	Advertiser	Expenditures ($ in millions)
6	K mart	349.6
7	Nabisco	341.0
8	R.J. Reynolds	321.3
9	American Telephone & Telegraph	297.0
10	Mobil	293.1
11	Ford Motor	286.7
12	Warner-Lambert	270.4
13	Colgate-Palmolive	260.0
14	PepsiCo	260.0
15	McDonald's	230.2
16	American Home Products	209.0
17	RCA	208.8
18	J.C. Penney	208.6
19	General Mills	207.3
20	Bristol-Myers	200.0
21	B.A.T. Industries	199.3
22	Coca-Cola	197.9
23	Johnson & Johnson	195.0
24	Chrysler	193.0
25	Ralston Purina	193.0

Reprinted with permission from the September 9, 1982, issue of *Advertising Age*. Copyright 1982 by Crain Communications, Inc.

Figure 14.1 Expenditures of some leading advertisers, 1981

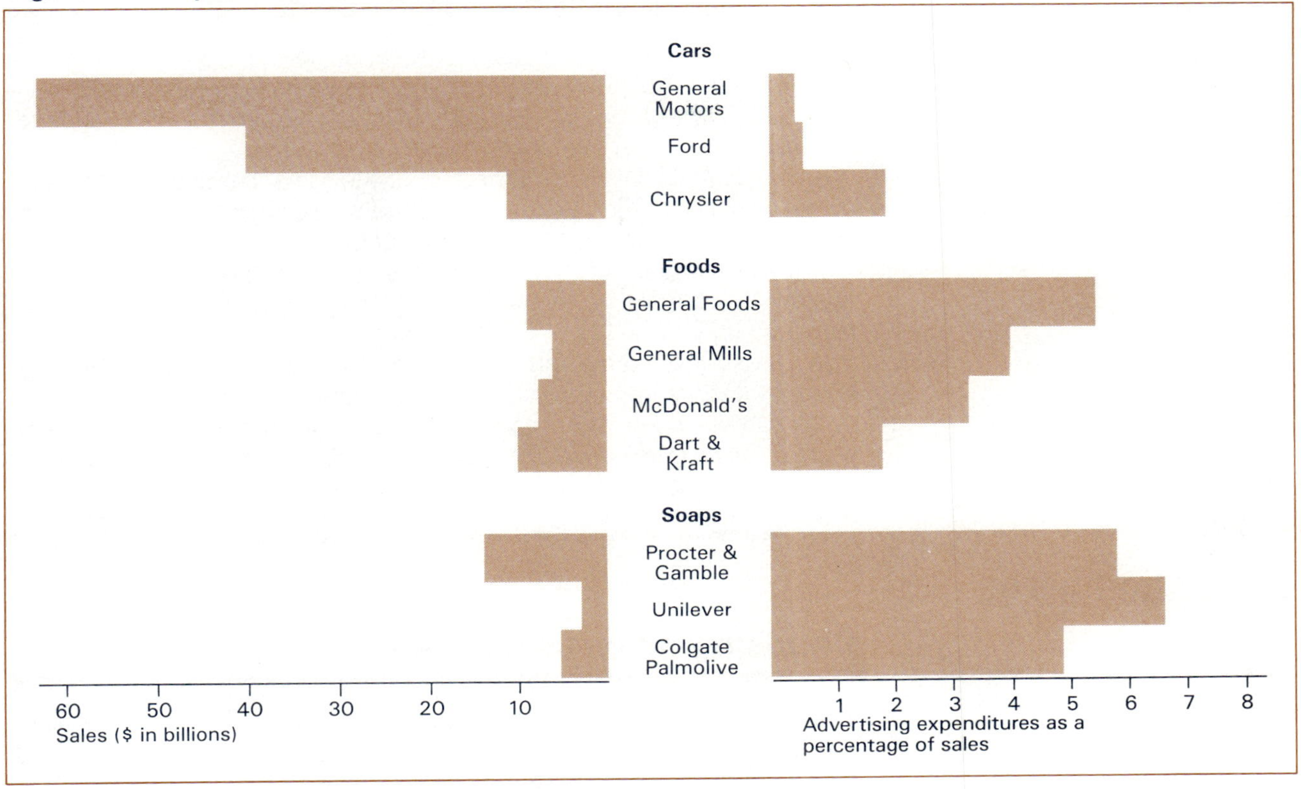

Cars: General Motors, Ford, Chrysler
Foods: General Foods, General Mills, McDonald's, Dart & Kraft
Soaps: Procter & Gamble, Unilever, Colgate Palmolive

Sales ($ in billions): 60, 50, 40, 30, 20, 10
Advertising expenditures as a percentage of sales: 1, 2, 3, 4, 5, 6, 7, 8

Reprinted with permission from the September 9, 1982, issue of *Advertising Age*. Copyright 1982 by Crain Communications, Inc.

Budget considerations

Wide-scale advertising can be very expensive. As shown in Table 14.2, Procter & Gamble, manufacturer of Crest toothpaste, Ivory soap, and many other consumer products, spent almost $672 million on advertising in 1981. To be effective, an advertising campaign must have repetition, coverage, and impact. Advertisements only work if they are run on a regular basis. They must appear in enough media to reach many potential buyers. And, ads must be large enough to attract attention. All this takes money.

Some advertisers spend as much as a fourth of their revenue on advertising. As shown in Figure 14.1, advertising expenditures vary greatly by industry. The amount of money budgeted for advertising greatly affects the scope of a campaign and the media that are used.

M&M/Mars: They upped their sales when they upped their size

In May 1980, Mars, the makers of M&Ms, Snickers, and Three Musketeers, and its advertising agency, the Ted Bates Group, started a new promotional campaign. Its underlying concept: improved value leads to increased sales.

Snickers, Milky Ways, and the rest of the Mars candy products were made bigger. But their prices stayed the same. This followed years of increasing prices and reducing candy bar sizes.

The candy lovers of America expressed their approval at the cash register. Mars sales hit record levels. As sales went up, so did productivity and efficiency. Mars' revenues increased.

In choosing this campaign, Mars counted on favorable reaction to their reward-the-consumer approach. Their gamble paid off.

Consumers don't often see the benefits of an advertising strategy passed on to them—certainly not as directly and simply as the Mars promotion, right at the cash register.

Choosing advertising media

The choice of media has important effects on an advertising campaign. The goal in choosing media is to communicate with the largest intended audience at the lowest possible cost.

Advertising media can be divided into two major categories based on technology. **The print media are newspapers, magazines, and direct mail. The electronic media are television and radio.**

Advertising in print media is sold by *space:* column inches, pages, or lines. The audience has a great deal of control over print media. Readers decide when it is most convenient to read a printed ad, which may be when there are few distractions or when they are looking for specific information. They can read it at whatever speed is comfortable. Printed ads can be saved, studied, clipped, and reexamined at a later date.

Advertising in electronic media is sold by *time:* 10-second, 30-second, or 60-second "spots." In these media, the advertiser controls the audience's exposure to the ad. Images or ideas can only be presented sequentially—one after another. The audience cannot review information that they missed. The message is instantaneous: once it is over, it is gone. Unless one has a video cassette or audio tape machine to record advertisements, no storage for later use is possible.

As a rule, the electronic media are better able to reach large masses of people at the same time. Except for *TV Guide* and *Reader's Digest,* no newspaper or magazine in the United States comes close to reaching as many people as a prime-time show or special sports event on television.

Each medium has unique features that lend themselves to advertisers' needs.

New life-styles alter Madison Avenue

American advertisers are recognizing that the traditional American housewife is becoming extinct. It's no news that more women are working outside the home. More households are also headed by either single men or single women. These changes in the average American household have challenged advertisers. They have had to rethink both their strategies and their messages.

Putting a briefcase in a woman's hand in an advertisement is not the whole answer. Neither is showing her husband, or her son, with laundry detergent and basket in hand. The difficulty for advertisers is that these changes in society cannot be automatically translated into easily identifiable market changes.

More women work today. But they may still do housework. Should advertisers of cleaning products gear their pitch toward the professional or the domestic side of the woman?

More men may be participating in house cleaning. To what extent do they shop for such products as detergent and bathroom deodorizer? Once these were thought of as purely women's purchases. Will men be offended if advertisements portray them not only as home owners, but as home *cleaners* as well?

Advertisers are faced with a tough challenge. Can they respond effectively to these significant demographic developments?

There are signs of progress:

- Products once considered men's purchases—such as tires, cars, and insurance—are now advertised in women's magazines, too.
- The once-stereotyped housewife is now portrayed as a more well-rounded, believable character in many commercials. She isn't as helpless and one-dimensional as she once seemed to be.
- More mini-appliances and single-serving portions of foods are now on the market. They are a response to the increased number of single, separated, widowed, and divorced consumers.

On the other hand, there are potential difficulties:

- Submarkets exist within the female consumer population. The attitudes of young, single, career women differ from those of older, married, working women. Thus, a trendy, "liberated" ad might sell well with one group but fail with the other.
- Efforts to avoid offending submarkets can result in overly simplistic ads that only substitute one stereotype for another.
- In directing attention to new trends, firms might lose sight of their fundamental strengths and successes. They might divert support and funds away from proven strategies and products that need not be altered in response to new developments.

Advertising is not an exact science. Its creative, emotion-oriented nature makes it difficult to analyze or judge. Thus, demographic changes offer advertisers some risky new opportunities to prove themselves.

Newspapers

Newspapers are the most common advertising medium. Every city and most smaller towns have their own newspapers, as do neighborhoods in most large cities. This allows advertisers to target their markets—at least geographically. A small department store can reach customers through the local newspaper. The corner record shop can advertise in weekly "shoppers"—free papers distributed in the neighborhood. Most retail advertising is placed in newspapers because they provide an effective and economical way of reaching many potential customers on a regular basis.

Magazines

Magazines are the most specialized mass medium. Among the approximately 9000 magazines published is one or more for almost every special interest. This variety makes it easy for advertisers to reach almost any market segment.

Consumer magazines are aimed at the general public. They include *Popular Photography, People, Newsweek, Good Housekeeping, Ebony, Smithsonian, Harper's,* and hundreds of others. Sellers of consumer goods and services commonly advertise in consumer magazines.

Trade magazines are published for the members of specific fields of work. Almost every occupation has its own trade magazine. *Advertising Age, Modern Medicine, Sales & Marketing Management, Computerworld,* and *Wisconsin Dairy Farmer* are all trade magazines. Advertisers buy space in trade magazines to promote specialized products and services used by people in specific fields: new drugs, accounting books, consulting services, tractors, and so forth.

Direct mail

Direct mail is one of the oldest and most common forms of advertising. In a direct-mail campaign, a seller mails advertisements directly to potential customers. This allows advertisers to carefully select their target audiences.

Some companies compile and sell categorized mailing lists. Advertisers can buy or rent lists of motorcycle owners, firms that use computer services, people who make more than $50,000, and many other general and highly specialized target markets.

Television

Television allows advertisers more creativity than any other mass medium. It comes as close to putting a personal salesperson in each viewer's home as technology permits. On television, advertisers can actively *demonstrate* a product, service, or idea. They can also use attention-getting gimmicks, humor, interesting story lines, strong personalities, and many other creative devices to sell their products.

Television is an excellent way to reach many potential buyers. About 98 percent of all U.S. households have at least one television set. A successful evening television show on a major network may reach 30 million homes and as many as 100 million viewers. Even news documentaries that appeal to more specialized audiences may reach 8 to 10 million viewers.

On television networks, advertisers can reach a national audience. On local stations, they can reach specific geographical market segments. The growth of cable television is increasing the alternatives for advertisers to reach smaller geographic areas and specialized target markets.

Radio

Radio is a unique mass medium because it offers no visual message. Since the eye absorbs information more efficiently than the ear, radio advertising is especially challenging.

Radio offers maximum geographical flexibility. There are 4600 AM and 3100 FM stations in the United States. Even communities without their own television stations and daily newspapers may have one or more radio stations. As a result, local advertisers can reach their audiences directly and efficiently.

In larger cities with many different radio stations, advertisers can achieve considerable demographic segmentation. For example, "Top 40" stations tend to attract teenagers, while "easy listening" stations have an older following. Still other stations have formats that tend to attract women, blacks, or speakers of foreign languages.

Other forms of advertising

Billboards are used to reach the motoring public and are often placed near the site of a buying decision. On the highway, billboards notify drivers of upcoming motels, restaurants, and gas stations. Or they might promote an idea, such as to quit smoking or to vote for a certain political candidate. Since traffic moves fairly rapidly, billboards can present only a small amount of information. Related forms of outdoor advertising are posters, neon signs, and sky writing.

Catalogs and directories can be very effective advertising tools. Catalogs enable customers to make purchases without leaving their homes or offices. Catalogs usually contain brief descriptions of products, along with pictures. But they are not well-suited for promoting products with which people may be unfamiliar. Sears began as a mail-order house and still uses catalogs today. Catalogs are expensive to print and mail. Large books like Sears' cost about $6 each. Sending out several million is a considerable expense.

The best-known directory is the Yellow Pages. Businesses must pay to be included in the listing. Many other directories cater to special interests, listing, for example, advertising agencies, universities and colleges, publishers of educational materials, and the like. Members of those industries are often asked to pay to be included in the directory or to have a larger display.

New media

Media options available for advertisers continue to evolve. This is most evident in the growth of new video formats. For many years, national television programming was limited to the three major networks, ABC, CBS, and NBC. The demand for limited advertising time on the networks helped keep TV advertising prices high.

Picture board from TV advertisement and print advertisement for the same product

MEMOREX

"GENRAD"

HIGH-BIAS AUDIO CASSETTE TAPE

1. MUSIC: (IN AND UNDER)

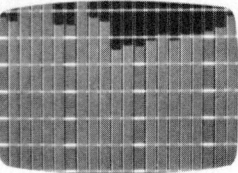
2. (Anncr VO): You are looking at live music.

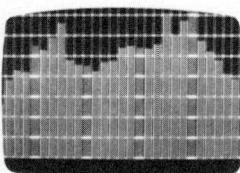
3. As seen through a computer.

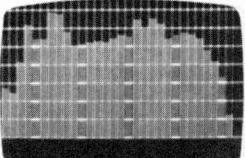
4. The computer can freeze an instant of the music.

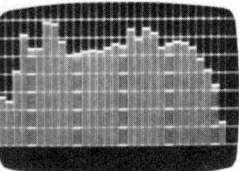
5. And mark it.

6. Now. . . MUSIC: (IN AND UNDER) (Anncr VO): . . .a Memorex High Bias II recording of the same music.

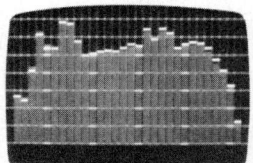
7. Compare Memorex to live.

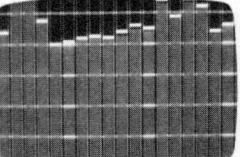
8. You will not hear truer reproduction on any high bias cassette. Not the first play. Not the one thousandth.

9. Not ever. Or we'll replace it. Free.

10. Is it live,. . .

11. or is it. . .

12. Memorex?

© 1983 Memtek Products

Presenting High Bias II and the Ultimate Tape Guarantee.
Memorex presents High Bias II, a tape so extraordinary, we're going to guarantee it <u>forever</u>.

We'll guarantee life-like sound.
Because Permapass,™ our unique oxide bonding process, locks each oxide particle—each musical detail—onto the tape. So music stays live. Not just the 1st play. Or the 1000th. But forever.

We'll guarantee the cassette.
Every facet of our cassette is engineered to protect the tape. Our waved-wafer improves tape-wind. Silicone-treated rollers insure smooth, precise tape alignment. Housing is made strong by a design unique to Memorex.

We'll guarantee them forever.
If you are ever dissatisfied with Memorex High Bias II, mail us the tape and we'll replace it free.

YOU'LL FOREVER WONDER, IS IT LIVE, OR IS IT MEMOREX®

© 1983 Memtek Products

Cable is now an alternative means of providing television programming to many homes. The various cable operators around the country use earth communications satellites. These circle the earth 22,300 miles above the equator. Programmers beam their shows up to a satellite, and cable operators receive the transmissions on dish-shaped antennae.

Most cable operators have 20, 30, 54, or more channels. So now there is room for many national television networks, and many have already started. They include Cable News Network, featuring all news; ESPN, specializing in sports; Black Entertainment Network, featuring programs of particular interest to black audiences; Galavision for Spanish speakers; and ABC's Alpha and Beta networks, showing programs oriented toward women or cultural interests, respectively. Bristol-Myers and Anheuser-Busch were among the first consumer goods' manufacturers to sign major advertising contracts with cable networks.

For advertisers cable TV means more outlets for sponsoring messages, greater geographical flexibility in choosing local markets, and great possibilities for reaching select special-interest audiences. For this last reason, television advertising may soon have some of the best advantages of special-interest magazines. Furthermore, advertisers will be able to afford products and services that were formerly uneconomical in the TV medium.

Videotex technology now enables text-like information to be sent to home TV sets from a computer. The user can tune to "pages" of information on a screen. Advertisers can sponsor such information. A beer company might have "pages" showing current sports scores. An airline can provide airline schedules or notices of flight conditions. Newspapers may provide classified advertising.

Video discs were introduced by Magnavox in 1978, using the first commercial video disc machine. This was followed in 1981 by the introduction of RCA's Selectavision video disc. Other companies have joined the market. In the beginning, the discs contained programs with movies that had already been box office hits. But some entrepreneurs see the possibility of marketers "sponsoring" discs. American Express might sponsor a disc about travel or restaurants. Then, much like today's magazines and newspapers, the discs could be sold for less than their full cost. In exchange for being exposed to an advertiser's message, the consumer gets a subsidized editorial product.

There have been several proposals to sell homeowners their own dish antennae to receive programming directly from satellites. This is *direct broadcast satellite*, or *DBS*. Advertisers may find this to be an attractive means for reaching audiences.

Summing up the media

As we saw in Chapter 6, any communication requires that a sender transmit a message over a conduit (or medium) to a recipient. This message must be interpreted and understood. The receiver may or may not respond to the message. If there is a response back to the sender, this is called "feedback." Without feedback there can be no assurance

The promotional mix may include grants to public television as well as normal, paid advertising.

"The following program is not made possible by a grant but by good old-fashioned advertising dollars."

From the *Wall Street Journal,* Permission—Cartoon Features Syndicate.

that communication has taken place, since the sender does not know if the transmitted message has been seen or heard.

In marketing terms, a firm may communicate by advertising on television, in magazines, newspapers, on radio, or some other medium. It may send out press releases to the media and hope they are used. A firm also may transmit its message through a sales force or in the form of labels on its products. How well the conduit works is not known unless there is some feedback. It may be in the form of increased sales, an order placed, suggestions of a more positive attitude toward that company, etc. Communication, therefore, is best viewed as a two-way process and is at the heart of contemporary marketing efforts.

"Noise" interferes with communication

Whether or not the intended message was received by the target audience depends in part on the amount of interference ("noise"). An advertisement shown on television is not generally seen or remembered by everyone watching that station at the moment the commercial was aired. Interfering with the message are other distractions. Some people go to the kitchen for a snack. Or perhaps the doorbell rang. We even seem to have developed a natural curtain which "filters out" messages we do not wish to receive. Other sources of noise are misunderstandings, lack of interest in the message, interference from the presence of other communications (like glancing at the newspaper while "watching" television), and similar other distractions.

A successful communicator must therefore anticipate these sources of interference and design messages and choose channels that overcome or offset them. A salesperson may therefore ask the customer questions to make sure the sales pitch is being understood. A newspaper ad may be composed with a bold headline. A television ad will start off with an entertaining line. All these are part of the attempt to make sure the potential receiver gets the message. But the effectiveness of the communicator is not known unless a means of feedback has been incorporated.

Many new media are developing that may prove useful for advertising purposes. They include cable TV, home computers, video discs, and direct broadcast satellites. The possibilities for advertising are limited only by advertisers' creativity.

Of course, there is no one best advertising medium. Advertisers must choose the media that can best reach the potential audience for their specific goods or services. As a result, most advertisers spend much effort on finding the best media mix for their products.

Publicity

Publicity is any form of unpaid message about a company or product presented through the media. Favorable publicity is a more effective sales tool than the same amount of paid advertising. Because publicity is not paid for and comes from neutral sources, people tend to be less skeptical about it.

For example, the attention a company receives for contributions to the community does more to enhance its image than could any amount of paid advertising. To foster such goodwill, many companies generously support the arts, educational institutions, and local and national charities.

Most companies actively seek out positive publicity and try to avoid negative publicity. Many have public relations departments or agents that issue press releases about company activities, including news about civic contributions, honors and awards, new products, and outstanding employees. If the company receives negative publicity, it will try to counteract it quickly by publicly offering to correct the situation or issuing denials.

Personal selling

Personal selling is the attempt to use personal contact to persuade a potential customer to make a purchase. Personal selling is usually done face to face. But it may also be done by telephone or personal letter.

Most companies highly value people with good sales skills. In addition to raising revenues, a salesperson represents the company to the outside world. If he or she treats a customer well, the customer tends to think well of the company.

There are many kinds of sales activities and potential customers. Salespeople are needed to sell to wholesalers, retailers, distributors, manufacturers, consumers, and industrial users. Often sales will not take place unless salespeople can service their customers' problems.

Figure 14.2 The selling process

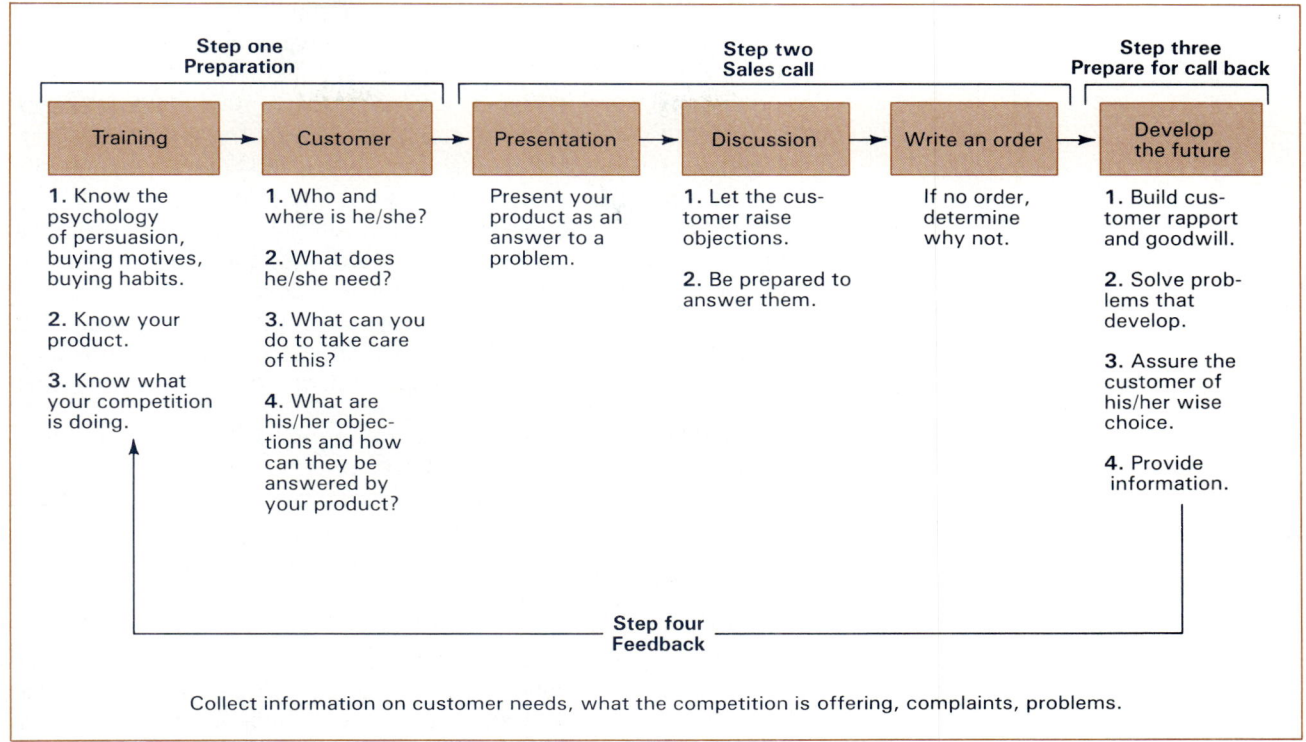

In addition, salespeople must be able to pass on useful information about new products and services, competitors' products, and new techniques of doing business. Some salespersons are given the sole job of building goodwill. They supplement the activities of middlemen or other salespersons who actually do the order-taking. A salesperson may do anything from simple across-the-counter retail selling to very complex industrial selling that involves long-term commitments and very expensive purchases.

The selling process

The selling process consists of four steps, as shown in Figure 14.2. First, a salesperson must carefully prepare a sales presentation. Preparation includes learning how to sell as well as understanding buying motives and habits and how to sell to a particular customer. By the time of a sales call, a salesperson should know the customer and his or her problems.

Most sales calls follow a fairly standard pattern. The salesperson presents the product and tries to persuade the customer to buy it. Listening and responding intelligently to customers' objections is a very important part of this step. The more a salesperson can tell prospects about their problems and how to solve them, the greater their interest.

Whether or not a sale is made, a salesperson should try to maintain the goodwill of every potential customer. Often this means staying in touch, providing additional information and service, and similar ongoing activities.

Selling to consumers, either door to door or in a retail store, presents similar problems. All sales personnel must know what they are selling. If it is clothes, they should know fabrics, styles, and color combinations. If it is stereo equipment, they must know the terminology, manufacturers, and features of various components. Although retail salespersons cannot prepare for each customer in advance, they can anticipate certain kinds of questions and have answers ready. If possible, they should try to find out about the customers with whom they will be dealing. Are they generally well informed about the products or services? Are they poor or wealthy? Is price usually important or do service, style, and performance matter more?

Advantages of personal selling

Most promotional activities are impersonal. The seller doesn't see or know exactly who has been contacted, and follow-up is difficult. Personal selling is very different. It allows the seller to accomplish the following:

1. Seek out and pinpoint good prospects. Sales personnel can go directly to the people who are most likely to buy. These may be regular customers or new prospects. For example, insurance salespeople know that newly married couples are often willing to consider buying life insurance. To make sales, they may get a list of people who have recently applied for marriage licenses and begin calling them. Companies often run advertisements offering information about a product or service to people who call or send in a coupon. A salesperson then follows up, knowing that the people who have expressed interest are more likely to buy than people who have not.

2. Tailor the presentation to the prospect and answer objections. Advertisements must reach many individuals. But a salesperson can try to anticipate the needs of a specific customer. If a couple with three small children walks into a furniture store and asks to see couches, the alert salesperson will emphasize features like durability, easy care, and simple cleaning. When a prospect raises questions, the salesperson can answer them. If a copy machine salesperson from IBM calls on an office manager using a Xerox machine, the office manager may ask, "Why should I change? I'm happy with my present copier." The salesperson can anticipate this question and present some strong arguments.

3. Demonstrate the product. A personal demonstration of a product can be very convincing. A stereo salesperson can show how one speaker has a deeper bass sound than another. A car salesperson can take a prospect for a test drive. An IBM representative can compare actual IBM copies with Xerox copies. When prospects can participate in a demonstration or experience its results firsthand, they can convince themselves of the product's desirability.

4. Develop a social relationship with customers. It is usually more difficult to say "no" to a friend than to a stranger. Salespeople who have regular customers may develop social relationships with them through lunches, repeated conversations, or helping to solve a problem. A good salesperson in a retail store can make sales more likely by showing personal interest in customers.

5. Close the sale. After making a sales presentation, a salesperson can give the final encouragement that helps a prospect decide to buy. Similarly, a personal call might encourage a purchase from someone who has seen a product advertised on television or by direct mail.

6. Obtain feedback. In many ways, a sales force acts as a marketing research department. As they work, salespeople learn what qualities customers seek in a product, what they like about the competition's goods, what their plans are for future purchases. Such information can help marketing managers in their product planning.

Sales promotion techniques

Sales promotion is any technique other than publicity and personal selling that is used to persuade people to buy a good or service. Sales promotion techniques usually support advertising and personal selling. Among the most common are the use of samples, cents-off coupons, trading stamps, premiums, contests, and giveaways. A popular form of sales promotion is to offer consumers a partial or full refund on their purchase of a product. Often users must collect several labels from the product in order to claim a cash refund or a coupon good on the next purchase.

Sales promotion techniques can be directed to both consumers and retailers. When promoting to retailers, the manufacturer hopes to motivate salespeople. A manufacturer may hold contests that offer retailers additional products, prizes, or cash for selling certain amounts of a product.

Sales promotions can also take place at the point of purchase. In such cases, manufacturers or retailers set up special store displays, racks, streamers, posters, and banners. In-store activities may be coordinated with direct-mail campaigns and/or newspaper, magazine, radio, or television advertisements.

In markets or industries where competition is strong, the use of sales promotion techniques to supplement advertising and personal selling increases. Several years ago, coffee prices rose rapidly due to crop failures in Brazil. In an attempt to counteract consumer resistance to high prices, coffee producers offered coupons and cents-off deals to maintain their sales.

14 Promotional decisions

Summary

Promotion is an organization's communication about itself to potential users of its goods and services. The *promotional mix* is made up of advertising, personal selling, publicity, and sales promotion.

Advertising is any form of paid message presented through the media by an identifiable sponsor. The five most common advertising media are newspapers, television, direct mail, radio, and magazines. About $61 billion was spent on advertising in 1981.

An advertising campaign should be based on a specific objective. Some common advertising objectives are to achieve *brand recognition* (consumer awareness of a specific brand name), to gain a trial purchase, to reach the buyer at a likely time, to add value to a product or service, to build distribution, and to aid in personal selling.

Most large-scale advertisers use more than one medium to reach their target markets. The most effective media mix depends on the nature of the product or service and its potential customers. The *print media* are newspapers, magazines, and direct mail; the *electronic media* are television and radio. Print media are controlled by their readers. Printed messages can be used at the reader's own pace, studied, and saved. Broadcast messages are instantaneous and cannot be saved. They are controlled by the advertiser and must be frequently repeated to achieve results.

Newspapers are used primarily by retailers in local communities to advertise branded merchandise available at their stores. Magazines are used more often by national advertisers. Direct mail is expensive but efficient in that it can reach a carefully selected audience. Television can reach large numbers of people at one time and is best for products that have a broad market. Radio offers great geographical and demographic flexibility, but it is the only medium that does not present a visual image. Outdoor advertising is limited to only the briefest messages. New media, such as cable TV, videotex, video discs, and direct broadcast satellites, will open up new opportunities for advertisers.

Publicity is any form of unpaid message about a company or product presented through the media. Favorable publicity is a more effective sales tool than the same amount of paid advertising because people are more likely to believe information from a neutral source.

Personal selling is the attempt to use personal contact to persuade a potential customer to make a purchase. It enables sellers to seek out and pinpoint prospective customers and tailor presentations to their specific needs. By meeting face to face with a customer, a salesperson can answer questions, demonstrate the product, and help close the sale.

Sales promotion is any technique other than advertising, publicity, and personal selling that is used to persuade people to buy a good or service. Among the most common sales promotion techniques are cents-off coupons, trading stamps, refunds, contests, and giveaways.

Review questions

1. What are the four elements of the promotional mix? Why does a company use promotion?
2. List and briefly explain the six specific objectives of promotion as described in this chapter.
3. Why can advertising be very expensive?
4. What is the main goal governing the choice of advertising media?
5. What are the two basic categories of advertising media? Name the advantages and disadvantages of each category.
6. What are the five most popular advertising media? Name several unique features of each medium.
7. What is the difference between advertising and publicity? Which one are people most likely to believe? Why?
8. What are the four steps in the personal selling process? What must a salesperson do at each step?
9. What are six advantages of personal selling?
10. What are five common sales promotion techniques?

Discussion questions

1. Some people say that advertising is wasteful and makes us purchase things we do not need or want. Do you agree? Why?
2. In trying to make a product distinctive, how far can, or should, an advertiser go?
3. Which media would probably be most effective for advertising each of the following goods and services? Why?
   a. a new educational toy for four- to six-year-olds
   b. heavy-duty shock absorbers
   c. low-calorie pickles
   d. career counseling
   e. a college play
   f. used die-casting machines
4. If you were the public affairs director for a large oil company, how would you use publicity to build a favorable image for your company?
5. Why is sales a good entry-level job in many companies? Why do so many companies consider sales experience an important qualification for top managers?

Chapter 14 case

The Green Grass Seed Company

Advertising a new product is different from advertising a well-known one. This case examines the problem of introducing something new to the marketplace.

In 1982, researchers at the Green Grass Seed Company presented Francis Mower, the marketing director, with the results of their latest efforts. It was a new form of grass that grew to a height of one inch and then stopped growing.

"Wonderful," proclaimed Mower. "This product is revolutionary. Every suburban homeowner is going to want this stuff. Think of all the afternoons that can be spent at the pool or watching baseball instead of cutting the lawn."

"Not so fast," warned the vice-president of manufacturing. "This is going to cost us more to produce than regular grass seed. It will have to sell for about twice the price of the other stuff."

"That's an important consideration," noted Mower, his enthusiasm only slightly dampened. "What we have to do now is come up with an advertising strategy that takes full advantage of the special characteristics of this product."

Mower appointed a task force to develop an advertising plan. They were given the following questions. If you were part of the task force, how would you answer them?

1. What makes this one-inch grass seed different from other grass seeds?
2. Besides the suburban homeowner, how many other markets exist for this product?
3. Which market would be most willing to pay extra for grass seed like this?
4. What would make a good advertising theme or slogan?
5. Which media would be most appropriate for advertisements?
6. What promotional techniques besides advertising could be used to focus attention on this revolutionary grass seed?

Business in perspective

Hello, Operator?
Send me a refrigerator

New technology may have a profound effect on the basic assumptions of marketing. High gasoline costs make consumers less willing to drive around shopping. As more wives join the work force, their cooking, cleaning, and shopping patterns change.

Spotting these trends, Federated Department Stores, one of the country's largest retailers, has teamed up with Comp-U-Card of America, Inc., a new marketing service. Comp-U-Card believes that its electronic shop-at-home service is the wave of the future. Federated, which owns Filene's and Bloomingdale's on the East Coast, Lazarus Stores in the Midwest, Bullock's in Southern California, and other traditional department stores, wants to be in the forefront of new technology.

Initially, Comp-U-Card offered its subscribers a simple service. The company had a computer that stores the price and delivery cost of about 30,000 items. Subscribers who called an operator on a toll-free number could get a price quotation for any of those items. If they liked the price, they could order the merchandise on the spot.

That service was useful, but not exactly revolutionary. Next, Comp-U-Card made its merchandise lists directly available to consumers who had personal computers. Subscribers could use their home computers to call the Comp-U-Card computer and browse through its product listings without calling the human operator.

The Comp-U-Card service is unique because it provides the ultimate in time and place utility. But it remains to be seen if subscribers will be satisfied by the delay in possession utility. How quickly can a product be delivered once it is ordered? And will consumers be willing to buy products without first seeing, touching, and trying them?

Federated Department Stores, a traditional retailer, is taking no chances and is experimenting with this investment. Comp-U-Card thinks it knows the answer and is betting its survival on it.

Chapter 15 — Channels of distribution

Key terms

channels of distribution
middleman
retailer
buying cooperative
broker
wholesaler
common carrier
contract carrier
private carrier
containerization

Chapter objectives

In Chapter 15, you will learn:

The participants in the distribution process

The channels of distribution available to manufacturers of consumer and industrial goods

How wholesalers serve both manufacturers and retailers

The role of retailers in the distribution process

How retailing has changed in response to changing life-styles

The role of transportation in the marketing process

The pros and cons of the five basic means of freight transportation

How containerization simplifies the transportation of goods

Overview

Channels of distribution are the paths goods and services follow from manufacturer to final buyer. There are two aspects to distribution. One is the middlemen who help goods move from manufacturers to consumers. The other is the means by which goods are transported from one location to another.

This chapter explores the channels of distribution available to manufacturers. In many cases, a product can follow more than one path to the ultimate user. We will look at how manufacturers choose their distribution patterns and the strengths and weaknesses of various forms of transportation.

Participants in the channels of distribution

Consumer goods and industrial goods follow somewhat similar channels of distribution, as shown in Figures 15.1 and 15.2. **A middleman is any person or firm that enters the distribution process between the manufacturer and the ultimate buyer.** Wholesalers, jobbers, distributors, and retailers are all middlemen.

Channels for consumer goods

As shown in Figure 15.1, consumer goods may follow several different paths from manufacturer to final buyer. The fewer the intermediaries, the shorter the marketing channel.

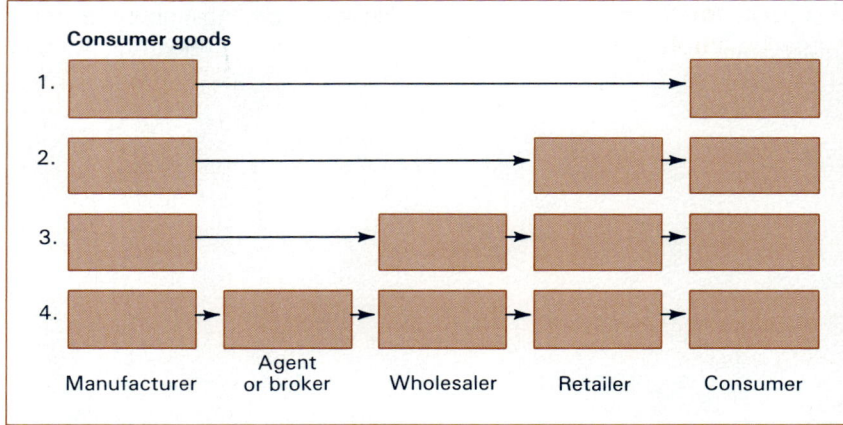

Figure 15.1 Channel alternatives in the marketing of consumer products

Chapter 15 Channels of distribution

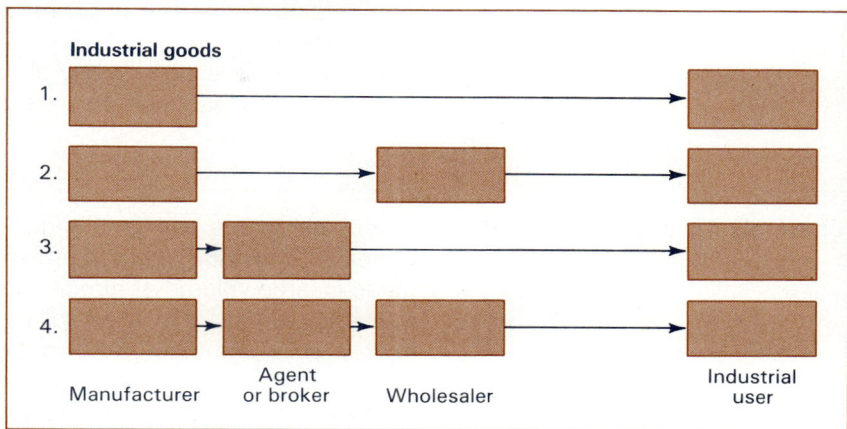

Figure 15.2 Channel alternatives in the marketing of industrial products

Directly from manufacturer to consumer

A manufacturer that sells its products through door-to-door sales or catalogs sells directly to the consumer. This is the least complicated distribution system. Fuller Brush and Avon distribute their products directly to consumers through door-to-door sales. Some encyclopedia publishers, such as World Book, also use this system. Other book publishers sell some or all of their books through direct mail, like the Time-Life Books' series on nature and photography.

One advantage of this system is that it gives the manufacturer great control over distribution. It may also increase profits because the company avoids giving discounts to middlemen. Consumers may find this method more convenient and less expensive than dealing through other channels.

Through retailers without wholesalers

A more common channel runs from manufacturer to retailer to consumer. Most consumer goods are bought in retail stores. **A retailer sells goods to buyers for their personal use rather than for resale.** Most large retailers, such as department stores and supermarkets, purchase their goods directly from the manufacturer. Auto dealers and franchises also operate this way. They can do this efficiently because they purchase in large quantities.

Through retailers using wholesalers

The most common distribution channel runs from manufacturer to wholesaler to retailer to consumer. This is the longest channel and requires the most markups. But it is often the most efficient, especially for dealing with small retailers.

Cooperatives

Some retailers band together into buying cooperatives. **A buying cooperative is a group of independent and competing store owners who form a wholesaling company that serves as their exclusive supplier.** This system gives small retailers the benefits of large-scale buying. In some cases, they all use the same name for their retailing operations so that benefits can extend to advertising and image building.

Channels for industrial goods

Industrial goods are usually distributed directly from manufacturer to user. This channel is most efficient because industrial goods are often sold in large volume or at high prices. When a firm buys a computer for several hundred thousand dollars from Control Data Corporation or an automobile manufacturer purchases tens of thousands of tires from B. F. Goodrich, the services of a middleman are unnecessary.

When this direct channel is not practical, distributors are used. They work in much the same way as wholesalers of consumer goods.

Multiple and modified channels

A manufacturer may use more than one channel of distribution at once. For example, a book publisher such as Random House or Holt, Rinehart and Winston may sell some of its potential best sellers directly to bookshop owners through its sales force. The publisher will also sell books to wholesalers who may resupply bookstores when their stocks of certain books run low. The publisher may also sell by direct mail to individuals.

Brokers

In some industries, such as food products, brokers are part of the distribution system. **A broker brings buyers and sellers together but does not actually take ownership of the goods.**

A retailer looking for a supplier may contact a broker who specializes in the desired product. The broker will then connect the retailer to an appropriate manufacturer. If the retailer and manufacturer can make a deal, the broker earns a commission.

In general, a manufacturer will use the channels of distribution that are least expensive and most efficient for getting its goods to potential customers.

The role of wholesalers

There are about 400,000 wholesaling establishments in the United States. **A wholesaler (or jobber or distributor) sells products to others for resale or for use in making other products.** The price the wholesaler charges is not part of the definition. Wholesalers perform a service for both manufacturers and retailers.

Wholesalers can provide a valuable service to their customers by supplying a range of goods from different manufacturers.

"Better let me have another gross of the #101 thunderbird ashtrays, two gross of #473 beaded souvenir moccasins, and two dozen #87 turquoise and silver runner pins."

Reprinted by permission from *Sales & Marketing Management* magazine. Copyright © 1977.

Services performed for manufacturers

Wholesalers perform five services for manufacturers: selling, market coverage, retailer contact, storage, and cost cutting.

Wholesalers sell manufacturers' products. For example, a pharmaceutical distributor has its own sales force to call on retail drugstores. This sales force takes orders, informs retailers of new products, and explains the benefits of carrying particular brands. Thus, the wholesalers actually sell the manufacturers' goods for them.

Wholesalers have direct contact with many different retailers. Thus, wholesalers personally reach more retail outlets than all but the largest manufacturers have the resources to reach themselves.

For example, there are about 80,000 places that sell sporting goods in the United States. It would be very difficult for every supplier of tennis balls or golf clubs to keep in touch with all those outlets. In some other trades, it is even worse: 94,000 places sell hardware, 195,000 sell automobile supplies, 271,000 sell groceries.[1] Wholesalers, being local

[1] U.S. Bureau of Census, *U.S. Census of Retail Trade, 1977.* Merchandise Line Sales, RC 77-L.

operations, can keep up with the retailers in their own area and provide the contact with them that manufacturers could not.

Wholesalers store goods for manufacturers. This reduces the amount of goods a producer must keep in stock, thus reducing warehousing costs. Goods that are not selling well do not clutter the manufacturer's plant.

Wholesalers save manufacturers money. Providing coverage and contact, selling, and warehousing are only four cost-saving functions that wholesalers perform. If there were no wholesalers, manufacturers would have to build larger sales forces and more store space. In addition, a manufacturer can ship a large order to jobbers rather than thousands of small orders to individual retail customers. This lowers the manufacturer's packing, shipping, and billing costs.

Services performed for retailers

Wholesalers also save retailers time, money, and effort.

Wholesalers can supply retailers with goods from many manufacturers. A retail drugstore must stock many different brands of many different items, each of which may come from a different manufacturer. Instead of dealing with each manufacturer individually, a retailer can rely on one or two wholesalers that carry all the brands needed. It is far more convenient and economical for the retailer to place one or two orders instead of the dozens that would be required if each supplier were contacted separately.

Wholesalers usually supply trade credit to their customers. They ship orders but do not require payment until 30 or more days later. Thus, retailers have free use of the merchandise for a period of time and may actually be able to sell it before they have to pay for it. Trade credit is like an interest-free loan.

Wholesalers can rapidly resupply retailers with stock. Most wholesalers operate on the local level. They are also prepared to handle small orders, which many manufacturers are not. As a result, they can rapidly deliver goods to retailers. This minimizes the amount of capital that a retailer must keep tied up in inventory and reduces the chance of lost sales due to out-of-stock merchandise.

The Ingram Book Company in Nashville, Tennessee, is a major book distributor. Ingram provides all its bookstore customers with a weekly computer printout of all the books it has in stock. Then, if a customer wants to special-order a book, the retail bookseller can learn immediately if Ingram has it. Or if a book suddenly becomes a best-seller, the retailer can quickly find out if additional supplies are close at hand. Both of these procedures would be difficult if the retailer had to call each publisher about each book. Moreover, Ingram can fill orders within three or four days—and sometimes overnight—even when orders include books from dozens of different publishers.

Figure 15.3 Manufacturers to retailers

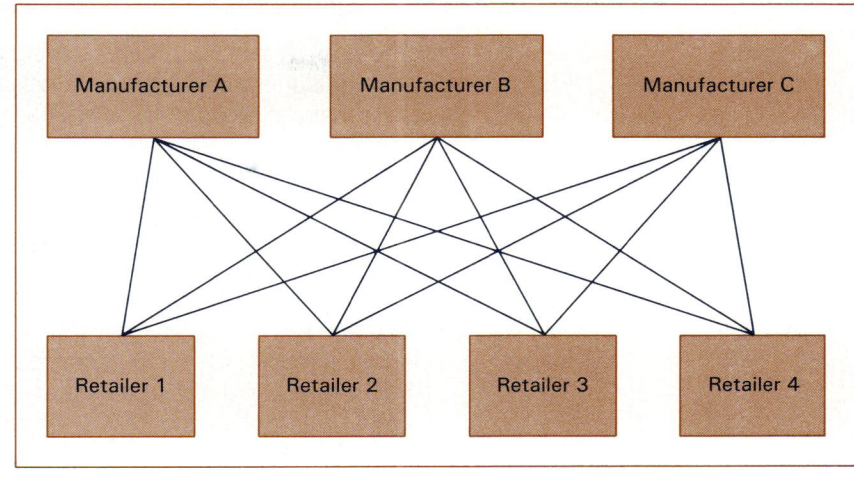

Figures 15.3 and 15.4 show how wholesalers simplify distribution channels for all parties. They act as "central switchboards," reducing the number of contacts among the retailers and manufacturers in a channel.

Adding a wholesaler to the channel of distribution means that an additional party must add to the markup of an item when it is sold to the customer. But simply eliminating the wholesaler will not necessarily result in savings that can be passed on to consumers. Someone—either the manufacturer or the retailer—will have to absorb the added costs of selling, shipping smaller orders, warehousing, and similar activities.

Part of these costs would be borne by the manufacturer, who must then raise the prices charged the retailer. But the retailer would also have higher expenses. All these expenses would eventually be reflected in the prices charged to consumers. As a result, in most industries, wholesalers are an integral part of the distribution network.

Figure 15.4 Manufacturer to wholesaler to retailers

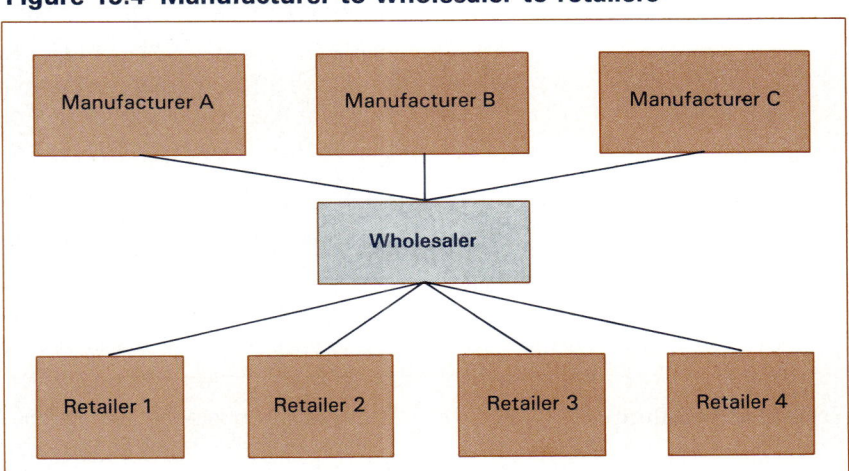

The role of retailers

There are almost 2 million retailing businesses in the United States. The retailer is the middleman who sells to the ultimate consumer. Americans spend about two-thirds of the money they have left after taxes in retail outlets.

The retailer's primary role is to provide consumers with the products they want when and where they want them. That is why there are so many retail stores and why retail competition is often so intense. Buyers want to take possession of a product at the time they buy it—or soon after. So a retailer who too frequently runs out of stock of popular items or sizes will quickly lose customers.

For some kinds of businesses, keeping a full range of goods has become more difficult in recent years. Men's clothing is one such example. Until the mid-1960s, most men's dress shirts were white. A store had to carry only one or two brands and collar styles in several different neck sizes and sleeve lengths. Today, men wear dress shirts in many different colors and styles. Stocking thirty different shirt styles in fifteen different sizes can cause serious inventory problems. But that is what consumers expect when they walk into a men's store, so that is what most stores must provide.

The retailer is the party that actually sells the consumer goods manufacturers make. Manufacturers may advertise or otherwise promote their products. But the goods must be present in retail stores, customers must be aware that the goods are there, and the retailer must have a pricing policy that encourages their sale.

Kinds and sizes of retail operations

Department stores carry a wide variety of products. Among the largest national department store chains are Sears, K mart, J.C. Penney, and Montgomery Ward. Locally based department store chains include Macy's, Gimbel's, Broadway, May Co., Marshall Field's, Wanamaker's, and Rich's.

Another kind of retail store is the specialty shop. These shops specialize in selling a particular line of goods, such as appliances, clothing, shoes, records, books, or cameras. There are also chains of specialty stores at the local, regional, and national levels. National specialty stores include The Gap, which sells jeans and accessories; B. Dalton, a chain of bookstores; and, of course, such fast-food operations as McDonald's, Pizza Hut, and Kentucky Fried Chicken.

Supermarket chains are among the largest retailers. Safeway and Kroger are the largest.

Table 15.1 identifies the 15 largest retailers in the United States.

Trends in retailing

The retailing business has undergone significant changes since the end of World War II. Many innovations have resulted.

Table 15.1 The 15 largest retailing companies, 1981 (by sales)

Rank	Company	Sales ($ in thousands)
1	Sears (Chicago)	$27,357,400
2	Safeway Stores (Oakland, Calif.)	16,580,318
3	K mart (Troy, Mich.)	16,527,012
4	J.C. Penney (New York)	11,860,169
5	Kroger (Cincinnati)	11,266,520
6	F.W. Woolworth (New York)	7,223,241
7	Lucky Stores (Dublin, Calif.)	7,201,404
8	American Stores (Salt Lake City)	7,096,590
9	Federated Department Stores (Cincinnati)	7,067,673
10	Great Atlantic & Pacific Tea (Montvale, N.J.)	6,989,529
11	Winn-Dixie Stores (Jacksonville, Fla.)	6,200,167
12	Montgomery Ward (Chicago)	5,742,491
13	Southland (Dallas)	5,693,636
14	Jewel Companies (Chicago)	5,107,614
15	Household Merchandising (Des Plaines, Ill.)	5,079,932

FORTUNE, July 12, 1982, p. 140. Reprinted from FORTUNE Magazine by permission; © Time Inc. All rights reserved.

Discounters Discount houses offer lower prices and fewer services than traditional retailers. They began by selling branded merchandise at discounts from list prices. For example, a General Electric radio that all retailers had previously sold for the same price was widely advertised by discounters at prices 20 percent lower (or more). Soon the discounters added clothing and other soft goods, sometimes under their own labels at prices lower than brand names. Specialty stores that sold toys, jewelry, or other products also began discounting their goods.

At first, traditional retailers looked on discount stores with contempt. The discounters offered little sales help to their customers and were often housed in large, brightly lit buildings with few of the services and amenities of retailers. They depended on low markups and overhead, with high turnover of goods. Today, discount stores are widely accepted members of the retail community. They are often hard to tell apart from the old-line, list-price stores.

Self-service Discounters were able to offer lower prices in part because they offered less service. Instead of salespeople to answer shoppers' questions, there were only a few clerks whose main job was to keep stock on the shelves. But the concept of self-service has spread to all areas of the retail sector because the use of fewer salespeople helps to keep down sales costs for everyone. The ultimate in self-service is the supermarket, which replaced the local grocery as the source for most food purchases.

A wider range of products The 1960s and 1970s saw unprecedented growth in the volume and kinds of goods and services. Thousands of new products, such as microwave ovens, electric carving knives, pocket calculators, home video recording machines, instant cameras, and ten-speed bicycles, were developed to satisfy the needs and wants of an increasingly affluent population. All have added to the variety of specialty stores and the diversity in department stores.

Credit sales Most consumers can now obtain credit. In the past, local shopkeepers sometimes offered charge accounts to regular customers and department stores provided some credit. But computerization has made it possible for firms to offer credit on a national—and even international—scale through such credit cards as Visa and MasterCard. Today, a tourist from Chicago can walk into almost any shop or restaurant in Philadelphia and pay for a purchase, no questions asked, with a credit card. This has encouraged sales with little risk to the retailer.

Computer controls Now, even small retailers can take advantage of computer-based programs to keep track of inventory, record sales, and figure profit margins. At first, only department stores and chains could afford computers. But by the 1970s, smaller and less expensive computers and computer-service companies made tighter internal controls possible for all retailers.

Shopping centers and malls As more people bought automobiles and moved to the suburbs, shopping centers and then completely enclosed malls arose. They drew business away from the older downtown shopping areas of towns and cities. One or two major department stores and several national chain stores often occupy large portions of a mall. Then specialty stores fill up the rest of the space.

Recently, similar shopping complexes have been built to revitalize downtown areas of large cities. Among the most successful are Ghirardelli Square in San Francisco, The Gallery in Philadelphia, Harborplace in Baltimore, Water Tower Place in Chicago, and Quincy Market in Boston.

Transportation and physical distribution

Transportation plays an important role in the marketing process. In the last century, railroads, interstate trucking, airlines, and pipelines have increasingly widened the market for goods. They have made it possible to sell freshly cut flowers in the northern states in the middle of the winter. Some restaurants in Chicago have fresh fish—not frozen—flown in from halfway around the world. This pattern is repeated throughout the country.

Improved transportation has also enhanced specialization. When it can sell its goods over a wider territory, a firm can grow large even if it manufactures only a few products. Without good transportation, the territory that a firm could serve effectively would be much smaller.

Finally, rapid lines of supply have made it possible for all members of a distribution channel to reduce inventories. Goods can be shipped much more quickly, so a wholesaler or retailer can quickly replace stock when it starts to run low.

Transportation companies

The product, the distance, the speed, and the cost determine the best transportation for a given situation. In general, the faster the service is, the more expensive it will be. Transportation companies fall into three categories.

Common carriers

United Parcel Service delivers small shipments at low cost

Courtesy United Parcel Service

A common carrier offers transportation services to the general public and has stated rates based on item, distance, and weight. These rates must be the same for all customers. United Parcel Service, North American Van Lines, Delta Airlines, and Conrail are all common carriers.

Common-carrier trucks and railroads are regulated by the Interstate Commerce Commission and airlines for many years were regulated by the Civil Aeronautics Board. Carriers that do not cross state lines are regulated by their state's public utility commission.

In the past few years, government progress toward deregulation has removed many of the rules that limited competition among common carriers.

Contract carriers

A contract carrier sells transportation services to individuals or firms on a per job or time basis. A contract carrier works exclusively for a particular client under a contract. It might be a one-time hauling arrangement or a long-term relationship. Many over-the-road truckers, for example, are independent contractors who will haul a client's trailer to a destination for an agreed-upon fee. Chartered jets are also contract carriers.

Table 15.2 The 15 largest transportation companies (by operating revenues)

Rank	Company	Operating revenues ($ in thousands)
1	CSX (Richmond, Va.)	$5,432,200
2	Trans World (New York)	5,265,468
3	UAL (Elk Grove Village, Ill.)	5,141,174
4	Burlington Northern (Seattle)	4,935,823
5	United Parcel Service (Greenwich, Conn.)	4,748,294
6	American Airlines (Dallas-Forth Worth)	4,108,699
7	Pan American World Airways (New York)	3,797,291
8	Eastern Air Lines (Miami)	3,727,093
9	Delta Air Lines (Atlanta)	3,533,326
10	Santa Fe Industries (Chicago)	3,366,900
11	Southern Pacific (San Francisco)	3,272,378
12	Missouri Pacific (St. Louis)	2,523,770
13	Northwest Airlines (St. Paul)	1,854,290
14	Norfolk & Western Railway (Roanoke, Va.)	1,801,655
15	Southern Railway (Washington, D.C.)	1,790,669

FORTUNE, July 12, 1982, p. 142. Reprinted from FORTUNE Magazine by permission; © Time Inc. All rights reserved.

Private carriers

A private carrier transports its own goods in its own vehicles. Many firms have their own trucking fleets, delivery vans, or corporate jets. Some mining operations even have their own private railroads. If you own your own automobile, you too are a private carrier.

A business may use all three kinds of carriers. A department store might depend on common and contract carriers to supply it with merchandise and use its own vans for local deliveries. Deliveries out of its immediate territory might be sent by United Parcel Service, a common carrier. Table 15.2 lists the 15 largest transportation companies in the United States. All are common carriers.

Figure 15.5 Percentage of domestic intercity freight by type of transport, 1943–1979

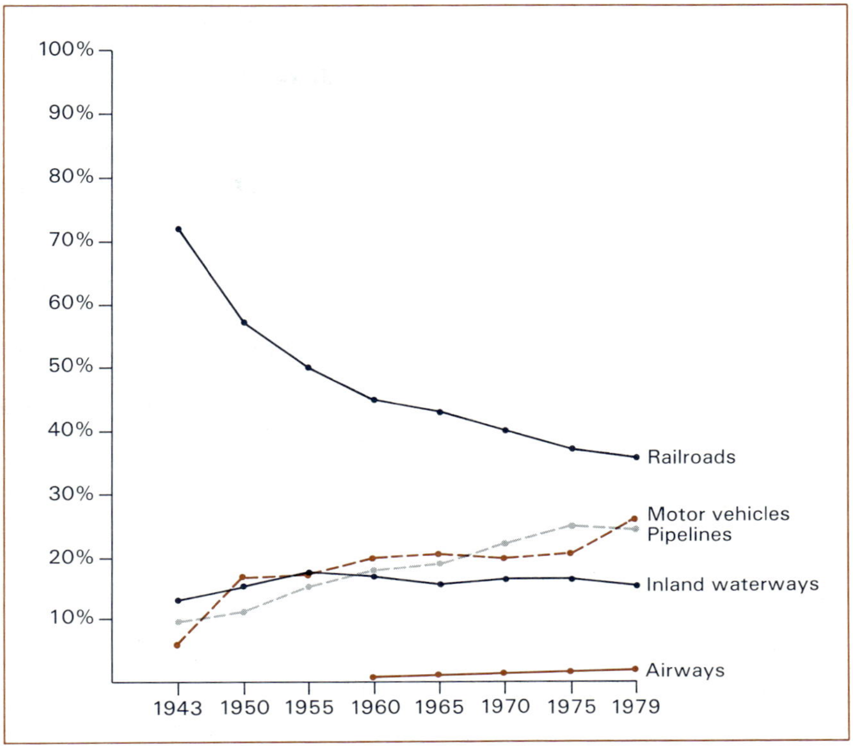

U.S. Interstate Commerce Commission, *Annual Report; Intercity Ton-Miles, 1939–1959; Transport Economics,* quarterly; and *Statistical Abstract of the United States 1981,* table 1063, p. 613.

Forms of freight transportation

A shipper may choose among five basic forms of transportation.

Railroads

More intercity freight is moved by rail than by any other means of transportation. As shown in Figure 15.5, however, in terms of all freight shipped, the proportion sent by rail slipped from more than 70 percent in 1943 to about 36 percent in 1979.

Railroads are the most efficient way to ship bulk goods over long distances. Large loads of a boxcar or more have a relatively low cost per ton. In addition, unlike trucks, ships, or planes, trains are easily expandable. Cars can be added as needed without having to call in added crews or engines. Finally, trains run on relatively regular and reliable schedules. They are unaffected by most traffic and weather conditions.

On the other hand, the greatest disadvantage of railroads is their inability to go directly to all destinations. Trains can run only where there are rails, so any shipper or customer not on a rail line will find trains less convenient. Rail transport is also relatively expensive for shipping quantities of less than a full boxcar.

Trucks

The major advantage of trucks is their flexibility. As a result, trucks account for about 25 percent of all intercity tonnage, as shown in Figure 15.5. Trucks can go anywhere there are roads, which means almost anywhere in the industrialized world. There are more than 3 million miles of paved roads in the United States alone.

In addition, trucks have been constructed to carry a wide range of special cargoes. Trucks come in various body styles: tanker, refrigerator, auto hauler, flatbed, cement, furniture, and many others.

Finally, trucks are particularly handy for intracity deliveries by retailers. Vans, stake trucks, and pickup trucks are used to deliver everything from groceries to furniture.

Trucks do have several drawbacks, however. The load of a truck is limited by its trailer size. Once a truck and trailer are full, further freight must go into a separate unit. And each new rig requires a driver, gas, oil, and maintenance. Trucks are also subject to delays. Bad weather, highway accidents, and traffic jams can all slow delivery of truck-borne goods.

Ships and barges

Waterways are one of the oldest means of transportation. Barges and ships traveled along canals, rivers, lakes, and oceans long before there were highways and railroads.

Ships are considerably less expensive than other means of transportation because they can carry large loads while utilizing relatively little energy. At the same time, in most cases, there is no right-of-way to be built and maintained. Unlike roads and railroad tracks, which must be constructed and repaired, oceans and rivers require no such investment.

Of course, ships can operate only where there are waterways. Therefore, many parts of the country do not have access to this alternative. Furthermore, ships are a relatively slow means of transportation and thus cannot be used when speed is crucial, as in shipping perishable products.

Pipelines

Pipelines are used to distribute some of our most basic necessities, such as oil, gas, and water. Because pipelines are virtually unaffected by weather and other outside conditions, it is a highly efficient transportation medium for certain kinds of products.

The usefulness of pipelines is limited because they can transport only liquids and gases. Furthermore, construction of a pipeline is extremely expensive. For example, the approximately 400-mile-long Alaskan crude-oil pipeline completed in 1976 cost $9 billion to construct. As a result, pipelines are built for the use of many shippers and are regulated as common carriers.

Containers on trucking rig

Courtesy of CAST North American, Ltd.

Airlines

Airlines carry only a small fraction of all freight shipped, but they are still an important alternative in the distribution process. Because of the great speed of air transportation, crucial parts and supplies can be quickly sent across great distances. The availability of jet transport can lower the inventory requirements for some businesses, such as dealers of fine gems. Services such as Federal Express and Emery Air Freight have created a booming market for overnight door-to-door delivery of messages and products.

The primary disadvantage of air freight is that it costs considerably more per pound than other methods of transportation. In addition, planes can only travel between airports. Motor vehicles must be used to get goods to and from the terminal. Thus, only high-priced or lightweight goods are regularly shipped by air. From 1960 to 1979, air freight tonnage increased by almost 500 percent.

Containerization: the systems approach to transportation

The handling of cargo is one of the most expensive parts of the shipping process. The loading and unloading of the goods, until they reach their final destination, is extremely inefficient and costly.

Manufacturers and transportation companies, therefore, have tried to find ways to reduce the handling. **Containerization is a systems approach to distribution that uses containers to package freight in order to minimize handling and repackaging as goods are moved from one form of transportation to another.** A container looks like a large truck trailer without wheels. Once packed and sealed, the container can be moved from truck to ship to train to truck without repacking the contents. The results are lower manpower costs, less delay, and greatly reduced breakage and theft.

The real cost of containerization

Containerization revolutionized the world's shipping industry. But it has also seriously threatened the future of longshoremen whose livelihoods have depended on repacking shipping cargoes.

Before the use of containers, productivity on the docks averaged one ton per man-hour. With containers, productivity can increase to 200 to 300 tons per man-hour. And loading and unloading times can be reduced from five days to as little as one day.

Containerization's benefits for both manufacturers and consumers are undisputed. But the practice is not without problems. To persuade the longshoremen's union to switch to containers, the shipping industry agreed to pay displaced longshoremen a guaranteed annual income. To fulfill this commitment, shippers added a charge on most cargoes in the Port of New York. This has increased the costs of shipping through New York.

Thus, despite the distinct advantages of containerization, costs have not been reduced as low as they might be. It is a fact of business life that economics must frequently be balanced with political and social realities. In this case, maximum savings have been balanced with the needs and power of the longshoremen's union.

15 Channels of distribution

Summary

Channels of distribution are the paths goods and services follow from producer to final buyer. For consumer goods, the participants in the channel may include *wholesalers, agents, brokers,* and *retailers*—all of whom are referred to as *middlemen.* In some cases, however, goods move directly from the producer to the consumer, as in direct-mail sales or manufacturer-owned outlets. For industrial goods, the channels are similar. But direct sales are more common, especially in the case of large-scale purchases.

Producers of goods and services must determine which channel is best for their products: which middlemen to use, where they should be located, the cost of alternatives, and how to keep in touch with middlemen during the distribution process.

A *wholesaler* sells products to others for resale or for use in making other products. Wholesalers perform many functions for both manufacturers and retailers. Thus, eliminating a wholesaler from the channel of distribution does not necessarily result in savings that can be passed on to consumers. A *buying cooperative* is a group of independent store owners who form a wholesaling company that serves as their exclusive supplier.

A *retailer* sells goods to buyers for their personal use rather than for resale. There are many kinds of retailers, including department stores, supermarkets, and specialty stores.

Retailing has seen some far-reaching changes in the last 25 years. Among them are discounting, self-service, wider product variety, credit sales, computer controls, and a move from downtown shopping districts to suburban shopping centers and malls.

Transportation plays a major role in the physical distribution of goods. Improved transportation has widened the mrket for goods and enhanced specialization. Rapid transportation has also reduced inventory needs.

There are three kinds of transportation companies: common carriers, contract carriers, and private carriers. The *common carrier* works for the general public at stated rates. A *contract carrier* sells its transportation services to firms or individuals on a per job or time basis. A *private carrier* transports its own goods in its own vehicles. A shipper may utilize any or all three.

Each form of transportation has distinct advantages and disadvantages. Railroads are still the primary hauler of intercity freight. Trucks are the second largest freight movers, aided by their extreme flexibility and variety. Ships offer the lowest cost per ton. Pipelines, expensive to build, are efficient for transporting gases and liquids. Airlines move a relatively small amount of freight, but they are extremely useful for certain products and firms that require fast delivery.

Containerization is a systems approach to distribution that minimizes the need for handling and repackaging goods as they are moved from one form of transportation to another.

Review questions

1. What are middlemen? What functions do they perform in the distribution process?
2. As a general rule, what does a manufacturer consider when choosing a channel of distribution?
3. What five services are performed by wholesalers?
4. Why is a distribution channel that goes from manufacturer to wholesaler to retailer to consumer often the most efficient?
5. Competition among retailers is very intense. What distribution-related factors can reduce a retailer's competitive edge?
6. What are three kinds of retailing operations? How do they differ from one another?
7. What are five recent developments in retailing?
8. How has improved transportation systems benefited manufacturers and consumers?
9. Explain the differences between common, contract, and private carriers.
10. Briefly discuss the pros and cons of each of the following means of transportation:
    a. railroads
    b. trucks
    c. ships
    d. pipelines
    e. airlines
11. What is containerization?

Discussion questions

1. Discuss the advantages and disadvantages of the alternative channels of distribution.
2. Describe the benefits of wholesalers in the marketing process. Under what circumstances might a wholesaler be most efficient? When might a wholesaler be unnecessary?
3. What channel of distribution might a Memphis-based manufacturer of expensive luggage use to get its product distributed in the United States and abroad?

Chapter 15 case

The Learned Publishing Company

Sometimes a newcomer in the market has to be willing to consider using innovative channels of distribution. What do you think are the chances of success in this case?

Sharon Smyth, the marketing manager of Learned Publishing Company, decided to propose something bold at the planning meeting. The company was about to introduce a new 18-volume encyclopedia. She thought it was time to try a new method of distributing encyclopedias to consumers. So, she was going to propose that Learned's new product be sold through bookstores.

Most encyclopedia publishers rely on personal selling to market their products. Usually, a salesperson comes to the home of a prospective customer and spends an hour or more explaining why the encyclopedia is a good purchase. *World Book* and *Encyclopaedia Britannica* are the two most successful users of this technique.

Most books, of course, are sold through bookstores. People come in "off the street" to search out specific titles or to just browse. Surveys have found that many books are bought either spontaneously or as gifts.

Encyclopedias are different. Because they cost hundreds of dollars per set, they are not just *bought*—they must be *sold*.

But direct sales has its drawbacks. The process is very time-consuming, and the salesperson must get a sizable commission for making a sale.

"By distributing our books through bookstores, we can get into the encyclopedia business much quicker than if we had to set up our own sales force," Smyth pointed out at the meeting. But not everyone was as confident as she about the effectiveness of selling through bookstores. The company president ordered a report on the advantages and disadvantages of the marketing manager's proposal.

Assume that you must present that report. Address these questions in particular:
1. What does Learned Publishing give up by having its encyclopedia sold through traditional bookstores?
2. What does the publisher gain by using the bookstores?
3. What other marketing tools will Learned Publishing need to make the bookstore channel work?
4. Would you recommend that the company adopt Sharon Smyth's proposal? Why?

5 Careers in marketing

A diverse group of occupations is available in marketing. There are jobs in sales, advertising, market research, and physical distribution. In many organizations, the best promotions are given to people who have worked in marketing. Often, new employees start in sales, regardless of where they will eventually work in the organization.

In general, the outlook for employment opportunities in marketing is favorable. Public relations, retail sales, and marketing research are expected to be among the fastest growing areas. Following are more detailed accounts of three broad categories of jobs: sales, marketing management, and marketing research.

Sales careers

Two jobs closely related to the distribution of goods are wholesale trade salespeople and manufacturer's representatives.

Wholesale trade salespeople represent wholesalers that distribute products for manufacturers. Most represent a specific category of goods, such as toys, consumer electronics, or sporting goods. Among the customers of wholesale trade salespeople are buyers for retail, industrial, and commercial firms as well as buyers for institutions (such as schools). Wholesale trade salespeople try to sell all products carried by the wholesaler. They do not focus on selling one particular brand.

As wholesaling has become increasingly competitive, wholesale salespeople have offered additional services in order to encourage customer loyalty. These services include checking retailers' inventories and advising buyers about items that are running low. The salesperson may also update inventory and ordering systems and advise on advertising, pricing, and window displays. If the wholesaler carries highly technical products, the salesperson might give technical assistance on installation and maintenance.

There are no specific educational requirements or licenses for wholesale trade representatives. Increasingly, however, a college degree is becoming the minimum credential. A survey of members of a sales executive's organization recommended courses in English, speech, psychology, marketing, public relations, economics, advertising, finance, accounting, personnel administration, and business law for people going into this area of sales.

An outgoing personality is an asset. A salesperson should also be aggressive, self-motivated, and able to anticipate public standards of style, design, and taste. In addition, a person interested in a sales career should be willing to put in long, irregular hours and endure a heavy travel schedule.

A typical entry-level position is that of sales trainee. Although sales is a highly competitive field, employment opportunities are expected to grow at about the average for other occupations during the 1980s. In particular, continued developments in high technology will place added value on people with some technical expertise. The key to success in any sales position is the ability to locate new customers and persuade them to buy.

Other occupations related to these are buyers, sales-service promoters, field contract technicians, and demonstrators.

Marketing manager

The responsibilities of a marketing manager vary from company to company. Basically, however, every marketing manager oversees those business activities that direct the flow of goods and services from producer to consumer. In addition, the marketing manager must provide objectives, strategies, and policies to promote the offerings of the firm. This means an involvement in all activities required to determine and meet customer needs from the time a product or service is conceived through its delivery and even after.

The nature and scope of the marketing manager's job are varied. Some of the duties that businesses assign to marketing managers include planning marketing programs; setting policies for prices, customer relations, and distribution channels; sales management; product management; marketing research; administration; sales forecasting; setting budgets; servicing customers; and sales promotion and advertising.

Marketing managers must be familiar with the marketplace and their competitors. They must also understand their potential customers' characteristics, such as income level, age, education, ethnic and religious background, and other factors that will affect the decision to buy.

Marketing managers must also understand the environment in which their company operates, including laws, social attitudes, and public concerns that will affect the success of their products.

REGIONAL MARKETING DIRECTOR

Burger King Corporation is seeking an assertive, take-charge business-oriented marketing professional to head up its marketing function for the metropolitan New York region, headquartered on Long Island.

To qualify for this demanding position you must possess a high degree of business acumen with a demonstrated ability to interact with all disciplines of a $2 billion corporation. Additionally, you should be able to combine an assertive goal-oriented approach with superior human relations skills at all levels.

The ideal candidate will have had some previous fast food or package goods experience and an MBA in marketing as a minimum. You must possess 10+ years marketing experience in a consumer business. We offer an excellent salary and benefits package which includes a company automobile. For confidential consideration, please send resume and salary history to: Roger Rendin, Burger King Corporation, 3 Huntington Quad, Suite 3N05, Melville, New York 11747.

An Equal Opportunity Employer M/F/H

BURGER KING

Marketing researcher

A professional engaged in marketing research collects, analyzes, and interprets data relating to consumer wants, needs, attitudes, and behavior. The result of this work is seen in decisions about pricing, distribution, advertising, packaging, and other parts of the marketing mix.

There are four general areas of marketing research. One is company services and products. Researchers in this field gather information on the company's products—their names, reputations, designs, and packaging. They also gather information about competitors' products and services.

A second area of marketing research is sales methods and policies. These researchers study the company's historical and geographical sales records. They seek trends that can serve as the bases for future sales campaigns, sales quotas, commissions, and the like.

Closely related to sales research is advertising research. Advertising researchers look at how consumers respond to particular advertising themes, concepts, designs, and media. Such data help to create ads that are most effective in accomplishing their objectives.

The fourth area of marketing research is in consumer demand and opinion. These researchers study consumers' wants, needs, likes, and dislikes. Such information is critical in planning new and improved products and services. It also helps in forecasting sales.

> **Market Research Executives**
>
> Expanding 20-year old marketing research firm seeks two executives to run its Washington D.C. and Ohio regional offices.
>
> You will be responsible for the complete operation and management of a regional office. You must have the following qualifications:
>
> Five or more years in market research firm management. Thorough knowledge of all consumer marketing research techniques. Experience in developing and maintaining contacts with top level management of existing and potential clients.
>
> If selected, you will report directly to the President. Compensation commensurate with experience.
>
> Send your resume to:
>
> Mr. Lee Weigle, President
> SMS Research
> 7710 Old Springhouse Road
> McLean, Virginia 22102
>
> **SMS RESEARCH**
> An Equal Opportunity Employer

Within these four basic marketing research areas are four kinds of jobs. The *project supervisor* plans a study and all that it entails. This person oversees the design of the questionnaire, the choice of participants, the analysis of the data, and the final recommendations.

The *statistician* develops samples and weighs questionnaire returns. *Tabulators* and *coders* examine the questionnaires when they return. They compile the answers for analysis, usually by computer. Finally, *field interviewers* are responsible for seeking out subjects for interviews and administering the questionnaire.

Among the skills that are highly sought in marketing researchers is a good understanding of electronic data processing. The project managers, and of course statisticians, must have a firm grasp of statistics and their application. In these areas, graduate training is almost always required.

For additional information, contact the following:

Sales & Marketing Executives International
Career Education Division
380 Lexington Avenue
New York, NY 10017

Council on Opportunities in Selling, Inc.
633 Third Avenue
New York, NY 10017

6

Financial concerns of business

Business in perspective

The cost of borrowing

The amount of money circulating in our economy—the money supply—is of great importance to businesses and individuals. As in any supply and demand equation, when the supply of money is greater than the demand, its price tends to go down. When the demand is greater than the supply, its price goes up. Interest is the price of money. Individuals pay interest when they borrow for a home, car, college tuition, or any other good paid for in installments. Businesses pay interest when they borrow money to purchase new equipment, build new plants and warehouses, or support added employees or expanded inventories.

Unlike private individuals, however, businesses tend to borrow money only when they believe that the return (profit) they can earn from these funds will exceed the cost (interest). When interest rates increase, a firm needs to make a greater return on its investment. So the higher interest rates go, the more projects businesses tend to postpone because the profit may not be high enough to justify the cost. Thus, when the interest rate is 9 percent, a retailer may be willing to borrow money to open a new store. But when the interest rate climbs to 16 percent, the retailer may feel that opening a new store will cost too much money.

High interest rates affect business in other ways. When interest gets too high, consumers hesitate to take a mortgage on a house or finance a new car. When families are unwilling or unable to buy houses, building contractors and construction workers lose work. Similarly, if consumers buy fewer new cars, some auto workers lose their jobs. Thus, high interest rates tend to lead to recession.

On the other hand, high inflation rates promote high interest. If the cost of goods and services rise at an annual rate of 10 percent, then $100 put in the bank today must be worth $110 a year from now or else it will have lost value. People will not invest their money unless they believe that the return will exceed the inflation rate. When inflation is high, the return (interest) must keep pace, and this creates high interest rates.

Ironically, one cause of inflation is rapid expansion of the economy. When many people spend a lot of money, their demand for goods and services helps keep prices high. Economists, therefore, recommend that in a period of inflation, businesses and individuals should be discouraged from borrowing. Then less money is spent (the money supply is smaller). Demand decreases and prices should come down, or at least stabilize.

One function of the Federal Reserve System is to keep the money supply at a level that encourages modest borrowing. When inflation rises too fast, the Federal Reserve tries to reduce the money supply. In a period of recession, when the economy's growth is sluggish, it tries to stimulate spending by expanding the money supply.

Chapter 16

Financial institutions and business

Key terms

money
cash
demand deposits
money supply
Federal Reserve System
reserve requirement
discount rate
commercial bank
life insurance company
savings and loan association
mutual savings bank
credit union
commercial finance company
investment bank
money market fund
electronic funds transfer (EFT)
negotiable order of withdrawal (NOW) account

Chapter objectives

In Chapter 16, you will learn:

How money differs from cash

What the money supply is and how it is controlled

How the Federal Reserve System is set up and what it does

How a bank deposit of $10,000 can cause the money supply to grow by nearly $40,000

The identity of the largest financial institution that deals with business

The role of insurance companies as financial institutions

How savings and loan associations differ from commercial banks

What an investment bank is

How electronic funds transfer sets the stage for a cashless and checkless society

How savings banks are becoming more like commercial banks

How credit cards have affected the financial structure of the United States

Overview

For most of us, money is the bills and coins in our pocket. Banks are places where we can store money or borrow for a car, home mortgage, or college tuition. But cash is only one kind of money, and banks do far more than just hold and lend our funds.

Consider this series of events: In 1978, inflation in the United States was running at about 10 percent annually. Overseas, currency traders were demanding more and more dollars to purchase foreign currencies. A U.S. dollar had been worth almost four German marks in 1970, but by 1978 it was worth only two marks. Thus, a German-made Volkswagen priced at 8000 German marks required the exchange of $4000 in 1978, as opposed to $2000 in 1970. Meanwhile, American companies were borrowing money to keep up with their expansion needs.

Suddenly, President Carter announced a program that included raising the discount rate from 8½ percent to 9½ percent. The value of the dollar immediately began to rise in overseas trading. Stock prices went up. And the news media started to predict impending recession, reductions in home building, and slower business expansion.

What happened? What is the discount rate? And why did a one percent increase in this rate have such a strong impact, even though it was only one aspect of the president's announcement?

This chapter identifies and analyzes the primary financial institutions in the United States, how they respond to the federal government's machinery for regulating the economy, and how business makes use of these institutions. By the end of this chapter, you will understand why President Carter's increase of the discount rate had such far-reaching effects.

Defining money

Money differs from cash. **Money is a medium of exchange.** It is anything that is widely accepted as an appropriate payment for goods or services. It may be pieces of gold or silver, sheets of printed paper, shells, stones, cattle, or anything else that is regarded as a legitimate basis of exchange for something else.

Cash is a form of money that consists of paper currency and coins. For much of our history, currency was backed by gold and silver (which would have been harder to carry around). But today, our paper currency has value only because the U.S. government stands behind it.

Likewise, coins were once made of metals that had about the same value as the coins' face value. The silver in a silver dollar, for example, was worth about one dollar. Today, like paper currency, coins have value only because the government says they do—and because people are willing to accept the coins as money.

Figure 16.1 Money stock, December 17, 1982

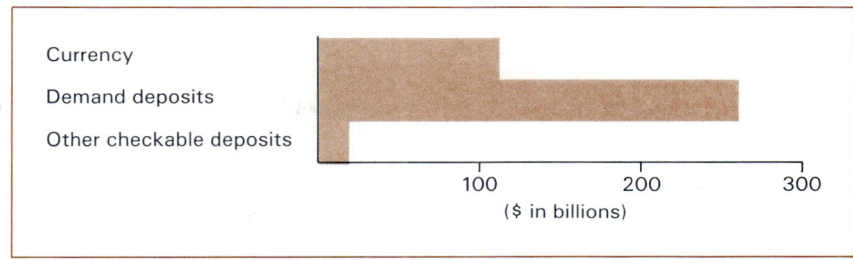

"Money Stock Measures and Liquid Assets (H-6)," Board of Governors of the Federal Reserve System, December 17, 1982.

But most money is not in the form of cash. It is in the form of **demand deposits, which is the money held in checking accounts.** Almost all businesses and most families keep the money they need for paying bills in a bank checking account. Then, instead of cash, they use checks to pay their bills. A check is a piece of paper that orders a bank to give the payee a specified amount of money.

The money supply is the total of all currency, coins, and checking-account balances. In mid-1983, the total money supply (called M-1) was $490 billion. Of this, about 28 percent was in the form of cash and the rest was in demand deposits (see Figure 16.1).

The Fed—more than the bankers' bank

The Federal Reserve System is the controlling mechanism of the financial structure of the United States. Created by Congress in 1913, "the Fed" is run by a seven-member Board of Governors. The members are appointed by the President and approved by the Senate, but they operate independently. Although the Fed's policies are set by the Board of Governors in Washington, much of the Fed's work is carried out by 12 regional Federal Reserve banks. Figure 16.2 shows the boundaries and headquarters for each region.

All federally chartered banks—which includes most of the largest banks—are members of the Federal Reserve System. State-chartered banks may join if they wish. By joining the Federal Reserve System, a bank gains certain services and may borrow from the Federal Reserve Bank. But it also becomes subject to requirements that limit the amount of money it can lend. Approximately 5400 banks belong to the Federal Reserve System.

How the Fed tries to control the economy

The Federal Reserve System promotes orderly and stable growth in the money supply and provides an orderly flow of money and credit. Monetary policy controls the supply of money. It is one tool the government

Figure 16.2 The Federal Reserve System

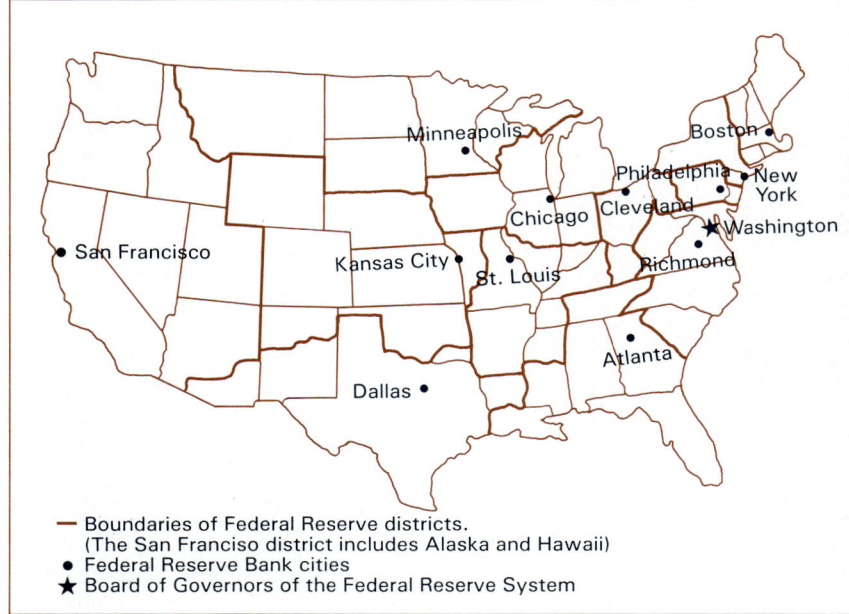

— Boundaries of Federal Reserve districts.
(The San Franciso district includes Alaska and Hawaii)
• Federal Reserve Bank cities
★ Board of Governors of the Federal Reserve System

can use to try to avoid serious recession and inflation. The Fed can exercise its monetary policy in three ways: through open-market operations, through the size of the reserve requirement, and through the discount rate.

Open-market operations

On a day-to-day basis, the Fed can affect the money supply by buying and selling short-term U.S. Treasury notes. Through U.S. Treasury notes, the federal government borrows from the public.

To *decrease* the amount of money available, the Fed *sells* notes. In doing so, it takes money out of circulation because purchasers pay for the notes with money from their checking accounts. The Fed might sell notes during times of unacceptably high inflation.

To *expand* the money supply, the Fed *purchases* Treasury notes. This puts money back in circulation, which may be desirable during a recession.

Treasury notes are sold in minimum amounts of $100,000. When Treasury notes are bought or sold, hundreds of millions of dollars either go into or come out of circulation.

Reserve requirements

A bank does not keep its money deposits in a vault. It loans most of its money to customers. They, in turn, deposit the money in their checking accounts until they are ready to spend it.

Chapter 16 Financial institutions and business

Why are banks quitting the Fed?

One of the Federal Reserve System's main tools for controlling the money supply is its reserve requirement for member banks. When the reserve requirement is increased, the supply of money is decreased. Although membership in the Fed is required for federally chartered banks, it is voluntary for state-chartered banks.

In the late 1970s, many banks began to rethink the cost of keeping funds in nonproductive reserves. As a result, many state banks began to withdraw their membership from the Fed. In doing so, they sacrificed such services as check processing, securities safekeeping, and access to Fed loans. On the other hand, they could invest the 20 percent or 25 percent of their deposits that had previously been tied up by the Fed's reserve requirements.

By pulling out, the banks faced some risks. But increasing competition and rising interest rates convinced many banks that the risks were worth taking.

The Fed faces some serious problems as its membership declines. For one thing, its ability to manage economic stability is being crippled. If banks continue to withdraw, the Fed's ability to control the money supply by raising reserve requirements could be seriously hindered. Furthermore, the Fed's ability to predict economic trends and take appropriate action requires careful monitoring of its member banks. If the portion of the money supply outside the Fed's control continues to grow, the Fed's predictions will lose precision. The consequences of this for future economic policy are still being debated.

However, a bank cannot lend all of the money deposited with it. The Federal Reserve System requires member banks to keep a specific amount of their funds in reserve. **The reserve requirement is a specific percentage of deposits member banks must set aside.**

The reserve requirement gives the Fed great control over the money supply. If the Fed wants to expand the money supply, it can lower the reserve requirements. Then banks can lend a greater proportion of their deposits. On the other hand, if the Fed wants to reduce the money supply, it can raise the reserve requirements. Then member banks must set more money aside and have less money available to lend.

The reserve requirement's impact on the money supply is even greater than it seems at first glance. Table 16.1 illustrates the multiplier effect of the reserve requirement. The money loaned from an initial deposit at Bank A, less the reserve requirement, becomes a deposit in Bank B. Bank B can then lend that money after deducting the reserve requirement. If these funds are deposited in Bank C, it too can lend them out. Thus, the original deposit of $10,000 feeds much more than $10,000 into the money supply.

If the reserve requirement is 20 percent, almost $50,000 in demand deposits can be generated from an initial deposit of $10,000. If the

Table 16.1 The multiplier effect of reserve requirements

	If 20% reserve requirement:			If 25% reserve requirement:
1.	$10,000	Initial deposit by Sarah Jones in Bank A		$10,000.00
	2,000	Reserve requirement		2,500.00
	8,000	Maximum amount Bank A can lend		7,500.00
2.	8,000	Borrowed by Jones Manufacturing company and deposited in Bank B		7,500.00
	1,600	Reserve requirement		1,875.00
	6,400	Maximum amount Bank B can lend		5,625.00
3.	6,400	Borrowed by Frank Smith and deposited in Bank C		5,625.00
	1,280	Reserve requirement		1,406.25
	5,120	Maximum amount Bank C can lend		4,218.75
4.	5,120	Borrowed by Ben's Pharmacy and deposited in Bank D		4,218.75
	1,024	Reserve requirement		1,054.69
	4,096	Maximum amount Bank D can lend		3,164.06
5.	4,096	Borrowed by John Doe and deposited in Bank E		3,164.06
		Etc.		

At this point, total demand deposits equal:

$10,000	Sarah Jones		$10,000.00
8,000	Jones Manufacturing Company		7,500.00
6,400	Frank Smith		5,625.00
5,120	Ben's Pharmacy		4,218.75
4,096	John Doe		3,164.06
$33,616			$30,507.81

reserve requirement is increased to 25 percent, a maximum of only $40,000 can be added to the money supply. Thus, the Fed's reserve requirement is a powerful tool in making major adjustments in the money supply.

The discount rate

One reason the Fed is called the "bankers' bank" is because it lends money to banks that they in turn lend to their customers. **The discount rate is the interest the Fed charges for the money it lends to banks.** A bank charges its customers higher interest than the discount rate in order to make a profit. Thus, if the discount rate is 8 percent, a bank might charge its very best customers about 10 percent (its prime rate). And it would charge smaller or less credit-worthy customers even more.

Chapter 16 Financial institutions and business

High interest rates can make it appear that banks do not want to loan money.

"If you have to ask the rate of interest, sir, then perhaps you can't afford the loan."

From the *Wall Street Journal,* Permission—Cartoon Features Syndicate.

The Fed can cause interest rates to rise and thus discourage some borrowing by raising the discount rate. When the discount rate rises, commercial banks raise the interest they charge, which makes loans less attractive to some potential borrowers. Higher interest rates, because they result in less borrowing, reduce the money supply and discourage businesses from expanding, buying new equipment, and adding employees.

Recently, the Federal Reserve has used the discount rate as its major tool in adjusting the money supply. As a result, the rate sometimes changes rapidly. The discount rate was 5½ percent in the summer of 1975, and it climbed by small increases to 8½ percent by October 1978. That was when President Carter asked the Fed to raise the discount rate all at once to 9½ percent, an unusually large one-time increase. This not only rapidly drove interest rates higher, but also signaled the government's intention to take serious steps to slow down the rate of inflation. (In 1981, the discount rate went so high that banks were charging their *best* customers as much as 21½ percent interest on loans. This drastically cut the amount of borrowing.)

Other Federal Reserve functions

The 12 regional Federal Reserve banks serve as clearing centers for nearly the 300 billion checks Americans write every year. As already noted, a check is a written authorization for a bank to withdraw a stated amount of money from the writer's account and give it to the payee.

Figure 16.3 How the Federal Reserve clears a check from Dallas to New York

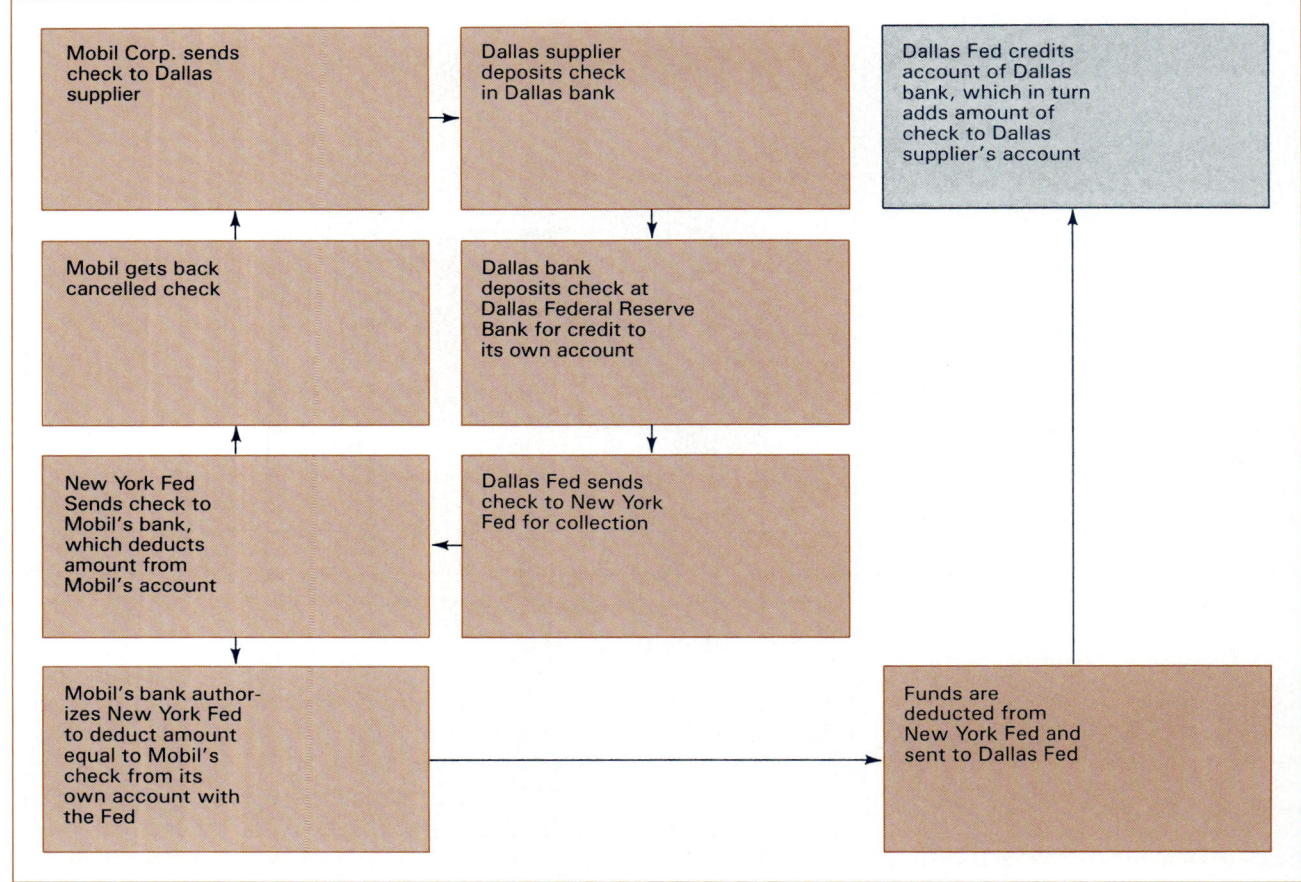

Making sure that the right account from the right bank is credited or debited with the transaction can be a complex task.

For example, suppose Mobil Corporation in New York buys some drilling equipment from a firm in Dallas. Mobil writes a check on its New York account and sends it to the Dallas supplier. The Dallas firm deposits the check in its account at a local bank. From there, the Federal Reserve System takes over, as diagramed in Figure 16.3. The Dallas bank sends the Mobil check, and all other checks it has received for deposit, to the Dallas Federal Reserve bank. They in turn send the check to the New York Federal Reserve bank. From there it goes to Mobil's own bank, which deducts the amount from Mobil's account. Meanwhile, the Federal Reserve banks make sure that the Dallas bank is credited with an equal amount. The process is aided immensely by computers, which can read figures encoded at the bottom of each check that identify the bank and the amount of the check.

The commercial banking system

Although the word *bank* is commonly used to refer to any institution that accepts money for deposit, the only true bank is the commercial bank. The largest category of financial institutions, the commercial banks have more than $1.7 trillion in assets and $1.3 trillion in deposits. **A commercial bank provides most of the checking accounts and business loans that create the money supply.** Commercial banks are at the heart of the financial network.

There are nearly 15,000 commercial banks. About one-third of them are nationally chartered. The rest are state-chartered. All banks operate under stringent regulations. Most insure the deposits of their customers through the Federal Deposit Insurance Corporation, a government organization. All banks, even national banks, can have offices to take deposits only in their home state. Some state regulations even prohibit banks from having branches within the state. But most of the largest banks do business with companies all over the United States and many seek out foreign customers as well.

Most commercial banks specialize in making loans and taking deposits from local customers. And most accept checking accounts and make loans to individuals. However, individual accounts make up only a small fraction of most banks' assets and loans.

The majority of commercial banks cater to business customers. A business may keep hundreds of thousands of dollars in demand deposit accounts and have lines of credit in the millions. Some commercial banks, especially in major money centers, such as New York, do not even handle personal accounts.

Life insurance companies

Life insurance companies, with about $525.8 billion in assets in 1981, are important members of the financial system. They do far more than merely provide insurance. **A life insurance company invests the millions in premiums it receives, much of it in commercial real estate mortgages.** Prudential, Metropolitan, Connecticut Life, and others derive about one-third of their income from such investments. In fact, they are the primary source of funds for builders of apartment and office buildings and shopping malls.

Savings and loan associations and mutual savings banks

Savings and loan associations are another kind of financial institution. **A savings and loan association primarily lends money to purchasers of residential real estate.** Until 1981, laws limited most savings and loan associations to lending funds only for residential mortgage loans.

Figure 16.4 Total assets and mortgage activity of banks, mutual savings banks, insurance companies, and savings and loan associations, 1979

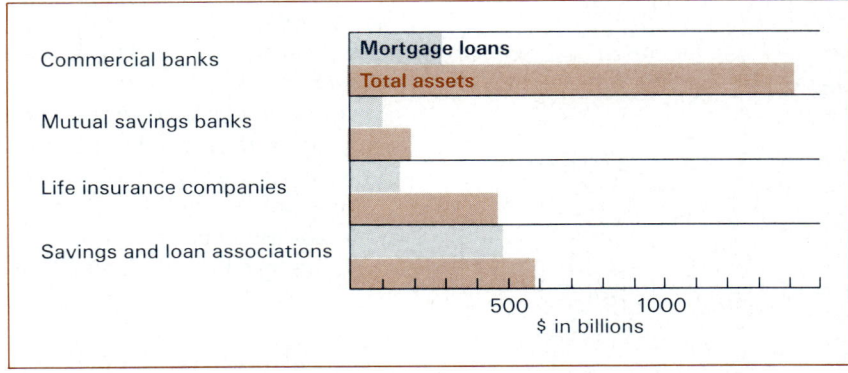

U.S. Department of Housing and Urban Development

In 1981, there were about 4300 savings and loan associations in the United States, with total assets of nearly $664 billion. About 82 percent of their funds were in home mortgages. As shown in Figure 16.4, this makes savings and loans the major source of mortgage money for individuals.

Mutual savings banks are found mostly in the northeastern section of the United States. **A mutual savings bank is similar in function to savings and loans, but it is technically owned by its depositors.** Rather than dividends, the owners get a share of the profits. In practice, profit distributions are limited to fixed dividend rates, and any surplus is used to expand the number of loans. Mutual banks are restricted to real estate loans, but they provide funds for apartments and commercial property as well as for residential mortgages.

To encourage individuals to use savings and loans and mutual savings banks, U.S. banking laws allow these institutions to pay slightly higher interest on passbook savings accounts and most certificates of deposit than commercial banks can pay.

Almost half of all new homes are financed from savings and loans and mutual banks. Yet these two financial institutions have been relatively unimportant to business because, until 1981, they could only lend money for real estate ventures. Due to federal legislation deregulating parts of the banking industry, however, the distinction between commercial banks and savings and loans is rapidly disappearing. Savings banks can now offer accounts that function just like checking accounts. And they can use some of their assets for loans that are not related to real estate.

Credit unions

A credit union is a financial institution that is usually sponsored by a labor union, employer, or other group for its members. It accepts deposits and pays interest. It also makes short-term loans to finance such common needs as automobiles, home improvements, and vacations. Since it is operated for the benefit of its members, interest rates on loans tend to be slightly lower than those at commercial banks. In 1981, there were about 21,000 active credit unions. With assets of about $77 billion, they are relatively small compared to other institutions. But they serve more than 45 million members.

Commercial finance companies

A bank does a thorough background check on any individual or business to which it intends to make a loan. It will not make a loan if it suspects that the lendee will be unable to repay the money.

Businesses that cannot get loans from banks can look to commercial finance companies. **A commercial finance company provides loans to business and takes tangible assets, such as inventory, accounts receivable, or machinery, as collateral.** Most finance companies, such as Commercial Credit and CIT, offer short-term loans. Because finance companies lend money to customers that are less likely to pay their debts, they tend to charge higher interest rates than commercial bank loans.

Investment banks

Investment banks are very useful to corporations that need to raise large amounts of money. They provide important financial advice and help firms raise money by selling securities. Many investment banks are also well known as stockbrokers, such as Merrill Lynch & Co. or E.F. Hutton and Company, Inc.

An investment banking house underwrites the securities issued by its client. That is, **an investment bank guarantees to buy newly issued securities from its corporate clients and then sell them to mutual funds, pension funds, foundations, and other major purchasers of securities, as well as to private individual investors.** Investment bankers are the middlemen between a corporation that wants to sell securities and the public that wants to buy them.

Investment bankers make a profit by keeping a small percentage of the total amount of an issue. However, if investors do not buy all the securities at the offering price, an investment banker may take a loss because it must keep the securities that remain unsold.

Money market funds

A money market fund is a mutual fund that pools the investments of many participants and purchases U.S. Treasury notes, bank certificates of deposit, and other interest-bearing securities. In early

Figure 16.5 A "tombstone" announcement by the underwriters of a security offering

This announcement is neither an offer to sell nor a solicitation of an offer to buy any of these Securities. The offer is made only by the Prospectus.

18,150,000 Shares

American Telephone and Telegraph Company

Common Shares

Price $57 a Share

Copies of the Prospectus may be obtained in any State from only such of the undersigned as may legally offer these Securities in compliance with the securities laws of such State.

MORGAN STANLEY & CO.
Incorporated
GOLDMAN, SACHS & CO.
E. F. HUTTON & COMPANY INC.
KIDDER, PEABODY & CO.
Incorporated
MERRILL LYNCH WHITE WELD CAPITAL MARKETS GROUP
Merrill Lynch, Pierce, Fenner & Smith Incorporated
DEAN WITTER REYNOLDS INC.

BACHE HALSEY STUART SHIELDS *Incorporated*	THE FIRST BOSTON CORPORATION
BEAR, STEARNS & CO. BLYTH EASTMAN PAINE WEBBER *Incorporated*	DILLON, READ & CO. INC.
DONALDSON, LUFKIN & JENRETTE *Securities Corporation*	DREXEL BURNHAM LAMBERT *Incorporated*
LAZARD FRERES & CO.	LEHMAN BROTHERS KUHN LOEB *Incorporated*
L. F. ROTHSCHILD, UNTERBERG, TOWBIN	SALOMON BROTHERS
SHEARSON LOEB RHOADES INC.	SMITH BARNEY, HARRIS UPHAM & CO. *Incorporated*
WARBURG PARIBAS BECKER *Incorporated*	WERTHEIM & CO., INC.

June 11, 1981

Courtesy of American Telephone and Telegraph Company.

1983, the public had more than $185 billion invested in money market funds.

Money market funds are run by professional money managers. They purchase short-term notes at current interest rates. To protect their investments, they usually purchase notes from only the most financially strong corporations, the U.S. Treasury, and government agencies like the Federal National Mortgage Association.

Major corporations and pension and trust funds use money market funds to "park" excess cash for short periods of time. For example, a pension fund might sell several million dollars' worth of stock without having chosen a suitable new investment. Rather than let the money sit in a non-interest-bearing checking account, the pension fund will temporarily invest its cash in a money market fund. The money market fund will pay a higher rate of interest than a conventional savings account. And the pension fund will have no trouble withdrawing its money when it is ready to make a new investment.

Some commercial banks and thrift institutions have complained that money market funds have seriously hurt them. Many people who had previously kept their savings in passbook accounts or certificates of deposit found that they could earn much higher interest rates from money market funds. So they withdrew their money from the banks and put them in money market funds. This is a process called *disintermediation*. To help stop this, in 1982, the bank regulators allowed banks and thrift institutions to offer savings accounts at unregulated interest rates. Now able to compete with money market funds, banks are experiencing a shift of funds back into savings accounts.

Banks and thrift institutions versus money market funds

As money for mortgage loans became scarcer in the early 1980s, banks and savings and loan associations mounted a battle against high-yield money market funds.

The banks and savings and loan associations decided that the money market funds were unfair competition because they were not as closely regulated by banking laws. (As mutual funds, they fell under the jurisdiction of the Securities and Exchange Commission.) The banks and savings and loans requested Congress to impose a reserve requirement on money invested with the funds. This would, in effect, lower the interest rates that money market funds could pay. Then the conventional savings institutions could remain competitive in the investment market. Opponents argued that this would force the small saver back to low interest rates, while corporations, pension funds, and the wealthy would be able to buy higher-yielding large-denomination securities.

Congress responded with a different idea. In 1981, it passed a measure providing for All-Savers certificates of deposit. Their rate of interest was 70 percent of the rate of certain Treasury notes. But savers did not have to pay federal income tax on the interest. Because savers *did* have to pay tax on income from money market investments, the All-Savers plan offered competitive returns for many people. However, Congress limited the amount of tax-free interest to only $1000 per individual (or $2000 for a married couple). The legislation expired at the end of 1982. In the meantime, it did help to bring an influx of funds to the banks.

Recent developments affecting financial institutions

Electronic funds transfer

Computers have greatly helped banks and the Federal Reserve cope with the ever-increasing number of checks in use today. Computers can also eliminate paper transactions altogether through electronic funds transfer (EFT). In its basic form, **electronic funds transfer is a computer-based method of taking funds from one checking account and crediting it directly to another account without having to process a check.** For example, many banks now have terminals outside their offices, at supermarkets, and at other convenient locations. Customers can not only make deposits at any time, but they can also withdraw cash. The automatic teller machine dispenses the money and deducts that sum from the user's account.

In stores in some cities, customers can pay for goods using a plastic card that looks much like a credit card. However, this card acts like cash. When a purchaser presents the card, the merchant inserts the card in a terminal that is connected to a bank's computer. The amount of the purchase is automatically deducted from the customer's checking account and credited to the merchant's account in that bank. This eliminates the need for processing a check and means that individuals do not need to carry large sums of cash. It also saves merchants from getting stuck with bad checks.

Commercial banks are also trying to encourage businesses to use EFT to pay their bills. At some large firms, for example, employees are paid through an EFT system.

The banking industry would like businesses to use this checkless payment system more often. According to one estimate, electronic transfers of corporate funds would eliminate up to 4 billion checks processed by banks each year.[1]

Blurring distinctions between commercial and savings banks

Until 1981, commercial banks were the only financial institutions allowed by law to offer demand deposit (checking) accounts. But in the mid-1970s, federal bank regulators began to allow savings and loans to experiment with negotiable orders of withdrawal (NOW) accounts. Since 1981, both savings and loans and mutual savings banks have been permitted to offer NOW accounts.

From the consumer's point of view, NOW accounts are just like checking accounts. Technically, **a NOW account is a time deposit (savings) account that permits the depositor to make withdrawals by writing**

---

[1] "Electronic Banking Aims at Business," *BusinessWeek,* January 24, 1977, p. 77.

out a checklike slip payable to a third party. Since NOW accounts are actually savings accounts, they have an advantage over commercial bank checking accounts in that they may pay interest. The changed law also allows commercial banks to offer NOW accounts. Most banks require customers to maintain a minimum balance in the account.

Savings banks are also being allowed to make a wider variety of loans. For example, they can now make loans to businesses for purposes other than real estate. Thus, the distinction between commercial banks and savings banks is gradually disappearing.

Credit cards

People in the United States currently own more than 600 million credit cards. In 1982, Americans owed over $343 billion in installment debt. The fact that so many people are buying now and paying later is causing profound changes in the U.S. economy and in business.

In 1976, only 390 commercial banks offered credit card plans. Today, more than 2300 banks have issued credit cards, primarily Visa and MasterCard (the two largest national credit card plans). They were initially offered free to customers, but today, many banks charge an annual fee. American Express, Diners Club, and Carte Blanche have been in business longer, but they tend to charge higher annual fees and have more stringent credit qualifications. They also demand payment in full each month, while the bank cards allow customers to pay only a portion of the balance.

Some believe that bank credit cards have greatly contributed to a steep rise in consumer debt. In 1970, Americans owed $5.1 billion in installments on their credit card purchases, but by 1980, that amount had increased ten-fold to $51.8 billion.

Today, credit cards are used to pay for everything from church donations and college tuition to dentists' and lawyers' bills. They eliminate the need to carry cash—and even the need to have the money to make the purchase. The bill for a charged purchase comes weeks or months later. Even then, bank cards require customers to pay only a portion of their amount due. Most banks add an annual finance charge of 18 percent or more to unpaid balances.

Advantage to business In many ways, credit cards are beneficial to businesses, especially retailers. First, the bank-issued cards eliminate the need for small businesses to offer their own credit services. Second, they lessen the number of bad checks passed, since it is the bank issuing the card that pays the business and must then collect from the cardholder. Third, credit cards have, for better or worse, encouraged people to buy more spontaneously.

Disadvantages The advantages of bank credit cards are somewhat offset by their costs. A business pays the bank a service charge, usually between 2 to 7 percent of each credit sale. Some critics claim that merchants then add these costs to their prices. But it is unlikely that merchants would lower their prices if bank cards were eliminated.

16 Financial institutions and business

Summary

Money is a medium of exchange. One-fourth of the U.S. money supply is in *cash* (bills and coins) and most of the rest is in *demand deposits* (checking account balances). Most financial transactions take place by check.

At the center of the financial structure of the United States is the *Federal Reserve* System. It consists of 12 regional Federal Reserve banks and a Board of Governors in Washington, D.C. The role of the Fed is to promote an orderly and stable growth in the money supply and to provide an orderly flow of money and credit. The control of the *money supply* is called monetary policy.

A tight money supply tends to lead to high interest rates and a decline in business borrowing. When interest rates are low, businesses and individuals are more likely to borrow money. This stimulates the economy, but it can also encourage unwanted inflation.

The Fed uses methods to keep the money supply in balance or to help keep inflation down. These include buying or selling Treasury notes in open-market operations, adjusting the amount of reserves banks must keep (the *reserve requirement*), and setting the *discount rate*—the interest banks pay to borrow from the Fed.

If the Fed is the brains of the banking system, then the 15,000 commercial banks are the heart. *Commercial banks* provide demand deposit accounts and make the majority of short- and medium-term loans to businesses. Although most commercial banks take deposits and make loans to businesses in the area they serve, the largest banks have customers all over the United States and in foreign countries.

Life insurance companies are also financial institutions. They earn about 33 percent of their income from investing in commercial real estate.

Until recently, *savings and loan associations* and *mutual savings banks* had severe restrictions on their lending activities. Almost all of their loans were for home mortgages, with some going to commercial real estate and apartment mortgages. Now, savings banks are no longer limited to making only real-estate-related loans.

Commercial finance companies make secured loans for business purposes, but they usually charge higher interest rates than commercial banks.

Credit unions are set up to take deposits and make short-term loans to their members. Although small in total assets, credit unions serve about 43 million individuals.

Investment banks serve as middlemen between investors and companies seeking funds through the sale of stocks and bonds. An investment bank underwrites a securities issue and usually takes a small percentage of the funds as a fee.

Money market funds have provided small investors the opportunity to pool their funds to buy Treasury notes and other high-interest-yielding securities.

Electronic funds transfer (EFT) is a recent development that allows individuals and businesses to complete financial transactions without using checks. In some cities, consumers can pay for merchandise by having a computer automatically deduct funds from their checking account and credit them to a merchant's account.

The widespread use of credit cards, especially the national bank-issued cards, has helped create a new method of debt finance for individuals. The cards have reduced the need to carry cash and have led to a steep rise in the level of consumer debt.

In recent years, the firm distinction between demand deposit and savings deposit accounts has been blurred. Savings and loan associations may offer *negotiable order of withdrawal (NOW) accounts,* which turn savings accounts into interest-bearing checking accounts. Commercial banks have responded by offering NOW accounts of their own. Since 1981, savings banks have also been allowed to make business loans for non-real-estate purposes.

Review questions

1. What three primary tools does the Fed use to try to control the growth of the economy?
2. What is a reserve requirement? How can the Fed use it to control the money supply?
3. Name the largest type of financial institution in the United States. What is the second largest type of financial institution? What is the basic misconception about these companies?
4. Describe the traditional basic difference between a bank and a savings and loan association. How is this distinction changing?
5. What are the two sources of financing for almost half of all new homes?
6. In what technical way is a mutual bank different from a savings and loan association?
7. Where can individuals or businesses go for a loan if their credit rating is not strong enough to get a loan from a commercial bank?
8. What is EFT? How may it change the way we get paid or pay our bills?
9. Name some advantages and disadvantages to the use of credit cards.

Discussion questions

1. In recent years, the United States has been plagued by a high rate of inflation. Suppose you were asked to brief the president before he met with the chairman of the Federal Reserve Board. What would you recommend that the Fed do?
2. Federal laws permit savings and loans and mutual savings banks to pay ¼ percent more interest on savings accounts and most certificates of deposit than commercial banks. Why do you suppose this difference exists?
3. If a small businessman does not have a strong enough credit rating to obtain a loan from a bank, he can go to a commercial finance company. If you were an officer of a commercial finance company, what information would you ask the businessman for? Name three requirements you would set for making loans to high-risk businesses.
4. Discuss the pros and cons of electronic funds transfer for commercial banks and their corporate and individual customers. Is EFT the beginning of a "paperless society"?
5. Credit card companies usually charge merchants a small percentage of each credit sale as their fee for assuming the credit and collection costs. Some merchants would like to *add* this charge to the price the customer pays for goods and services. The credit card industry has opposed such surcharges as unfair. Should those who use credit cards be expected to pay extra for the privilege? Why might a business be willing to *absorb* the extra cost itself?

Chapter 16 case

Starting an IRA

A new tax law took effect in 1981. One of its most important features was that it allowed anyone with earned income to open an Individual Retirement Account (IRA). Competition among financial institutions for IRAs became fierce. Some factors that affect an individual's decision to open an IRA are examined in this case.

Domenic D'Antonio and Sharon Galinski were discussing Individual Retirement Accounts. Both have full-time jobs and pay Social Security. But they doubt that Social Security will provide them with enough money when they retire in 40 years. Domenic said he was thinking of opening an IRA at his bank. "I guess that's a pretty safe approach," answered Sharon. "But I think I'd rather start my IRA with a stockbroker and invest in stocks. That way my money can do more than just collect interest."

An IRA is a personal retirement plan. Basically, an individual worker can save up to $2000 per year in an IRA. An IRA differs from a more traditional savings plan in that the interest, dividends, or capital gains it yields are not subject to income tax until its owner retires and starts to draw money out of the account. Presumably, the retired individual will then be in a lower tax bracket, so taxes will be lower on the money from the IRA. Perhaps more importantly, the tax-free interest, dividends, and capital gains are compounded each year. The impact is significant, as shown in the following table:

	Marginal tax bracket			
	25%	40%	50%	IRA
Amount available to invest	$ 2,000	$ 2,000	$ 2,000	$ 2,000
Tax	$ 500	$ 800	$ 1,000	-0-
Amount available after taxes	$ 1,500	$ 1,200	$ 1,000	$ 2,000
Earnings rate after tax	9%	7.2%	6%	12%
Amount at the end of 30 years	$222,863	$125,976	$ 83,802	$540,585

Note that a worker in the 25 percent income tax bracket would have $222,863 after 30 years if he or she saved $2000 annually in an investment that paid 12 percent interest. But by putting $2000 in an IRA, the $2000 is not taxed as income. The entire $2000 could earn interest. After 30 years, the account would have more than $540,000. This is a difference of more than $317,000. For a worker in the 50 percent tax bracket, the difference would be even more—$467,000.

Anyone with earned income can open an IRA. And virtually any type of financial institution can manage IRAs. Banks, savings and loan associations, and credit unions all offer IRAs that pay interest. Stockbrokers offer IRAs that invest in stocks and bonds. Money market fund managers advertise IRAs that put money into certificates of deposit, Treasury notes, and commercial paper. Mutual funds are eager to sell their shares as part of an IRA. And life insurance companies combine IRAs with insurance programs.

If you were Domenic or Sharon, how would you evaluate the financial institutions that could help you with an IRA? Consider:

1. Where would the investor's money be safest?
2. Which might be the best alternative if interest rates stay very high?
3. Which might be best if there is a high rate of inflation?
4. How do IRAs benefit the U.S. economic system?

Business in perspective

How to improve your chance of getting a loan

Fewer than 10 percent of prospective borrowers come to a bank adequately prepared. And bankers don't have the time to dig for the facts they need. Here are a few tips to increase your possibility of success if you ever need a loan.

Pick your bank carefully. Does it deal mostly with larger corporations? Or does it aim to serve consumers and smaller businesses? If you pick the wrong one and wind up getting rejected, you'll have a harder time getting a loan from the next bank you choose.

Have a good accountant prepare a complete set of financial statements for your business, as well as a business plan and a personal balance sheet. If possible, have the accountant accompany you to the bank. If you come into the bank with an accountant and all the necessary financial information, it improves your odds of getting a loan by 75 percent.

Make an appointment. Many people don't seem to realize that you can't just walk in off the street and ask a banker for $100,000. People who ask for appointments show they are business-oriented.

Demonstrate that you're a person of good character, especially if it's the first time that you're applying for a loan. A banker likes to know that you're civic-minded and respected in business and community circles.

Show that you don't have your head buried in the sand. Pick up the Wall Street Journal and read trade journals so that you're knowledgeable about your entire industry and the economy as well as your own business.

Be honest with your banker and ask for the amount of money you really need.

Even the best credit prospects must be prepared to guarantee their loans personally. If businesspeople aren't willing to put their assets on the line, why should a bank?

Adapted from Michael Celello, "Tips From a Banker," INC., November 1981, p. 44. Reprinted with permission, INC., November 1981. Copyright © 1981 by INC. Publishing Company, 38 Commercial Wharf, Boston, MA 02110.

Chapter 17 — Raising and managing capital

Key terms

revenues
expenses
finance
assets
liabilities
financial-management process
short-term finance
unsecured loan
collateral
promissory note
prime interest rate
line of credit
revolving credit agreement
secured loans
long-term finance
debt financing
bond
indenture
equity financing
par value
common stock
dividends
preemptive rights
preferred stock

Chapter objectives

In Chapter 17, you will learn:

The nature of the finance function

The steps in the financial-management process

How a company may use short-term funds

The most common sources of short-term business financing

How the four basic kinds of bonds are issued and retired

The factors that affect bond values

The characteristics of equity financing

How common and preferred stock differ

Overview

In other chapters, we have discussed the four factors of production: land, labor, capital, and entrepreneurial ability. Businesses combine the four factors of production to provide the goods and services that consumers demand.

These resources are limited, so business managers must give careful attention to their use. Obtaining and using capital to acquire the other factors of production is a crucial business function. The survival of a business depends on sound financial management. How funds are managed often makes the difference between a profitable business and a bankrupt one.

This chapter considers the basic elements of financial management. It describes the characteristics of short-term and long-term financing. And it explains how managers decide which form of long-term financing to use in raising capital: equity (owner) financing or creditor (debt) financing.

What is finance?

In operating a business, money regularly flows through the firm. **Revenues are all funds an organization raises from the sale of its goods or services and from other business activities. Expenses are the costs a business incurs in acquiring resources, producing goods or services, and marketing.**

Finance is the business function of obtaining and using money (capital funds) efficiently. Every business needs money to accomplish its objectives. Nearly every business decision, from hiring an employee to choosing the computer that best fits company needs, has a financial effect on the firm. Thus, finance is a crucial management function.

Assets and liabilities

Assets are everything of value that a company owns. They typically include such things as cash, buildings, machinery, and inventory.

Liabilities are the financial obligations, or debts, a firm has incurred in buying goods and services from others. Liabilities include such things as accounts payable, loans outstanding or taxes due. Chapter 19 describes in detail the various classes of assets and liabilities.

The financial-management process

To carry out its goals and objectives, a company must be able to acquire funds to purchase the factors of production. **The financial-management process attempts to assess the firm's financial needs, acquire needed funds, and oversee the use of funds.**

Chapter 17 Raising and managing capital

Figure 17.1 The financial-management process

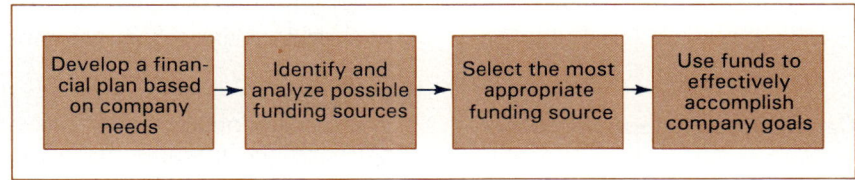

The financial-management process includes the following steps:
1. Develop a financial plan based on company needs
2. Identify and analyze possible sources of funds
3. Select the most appropriate source of funds
4. Use the funds effectively to achieve company goals.

Financial managers must perform these tasks while keeping in mind the unique needs and circumstances of their particular company. They must consider company objectives, profit projections, and current financial conditions, among other things.

Short-term financing

To get the most use from each business dollar, the finance manager must balance short-term revenues and expenses. **Short-term finance refers to revenues and expenses that will arise within one year.**

Three areas are often considered. First, if the firm extends credit to its customers, how generous should it be? Making credit available may attract customers, but allowing too much credit can mean the company does not have ready cash to meet expenses.

Second, at what level should the inventory of goods be maintained? Having a large inventory on hand ties up cash resources. Does current demand warrant it?

Third, if there is extra cash on hand, what should be done with it? Cash has important effects on short-term operations. If a firm has too little cash on hand, it will be unable to meet its immediate obligations. But if a firm keeps too much cash on hand, it loses the opportunity to earn interest through short-term investments.

Uses of short-term funds

A company holds some cash in its checking account to meet current bills and expenses. But, because cash on hand does not earn interest, managers often seek income-producing uses for the cash left over after short-term needs are met.

Common investments for short-term cash include U.S. Treasury bills, certificates of deposit (CDs), and commercial paper.

U.S. Treasury bills

Treasury bills are short-term notes issued by the U.S. Treasury, usually for periods of three to six months. They are sold at a weekly auction with competitive bidding. Their face value ranges from $10,000 to $1 million. Because they are backed by the U.S. government, Treasury bills are an almost riskless investment.

Certificates of deposit (CDs)

Certificates of deposit are short-term notes issued by commercial banks. Their size and maturity are often negotiated on a case-by-case basis. Usually, the minimum is 30 days. CDs pay relatively high interest rates and are easily resold.

Commercial paper

Commercial paper is short-term notes issued by companies that have an excellent credit rating. In effect, they are corporate IOUs used to raise money for short-term cash needs. Commercial paper may be issued for periods as short as one day or up to nine months. Large companies may prefer to use commercial paper to raise funds because its interest rates are usually lower than those of short-term bank loans.

Short-term needs for funds

Many businesses depend on short-term borrowing to finance day-to-day operations. Agriculture provides a case in point.

Many farmers need seed, fertilizer, labor, and machinery during the months of March, April, and May. These are very large expenses, and the farmers may lack funds to pay for them immediately. So they often borrow short-term capital to pay for their factors of production. They prepare for their needs by borrowing money in January and February.

In June, July, and August, farmers harvest and sell their crops. With the money they earn from crop sales, they can repay their loans during September through December. Figure 17.2 illustrates this annual process.

Figure 17.2 A short-term farm loan

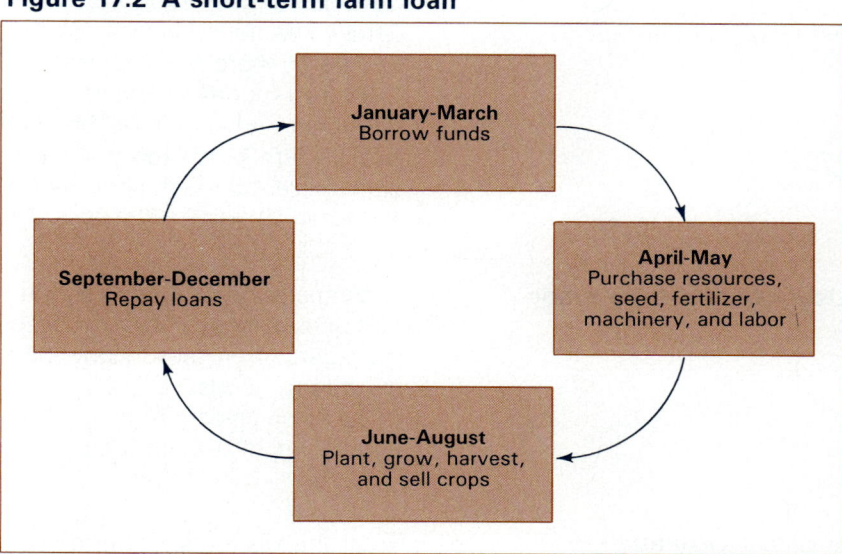

Chapter 17 Raising and managing capital 365

Sources of short-term financing

Businesses have three major sources for short-term financing: (1) their resource supplier, (2) commercial banks and other lending institutions, and (3) loans from investors or other businesses.

Credit from resource suppliers

Trade credit is an arrangement in which a business purchases goods or services from suppliers without immediately paying for them. Trade credit is not usually based on a formal, written contract. Instead, the supplier indicates the repayment terms on the bill submitted to the buyer.

Payment is usually due in 30 or 60 days from the date of the bill. To encourage payment before that time, a supplier may offer a cash discount. You may recall from Chapter 3, for example, that a notation of 2/10, n/30 on a bill means that it may be paid in two ways: (1) with a 2 percent discount if paid within 10 days from the date of the bill, or (2) with the full amount if paid after 10 days from the billing date but within 30 days.

A local paint store buys $2,000 worth of varnish from its supplier with credit terms stated at 2/10, n/30. If the paint store pays within 10 days, it will send $1,960 ($2,000 less 2 percent). Otherwise, it must pay the full $2,000 by the end of the 30-day period.

Trade credit is a major source of short-term business financing. Without trade credit, many small business owners would find it difficult or impossible to start a business and keep it operating.

A supplier usually investigates the credit standing of new customers before providing them trade credit. The supplier may ask for the company financial statements and contact the potential customer's bank and other references.

Suppliers also benefit from extending trade credit. Their sales would probably be much lower if they sold only for cash on delivery. Suppliers' credit policies, however, may not be the same for all their customers. Clients with excellent credit ratings may be given liberal credit terms. Less-established customers may be required to pay for their goods upon delivery or within a very short time.

Credit from commercial banks

A second major source of short-term business funds is commercial banks. Short-term bank loans to businesses are often unsecured. **An unsecured loan is a loan for which the borrower is not required to pledge any assets as collateral.** Collateral is anything of value that a borrower may pledge to a lender to back up the repayment of a loan. If the borrower fails to pay the loan, the lender may take possession of the collateral.

In Santa Ana, flop houses give way to banks

Barbara Mathewson, a former high-school guidance counselor, learned rehabilitation skills from renovating her 1920s house on Balboa Island, Calif., where "ivy grew through the walls." Now, with the help of a unique government financing program, she is helping turn a "borderline retail area" in Santa Ana, Calif., into a thriving business district.

"Not long ago the area included a number of rescue missions, 17 thrift shops, liquor stores, and flop houses," says Bob Clayton, the city's commercial rehabilitation coordinator. "Now we are building banks where the cheap bars once were. We've got photo studios, law firms, offices, and a wide range of retailers."

Mathewson's $1 million restoration of the Builder's Exchange, a building replete with marble columns and pilasters decorating early California brick, has been greeted with enthusiasm. A law firm has signed on to lease the top floor of the three-story building at a monthly rate of $1.19 per square foot, and has taken a one-eighth ownership interest in the building. Ground-floor retail and a mezzanine remain to be leased. Mathewson plans a gym with racquetball courts, saunas, and a Jacuzzi in the basement.

"Instead of using tax money, we've used the city's ability to borrow at preferential rates," explains Clayton. "Banks accept a property's deed of trust as security and are eager to lend to us because they get a tax-exempt loan by dealing with a municipality." What happens is that the city funnels the money to developers who pass muster—at an average 11½ percent interest rate.

Since February 1981, the city, which is the county seat of populous Orange County, Calif., has loaned some $15 million to 29 projects, and expects another $15 million will complete the area's renovation within the next 18 months.

Pamela Bayless, "New Life For the Cities," *Venture*, August 1982, pp. 26–29, 32–36, 38. Reprinted from the August 1982, issue of VENTURE, The Magazine for Entrepreneurs, by special permission © 1982. Venture Magazine, Inc., 35 West 45th Street, New York, NY 10036.

The basis of unsecured loans is the credit reputation or experience the bank has had with the company. The three major forms of unsecured loans are promissory notes, lines of credit, and revolving credit agreements.

A promissory note is a written agreement in which a business promises to repay a bank a sum of money it has borrowed on a specified future date at a specified interest rate. The interest rate is expressed as a percent of the amount borrowed.

The interest rate charged for the loan depends on the credit rating of the borrower. For large companies with excellent credit ratings, the interest rate may be at or near the prime interest rate. **The prime interest rate is the lowest rate of interest charged by commercial banks to their best credit risks.** Other interest rates may be higher, depending on the availability of funds and the creditworthiness of the company.

Chapter 17 Raising and managing capital

A line of credit is an agreement between a company and a commercial bank that establishes the maximum amount of unsecured short-term credit the bank will make available to the company if the funds are available. A line of credit is usually negotiated on a yearly basis. The company can then borrow funds, up to its credit limit, without filing a formal loan application each time.

For individual consumers, bank credit cards provide a service similar to the line of credit. MasterCard and Visa, for example, assign an individual a maximum credit limit.

A revolving credit agreement is a guaranteed line of credit. It is similar to a line of credit except that the bank promises to make the money available. In return for this guarantee, the bank usually charges the borrower a fee, even if all or part of the agreed-upon amount of credit is not used.

Loans from investors or other businesses

A company may need other loans besides trade credit and loans from commercial banks. In such cases, it may issue commercial paper or take out secured loans.

A secured loan is a loan that requires the borrower to pledge assets as collateral. Assets commonly pledged as collateral include accounts receivable, inventory, and machinery.

Long-term financing

Businesses may need large amounts of capital to acquire expensive machinery. Or they may wish to expand operations by building a new manufacturing plant. A company may be able to use some of its profits for these purposes. But few firms have enough profits to meet all of their long-term financial needs. **Long-term finance refers to revenues and expenses that will extend more than one year into the future.**

Most corporations that need long-term capital funding use either debt financing (bonds) or equity financing (preferred and common stock).

Debt financing: bonds

Debt financing is the raising of funds through borrowing. A firm is obligated to repay the funds borrowed and to pay interest for their use. A company with a high credit rating is able to borrow at lower rates of interest. The rate of interest on loans is directly related to the level of risk involved. If a company is in weak financial condition, it must pay higher interest rates to compensate creditors for the risk that the loan may not be repaid.

Those who lend the money—the firm's creditors—are promised a fixed return. If a company dissolves, creditors can claim the company's assets before the stockholders can.

Figure 17.3 Sources of long-term funds

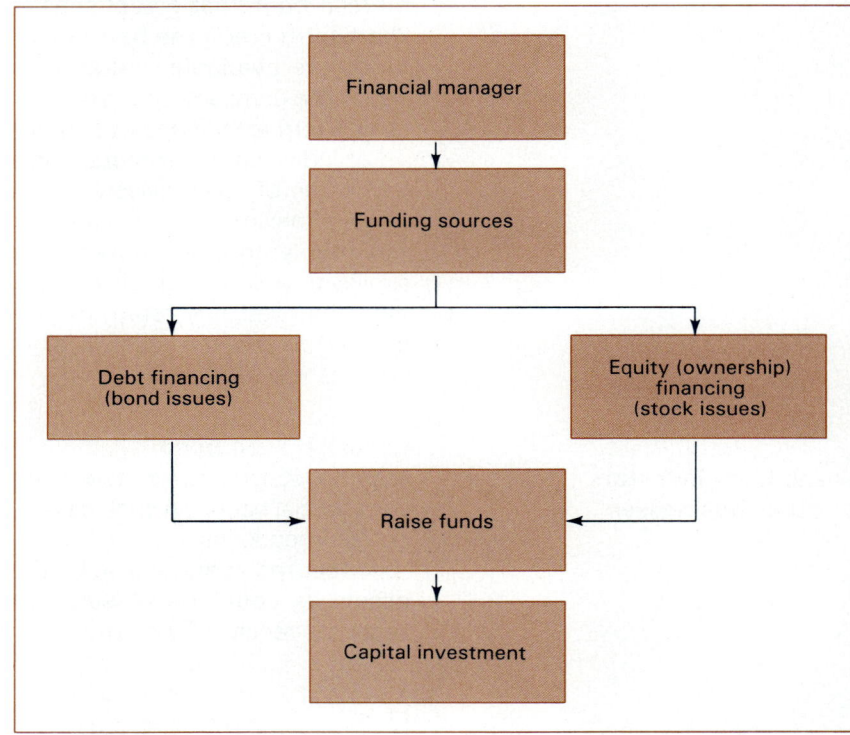

Bonds are an important source of capital funding for businesses. The people who buy bonds must have trust in the company's ability to repay the debt over a period of 20 to 30 years.

A bond is a certificate of indebtedness that is sold to raise long-term funds for a corporation or a government agency. It is a fixed obligation that represents a loan to the company. The obligation includes the principal (the amount borrowed) and the interest rate expressed as an annual percentage.

For example, suppose that General Motors issued a 14 percent, $5 million bond on March 1, 1983, due on March 1, 1998. General Motors would agree to pay bondholders 14 percent interest each March 1 from 1984 through 1998. On March 1, 1998, the company would also return the principal of $5 million.

An indenture is a legal contract in which the full terms of a bond issue are set forth. The indenture states such information as the following:

1. The rate of interest, with time and means of payment
2. The date of maturity and any conditions for repayment of the principal before maturity
3. A description of any collateral pledged, with priorities for bondholder reimbursement in the event of default
4. The name and address of the party responsible for supervising the terms of the agreement (the trustee).

Under the federal Trust Indenture Act of 1939, for public offerings of debt securities, an independent trustee must be appointed to protect creditors and ensure that the company meets the terms of the indenture. The trustee is usually a commercial bank.

Kinds of bonds

There are four kinds of bonds, each with different forms of investor protection: (1) mortgage bonds, (2) collateral trust bonds, (3) equipment trust bonds, and (4) debenture bonds.

Mortgage bonds Mortgage bonds are secured by the corporation's real assets, such as land and buildings. They are the most common form of secured obligation. The property pledged must be worth more than the amount of money borrowed so that the bondholders will be protected.

Collateral trust bonds With collateral trust bonds, the company pledges a group of securities that are held in trust by a commercial bank. The securities could be shares it owns in another corporation, including shares of a subsidiary. Collateral trust bonds are usually considered very safe investments.

Equipment trust bonds Equipment trust bonds are used to finance machinery or equipment that the company uses in its everyday operations. The machinery or equipment is then pledged as collateral for the loan. Railroads, trucking lines, airlines, and oil companies are among the companies that commonly use this form of financing. Equipment pledged may include locomotives, trucks, aircraft, and oil-drilling rigs.

Financing terms usually require that the company issuing the bonds make a down payment on the equipment and that a trustee hold title to the equipment until the debt is repaid. Equipment trust bondholders are protected because the assets pledged are common among firms in the issuer's industry. Thus the equipment can be sold if the company defaults on payments.

Debenture bonds A debenture bond is an unsecured debt based on the credit reputation of the issuing corporation. Because they are unsecured, debenture bonds give less protection to investors. If a company dissolves, creditors with secured claims are paid off before creditors with unsecured claims. Most investors will buy debenture bonds only from companies with excellent credit ratings.

Table 17.1 summarizes the kinds of bonds that are commonly issued.

Paying off bond issues

Almost all bonds have a definite date of maturity. On that date, the corporation must pay bondholders the principal due plus any interest accumulated since the last interest date.

There are four common ways of retiring, or paying off, a bond issue: (1) sinking funds, (2) call provisions, (3) debt refunding, and (4) conversion rights.

Table 17.1 Kinds of bonds

Bond	Bondholder protection	Degree of risk
Mortgage	Pledges real assets, such as real estate	Lowest
Collateral trust	Pledges corporate securities in other companies	Low
Equipment trust	Pledges equipment and machinery, such as trucks, locomotives, and aircraft	Low
Debentures	Pledges no company assets; based on overall credit rating of company	Highest

Sinking fund When a company establishes a sinking fund, it sets aside a portion of money each year so that it will have enough cash to repay the entire issue on its maturity date. If a company must set up a sinking fund, the terms are usually stated in the indenture agreement when the company issues the bonds. For example, if a company had a 30-year, $60 million bond issue, it would set aside 1/30th of $60 million—$2 million—in its sinking fund each year. Of course, the company must also pay interest to bondholders in the meantime.

Call provisions If a call provision is included in an indenture agreement, a company can pay off its bonds before maturity. A call provision allows a company to repay its bondholders early if it is advantageous to do so.

For example, suppose an 11 percent callable bond was issued in 1983 with a maturity date of 2003. If bond interest rates fall to 8 percent in 1990, the company may decide to redeem the bond right away rather than wait until 2003. That way the company could avoid paying 11 percent interest when the going rate was only 8 percent.

A change in the prime rate is important news.

"This alarm clock is a real eye-opener! Instead of a buzzer, it zaps you with the latest prime interest rate!"

From the *Wall Street Journal,* Permission—Cartoon Features Syndicate.

Chapter 17 Raising and managing capital

Refunding A company may decide to pay off a high-interest bond issue by issuing new bonds at a lower interest rate. This is called refunding. In the previous example, the corporation may decide to retire its 11 percent bond obligation by issuing new bonds at 8 percent. The proceeds from the new bonds would then be used to pay off the older ones.

Conversion rights A bond indenture agreement may specify that the bonds are convertible. Holders of convertible bonds can exchange their bonds for a specific number of shares of the company's common stock. This may have advantages for both bondholders and bond issuers. It gives bondholders the opportunity to share in potential increases in stock value. And it gives the company the opportunity to remove a fixed debt obligation.

Default on bond payments

A corporation defaults if it is unable to pay interest on the date set in the indenture agreement or if it is unable to repay the principal on the maturity date. In either case, the bondholders' trustee can take legal steps to obtain the assets that secure the loan.

The company may respond by asking a federal court for continuing control and protection from its creditors under Chapter XI of the Bankruptcy Act. If the court denies the Chapter XI petition, the company has two options left. It may sell company assets to meet its debts, or it may try to continue in business by reorganizing and deferring debt payments, if creditors will agree.

Factors affecting bond values

The interest rate on bonds is affected by two factors: the availability of credit and the company's ability to meet the financial terms of the indenture agreement.

Availability of credit for bond funds is influenced by the money and credit policies of the Federal Reserve Board. When money is scarce, interest rates rise. (This concept is explored in more detail in Chapter 16.)

Three major rating services evaluate companies' abilities to meet their debts. Each service issues ratings that indicate its assessment of the quality of company investments. Since each rating service uses its own criteria, their ratings do not always agree. The rating firms are Standard & Poor's, Moody, and Fitch. Investors use these services' ratings to gauge a bond's degree of risk.

Information commonly used in rating a bond includes the firm's past earnings record, its current financial position, the nature of the firm's business, and its relative position in the industry. Table 17.2 describes the scales used by the three rating organizations.

A bond offering's ratings will affect its market price. In general, bonds with lower ratings carry higher interest rates. This reflects the increased risk associated with them.

Table 17.2 Bond-rating systems

Investment category	Standard & Poor's	Moody	Fitch
Top quality	AAA	Aaa	AAA
	AA	Aa	AA
	A	A	A
Medium quality to speculative	BBB	Baa	BBB
	BB	Ba	BB
	B	B	B
Poor quality	CCC	Caa	CCC
	CC	Ca	CC
	C	C	C
Value is questionable	DDD		DDD
	DD		DD
	D		D

Equity financing: stock

Equity financing is the raising of long-term funds by selling stock. Stock is shares of ownership (equity) in a corporation. When a corporation is formed, its board of directors specifies in its charter the maximum number of shares that it intends to issue. This is called the authorized stock.

Issued stock is the portion of authorized stock that has actually been sold to investors. Unissued stock is the portion of authorized stock that is retained by the company for future use. Typical uses include (1) sale to raise capital, (2) payment for shares of another corporation the firm wants to acquire, (3) distribution to current stock owners as a stock dividend or stock split, and (4) bonuses to key employees.

Par value is the face value per share printed on each stock certificate. It usually is an arbitrary value, often $1, given to each share. Par value is sometimes used to compute dividends or assign value for state incorporation taxes. No-par stock has no stated value printed on the stock certificate.

There are two forms of stock: common and preferred. All corporations issue common stock. Only some issue preferred stock.

Common stock

Common stock is the most basic form of ownership in a corporation and includes voting rights and dividends as declared by the board of directors. Holders of common stock are the true owners of a corporation. In return for their investment, they expect to earn profits from dividend payments and increased stock values.

Common stock has five important characteristics: (1) voting privileges, (2) dividends, (3) easy transfer of ownership, (4) proportionate shares of assets in liquidation, and (5) preemptive rights.

Specimen of common stock, face

Specimen of common stock, endorsements

Courtesy of Wisconsin Power & Light Company.

Voting privileges As owners, common stockholders have a voice in deciding important company business. They always participate in electing the board of directors. Stockholders may also be asked to vote on mergers, reorganizations, bonus plans for management, and other important issues.

Dividends Dividends are the portion of its earnings a company distributes to its stockholders. The amount of dividends must be declared by the board of directors. Dividends may be paid in cash or stock. A company usually gives its stockholders only a portion of its earnings. The remainder is used for expansion, capital, or other operating needs.

Easy transfer of ownership Stock ownership can be transferred through stockbrokers and securities exchanges such as the New York Stock Exchange and the American Stock Exchange. A firm makes money only on the initial sale of stock. When stock ownership is transferred through a stockbroker, the firm does not receive any of the proceeds.

Proportionate share of company assets If a company is dissolved, holders of common stock are entitled to a share of its assets based on the amount of stock they own. Such distribution, however, takes place only after all other debts and obligations have been satisfied.

Preemptive rights Preemptive rights are the rights of stockholders to maintain their proportionate share of company assets when new stock is issued. Because of their preemptive rights, stockholders can purchase any new shares of common stock the company plans to sell before they are made available to the general public.

Stock dividends and ownership

If a stock dividend is paid, each common shareholder's percentage of ownership remains the same. The same is true when a stock splits. If XYZ Corporation has 50,000 shares outstanding and declares a 10 percent stock dividend, an owner of 1000 shares of common stock would own the same proportion of stock after the dividend is paid.

$$\text{Before dividend: } \frac{1000 \text{ shares owned}}{50,000 \text{ shares issued and outstanding}} = 2\% \text{ ownership interest}$$

$$\text{After dividend: } \frac{1100 \text{ shares owned}}{55,000 \text{ shares issued and outstanding}} = 2\% \text{ ownership interest}$$

Preferred stock

Preferred stock gives its owners preference in the payment of dividends and an earlier claim on company assets in the event of liquidation but does not usually include voting rights. Like common stock, preferred stock represents ownership in a corporation.

The dividends that preferred stock pays are usually fixed and stated at the time of issue. But a company is not legally obligated to pay preferred stock dividends. It may skip paying dividends to all stockholders with no penalty. If the company does declare a dividend, however, it must pay its preferred stockholders before it can pay its common stockholders.

A company may add features to preferred stock to make it even more attractive to potential investors. As a result, a company may offer cumulative preferred, convertible preferred, or participating preferred stock.

Cumulative preferred stock Cumulative preferred stock entitles its owners to back payment of dividends for years in which dividends were not paid. Owners can collect their back dividends before any dividends can be paid to common stockholders. Thus, if a company misses a $3.50 per share dividend payment on cumulative preferred stock one year, the next year, if it has enough money, it must pay $7.00 per share to preferred stockholders before common stock dividends can be authorized. Noncumulative preferred stock does not require payment of missed dividends. Unpaid dividends from one year do not carry over to the next.

Convertible preferred stock Owners of convertible preferred stock can exchange their preferred shares for a specified number of common shares. Convertible preferred stock may be attractive to an investor because it provides flexibility.

Table 17.3 Comparison of income, risk, and control for basic securities

Security	Income	Risk	Control over corporation
Bonds	Fixed: in form of interest	Relatively low; early claim to assets if company liquidated	None or little
Preferred Stock	Fixed: in form of stated dividend	Moderate; dividend may be skipped; stock may change in price	Usually little
Common Stock	Variable: in form of dividends, when and if declared	Relatively high; last claim on corporate assets; stock price changes	High, depending on percentage of stock owned

Participating preferred stock Owners of participating preferred stock may receive more dividends than the amount fixed in the stock agreement. Once preferred stockholders have been paid their fixed dividends and common stockholders have been paid an acceptable dividend, any additional dividends that are declared must be shared equally between participating preferred stockholders and common stockholders.

17 Raising and managing capital

Summary

A business has limited resources and must use them efficiently. Sound financial management is important for business survival.

In operating a business, money flows into and out of a firm. *Revenues* are the funds a firm raises from the sale of its goods or services and from other business activities. *Expenses* are the costs incurred by a business in its sale of goods or services and all other business activities.

Capital funds are needed to acquire the factors of production to produce goods or services. *Finance* is the business function of obtaining and using money (capital funds) efficiently.

Assets are everything of value a company owns. *Liabilities* are the debts a company has incurred in buying goods and services from others.

The *financial-management process* attempts to assess the firm's financial needs, acquire the funds, and oversee the use of the funds. It includes the following steps: (1) developing a financial plan based on company needs, (2) identifying and analyzing possible funding sources, (3) selecting the most appropriate funding sources, and (4) using the funds effectively to achieve company goals.

Short-term finance deals with revenues and expenses that will arise within one year. For the short term, firms commonly invest their excess cash in U.S. Treasury bills, certificates of deposit (CDs), and commercial paper.

Many businesses depend on short-term loans to finance day-to-day operations. Sources of short-term financing include trade credit, loans from commercial banks, and loans from investors or other businesses.

An *unsecured loan* is one that does not require assets to be pledged as collateral. The loan is granted on the basis of the borrower's reputation. A *promissory note* is a written agreement in which a business promises to repay a sum of money by a specified date at a specified interest rate. The *prime interest rate* is the lowest rate of interest, usually that which banks charge their best credit risks. A *line of credit* is an agreement between a company and a commercial bank, in which the bank stipulates a maximum amount of money it will lend to the firm as an unsecured loan (if funds are available). A *revolving credit agreement* is a guaranteed line of credit. A *secured loan* is one that requires the borrower to pledge assets as collateral.

Long-term finance deals with revenues and expenses that will extend more than one year into the future. The two usual sources of large amounts of long-term capital are *debt financing* (bonds) and *equity financing* (preferred stock and common stock).

A *bond* is a long-term debt that includes the principal amount borrowed and the annual interest for the use of the funds. There are four common kinds of bonds, each offering different creditor protection: mortgage bonds, collateral trust bonds, equipment trust bonds, and debenture bonds. Bonds are rated according to the company's financial reputation and the availability of credit funds. An *indenture* is a legal document setting forth the terms of the bond's issue.

Bond obligations may be retired through sinking funds, call provisions, refunding, and/or conversion rights.

If a company is dissolved, its bondholders may claim company assets before its stockholders can. Bondholders are creditors; they have no ownership rights.

Equity financing is the raising of long-term funds by selling shares of ownership (stock) in a corporation. There are two kinds of stock: preferred and common. *Par value* is the face value per share printed on the stock certificate. Owners of *preferred stock* have preference over common stockholders in receiving *dividends* and in claiming company assets in the case of bankruptcy. There are three forms of preferred stock: cumulative preferred, convertible preferred, and participating preferred.

Common stock is the most basic form of ownership in a corporation. The advantages of common stock are voting privileges, dividend payments, easy transfer of ownership, proportionate share of company assets in liquidation, and *preemptive rights*—the right of a stockholder to maintain a proportionate share of company assets when new stock is issued.

Review questions

1. What is finance? Why is it important to a company?
2. What are assets? What are liabilities? Give three examples of company assets and three examples of company liabilities.
3. What is the goal of financial management? What are the four steps in the finance-management process?
4. What are the three most common uses of short-term funds?
5. What are the most common sources of short-term business funds?
6. What is a line of credit? Why is it useful for a business?
7. What is the difference between a secured loan and an unsecured loan?
8. What is a bond? What is an indenture?
9. Identify the four kinds of bonds and the nature of investor protection each offers.
10. What two preferences are given to owners of preferred stock? What other special features of preferred stock may attract investors?
11. Explain the difference between (a) authorized stock, (b) issued stock, and (c) unissued stock.
12. What are the special advantages of common stock?

Discussion questions

1. A business uses trade credit to obtain $4000 in goods, with the terms 2/10, n/30. What are the two possible costs for the goods? What cost represents the actual cost of the goods? Why?
2. If you were seeking a $10,000 loan from a bank, why would you rather have an unsecured loan than a secured loan? What does each kind of loan represent?
3. A company may retire its bonds using four methods. Explain how each method might be used to the company's advantage.
4. Explain how special preference given to preferred stockholders may have a negative impact on common stockholders.
5. Why is it important for common stockholders to retain the preemptive right?
6. Evaluate the major advantages and disadvantages of long-term credit financing and equity financing. Which is the most desirable to use?

Chapter 17 case

Oakland A's: financial forecast

Professional sports teams are businesses having special financial problems. The Oakland A's baseball team's financial forecast shows that profitability in professional baseball is by no means guaranteed.

Perhaps the only thing that's conservative about the Oakland A's these days is owner Roy Eisenhardt's 1982 financial forecast. Some expenses have been exaggerated and some revenue estimates understated, admits Eisenhardt, "just to be on the safe side."

Eisenhardt has budgeted total paid home attendance for the club at 1.8 million people. With an average unit sale of $4.30, projected ticket revenues for the season are $7.74 million.

Despite aggressive marketing off the field and aggressive play on it, Eisenhardt still expects the A's to lose about $5 million on revenues of about $14 million. Oakland's situation points out how difficult and sometimes deceiving the world of professional-sports management can be.

"Profitability in professional baseball is by no means guaranteed," says Eisenhardt.

Income		Expenses	
Tickets	$7,740,000	Players' salaries	$6,300,000
Local television	1,200,000	Management/office personnel salaries	800,000
Local radio	750,000	Travel/hotels	720,000

National television	1,200,000	Ticket operations	1,000,000
Novelty sales	750,000	Marketing	2,900,000
Program and publications	800,000	Scouting	1,200,000
Coliseum concessions and parking	1,500,000	Minor-league salaries and operations	3,000,000
		Coliseum rent	1,350,000
		Miscellaneous	250,000
		American League fee	232,000
Total	$13,940,000	Total	$17,752,200

1. Why do you think Eisenhardt exaggerated some expenses and understated some revenue estimates?
2. If the A's have a poor season on the field, explain its impact on specific income figure projections. How can this affect the club's financial health?
3. Comment on the following statement by Eisenhardt: "I don't really view the players as labor. They're part of a business team. Considering their salaries, I'd put players about on a parity with owners. I believe players are entitled to a certain share of the pie, the same as the invested capital side should be rewarded.... The reality is that the players are already partners."

Jay Stuller, "For Roy Eisenhardt, Business Is a Ball," *INC.,* June 1982, pp. 31–36. Reprinted with permission, *INC.* Copyright © 1982 by INC. Publishing Company, 38 Commercial Wharf, Boston, MA 02110.

Business in perspective

Western Union's new message

For years, observers of the business world have expected Western Union to come alive, ending decades of lackluster performance. But Western Union, the country's oldest communications company, keeps falling short of the promising predictions.

Western Union owns a nationwide communications network that transmits both data and voice by both satellite and land-based facilities. This long-distance network ties into the company's cable systems in major metropolitan areas. Its telex system—the largest in the United States—has 140,000 subscribers. (Telex is a message service by which typewriterlike devices "talk" to each other.) The company launched its first two satellites in 1974, added another in 1979, and two more in 1982.

In the early 1970s, Western Union introduced Mailgram, an overnight service that relies on the U.S. Postal Service to deliver messages transmitted by Western Union. It is one of the company's fastest-growing businesses.

Western Union was the first company to sell satellite transponders to users. Transponders are devices that receive and retransmit signals from earth and are used for video broadcasting and voice and data communications.

Western Union has also recently been given permission to reenter the international telex market, which is growing three times as fast as the U.S. domestic market. In the United States, Western Union hopes to be the first to offer "super telex," which operates at more than 20 times regular telex's maximum of 100 words a minute.

The company also offers telex subscribers an additional service called FYI that allows a customer to dial up information on a terminal, ranging from ski conditions to stock quotes. Another new business is a system allowing airline passengers to make telephone calls in flight. Western Union owns 50 percent of AirFone Inc., and 12 airlines have already signed up for the service.

With all of this high technology going for it, analysts on Wall Street are hopeful that Western Union might finally become a "hot" buy.

Adapted from Lisa Miller Mesdag, "Western Union's New Message," *FORTUNE,* February 8, 1982, pp. 63–64. Reprinted from *FORTUNE* Magazine by permission. © 1982 Time Inc.

Chapter 18 — Securities markets

Key terms

venture capital
securities market
stock exchange
over-the-counter market (OTC)
Securities and Exchange
 Commission (SEC)
yield
speculator
bull market
bear market
underwriting
price-earnings ratio
round lot
odd lot
discount bond
premium bond
market order
bid
offer
limit order
buying on margin
selling short

Chapter objectives

In Chapter 18, you will learn:

Why investment capital is vital for business development

What securities markets are

How and why the federal government regulates securities markets

Investors' three most common objectives

How securities are bought and sold

How to read the stock market reports in the newspaper

How to place an order for securities

Overview

A major advantage of the corporate form of business structure is the ability to raise capital. Behind most successful businesses is a strong financial base.

Investors willing to risk their money by buying stocks and bonds are important contributors to business's growth and development. These funds enable people with imagination, creativity, determination, and desire to develop goods and services that raise the standard of living.

This chapter explains the role and operation of the securities markets where stocks and bonds are bought and sold. Wall Street in New York City is the symbolic center of this financial activity.

The chapter looks at individuals' investment goals, as well as the major kinds of stock market transactions. It also covers legislation regulating securities transactions and how to read the stock pages of the newspaper.

The importance of investment

There are many kinds of capital. Working capital, for example, is used for day-to-day operations. Another very important form of capital is venture capital. **Venture capital is money used to form new businesses, products, and industries.** Venture capital was used to colonize North America, develop the oil industry, construct the railroads, and pioneer computers. The United States still needs venture capital to enable industries to get started, operate, and expand.

Securities exchanges provide a marketplace where capital can be invested. The funds come from insurance companies, trust funds, pension funds, and individuals. Through the securities exchanges, investors finance and thereby participate in the growth of business.

The securities exchanges

A securities market is a place where investors buy and sell securities, mostly stocks and bonds. A stock exchange is a formal organization whose members come together in a specific location to buy and sell securities for their customers.

Stock exchanges operate much like an auction, with buyers and sellers competing to make the best bargain. The buyer who makes the highest bid purchases from the seller who makes the lowest offer, when the two agree on a price. The law of supply and demand affects these transactions.

Chapter 18 Securities markets

Characteristics of stock exchanges

Stock exchanges provide a place where brokers representing buyers and sellers can meet and do business. Exchanges do not own the stock traded, nor do they set stock prices. Their only role is to ease the exchange of securities and monitor activities to prevent unfair manipulation of prices.

Stock exchanges offer investors the following advantages:

- Ease of marketing securities
- Efficient market operations
- Information about corporations listed on the exchange
- Screening of companies listed on the exchange
- Liquidity for listed companies.

There are several stock exchanges in the United States and overseas.

The New York Stock Exchange (NYSE)

The New York Stock Exchange, also known as the Big Board, is considered the most important marketplace for buying and selling securities. A membership in the NYSE is called a *seat*. Membership requirements are strict. Individuals must satisfy rigid personal requirements, including approval by the NYSE's board of governors. Member integrity is important because the buying and selling of securities on the exchange is done by verbal agreements. A member's word must be trustworthy.

NYSE membership is set at 1,366 seats. Ownership of a seat may be transferred or sold, but the potential member must be approved by the NYSE board of governors.

Only members of the NYSE can actually buy and sell securities on that exchange.

Listing of securities on the New York Stock Exchange

Before a security can be traded on the NYSE, it must be registered with the Securities and Exchange Commission, a federal agency. If the company meets SEC and NYSE requirements, it may be *listed,* or traded, on the exchange.

To be listed on the NYSE, a corporation's stock must meet the following minimum requirements:

1. Profit for the most recent year must be at least $2.5 million before taxes. Profit for each of the two preceding years must be at least $2 million.
2. At least 1 million shares must be publicly held.
3. At least 2000 investors must hold 100 shares or more.
4. The outstanding common stock must have a market value of at least $6 million.
5. The company must have net tangible assets of at least $16 million.

Figure 18.1 shows the listed companies with the largest number of shareholders.

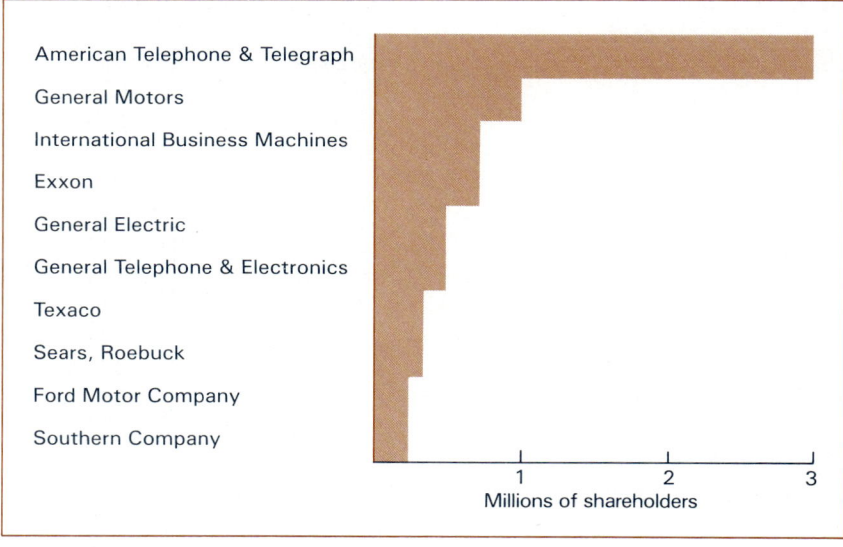

Figure 18.1 NYSE-listed companies with the largest number of shareholders

New York Stock Exchange, *Fact Book 1981,* p. 35.

The American Stock Exchange (AMEX)

The American Stock Exchange is the nation's second-largest securities exchange. It offers many of the same advantages as the NYSE. It operates similarly to the Big Board, but its listing requirements are not as strict. Thus, it has traditionally been a marketplace for smaller companies and new stock issues. The AMEX is also located in New York City.

Other stock exchanges

Besides the two major New York exchanges, there are several regional and local exchanges throughout the United States. Two of the largest are the Midwest Stock Exchange in Chicago and the Pacific Coast Stock Exchange in San Francisco. Another significant one is the Philadelphia-Baltimore-Washington Stock Exchange in Philadelphia.

Prominent among foreign stock exchanges is the London Stock Exchange. The Tokyo Stock Exchange has the largest trading volume in the world. Active stock exchanges operate in Montreal, Toronto, Paris, Frankfurt, Brussels, Milan, Zurich, Amsterdam, and Johannesburg. For the most part, each trades the stock of firms headquartered in its own country.

The over-the-counter market (OTC)

Only a small percentage of the thousands of corporations in existence are listed on registered stock exchanges. **The over-the-counter market (OTC) is a securities market where unlisted securities are traded.**

The over-the-counter market has no single building or trading center. It consists of a network of more than 4,000 securities dealers throughout the country who trade with each other by telephone and teletype.

This market deals primarily with unlisted securities, although it may trade some listed securities. Typically, the OTC market handles stocks of smaller companies, mostly bank and trust companies, insurance companies, and government bonds.

The National Association of Securities Dealers (NASD) establishes and enforces rules of conduct for member brokers and dealers. It seeks to protect investors by maintaining high standards of conduct and ethical practices.

Regulating the securities exchanges

During the 1920s, the American economy expanded rapidly and stimulated the securities markets. Ruthless dealers abused the system, using misrepresentation and fraud to sell securities. Many of these excesses contributed to the 1929 stock market crash. Investors lost billions of dollars. As a result, the public lost confidence in the securities market.

During the 1930s, several federal securities laws were passed to correct earlier abuses. These laws, commonly called the truth-in-securities laws, were intended to renew investor confidence. In addition to these laws, the securities industry adopted stronger self-policing policies.

The Securities Act of 1933

The Securities Act of 1933 is a federal law designed to protect the public against the sale of fraudulent securities. It requires corporations to disclose important financial information about securities offered for public sale in interstate commerce or through the mails. And it requires that corporations offering securities to the public file a registration statement with the Securities and Exchange Commission (SEC). The registration statement must also be condensed into a *prospectus,* a document summarizing important financial information about the securities that must be given to every potential buyer of the securities.

The Securities Exchange Act of 1934

The Securities Exchange Act of 1934 created the **Securities and Exchange Commission, a federal agency established to ensure that corporations that sell their stocks and bonds to the public provide truthful information about their activities and securities.** Investors need complete and accurate information in order to decide what stocks to buy. Registration with the SEC does not necessarily mean that a stock is a "good" investment, but it does mean that the company has supplied the information required by the SEC. The SEC is administered by five commissioners appointed for a fixed term by the president of the United States. Commissioners must be approved by a two-thirds vote of the Senate. They cannot be removed by the president during their term.

The act also gave the SEC the authority to regulate trading practices on national stock exchanges and in the over-the-counter market. National securities exchanges and OTC brokers and dealers must be registered with the SEC. The act also requires that all companies listed on stock exchanges file registration statements with the SEC and submit periodic update reports.

The Maloney Act of 1938

This act requires all national securities associations to register with the SEC. The securities associations are empowered to establish operating standards that promote ethical trading standards. Under this act, the National Association of Securities Dealers (NASD) was formed in 1939. NASD is responsible for regulating over-the-counter securities operations.

The Trust Indenture Act of 1939

The Trust Indenture Act of 1939 is a federal law that requires companies issuing bonds to appoint one or more trustees to ensure that the terms of the bond indenture agreement are followed by all parties.

The Investment Company Act of 1940

The Investment Company Act of 1940 is a federal law designed to protect investors by placing investment companies (such as mutual funds) under the jurisdiction of the Securities and Exchange Commission. A key portion of the protection concerns company disclosure requirements. Every investment company is required to inform stockholders about its financial dealings.

Buying and selling securities

Both stocks and bonds are considered securities. The basic difference is that stock represents ownership in a corporation, while a bond represents a debt.

People invest their money in securities for a variety of reasons. Some investors want to preserve their capital. They tend to restrict their investments to well-established companies with long records of profitable operation. They might be especially likely to buy the preferred stocks or bonds of such companies. These are sometimes referred to as "blue chip" investments. Other investors are willing to take greater risks, with the expectation of greater rewards.

Investment goals largely depend on an individual's financial situation. Young investors with years of increasing earnings ahead may seek long-term gains (called *capital appreciation*). Individuals in their middle or later years may prefer more immediate returns in the form of interest or dividends. An individual who inherits a substantial amount of money may be willing to take added risks.

Before investing in securities, an individual should have adequate savings and insurance protection. Money that is needed to pay the rent or mortgage is not appropriate for investing in speculative ventures. The New York Stock Exchange offers five basic rules for anyone considering buying stock:

1. Remember the risks as well as the rewards.
2. Get the facts about the stock or bond.
3. Seek advice from a reliable financial adviser.
4. Always keep a cash reserve handy.
5. Tailor investments to personal goals.

Three investment strategies

A combination of three goals usually forms the basis of any person's investment strategy. They are: (1) seeking current income, (2) investing for long-term appreciation of the principal invested, and (3) providing maximum safety for the invested principal. All three goals cannot usually be achieved in a single investment. But a group of investments can form a *portfolio* that balances them.

Investing for income

An investor who seeks income from a stock investment looks for a company that has a favorable record of dividend payments. Dividends are not guaranteed. They are declared by the company's board of directors. Some years may see higher dividends than others.

An investor who has income as a primary goal will be concerned about a stock's yield. **Yield is the income from an investment, calculated by dividing annual dividends by the market price.** For example, if an investor bought a share of stock selling for $80 that pays a dividend of $4 per year, the yield would be 5 percent. This is computed as follows:

$$\text{Yield} = \frac{\text{Annual dividend}}{\text{Market price}} = \frac{\$4}{\$80} = .05 = 5 \text{ percent.}$$

Over time, however, the dividend may increase. If it goes up to $6 per share, the investor would get a yield of 7.5 percent on the $80 investment. The price of the stock may also increase, which would lower the yield for new purchasers. But the basis for the yield of an investor who bought at $80 would not change.

Investing for growth

Investors whose primary goal is to increase their capital investment will seek stocks that are likely to increase in price. A growth-oriented investor hopes to make a profit in the future by selling the stock at a price that is higher than the current purchase price.

For example, a stock purchased at $50 per share in 1982 may increase in value to $90 per share by 1985. An investor can sell the stock at a profit of $40 per share, before stockbrokers' commissions and taxes are deducted. A company's stock price is affected by many factors. But over the long run, it is tied closely to current profits and investors' expectations for its future profits.

Many companies whose stock increases in price do not pay large dividends. Some pay no dividends at all. They may choose instead to use their profits to expand and increase their business. Growth investors are less interested in dividend income than in the potential for future profits.

Investing for safety

In general, the potential for gain from an investment is directly proportional to the amount of risk that the investor's money may be lost. Investing for capital appreciation carries the risk that the firm may not grow and that the value of the stock may decrease. The interest paid on bonds is tied to the risk that the firm may default on its payments.

The safest investments are in federally insured bank accounts or U.S. Savings Bonds. Neither offers any chance for appreciation and their interest rates are below other investments. But there is almost no risk that the value of the principal will decrease. Bonds of other government bodies and blue-chip corporations have slightly more—but still low—risk. People who are very concerned about the safety of their principal are well advised to put most or all of their investment money in such securities. The three investment strategies are summarized in Figure 18.2.

Figure 18.2 Three investment strategies

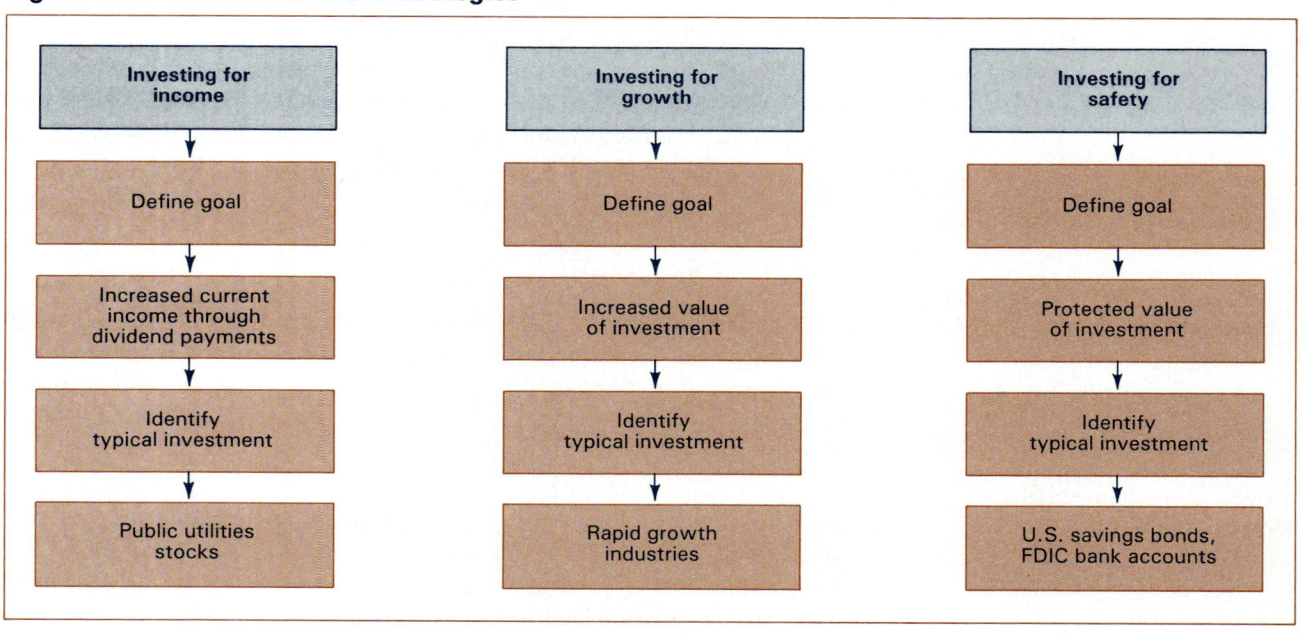

Chapter 18 Securities markets

Speculators

A speculator is an investor who takes large risks in the hope of making a quick profit through relatively short-term ups and downs in the prices of securities. Speculators tend to invest in high-risk companies, often buying shares at relatively low prices. They may invest heavily in the stock of a company that is the target of an acquisition. Or they may invest with the belief that the company will soon announce a dramatically new product that will lead to big profits.

Changes in stock prices

Stock prices reflect changes in supply and demand. The price at which a stock changes hands is determined by the buyer and seller.

If the market price of Walt Disney Productions, for example, was 53½ ($53.50) on a particular morning, this means that someone bought and someone else sold Disney at that price. Later in the day, the market price for Disney might rise to 55½ ($55.50). This rise in price does not necessarily mean that within a few hours the company earned larger profits or had a greater potential for growth. Rather, it most likely means that in the morning an investor agreed that 53½ was a fair price per share for Disney. Later in the day, another investor felt that the stock was worth a price of 55½.

As a general rule, a stock's market price rises most when there are more investors trying to buy than there are owners willing to sell. On the other hand, prices decline when there are more investors trying to sell than there are willing to buy.

This applies to supply and demand for individual stocks. But overall stock prices are also affected by the confidence investors as a group have in the market. **A bull market occurs when investors are in a buying mood and overall stock prices are rising. A bear market occurs when investors are in a selling mood and overall stock prices are falling.**

Many factors influence people's judgment of a fair price for securities. Investors react to the general business outlook, the outlook for a particular industry, a company's past earnings, and a company's future prospects.

Underwriting securities

Underwriting is the process used by a corporation to sell a new issue of stocks or bonds through an investment banking firm. The underwriter purchases the securities from the company and offers them for sale to the public.

Figure 18.3 shows the underwriting process.

Figure 18.3 Underwriting a stock issue

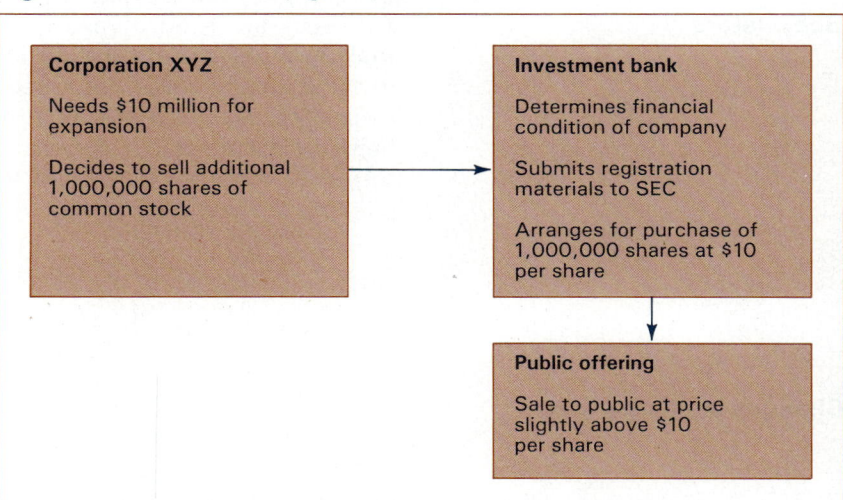

Understanding the financial news

Investors can find much information about activity on the major stock and bond exchanges. The single most common source of information is probably daily newspapers, including the *Wall Street Journal*. Several publishers and brokerage houses also offer newsletters and reports with financial information for investors.

The news media also report daily on the *Dow-Jones Industrial Average* and the *Standard and Poor's Index of 500 Stocks*. These are indexes made up of stocks whose activity is supposed to reflect the tendencies of the market in general. Both indexes are based on an averaging system. (For the operation of the *Dow-Jones Averages,* see box.)

New York and American exchanges

After each day's activities, the major news services provide a report of stocks traded on the exchanges. Such a newspaper report is shown in Figure 18.4.

Let's look at how Xerox performed on March 9, 1983. Columns 1 and 2 show the highest and lowest prices that one share of Xerox stock traded at during the past year. Xerox's stock price ranged from a high of $42.50 to a low of $27.125. (Note that prices are always given in fractions.) Each eighth is 12.5 cents, so 27⅛ = $27.125. Column 4 lists the annual dividend payment based on the last dividend declared by Xerox's board of directors. It is $3.00, providing a yield (column 5) of 7.5 percent, based on the closing market price of $39.875 (column 10).

Chapter 18 Securities markets

Figure 18.4 Stock quotations

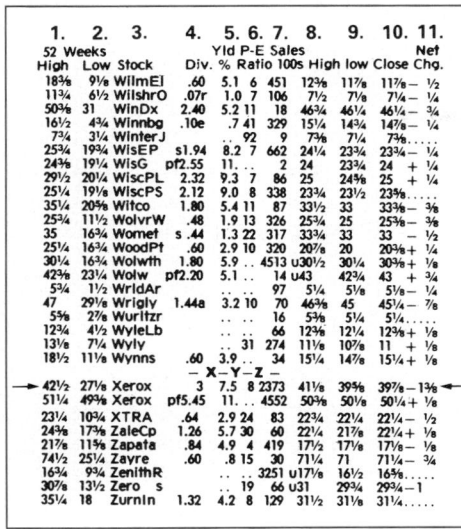

(1) Highest price paid for a share in past 52 weeks.
(2) Lowest price paid for a share in past 52 weeks.
(3) Abbreviated name of corporation.
(4) Current dividend per share. Stock is assumed to be common unless marked *pf,* which means "preferred." Other abbreviations are explained in the footnotes at the end of the table.
(5) Yield based on closing price.
(6) Price-to-earnings ratio. Also referred to as the stock's *multiple.*
(7) Number of shares sold (in hundreds).
(8) Highest price paid for a share traded that day.
(9) Lowest price paid for a share traded that day.
(10) Price of a share at the last trade of the day.
(11) Change between today's closing price and the previous day's closing price.

Reprinted by permission of the *Wall Street Journal.* © Dow Jones & Company, Inc., 1983. All rights reserved.

A closer look at Dow Jones average

To most people, the Dow Jones is considered "the market." It consists of stocks of 30 major U.S. corporations listed on the New York Stock Exchange. The ups and downs of these issues are tabulated daily to make up the overall average.

How is this average computed?
The price per share of each of the 30 stocks is added up, then divided by 1.359.

Why such a strange number?
This compensates for numerous stock splits over the years that would otherwise distort the average. Moreover, it takes into account periodic substitutions in the listed stocks.

How often do substitutions occur?
Infrequently. American Express Company on August 30 replaced Manville Corporation, which filed for bankruptcy. Prior to that, the last switches were in June 1979, when IBM and Merck were added. Two companies have been listed for 86 years—General Electric and American Tobacco, now American Brands.

Why does the Dow get such notice?
While there are several other measurements of stock prices, the Dow Jones is the oldest continuous barometer of Wall Street activity. Compiled by Dow Jones & Company, a financial-publishing firm, it began with 12 stocks in 1896, when Grover Cleveland was president. It was expanded to 20 stocks in 1916 and to 30 in 1928.

What about other stock-market indexes?

The two most prominent are Standard & Poor's index of 500 stocks and the NYSE's index of all listed common stocks, currently more than 1,500. The movements of shares in the smaller, generally more-speculative companies are measured by the American Stock Exchange index and by the National Association of Securities Dealers Automated Quotations (NASDAQ) index.

Do these other indexes give a more accurate reading of the market than the Dow Jones?

Not really. The NYSE and S&P indexes are broader based, thus more representative of all stocks traded. Standard & Poor's index, for instance, encompasses about 80 percent of the market value of all common stocks listed on the NYSE, compared with only 23 percent for the Dow Jones. Still, the fluctuations of the Dow and the two other major indexes are usually quite similar. More important, Dow Jones issues usually set the market's pace. Says one analyst: "When the Dow moves, the overall market responds."

Does the Dow have shortcomings?

Critics say it does. They contend—

• The Dow fails to reflect the changing American economy. It contains too many "smokestack" issues—older, heavy-manufacturing companies whose heyday may be past. An abundance of blue-chip corporations that pile up year after year of steady growth and consistent dividend payments are included, too. At the same time, the average does not take into account the nation's emerging reliance on service industries. Excluded are many glamour issues—companies that devise and market new technologies.

• The average is subject to distortion. For instance, a 10 percent gain in Procter & Gamble, priced near $100 per share, would have twice as much effect on the Dow Jones as would the same move for General Motors at $48 and 10 times the effect of Inco at $10.

The 30 stocks in the DJ Average

Allied Corporation	General Electric	Owens-Illinois
Alcoa	General Foods	Procter & Gamble
American Brands	General Motors	Sears, Roebuck
American Can	Goodyear	Standard Oil of California
American Express	Inco	Texaco
AT&T	IBM	Union Carbide
Bethlehem Steel	International Harvester	U.S. Steel
Du Pont	International Paper	United Technologies
Eastman Kodak	Merck	Westinghouse Electric
Exxon	Minnesota Mining	F.W. Woolworth

Reprinted from *U.S. News & World Report*, Sept. 13, 1982. Copyright 1982, U.S. News & World Report, Inc.

Some stock-market fortunes have been made on hunches, but not many.

"Don't laugh—she's called the last five Dow Jones turn-arounds right on the nose."

From the *Wall Street Journal,* Permission—Cartoon Features Syndicate.

Column 6 gives the price-earnings ratio (P-E ratio). **The price-earnings ratio is the relationship between the stock's market price and its earnings per share.** Earnings per share are calculated by taking the net income available for common stock and dividing it by the number of shares of common stock outstanding. Xerox has a P-E ratio of 8. It is selling in the market at 8 times its earnings. This is the *multiple* of its earnings.

The figure in column 7, 2373, represents the number of shares, in hundreds, traded during that particular day. Multiplying 2373 by 100 means that there were 237,300 shares of Xerox traded that day. Stock is sold only in round lots. **A round lot is a group of 100 shares.** Some brokers will buy and sell odd lots for an extra fee. **An odd lot is a group of less than 100 shares.**

Columns 8, 9, and 10 provide information about changes in the stock price during the trading day. The highest price paid for Xerox was 41⅛ ($41.125). The lowest price paid was 39⅝ ($39.625). The closing price

Figure 18.5 Over-the-counter quotations

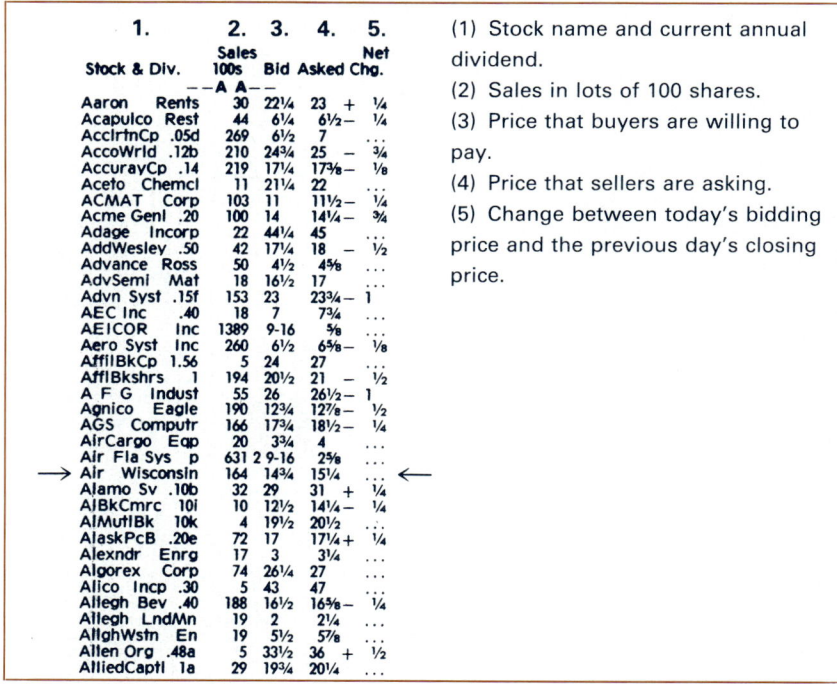

(1) Stock name and current annual dividend.
(2) Sales in lots of 100 shares.
(3) Price that buyers are willing to pay.
(4) Price that sellers are asking.
(5) Change between today's bidding price and the previous day's closing price.

Reprinted by permission of the *Wall Street Journal*. © Dow Jones & Company, Inc., 1983. All rights reserved.

showed a net change of $1.375 (column 11) below the closing price on the previous business day. That means that Xerox closed at $39.875 on Wednesday, March 9, 1983.

Over-the-counter stocks

Newspaper information about over-the-counter stocks is less detailed than the reports on the formal stock exchanges. Figure 18.5 shows a typical OTC listing. We will look at Air Wisconsin.

Air Wisconsin is apparently paying no dividend, as none is shown in column 1. It had 164,000 of its shares traded (column 2). The bid price is the amount a purchaser offered to pay for a share, in this case, $14.75. The asked price, as shown in column 4, was $15.25. These figures are based on round lot sales made at about 4 p.m. on the previous trading day. There was no net change in the bidding price (column 5) from the previous day. Therefore, the bidding price at the end of the previous day was $14.75.

Bond price quotations

The bond market provides liquidity for investments that otherwise would not mature for 20 years or more. Many newspapers carry trading reports for bonds. To find the price at which a bond is selling, multiply the reported figure by 10. For example, if the newspaper shows a bond

Figure 18.6 Bond market quotations

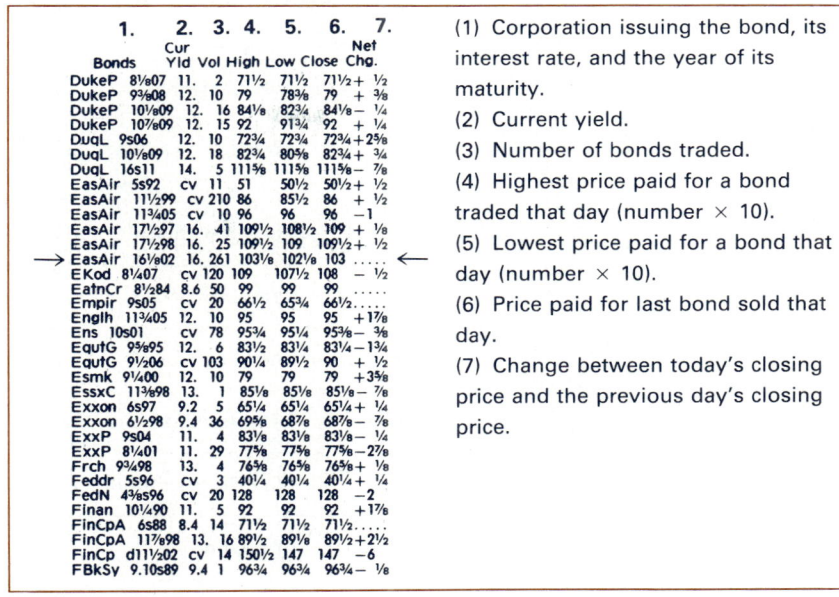

(1) Corporation issuing the bond, its interest rate, and the year of its maturity.
(2) Current yield.
(3) Number of bonds traded.
(4) Highest price paid for a bond traded that day (number × 10).
(5) Lowest price paid for a bond that day (number × 10).
(6) Price paid for last bond sold that day.
(7) Change between today's closing price and the previous day's closing price.

Reprinted by permission of the *Wall Street Journal.* © Dow Jones & Company, Inc., 1983. All rights reserved.

selling for 93, its actual price is $930. Similarly, a bond quoted at 91½ would be selling at $915 (91.5 × 10).

The face value of most bonds is $1000. **A discount bond is a bond selling at a price below its face value. A premium bond is a bond selling at a price above its face value.** When a bond matures, a bondholder is entitled to receive its face value. Thus, an investor can buy a discount bond for $930 and receive $1000 when it matures. And a premium bond priced at $1072.50 will also yield $1000 at maturity.

Figure 18.6 illustrates bond quotations. We shall read quotes for one of the Eastern Air Lines bond issues.

As shown in column 1, an Eastern Air Lines bond was issued at 16.125 percent interest and matures in 2002. Note that Eastern has other bond issues maturing at other times and paying different interest rates. This bond's current yield, listed in column 2, is 16 percent. On the day quoted, there were six bonds sold (column 3). Its high and low prices for the day were $103.125 and $102.125 (columns 4 and 5). The last bond sold that day sold for $103 (column 6). Column 7 shows that there was no net change for the day. This means that the closing price on the previous trading day was $130.

Reading the ticker

The ticker tape—which today is usually electronic rather than printed on paper tape—reports securities transactions. An important source of information for investors, the tape is updated continuously as securities

Table 18.2 Ticker tape symbols for well-known companies

Ticker symbol	Company	Principal business
AMO	American Motors	AMC and Jeep vehicles
T	American Telephone & Telegraph	Telephone service, electronics
BUD	Anheuser-Busch Companies	Beer
CPS	Campbell Soups	Canned soup and other foods
KO	Coca-Cola	Soft-drink syrup, juices
DAL	Delta Air Lines	Domestic, Caribbean air transportation
DIS	Walt Disney Productions	Amusement parks, films, TV
DOC	Dr Pepper	Soft-drink concentrate
XON	Exxon	Petroleum
LVI	Levi-Strauss	Apparel, jeans, slacks, shorts
OAT	Quaker Oats	Food, consumer products
S	Sears, Roebuck	Retailing general merchandise, insurance
XRX	Xerox	Copiers, duplicators, service

Standard & Poor's Corporation, *Stock Guide*, New York.

trades are made. The tape usually shows a sale within minutes of its completion on the stock exchange floor. Brokers all over the country—and the world—can subscribe to the ticker service.

A portion of the tape may look like the illustration in Figure 18.7.

Placing a securities order

An individual who decided to begin investing in the stock market would ordinarily follow these steps:

1. The investor contacts and meets with a stockbroker representing a brokerage firm to discuss investment goals and objectives.

2. Based on personal investment goals and objectives, and with advice from the broker, the investor makes a decision about the kind and quantity of stocks to purchase.

Figure 18.7 Reading the ticker

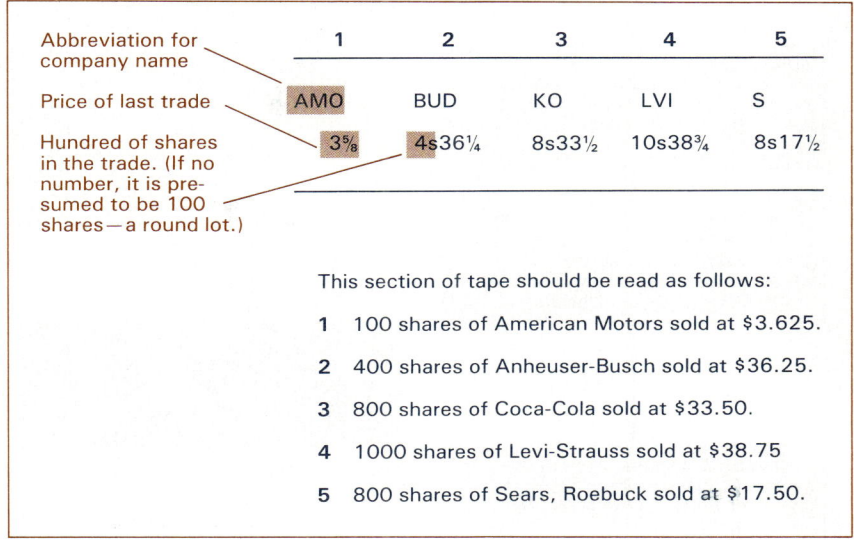

3. The stockbroker executes a purchase order by giving the order to the brokerage firm's representative on the floor of the exchange where the purchase will be made.
4. When the stock is purchased, a confirmation is teletyped back to the broker's office.
5. The broker notifies the investor to confirm that the purchase has been made.

Figure 18.8 illustrates a simultaneous sale and purchase on the New York Stock Exchange.

There are two kinds of brokers. First, there are the traditional retail brokers at the many old-line brokerage firms, such as Merrill Lynch, Pierce, Fenner & Smith (the largest); E. F. Hutton; and Bache & Company. Besides executing buy and sell orders for customers, they analyze investment opportunities and offer advice to their clients. They suggest when a security is overpriced or looks like a good deal.

Remember, however, that brokers are in the sales business. Their pay is based on commissions from the securities they trade for customers. In the end, the investor must decide what to buy or sell and when.

A different kind of broker works for the relatively new discount brokerage houses, such as Quick & Reilly, Source, and Charles Schwab, Inc. These firms often charge much lower commissions than the traditional brokers do. But they generally do not provide investment advice or analysis. They simply act as intermediaries between those who want to buy or sell and the stock exchanges. Discount brokers are best used by investors who do their own analysis.

Figure 18.8 How an order is placed on the New York Stock Exchange

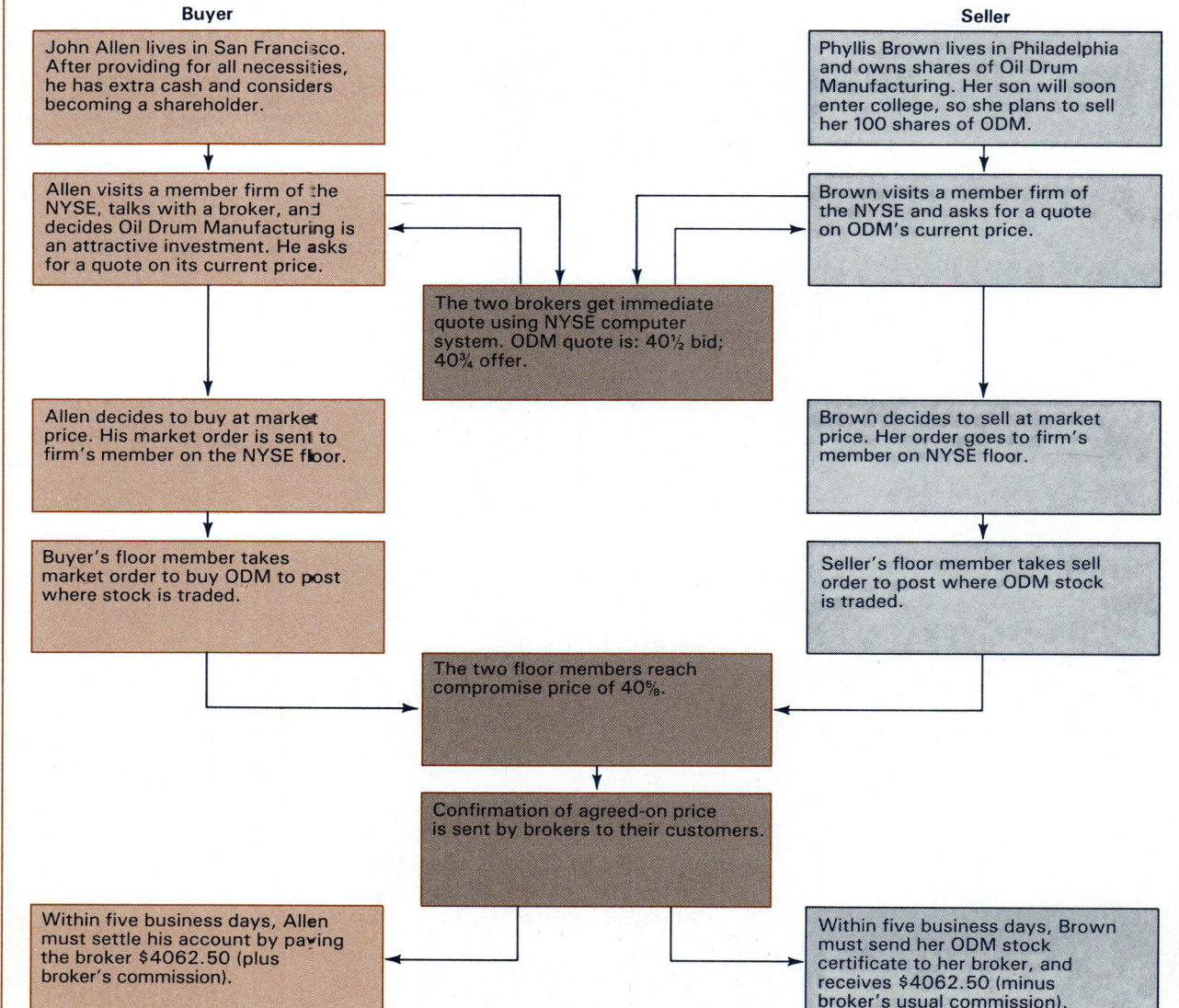

Adapted from New York Stock Exchange chart, "How an order is executed on the New York Stock Exchange."

Kinds of securities orders

There are four basic ways in which people buy or sell stock. They are market orders, limit orders, margin buying, and selling short.

A market order is an order to either buy or sell a security immediately at the best available market price. For example, a market order to buy requires a purchase at the lowest offering price available at the time. A market order to sell requires a sale at the highest bid price available at the time.

Newspapers publish prices at which stocks change hands. But trades develop only after prices have been bid and offered. Prospective buyers make bids. **A bid is the price a buyer is willing to pay to buy a stock.** Prospective sellers make an offer. **An offer is the price at which a seller is willing to sell a stock.** This is the *market*.

If a customer calls a stockbroker and asks for the market in Exxon, the broker would quote the best existing bid and offer, and possibly the last price at which a sale took place. The broker might say: "Exxon, 34¾ to 35¼, last 35." This means that someone is ready to pay $34.75, someone else has entered an order to sell at $35.25, and the last actual trade was at $35.

When a customer places a market order, action is taken immediately. If a client wants to buy and the best offer at the time is 35¼, that is what the customer pays. If a customer wants to sell, the order would get the best bid—34¾. A broker is supposed to try to get a better price than the quoted price.

A limit order is an order in which an investor sets a maximum buying price or a minimum selling price for a desired trade. Under no circumstances may a broker pay more or sell for less than this price. It is possible, of course, for the stock to be purchased for even less than the stated maximum or sold for more than the acceptable minimum.

For example, a limit order to sell shares of Exxon at 35½ might be transmitted to the trading room of the New York Stock Exchange. It is possible that no one is willing to pay that much for Exxon. In that case, the shares would not get sold that day.

Buying on margin occurs when an investor borrows part of the purchase price of a stock from the broker. The Securities Exchange Act of 1934 gives the Federal Reserve Board responsibility for setting the margin rate. The margin rate is the percentage of cash that must be put up when buying stock on credit.

For example, assume the margin requirement is 50 percent. To invest in securities on margin, an investor must deposit a minimum of 50 percent of the purchase price with a broker. To buy a stock at $20 per share, an investor must pay at least $10 for each share. The remaining $10 could be borrowed. The investor must pay a market rate of interest on the borrowed funds.

Since 1934, margin rates have fluctuated between 40 percent and 100 percent. At a 100 percent margin rate, an investor must put up all the money in buying a security.

When buying stock this way, investors are subject to *margin calls* if the stock decreases in value. If a $20 stock dropped to near $10, the broker would ask the investor to put up more of the money. If the investor did not have the money or did not want to meet the margin call, the broker would sell the stock. The proceeds would be used to pay off the margin loan. Anything remaining would be returned to the investor.

Selling short occurs when investors sell shares they do not own in anticipation of the stock price declining. They expect to buy more shares at a lower price to cover for the ones they previously sold.

For example, assume that an investor believes that a stock selling for $20 per share is going to decline in price. The investor arranges to sell shares at $20, and the investor's broker borrows the shares that are sold. Then if the price indeed does decline to $12 per share, the investor buys the shares at $12 and returns them to the lender. Having sold at $20 and bought at $12, the investor makes a profit of $8 per share, minus the broker's commission and taxes.

However, if the price of the security goes up, the investor would lose money. For example, if the $20 share rose to $25, the investor would then have to buy at $25 per share, with a loss of $5 per share, plus commission and taxes.

Buying on margin and selling short are not activities for the inexperienced investor.

18 Securities markets

Summary

Corporations can raise capital to finance their operations by selling stocks and bonds. *Venture capital*—money used to form new businesses, products, and industries—has been an important feature of American business development.

Securities markets and *stock exchanges* provide a place for buyers and sellers of securities to come together and conduct business. Exchanges operate much like auctions, with sales made to the highest bidder.

The New York Stock Exchange (NYSE) is the major marketplace for buying and selling securities. Only members of the NYSE, who must satisfy rigid personal requirements, can actually buy and sell securities there. Corporations whose stocks are listed on the NYSE must meet specified financial requirements.

Other important domestic stock exchanges include the American Stock Exchange (AMEX) in New York, the Midwest Exchange in Chicago, and the Pacific Coast Stock Exchange in San Francisco. Important foreign stock exchanges include the London Stock Exchange and the Tokyo Exchange.

The many thousands of corporate stocks not listed on formal stock exchanges are traded in the *over-the-counter market* (*OTC*). The OTC is composed of a network of more than 4000 securities dealers throughout the country who communicate with each other by telephone and teletype. The National Association of Securities Dealers (NASD) enforces standards for member brokers and dealers.

During the 1930s, several federal securities laws were passed to prevent fraudulent and misleading marketing of securities. These federal laws include the Securities Act of 1933, the Securities Exchange Act of 1934, the Maloney Act of 1938, the Trust Indenture Act of 1939, and the Investment Company Act of 1940. The Securities and Exchange Commission (SEC) is the federal agency charged with regulating securities markets.

The New York Stock Exchange recommends five basic rules for investors: (1) remember risks as well as rewards; (2) get facts about the security; (3) seek advice from a reliable financial adviser; (4) always keep a cash reserve; and (5) tailor investments to personal goals.

The three most common investment goals are investing for income, investing for growth, and investing to preserve the principal.

Yield is the income from an investment. It is calculated by dividing annual dividends by the market price. A *speculator* is an investor who takes great risks in the hope of making a quick profit through relatively short-term fluctuations in securities prices. A *bull market* is one in which investors are buying and overall stock prices are rising. In a *bear market,* investors are in a selling mood and stock prices overall are falling.

Underwriting is the process a corporation uses to sell a new issue of stocks or bonds through an investment banking firm. The *price-earnings ratio* is the relationship between a stock's market price and its earnings per share. A *round lot* of stock is a group of 100 shares. An *odd lot* is a group of less than 100 shares.

A *discount bond* is one that sells below its face value. A *premium bond* is one that sells above its face value.

The four basic ways in which people buy or sell securities are *market orders, limit orders, buying on margin,* and *selling short.*

To make sound decisions, investors must have good information about securities. Electronic communications systems, as well as ticker tapes, are used to transmit securities transactions and other financial information. Most daily newspapers also present a wealth of information on securities.

Review questions

1. What is venture capital? Why is it important for corporations?
2. What major benefits do stock exchanges offer investors?
3. What are the minimum requirements for listing a corporation's stock on the NYSE?
4. Explain the most important elements of the federal securities laws passed in the 1930s.
5. Describe the differences between the three basic investment objectives.
6. Explain each of the following:
   a. market order
   b. limit order
   c. buying on margin
   d. selling short
7. Describe how a securities order is placed.
8. What is a round lot?

Discussion questions

1. Interpret the following ticker tape information:

T	LVI	DAL	OAT
6s59	39½	4s65¼	2s37⅞

2. Compute the yield for the following stocks:

Company	Share price	Dividends per share
KO	35⅞	$2.16
DAL	67¼	1.20
S	15¼	1.34

3. Discuss the advantages and disadvantages of the following investment objectives:
   a. investing for income
   b. investing for growth
   c. investing for safety
4. What current events might cause stock prices to rise? What current events might cause stock prices to fall?

Chapter 18 case

Which way to invest

Individual personal needs affect investment decisions. This case presents three people having different personal needs as they each seek to invest their $50,000 inheritance.

About six months ago, Charles Humphries, a bachelor, died, leaving in his will $50,000 to each of three relatives. His brother John, 57, is an electrical engineer, is married, and has two grown children. His sister Mary, 43, is unmarried, and is a pediatrician. Jerry, his nephew, is 23, married, and has a small child. He works as a computer programmer.

If each of these individuals asked you for advice about investing their $50,000, what investment strategies would you advise? Why?

Business in perspective

The rise of the corporate controller

For most of industrial history, the company controller was the person who kept the accounting books. The controllership was not a glamorous position. Nor was it considered a good rung for climbing the corporate ladder.

However, inflation, uncontrolled corporate growth, and the need to measure the cost of doing business have helped raise the controller from obscurity. Many companies now give their controllers significant power and influence in corporate policy making. And controllers are involved with all facets of their companies' operations. Their advice is demanded on such diverse matters as production, marketing, investment decisions, and strategic planning. As a result, the controller is now reporting directly to top management.

The major advantages of the job—and the reason it has the attention of top management—is that the controller is the only one who knows how every part of the organization operates. As a result, the controller can spot trouble and pinpoint where costs are rising and why. The controller can help improve the company's profits by reducing excessive costs and tightening financial controls.

The controller's office has now become a primary breeding ground for rising executives. Such companies as Cooper Industries, Singer, FMC, General Motors, Fruehauf, and CPC International have had controllers at the helm in recent years. In fact, companies that are known for their excellent controller training are being raided by other firms looking for candidates to fill top executive positions.

Adapted from "The Controller: Inflation Gives Him More Clout with Management," *BusinessWeek*, August 15, 1977, pp. 84–95.

Chapter 19

Accounting: understanding financial statements

Key terms

income statement
revenues
expenses
net income
balance sheet
assets
current assets
fixed assets
intangible assets
liabilities
current liabilities
long-term liabilities
owners' equity
statement of changes in financial position
working capital
ratio analysis
vertical analysis
liquidity

Chapter objectives

In Chapter 19, you will learn:

The function of accounting and the role of the accountant

What an income statement tells about a company

The basic information presented in a balance sheet

Why investors may be especially interested in a company's statement of changes in financial position

Some basic techniques for interpreting a company's financial statements

Overview

Accounting is history and accountants are historians. Accounting records analyze and interpret the results of an organization's financial transactions. The bookkeeping function—the recording—is only a small portion of the accountant's job. Just as the memorizing of dates is only a first step toward learning history, so the recording of financial data is only the start of the accounting function.

This chapter explains the role of accounting in a business firm. It does not present the mechanics of bookkeeping—debits, credits, and journal entries—which can be learned in an introductory accounting course. Instead, this chapter considers the issues that accountants must deal with to ensure that their reports will be useful to management, stockholders, and the public. It also discusses the three most common financial statements and their interpretation.

The need for accounting

Managers' needs for organized financial reports grow directly as the company grows. The owner/manager of a very small business may be able to tell from direct observation and participation how well things are going, where inefficiencies are, and what areas need correcting.

But a large corporation—or government body—often has operations in many locations with many different products or services. In such cases, accounting must be systematically gathered, compiled, and distributed in forms that are easily understood by many people.

Furthermore, most large corporations are owned by stockholders who expect to be informed of company performance. The law requires that stockholders be given accurate financial statements organized under a set of well-defined rules.

Finally, banks and suppliers base their credit decisions on a company's accounting reports. They want to be sure that a company has enough sales, profits, and assets to repay any loan they may decide to make.

Fundamentals of accounting

The sum of all businesses' transactions can be summarized into three basic financial reports:
1. The income statement (also called a profit and loss statement)
2. The balance sheet
3. The statement of changes in financial position.

Rapidly rising interest rates can bring about drastic consequences for businesses.

"Interest rates are peaking . . . interest rates are peaking . . ."

From the *Wall Street Journal,* Permission—Cartoon Features Syndicate.

The income statement

An income statement summarizes a company's revenues and expenses over a specified period of time. It is probably the most frequently studied of all financial statements.

Revenues are all funds an organization raises from the sale of its goods and services and all other business activities. Expenses are the costs a business incurs in acquiring resources, producing goods and services, and marketing. Net income is the amount of money that remains after all expenses have been subtracted from all revenues. If the income statement shows that revenues were greater than expenses, the company made a profit. If expenses were greater than revenues, the company suffered a loss.

Net income is the final figure on the income statement. It is often referred to as the "bottom line." This figure is the end result of all the firm's financial dealings. Many people use it to judge whether a firm is doing well, improving, declining, or stagnating.

An income statement always sums up financial transactions for a specific period of time. For example, the income statement in Figure 19.1 covers the year ending December 31, 1983. Income statements are also frequently drawn for three-month periods (quarters) and six-month periods (halves).

Figure 19.1

Income statement
Consolidated Bopler Company and subsidiaries
Year ending December 31, 1983

	($ in thousands)	
Revenues		
Boplers	$193,338	
Finsters	88,048	
Winklers	73,006	
Fanortons	6,804	
Other	28,408	
Total revenue		$389,604
Costs of goods sold		205,095
Gross profit		$184,509
Other expenses		
Salaries and wages	20,060	
Employee benefits	19,172	
Depreciation	6,222	
Other production, distribution, and operating costs	113,482	
Total		$158,936
Net income before taxes		$ 25,573
Income taxes		
State and city, etc.	2,416	
Federal	10,153	
Total		$ 12,569
Net income		$ 13,004

Components of the income statement

Figure 19.1 presents a typical income statement. First, it *identifies the amount of revenue* for the company—in this case, the Consolidated Bopler Company, an imaginary manufacturer. A firm that sells only a few similar products or services may have a single line for revenue. But other companies, as in this example, have a variety of operations. Their income statements may show how much revenue each product provided. Consolidated Bopler has five main product lines: boplers, finsters, winklers, fanortons, and other. Total revenue in 1983 was $389,604,000.

Revenues are followed by a list of costs and expenses. These are broken down into categories. For many manufacturing firms, the largest is *cost of goods sold*. This includes the materials and direct labor that went into making the products that were sold. Subtracting cost of goods sold from revenue yields the *gross profit.*

Other expenses are subtracted from gross profit. These include salaries for office staff, sales force, and other personnel and depreciation of equipment, among others. In most service businesses, cost of goods sold is replaced by a more detailed listing of expenses by category.

Subtracting all expenses from total revenue yields *net income before taxes.* This figure may be either positive or negative. If negative, the company lost money, and the income statement ends at that point.

When there is a profit, the firm must pay state and federal income taxes. These taxes are subtracted, and the end result is net income—or profit. The basic equation for the income statement is:

Net income = Revenue − Expenses.

The balance sheet

A balance sheet shows a company's financial condition at one point in time by reporting its assets, liabilities, and owners' equity. It shows a single date on it—such as December 31, 1983—and provides information about that date only. Unlike an income statement, which spans a specified period of time, a balance sheet reports information as it stood on one particular day.

In reality, the details of a company's financial condition constantly change. Every day a company sends out bills and receives payments. It uses up inventory and orders new supplies. The value of its plants and equipment change as machines grow old and new ones are bought.

So a balance sheet is like a stop-action frame in the midst of a fast-moving game. It is based on the assumption that the date it "captures" is typical of recent weeks and months.

To get a good notion of a company's financial condition, it is helpful to compare balance sheets from month to month and year to year, looking at changes. This comes closer to showing the constant change that really exists.

On any balance sheet, assets must equal liabilities and owners' equity. That is, assets *balance* with the other two figures. This is summarized as the balance sheet equation:

Assets = Liabilities + Owners' equity.

The balance sheet for Consolidated Bopler is presented in Figure 19.2.

Assets

Assets are everything of value that a company owns. They are often classified as current or fixed.

Current assets are cash, or anything that could be converted into cash within one year. Current assets include accounts receivable, inventory, and marketable securities (investments that can be quickly changed to cash if the need arises). Fixed assets are buildings, machinery, land, and other tangible goods that are used in the conduct of the business, rather than for resale or consumption.

A company may also have intangible assets. Intangible assets are things of value that lack concrete, physical properties. For example, patents, copyrights, brand names, and trademarks are all intangible assets. Sometimes they are listed on the balance sheet as "good will." Their importance to a firm is undeniable, but their true value may be very hard to ascertain. What is the name *McDonald's* worth, for instance? Sometimes, the owner of a trademark or brand name licenses its use to others for a fee. Then the intangible asset gains a true value.

Figure 19.2

Balance sheet
Consolidated Bopler Company and subsidiaries
December 31, 1983

Assets	($ in thousands)		Liabilities and owners' equity	($ in thousands)	
Current assets			**Current liabilities**		
Cash	$ 6,193		Accounts payable	$35,267	
Short-term investments	10,196		Payrolls	10,489	
Accounts receivable	42,683		Accrued expenses	5,594	
Inventories	24,945		Federal income taxes	1,752	
Prepaid expenses	4,853		Current portion of notes payable	3,020	
Total current assets		$88,870	Total current liabilities		$56,122
Fixed assets			**Other liabilities**		
Property, plant, and equipment		54,975	8½% mortgage notes	7,200	
			Deferred income taxes	3,204	
			Other noncurrent notes payable	5,679	
Intangible assets		28,249	Total other liabilities		16,083
Total assets		$172,094	**Owners' equity**		
			Preferred stock	3,863	
			Common stock	1,093	
			Earnings reinvested in the business	94,933	
			Total owners' equity		99,889
			Total liabilities and owners' equity		$172,094

Liabilities

Liabilities are the obligations, or debts, a firm has incurred in buying goods and services from others. Similar to assets, they are classified as either current or long term.

Current liabilities are debts that must be paid within one year of the date of the balance sheet. They include accounts payable (usually owed to suppliers for materials or services), notes payable (short-term borrowing), the current portion due on a long-term loan, taxes payable, and accrued wages (money owed workers but not yet paid).

Long-term liabilities are debts that will not fall due for a year or more. Mortgages on land and buildings, certain bank loans, and bond issues with due dates more than a year away are all long-term liabilities.

Owners' equity

Liabilities are the claims that creditors have against a firm's assets. **Owners' equity is the claim that owners (stockholders) have against a firm's assets.** Liabilities and owners' equity always equal assets. A quick way to determine equity is to subtract liabilities from assets.

A balance sheet for your own business

Suppose you and three friends start a business selling T-shirts with your school's name on them. The four of you invest a total of $1000 into the business. Your manufacturer sends you an initial shipment of the shirts and a bill for $500 payable in 30 days. Your balance sheet might look like this on March 15:

The T-Shirt Company
Balance sheet, March 15, 1983

Assets		Liabilities	
Cash	$1,000	Accounts payable	$ 500
Merchandise	500		
		Owners' equity	
		Paid-in capital	1,000
Total assets	$1,500	Total liabilities and equity	$1,500

As you have probably noticed, your balance sheet shows that your assets are greater than the amount of money you invested. But the $500 increase is not really all yours. It arises because you bought $500 worth of T-shirts on credit. This $500 in merchandise is an asset that is balanced by the manufacturer's bill for $500 (accounts payable). If you pay for the merchandise on March 16, before you sell any shirts, you will have $500 less in your cash account and no accounts payable:

The T-Shirt Company
Balance sheet, March 16, 1983

Assets		Liabilities	
Cash	$ 500	Accounts payable	$ 0
Merchandise	500	Owners' equity	
		Paid-in capital	1,000
Total assets	$1,000	Total liabilities and equity	$1,000

Statement of changes in financial position

A statement of changes in financial position explains the changes in the balance sheet items from one accounting period to another. Like an income statement, it covers a stated period of time. An example is presented in Figure 19.3.

This statement has gained importance because stockholders and analysts want to know where a company's money comes from and how it is used. The statement of changes in financial position is sometimes called a *sources and uses of funds statement* or a *statement of changes in working capital*.

The report focuses on working capital. **Working capital is the amount of money left when current liabilities are subtracted from current**

Figure 19.3

Statement of changes in financial position	
Consolidated Bopler Company and subsidiaries	
Year ending December 31, 1983	

Source of funds	($ in thousands)	
From operations		
Net income	$13,004	
Add items not requiring funds		
Depreciation	6,222	
Deferred income taxes	3,204	
Other	125	
Total		$22,555
Sale of property, plant, and equipment		730
Total sources		$23,285
Uses of funds		
Additions to property, plant, and equipment	$ 9,141	
Cash dividends declared	5,508	
Increase in miscellaneous assets	353	
Repayment of notes payable	4,207	
Other	432	
Total uses		$19,641
Increase in working capital		$ 3,644

assets. It is the money a business has available to invest in additional inventory, pay employees, buy advertising, and finance other business activities. Working capital is the pool of funds a company is able to spend on everyday operations and expansion.

A statement of changes in financial position shows the increase or decrease in working capital by identifying all sources of working capital and all uses to which it was put during the period. Subtracting uses from sources yields the change—positive or negative—in working capital. Among the sources of funds are *current operations,* such as net profits, and depreciation.

Depreciation is shown on an income statement as an expense. But it is not really an outlay of cash. It is simply a bookkeeping entry that recognizes the gradual loss of value in fixed assets. Another source of funds is a *deferral* from paying a current liability. For example, if taxes would normally be due but the due date has been extended, the amount of the taxes would be considered a source of funds.

Cash and other current assets may also come from the sale of fixed assets or perhaps from licensing a company or product name (an intangible asset). Finally, a long-term loan or the sale of stock could be sources of funds.

Current operations use funds as well as raise funds. A company must use funds to purchase fixed assets, repay long-term debts, pay dividends to stockholders, and so forth.

Figure 19.3 shows the statement of changes in financial position that accompanies the income statement and balance sheet of Figures 19.1 and 19.2. It shows that Bopler had a net increase in working capital in 1983.

Interpreting financial statements

The numbers reported in financial statements are best understood when placed in some context. That is, by some measures a company with net profits of $5 million may be more profitable than a company with a net profit of $100 million. Profits, assets, and other accounting measures must be related to each other in order to derive their true meaning.

Most techniques for interpreting financial statements involve ratios. **Ratio analysis is a means of examining the relationship between figures on financial statements.** A basic evaluation of any firm's financial health can be made using ratio analysis.

Comparisons from period to period

One of the easiest forms of analysis is to compare financial results from one period to the next. Figures 19.4 and 19.5 show the income statement and balance sheet for Communications Enterprises, Inc. (ComEnt), a hypothetical owner of newspapers and broadcasting stations, for 1982 and 1983. Total revenue increased from $82,448,000 in 1982 to $104,690,000 in 1983. This was an increase of $22,242, or 27 percent ($22,242 ÷ $82,448,000). Even if higher prices produced some of the increase, 27 percent may be considered a healthy one-year growth.

Ordinarily, we would expect net income (profits) to increase at about the same rate as revenue. That is, Communications Enterprises should have had about 27 percent more profit in 1983 than in 1982 because its revenue was up that amount. In fact, ComEnt had a 36 percent growth in income ($15,914,000 − $11,670,000 = $4,244,000; $4,244,000 ÷ $11,670,000 = 36%). There are many possible reasons for the greater profitability ratio, including improved operating efficiency and the production of more profitable products.

Almost any item on an income statement or balance sheet can be compared from accounting period to accounting period. The goal is to look for trends that indicate whether a company is growing, declining, or holding steady.

Measures of profitability

One highly useful technique for analyzing an income statement is vertical analysis. **In vertical analysis, all income and expense figures are expressed as percentages of total revenue.** Vertical analysis for ComEnt for 1982 and 1983 is shown in Figure 19.4.

Figure 19.4

Income statement
Communications Enterprises, Inc.
Years ending September 30, 1982 and September 30, 1983

	1983 ($ in thousands)	Percent of revenue	1982 ($ in thousands)	Percent of revenue
Revenue				
Newspaper advertising	$ 47,588,000	45%	$41,665,000	51%
Newspaper circulation	14,869,000	14	$13,633,000	17
Broadcasting	28,574,000	27	15,233,000	18
Other	13,659,000	13	11,917,000	14
Total revenue	$104,690,000	100	$82,448,000	100
Expenses				
Wages and salaries	$ 35,648,000	34	$30,095,000	37
Newsprint and ink	9,551,000	9	8,071,000	10
Depreciation and amortization	5,348,000	5	4,433,000	5
Other operating costs	27,345,000	26	19,849,000	24
Total expenses	$ 77,892,000	74	$62,448,000	76
Operating income	$ 26,798,000	26	$20,000,000	24
Interest income (expense), net	(2,022,000)	(2)	(85,000)	—
Income before taxes on income and gain on sale of properties	$ 24,776,000	24	$19,915,000	24
Gain on sale of properties	4,590,000	4	933,000	1
Income before taxes on income	$ 29,366,000	28	$20,848,000	25
Income taxes	13,452,000	13	9,178,000	11
Net income	$ 15,914,000	15	$11,670,000	14
Weighted average number of common stock and common stock equivalent shares	7,371,000		7,461,000	
Earnings per common and common equivalent share	$ 2.16		$ 1.56	

The percentages show the relative weight of each revenue item or expense item in comparison to that year's total revenue (revenue item ÷ total revenue or expense item ÷ total revenue). For example, it may be useful to know that revenue from newspaper advertising increased from $41.7 million to $47.6 million. But it is probably more useful to know that as a percentage of total revenue, advertising revenue fell from 51 percent to 45 percent. On the other hand, broadcasting revenue jumped from 18 percent to 27 percent of total revenue. This may suggest that the firm added some new television or radio stations or that it made its existing stations more profitable. It may also mean that newspaper advertising was not increasing as fast as the broadcasting segment.

In general, such figures can indicate when an analyst should seek further information. Is the company actively trying to diversify into new fields? Is one segment of the business suffering from new competition, labor problems, or other such concerns?

Figure 19.5

Balance sheet
Communications Enterprises, Inc.
Years ending September 30, 1982 and September 30, 1983

Assets	1983	1982	Liabilities and owners' equity	1983	1982
Current assets	($ in thousands)		**Current liabilities**	($ in thousands)	
Cash and marketable securities	$ 10,818	$ 4,028	Current portion of long-term debt	$ 5,446	$ 1,455
Accounts receivable, less allowance for doubtful accounts	11,521	8,167	Accounts payable	3,444	3,201
Inventories	3,080	2,208	Accrued wages	7,954	6,742
Prepaid expenses	3,176	1,886	Income taxes payable	5,060	2,449
Total current assets	$ 28,595	$16,289	Total current liabilities	$ 21,904	$13,847
Investments	$ 17,389	$12,004	**Long-term debt**	$ 23,524	$ 4,262
Fixed assets			**Deferred items**		
Land and buildings	$ 21,159	$19,344	Retirement and compensation	$ 5,630	$ 4,533
Production and other equipment	33,619	30,846	Investment tax credit	656	640
Total fixed assets	$ 54,778	$50,190	Total deferred items	6,286	5,173
Less accumulated depreciation	25,178	22,086	**Total liabilities**		
Total fixed assets	$ 29,600	$28,104	Owners' equity	$ 57,714	$23,282
Intangible and other assets	$ 50,467	$31,048	Common stock	15,112	10,075
Total assets	$126,051	$87,445	Additional paid-in capital	2,447	3,376
			Retained earnings	56,778	50,721
			Total owners' equity	$ 74,337	$64,163
			Total liabilities and owners' equity	$126,051	$87,445

Net income to revenue

At the bottom of the statement, the vertical analysis shows one of the most important measures of profitability: net income as a percentage of revenue. This is a common percentage for expressing how profitable a firm is. A businessperson who mentions "a 10 percent profit" is usually referring to the calculation of net profit divided by total revenue.

The calculation is

$$\text{Percent profitability} = \frac{\text{Net income}}{\text{Total revenue}} \times 100.$$

The amount for a "good" profit varies from industry to industry. ComEnt had a 15 percent profit in 1983, an improvement from 14 percent in 1982. Compared to other firms that derive all or most of their revenue from newspapers, this was well above average. For a firm engaged in mining or oil production, it might have been just average. Supermarket companies, on the other hand, tend to rate any profit above 1 or 2 percent as excellent.

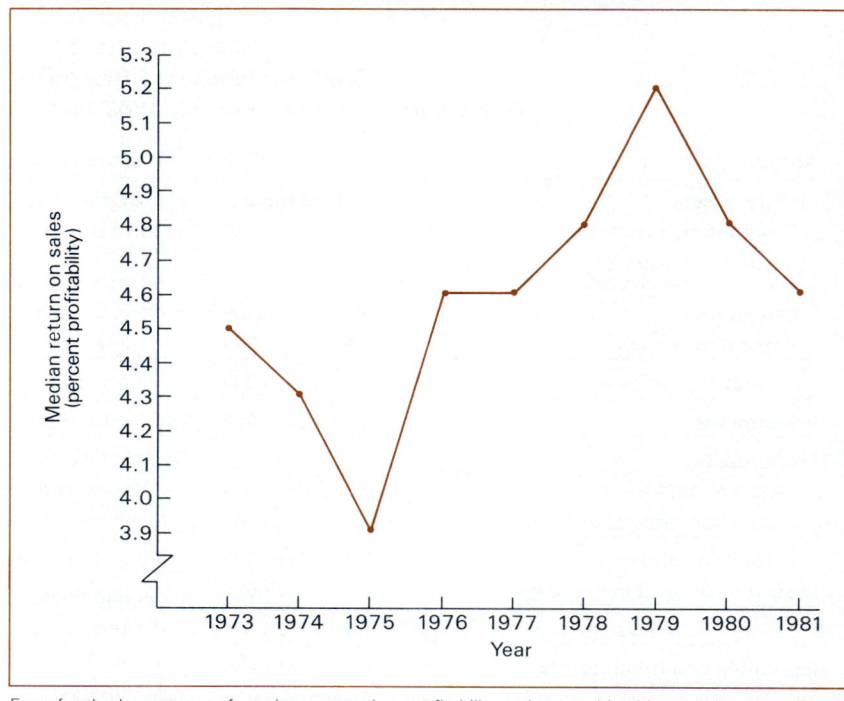

Figure 19.6 Return on sales for Fortune 500 companies

Even for the largest manufacturing companies, profitability varies considerably over the years. The median figure means that half the companies were equally or more profitable, while the other half were equally or less profitable.

Fortune 500 listings in FORTUNE, 1974–1982. Information reprinted from the FORTUNE Directory by permission; © 1982 Time, Inc. All rights reserved.

Net profits to assets

Another way of evaluating net income is to divide it by total assets. This measure recognizes that the most efficiently employed assets should yield the greatest profit. The calculation is

$$\text{Percent return on assets} = \frac{\text{Net income [from income statements]}}{\text{Total assets [from balance sheet]}} \times 100.$$

For ComEnt in 1983, that would be

$$\frac{\$15,914,000}{\$126,051,000} = .126, \text{ or } 12.6\%.$$

A return of 12.6 percent is significantly more than the firm could earn if it placed all its assets in a bank savings account.

Notice that in this measurement, as in many others, information must be taken from both the income statement and the balance sheet.

Net profit to equity

A third measure of profitability is calculated by dividing net income by average stockholders' equity:

Percent return on equity

$$= \frac{\text{Net income [from income statement]}}{\text{Average stockholders' equity [from balance sheet]}} \times 100$$

where

$$\text{Average stockholders' equity} = \frac{\text{Equity at start of period} + \text{Equity at end of period}}{2}.$$

Return on equity shows the rate of return on the money that stockholders have invested. These figures may be compared from year to year within the same company and against return of equity figures for other companies in the same industry.

For ComEnt, the ratio for 1983 was

$$\text{Average stockholders' equity} = \frac{\$64{,}163{,}000 + \$74{,}337{,}000}{2} = \$69{,}250{,}000$$

$$\text{Percent return on equity} = \frac{\$15{,}914{,}000}{\$69{,}250{,}000} = .23, \text{ or } 23.0 \text{ percent.}$$

Earnings per share

Investment analysts look closely at earnings per share (EPS) because it is useful in determining the value of a corporation's stock. Earnings per share is usually included only on income statements for public firms. In its simplest form, EPS is the net income of the company for the period divided by the number of common shares held by all stockholders. Thus,

$$\text{Earnings per share} = \frac{\text{Net income [from income statement]}}{\text{Number of common shares outstanding [usually on income statement]}}.$$

Communications Enterprises has already made the calculation at the bottom of its income statement (Figure 19.4). It was $2.16 in 1983 and $1.56 in 1982. The increase was 38.5 percent.

Measures of liquidity

Liquidity is the ease with which a company can convert its assets to cash. It indicates the firm's ability to pay its current liabilities. A firm may have many valuable assets in the form of buildings, land, and machinery that are necessary for production. But such assets cannot be quickly sold and converted to cash. So despite its many fixed assets, the firm may lack the cash to pay for supplies, wages, or other operating expenses. The Penn Central Railroad went into bankruptcy in the 1970s even though it had hundreds of millions of dollars in fixed assets. Most had to be sold to pay creditors.

Current ratios

Liquidity ratios indicated a firm's ability to meet current liabilities without having to sell fixed assets. All the needed figures are found on the balance sheet.

One of the most commonly used ratios is the current ratio, which is current assets divided by current liabilities.

$$\text{Current ratio} = \frac{\text{Current assets}}{\text{Current liabilities}}$$

ComEnt's current ratio for 1983 is:

$$\frac{\$28,595,000}{\$21,904,000} = 1.31.$$

This means that ComEnt has $1.31 in cash or short-term assets for each $1.00 in liabilities that will be due within the year. In general, the current ratio for a manufacturing company should be about 2:1, but this varies greatly among industries. ComEnt's 1983 current ratio improved from 1.18 in 1982.

Quick ratio

A stricter test of liquidity is the quick ratio (sometimes called the acid test), which does not count inventories as current assets:

$$\text{Quick ratio} = \frac{\text{Cash + Marketable securities + Accounts receivable}}{\text{Current liabilities}}$$

This calculation recognizes that inventories may not actually get sold. Back in the late 1960s, the men's clothing industry was hit by a fad for Nehru jackets, a style influenced by the late prime minister of India. The fad died as quickly as it started and many manufacturers were stuck with warehouses full of unsold inventory. Since the jackets couldn't be sold, the manufacturers couldn't consider them as assets.

In 1983, the quick ratio for ComEnt was

$$\frac{\$10,818,000 + \$11,521,000}{\$21,904,000} = \$1.02.$$

The rule of thumb for a quick ratio is about $1.00 in quick assets to $1.00 in current liabilities.

Accounts receivable collection period

When a business sells something and accepts payment at a later date, it in effect gives the buyer a loan. Manufacturers, wholesalers, and retailers commonly do business on credit, with payment usually due within 30 days, or sometimes 60 days, of billing.

In the meantime, the business has its cash tied up. It has to pay wages, overhead, and suppliers for the raw materials involved in the product or service. But it does not yet have the cash. In addition, a business must be careful that it does not sell to customers who will be

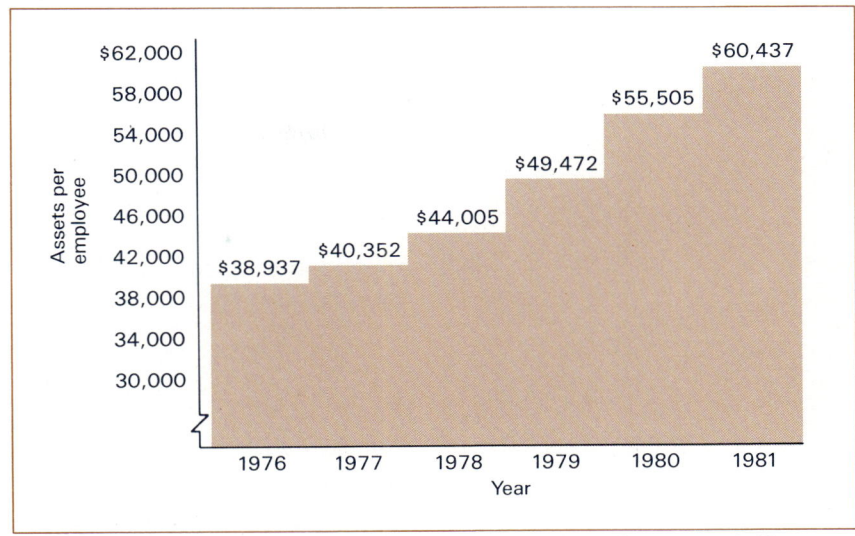

Figure 19.7 Assets per employee, Fortune 500 companies

Increased assets per employee reflect inflation (greater dollar value on new assets) as well as automation—using more capital to replace labor, thus making labor more productive.

Information reprinted from the FORTUNE Directory by permission; © 1982 Time Inc. All rights reserved.

unable to pay or who will take a long time to pay. Thus, it is important to know the average length of time it takes a company to collect accounts receivable. The calculation is a two-step process:

$$\text{Collection period} = \frac{\text{Accounts receivable}}{\text{Average daily sales}}$$

where

$$\text{Average daily sales} = \frac{\text{Total sales [from income statement]}}{365 \text{ [days in year]}}$$

The result can be used two ways. First, managers can see if the average collection period is close to their stated collection terms. Second, they can compare collection periods over time to see if the span is getting longer or shorter. The more days it takes to collect the bills, the more cash is tied up in "loans" to buyers. To generate more cash, a firm can get stricter with its customers and shorten the collection period.

In 1983, ComEnt had a 40-day collection period:

$$\text{Average daily sales} = \frac{\$104{,}690{,}000}{365} = \$286{,}820$$

$$\text{Collection period} = \frac{\$11{,}521{,}000}{\$286{,}820} = 40.2 \text{ days.}$$

How inventory turnover increases profit

As an owner of The T-Shirt Company, you can buy T-shirts for $2.50 each. So you invest $500 in inventory and purchase 200 shirts. Over the next six months, you sell all 200 T-shirts for $5 each. Your total revenue is $1000.

When you run out of inventory, you purchase 200 more shirts for $500 and sell them over the next six months. Your revenue would be another $1000.

You run your business out of your basement and have no other expenses. After your first year in operation, your income statement would look like this:

The T-Shirt Company
Income statement
Year ending March 31, 1983

Total revenue	$2,000
Cost of goods sold	1,000
Net income	$1,000

Dividing income by revenue shows a 50 percent return on sales. Since you sold out your inventory twice during the year, your inventory turnover rate was 2.

Now, suppose that by reducing your price to $4.50, you could sell your shirts more quickly. You start the next year with 200 more shirts at a cost of $500. But you sell them all in four months. Another order sells out in four months, as does a third order. At the end of the second year, you have sold three orders of T-shirts, or 600, compared to 400 the first year. Although you lowered your price, your total revenue increased: 600 × $4.50 = $2700. Your total cost was $1500. So your income statement would look like this:

The T-Shirt Company
Income statement
Year ending March 31, 1983

Total revenue	$2,700
Cost of goods sold	1,500
Net income	$1,200

Return on sales decreased to 44 percent ($1200 ÷ $2700), but net income was up 20 percent ($200 ÷ $1000). Both years, the total amount invested in inventory at any one time was $500. But in the second year, the business used a lower price to increase sales. Inventory turned over three times. And you and your fellow students shared a greater profit.

Chapter 19 Accounting: financial statements

Thus, an average of 40 days' sales had not been paid for on the date of the balance sheet. A year earlier, the collection period was about 36 days. The collection period tends to grow longer during periods of recession or high interest.

Inventory turnover

The quicker and more often a business can convert its inventory of raw materials into finished goods and sell them, the more efficiently it is using its assets. The typical rate of turnover varies by industry. Supermarkets, with their high volume of sales, might expect inventory to turn over an average of 15 times per year. On the other hand, a retailer of diamonds and other fine jewels might be doing well if inventory turns over once per year. In general, a higher rate of turnover is desirable. The inventory turnover rate also indicates how long it might take the inventory figure on the balance sheet to be turned into cash. Inventory turnover has a two-step calculation:

$$\text{Inventory turnover} = \frac{\text{Cost of goods sold}}{\text{Average inventory}} \left[\text{from income statement} \right]$$

where

$$\text{Average inventory} = \frac{\text{Starting inventory}[1] + \text{Ending inventory [from balance sheet]}}{2}$$

In ComEnt's case, cost of goods sold would be the paper and ink used to print the newspaper. The income statements of other retail and manufacturing firms may show a separate line for cost of goods sold. Of course, a service business would not find this ratio very applicable.

$$\text{Average inventory} = \frac{\$2,208,000 + \$3,080,000}{2} = \$2,644,000$$

$$\text{Inventory turnover} = \frac{\$9,551,000}{\$2,644,000} = 3.6 \text{ times.}$$

This means that ComEnt has about a three-and-a-half-month supply of inventory at this time.

Use of borrowed funds versus ownership funds

Finally, an investor, creditor, or analyst may want to know how much debt a company has. Most businesses rely to a considerable extent on borrowed money. In fact, the use of borrowed money actually improves the profit from the owners' investment.

---

[1] Starting inventory is equal to inventory at end of previous year—in this case, September 30, 1982. Ending inventory is amount of inventory at end of current year—September 30, 1983.

On the other hand, increased debt implies greater risk because the money must eventually be repaid. There is also uncertainty about interest rates. If interest rates rise steeply, as they did in 1980 and 1981, the cost of borrowing funds can significantly lower a firm's profits.

The *debt to assets* ratio is commonly used to measure the percentage of total assets provided by creditors. The formula is

$$\text{Debt to assets} = \frac{\text{Total debt}}{\text{Total assets}} \times 100.$$

For ComEnt in 1983, this was

$$\frac{\$23,524,000}{\$126,051,000} = .187, \text{ or } 18.7\%.$$

In 1983, 19 percent of ComEnt's assets were funded by borrowed money, up from just 5 percent in 1982. This ratio shows increased reliance on outside lenders in 1983. From a creditor's viewpoint, the lower the percentage of debt financing to total assets, the better.

Limitations of ratio analysis

Ratios are extremely useful tools for analyzing the raw numbers presented in accounting statements, but they cannot stand alone. The analyst must understand the individual firm as well as its industry and its environment. The trend of a given ratio over a period of years and its value compared to overall industry standards are only starting points. Managers, investors, and creditors must look further into causes of problems, areas for improvement, and possible warnings of financial troubles. They are an aid, but they do not provide all the information needed to make important decisions.

19 Accounting: understanding financial statements

Summary

An accountant is a financial historian who compiles a mathematical record of a firm's business transactions. But this is only the start of the accounting process. The end products are a series of financial reports. These include the income statement (or profit and loss statement), the balance sheet, and the statement of changes in financial position. These and other accounting statements provide owners, managers, investors, and other interested parties with information that can be used in decision making.

An *income statement* summarizes a company's income and expenses over a specific period of time. By subtracting *expenses* from *revenues,* it shows whether the company had a profit or loss.

A *balance sheet* shows a company's financial condition at one point in time. In every case, the company's assets must balance *liabilities* and *owners' equity.*

Another important report, the *statement of changes in financial position,* explains the changes in items on the balance sheet from one accounting period to another. Specifically, it identifies the source of *working capital* and the uses to which it was put. Working capital is the amount of money left when *current liabilities* are subtracted from *current assets.*

The size of a company's profit or the amount of its assets does not tell the whole story. An organization's financial position must be examined in terms of past performance and the performances of other companies in the same industry. *Ratio analysis* is an important tool in this process. Using figures from the income statement and balance sheet, an analyst is able to compare *profit ratios, liquidity measures,* and *debt proportions* to similar calculations for previous periods or to industry standards. This allows managers to spot trends or problem areas and investigate further so that corrective action can be taken. Ratios are also useful for investors and lenders who wish to examine a company's financial health before they invest or lend money.

Among the most useful ratios are net income to sales, earnings per share, current and quick ratios, inventory turnover, average collection period for accounts receivable, and debt to assets.

Review questions

1. What are the fundamental differences between a balance sheet and an income statement? What is each used for?
2. What is the difference between current and fixed assets? Current and long-term liabilities? What are intangible assets? Name two items that might be found in each category.
3. What is working capital? Why is it important?
4. Why would potential investors be interested in seeing a company's statement of changes in financial position?
5. Why would investors want to know more about a company than its profitability? What would they want to know? How would they find it out?
6. What is vertical analysis? What kind of information does it provide?
7. What is ratio analysis? Why are managers, creditors, and investors all interested in a company's ratios?
8. What is liquidity? Why is it important?

Discussion questions

1. Use the financial statements of Consolidated Bopler to analyze the financial health and appropriate ratios of the company.
2. Raising questions is as important as making observations about a company's performance based on its financial statements. As you discuss Consolidated Bopler, what questions arise that call for additional information?
3. Suppose you are starting your own business. You may sell your product for either $1.00 or $1.50. At the lower price, you will have a lower return on sales than at the higher price. But inventory will also turn over faster. Which pricing policy would you choose? Why?
4. Discuss the importance and limitations of each of the following frequently used ratios: current ratio, quick ratio, profit to sales ratio, profit to total assets ratio, inventory turnover, earnings per share, debt to asset ratio, and average collection days for receivables.
5. Assume your boss is going to evaluate your performance over the past year based on the profit and loss statements of your department. Discuss the limitations of basing a performance evaluation on profit alone.

Chapter 19 case

Southwest Fast Foods, Inc.

At the heart of financial analysis is the ability to make sense of the figures presented in financial statements. In this case, you are asked to analyze the financial data of a fast-food chain.

Several years ago, Bernard Escabar bought some shares in

Southwest Fast Food, Inc. The company operates a chain of restaurants in high-traffic locations and specializes in Mexican-style food. Escabar bought the stock because some of his friends worked for the company. They thought it was well run and would be successful. Now Escabar has a little more money to invest. He's thinking of buying more shares of Southwest. But first he wants to take a closer look at how well the company is really doing.

He got out Southwest's most recent annual report and turned to the income statement and balance sheet (shown in Case Figures 19.1 and 19.2). Then Escabar called you, his accountant, for help. You got out your calculator and began your analysis.

1. How do 1983 sales and profits compare to those for 1982?
2. Based on measures of liquidity and debt, what changes occurred between the two years? Are these measures healthy in 1983?
3. What other information would you want that cannot be found on these financial statements?

Case Figure 19.1

Balance sheet
Southwest Fast Foods, Inc.
Year ending December 31, 1982, and December 31, 1983

Assets	1983	1982
Current	($ in millions)	
Cash	$ 50.5	$ 60.0
Accounts receivable	60.0	42.0
Inventory	80.0	74.6
Marketable securities	9.5	3.4
Total current assets	$ 200.0	$ 180.0
Fixed assets		
Buildings and land	440.5	385.9
Equipment	69.5	74.1
Less: accumulated depreciation	180.0	160.0
Total fixed assets	$ 330.0	$ 300.0
Total assets	$ 530.0	$ 480.0
Liabilities		
Current		
Accounts payable	$ 50.0	$ 40.0
Accrued wages	25.0	20.0
Taxes due	18.7	15.5
Note payable	36.3	34.5
Total current liabilities	$ 130.0	$ 110.0

Case Figure 19.1 (continued)

Balance sheet
Southwest Fast Foods, Inc.
Year ending December 31, 1982, and December 31, 1983

Assets	1983	1982
Current	($ in millions)	
Long-term liabilities		
Long-term debt	$ 100.0	$ 110.0
Total liabilities	$ 230.0	$ 220.0
Owners' Equity		
Common stock	$ 170.0	$ 165.0
Retained earnings	130.0	105.0
Total stockholders' equity	$ 300.0	$ 270.0
Total liabilities and stockholders' equity	$ 530.0	$ 490.0

Case Figure 19.2

Income statement
Southwest Fast Foods, Inc.
Years ending December 31, 1982, and December 31, 1983

	1983	1982
	($ in millions)	
Revenue	$1,200.0	$900.0
Cost of goods sold	1,000.0	740.0
Gross profit	200.0	160.0
Selling, general and administrative expense	100.0	80.0
Interest	10.0	9.5
Profit before income tax	$ 90.0	$ 70.5
Income tax	40.0	30.5
Net income	$ 50.0	$ 40.0

Business in perspective

Product liability threatens small business

Can you be held liable for a product that was built before you were born?

The answer is yes.

Consider the recent product liability case of a small equipment manufacturer who bought the assets of an old company. It consisted mostly of an existing brand name and the equipment to make printing machines. The product name had a prestigious and reliable reputation, but the former company made machinery that was potentially dangerous to employees. The machines, if handled incorrectly or without proper safety precautions, could and did cause disfiguring and expensive injuries.

Soon after the new owner took over, 20 people who were injured with the old machinery sued the company. The new owner had not even been associated with the company at the time the injuries occurred.

The law, however, did not find the new company innocent. Using the philosophy of "taking the good with the bad," the court ruled that the company assumed the risks as well as the goodwill of the previous company's history. That is, if a company profits from a predecessor's reputation, it also must assume responsibility for the problems.

Increasingly, judges are trying to ensure that an injured party will have someone from whom to collect damages. This certainly benefits the injured parties, but small companies are suffering some serious consequences. They often can't buy liability insurance because it is either too expensive or not available.

This small printing machine company did have insurance, but its insurance company cancelled its policy after a number of suits. Unable to find another policy with a reasonable premium, the company owner decided to insure himself. During the next three years, he paid out legal fees of about $50,000. The company finally found an insurer that offered a $5-million product liability policy for a $20,000 annual premium. But the firm was still liable to be sued for any injuries that had occurred during the years without insurance.

The best advice for this situation came from a Kansas City lawyer. He told the small company to notify owners of machines that were bought before the company changed hands that the machinery was unsafe. The new company should also refuse to service or sell parts for the old equipment if it does not meet today's safety standards.

Adapted from Sanford L. Jacobs, "Changes in Product Liability Jeopardize Small Companies," *Wall Street Journal,* November 30, 1981.

Chapter 20

Risk management and insurance

Key terms

risk
pure risk
speculative risk
risk management
insurance
law of large numbers
casualty insurance
liability insurance
key person insurance
life insurance
face amount
premium
beneficiary
insured
cash value
loan value
paid-up policy

Chapter objectives

In Chapter 20, you will learn:

The kinds of risks businesses face

Four approaches to risk management

What kinds of risks are insurable

How the law of large numbers affects insurance

The three rules of risk management

The purposes of casualty, liability, and key person insurance

The forms of coverage available to buyers of automobile insurance

Why it's important to have health insurance

The things to consider when choosing a life insurance policy

Overview

Life is full of risks. Some, such as disease, we can do little about. Some, such as household accidents, we can minimize by being especially careful. And others, such as dangerous sports, we can avoid altogether.

We know that business involves risk. There is the obvious risk of lost capital if a business fails. There are major catastrophes, such as the risk of fire. But there are also many less drastic risks, such as losses due to shoplifting. Managers, therefore, must make plans for dealing with risk. They must understand the nature of risk and anticipate the kinds of losses they may face. This chapter first examines what risk is. Then, it looks at insurance, one of the most common ways of handling possible losses.

Kinds of risk

Risk is the possibility of loss. Losses may include money, property, and physical health. There are two kinds of risk: pure risk and speculative risk.

A pure risk involves only the chance of loss; there is no chance for gain. Fires, burglaries, and auto accidents are pure risks. If they occur, someone suffers a physical and/or financial loss. But if they don't happen, there is no gain.

A speculative risk offers the possibility of either a gain or a loss. Buying lottery tickets, investing in common stocks, and owning a business are all speculative risks. In each case, individuals take a calculated risk. They know there is a chance of loss. Yet they choose to face the risk because of the chance for gain. Often the greater the risk, the greater the potential gain.

Managing risk

Risk management is the attempt to reduce the possibility of loss. It is an essential part of business. Managers must be aware of potential risks and take steps to cope with them. There are four general approaches to managing risk: avoid risk, assume risk, reduce risk, and shift risk.

Avoid risk

The ultimate way to avoid risk is to stay at home. Someone who never goes outside avoids the risks of daily life. (Of course, there is still the possibility of slipping in the bathtub.) More realistically, it is possible to avoid speculative risks. That is why some people put their savings in the bank, while others invest in stocks and still others take their spare cash to the racetrack. Any situation that gives an individual a choice of actions provides an opportunity to avoid a speculative risk. Unfortunately, there is no sure way to avoid pure risk.

Reduce risk

Pure risks cannot be avoided. But certain aspects of pure risk can be reduced through smart management. For example, the risk of fire can be reduced by attacking the causes of fire: flammable materials can be kept in appropriate containers; a lightning rod can be mounted on a building; smoke detectors and sprinkler systems can be placed around areas of potential fire; and so forth. Similarly, we can reduce our risk of premature death by improving our health through exercise, diet, not smoking, and the like. When workers must use potentially dangerous equipment, safety goggles, hard hats, and guards on machines can provide protection. Wherever possible, reduce the *hazard* that is the source of risk.

Assume risk

Self-insurance is a way of assuming risk. Large firms sometimes set aside funds to compensate for financial loss due to risks. The federal government assumes its own risks. As individuals, most of us have some degree of self-insurance. It is the deductible amount in our automobile or home insurance. For example, you may have $200 deductible collision insurance. If you are in a car accident, you must pay the first $200 in damages before your insurance company will give you any money. Businesses and individuals who decide to self-insure must be certain that they have the financial ability to pay for unexpected losses.

Shift risk

The primary way to shift risk is to buy insurance. **Insurance is a business arrangement in which an outside firm agrees to compensate an individual or company for losses resulting from pure risk.** In effect, the purchaser of insurance exchanges a certain but small loss—the insurance payment, or premium—for protection from a more uncertain but perhaps greater loss. The risk is then shifted to the insurance company. For many business risks, the insured firm will never collect any money.

Requirements for an insurable risk

Insurance is not available against all possible risks. For example, there is no insurance that pays off if a company has an unprofitable year. You could not buy a policy that protects you from failure to get the job of your choice. Insurable risks meet specific conditions: A large group or population must be exposed to the same risk. The loss must be definite. The loss must be accidental in nature. The potential loss must be sizable. And an insurance company's assuming the risk must be economically practical.

Large groups

Insurance is based on the law of large numbers. **The law of large numbers means that when a large number of identical units (such as people or clothing retailers) are involved, it is possible to predict the statistical likelihood of the occurrence of any kind of peril.** For example, out of thousands of businesses, an insurance company can predict quite accurately how many will be burglarized per year and how much their losses will be.

This knowledge is based on experience. Based on statistics gathered over many years, insurers know *on average* what will happen. Note that insurers do not know exactly *which* firms will be burglarized. But they can estimate quite well how much the firms will lose. The larger the size of the group that is exposed to a particular peril, the more accurate the estimates will be.

This can be illustrated by the mortality tables used to set life insurance rates. Table 20.1 shows that, based on past experience, for every 1000 white males who are now 25 years old, 1.79 will die within a year. For males who are now 43 years old, the death rate per 1000 is about twice as high, 3.58. That means that to make a profit, a life insurance company must charge 43-year-olds a higher premium because being part of that age group indicates a greater risk of death in the coming year than for younger people. Insurance companies use similar methods to determine the chance of a fire in a building located in a congested part of a city or the chance of an accident in a coal mine.

Table 20.1 Mortality table for men and women, birth to age 50[a]

Age	Males deaths per 1,000	Expectation of life (years)	Females deaths per 1,000	Expectation of life (years)
0	13.37	70.2	10.58	77.8
1	1.01	70.1	0.71	77.6
2	0.75	69.2	0.56	76.7
3	0.59	68.3	0.46	75.7
4	0.49	67.3	0.38	74.8
5	0.43	66.3	0.33	73.8
6	0.40	65.4	0.29	72.8
7	0.37	64.4	0.26	71.8
8	0.33	63.4	0.23	70.8
9	0.28	62.4	0.21	69.9
10	0.24	61.5	0.19	68.9
11	0.24	60.5	0.18	67.9
12	0.33	59.5	0.21	66.9
13	0.51	58.5	0.26	65.9
14	0.77	57.5	0.34	64.9

[a]The numbers in this table are for white males and females. For blacks and others, the number of expected deaths per 1,000 is somewhat higher, and the expectation of life is somewhat lower.

Table 20.1 (continued)

Age	Males deaths per 1,000	Expectation of life (years)	Females deaths per 1,000	Expectation of life (years)
15	1.06	56.6	0.44	64.0
16	1.33	55.6	0.52	63.0
17	1.55	54.7	0.58	62.0
18	1.69	53.8	0.61	61.1
19	1.78	52.9	0.61	60.1
20	1.85	52.0	0.61	59.1
21	1.93	51.1	0.61	58.2
22	1.96	50.2	0.61	57.2
23	1.93	49.3	0.61	56.2
24	1.87	48.4	0.62	55.3
25	1.79	47.5	0.62	54.3
26	1.72	46.5	0.62	53.3
27	1.66	45.5	0.62	52.4
28	1.62	44.7	0.64	51.4
29	1.61	43.8	0.66	50.4
30	1.60	42.8	0.69	49.5
31	1.60	41.9	0.72	48.5
32	1.63	41.0	0.76	47.5
33	1.68	40.0	0.80	46.6
34	1.76	39.1	0.85	45.6
35	1.86	38.2	0.90	44.6
36	1.99	37.2	0.98	43.7
37	2.13	36.3	1.07	42.7
38	2.29	35.4	1.19	41.8
39	2.47	34.5	1.33	40.8
40	2.68	33.6	1.49	39.9
41	2.93	32.6	1.66	38.9
42	3.22	31.7	1.85	38.0
43	3.58	30.8	2.06	37.1
44	3.99	29.9	2.28	36.1
45	4.44	29.1	2.52	35.2
46	4.93	28.2	2.78	34.3
47	5.48	27.3	3.06	33.4
48	6.08	26.5	3.34	32.5
49	6.73	25.6	3.65	31.6
50	7.46	24.8	3.98	30.7

Due to the law of large numbers, it is difficult to obtain insurance for certain risks. You may have read stories about concert pianists who have insured themselves against damage to their hands. Since there is a very small group of people in that occupation, it is difficult for insurance companies to estimate the chance of having to pay for such a loss. Many insurance companies do not provide policies on such specialized perils.

Definite loss

An insurable loss must have a real value, and it must be possible to determine that a loss actually occurred. This is not always easy. Suppose a customer shopping in a food store slips on a wet floor and injures his back. The store's insurance company will no doubt pay the cost of the customer's medical treatment. But what if the injured customer wants additional payment for pain and suffering? Or what if the customer claims that the injury has reduced his ability to perform his job? How can compensation for such claims be determined?

Accidental loss

A loss resulting from an insurable risk must be accidental when it does occur. It cannot occur in the normal course of business. For example, the depreciation of machinery is a loss. But it is something that is expected to happen. So it is not insurable. Similarly, while burglary (breaking and entering) can be insured, shoplifting cannot be insured because shoplifting has become an expected part of retail business. Furthermore, it is difficult to prove that shortages are due to shoplifting. Missing goods could have been accidentally thrown out, not properly recorded when they first arrived, and so forth.

Large loss

In general, businesses tend to self-insure against minor risks. They buy insurance against major risks involving losses that could threaten their survival. The administrative costs of writing and administering insurance policies often make insurance for potentially small losses uneconomical.

Economically feasible cost

A risk must have an economically practical cost to make it insurable. For example, an insurer would have to charge a very high rate for flood insurance if a factory was built next to a river that flooded every spring. Similarly, because there are so many minor automobile accidents, no-deductible collision insurance must be quite expensive. In such a policy, any minor scrape or dent would result in an insurance claim. The cost of collision insurance is reduced by deductibles.

The rules of risk management

Insurance is one way to shift the risk of potential hazards, but it can be expensive so a business needs to practice intelligent risk management. This includes learning what kinds of insurance are needed and how much insurance to buy. These factors have given rise to three rules of risk management.[1] These are: (1) don't risk more than the business can afford to lose; (2) don't risk a lot for a little; (3) consider the odds.

Don't risk more than the business can afford to lose

Businesses must constantly balance the risks they wish to assume with those they wish to shift to an insurance company. One approach is to consider the maximum potential loss that may result from a risk. If it would gravely cripple the firm—perhaps send it into bankruptcy—then it would be too dangerous to assume.

Don't risk a lot for a little

This rule reinforces the previous one. A risk manager must decide whether the amount saved by not buying insurance will compensate the company in the long run if a loss should occur. A business should insure its most important assets, such as buildings, machinery, inventory, and key people. The risk of losing any one of them may be small. But if a loss did occur, the impact on the firm would be great and the cost of the insurance would be small by comparison.

Consider the odds

It may seen obvious that insurance should be bought for the perils that are most likely to happen. But just the opposite is true. First, losses that occur fairly frequently are usually predictable. These include shoplifting and nonpayment of debts by customers. Second, the most common losses tend to be relatively small. Since most common losses are predictable and small, companies can assume or reduce their risks. For example, a store may cope with shoplifting by charging slightly higher prices and installing theft-detection equipment. Companies deal with bad debts by setting up an accounting reserve and carefully checking their customers' credit ratings.

---

[1] Robert L. Mehr and Robert A. Hedges, *Risk Management in the Business Enterprise* (New York: Richard D. Irwin Co., 1963), pp. 16–19.

Risks and insurance

Businesses face many kinds of risks. A large number of business risks are speculative and cannot be insured against. A business cannot buy insurance against the failure of a new product, the building of too much production capacity, or the ineffectiveness of an advertising campaign.

But there are also many pure risks that can be covered by insurance. These include damage or loss of property, liability to employees and the public, and the death of key employees.

Casualty insurance

Casualty insurance protects a business from damage or loss of property through fire, theft, and other unexpected circumstances. The three most common forms of casualty insurance are fire insurance, business interruption insurance, and comprehensive insurance.

Fire insurance and extended coverage A business's buildings, equipment, inventory, and records are primary candidates for protection by insurance. The basic form of protection is fire insurance. But most fire policies include a provision for extended coverage. This provides additional insurance beyond the basic fire policy. It covers damage caused by smoke or explosion that may accompany a fire. It also covers water damage because the water used in extinguishing a fire can cause great damage. Extended coverage may also apply to damage due to wind, hail, civil disturbances, automobiles, aircraft, and vandalism.

Business interruption insurance It is not enough to have insurance protection against the immediate effects of an event. After a fire, a company may have expenses for finding temporary facilities, continuing to pay valued employees, and the like. These are known as consequential losses. They are the consequence, or result, of the damage. Business interruption insurance covers consequential losses. Such a policy covers the fixed costs that would continue if any part of a business were forced to close down temporarily. This includes taxes, lease payments, depreciation, utilities, salaries, and estimated profits. The policy would also pay for temporary quarters.

Comprehensive insurance Burglary and robbery are two common ways in which property can be lost. Burglary is forced entry onto property that results in missing money, goods, or securities. Robbery involves similar losses, but includes losses by force, trickery, or the threat of violence. Robbery may also take place off the business premises, as when a delivery truck is hijacked. In most cases, a business would purchase a comprehensive dishonesty, disappearance, and destruction policy to cover losses from burglary and robbery, as well as from counterfeit currency and forgery.

Figure 20.1 Property and liability insurance premiums, 1979

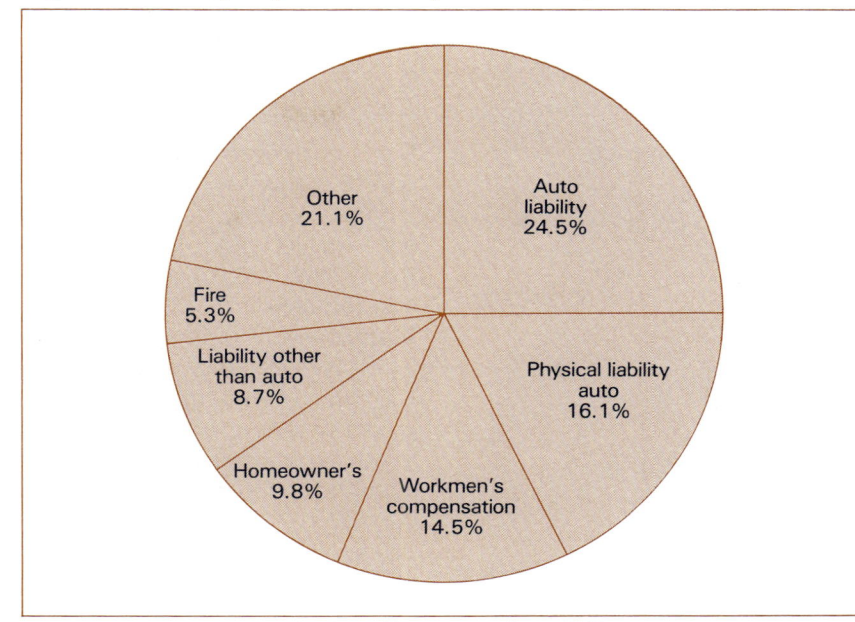

Insurance Information Institute, New York, NY, *Insurance Facts*, 1980.

Liability insurance

Liability insurance protects a company from losses due to an individual's injury or death and damage to other's property. There are several kinds of liability insurance.

Workers' compensation By law, employers are liable for injuries that employees suffer while on the job. In about half the states, employers are required to carry workers' compensation insurance that provides payments to injured workers. In other states, most businesses carry such insurance voluntarily.

Third-party liability insurance Businesses may also be liable when nonemployees are injured on company property. This could happen if a pedestrian slips on the ice outside a store, if a stack of cans at a supermarket tumbles onto a shopper, or if a bar patron is cut by broken glass. These and similar accidents are covered by third-party liability policies.

Other liability policies Doctors and some other professionals carry professional liability policies as protection from malpractice claims.

A company also needs a separate policy for automobile liability. This covers injuries and property damage caused by employees while performing the duties of their employment. In such cases, it doesn't matter whether an employee was using a personal or company vehicle.

Most often, businesses buy comprehensive general liability insurance combined with a standard worker's compensation policy and comprehensive automobile liability.

Key person insurance

Many businesses, especially small ones, are built around the talents of one or a few key employees. A key person may be the entrepreneur who started the business and remains the guiding force behind it. Or some valued executives who have been especially effective in making the business successful may be considered key persons. **Key person insurance is a life insurance policy in which the company is the beneficiary.** The business collects the benefits if the key person dies or is disabled. Such a policy protects the company from the hardships that would result from the loss of a key employee. The insurance money would provide the resources to seek out and hire an appropriate replacement. Or it could provide a financial cushion to buy the firm time to adjust to the loss.

Other kinds of insurance

There are numerous other kinds of insurance. Many apply only to businesses with highly specialized needs. Others are so common that you might already be familiar with them.

Marine insurance is one of the more specialized forms of coverage. As its name implies, it insures ships and their cargoes. Ocean marine insurance covers ships and their contents while at sea or in port. Inland marine insurance covers the goods while they are transported by airplane, truck, and railroad as well as by ship.

Bonding is a form of insurance. A bond is a written obligation on the part of the insuring company to pay for losses under specific circumstances. For example, an employer may buy a fidelilty bond on employees who handle large amounts of money. The employer is then protected from dishonesty in those employees. If any of them embezzle funds, the bonding company must reimburse the company for the amount of the loss, up to the limit of the policy. Unlike robbery insurance, a bond protects a company against damage from specifically named individuals.

A *surety bond* protects its holder from losses resulting from nonperformance of a contract. For example, a traveling carnival may wish to use a town park for a week. To make sure that the carnival operator cleans up and repairs any damages to the park, the town may require the carnival to post a surety bond in an amount equal to the clean-up costs. A firm that has a poor record for cleaning up in the past may find that a bonding company will not issue the surety bond or will charge a very high price.

Title insurance protects a real estate purchaser against later claims to the title on the property. Thus, if the seller did not really have clear title to the property, the new owners would be protected. A title insurance company in effect takes on the risk.

Credit insurance protects businesses from unusually high bad debts. This is particularly important for firms that do most of their business on credit. Since some bad debt is an expected part of business, credit insurance covers only abnormally high losses. This might occur if a major customer went out of business, leaving behind a sizable unpaid account.

Automobile insurance

Most of the insurance discussed so far applies only to businesses. Other forms of insurance apply to individuals as well. Automobile insurance is one common form. Most automobile policies actually provide three forms of coverage: liability, collision, and comprehensive.

Automobile liability insurance covers payments to others for bodily harm or property damage resulting from a car accident. Liability limits are typically expressed as $25,000/$50,000 or $100,000/$300,000. The first number in each pair refers to the most that the insurance company will pay to any one individual for injury or death. The second figure is the total the company will pay for all the claims from a single accident. It is relatively inexpensive to increase the limits of liability insurance.

Collision insurance is usually the most expensive form of coverage. It covers the cost of repairing the vehicle when the accident is the driver's fault or when damage is caused by an unknown or uninsured driver. Raising the collision deductible to $200 or $500 cuts the premium substantially because the owner assumes the cost of small accidents. The insurance is then used only in the case of major damage.

Comprehensive fire and theft insurance covers damage due to fire, falling objects, and similar perils. If a car is stolen, the policy pays the owner the value of the car if it is not recovered or the cost of repairs if it is recovered. The policy will also compensate the owner if anything is stolen from inside the vehicle. (Very often, CB radios and stereo cassette decks are excluded from standard insurance policies because they are so commonly stolen. A separate policy may be necessary to cover these.)

Health insurance

Health insurance has become one of the most important kinds of coverage an individual can buy. Today, most employers provide some amount of health insurance for their employees. It is expensive. But the huge cost of health care makes insurance necessary to protect a family's financial stability. About 90 percent of all families in the United States have some form of health insurance. In 1979, institutions and individuals paid a total of $55.9 billion in health insurance premiums, and health plans paid out $50.2 billion in benefits. Figure 20.2 shows the huge increase in the premiums paid for health insurance plans and the benefits paid out since 1960 by insurance companies.

Health insurance can be divided into three basic segments: hospital coverage, medical coverage, and disability. Hospital coverage pays for the costs of a hospital stay: room, food, laboratory tests, operating room

Figure 20.2 Health insurance premiums and benefits, 1960–1978

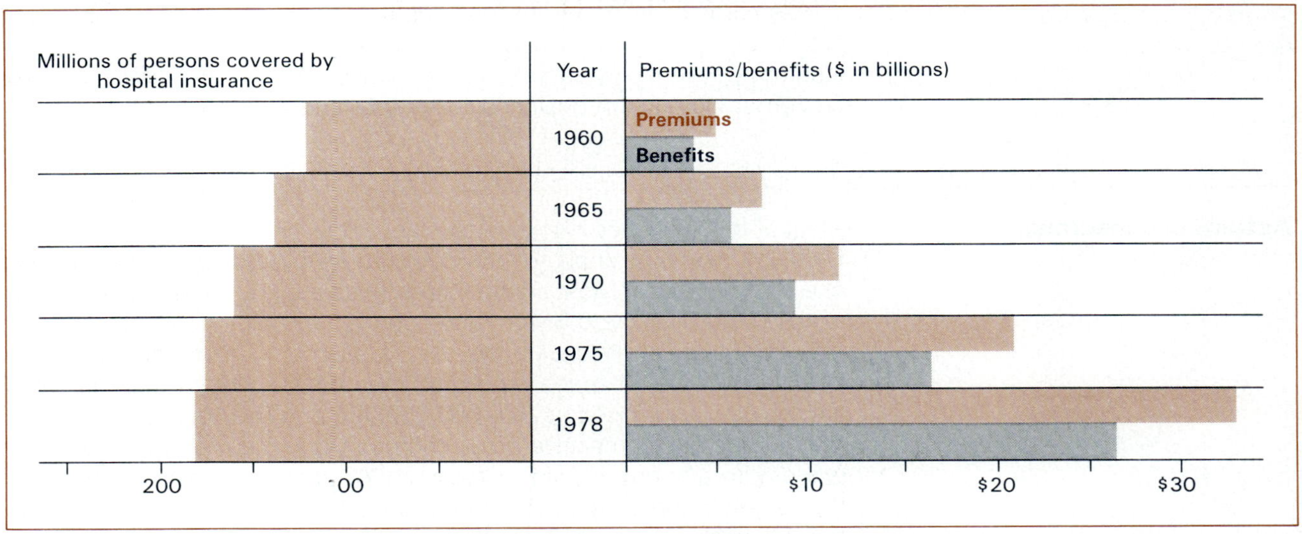

Millions of persons covered by hospital insurance	Year	Premiums/benefits ($ in billions)
	1960	Premiums / Benefits
	1965	
	1970	
	1975	
	1978	

Health Insurance Institute; and Health Insurance Association of America

fees, and the like. Medical coverage pays for doctors' charges. It may cover visits to a doctor's office and care in a hospital. Disability insurance protects individuals from loss of income during extended illness, injury, and recuperation. It pays the patient a percentage of lost income.

Life insurance

The most widespread form of insurance is life insurance. In 1980, there were 402 million life insurance policies in force in the United States. They had a value of $3.5 trillion.

Unlike other forms of insurance, **life insurance covers a sure risk—death.** The only uncertainty about death is when it will occur. As a result, the cost of life insurance is based on the expected rate of death for all people at a given age in accordance with the law of large numbers.

Businesses frequently purchase life insurance as a fringe benefit for their employees. Many individuals also buy insurance on their own. The purpose of life insurance is to provide financial security for a family if one or both of its wage earners die. The amount of insurance needed depends on the size of the family, its living standards, and the age and number of its children. For example, a family with two young children, a large mortgage on a house, and a nonworking spouse needs a different insurance package than does a couple with grown children and no house mortgage.

The terminology of life insurance

Certain basic terms are used to describe life insurance policies and their provisions.

The face amount of a policy is the amount of money the insurance company promises to pay if the insured person dies. On a $50,000 policy, the face amount is $50,000.

A premium is the annual cost of a policy. The amount of a life insurance premium depends on the policy's face amount, the kind of coverage, and the specific insurance company.

A beneficiary is a person or institution who is named to receive the face amount of the policy when the insured person dies.

An insured is the person (or institution) covered by the policy.

Some forms of life insurance have a cash value. **The cash value** of a life insurance policy is the amount of money the insurance company will pay back if the policy is cancelled before the insured dies.

The loan value of a policy is the amount that the insurance company will lend the insured, with the cash value used as security.

A paid-up policy is one for which no further premium payments are necessary to maintain the face value.

Forms of life insurance

Life insurance comes in several forms. The most basic is term insurance. There are also several kinds of whole life policies and endowment policies.

Term life insurance

The least expensive kind of life insurance is term insurance. Policies usually span from one to twenty years. Most typical is a five-year policy. The premium is based on the insured's age at the time the policy is written and stays the same for the term of the policy. At the end of the specified term, a new policy must be taken out. But premiums are increased because of the higher death risk with an older person. Term policies do not have cash or loan values.

A variation of term life insurance is decreasing term insurance. In such cases, the face value of the policy decreases each year until it has no face value at all. The attraction of decreasing term is that it offers the highest amount of insurance for the money in the short run. It can be used to protect the mortgage on a house, which will decline over the years. It also benefits young families. Families in their early years often have little money to devote to insurance. But they need insurance to make sure small children will be cared for in case the wage earners die. As the children grow older, the time span over which they will need care decreases, so less insurance is needed. Decreasing term insurance adapts to such families' changing needs.

The new kid on the block: universal life

One way the life insurance business has tried to adapt to the decline in whole life policies has been through a plan called *universal life*. These policies offer all the benefits of whole life insurance. But they add a feature that enables higher interest rates. The portion of the premiums not used to buy basic insurance are placed in investments that allow an insurance company to offer an interest rate closer to the current rate being paid in money market funds. Of course, this rate can go up and down over time.

In 1982, New York Life, the nation's fifth largest insurance company, reported that it was experiencing an increased rate of surrenders of policies. That meant that policy-holders were willing to stop their insurance, so that they could invest their premiums in investments that were equally safe but paid more. The universal life option was the insurance industry's attempt to lure back lost business. It gave insurance salespersons a response to the criticism that whole life policies paid an interest rate that was far below the rate of inflation.

Whole life insurance

For most of its existence, the life insurance industry has concentrated on selling whole life insurance. The premium for whole life is based on the face value of the policy and the age of the insured at the time the policy is written. For the form of whole life called *ordinary life,* the insured pays the same premium every year until death. The advantage of whole life is that its cash and loan values build up over the years. Loans on a whole life policy are usually available at much lower rates than bank interest. The premiums for whole life are always the same, year after year, while the premiums for term life increase with each new term of the policy.

Another form of whole life is *limited pay whole life*. For this coverage, the insured pays premiums only for a specific number of years, usually 20 or 30. Then the policy is paid up. It remains in force, but no further payments need be made. Such insurance is bought by people who prefer to pay up their policy within a given number of years. Naturally, annual premiums for limited pay whole life are higher than for ordinary life.

Endowment life

Endowment policies combine whole life insurance with savings. Premiums are paid for a fixed number of years, or sometimes until age 65. At that time, the face value of the policy is returned to the insured. Thus, endowment policies are really a form of enforced savings and are usually used as part of an overall retirement plan.

There are variations on all these forms of insurance. The high rate of inflation in the 1970s coupled with the low rates of return insurance companies paid off on their whole life and endowment policies reduced the attraction of these forms of insurance. As a result, life insurance

Figure 20.3 Percentage of ordinary whole-life policies compared to group term insurance, 1950–1979

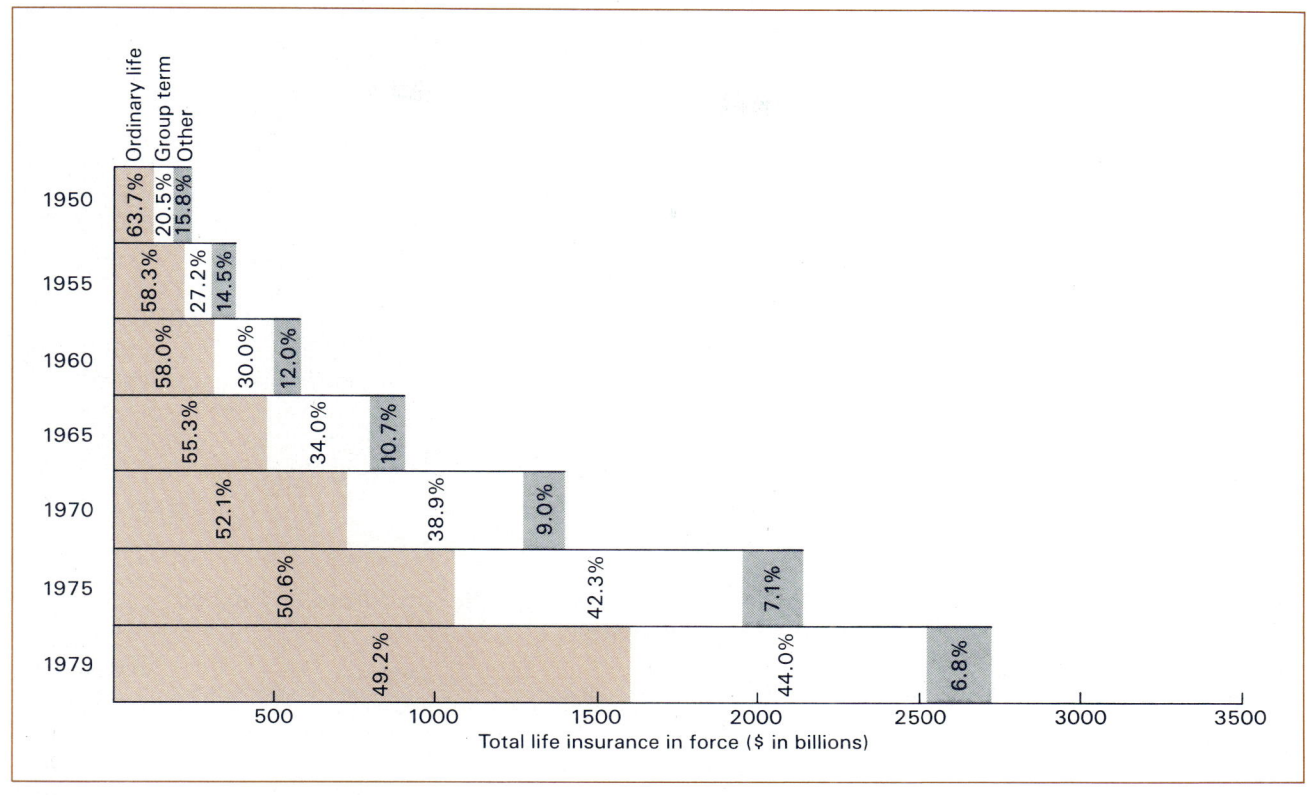

American Council of Life Insurance, Washington, D.C., *Life Insurance Fact Book,* 1950 to 1979.

companies have introduced new kinds of policies that pay higher yields as interest rates rise. Figure 20.3 shows that since 1950 there has been a steady decline in whole life. The percentage of term life, usually in the form of group insurance purchased by businesses for employees, has more than doubled.

Which kind of insurance is best?

The best kind of life insurance for a given person depends on many individual factors, including income, financial responsibilities, and age. Term insurance is quite inexpensive when the insured is young, but it gets more expensive as the insured grows older. Moreover, some term policies do not guarantee that they can be renewed without a physical examination. Thus, if the insured develops a disease, the insurance company may refuse to renew the policy. The individual may then be without insurance when it is most needed. A whole life policy, on the other hand, cannot be cancelled so long as the premiums are paid on time, even if the insured develops health problems. Some policies even guarantee the insured the right to buy more insurance in later years without a physical exam.

Term insurance is by far the most economical, especially in early life. Table 20.2 compares the cost of $50,000 worth of life insurance provided by different kinds of policies. It also shows the increase in premiums for older people. Note that women pay less for any policy than do men of the same age. This is based on the higher life expectancy for women at any age. It is also important to recognize that in the two whole life options, the premium that is set when the policy is written is based on the insured's age at that time. The premium will always be the same. For the term insurance, the premium will vary according to the insured's age each time the policy is renewed.

For example, at the age of 25, a male who bought a $50,000 ordinary life policy would pay $603.50 per year until he died. The same person purchasing the same amount of five-year renewal term insurance would pay only $129 annually. But in five years, he would have to renew the term policy and pay the rate of a 30-year-old, $144. Every five years, the policy would be renewed at a higher rate. At age 60, he would have to pay $1,351.50 per year to keep the policy in force. Under ordinary life, he would still be paying $603.50.

Table 20.2 Annual costs of different forms of $50,000 life insurance policies[a]

Age		5-year renewal term	15-year decreasing term[b]	Whole life: ordinary	Whole life: 30-year pay
Male	Female				
20	25	$ 118.50	$ 77.00	$ 506.50	$ 642.50
21	26	120.00	78.50	525.00	661.50
22	27	122.00	79.50	543.00	680.50
23	28	125.00	81.50	563.00	701.00
24	29	127.50	83.50	584.00	721.00
25	30	129.00	85.50	603.50	741.00
26	31	131.00	87.50	623.50	760.00
27	32	133.50	90.00	645.00	781.00
28	33	136.50	93.50	667.00	802.50
29	34	139.00	97.50	690.50	825.00
30	35	144.00	101.50	715.00	849.00
35	40	186.50	136.50	859.00	984.00
40	45	265.00	201.00	1,047.00	1,156.00
45	50	387.00	306.00	1,295.50	1,383.00
50	55	608.00	484.00	1,655.00	1,717.50
55	60	977.50	767.00	2,147.50	2,184.50
60	65	1,351.50	—	2,626.00	2,640.05

[a]This is for illustration only. It shows the cost in 1979 from one insurance company. Actual premiums are likely to be reduced by dividends.

[b]Would have a face value of $50,000 in the first year, $41,450 in the fifth year, $26,600 in the tenth year, and $5250 in the fifteenth year.

Source: Teachers Insurance and Annuity Association, New York.

Chapter 20   Risk management and insurance

In fact, under the whole life option, the 25-year-old would pay premiums totaling $24,140 by the time he is 65 years old. Using the term plan, he would pay only $20,242 by age 65. When the insured was 65, the whole life policy would have a cash value, but the term life policy would not. On the other hand, the insured may decide at age 55 that he does not need the policy anymore. In that case, he will have paid only $8,599.50 on the term policy, compared to $18,105 on the whole life policy.

Kinds of insurance companies

Insurance firms tend to specialize in one or two areas. The largest are primarily life insurance companies, such as Prudential, Metropolitan Life, Equitable Life Assurance, and Aetna Life. Other firms concentrate on casualty and liability insurance. Leading firms in this field include Travelers, INA, and Transamerica.

Regardless of their field of specialty, insurance companies take one of two legal forms. They may be either stock insurance companies or mutual insurance companies.

Stock companies

Insurance firms organized as stock companies operate for the profit of their stockholders. The stockholders do not necessarily have policies issued by the insurance company in which they own stock. They invest for the dividends and the possible appreciation of the insurance company's stock.

Mutual companies

Mutual insurance companies are owned by their policyholders. They do not earn profits. All income left over after expenses, claims, and reserves is returned to policyholders in the form of reduced premiums or dividends. The board of directors is elected by policyholders.

Insurance companies' earnings and profits

Four of the five largest life insurance companies are mutual companies, as are thirteen of the largest twenty. Table 20.3 lists the 25 largest firms. Prudential, the largest, is a mutual company with nearly $60 billion in assets.

Both stock and mutual insurance companies function in about the same way. In each case, they have two sources of income. First, there are the premiums paid by the policyholders. Second, there is the income earned from investing the premiums. Life insurance companies, for example, are a major source of mortgages for commercial real estate. In 1980, about 38 percent of the revenue of the largest life insurance companies came from their investments.

Table 20.3 The 25 largest life insurance companies (by assets)

Rank	Company	Assets ($ in thousands)	Premium and annuity receipts ($ in thousands)	Net investment income ($ in thousands)	Life insurance in force ($ in thousands)
1	Prudential (Newark)*	$59,778,470	$8,668,858	$3,561,970	$406,571,823
2	Metropolitan (New York)*	48,309,771	6,010,574	3,449,368	349,192,320
3	Equitable Life Assurance (New York)*	34,599,737	4,163,345	1,959,052	197,338,258
4	Aetna Life (Hartford)	22,270,634	5,412,032	1,392,105	144,214,809
5	New York Life*	19,725,325	2,682,329	1,345,953	122,764,294
6	John Hancock Mutual (Boston)*	18,760,598	2,436,403	1,231,265	133,703,479
7	Connecticut General Life (Bloomfield)	13,776,921	1,861,488	956,218	80,402,921
8	Travelers (Hartford)	13,351,227	3,955,025	934,764	104,402,349
9	Northwestern Mutual (Milwaukee)*	11,350,786	1,193,496	789,624	61,308,461
10	Teachers Insurance & Annuity (New York)	9,748,371	1,315,944	811,601	7,587,077
11	Massachusetts Mutual (Springfield)*	9,145,484	1,239,769	614,954	50,934,797
12	Mutual of New York*	8,005,708	891,919	559,314	37,968,654
13	Bankers Life (Des Moines)*	7,988,996	1,536,613	571,707	35,051,210
14	New England Mutual (Boston)*	6,823,015	991,410	465,489	31,672,479
15	Mutual Benefit (Newark)*	5,872,814	1,093,035	396,912	40,241,181
16	Connecticut Mutual (Hartford)*	5,384,922	683,008	353,202	26,223,401
17	Lincoln National Life (Fort Wayne)	4,960,720	1,138,649	339,062	59,931,472
18	Penn Mutual (Philadelphia)	3,866,281	419,127	254,832	18,061,591
19	State Farm Life (Bloomington, Ill.)	3,329,539	536,115	238,382	50,955,938
20	Continental Assurance (Chicago)	3,259,254	1,034,807	171,094	27,791,432
21	Western & Southern (Cincinnati)*	3,062,024	315,904	211,185	14,415,905
22	Phoenix Mutual (Hartford)*	3,038,195	543,621	202,182	29,059,755
23	National Life & Accident (Nashville)	2,906,963	368,718	213,724	16,639,025
24	Pacific Mutual (Newport Beach, Calif.)*	2,903,753	889,612	202,480	18,581,590
25	Occidental of California (Los Angeles)	2,674,866	1,097,020	159,434	67,965,680

*Mutual company

Reprinted from the 1982 FORTUNE Directory by permission; © 1982 Time Inc. All rights reserved.

20 Risk management and insurance

Summary

Risk is the possibility of loss. A *pure risk* involves only the chance of loss: there is no chance for gain. A *speculative risk* offers the possibility of either a gain or a loss. The possibility of fire is a pure risk. The possibility of winning a lottery is a speculative risk.

Risk management, the attempt to reduce the possibility of loss, is an essential part of business. There are four general approaches to managing risk: (1) avoid the risk, (2) reduce the risk, (3) assume the risk, or (4) shift the risk. The primary way of shifting the risk is to purchase *insurance,* a business arrangement whereby a firm agrees to compensate an individual or company for losses resulting from pure risk.

It is impossible to buy insurance against all possible risks. Specific conditions describe insurable risks. A large group of people must be exposed to the same risk. Any loss must be definite, accidental, and sizable. And it must be economically practical for someone to assume the risk.

Insurance is based on the *law of large numbers*. Thus, in a large number of nearly identical units (such as people or clothing retailers), it is possible to predict how many will suffer any kind of peril.

Insurance is a way to shift the risk of potential hazards, but it can be expensive. Smart managers observe three rules of risk management: (1) don't risk more than the business can afford to lose, (2) don't risk a lot for a little, and (3) consider the odds.

Among the major kinds of insurance are casualty, liability, and life insurance. *Casualty insurance* covers damage to property. Fire insurance with extended coverage is a casualty policy. Casualty insurance may also cover loss of property from burglary and robbery. These would be covered by a comprehensive dishonesty, disappearance, and destruction policy.

Liability insurance protects a company from losses due to an individual's injury or death and damage to others' property. Most businesses carry workers' compensation insurance, which provides payment to workers injured on the job. Third-party liability protects the business from injuries suffered by customers or others while on the business premises.

Key person insurance is a life insurance policy taken out by a business on the life of one or a few key employees. Depending on its individual needs, a business may also have marine insurance, fidelity or surety bonds, title insurance, and credit insurance.

Most businesses, as well as most individuals, also buy automobile insurance. Most automobile policies provide three forms of coverage: liability, collision, and comprehensive.

Health insurance has become one of the most important forms of coverage. Most employers include some health insurance as a fringe benefit for employees. Health insurance can be divided into three basic segments: hospital coverage, medical coverage, and disability.

Unlike other forms of insurance, *life insurance* deals with a certain risk—death. In 1980, life insurance policies in the United States had a face value of $3.4 trillion. The best kind of life insurance depends on many individual factors, including income, financial responsibilities, and age.

The *face amount* of a policy is the amount the insurance company promises to pay if the insured person dies. The *premium* is the annual cost of the policy. A *beneficiary* is the person or institution named to receive the face amount of the policy if the insured person dies. The *insured* is the person or institution covered by the policy.

The *cash value* of the policy is the amount the company will pay back if the policy is cancelled before the insured dies. The *loan value* of the policy is the amount that the insurance company will lend the insured, with the cash value used as security. A *paid-up policy* is one for which no further premiums are owed to maintain the face value.

Life insurance comes in several forms. Term insurance is the most basic, and whole life insurance is the most common. Endowment life combines whole life insurance with savings. At the end of the fixed payment period, the face value of the policy is paid to the insured.

Insurance firms may be either stock companies or mutual companies. Stock companies have stockholders, and the company's profits may be paid out as dividends. In mutual companies, the policyholders own the company. Any profits are returned to the policyholders in the form of dividends or reduced premiums.

All insurance companies receive their revenue from two sources, insurance premiums and income from investing the premiums. About 38 percent of insurance company revenue comes from investment income.

Review questions

1. What are the four most common ways of managing risk?
2. Name the pure risks that can be insured. How does pure risk differ from speculative risk?
3. Why might a pianist have difficulty insuring his or her hands? In your answer, explain the specific conditions that describe insurable risks.
4. To avoid spending too much money on insurance, entrepreneurs must learn what kinds of insurance are needed and how much to buy. What rules should they consider?
5. Describe the three most common forms of insurance coverage for automobiles.

Chapter 20 Risk management and insurance

6. Define the following insurance terms: (a) face amount, (b) premium, (c) beneficiary, (d) insured, (e) cash value, (f) loan value, and (g) paid-up policy.
7. What is the difference between term insurance, whole life insurance, and endowment life insurance?
8. What factors should you consider in choosing life insurance?

Discussion questions

1. Should the following three people get life insurance? If so, what kind?
   a. Susan, a single 32-year-old, has her own consulting business. She just bought a house, and she earns about $30,000 a year.
   b. Barry, 27, is a computer programmer whose wife, Judy, a biochemist, is about to have a child. Their combined income is about $40,000.
   c. Saul, 55, is a dentist with three children. His wife died last year, and his youngest child is finishing college this year. He makes about $80,000 a year.
2. You just bought a used car—a 1977 Datsun—and you need to buy insurance. Considering varying deductibles, how can you get adequate yet economical insurance?
3. A friend of yours just bought a craft store in partnership with the woman who makes the very popular stained-glass mirrors the store sells. The owners are considering different kinds of insurance. What would you suggest?
4. You have contact lenses, and your doctor has suggested that you buy insurance for their loss. A pair of lenses cost $200. Insurance costs $35 per year, and replacement cost for one lens—with the insurance—is $20. Would you buy the insurance or self-insure? Why?

Chapter 20 case

Frank Brothers Telecom, Inc.

Before an insurance agent comes to call, company managers should be aware of their basic insurance needs and the risks they may be exposed to. In this case, the owners of a young business need to do just that kind of thinking.

Simon and Harry Frank started Frank Brothers Telecom after many years of pursuing separate careers. Simon was a stockbroker, sold automobiles, and most recently worked as a salesman of small computers. Harry had managed a toy store and then became a district manager for a chain of furniture stores. Both were good at what they did. Simon was an excellent salesman; Harry was a good manager. With these qualities, they decided to team up. They started a small business that sold telephone equipment to businesses.

From a Japanese firm, the Frank brothers bought telephones and the special computers that connected them. Then they tried to convince businesses to buy their equipment rather than continue to rent from the telephone company or buy from competitors.

Frank Brothers Telecom consisted of the two owners and twelve employees. Simon was the sales manager and directed four other salespersons. Each was given a company car. Harry handled the "inside" part of the business. He supervised the two office workers, four warehousemen, and two repairmen. The repairmen used company vans while making their calls.

The company worked out of a small building it leased on the outskirts of Dayton, Ohio. The offices were not fancy, as customers did not call there. The company handled little cash, as most of its business was conducted by billing clients for equipment and service. The business did have an inventory of telephone equipment worth about $300,000.

Although the brothers were equal partners in the corporation, Simon's role was considered more critical. He was an excellent salesman, and he had numerous contacts with firms of all sizes in the Dayton area. The key to success for the brothers lay in Simon's ability to land major accounts.

When the brothers started the business, they took out a basic comprehensive insurance package that included fire, theft, and robbery insurance. Now that they had a going concern, they wanted to take a more serious look at their insurance needs. A broker representing an independent insurance agency was going to come by, and Simon and Harry wanted to evaluate their needs before she arrived.

1. What risks do the Frank brothers face? Which are pure risks? Which are speculative?
2. Are there any risks that can be handled without insurance?
3. What forms of insurance would you recommend they buy for themselves, the business, and their employees? Are there any kinds of insurance they *must* carry?

Careers in banking, finance, investments, accounting, and insurance

Nearly every business and individual uses financial services. Employment in finance, banking, and insurance has grown steadily and has not been greatly affected by changes in economic conditions. A broad range of job opportunities exists in both the private and public sectors.

Through the 1980s, employment in financial services is expected to grow faster than average for all industries. Changes in technology and increasing use of data processing is expected to stimulate demand for skilled workers.

Selected careers available in this area are described below.

Credit analysts

Credit analysts analyze credit data to estimate how much risk is involved in extending credit to firms and individuals. They contact banks, trade and credit associations, and other sources to obtain credit information, and they study economic trends. They also visit firms to evaluate the condition of plants and machinery and prepare reports of their findings.

Credit analysts need mathematical ability, memory for detail, concentration, and accuracy. Their college courses should include business, accounting, economics, and math. A bachelor's degree is usually required. Three-fourths of all credit analysts are employed by credit agencies other than banks.

Stockbrokers

Stockbrokers buy and sell stocks and bonds for individuals and organizations. Stockbrokers use their knowledge of securities, market conditions, government regulations, and clients' needs to advise clients about investments. They need verbal, mathematical, and clerical skills, as well as tact, initiative, and persuasiveness.

Stockbrokers must pass an industry, state, or federal exam, with licensing required in most states. College courses in business, economics, English, and math are helpful.

Accountants

Accountants apply accounting principles to plan and put into effect a system for general accounting. Accountants gather and analyze financial information to help managers make decisions. They prepare balance sheets to reflect a company's assets, liabilities, and capital. They audit contracts, orders, and vouchers, and prepare profit and loss statements and reports to verify transactions.

Accountants are employed by accounting firms, business firms, and government agencies. They need mathematical and organizational skills, attention to detail, and independent judgment. Their college courses should include business, accounting, mathematics, English, and social studies. Larger firms require a bachelor's degree. Becoming a certified public accountant is also useful for advancement.

Actuaries

Actuaries apply knowledge of mathematics, probability, statistics, finance, and business to solve insurance, annuity, and pension problems. Actuaries design or review insurance and pension plans and calculate premiums. They construct probability tables for the occurrence of fire, natural disasters, unemployment, and other insurance risks. They work to ensure payment of future benefits.

Actuaries are typically employed by insurance companies. Others work for the state or federal government, consulting firms, and rating bureaus. They must have the ability to use mathematical and statistical concepts. They should take college courses in business, economics, calculus, and statistics. To be an actuary requires a bachelor's degree, with examinations offered by professional societies.

Additional information can be obtained from:

National Association of Accountants
919 Third Avenue
New York, NY 10022

National Association of Credit Managers
475 Park Avenue South
New York, NY 10018

National Association of Securities Dealers
1735 K Street NW
Washington, DC 20006

Society of Actuaries
208 South LaSalle Street
Chicago, IL 60604

7 From mom-and-pop stores to multinationals

Business in perspective

Two guys and their Umbroller

Most small business ventures are based on trial and error for at least the first two years. This was certainly the case for Alexandre Goodwin and Deaver Brown. The two worked together to produce and market the Umbroller and the baby backpack.

Goodwin and Brown were dissatisfied with their well-paying jobs in large organizations. Restless for a job over which they had more control and searching to revive the spirit of their high school adventures, the two young men launched Cross River Products in 1969.

Brown, who had earned a master's degree in business administration, knew that the first step was to decide which industry to enter. Dismissing the popular high-technology industries because of the already established giants, they decided on the traditionally fragmented and slow-moving juvenile-equipment industry. Then they persuaded an old family friend who was an engineer to design their first product—the Umbroller, a lightweight, collapsible stroller.

Their first effort to actually sell the product was a disaster. In the first six months, they sold only 1500 strollers. The problem, they concluded, was that buyers in the juvenile-equipment industry are very reluctant to adopt a new product before it has been proven. The higher price that they had to charge for their collapsible stroller was also an obstacle to sales.

Goodwin and Brown also had problems with their manufacturer. He had not purchased the necessary equipment for assembling the strollers and was so poorly organized that he was producing only seven strollers a day. This caused a two-month delay in the delivery of their first orders—not a very strong beginning in an industry where all the buyers know each other and where punctuality is crucial.

In spite of these setbacks, sales began to pick up. An improved economy helped. But most of the credit goes to the tireless efforts of Goodwin and Brown. They hired sales representatives who were already acquainted with buyers, and opened their own assembly plant.

Both men concede that the risks and pressures of running their own business are enormous. But they also agree that for them the rewards far outweigh the risks.

Adapted from Barbara Davidson, "Two Guys Who Made It with Their 'Umbroller,'" *New York Times Magazine,* January 7, 1973, pp. 38–48.

Chapter 21

Small business management

Key terms

entrepreneur
small business
venture capitalist
Small Business Administration
 (SBA)
franchise

Chapter objectives

In Chapter 21, you will learn:

What a small business is

The role of small business in the private-enterprise system

The special problems that owners of small businesses face

The personality traits that entrepreneurs have in common

Some basic decisions a prospective entrepreneur must make

How to choose a location

Some sources of funds for small business owners

How the Small Business Administration helps entrepreneurs

The pros and cons of owning a franchise

Overview

Being in business for yourself can be highly rewarding and challenging. **An entrepreneur is someone who takes on the personal and financial risk of starting a business and keeping it going.** But entrepreneurship is not for everyone. It takes a special kind of person—one who is willing to take some risks, is determined to keep working when things go poorly, and has the desire and motivation to work long hours to see his or her dream succeed.

This chapter will look at the unique place of small business in the American economic structure. It will briefly explore the nature of small business and its special problems. The chapter will also look at what makes a good entrepreneur and suggest some things to consider before starting a small business.

The nature of small business

There are about 15 million business firms of all kinds in the United States. About three-fifths of them have annual revenues under $25,000. Thus, in total numbers, most enterprises in this country are quite small.

What is a small business?

Most people would agree that a hot dog vendor with a pushcart is a small business. So is the neighborhood grocery store. These are often called mom-and-pop operations because they are run by one family with little or no outside help.

On the other hand, General Motors, Exxon, and Sears are big businesses. Thousands of individuals share ownership in them through common stock. These companies are run by professional managers, have tens of thousands of employees, and conduct business all over the country and the world.

But many other businesses are not so easily classified. Is a local manufacturing plant that employs 200 workers a large business or a small one? Is a supermarket chain with many outlets in a particular locality a big business? Both may be quite small when compared with such giant firms as General Electric and Safeway. According to the Small Business Administration (SBA), **a small business is one that is independently owned and operated, is not dominant in its field, and does not exceed specified standards of size.**

Measuring size

Some experts set absolute criteria for measuring size. For example, the SBA says that a retail operation can have no more than $7.5 million in sales to be considered a small business. A more flexible and useful set of guidelines has been adopted by the Committee for Economic De-

Chapter 21 Small business management

Figure 21.1 Number of self-employed workers
A long-term trend of reduced self-employment turned around in 1972, as the number of self-employed Americans grew by 19 percent by 1980.

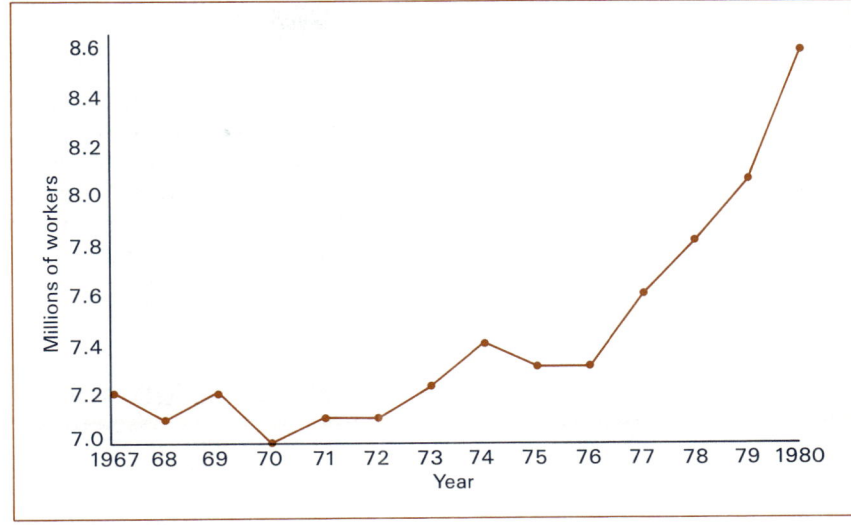

U.S. Bureau of Labor Statistics

velopment. It identifies four characteristics that may apply to a small business. A business with any two of the characteristics can be considered small. The characteristics include these:

1. Management is independent. In most cases, the managers are the owners of the business.
2. Capital is provided by a single person or a small group of persons.
3. The area of operation is mainly local in that the owners and workers all live nearby. The products or services of the firm, however, may be sold regionally or nationally.
4. The size of the firm is small compared to other firms in its industry. Size may be measured in assets, number of employees, or sales revenue.

The roles of small business

Because large national chain stores and manufacturing firms are so prominent, it is easy to forget that small businesses still provide many essential goods and services at all levels of our economy.

Small businesses provide specialized goods and services to big businesses. Even the largest manufacturers depend on relatively small firms to manufacture many subassemblies and parts. A national franchise like McDonald's still depends on numerous local suppliers for its fresh meat, beverages, and baked goods. Large national operations often depend on small service businesses, such as advertising agencies, accounting firms, and printing plants.

Small businesses often offer personalized services not available from large businesses. At one time, some people were predicting that the large national discount department stores would mean the end of the local retailer. They doubted that consumers would want to pay full price for an item at a retail store when they could pay less at a discount chain. In fact, however, many consumers are willing to spend more money to get the personalized service, expert advice, and individual recognition they often receive from a neighborhood specialty store.

Small businesses are sources of new ideas and innovation. Many new products and trends are introduced by entrepreneurs who are free from the fixed budgets, large bureaucracies, and entrenched managers that often slow creativity at larger businesses. The Polaroid camera and the photocopying process popularized by Xerox are well-known examples of products created by small businesses that grew into big businesses.

Special problems of small business

Entrepreneurs face unique problems that do not trouble managers of larger firms. Before starting a business, an entrepreneur must anticipate such problems and have plans for dealing with them. Among the major problems are lack of varied managerial skills, weak financing, and difficulty in attracting and keeping talented employees.

Managerial depth

Big business firms have the resources to hire many specialists. But small business owners must be prepared to take on a wide variety of tasks themselves. This might include supervising employees, hiring and firing, advertising, selling, bookkeeping, and production. Small business owners must also make up the budgets and financial plans needed for internal use and for presentation to lenders and potential investors. Thus, an entrepreneur needs many skills and a wide range of experience.

Most entrepreneurs also hire outside consultants when they need expert help. Lawyers, accountants, advertising agencies, and other such specialists may save entrepreneurs money in the long run. Some entrepreneurs also work with one or more partners whose skills differ from their own.

Lack of adequate financing

Financing is a major obstacle for many would-be entrepreneurs. As a result, many people start business operations without adequate capital. This can cause several problems.

First, lack of money allows little margin for error. One or two costly mistakes can force a business to fail. The owner may buy some merchandise that doesn't sell well or spend too much on an advertising campaign that doesn't work. In such ways, the owner's money is quickly used up and the enterprise fails.

The hidden costs of entrepreneurship

Many owners of small businesses complain about the mass of rules and regulations imposed on them by government legislation.

The biggest financial drains on small businesses are workers' compensation, unemployment compensation, pollution-control regulations, minimum wage scales, and Occupational Safety and Health Administration (OSHA) standards. All of these stem from social legislation to protect workers and counteract industrial dangers.

Some people believe that these government regulations actually hurt the economy and, consequently, the very people they are supposed to protect. Many small businesspeople complain that the costs of filling out the many government forms are too high to calculate. One entrepreneur estimated that he was losing $1000 a month in revenues because he could not take time away from his form-filling obligations to set price increases for his products. Another complained that he had to fill out 110 tax-related documents in one year.

Small businesses spend a staggering $20 billion every year on federal paperwork. State and local governments also require paperwork. And the government itself is spending about $30 billion to regulate small business.

The end result is that all consumers pay twice: once through increased prices and once through high taxes. Some former small business owners claim that they were forced to close because they were drowning in a sea of paperwork.

Second, an entrepreneur who lacks capital cannot afford to hire the kinds of employees who are necessary for success. A business owner who does not have enough money to pay skilled workers may have to hire less competent people at lower wages. This can be self-defeating in the long run.

Third, undercapitalized businesses often suffer from a lack of inventory. A firm cannot sell merchandise that it does not have on the shelves or manufacture goods if it cannot stock raw materials. A clothing retailer, for example, who does not have the funds to offer a large selection of styles and sizes may find that shoppers stop coming to the store. Underfinanced business owners also cannot take advantage of quantity discounts when ordering merchandise and they may be unable to pay invoices in time to gain the cash discount many suppliers offer.

Fourth, an undercapitalized business may have to close down even though its product or service is basically sound. New entrepreneurs often expect to start earning a profit shortly after they begin business. But in reality, an entrepreneur may have to live with little or no salary for a year or more.

Canvas bags from Cornish, Maine

More and more women are becoming entrepreneurs. In most cases, they run the same risks as men. But in addition, they sometimes have more trouble getting the capital to start a business because they have not established a credit rating for themselves.

One woman who developed a successful business in spite of her lack of capital was Chris Birchfield from Cornish, Maine. Her husband had lost his job and they needed money. While driving a bus—the only job she could get—she was seized by an entrepreneurial brainstorm. She decided to manufacture canvas bags similar to the ones that were so popular at L. L. Bean, the famous sporting equipment store.

Convinced that she could make more attractive bags, she rented a huge building and equipped it with a small sewing machine. By simply displaying her product in the window of her building, she attracted buyers for her bags.

With success came sizable rent increases on the factory. At the same time, she and her husband decided to abandon their rustic farm and find a home with plumbing and electricity. So they bought a house with a barn that became the new Birchfield canvas bag shop.

Birchfield was then able to borrow from the bank to establish a credit rating. Her sales steadily increased. To cope with the growth, she hired sales representatives to cover other areas of the country and added some additional machines and people.

Like other entrepreneurs, Birchfield leads a hectic life but feels that the sacrifices are well worth the freedom and control she gains from having her own business.

Adapted from Terri P. Tepper, "Three Women Who Started from Scratch," *New York Times Magazine*, September 14, 1980.

Attracting key personnel

Entrepreneurs may be willing to forgo high salaries in order to build up their business. But their employees do not have the same motivation. Employees expect fair wages and fringe benefits. Yet new businesses can rarely compete with established corporations in offering competitive salaries, overtime pay, medical coverage, life insurance, and vacation time.

For example, a small publishing house was looking for an editor. It could offer no more than $12,000 a year and few fringe benefits, even though it needed an experienced person who could take charge of many responsibilities. Because this kind of person could make 30 to 40 percent more money at a major publishing house, the publisher had to settle for someone with less experience and know-how. This caused long delays in publication schedules, uneven quality, and lost sales due to disgruntled customers.

Clever entrepreneurs often find ways to attract good employees, however. Some purposely set aside enough money to hire one or two key employees. They may also offer key employees opportunities that they could not find in large organizations.

For example, they may give a valued employee greater authority and responsibility for the final product. In a large business, an employee often feels anonymous and powerless. In a small business, an employee can feel a greater sense of participation.

An employee of a small business may also have greater opportunity for creativity and freedom of action. Instead of being boxed in by corporate policy and bureaucracy, an employee can have the chance to put personal ideas directly to work.

Small businesses also offer ready recognition of accomplishments and rapid advancement. Whereas employees in large organizations often feel lost or unnoticed, employees in small businesses can be assured of high visibility. Moreover, as the business grows, they have a chance to move up quickly. A small wholesaler with one or two salespersons may soon expand its sales force. Those first employees can become sales managers and, with further growth, vice-presidents.

Finally, to attract or keep a very valuable employee, an entrepreneur can offer profit sharing or part ownership in the business. For example, owners of small restaurants know that good chefs are in great demand and are frequently hired away by competitors. To ensure continued success, an owner may offer a good chef a share of the business. This helps create a loyal employee (and one who will avoid waste and guard quality even more than before).

The entrepreneurial role

The acceptance of personal and financial risk distinguishes an entrepreneur from other people in the business world. An entrepreneur can never be sure that a new venture will be successful, so a degree of risk is always involved. But unlike a gambler, an entrepreneur has considerable control over success or failure.

The pros and cons of entrepreneurship

Not everyone is comfortable in the role of entrepreneur. Many people like the security of a regular paycheck and the limited responsibility that comes from working for someone else. Therefore, persons thinking of starting their own business should carefully analyze themselves and their situation. They should look at the advantages of entrepreneurship and compare them to the advantages of being a salaried manager.

Pros

An entrepreneur gets all the rewards of success. If a business does well, not only can the entrepreneur draw a comfortable salary, but the business will increase in value. Someday it may be sold for an attractive profit.

In the 1960s and 1970s, for example, many computer specialists in southern California started their own firms to make mini- and microcomputers. Through a combination of good engineering and successful marketing, many of the firms grew rapidly into multimillion dollar operations. After a time, the founders were able to offer company stock to the public. Their initial investment of time and money multiplied in value many times, so that today each founder has stock worth millions of dollars. And this is in addition to the large salaries they have been able to pay themselves since their firms became profitable.

An entrepreneur may also gain security. If a business is successful, its owner achieves far more than is possible for an individual who works for someone else.

Third, an entrepreneur is free to put personal ideas into action. Such independence is rarely obtainable when working for someone else.

Fourth, many small business owners enjoy a great deal of prestige. Successful entrepreneurs are often called on to participate in civic affairs, address school or charity groups, and run for political office. All this can be as personally satisfying as financial rewards.

Cons

Some negative factors balance out the advantages of self-employment. One is the possibility of financial loss if the business fails. The vast majority of business failures are not legal bankruptcies. More often a struggling owner simply decides to pay off all creditors and close shop. As a result, accurate statistics about small business failures are difficult to calculate. But it is estimated that two out of three new businesses do not last beyond their third year of operation. Thus, entrepreneurs must go into business knowing that all or most of their investment may be consumed by the venture.

Also, many people have the mistaken impression that being self-employed allows more free time. Just the contrary is the case. Almost invariably, successful entrepreneurs must put in 50, 60, or more hours per week. Business owners usually are the first to arrive each morning and the last to leave at night. They must often do paperwork at home in the evening. In retail operations, Saturday and Sunday hours may also be required. During particularly busy seasons, an owner may work seven days a week. Only after years of work and the development of trusted employees do some owners find it possible to take a vacation without closing the entire operation.

Finally, potential entrepreneurs must be prepared for little or no pay during the first months or years of operation, especially if starting a business from scratch. A business owner may have to put all business income into operating expenses, expanded inventory, and promotion.

The pros and cons of salaried employment

Pros

An established employee is likely to earn a higher wage than a newly self-employed individual. This is one reason that many would-be entrepreneurs never actually start their own businesses. An executive may become too comfortable on a salary and not wish to accept the cut in pay that self-employment might entail.

Figure 21.2 The number of new businesses has been increasing... ...while the failure rate declines

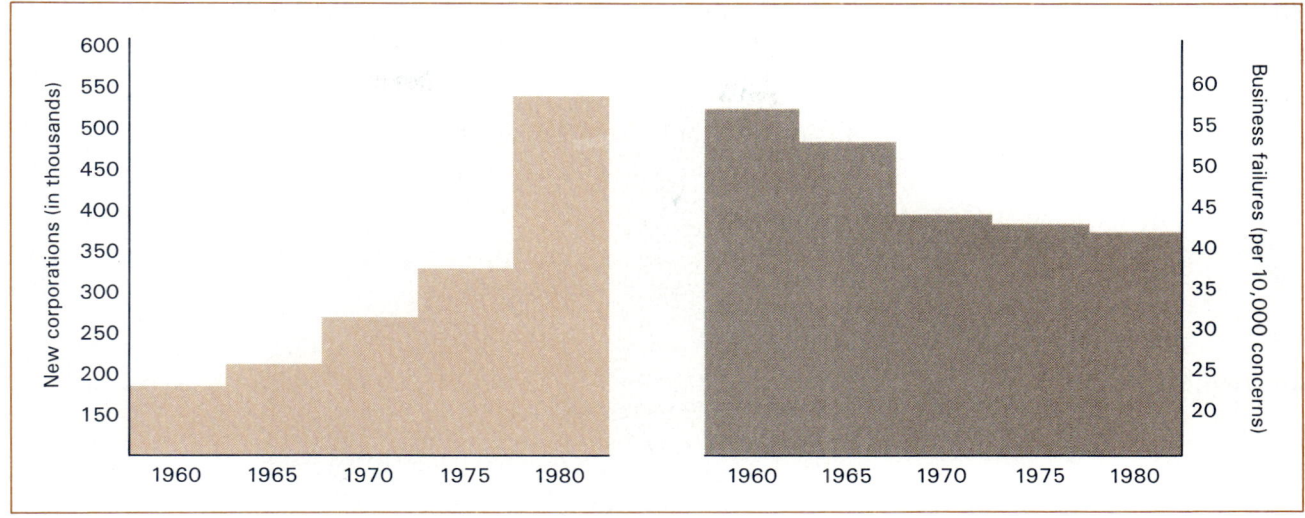

Statistical Abstract of the United States, 1981. Data compiled from Dun & Bradstreet, Monthly New Business Incorporation Report.

Also, an employee can count on being paid a fixed amount of money at regular intervals. In a new small business, the owner's salary may depend on how much revenue was produced that week. But an employee receives a paycheck regardless of the firm's immediate performance.

In addition, salaried employees usually receive numerous fringe benefits. These may include medical insurance, paid vacations, and even a company car. Some employees also earn overtime and other bonuses. But entrepreneurs only receive fringe benefits if they pay for them themselves. And many new businesses lack the capital to pay for such benefits.

Salaried employees often have less responsibility and are not required to work more than a fixed 40-hour work week. At the end of the day, they can forget business problems and relax. Most entrepreneurs, on the other hand, find that their business takes up all their free time.

Finally, salaried employees have no personal financial investment at risk.

Cons

Although salaried employees may look forward to a fixed work week and less responsibility, that is not always the case. Managerial and executive positions are especially likely to demand more time. Workers in these categories receive a fixed salary, but their jobs may demand many more than 40 hours a week. Managers who aspire to promotions often come into the office on Saturdays and take work home at night.

Managers may have a great deal of responsibility and concerns that cannot be forgotten at five o'clock. A salaried employee may be

Entrepreneurship versus salaried employment

Entrepreneurship

Pros
1. Financial rewards of success
2. Security
3. Opportunity to be creative
4. Social stature in the community

Cons
1. Risk of financial loss
2. Long hours and hard work
3. Little or no pay in early stages

Salaried employment

Pros
1. Salary likely to be higher at first
2. Fixed salary paid at regular intervals
3. Fringe benefits
4. Less responsibility
5. No personal financial risk

Cons
1. Long hours required to get ahead
2. Great responsibility with benefits going to the company
3. Bureaucratic policies and procedures
4. Job security dependent on others
5. Need to accept transfers and other company decisions

responsible for increasing sales or profits, maintaining strict standards of production, or meeting deadlines on which millions of dollars depend. Yet despite the responsibility, the major financial benefits go to the owners of the business.

Some employees find it hard to work in a large bureaucracy. They may feel that their creative ideas get buried in too much paperwork or cannot be implemented because they conflict with company policy. They may feel that no one listens to them or cares about their work. Or they may feel that there is too much emphasis on profits and not enough on human values.

Salaried employees have limited job security. Their ongoing employment depends on company decisions. In times of recession, corporate managers may be laid off along with production workers. This happened in the automobile industry in 1980 and 1981. Chrysler executives were particularly hard hit. Even vice-presidents and middle-level executives were affected. They were fired not because they were doing a bad job, but because company expenses were too high and business had dropped. Even a strong union cannot prevent permanent layoffs if business declines.

Finally, employees of large firms may have to accept such corporate decisions as transfers to other geographic locations if they wish to advance steadily. People who refuse to make such moves may be left to stagnate in their present jobs.

Persons considering self-employment should consider all of these points. Then they should ask themselves if they have the personal characteristics of an entrepreneur.

The entrepreneurial personality

Many researchers have studied the personal characteristics of entrepreneurs. In the process, they have identified certain key traits that set entrepreneurs apart. These include intense desire to succeed, self-discipline, perseverance, drive for independence, need for achievement, assertiveness, action-orientation, goal-orientation, and high energy levels. These characteristics are not commonly found in the general population.

Entrepreneurs have a strong need to succeed on their own rather than work for an existing organization or employer. They have an overwhelming desire to succeed combined with a willingness to work hard for long hours. Many express a desire for control over their own fate and a belief that control is within their grasp. Energetic, self-disciplined, and self-motivated, they show an aggressive determination to make things happen and the ability to endure high levels of stress. In fact, many entrepreneurs actually seem to be energized by the stress of creating their own business lives.

Starting a business

A person who decides to become self-employed must set up a plan of action. Basic decisions must be made, including (1) the legal form the business will take, (2) whether to buy an existing business or start from scratch, (3) where the business will be located, and (4) how to obtain financing.

Legal forms of business

All businesses take one of three possible legal forms: sole proprietorship, partnership, or corporation. These legal forms are discussed in detail in Chapter 2. Each form has its own advantages and disadvantages. The best form for a given business depends on the personal preferences of the owner, as well as on certain tax considerations.

Because of the added expense, taxes, and paperwork involved in incorporation, many entrepreneurs start their businesses as proprietorships or partnerships. They don't incorporate until the business grows larger and can take advantage of the limited liability and stock financing benefits of that legal form.

A turnaround entrepreneur

Some people like to buy failing businesses and turn them into profitable operations. One man who has had tremendous success at this is Percy Ross of Minnesota.

Raised in a poverty-stricken family, Ross opened a fur and scrap-metal business immediately after his graduation from high school. Next he became the middleman between fur ranchers and fur buyers on the East Coast. Although that business failed, he rebounded quickly and became a successful equipment auctioneer.

However, the mark of a true entrepreneur is the need for new challenges. So in 1958, he purchased a faltering plastic-bag company for $30,000. By 1963, the company was a half-million dollars in debt and operating under Chapter XI of the Federal Bankruptcy Act.

When the outlook was least promising, Ross became the most creative. He pawned his wife's valuables to raise capital. He used his son's mathematical expertise to figure out how to earn a greater profit. With some commercial financing and some quick talking to persuade suppliers to provide favorable terms, Ross began producing his bags with recycled resin.

Then he had to devise a way to conceal the imperfections that resulted from using recycled materials. The answer was to color the bags.

With his production problems solved, Ross's next challenge was to increase sales. He reasoned that by replacing his traveling sales staff with a telephone sales staff, he could increase his contacts from five a day to forty a day.

In 1969, Ross was in excellent financial condition. He sold his plastic-bag business for $8 million. By 1979, he owned close to 90 companies, a Lincoln, two Cadillacs, a Jaguar, and a Mercedes-Benz. He also claimed to have given away two-thirds of his wealth during the 1970s.

Adapted from Michael W. Fedo, "A Millionaire in the Unmaking," *New York Times,* April 9, 1979.

Buying an existing business or starting from scratch

The quickest way to get into business is to buy an ongoing concern. Among the advantages of this approach are that customers and suppliers are immediately available, inventory is on hand, an organization and staff are in place, and a reputation is established. Best of all, buying an existing business reduces uncertainty and risk. An existing business has a history of performance that the purchaser can examine through its financial records.

Sometimes, however, there is no existing business available. This would be the case for a business based on an altogether new product or service or located in a growing area.

Under these circumstances, the entrepreneur would need to start from the ground up. This gives the owner the opportunity to shape the business to meet personal needs, buy the supplies that are really wanted, hire the best people, and establish a personal reputation. In the short run, it may also take less capital because the entrepreneur would not need to pay for the goodwill built up by someone else.

Choosing a location

The owner of a small pottery shop, when asked the three most crucial decisions about a new business, replied, "First, location; second, location; third, location." For a retail business such as his, the emphasis on a well-considered location may be warranted. For some other kinds of operations, however, location may be relatively unimportant.

Retailers

Of course, there can be only a limited demand for a snowmobile shop in Florida or a hamburger stand in the Utah desert. But other factors that affect the location of a business may be less obvious.

Most retailers should look for spots where potential customers will be. That is why two or three different women's clothing stores, for example, may operate in the same shopping mall, despite the presence of a popular department store as well. In many large cities, there are strips of specialty stores. There are concentrations of jewelry stores, antique shops, or clothing stores. In the suburbs, it is common to find a section of a major highway lined with competing automobile dealers. A store owner who chooses a location that is isolated from competition may be isolated from potential customers as well.

Manufacturers

Most manufacturers do not need to be located near their customers. Instead, they can locate in the low-rent districts of cities or in suburban industrial parks. Manufacturers are more concerned with being near a pool of appropriately skilled workers. Thus, an entrepreneur in the garment-manufacturing business might think of locating in the Philadelphia area. An electronics firm might consider San Francisco, Dallas, or Boston, while a furniture maker would find craftsmen in North Carolina or Tennessee.

Manufacturers also look for locations with good transportation links, access to raw materials, and, if their products are perishable, nearness to their markets.

Wholesalers

Wholesalers serve as middlemen between manufacturers and retailers. Like manufacturers, they do not have to locate in high-rent territory. But since much of their success depends on the speed and service they provide their retail customers, they must be within reasonable shipping distance. They need access to a good highway system or other appropriate transportation links.

Providers of services

Some providers of services, such as accountants, window washers, and plumbers, work on their clients' premises. Thus, their business location is important only to the extent that it favors the service they provide. For example, a landscaping and gardening business might be most profitable if located in a southern climate with a year-round growing season. As these service providers do not depend on walk-in trade, they can frequently work out of their own homes or other low-rent facilities. Other service providers, such as lawyers or marriage counselors, may have more in common with retailers in choosing a location.

Financing

One of the most perplexing aspects of self-employment is raising the money to get started. First-time entrepreneurs may have an especially difficult time persuading lenders and investors to provide start-up funds. The sources they may call on include these:

1. Personal resources. An entrepreneur should plan on investing a substantial amount of personal savings in a new venture. Few outsiders will be willing to invest money without proof that the entrepreneur has committed his or her own money to the venture. A partnership multiplies the personal funds available to the business.

2. Friends and relatives. The people who are closest to the entrepreneur may be good sources of personal loans or investments (especially if the operation incorporates and can offer stock with limited liability).

For most people, personal savings and funds from friends and relatives form the basis of their start-up cash. If a venture is particularly well planned, however, other sources may be approached.

3. Commercial banks. Banks do not usually lend start-up money to a new business. However, they may lend money to the purchaser of an existing successful business. The assets of the business or of the borrowers can serve as collateral. If a business has valuable fixed assets, such as machinery, buildings, or trucks, a bank may give it a mortgage or use its assets as collateral.

4. Private venture capitalists. **A venture capitalist is an individual or business that seeks out promising new ventures in which to invest.** Venture capitalists are especially interested in innovative enterprises with proven track records and great potential for growth. They do not usually consider extremely small proposals. Venture capitalists typically buy an equity share in the business, from as little as 10 percent to as much as 90 percent.

5. Small Business Investment Corporations (SBICs). Small Business Investment Corporations operate in much the same way as private venture capital firms, but they are chartered by the federal government through the Small Business Administration. They are, however, privately owned and operated. SBICs may either lend money or make an equity investment. And they are more flexible than banks in the kinds of collateral they will accept. Minority Enterprise Small Business Investment Corporations (MESBICs) are special forms of SBICs. MESBICs were created to provide capital to entrepreneurs from minority groups who may have trouble obtaining conventional financing.

6. Corporate venture capital activities. Many large corporations make investments to encourage the private development of products and processes. They are especially likely to invest in new enterprises that may eventually become either suppliers or customers.

7. The Small Business Administration (SBA). **The Small Business Administration is a federal agency that promotes small business development.** It was created by Congress in 1953. The SBA provides many useful services to businesses and their owners. Besides publishing useful booklets describing many different kinds of businesses, it conducts frequent seminars on subjects ranging from how to start a business to accounting practices and inventory control.

The SBA may also provide financial assistance. First, it may help an entrepreneur to prepare the financial presentation needed to apply for a commercial bank loan. Then, if the entrepreneur is turned down by several commercial lenders, the SBA may agree to guarantee the loan. In such cases, a bank makes the loan to the individual and the SBA guarantees that the federal government will pay back the bank if the business fails. In still other cases, the SBA may actually lend part of the needed money, with the remainder coming from a bank. Finally (albeit rarely), the SBA has the option of making the entire loan itself.

The SBA requires all applicants to submit a plan for the use of the money and to show that they are reasonably capable of repayment. Moreover, SBA loans are generally available only to businesses that are already established. One drawback that many applicants for SBA loans cite is the large amount of paperwork and the relatively long waiting period for processing.

Franchising

A franchise is the right to use an established name or idea to sell products or services. Franchising is primarily a means of distribution. A manufacturer of pottery, for example, may wish to have more outlets for its products. But to open many retail stores would be very expensive. As an alternative, the manufacturer may find many independent entrepreneurs who will agree to sell the pottery using the manufacturer's name. The pottery manufacturer thus becomes a franchisor.

Each store is owned by an independent franchisee (although sometimes a single person or firm will buy several franchises). All franchisees do business under the same name and usually have similar store layouts, prices, and policies. They benefit from the well-known name and reputation of the franchisor and gain business through the advertising of the entire franchise chain. Each franchisee is usually given exclusive rights to sell the franchised product in a specific territory. In return, the franchisee agrees to sell only or primarily the franchised products and pay the franchisor a fee for the use of the name.

Wendy's

Combining entrepreneurial instinct with franchise experience can be a winning formula. So says R. David Thomas, former Kentucky Fried Chicken franchisee and founder and owner of Wendy's, the hamburger franchisor. By doing his homework and building on his fast-food experience, Thomas discovered that consumers wanted a fast-food operation that served hamburgers in a variety of ways, and a special kind of chili.

Thomas sold broad franchise territories rather than individual franchises. And he sold primarily to experienced fast-food operators. This strategy resulted in fewer failures and tighter control because there are fewer franchisees to deal with.

Selling the franchises was part of a larger scheme that Thomas had in mind. With the money his company retained from selling stock, he started buying back his franchise operations. By running them himself, he could increase his control even more.

Adapted from "A New Hamburger Chain Built on Hindsight," *BusinessWeek,* September 20, 1976.

The advantages of buying a franchise

Entrepreneurs may gain many advantages by becoming franchisees.
1. They immediately gain an established reputation.
2. Franchisors often provide proven products and practices that eliminate many of the problems an independent business owner might have.
3. Franchisors may also have training courses for new owners and provide ongoing consulting services that would otherwise have to be purchased from outsiders.
4. Franchisors often provide financial backing or can help an eligible entrepreneur raise capital through their own banking connections or reputation.

The costs of buying a franchise

An entrepreneur pays an initial fee to acquire a franchise. This may vary from a few thousand dollars for a franchise in a little-known chain to hundreds of thousands of dollars for the rights to a Holiday Inn or McDonald's. Although a franchisor may include specific equipment, a building, or other tangible assets as part of the fee, some of the money pays for the goodwill a top reputation provides. For example, an entrepreneur could build a hotel that was identical in every respect to a Holiday Inn for less than it would cost to build the same facility with the right to use the Holiday Inn name. The difference in costs would be the true price of the franchise.

Most franchisors also require each owner to pay a continuing franchise fee based on a percentage of gross sales or other measure of dollar volume. They may also charge an annual advertising fee and other assessments. Such expenses can decrease the owner's profits.

Franchisees are often required to buy supplies and services from the franchisor. In many instances, they are not free to find their own suppliers at cheaper prices.

In most cases, franchisors have rules about decor, facilities, and operating practices. One hamburger franchisor, for instance, has even established how often the floor must be swept. It also requires that hamburgers not sold within 30 minutes of being produced must be thrown out.

Finally, franchisees may not be free to sell their businesses to whomever they choose. Some franchisors demand approval of a new owner.

Is a franchisee an independent entrepreneur?

Being part of a franchise may not provide the opportunity to be creative and fulfill the need for achievement that many entrepreneurs value. Success may be due less to the labors of the individual owner than to the franchise's corporate management.

On the other hand, a franchise does give an owner the rights to operating profits and any increase in value when the business is sold—different rights from those of a manager. Moreover, a franchisee has a chance to enhance the business. Like any self-employed businessperson, a franchise owner is free to select and direct personnel, provide superior service, and add other personal touches.

The dangers of buying a franchise

A potential franchisee should take great care in investigating the character and reputation of the franchisor. Although there are hundreds of franchisors, few have the stature of the major car dealerships, fast-food restaurants, and hotel chains.

Many con artists prey on gullible entrepreneurs. They promise attractive profits and services. But once they have collected the franchise fee, they either deliver much less than promised or disappear altogether. Other franchisors may have legitimate intentions but fail to fulfill their obligations. Entrepreneurs can make a lot of money by buying into young franchises that eventually become successful. But they stand to lose a lot of money if they don't choose wisely.

It is especially important for a potential franchisee to visit existing franchised locations and talk to their owners. It is an excellent way to find out if the franchisor's promises are likely to come true.

A potential franchisee should read the franchising agreement carefully with the help of a lawyer. Franchising may be a shortcut to getting into small business, but it still requires analysis, diligence, and hard work.

"I guess the fast-food business has pretty much reached the saturation point."

Source: Drawing by Guindon. Copyright © 1978, Los Angeles Times Syndicate. Reprinted with permission.

A few words of advice

Being self-employed can be extremely rewarding, both financially and personally, but it is not a step to be taken lightly. Experienced entrepreneurs agree on two points.

First, to ensure success, you must be well prepared for your intended venture. You must know the business that you will be operating. This may require an apprenticeship in the field you wish to enter. As someone else's employee, you can learn the secrets of a successful operation without losing your own hard-earned capital on costly mistakes.

Second, be ready to make many sacrifices to build your business. It costs time and energy, as well as money, to keep a business going. And an entrepreneur can never afford to get lazy or rest on past successes. Even very successful entrepreneurs can suddenly fail if they get careless, stop watching the competition, pay less attention to detail, and start missing important trends. People who own their own businesses must constantly strive to stay successful.

21 Small business management

Summary

An *entrepreneur* is someone who takes on the personal and financial risk of starting a business and keeping it going.

Such activities are highly rewarding for some people. But entrepreneurs must cope with problems that salaried employees never have. In particular, entrepreneurs must accept financial risk and long hours of hard work. Nonetheless, if they are successful, they can enjoy financial rewards and the satisfaction of having succeeded on their own.

A *small business* is one that is independently owned and operated, does not dominate its field, and does not exceed specific standards of size.

Small business plays a major role in our economy. It provides specialized goods and services to big business. It provides the personalized services that many consumers seek. And it provides new ideas and innovations that may get overlooked or buried in the bureaucracy of large organizations.

Small business owners have some special problems. These include weak financing, lack of specialized management skills, and difficulty in attracting key personnel. These obstacles can be overcome, however, by creative approaches to obtaining capital, employing outside consultants when necessary, and offering employees opportunities that cannot be matched by big business.

An enterprise may be legally set up as a proprietorship, a partnership, or a corporation. A sole proprietorship is the simplest, but its owner may suffer from limited resources and unlimited financial liability. Forming a partnership can give owners more capital and broader skills, but partners may also suffer from unlimited liability. A corporation is the most expensive and complex form of business to set up, but it is the best form for raising large sums of equity capital and may provide a shield from personal liability.

There are many other decisions to make when starting a business, including whether to buy an existing operation or start from scratch, the choice of location, and how to raise capital. Most first-time entrepreneurs depend on personal savings and investments from friends and relatives for start-up capital. Some entrepreneurs may receive help from a *venture capitalist,* an individual or business that seeks out promising new ventures for investment. *The Small Business Administration,* a federal agency that provides technical assistance to small businesses, can also help entrepreneurs get bank loans. Buying a *franchise*—the right to use an established name or idea to market a product or service—is another way to become self-employed. But entrepreneurs must carefully consider the pros and cons of entering into a specific franchise agreement.

Entrepreneurs must be knowledgeable about their intended business fields. And they must be ready to put in long hours of hard work.

Review questions

1. What four characteristics help define a small business?
2. What are three functions performed by small business?
3. What four benefits can a small business offer its owner that a large corporation cannot offer a manager?
4. What are three common problems for small enterprises?
5. What problems can occur when a small business is undercapitalized?
6. List four advantages and three disadvantages of owning your own business.
7. What personality traits are common among entrepreneurs?
8. What are the most important considerations in determining the location for the following kinds of businesses? (a) retail store, (b) manufacturing plant, (c) wholesale operation, and (d) service business
9. Name at least five potential sources of financing for a small business.
10. What services are offered by the Small Business Administration?
11. What are the differences between a franchisee and an independent entrepreneur?

Discussion questions

1. Which of the entrepreneurial personality traits identified by researchers do you consider most important? Why?
2. Assume that you have just opened a small clothing store. What job skills would you look for in the first three employees you would hire? Why?
3. A strong advantage of self-employment is the freedom to operate independently. A strong advantage of salaried employment is the presumed security of being in someone else's employ. Which situation do you find more desirable? Why?
4. Working with a classmate, make plans for going into partnership together and starting a new business. What kind of business would you start? Where would you locate and why? What kinds of financing would you seek?
5. You have received two unique business opportunities. Mr. Schuss is getting ready to retire and wants to sell you his ski shop, which is located in Aspen, Colorado. The store is highly profitable and its reputation superb. Ms. Mogul owns a newly established but rapidly growing ski-equipment company seeking to sell franchises. The company already has a number of very profitable franchises in several eastern states where skiing is popular. Mogul wants to expand heavily into the western ski states and offers you the opportunity to buy a franchise in Colorado. Which offer would you take? Why?

Chapter 21 case

Cynthia Creations

It is not uncommon for a small business to grow out of an individual's hobby or sideline. The problem is to transform an activity that was fun into a businesslike operation and still maintain some of the fun. Here is one woman's experience.

Cynthia Steinmetz had no idea she would become an entrepreneur when she received her college degree in textiles and clothing. She went to New York and took a job as an educational representative for a firm that made fabrics for home sewing. She traveled throughout the United States and Canada promoting fabrics and teaching sewing techniques. After a few years, she tired of the constant travel and began thinking about a business of her own. That year, she made some Christmas cards for her friends by pasting cut-out fabric on colored paper. "My friends loved them and I enjoyed doing it," she remembers.

As a result, she decided to build a business around her unique cards. "I developed a dozen designs and began production on the dining-room table." Her first sale was for 60 cards at a wholesale price of $.75 each. The store then sold them for $1.50.

"In the beginning, it was hectic," says Steinmetz, "but I loved it. I would go out and sell cards for a week, then come back home and manufacture the cards myself. When the orders were filled, it was back out on the road." In her first year, she sold 8000 cards, each hand-signed.

Eventually, Steinmetz had too many orders to handle everything herself, and she had definitely outgrown the dining-room table. She finally had to move to her own factory. She invested her profits in machinery to speed up the production process. Soon she had two full-time employees and a network of stores selling her cards all over the east coast.

Next, she rented a booth at the National Stationery Show in New York. "That was a turning point for the business because a lot of sales representatives were impressed with my idea. Business picked up considerably."

As her business expanded, Steinmetz had to cut back on her travel to supervise production. She also had to stop signing each card personally. Instead, she bought a small printing press that duplicated her signature on each of the 70,000 cards she sold. Orders now come in from all over the world. "I love to pick up the mail and see where the orders come from," she notes, adding that she has had requests from as far away as Saudi Arabia.

From Steinmetz's point of view, Cynthia Creations is not really work. "I think of it as a full-time hobby that I've become deeply involved with."

Evaluate Steinmetz and her business.

1. What entrepreneurial personality traits does Steinmetz exhibit? How do they help her in her business?
2. What problems are likely to threaten the growth of Cynthia Creations? How can they be avoided or otherwise handled?

Business in perspective

Asia's little dragons

Singapore, South Korea, Taiwan, and Hong Kong, known as the little dragons in Asia, are becoming increasingly competitive international traders. Taiwan and Hong Kong, long notable as garment makers and assemblers of simple electronics instruments, are graduating into more sophisticated telecommunications and computer gear. South Korea shipyards are underbidding the Japanese for major contracts. Hong Kong technicians are copying Japan's latest designs for electronic watches, then manufacturing and exporting them at lower prices.

For the United States, the dragons pose both opportunities and risks. Digital Equipment Company, for example, is one of many U.S. firms with plants in Taiwan, Hong Kong, and Singapore. The overseas plants manufacture both components and entire sections of minicomputers that are later assembled in facilities near Boston.

As Asian manufacturers build up their technical skills, however, they threaten U.S. products. The United States has already imposed limits on color television shipments from Korea.

The little dragons promote key industries with low taxes and export incentives. When private capital is lacking for big ventures, such as steel mills, the government helps out.

Like Japan, the dragons have concentrated on a few products at a time, gradually progressing from basic consumer items to machine tools. One common thread through all four nations is a residue of Confucian values that spur achievement. Notes Kim Kyung Won, secretary general to Korea's Harvard-educated president: "It's the culture of discipline and postponing immediate satisfaction for the future—even for posterity."

Louis Kraar, "Make Way for the New Japans," *FORTUNE,* August 10, 1981, pp. 176–184. Copyright 1981 by Time Inc. All rights reserved.

Chapter 22 International trade

Key terms

specialization
labor-intensive economy
capital-intensive economy
theory of comparative
  advantage
exporting
importing
balance of trade
balance of payments
tariff
protective tariff
revenue tariff
import quota
embargo
monetary exchange controls
European Economic
  Community (EEC)
international cartel
multinational corporation

Chapter objectives

In Chapter 22, you will learn:

Why countries trade with each other

How the theory of comparative advantage relates to the concept of specialization

The meaning of a country's balance of trade and balance of payments

How government policies can restrict or encourage international trade

How multinational trade agreements, international cartels, and multinational corporations affect world trade

The various forms of international trade

The strengths and weaknesses of multinational companies

The special problems that face managers working overseas

Overview

A company's business activities and markets are not limited to its nation's borders. The United States' large domestic market is the envy of much of the world. Perhaps due to the nation's great size, exports account for only about 8 percent of the U.S. gross national product. This compares to about 14 percent for Japan and 21 percent for Great Britain.

Foreign trade is very common today. We need only look in our stores to see how much we trade with other nations. Japanese cameras and videotape recorders, French and Italian wines, and German mopeds compete side-by-side with American-made products. Foreign cars now account for more than 20 percent of all automobiles sold in the United States.

This chapter looks at the reasons businesses become involved in foreign trade and the various levels of such trade. The chapter also explores the basis for international trade and the theories of comparative advantage and specialization. It also considers the important economic concepts of balance of trade and balance of payments between trading nations. Finally, this chapter considers the multinational corporations that operate in many foreign countries, the important role played by governments in promoting or restricting trade flows, and the unique demands made on managers of foreign trade.

Why is foreign trade important?

Despite the tremendous productive output of the American economy, we lack many goods. These include such common items as bananas, coffee, tea, nickel, tin, and diamonds. Since 1973, we have all felt the economic impact of the U.S. dependence on imported oil.

On the other hand, many American industries depend on the sales of their products in foreign markets. Agriculture relies heavily on sales of wheat, tobacco, rice, and cotton to other countries. In addition, such important American industries as aircraft, chemicals, automobiles, and computer hardware sell much of their output in foreign markets.

Companies such as General Motors, Ford, DuPont, IBM, and Eastman Kodak each export well over $1 billion of goods annually.

Specialization

International trade allows countries to get maximum use from their limited resources through specialization. **Specialization is the practice of producing and trading the products that one can supply most efficiently and cheaply.** By providing the goods that it can produce most efficiently and cheaply, a nation can obtain the goods that it cannot produce efficiently and cheaply.

A **labor-intensive economy uses production processes that rely on a labor force that is plentiful and relatively inexpensive.** As a result, South Korea is able to efficiently produce labor-intensive products such as textiles, transistor radios, and television sets more cheaply than would be possible in the United States.

A **capital-intensive economy uses production processes that rely on large amounts of capital equipment.** The United States, for example, produces items such as automobiles, machinery, chemicals, and computer hardware, which require expensive plants and equipment. The United States has a capital-intensive economy.

The theory of comparative advantage

The theory of comparative advantage holds that each nation should specialize in producing those goods that it can supply most easily and cheaply and trade for those items that other countries can produce most easily and cheaply. As a result, everyone gains a higher standard of living. More goods will be available at lower prices for all nations.

Japan has an abundant supply of skilled workers, but lacks petroleum and agricultural products. American farmers help feed Japan at prices that are economical for both countries. It is efficient for the United States to sell Japan agricultural products, and in turn buy color televisions and automobiles from Japan.

Due to comparative advantages, resources and goods tend to move from places where they are plentiful to places where they are scarce. Coffee from Brazil, TV sets from Japan, and computer hardware from the United States are traded to countries that cannot produce them efficiently.

Every country has limited resources. Therefore, no country can expect to produce everything it desires. Specialization allows a nation's resources to be concentrated on efficient production.

Exports and imports

When a country has a comparative advantage in producing certain products, it is to that nation's advantage to produce large quantities of those products and sell them to other countries. **Exporting is the selling of goods and services in other countries.**

At the same time, other nations have a comparative advantage in producing other products, and it is to the nation's advantage to buy those items. **Importing is the buying of goods and services from other countries.**

Balance of trade and balance of payments

Countries that participate in international trade pay particular attention to their balance of trade and balance of payments.

Figure 22.1 U.S. exports and imports, 1982
When imports exceed exports, a trade deficit results, increasing indebtedness of U.S. public and private sectors to foreign countries.

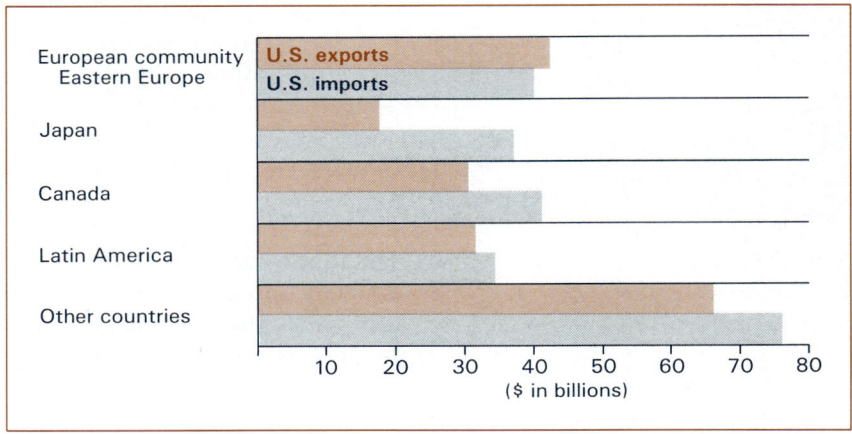

Estimates based on U.S. Department of Commerce figures through August 1982.

The balance of trade

A country's balance of trade is the relationship between the value of its exports and the value of its imports. A favorable balance of trade occurs when exports are greater than imports. An unfavorable balance of trade occurs when imports are greater than exports. Ideally, a nation tries to maintain a balance between its exports and imports.

In 1982, the U.S. had an unfavorable balance of trade. That is, imports exceeded exports by $38.4 billion (see Figure 22.1).

The balance of payments

The balance of payments is a measure of the flow of money into and out of a country. International trade has a strong effect on a country's balance of payments. The balance of payments reflects the difference between the total payments made to foreign countries and the total payments received from foreign countries. When a nation has a favorable balance of payments, more money has flowed into the country than has flowed out. When a nation has an unfavorable balance of payments, more money has flowed out of the country than in.

A country's balance of payments reflects other international activities besides imports and exports. For example, the U.S. balance of payments is affected by military spending abroad, long-term investments overseas, foreign aid, and tourism.

Nissan is driven

Photo courtesy of Nissan Motor Corp. of America.

Japan's Nissan Motor Co., Ltd. last year sold 1.5 million cars and trucks in 130 countries under the name Datsun. Now, in a move that has stunned its dealers around the world, the company has decided to phase out the Datsun nameplate by the end of 1983 as part of the company's 50th anniversary celebration. After that, Datsun cars will be called Nissan, just as they now are in Japan.

Datsun Dealer Lou Porreco of Erie, Pa., feels betrayed by the change. Says he: "The Datsun name already has a lot of recognition and respect. I don't know if we can ever develop the same confidence in the new name." A Detroit auto executive agrees, saying, "Any time you pull the rug out from under a brand name, you kiss off years of marketing."

Nissan explains that it is changing its name because of a corporate identity problem. The company has been borrowing on world money markets to finance its expansion, but President Takashi Ishihara discovered three months ago in London that many potential lenders were not aware that his firm made Datsuns.

Company officials also note that the Datsun name is meaningless. Dat, the word for rabbit in Japanese, comes from the initials of the company's three chief financial backers. It was originally lengthened to Datson or "son of rabbit." But the word son had an unlucky connotation in Japanese, which was seemingly proved correct when a typhoon hit a Datson plant in 1933. Therefore, the company changed the marketing name to Datsun. Executives at Nissan are convinced that despite the worries of their dealers, a Datsun by any other name will sell as swiftly as ever.

Reprinted with permission from *Time,* September 14, 1981.

Government involvement in foreign trade

Governments become involved in foreign trade for three basic reasons: (1) generating income through taxes on imports; (2) protecting domestic interests, including businesses, national defense, and natural and human resources; and (3) encouraging domestic growth.

Through imports, foreign nations obtain the currency with which they can purchase exports. *To export, a country must import.* Most countries hesitate to buy the products of a nation that will not return the favor by buying their products.

Government trade policies affect the freedom of trade between nations. Some countries have more regulations than others. Governments may encourage or discourage foreign trade through tariffs, import quotas, embargoes, monetary exchange controls, government subsidies and assistance to domestic industries, and "buy domestic" campaigns.

Table 22.1 Regional economic associations

Name	Membership	Date of origin
ANCOM: Andean Common Market	Bolivia, Colombia, Ecuador, Peru, Venezuela	1967
ASEAN: Association of Southeast Asian Nations	Indonesia, Malaysia, Philippines, Singapore, Thailand	1967
CACM: Central American Common Market	Costa Rica, El Salvador, Guatemala, Honduras, Nicaragua	1960
CARICOM: Caribbean Common Market	Antigua, Barbados, Domenica, Grenada, Guyana, Jamaica, Montserrat, St. Christopher, St. Lucia, St. Vincent, Trinidad, and Tobago	1973
CMEA: Council for Mutual Economic Assistance	Bulgaria, Czechoslovakia, German Democratic Rep., Hungary, Mongolia, Poland, Romania, USSR, Cuba, Vietnam	1949
EC: European Community	Belgium, France, West Germany, Italy, Luxembourg, The Netherlands, Denmark, Ireland, United Kingdom, Greece	1958
EFTA: European Free Trade Area	Austria, Norway, Portugal, Sweden, Switzerland, Iceland, Finland (associate)	1960
LAIA: Latin American Integration Association (replaced LAFTA)	Argentina, Bolivia, Brazil, Chile, Colombia, Ecuador, Mexico, Paraguay, Peru, Uruguay, Venezuela	1980

Vern Terpstra, *International Marketing*. 3d ed., p. 42. © 1983 CBS College Publishing. Reprinted by permission of CBS College Publishing.

Figure 22.2 Industrial-world oil consumption, 1977–1981

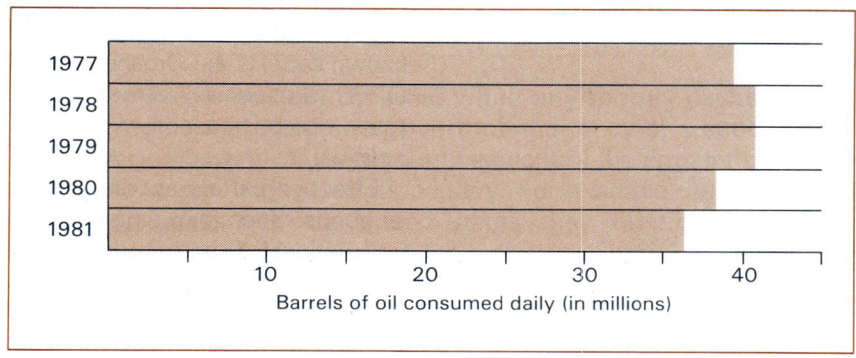

Reprinted with permission from *FORTUNE* Magazine, August 10, 1981.

Table 22.2 The ten largest industrial companies in the world (by sales)

Company	Headquarters	Sales ($ in thousands)	Net income ($ in thousands)
Exxon	New York	$103,107,688	$5,567,481
Royal Dutch/Shell Group	The Hague/London	82,291,728	3,642,142
Mobil	New York	64,488,000	2,433,000
General Motors	Detroit	62,698,500	333,400
Texaco	Harrison, NY	57,628,000	2,310,000
British Petroleum	London	52,199,976	2,063,272
Standard Oil of California	San Francisco	44,224,000	2,380,000
Ford Motor	Detroit	38,247,000	(1,060,100)*
Standard Oil (Indiana)	Chicago	29,947,100	1,922,000
ENI	Rome	29,444,315	383,234

*Net loss

"The Largest Industrial Companies in the World," FORTUNE, August 23, 1982, p. 181. Reprinted from the FORTUNE Directory by permission; © 1982 Time Inc. All rights reserved.

Multinational corporations (MNCs)

A multinational corporation is a company with business investments, production operations, and management personnel in several countries. Multinational corporations seek to use available resources as efficiently as possible, without regard to national boundaries. A true MNC actually owns businesses in many countries. And each business is usually run by managers from that country. For example, Saks Fifth Avenue, the clothing store, is a subsidiary of British American Tobacco Company, a British firm. Many European, Asian, and Canadian companies are owned by American-based firms. Table 22.2 shows the ten largest industrial companies in the world, ranked by sales.

Multinational corporations are growing for three reasons. First, costs may be reduced by locating production facilities close to sources of lower-cost raw materials and labor. If productivity can be maintained, closeness to resources can be a definite advantage. Second, profits in foreign markets may be greater than at home, with foreign demand growing more rapidly. Finally, producing demand products for foreign consumption may be efficient if domestic production costs decrease as volume of output increases. Within limits, producing more goods leads to lower unit costs.

Figure 22.3 Forms of international trade

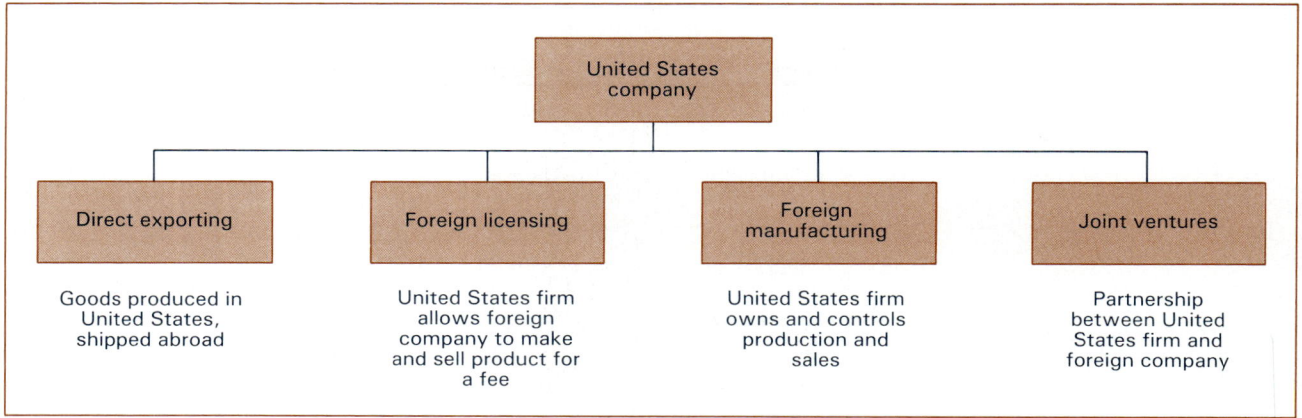

The strengths and weaknesses of MNCs

Multinational corporations can play an important role in developing countries. They supply technology and capital that would not otherwise be available. They also generate new jobs and become important suppliers of export revenues. By purchasing resources at lower costs and selling products in emerging foreign markets, MNCs promote improved living standards throughout the world.

On the other hand, some developing countries are suspicious of the power of MNCs. They fear that foreign-owned MNCs may be able to dominate their economies. And they worry that the MNCs may interfere in domestic political and social affairs to influence government decisions.

There are many advantages and disadvantages to the growth of multinational companies. Each multinational company is a unique entity that should be evaluated in terms of its own record.

Other forms of international trade

Companies may engage in various forms of international trade without being true multinationals. They may participate in direct exporting, foreign licensing, foreign manufacturing, and joint ventures (see Figure 22.3).

Direct exporting

A direct exporter seeks orders from foreign buyers for goods that are domestically produced. This is the most basic level of international trade.

Big Mac attack

> When McDonald's golden arches appeared in Paris nine years ago, the fast-food chain seemed to acquire a new international cachet. What better testimony to its cuisine than crowds of finicky Frenchmen munching Big Macs along the Champs Elysées?
>
> But McDonald's claims that its Paris licensee, Raymond Dayan, has spoiled the company's image by serving food in grimy surroundings. Says a McDonald's spokesman: "Dayan's restaurants were so filthy that your clothes would be covered with grease if you stayed in there too long." The firm wants to take away Dayan's right to use McDonald's name for his 14 restaurants.
>
> Dayan, in turn, has filed two suits in Chicago, seeking to protect his franchise and collect $500 million in damages. He says that he was given the French franchise on unusually favorable terms, and that the corporation now wants to get it back. Dayan admits that he had trouble matching the firm's American standards at first, but insists that both food and cleanliness in his restaurants are now comparable to those in the U.S. Thousands of Parisians who have given up long lunches for *le snack* at McDonald's seem to agree.

Reprinted with permission from *Time*, September 14, 1981, p. 68.

Foreign licensing

Under a licensing agreement, a domestic company allows a foreign company to produce and sell its product in the foreign market in return for a fee. The fee is usually a specified percentage of sales. Licensing agreements typically try to ensure that product quality will be maintained in the foreign market.

Such well-known companies as Coca-Cola, Pepsi-Cola, and McDonald's have foreign licensees. Licensing may be the only way a company can enter a foreign market due to tariffs, labor laws, or other restrictions.

Foreign manufacturing

Some companies directly own facilities and control the production and sales of their goods in foreign countries. General Electric, for example, established plants in Brazil. From there it exports items such as locomotive engines and electrical appliances. These are sold worldwide using GE distributors.

Joint venture

A joint venture is a business partnership involving a foreign company and a domestic company. This arrangement is often used when a country does not allow foreign companies to hold controlling interests in domestic companies. A joint venture provides a foreign company with

Table 22.3 The ten largest foreign corporations

Company	Country	Industry
Royal Dutch/Shell Group	Netherlands/Britain	Petroleum
British Petroleum	Britain	Petroleum
ENI	Italy	Petroleum
Unilever	Britain/Netherlands	Food products
Francais des Petroles	France	Petroleum
Kuwait Petroleum	Kuwait	Petroleum
Elf Aquitaine	France	Petroleum
Petroleos de Venezuela	Venezuela	Petroleum
Fiat	Italy	Motor vehicles
Petrobas (Petroeo Brasileiro)	Brazil	Petroleum

"The Foreign 500," FORTUNE, August 23, 1982, p. 183. Reprinted from the FORTUNE Directory by permission; © 1982 Time Inc. All rights reserved.

part-ownership of an operation. Control remains with the domestic firm. Both Mexico and Japan prohibit foreign-controlled businesses but allow joint ventures.

Table 22.3 shows the ten largest industrial corporations in the world outside of the United States.

Foreign exchange

All firms engaged in international trade are affected by currency exchange rates. These rates constantly rise and fall in response to economic conditions.

Currency values are determined in foreign exchange markets, much like the value of stock is determined on stock exchanges. Increases or decreases in the value of the dollar compared to currencies such as the British pound, French franc, or Japanese yen are crucial to international business operations.

For example, suppose that a U.S. manufacturer buys some steel from a Japanese company for 150 million yen. If the exchange rate that day is 240 yen to the dollar, the U.S. manufacturer would need to exchange $62,500 into yen to make the purchase. But if the yen falls to 210 yen per dollar, it will cost the U.S. purchaser $71,429 to get the same number of yen and buy the same amount of steel.

Managing international business

American managers working in a foreign nation must recognize how that country's culture differs from their own. Managers abroad must deal with different languages, social and religious customs, legal systems, educational levels, and government policies.

Each cultural difference can easily lead to misunderstanding and miscalculation, so managers must be sensitive to, and knowledgeable about, the ways of the country in which they work. For example, in the Middle East, punctuality has a different meaning than in the United States. A person may arrive two or three hours past the time of an appointment without being considered rude. In the United States, however, being five or ten minutes late usually requires a word of explanation.

More and more multinational companies are employing native-born management personnel. Expanding operations in foreign countries require such managers who can employ their own cultural perspectives and experiences to meet business challenges. Effective use of management, marketing, and financial resources is required to sustain and promote international growth.

22 International trade

Summary

Trade between nations is becoming increasingly important. No nation has all the goods and resources it needs. So all nations must trade among each other to obtain the goods they lack. *Specialization* is the practice of producing and trading the products that one can supply most efficiently and cheaply.

A *labor-intensive economy* uses production processes that rely on a labor force that is plentiful and relatively inexpensive. A *capital-intensive economy* uses production processes that rely on large amounts of capital equipment. *Exporting* is the selling of goods and services in other countries. *Importing* is the buying of goods and services from other countries.

The *theory of comparative advantage* holds that nations should specialize in producing goods that they can supply most efficiently and inexpensively. They should trade with other nations doing the same thing. The results benefit all parties because resources will move from places where they are plentiful to places where they are scarce.

A country's *balance of trade* is the relationship between the value of its imports and the value of its exports. The *balance of payments* is a measure of the flow of money into and out of the country.

Governments want to use their nation's resources as efficiently as possible. They are interested in generating income through taxes on foreign imports, protecting domestic interests, and encouraging domestic growth. Government policies affect the freedom of trade between nations. A government may encourage or discourage trade through *tariffs, import quotas, embargoes, monetary exchange controls,* and government subsidies and assistance to domestic industries.

Many nations enter into *multinational trade agreements* to lower trade barriers with neighboring countries. The *European Economic Community (EEC),* often called the Common Market, is based on multinational trade agreements.

An international cartel is a group of nations or producers who band together to control the price and flow of certain goods. The Organization of Petroleum Exporting Countries (OPEC) is an example of a cartel.

A *multinational corporation* is a company with business investments, production operations, and management personnel in several countries. These companies seek to produce more efficiently by locating facilities near sources of lower-cost raw materials and labor. Profits in foreign markets with increasing demand provide a strong incentive for MNCs.

Multinational companies can supply developing countries with capital and technology. They also generate new jobs and provide products in emerging foreign markets. Some nations view MNCs with suspicion. They fear that the companies may be powerful enough to influence and alter their national political, social, and economic structures.

Other forms of international trade include direct exporting, foreign licensing, foreign manufacturing, and joint ventures.

Management in a foreign environment requires sensitivity to differences in language, social and religious customs, legal systems, educational levels, and government policies.

Review questions

1. What are the differences between a labor-intensive economy and a capital-intensive economy?
2. Why do nations trade with each other?
3. How does the theory of comparative advantage result in foreign trade?
4. What is a country's balance of trade? What causes a favorable balance? What causes an unfavorable balance?
5. What is a country's balance of payments? When does a country have a favorable balance? When does it have an unfavorable balance?
6. What are the three basic reasons that governments become involved in foreign trade?
7. Briefly distinguish between the following government policies: (a) tariffs, (b) import quotas, and (c) embargoes.
8. What is the European Economic Community? How does it operate?
9. What are three major reasons that multinational corporations are growing?
10. Briefly explain the difference between a foreign licensing agreement and a joint venture.

Discussion questions

1. Why will international business become increasingly important?
2. The Organization of Petroleum Exporting Countries (OPEC) is an international cartel. What impact has OPEC had on your personal economic condition?
3. In your shopping area, identify six items imported from a foreign country. Which countries do these items come from?
4. Are there any foreign companies in your area? What goods or services do they provide? Why do you think they located in your region?

Chapter 22 case

U.S. mushroom capital battered by China imports

Cheap foreign imports often damage U.S. industries. The U.S. mushroom-growing industry's problems show the dramatic effects of Chinese imports.

The U.S. mushroom-growing industry, which had huge profits as recently as three years ago, is being battered by cheap imports.

"We're just trying to breathe, trying to hold on," says Charles Nigro, a mushroom farmer in Pennsylvania, where half of the nation's $350 million crop is grown. "I've got an 18-year-old son, and I don't want him in the business," he says.

The outlook for growers is particularly grim in southeastern Pennsylvania's Chester County, which produces about 60 percent of the state's mushroom crop. Kennett Square (population: 5000) still proudly calls itself the mushroom capital of the world, but Nigro predicts, "If we have another year like this, Kennett Square will be a ghost town."

The farmers blame most of their trouble on the mass of imports from the People's Republic of China. China shipped 27.4 million pounds of mushrooms here last year, and that number will nearly double this year. China is also expected to send nearly 25 million pounds of mushrooms to the United States by way of middlemen in Hong Kong and Macao.

The problems for U.S. growers began in early 1980, shortly after China received special trade status from the United States. The growers say that the People's Republic quickly targeted mushroom farming, which is very labor-intensive, as an ideal export industry through which to acquire foreign exchange.

"I wish they'd picked string beans," says Jack Kooker, the Mushroom Institute's executive director. Chinese embassy officials refuse to comment on the dispute.

1. Why are Chinese mushrooms probably cheaper than American mushrooms?
2. What government policies might help the American mushroom-growing industry?
3. What choices does an individual American mushroom grower have in this situation?

Paul A. Engelmayer, "U.S. Mushroom Growers Getting Mauled by Flood of Low-Cost Imports from China," *Wall Street Journal*, July 23, 1982. Reprinted by permission of the *Wall Street Journal*, © Dow Jones & Company, Inc., all rights reserved.

7 Careers in small business and international trade

Small business

Small business continues to be a vital portion of the economy and an area of great opportunity. Between 1966 and 1976, for example, 9 million new jobs were created in the United States. Of that number, 6 million—two-thirds—were developed by small businesses.

Career opportunities in small business follow the same pattern as those in business in general. That is, service rather than manufacturing is the area of greatest growth. Businesses relating to computers and telecommunications, certain areas of retailing, and service establishments of many types offer the greatest opportunity.

Among the businesses that have the lowest failure rates are small motels and inns and small eating and drinking places. On the other hand, book and stationery stores, sporting goods stores, and camera shops have traditionally had the highest failure rates.

Ideas for small businesses

Imagination and the ability to spot an unfilled niche have led to success for many entrepreneurs. In Boulder, Colorado, one entrepreneur recognized that with both husbands and wives working full-time, the weekly shopping was becoming a frantic chore. So, for $20 or less, he performs weekly shopping expeditions for busy people.

In San Francisco, a former advertising saleswoman founded a wardrobe-consulting service. She charges $40 an hour to select clothes for men and women. She is reportedly booked up two months in advance.

The high cost of buying a house provided an opportunity for a New Jersey firm. It inspects houses and their components for prospective buyers.

When is the best time to launch a new venture? Ironically, there is often an upsurge in small businesses during recessions. At the same time that many small businesses are failing, many are getting underway. This occurs because laid-off workers use their energy to start businesses that they hope will become permanent jobs. Moreover, during a recession, many existing businesses are available at bargain prices.

Careers in international trade

There are two kinds of jobs in international business. One involves working in the United States for a firm that engages in international trade but requires little foreign travel. The second kind of job requires either extensive travel overseas or working full-time abroad.

Although overseas assignments may seem glamorous, they do have their drawbacks. According to one survey, managers assigned to overseas posts have found that even with additional financial compensation, high living expenses may result in an overall financial setback. Some employees felt that while they were overseas, their company forgot about them, which reduced their chances for promotion. Nonetheless, such assignments do have their attractions. It is a chance to live in and experience a different culture. And it is the best way to perfect the speaking of a foreign language.

Both large and small companies offer opportunities in international business. Many import businesses operate on a small scale. For example, a New York man who traveled to Nepal on a vacation brought back a few rugs for himself. His friends liked them a great deal. So he sold them for enough money to finance another trip to Nepal. Now he travels there twice a year to buy rugs for his import business.

Jobs in international trade
International managers

Firms with international operations often appoint one or two top executives to work in each subsidiary that they have abroad. The rest of the managers and employees are often from the host country. Firms in banking, textiles, appliance manufacturing, and mining are among those stationing Americans overseas.

Importers

Importers buy goods overseas for resale in their own country. As a result, importers may travel extensively. In such cases, knowledge of foreign languages is an asset. Importers must also be sensitive to the customs and ways of doing business in other countries.

Export managers

Export managers are important to firms that sell their products abroad. They oversee international marketing, transportation, arrangement of credit terms, and customer relations. Like importers, export managers may have to travel extensively.

8 ... And toward the 21st century

Business in perspective

Worker stabbed to death by robot
The first recorded incident of a person being fatally injured by a computer-controlled robot was reported in Japan in 1981. A 37-year-old factory maintenance worker was stabbed to death when a robot suddenly started up and pinned him against another machine. At the time, Japan had about 70,000 robots in use.

As reported by the government, the victim stepped across a safety barrier, thereby accidentally starting up the robot. The robot's arm stabbed the worker in the back. The government investigation blamed the accident on the worker's carelessness. But it also decided that safety measures in the plant were inadequate.

Chapter 23

Business and the future

Key terms

genetic engineering
baby boom
baby bust
Third Wave

Chapter objectives

In Chapter 23, you will learn:

The major forces that will shape business and society in the coming decades

How technology will affect the price and availability of energy in the years ahead

What lies ahead in the application of computer technology

The contributions that genetic engineering can make to society

The challenges and opportunities that increasing business competition from Western Europe, Japan, and less-developed countries present to American industry

How the baby boom will affect our nation

The probable role of government in the coming years

What the future holds for large corporations

The effects of technology on workers of the future

How the Third Wave will affect individuals

How an individual can cope with the future even though it cannot be accurately predicted

Overview

Humans have never been successful in predicting the future. For example, Thomas Edison predicted early in this century that film would shortly spell the end of books in the classroom. Karl Marx, on the other hand, predicted that workers in the most industrialized countries would be the first to rebel against the existing social and economic order. Obviously, both were wrong.

Thus, it may be futile to try to predict the future. But we can look at the forces of change at work today and try to anticipate their likely directions. This might help us prepare for changes that may take place during our working lifetimes.

Identifying forces and trends

Among the factors that will have the greatest impact on society and business are the following:
1. Developments in technology
2. Increasing foreign competition
3. Changing population characteristics
4. The changing role of government.

Developments in technology and their outcomes

While there are many areas of technological change, the three most likely to strongly affect business and society are in energy, information, and biology.

Energy

The 500 percent increase in oil prices in the 1970s seriously slowed U.S. investment and productivity. It led to reduced demand for petroleum products and encouraged a shift to other fossil fuels, such as coal. But all fossil fuels will eventually dry up. Thus, in the long term, many analysts believe we need a major technological breakthrough to make solar power and nuclear fusion the low-cost energy sources of the twenty-first century.

The cost of solar power has dropped dramatically. Not long ago, it cost $50 to produce one watt of capacity from the sun. By 1980, the cost had fallen to $10. But to be competitive, the cost would have to fall to about $.50 per watt of capacity. Researchers are working on ways to make solar cells more efficient and less expensive.

Fusion is another long-term possibility as a major energy source. Unlike today's nuclear fission processes, fusion produces only a small amount of radioactive by-products. Nor does it require the dangerous fuels that fission does. Because it is so efficient, fusion may account for the majority of our electricity in 50 years. But due to the technological complexity of this process, the first prototype plants will probably not be in operation until the early 1990s.

Information

Computers have already had a profound effect on both our business and our personal lives. And their impact is likely to grow. But the computer is really only a tool. The resource that the computer manipulates is information. As computers get smaller and more powerful, they are able to handle greater quantities of information. In the not-too-distant future, experts expect to make a major breakthrough in artificial intelligence. Then computers would no longer be the "dumb" machines we use today. Rather, they would be capable of humanlike reasoning. As one study reported:

> If artificial intelligence can be created at all, there is little reason to believe that [it] could not swiftly lead to the construction of superintelligences able to explore significant mathematical, scientific, or engineering alternatives at a rate far exceeding human abilities.[1]

The possible applications of artificial intelligence are almost endless. Thinking computers can already diagnose patients' lung conditions. Physicians accept the computer's analysis without challenge 85 percent of the time. In factories, artificial intelligence coupled with robots will increasingly take over boring and dangerous tasks.

Biology

Genetic engineering is the modification of microorganisms, such as bacteria, for a predetermined purpose. The implications of this form of biotechnology may be as far-reaching as those of computerization.

Scientists have already created valuable hormones and drugs using genetic engineering. One bacterium can turn wood waste products into alcohol. A growth hormone can combat dwarfism.

But genetic engineering may hold much more for business in the future. Researchers are working on new strains of plants and livestock that can grow in harsh environments and produce their own fertilizer. They may also be able to create plants that are resistant to certain herbicides. Then a farmer could spray a field and kill everything except the desired crop plant. Livestock in the future may be more resistant to disease and yet produce far more milk or meat.

---

[1] *BusinessWeek,* July 6, 1981, p. 50.

"A whole new way of making tires"

Armstrong Rubber Company's new Tredloc tires make an end run around an awkward fact that has bedeviled tiremakers for decades: rubber won't stick to the material used to reinforce belts—polyester, glass fiber, steel, or even Kevlar. Adhesives must be added to create a bond. Up to now, the belts have been cut from huge rolls and hand-laid on each tire before it is cured in massive presses using superheated steam and high pressure. But the cutting removes the adhesive from the edges and ends of the belts, leaving a steel radial tire weakest on the shoulder, where it flexes with every bump in the road.

By contrast, the Tredloc process is "a whole new way of making tires," says John A. Breslin, vice president for marketing at Armstrong. Two Kevlar threads, each about as thin as a small paper-clip wire, are twisted into a cord. An adhesive is applied and six or eight cords are encased in rubber-covered strips ⅜ inch wide. Computer-controlled machinery weaves two strips into a light but tough two-ply belt around each "green" tire carcass, leaving no cut edges. "It looks simple but it isn't," says Chairman James Walsh.

At $6.50 a pound, Kevlar costs nearly six times as much as steel, but it has five times the tensile strength, so less of it is needed. A steel-belted radial tire contains 2½ to 2¾ pounds of wire, as against ¾ of a pound of Kevlar in a Tredloc tire.

Gurney Breckenfeld, "The Niche Pickers at Armstrong Rubber," FORTUNE, September 6, 1982, pp. 100–102; © 1982 Time Inc. All rights reserved.

Biotechnology will also benefit human health. Vaccines against malaria and hepatitis are under development. Work with human proteins may help show how the body fights disease. And some scientists hope that a substance could be formed that would help the body regenerate lost limbs.

Finally, biotechnology may play a role in energy production. Modified organisms may help convert coal into synthetic gas. They may help split water into hydrogen and oxygen, with energy as the by-product. Scientists have already found bacteria that can reduce air pollution caused by oil.

Implications

These and other technological developments have long-range implications for individuals as well as for business. For individuals, they suggest opportunities for better and longer life. Many of these trends should help combat higher prices and decreasing supplies of food and energy. They also offer many promising career opportunities.

Business, of course, has a major stake in all trends that affect the U.S. and world economy. Obtaining adequate supplies of inexpensive energy is extremely important to many manufacturers. Smaller, cheaper,

Figure 23.1 A completely automated Japanese factory

Time, November 16, 1981, p. 127.

and easy-to-use microcomputers have wide-ranging implications for all kinds of businesses, from local retail stores to the largest banks and military organizations.

Technology creates many opportunities for individuals and business. The challenge is to recognize them and act on them from a position of strength and knowledge.

Increasing foreign competition

American industry is already feeling the effects of foreign competition. Japan and Western Europe have become strong competitors in the automobile and steel industries. Most of the television sets and sewing machines in the United States come from abroad. Less-developed nations are using their lower-cost labor pools to compete in such labor-intensive industries as textiles and electronics. As more nations improve their living standards and industrial strength, they too will compete in world markets with U.S. manufacturers. Only the high-technology portions of U.S. industry may survive without government intervention.

U.S. exports are expected to continue to grow. But foreign competition will be strong. Thus, U.S. exports will actually account for a much lower percentage of world trade by the year 2025.

Industries threatened by foreign competition tend to seek protection from their government. In response, the government may set quotas or taxes on imports. Or it may place restrictions on foreign firms that wish to do business within its borders. American businesses often complain, for example, of Japanese government regulations that make selling in Japan very difficult. At the same time, U.S. auto manufacturers have convinced government regulators to restrict the number of Japanese cars imported into the United States.

Some economists predict that more and more countries will restrict imports. The less-developed countries argue that they must protect their young industries from foreign competitors whose well-established industries can produce goods at lower costs. In the industrialized countries, it is often the slowest-growing but most powerful industries, such as steelmaking, that demand protection from overseas firms with newer, lower-cost plants.

The challenge to American industry and labor is to remain efficient and avoid the temptation to protect industries that produce goods we can buy cheaper elsewhere. And we must persuade other nations that it is in their best interests to buy from us the goods that they cannot efficiently produce themselves.

Changing population characteristics

Perhaps the most certain predictions can be made about population characteristics. Based on the number and ages of people now alive, we can quite accurately calculate the make-up of the population well into the next century. This is important for both business and government.

Businesses want to know what goods and services will be in greatest and least demand. We know, for example, that young families spend proportionately more than other age groups for things like appliances and furniture. Older people have relatively higher amounts of money to spend on vacations or to use for savings.

Government needs to know population trends, too. Lower birthrates mean a declining need for schools, teachers, and playgrounds. An aging population requires medical services, special transportation facilities, and the like.

Baby boom to baby bust

The characteristics of tomorrow's population can be traced to the shifts in population patterns that have occurred since the end of World War II. First, there was the baby boom. **The baby boom was a period of high birthrates that started in 1946 and ended in the early 1960s.** People born during the baby boom are now in their 20s and 30s. The baby boom was followed by an extended baby bust. **The baby bust is the current period of low birthrates occurring because the baby boom generation has put off having children until much later in their lives.** Therefore, today's families are smaller than demographers would have predicted from past trends.

The average age of the U.S. population is also getting higher. The number of Americans 65 years old and over doubled between 1950 and 1980. More significantly, this age group rose from only 8 percent of the population to 11 percent. And the most dramatic shift is yet to come. According to the U.S. Bureau of the Census, in 1979 there were only 26 people 62 years or older for each 100 people of working age (21 to 61). But the baby boom will cause that ratio to shift dramatically. In 2029, there will be 43 persons 62 or older for 100 working-age adults.

Implications

The entry of the baby boom generation into young adulthood caused many social problems. One problem was high teenage unemployment. Some sociologists blame high crime rates on the large numbers of people who hit the job market in a short period of time. Many couldn't find work. Crime, the sociologists say, was one response to the frustration of not finding employment.

In the future, growth of the labor force will slow. Because the baby bust generation has fewer members, the unemployment rate should drop. And for those born since the mid-1960s, the future holds the promise of better entry-level jobs and a higher standard of living. Promotion should come fast to them due to their sparser numbers.

Meanwhile, members of the baby boom generation will continue to find stiff competition for jobs and promotions. Business and government organizations will face the challenge of keeping many talented middle managers satisfied when there is little chance for promotion. At the same time, this situation will give business the opportunity to choose its executives from a large pool of capable and well-educated talent.

Both business and government must also begin to plan for the pension needs of the baby boom generation. These people will live longer after retirement than previous generations. Yet the number of workers per retiree will be decreasing. Unless other sources of funds are found, those who remain employed will have to pay increased payroll tax to pay Social Security benefits for the many who will be retiring. A major overhaul of the Social Security system by Congress in 1983 was in response to these trends.

Trends in government

Despite moves toward deregulation of certain industries in the late 1970s and early 1980s, many people still believe that the U.S. government is too deeply involved in business. Yet the very forces that promote bigness in our economy will continue to demand government participation in the role of watchdog.

A broker's scenario with electronic mail

The notion of electronic mail is so new, and so difficult for the initiate to conceptualize, that some consultants and vendors have adopted a storybook approach, outlining a day in the life of a fictitious EM user to illustrate the process. Susan K. Kubany, president of Omnet Inc., a Boston-based company that helps set up and administer EM systems, has penned a scenario for prospective clients: the tale of Edgar Mills.

Edgar Mills is in charge of the Boston office of a nationwide brokerage firm. He sneaks out of bed at 6 a.m. past his sleeping wife, brews coffee in the kitchen, and plugs his portable phonewriter—a keyboard and display unit the size of a briefcase—into the wall near the kitchen table.

Edgar dials a local phone number and attaches the phone to his phonewriter. When the electronic mail system is activated, he types his name and password. The system tells him that three messages have arrived since he checked his "mailbox" at 7 p.m.

Two of the messages are from the vice-president in the Los Angeles office. The first answers Edgar's request for information about a new issue being handled from the L.A. office. Edgar reads the message and files it electronically.

The second message is a request sent to all vice-president/office managers asking their opinion of a medical insurance policy the L.A. vice-president has just heard about. Edgar comments on the insurance option. He also forwards the message to his assistant, asking: "Do you have any thoughts on this?"

The third message is an order from one of Edgar's few, but very special, customers to buy 500 shares of a certain stock. Edgar enters this message electronically in the customer's file and also forwards the message to the trading department, with instructions to fill the order.

Edgar is off to a day-long seminar, so he packs his lightweight phonewriter in the car. During the morning coffee break, he checks his messages again. There is one message, marked "private," from a broker in his office. Edgar needs a special, additional password to read this message. Even his assistant cannot read messages that are marked "private." The message reads: "Got a priblem I must discuss with you immediately. Please give me a call befroe lunch." (Many messages sent on electronic mail contain typos; it is generally understood that the message was composed directly by an executive. It is, of course, assumed that the message makes some sense.) Edgar makes the call immediately, and the problem is straightened out.

At the office, a broker receives a message from the New York office that a customer agreement form submitted the previous day is incomplete. The broker is asked for the missing information. Another broker sends a message to the company's research department requesting background on a specific stock. A third message is posted on the Brokers' (electronic mail) Bulletin Board for all brokers across the country. It concerns a corporate change in commission policy. Hundreds of other messages are sent and received through the day.

> At the end of the day, Edgar goes home and checks for messages once again. There is a reminder to check the Stocks Bulletin Board for information about the total number of shares of stock the firm traded that day, as well as the Dow Jones closings. Edgar's assistant posted a message to all employees of the Boston office reminding them of the staff meeting the next afternoon. Edgar composes a message to one of his brokers and signs off the electronic mail service.
>
> In the middle of the night, Edgar remembers an open order to buy that he forgot to place two days earlier. He jumps out of bed, turns on his phonewriter, composes the order in the form of a message to the trading department, and falls back to sleep.
>
> Using EM, Edgar saved about $30 worth of his salary, plus secretarial, telephone, postage, and other expenses. The cost of EM is estimated at $3 for the day.

Reprinted with permission, *INC*, August 1982. Copyright © 1982 by INC. Publishing Company, 38 Commercial Wharf, Boston, MA 02110.

The challenge of government regulators in the coming decades will be to ensure cooperation from those they regulate. The size of the industries will make regulation difficult unless the business community itself assumes an attitude of compliance. There is reason to believe this is possible. Most Americans voluntarily comply with tax laws. By and large, they report their income and pay their taxes, even though there is very little chance that they will ever be audited.

So it might be argued that business can police itself, with government acting as a referee. Or government might focus on only the most serious violations of environmental, antitrust, safety, and other regulations.

Some people believe that private individuals and the business community can act as a balance to big business. For example, the federal government used to bring most antitrust actions. But today, most antitrust suits are brought by private individuals or other businesses. We can anticipate similar trends in other areas of business regulation.

The future of the corporation

There are two major schools of thought about the future of corporations. The doomsayers believe that U.S. corporations have become too large and bureaucratic. They say that businesses can no longer innovate because they have lost their creativity and flexibility. Jay Forrester, a professor at the Massachusetts Institute of Technology, thinks large corporations will be replaced by entrepreneurs who are not hampered by complicated organizational structure. Less radical forecasters see a smaller role for corporations. Big business will exist, but the major force for change will come from smaller organizations.

The other school of thought, the adapters, believe that today's large corporations have some built-in advantages. Size is often accompanied by economic efficiency. This includes the reduced costs of mass purchasing and manufacturing. As a result, large companies can afford to fund the extensive research and development needed to bring technology to the marketplace.

Forecasters from this school of thought say that technology will enable corporations to adapt. Widespread use of low-cost computers and telecommunications will make information available to people at lower levels of the organization. Instead of decisions being made by top executives at corporate headquarters, they will be made by managers at the division level. This decentralization of decision making will enable large corporations to operate like smaller businesses.

Will corporations adapt or die?

Both the doomsayers and the adapters can cite forces in their favor. As is often the case, the outcome will probably be somewhere between the two extremes. American society tends to distrust bigness. Government will continue to set regulations for hiring and firing, environmental standards, safety, health, and the like to restrain business excesses. But business may also move on its own to avoid legislation in certain areas.

To compete internationally, the United States must have large corporations. Businesses, in exchange for being allowed to be large, will make some concessions. For example, workers may get a greater voice in management. Government agencies may acquire minority interests in some corporations and place representatives on their boards of directors.

At the same time, we can expect small businesses to continue to prosper. The entrepreneurial spirit does not thrive in most large organizations. And the importance of the independent entrepreneur is unlikely to diminish. For the many reasons discussed in Chapter 21, small business will continue to be necessary to the U.S. economy. And its ability to compete is likely to be enhanced by the same technology available to big business—low-cost computers and telecommunications.

The role of workers

Most forecasters believe that employees at all levels will gain more say in how they do their jobs. Although management is unlikely to yield all control to workers, corporate democracy will grow.

Management will face more and more pressure to increase efficiency and productivity. To achieve this on a broad scale, management will need workers to assume more responsibility. But employees cannot simply be ordered to be more responsible and productive. In order to get workers to cooperate, management will have to let them participate in the decision-making process.

Top management will probably retain responsibility for long-range policies. But workers will be regularly consulted and decisions will tend to reflect their viewpoints. As a result, many expect that workers will be more willing to implement decisions.

Moreover, many of the fringe benefits now reserved for senior management may become more widely available. Programs such as tuition assistance for children, low-cost home loans, access to recreational facilities, and the like will become more common. Such benefits will be used to create greater worker loyalty and reduce employee turnover.

It is unclear whether workers will actually want representatives on boards of directors, however. Organized labor has been especially opposed to this. In Western Europe, union participation in management is common. But U.S. labor unions fear this would compromise their ability to criticize company policy from the outside. Once they were on the board, some say, they would be part of management. How could they then negotiate as an opposing force? The experience of the president of the United Auto Workers, elected to the board of Chrysler Corporation during the time of its greatest financial difficulty, may be educational for both union and management.

The role of the individual

How individuals will fit into future society is unclear. Technological developments seem to suggest longer life spans and more leisure time. Computers and telecommunications will allow more people to work from their homes. They will also bring people home shopping, banking, and entertainment.

At the same time, possible energy, water, and food shortages could make society much more conservation-minded. "Small" and "efficient" may become more important than "large" and "showy." And the human desire for social contact may counteract the technological capability of being able to work and shop from home. Can purchasing a sofa from a video picture replace the experience of visiting furniture stores, sitting on various sofas, and asking questions? Can two-way television hookups between employees working at home replace the spontaneity of the common workplace?

What is rather certain, however, is that society will place increasingly greater emphasis on the ability to handle information. Everyone will be affected. Farmers, for example, will have access to improved weather forecasts. They will have more up-to-date information on current prices and demand for their crops. They will be able to discover what pests are in the area and what remedies are available. Their ability to receive, analyze, and act on this information can affect their productivity and hence their profit.

Technology may make some skills unnecessary. But it will also make it easier for individuals to find new jobs through computer searches of "skill banks." Technology may also make it easier to train for new jobs and improve knowledge in existing jobs.

Figure 23.2 1990 jobs There will be plenty of jobs by 1990, but they'll be spread unevenly across the market. Nobody can be sure how it will all shake out, but in this new forecast by the Bureau of Labor Statistics, fast-food chains, for example, will add nearly 800,000 jobs, while the number of teachers will continue to drop.

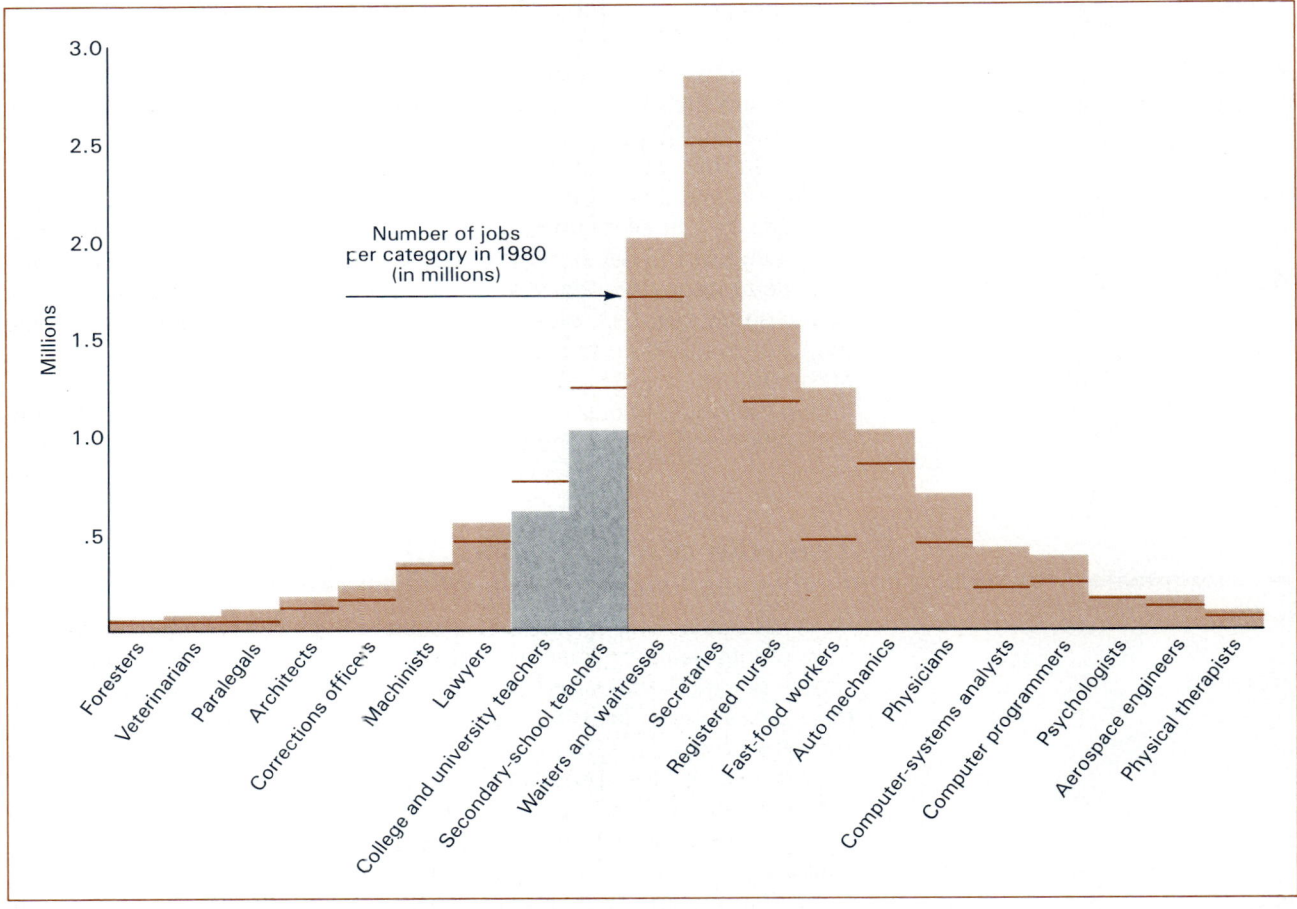

Reprinted with permission from FORTUNE Magazine, June 28, 1982.

The Third Wave

Futurist Alvin Toffler has predicted that the industrial society of the mid-twentieth century will be replaced by a new era. **The Third Wave is a new era in which the key to civilization will be diversity rather than the uniformity that accompanied the mass production of the industrial age.** Toffler suggests that the businesses that prosper in the future will be those that are best at customizing their products and services at the lowest cost.

Chapter 23 Business and the future

Mass production will be replaced by the technology of information processing. Factories will employ robots instead of people. But more people will work in service industries. Thus, more people will be working with other people instead of with machines.

Implications for you

How will the future affect you? Toffler's and other futurists' predictions may not come true. But dramatic changes of some kind definitely will occur during your lifetime. As individuals, we must all be prepared to understand these changes, grow with them, and act rather than react. Just as businesses will have to look for new opportunities or face gradual decay, so individuals will have to stay alert to new developments.

Given the uncertainties of change, perhaps the most useful career question you can ask yourself is, "What skills or talents can I develop and use regardless of how future shifts in technology and the economy affect business and society?"

For example, some people look forward to becoming clothing buyers for department stores. But what if future technology makes it possible for consumers to shop for clothing by using their home video terminals? That would greatly reduce the need for retail stores and the buyers who work in them. Buyers could, however, exploit their ability to anticipate styles. Such skill is applicable to far more jobs than the limited one of clothing buyer.

Skills that involve analysis, reasoning, and information processing are likely to be most versatile in the long run.

In the end, the most successful people will be those who do not fear or deny change. Change can carry threats, but it can also signify progress. Change by itself is neither good nor bad. Its quality depends on how it is employed by individuals and societies.

23 Business and the future

Summary

The future is all but impossible to predict with much certainty. Nonetheless, some forces and trends at work today suggest what the future may hold.

Technology is a very powerful force of change. It will shape the availability and cost of energy well into the twenty-first century. Information technology will develop new applications for computers and telecommunications. And the technology of *genetic engineering,* the modification of microorganisms for a predetermined purpose, has long-range implications for human health.

A second trend to watch is the growth of foreign business competition. The era of U.S. dominance has ended. The industrialized nations are proving to be strong competitors for the sale of goods and services around the world. The less-developed countries are using their low-cost labor pools to manufacture products at far lower costs than American manufacturers can achieve. The United States will have to seek out markets in the goods and services it can provide most efficiently.

A third trend, changes in the characteristics of U.S. population, is the most predictable. Our population is aging as the children of the post-World War II *baby boom* reach adulthood. This has created a large pool of individuals competing for jobs. It has also provided businesses with large and profitable markets for their products. But the baby boom was followed by the *baby bust.* Due to their smaller numbers, the baby bust generation will have opportunities for rapid career advancement. But they will also bear the burden of supporting the baby boom generation when that group reaches old age.

The role of government in private enterprise will probably not change significantly. The need for technological research and development will require the resources of large corporations, as will the challenge of doing business on a world-wide scale. But in return for being permitted to grow larger and potentially more powerful, big business will have to accept continued government regulations in areas of health, safety, environmental protection, and antitrust. Some people believe that, to some extent, businesses will end up policing themselves.

There are two schools of thought about the future of the corporation. The doomsayers believe that large corporate bureaucracies will not be able to compete with smaller entrepreneurial firms. The adapters think that large corporations will adjust to changing conditions. The final outcome will probably be somewhere between the two extremes.

Chapter 23 Business and the future

The role of workers is expected to shift somewhat. In order to get workers' cooperation in implementing decisions, management is more likely to consult them before making major decisions. Workers are also more likely to be given some fringe benefits that were once reserved for top management. And more workers than ever will work with other people rather than with machines.

All this speculation may make the individual feel very uncertain about the future. Technology holds out the promise of longer life, a higher standard of living, and more rewarding jobs. It also suggests loss of some jobs, less social contact with fellow workers, and fewer opportunities for the unskilled. An individual can prepare for the future by anticipating the general skills that are likely to be needed. These include strength in reasoning, analysis, and information processing.

Review questions

1. What factors will have the greatest impact on society and business in the coming decades?
2. What are the effects of foreign competition on the United States? How can the United States respond to foreign competition?
3. What problems does the aging of the post-World War II baby boom generation pose for society?
4. What is the biggest challenge for government regulators in the future?
5. Describe the two schools of thought about the future of the corporation in the United States.
6. How might the role of workers change in the coming years?
7. What is the Third Wave and what might it mean to you as an individual?

Discussion questions

1. Why has it been difficult to predict the future?
2. How do computers affect your life now? How might they affect you in the future?
3. The baby boom generation produced many teaching professionals who are now unemployed or working in other professions. Why did this happen? How could you avoid the dilemma of those teachers?
4. Due to budgetary pressures, your school has decided not to buy a new computer for the use of students. Do you think that is a wise decision? Why?
5. There is a proposal to build a nuclear energy plant about ten miles away from you. You've been invited to a hearing where you can express your views. What would you say?
6. You've been given two options to invest your money. You may go into partnership in a new gas station near the center of town, or you may go into partnership with a solar-energy equipment supplier. Which would you choose? Why?
7. Your friend is fascinated by biotechnology. Would you encourage him or her to pursue a career in that field? Why?

Chapter 23 case

All the news that's fit to . . .?

Many industries will have to adapt to evolving technology. Until recently, the way that newspapers were printed had barely changed in 150 years. Now publishers must be alert to major changes.

The newspaper that is sold today would be easily recognized by a publisher from 1900. In fact, it would even look familiar to Ben Franklin. Although much of a newspaper's production process today is handled by electronics and computers, it is still printed by huge presses that smear about a fifth of an ounce of ink over 60 pages of paper.

The printing press is the most expensive piece of equipment a newspaper publishing company owns. But the paper itself has become a major expense. The manufacturing of paper requires a great deal of energy in the form of oil or gas. The steep rise of energy costs caused paper prices to rise, too. The paper alone costs more than what a publisher receives from a paying reader—and that's before anything is printed on it. Then, the publisher must distribute the newspaper using trucks that also use much high-priced gasoline. Thus, the cost of distributing information that is printed on paper is getting more expensive.

On the other hand, rapid advances in technology have made computers cheaper than ever. And computers can transfer their information using telephone lines or cable lines that go into almost every home. As a result, the newspaper of the future may depend on computers and transmission lines.

This would produce an "electronic newspaper." Customers at home could turn on their new enhanced television sets and "dial-up" a computer. The computer would then provide any kind of information they wanted—sports scores, news events, recipes, closing stock quotes, classified advertising, and the like.

If you were a newspaper publisher today:
1. How would you prepare for the future where the traditional newspaper could be replaced by electronics?
2. What opportunities might there be for continuing the ink and paper newspaper? What opportunities are there for an "electronic newspaper"?
3. What industries may be the potential competitors of today's newspapers?

8 Careers with new opportunities

Many jobs that provide employment for tens of thousands of people today did not even exist 40 or 50 years ago. Technological advances that brought us television, for example, created the need for people who could manufacture, sell, and service TV sets. Xerox and other copying machines, computers, integrated circuits, and all sorts of electronic developments have created industries and jobs that did not exist a generation or two ago. Economic growth and prosperity have created a rapid expansion of the service work force in fast-food establishments like McDonald's, at mass merchandise retailers like Kmart, in rapidly expanding government and social services, and in education.

High technology is one key to anticipating opportunities for future jobs. Massachusetts, for example, lost thousands of jobs in manufacturing textiles and shoes in the 1950s and 1960s. But now, high-technology firms like Wang and Digital Equipment Corporation employ 250,000 people—one-third of the state's manufacturing labor force—which more than makes up for the old losses. In the San Francisco area, electronics plants provided jobs for 161,000 workers in 1982.

While many new jobs in the future will be tied to new technological developments, there will be fewer opportunities in such traditional areas as automobile or steel manufacturing. The president of General Motors has said that by 1988, 90 percent of GM production machinery will be computer controlled. Thus, there will be trade-offs: technology will increase productivity and result in lost jobs. But it will also create new jobs.

New jobs for new demands

Trends in business indicate that new jobs will be required to meet new demands. Dr. J. Ray Watson, assistant dean for executive education at Duke University's business school, suggests at least five areas that will either be new or will acquire greater importance in businesses.[1] These include information systems, quality control, human resources, distribution, and government relations.

[1] Elizabeth M. Fowler, "New Titles for New Demands," *New York Times*, December 9, 1981.

Information systems	This is a logical outgrowth of the development of computers in so many parts of company operations. Review the chapters and careers section of Part 3 to see the many employment opportunities available in this field.
Quality control	Concerns about productivity in the work force have raised the importance of quality control. Some people believe that many foreign competitors have outperformed U.S. companies in this regard. Many American companies may turn to robots to help improve the quality of their products.
Human resources	Human resources specialists are far different from traditional personnel managers. In human resources management, the emphasis is on strategic planning for personnel needs in the future. At some companies, this job is considered so important for advancement that all top managers are expected to spend some time as a human resources manager.
Distribution	In our fast-paced society, it is becoming increasingly important to ship goods where they are needed, when they are needed, at the lowest possible cost. This requires experience in purchasing, traffic management, and inventory control. In most companies, these departments have operated separately. In the future, they are more likely to be viewed as parts of a single function.
Government relations	The increasing role of government regulation in so many areas of business has already led many companies to hire government affairs specialists. Many firms have an office in Washington, D.C. From there they can keep track of legislation and attend hearings. In many cases, government affairs specialists lobby Congress for or against legislation that affects their employers.

Getting a job

Getting a job is hard work. Getting a job that you will enjoy and that will provide opportunities for personal development is a challenge. In many ways, job hunting is a marketing job. You must package, promote, and price yourself right and get to the place that has the opportunities. This requires careful self-evaluation.

Before you set out on a job hunt, you must prepare yourself. You can begin by reading one of the many good books of advice on job searching. These will tell you how to dress, what to expect in a job interview, what to say (and what not to say), how to get leads on job openings, and the like. Several of these books and some other resources are listed at the end of this section.

Careers Figure 8.1 Sample resume of Benjamin M. Compaine

```
5 Ellery Square
Denver, CO 12345
(555) 495-4114
```

Job Objective	Entry-level position in brand management or as account executive for advertising agency.
Work Experience	
	Franklin Advertising Agency Denver, CO
Part-time 1982-Present	Started as messenger and errand boy. Then assisted in copy writing. Currently an assistant to account executive for two local retail stores. Responsibilities include meeting with client representatives to work out ad campaign themes. Also work with account executive in planning media buys.
Summers	May Co. Denver, CO
1981	Men's clothing department. At beginning of summer, started as stock clerk. Was promoted to salesman. Earned highest commission of any summer salesman. Suggested sales promotion to men's clothing buyer that was eventually used.
1980	Self-employed Denver, CO
	Designed T-shirts for rock concerts coming to Denver. Arranged for artist to draw design, then had it silk-screened onto T-shirts. Hired commissioned salespeople to sell T-shirts before and after concerts. Sold over 3,000 shirts at $5.95 each in 10 weeks.
Education	
	Frankmont Community College Somewhere, CO
1983-Present	Candidate for Associate of Arts degree, June 1984. Major in business administration, with concentration in marketing. Dean's list each semester. President, Advertising Club. Member, Computer Society. Took courses in creative writing, computer programming (BASIC).
	South Rim High School Somewhere, CO
1979-1983	Completed academic program with honors diploma. Elected treasurer, senior class. Varsity soccer.
Other Interests	Photography and music, including playing guitar. Won regional Pac-Man video game prize, which included trip to San Francisco for national contest (came in 10th).
	Excellent health. Willing to relocate.

The resume

Basically, a resume is a sales tool. It tells employers about you in a brief series of statements that highlight your experience, skills, and education. Your resume should be honest, but it should tell about you in the most favorable light.

Figure 1 shows a sample resume. Writing a good resume can be very time consuming. In your resume, you want to show prospective employers that you have gained experience, skills, and responsibility over the years. This holds true even if you have held only summer and part-time jobs. For example, say that one summer you worked as an order taker for a fast-food restaurant. The next summer you were hired back to make hamburgers. Your job included judging how many hamburgers to make so that there were enough during busy periods but no leftovers during slow periods.

In that case, you might write this entry in your resume:

Summers 198– and 198–   XYZ Fast Foods, Inc.

Started as order taker. Responsibilities included taking customer orders, filling them, making change. Next summer was promoted to hamburger cook. This included responsibility for quality, determining production levels, and maintaining appropriate inventory.

Your resume is an important sales tool. It may be all that a prospective employer sees before deciding whether to invite you for an interview. It is worth the time to make a document that helps you get your foot in the door.

The interview

The face-to-face meeting with a company interviewer is the most critical step in your job search. Successful job interviews have three steps: a plan, an interview performance, and an interview follow-up.

Interview plan

Review your qualifications Key areas that employers consider include leadership skills, initiative, decision-making skills, written and oral communication skills, adaptability, appearance, dependability, maturity, and self-confidence.

Prepare questions about the company Gather information about the company, including products made, plant locations, job types, and future growth prospects.

Anticipate interview questions Common questions interviewers ask include: Why would you like to work for our company? What qualifications do you have for this job? What jobs have you had? Why did you leave your last job? What do you know about our company? Are you willing to relocate? What are your special abilities? What salary do you expect?

Consider your appearance First impressions *do* count and selection is influenced by physical appearance. Generally, you should dress as you would in the job situation.

Interview performance

Arrive early or on time Promptness shows interest in the position. If you must be late, call and explain why. Consider making a "trial run," before the interview date to determine travel time, parking facilities, and exact location of the interview.

Have a firm handshake Extend your hand as you approach the interviewer. A firm handshake is an accepted business greeting.

Establish and maintain eye contact with the interviewer Lack of eye contact with the interviewer gives the impression of a weak personality.

Consider your posture Create a positive image by sitting erect and facing the interviewer. Avoid crossing your arms or legs.

Avoid fiddling with objects Playing with objects—pens or pencils, for example—during the interview may communicate unusual nervousness and cause the interviewer to feel that you cannot perform well in stressful situations.

Don't criticize previous employers Criticizing past employers can give the impression that you are a complainer.

Don't evaluate previous jobs—simply describe them No matter how unimportant you may think your previous jobs have been, an interviewer will ask questions about them in order to evaluate such qualities as dependability, leadership skills, and initiative. Be prepared to respond.

Ask questions about the company Use the questions about the company you have prepared.

Express appreciation for the interview As the interview ends, thank the interviewer for discussing employment opportunities with you.

Interview follow-up

Within a few days after the interview, contact the interviewer. This may be done by letter, return visit, or a telephone call. This follow-up shows your interest in the job and could make all the difference in whether you get the job.

Glossary

accountability an individual's liability for performing assigned activities

advertising any nonpersonal form of paid message presented through the media by an identifiable sponsor

agency a relationship that exists when one party—the principal—authorizes another—the agent—to represent the principal in business transactions

agency shop a work place in which nonunion members may be hired, but they must pay the union an amount equal to dues paid by union members

analytic process the process of breaking down raw materials into their component parts

arbitration a process in which an impartial third party listens to the arguments of both labor and management and renders a final, binding decision

assets everything of value that a company owns

authority the right to act and make decisions in carrying out assignments

automated teller machine (ATM) a computer terminal that performs many banking transactions in place of human tellers

automation the use of machines to perform production processes without direct help from humans

baby boom a period of high birthrates, starting around 1946 and ending in the early 1960s

baby bust a period of low birthrates, beginning in the middle 1960s and continuing through the 1970s

balance of payments a measure of the flow of money into and out of a country

balance of trade the relationship between the value of a country's exports and the value of its imports

balance sheet a financial statement showing a company's financial condition on a particular date by reporting its assets, liabilities, and owners' equity

bankruptcy a legal process in which debtors who are unable to meet their financial obligations have their assets divided among their creditors

bargaining unit the specific group that the union will represent

BASIC (Beginners' all-purpose Symbolic Instruction Code) a computer language used extensively in instruction and with microcomputers

batch process the production of many identical products from a single machine set-up

bear market a market situation where investors are in a selling mood and overall stock prices are falling

beneficiary a person or institution named to receive the face amount of an insurance policy when the insured person dies

bid the price a buyer is willing to pay to buy a stock

binary number system a two-digit system (0 and 1) used to express numbers entered into the computer

board of directors a group of people, elected by the stockholders of a corporation, that develops broad company policy and goals and has overall legal responsibility for managing the corporation

bond a certificate of indebtedness that is sold to raise long-term funds for a corporation or a government agency

boycott an attempt to discourage people from buying goods or services from a particular firm

brand a name, symbol, design, or term used singly or in combination to identify the goods or services of a specific producer and to distinguish these products from those of competitors

brand recognition the consumer's awareness of a specific brand name

breakeven the point at which the number of units sold balances the amount of money invested in developing, manufacturing, and marketing a product

broker an individual who brings buyers and sellers together but does not actually take ownership of the goods; earns a commission for services

bull market a market situation where investors are in a buying mood and overall stock prices are rising

business an organization that attempts to earn a profit by providing goods and/or services society needs and wants

business unionism the belief that a union should concentrate on matters of direct interest to workers—wages, working conditions, and hours

buying cooperative a group of independent and competing firms that form a wholesaling company that serves as their exclusive supplier

buying on margin the practice of borrowing part of the purchase price of a stock from a stockholder

capital funding—usually money or credit—that enables a business to operate

capital goods buildings, equipment, machinery, and tools that are used to produce goods and services

capital-intensive economy an economy using production processes that rely on large amounts of capital equipment

capitalism an economic system based on the concept that society is best served by free competition among individual businesses (also called private enterprise system)

cash a form of money consisting of paper currency and coins

cash value the amount of money an insurance company will pay back if the policy is cancelled before the insured dies

casualty insurance a type of insurance protecting a business from damage or loss of property through fire, theft, and other unexpected circumstances

cathode ray tube (CRT) a computer output device similar in appearance to a television screen

centralized authority the retaining of most decision-making authority and responsibility at upper-management levels

central processing unit (CPU) the part of a computer where all arithmetic and logic functions are performed

channels of distribution the route or path goods and services follow from manufacturer to the final user

closed shop a work place in which every eligible worker must belong to the union, and in which the employer can hire only people who are already union members

COBOL (Common Business-Oriented Language) a specialized business data processing language

collateral anything of value a borrower may pledge to a lender to back a repayment of a loan

collective bargaining a process in which an employer and union representatives meet as equals to agree on the provisions of an employment contract

commercial bank a privately owned, profit-seeking company providing most of the checking accounts and business loans that create the money supply

commercial finance company a firm providing loans to businesses, taking tangible assets such as inventory, accounts receivable, or machinery as collateral

commercial paper a company's written promise to pay a specified sum of money

committee organization the organization structure composed of groups of individuals sharing authority and responsibility, usually for specific activities (also called project management, team management, and group management)

common carrier a company offering transportation services to the general public at stated rates based on item, distance, and weight

common law law based on custom and previous judicial decisions

common stock the most basic form of corporate ownership, including voting rights and dividends as declared by the board of directors, after other forms of debt and ownership have been paid (residual claim)

communication a process by which information and understanding are transmitted from a sender to a receiver

communism an economic system in which almost all the factors of production are owned by the government

computer a programmable machine that can store, retrieve, and process data with great speed and accuracy

computer-aided design (CAD) the process of designing, drafting, and analyzing with computer graphics displayed on a screen

computer-aided manufacturing (CAM) the use of computer-controlled machines in production processes

consumer goods products and services purchased by individual consumers for their own use

consumers individuals or businesses who buy goods and services

consumer services activities providing consumers with personal need satisfaction; includes industries such as restaurants, hotels, resorts, laundries, and dry-cleaning establishments

containerization a systems approach to distribution using standard container units to package freight to minimize handling and repackaging of goods

continuous process the production of large quantities over long periods of time without adjusting machines

contract an agreement between two or more parties regarding specific activities that a court will enforce

contract carrier a firm selling transportation services to individuals or firms on a per-job or time assignment

controlling the management function of measuring actual behavior or output against established goals and objectives

convenience goods relatively low-cost, widely available products that consumers purchase quickly and often

cooperative a group of persons who pool resources to carry out specific business activities and share in the profits

corporation a business form created by law in which a business's indemnity and liability are separate from those of its individual owners

craft union a union made up of workers from a single trade: plumbers, machinists, carpenters, etc.

credit union a financial institution that is usually sponsored by a labor union, employer, or other group for its members

critical path the sequence of operations in a PERT chart that takes the longest time to complete if no time is wasted

current assets cash, or anything that could be converted into cash within one year

Glossary

current liabilities debts that must be paid within one year

customer departmentalization the grouping of a firm's resources based on special groups of customers having unique requirements and characteristics

debt financing the raising of funds through borrowing

decentralized authority the delegation of substantial authority and responsibility to middle and supervisory managers

decision a choice made about what should or should not be done in a given situation

deed a written document representing ownership rights in real property

delegation the assigning of a portion of authority to a subordinate along with the accompanying responsibility for performing assigned tasks

demand a situation in which consumers have both the desire for a good or service and the ability to pay for it

demand deposits money held in checking accounts

departmentalization the grouping of job activities and functions into specific, related areas

directing the management function of coordinating, guiding, and motivating people in the tasks and responsibilities necessary for the production of goods and services

discount a reduction in the price of a product

discount bond a bond selling at a price below its face value

discount rate the Federal Reserve System's interest rate on loans to member banks

dispatching the production control function of sending instructions to every department stating when and how that department must perform its part of the production process

distributive services activities that bring needed services to consumers, including wholesale and retail trade, communications, transportation, and public utilities

dividends the portion of its earnings a company distributes to its stockholders

electronic funds transfer (EFT) a computer-based method of taking funds from one checking account and crediting it directly to another account without having to process a check

electronic media advertising sources (such as television and radio) sold by amount of time used

embargo a complete ban on the importation of certain products into a country

employer association a group of employers that join together to deal with labor unions

endorsement the signature of the person to be paid, usually written on the back of a negotiable instrument

entrepreneur someone who takes on the personal and financial risk of starting a business and keeping it going

equity financing the raising of long-term funds by selling stock or ownership shares in a corporation

esteem needs needs for respect from other people and respect for oneself

ethics a group of principles that define how individuals should and shouldn't behave

European Economic Community (EEC) a regional economic association that seeks to establish and maintain for the free movement of goods, capital, and raw materials among its member countries (also called the Common Market)

expenses the costs a business incurs in acquiring resources, producing goods and services, and marketing

exporting the selling of goods and services in other countries

external data facts obtained from sources outside the firm

extractive process a manufacturing process that withdraws or separates a substance from its natural form

fabricating process a manufacturing process that changes the shape or form of a material without changing its basic nature

face amount the amount of money an insurance company promises to pay if the insured person dies

Federal Reserve System the financial system regulating banking and the money supply in the United States; consists of 12 regional banks controlled by a board of governors

finance the business activity of obtaining and using money (capital funds) efficiently

financial-management process a process that attempts to assess the firm's financial needs, acquire needed funds, and oversee the use of funds

fixed assets items of value that are not likely to be converted to cash within a year; includes tangible goods such as building, machinery, and land

flextime a scheduling that gives employees some control over the hours they work

form utility utility created when a product is extracted, grown, or manufactured

FORTRAN (Formula Translating System) a programming language used primarily to express computer programs in arithmetic formulas

franchise operation a business arrangement in which a firm sells to others the exclusive rights governing the use of its idea and name under a licensing agreement

functional organization an organizational structure that gives authority to an individual or department based on a specific task or process

functional (process) departmentalization the grouping of people according to job functions

general partner a partner with unlimited responsibility for the firm's debts who actively participates in operating the business

genetic engineering the modification of microorganisms, such as bacteria, for a predetermined purpose

geographic departmentalization the grouping of a firm's resources and activities by location

goods tangible items that can be seen, touched, and/or held

grapevine an informal communication system that transmits both personal and business-related news and information

grievance an individual or union complaint that management has violated a provision of a union contract

grievance procedure a formal process set forth in a union contract that is used to settle disputes between union and management

hard copy a computer-produced document that is printed in ordinary language

hardware the physical components of a computer system

Hawthorne effect the positive influence a change in the work environment has on increasing employee output

human capital the skill and knowledge possessed by a population

importing the purchasing of goods and services from other countries

import quota represents a limit set on the quantity of a particular good that can be imported into a country

income statement a financial statement that summarizes a company's revenues and expenses over a specified period of time

indenture a legal contract in which the full terms of a bond issue are set forth

industrial goods products and services purchased by businesses for use in producing other goods and services

industrial union a labor union composed of groups of workers from the same industry, including skilled and unskilled workers

informal organization the network of interpersonal relationships that develop within the formal organization structure of a firm

injunction a court order prohibiting a certain activity from taking place

input devices computer components that feed instructions and data into the memory for processing by the central processing unit (CPU)

insurance a business arrangement in which an outside firm (usually an insurance company) agrees to compensate an individual or company for losses, in exchange for payment of premium fees

insured the person (or institution) covered by an insurance policy

intangible assets things of value that lack physical properties, including patents, brand names, copyrights, and trademarks

interest payment for the use of capital as a factor of production

internal data facts obtained directly from a firm's own records

international cartel a group of nations or producers who band together to control the price and flow of certain goods

inventory the supply of goods not yet used or sold

inventory control the balancing of the need to keep adequate supplies of raw materials with the cost of buying and storing raw materials

investment bank a financial institution that buys newly issued securities from its corporate clients and sells them to major purchasers of securities, such as mutual funds, foundations, pension funds, and private individual investors

job enrichment programs giving employees increased authority and responsibility for their work

job shop adjusting the production process to suit individual customer orders

key person insurance a life insurance policy in which a company is the beneficiary in the death or disability of a key employee

labor the physical and/or mental efforts that people contribute as a factor of production

labor-intensive economy an economy using production processes that rely on a labor force that is plentiful and relatively inexpensive

labor union a group of workers who have joined together to work toward common job-related goals such as improved wages, benefits, and working conditions

land a factor of production that includes all natural resources

Landrum-Griffin Act a federal law passed in 1959, amending the Taft-Hartley Act, requiring that union officials who handle funds be bonded and establishing federal penalties for embezzlement of union funds

law an enforceable set of rules governing the relationship of individuals and institutions to each other and to an organized society

law of large numbers a probability calculation predicting the statistical likelihood of the occurrence of any kind of peril when a large number of identical units are involved

leadership a manager's ability to stimulate people to perform well by creating an environment that inspires them to achieve

liabilities financial obligations or debts a firm has incurred in buying goods and services from others

liability insurance insurance protecting a firm from losses due to an individual's injury or death and damage to another's property

life insurance an insurance policy paying a stated cash amount to a beneficiary upon the death of the insured person

life insurance company a firm that sells insurance protection; invests much of its revenue in commercial real estate mortgages

limit order an order in which an investor sets a maximum buying price or a minimum selling price for a desired trade

limited liability legal liability that is limited to the amount of an owner's financial investment in a business (applies to corporation stockholders and limited partners)

limited partner a partner whose contribution and legal liability are limited; does not actively participate in the management of the firm

Glossary

line-and-staff organization the organization structure combining direct-line authority with staff departments providing advice, assistance, and support in specialized areas

line of credit an agreement between a company and a commercial bank that establishes the maximum amount of unsecured short-term credit the bank will make available to the company if the funds are available

line organization the organizational structure in which direct authority flows from upper management levels to lower management levels

liquidity the ease with which a company can convert its assets to cash

loan value the amount of money the insurance company will lend the insured, with the cash value used as security

lockout a management method of exerting pressure on workers, by closing down the company until the union agrees to management demands

long-term finance revenues and expenses that will extend more than one year into the future

long-term liabilities debts that will not be due for a year or more

loss when a firm's expenses are greater than its income

management a process through which people seek to meet goals and objectives by efficiently coordinating available resources

management by objectives (MBO) a process by which managers and subordinates work together to set employee goals and to evaluate performance

management information system (MIS) an organized method of providing past, present, and projected information about a business's internal operations and external environment

managerial skills the skills possessed by effective managers; includes technical, human, and conceptual skills

manufacturing the process of coordinating material, people, machines, and money to create finished goods (also called production)

market a group of potential buyers with the authority and ability to make purchases

market order an investor request to either buy or sell a security immediately at the best available market price

market segment a subgroup of individuals with distinct characteristics within a total market

market skimming the setting of high prices in order to attract only the most select customers

marketing a system of activities that businesses use to plan, price, promote, and distribute goods and services that consumers will want and need

marketing concept a total company-wide effort to find out what customers need or want and to develop products that will fill those desires

marketing mix the combination of product, price, promotion, and distribution strategies a company uses to reach a specific target market

marketing research the systematic gathering and analysis of information about marketing problems

marketplace where buyers and sellers come together to exchange goods and services, usually for money

markup the difference between the cost of producing a product and its selling price

mass production the process of manufacturing an item in large quantities, resulting in lower costs per unit than small-scale production

mean the arithmetic average of a group of numbers

mechanization the use of human-operated machines to do work that was previously performed by humans alone

median the middle number when data are ordered from highest to lowest

mediation a process in which an impartial third party attempts to assist labor and management by recommending possible areas of agreement to resolve a dispute

memory the part of a computer in which instructions and data are stored

middleman any person or firm that enters the distribution process between the manufacturer and the ultimate user

middle management the second management level, which includes individuals who develop plans and procedures for carrying out the decisions made by top management

mode the number that appears most often in a series of data

monetary exchange controls regulation of money exchanged in trade, either by a government agency or a specific central bank, in order to control the amount of foreign money flowing in and out of a country

money a medium of exchange, anything that is widely accepted as an appropriate payment for goods and services

money market fund a mutual fund that pools the investments of many investors and purchases U.S. Treasury notes, bank certificates of deposit, and other interest-bearing securities

money supply the total of all currency, coins, and checking-account balances

monopolistic competition an economic situation in which there are many sellers, whose products differ from those of their competitors

monopoly an economic situation in which there is only one seller

morale employee attitudes toward their employer and their jobs

motivation a response to a need that makes an individual work toward achieving a particular goal

multinational corporation a company with business investments, production operations, and management personnel in several countries

mutual savings bank a financial institution that lends money to purchasers of residential real estate; technically owned by its depositors

National Labor Relations Act legislation passed in 1935 that gave legal recognition to labor unions; has been called labor's Bill of Rights (also known as the Wagner Act)

Glossary

silent partner a partner who does not actively participate in a firm's operation, but whose name may be associated with the firm

slowdown a job action in which union members come to work but stall production

small business a business that is independently owned and operated, is not dominant in its field, and does not exceed specified standards of size

Small Business Administration (SBA) a federal agency that promotes small business development through providing financial assistance, management training, and consulting, and other services

socialism an economic system in which the government controls the major industries

social needs needs for friendship, belongingness, and love

social utility the level of importance that society attaches to a good or service

software the instructions or programs that make a computer work

sole proprietorship a business that is owned and operated by a single individual

span of control the optimal number of people a manager can effectively supervise

specialization the practice of producing and trading the products that one can supply most efficiently and cheaply

specialization of labor the breaking down of an assembly process into individual tasks, each of which is performed by a different worker

specialty goods products that consumers perceive as unique and will make a special effort to seek out

speculative risk a situation offering the possibility of a gain or a loss

speculator an investor who takes large risks in the hope of making a quick profit through relatively short-term ups and downs in the price of securities

standardization the use of uniform methods to produce uniform goods

statement of changes in financial position a financial statement explaining any changes in balance sheet items from one accounting period to another

statistic a fact expressed as a number

statistics a field of mathematics that deals with the collection, analysis, interpretation, and presentation of numerical information

statutory law written laws passed by local, state, or federal legislative bodies, including state and federal constitutions and treaties

stock exchange a formal organization whose members come together in a specific location to buy and sell securities for their customers

stockholders investors who become part-owners of a corporation by buying shares of its stock (also called shareholders)

strike the refusal to work, made by members of a bargaining unit, until a dispute is settled or an employment contract is signed

Subchapter S corporation a small corporation electing to be taxed as a partnership while keeping advantages of incorporation

supervisory management the lowest management level, which includes individuals directly responsible for accomplishing specific, narrowly defined tasks performed by nonmanagement employees

supply the amount of a good or service that is available in the marketplace

synthetic process the combining of two or more raw materials into a new and different finished product

Taft-Hartley Act a federal law passed in 1947 to maintain a balance in the collective bargaining process by prohibiting certain unfair union activities

target market the group of consumers at which a company aims its marketing efforts

tariff a tax on goods imported into a country

theory of comparative advantage a theory holding that each nation should specialize in producing those goods it can supply most easily and cheaply, and trade for those items other countries can produce most easily and cheaply

Theory X a managerial assumption that employees basically dislike work and must therefore be closely supervised and controlled

Theory Y a managerial assumption that employees are individuals who have ability and potential that should be encouraged in the work place

Third Wave a new era, described by futurist Alvin Toffler, in which the key to civilization will be diversity rather than the uniformity that accompanied the mass production of the industrial age

time utility utility created when a product is available when consumers want or need it

title legal ownership of property and the right to use the property

top management the highest level of management, including the president and other high-level executives, who spend the largest portion of their time on the planning function

tort an act that injures another person or another person's property

trademark a brand or any art or symbol associated with it that is legally registered with the federal government

underwriting the process used by a corporation to sell a new issue of stocks or bonds through an investment banking firm

union shop a work place in which the employer is free to hire anyone, but after a specified time period, new workers must join the union

unity of command a chain of management command in which each person has only one supervisor to whom he or she is accountable

unlimited liability legal responsibility for business debts, which can extend to a business owner's personal assets (applies to sole proprietors and general partners)

Glossary

unsecured loan a loan for which the borrower is not required to pledge any assets as collateral

utility the satisfaction consumers gain from having goods and services

venture capital money invested to form new businesses, products, and industries

venture capitalist an individual or business that seeks out promising new enterprises in which to invest

wages payment for the use of labor as a factor of production

wholesaler individuals or firms selling products to others for resale or for use in making other products; primarily located between producer and retailer

working capital the amount of money left when current liabilities are subtracted from current assets

yield the income from an investment, calculated by dividing annual dividends by the market price of a stock

Index

Accountability, 104
Accountants, 454
Accounting:
　fundamentals of, 408–415
　need for, 408
　See also Financial statements
Accounts receivable collection period, 420–423
Actuaries, 454
Advertisers, largest, 295–296
Advertising, 294–298
　budget and, 297
　life-styles and, 299
Advertising expenditures, 295, 297
Advertising media, 298–306
Advertising personalities, 290
AFL-CIO, 140
Agency, 53
Agency law, 53
Agency shop, 146
Airlines, 221, 329
All-Savers certificates of deposit, 353
Alyn, Scott, 2
American Airlines, 221
American Federation of Labor (AFL), 139–140
American Federation of State, County, and Municipal Employees (AFSCME), 152–153
American Stock Exchange (AMEX), 386
Analytic process, 214
Andean Common Market (ANCOM), 488
Anheuser-Busch Companies, 271
Appellate courts, 50
Arbitration, 151
Arel, Maurice, 96
Armstrong Rubber Company, 506
Artificial intelligence, 505
Artificial sweeteners, 65
Asher, Jerrold, 193
Asian industries, 480
Assets, 362, 411
Association of Southeast Asian Nations (ASEAN), 488
Attorney:
　power of, 53
　selection of, 51

Authority, 103
　centralized vs. decentralized, 104–105
　functional, 109
　line, 106
　line-and-staff, 107–108
Authority relationships, 105–109
Autocratic leaders, 82
Automated teller machine (ATM), 198
Automation, 177, 210–211
Automobile insurance, 441

Baby boom, 508
Baby bust, 509
Balance of payments, 484
Balance of trade, 484
Balance sheet, 411–413, 417, 427–428
Banking, 198, 247–248
Bankruptcy, 56
Bankruptcy law, 56–57, 371
Banks:
　commercial, 349, 354–355
　credit cards and, 355
　electronic funds transfer and, 354
　Federal Reserve System and, 345
　investment, 351
　money market funds vs., 353
　mutual savings, 350, 354–355
Bargaining unit, 144
Barges, 328
Bar graph, 196
Baseball, 379–380
BASIC, 176
Batch process, 179, 224
Bear market, 391
Bears, toy, 279
Beers, light, 271
Beneficiary, 443
Benefits managers, 160–161
Bic pens, 262
Bid, 401
Billboard advertising, 301
Binary, 169
Binary number system, 178
Biotechnology, 505–506
Birchfield, Chris, 464
Bishop Graphics Inc., 193
Bits, 178

Blacklists, 142
Blank endorsement, 55
Board of directors, 34
Bonding, 440
Bonding price quotations, 396–397
Bonds, 368, 375
　default on, 371
　kinds of, 369, 370, 397
　payoff of, 369–371
　ratings of, 371, 372
　values of, 371
　See also Securities
Bonus system, 116
Borrowing, cost of, 340
　See also Credit; Loans
Boycott, 149
Brand names, protection of, 276–277
Brand recognition, 292
Brands, 276–280
Breakeven, 282
Breakeven analysis, 282–283
Breslin, John A., 506
Broker, 318, 398–399
Brokerage firms, 399
Brown, Deaver, 458
Budweiser beer, 271
Builder's Exchange, 366
Building renovation, 366
Bull market, 391
Burghardt, Kurt, 186
Business, 5
　basic definitions in, 5
　careers in, 67–71
　choices in, 22
　federal regulation of, 60–62
　international, 487–493
　in U.S., 4
　See also Small business
Business ethics, 57–59
Business interruption insurance, 438
Business managers (amusement and recreation), 251
Business organizations:
　cooperatives, 39
　corporation, 33–39
　factors affecting choice of, 28
　franchises, 40
　management of, 42–43
　partnership, 31–33

　sole proprietorship, 29–31
Business unionism, 139
BusinessWeek, 193
Buying cooperative, 318
Buying on margin, 401
Bytes, 178

Cable advertising, 304
Call provisions, 370
Canvas bags, 464
Capital, 19
　venture, 384
　working, 413–414
Capital appreciation, 389
Capital goods, 19
Capital-intensive economy, 483
Capitalism, 13, 21
Careers:
　in accounting, 454
　in banking, 453–454
　in computers, 204–205
　in finance, 453–454
　in the future, 519–520
　in information systems management, 204–205
　in insurance, 454
　in international trade, 498
　in investments, 453–454
　in management, 160–163
　in manufacturing industries, 249–251
　obsolescent, 68
　in sales, 334–337
　in service industries, 249–251
　in small business, 497–498
　steps in choosing, 67–68
　women in, 69–71
Caribbean Common Market (CARICOM), 488
Car rental business, 74
Cartels, 487
Carter, Jimmy, 154–155
Cartier, pens, 262
Cash, 342
Cash discount, 286
Cash value, 443
Casualty insurance, 438
Catalogs, 301
Catalog shopping, 184–185
Cathode ray tube (CRT), 173
Celler-Kefauver Antimerger Act, 60

Index

Cenowa, Ronald A., 198
Central American Common Market, (CACM), 488
Centralized authority, 105
Central processing unit (CPU), 169
Certificates of deposit (CDs), 364
Chandler, James, 96
Channels of distribution. *See* Distribution channels
Chapter XI, 371
Charts, 196–197
Child Protection Act, 61
Chinese imports, 496
Chrysler Corporation, 149, 225
Clark, Grieg, 122
Clayton, Bob, 366
Clayton Act (1914), 60, 283
Closed shop, 145–146
Clothing business, 95
Clough, Charles, 96
COBOL, 176
Collateral, 365
Collateral trust bonds, 369, 370
Collective bargaining, 147–150
College Pro Painters Ltd., 122
Command, unity of, 106
Commercial banks, 349, 354–355, 365–367
Commercial finance companies, 351
Commercial paper, 55, 364
Committee organization, 109
Common carriers, 325
Common law, 48
Common Market, 487
Common stock, 372–374, 375
Communication, 129
  development of listening skills, 132
  "noise" and, 305–306
  process of, 129–130
Communications, 181–182
Communism, 22
Company image, 284
Comparative advantage, theory of, 483
Competition, 14
  foreign, 507–508
  forms of, 15–16
  government regulation of, 16
  nonprice, 286
Competitors, as sources of information, 193
Compiler, 175
Comprehensive insurance, 438
Comp-U-Card of America, 314
Computer-aided design (CAD), 198–199
Computer-aided manufacturing (CAM), 199
Computer applications, 197–198
Computer programmer, 182, 204
Computers, 168–182
  components of, 169–174
  costs of, 179
  in the future, 179–182
  information and, 505
  jobs and, 166, 177
  limitations of, 176
  programming and software for, 175–176
  retailers and, 324

workings of, 176, 178
Computer service technician, 205
Conceptual skills, 91–92
Congress of Industrial Organizations (CIO), 140
Considine, Richard, 8–9
Consumer Credit Protection Act, 61
Consumer goods, 259–260
Consumerism, 258
Consumer Product Safety Act, 61
Consumer protection statutes, 61–62
Consumers, 5
  income and, 7
  price and quality and, 7
  role of, 6
  satisfaction and, 7
Consumer services, 234
Containerization, 329–330
Continuous process, 224
Contract, 50
  breach of, 52
  elements of, 51–52
Contract carrier, 326
Control, span of, 104
Controllers, 406
Controlling, 77, 83
Convenience goods, 260
Conversion rights, 371
Convertible preferred stock, 375
Cooperatives, 39, 318
Corporate controllers, 406
Corporations, 33
  advantages of, 34–36, 38
  board of directors of, 34
  delegation of authority in, 38
  disadvantages of, 36–37, 38
  formation of, 33–34
  future of, 511–512
  largest in U.S., 35
  multinational, 489–490
  Subchapter S, 37
Cost of goods sold, 410
Council for Mutual Economic Assistance (CMEA), 488
Court system, 49–50
Craft union, 139
Credit:
  from commercial banks, 365–367
  from investors, 367
  line of, 367
  from resource suppliers, 365
  revolving, 367
  secured, 56, 367
  unsecured, 56, 365–366
Credit analysts, 453
Credit cards, 355
Credit insurance, 441
Credit sales, 324
Credit unions, 350–351
Critical path, 218–219
Cross River Products, 458
Cumulative preferred stock, 375
Current assets, 411
Current liabilities, 412
Current operations, 414
Current ratios, 420
Customer departmentalization, 102
Cyclamates, 65
Cynthia Creations, 478

Data:
  external, 192–193
  internal, 191–192
  presentation of, 196–197
  primary, 194
  secondary, 194
Data analysis, 267
Data base manager, 205
Data collection, 267
Datsuns, 485
Debenture bonds, 369, 370
Debt financing, 367
Decentralized authority, 105
Decision, 87
Decision making, 87, 89–90
Deed, 54
Deferral, 414
Delaney Amendment, 65
Delegation, 104
Demand, 5, 7
Demand deposits, 343
Democratic leaders, 82
Departmentalization, 102
Diapers, disposable, 254
Diet franchises, 30
Digital Equipment Corp., 177
Direct broadcast satellite (DBS), 304
Direct exporting, 490
Directing, 77, 82
Direct mail advertising, 300
Directories, 301
Discount bond, 397
Discounters, 323–324
Discount rate, 346–347
Discounts, 285–286
Discs, computer, 171–172
Disintermediation, 353
Disney World, 232
Dispatching, 217
Distributed processing, 180
Distribution:
  jobs in, 520
  transportation and, 325–330
Distribution channels, 316
  participants in, 316–318
  retailers, 317, 322–324
  wholesalers, 318–321
Distributive services, 234
Dividends, 374
Dow-Jones Industrial Average, 392, 393–394
Dun and Bradstreet, 193

Earnings per share, 419
Eaton-Swain Associates, 101
Economic associations, 487, 488
Economic systems, 20, 21–22
Economy:
  government involvement in, 12–13
  workings of, 13–14
Eisenhardt, Roy, 379
Electronic funds transfer (EFT), 354
Electronic mail (EM), 510–511
Electronic media, 298, 300–301, 303, 304
Embargo, 486
Emens, Kenneth, 186
Employees:
  communication with, 129–132
  flextime and, 127–128

job enrichment and, 128–129
management by objectives and, 127
managers and, 119
morale of, 126
of small businesses, 464–465
  See also Labor; Workers
Employer association, 150
Encyclopedias, 333
Endorsements, 55–56
Endowment life insurance, 444–445
Energy technology, 504–505
Entrepreneurs, 19, 460, 470
  moonlighting, 26
  as producers, 11
  qualities of, 10–11, 469
Entrepreneurship:
  hidden costs of, 463
  pros and cons of, 465–466
  workings of, 18
Equal Credit Opportunity Act, 61
Equipment trust bonds, 369, 370
Equity financing, 372
Esteem needs, 124
Ethics, 57
  See also Business ethics
E.T. The Extra-Terrestrial, 244
European Economic Community (EEC), 487, 488
Executives, 84–85, 101
Expenses, 362, 409
Exporting, 483, 484, 490
  See also Trade
Export managers, 498
External data, 192–193
Extractive process, 214

Fabricating process, 215
Face amount, 443
Fair Credit Reporting Act, 61
Fair Debt Collection Practices Act, 61
Fair Packaging and Labeling Act, 61
Fast-food businesses, 237, 426–428, 474, 514
Federal Communications Commission (FCC), 244
Federal Mediation and Conciliation Service, 151–152
Federal Power Commission, 244
Federal Reserve System, 340, 343
  bank withdrawals from, 345
  check clearance and, 347–348
  discount rate of, 346–347
  open-market operations of, 344
  reserve requirements of, 344–346
Federal Trade Commission, 46, 60, 62
Federal Trade Commission Act, 60, 62
Federated Department Stores, 314
Finance, 362
Finance companies, 351
Financial institutions:
  commercial banks, 349, 354–355
  commercial finance companies, 351

Index

credit unions, 350–351
investment banks, 351
life insurance companies, 349, 350
money market funds, 351–353
mutual savings banks, 350, 354–355
recent developments affecting, 354–355
savings and loan associations, 349–350, 354
Financial-management process, 362–363
Financial news, understanding of, 392–397
Financial position, statement of changes in, 413–415
Financial statements:
balance sheet, 411–413, 417, 427–428
income statement, 409–411, 416, 428
interpretation of, 415–424
statement of changes in financial position, 413–415
Financing:
long-term, 367–376
short-term, 363–367
of small businesses, 462–463, 472–473
Fire insurance, 438
Fixed assets, 411
Flammable Fabrics Act, 61
Flextime, 127–128
Food and Drug Administration (FDA), 65
Food, Drug and Cosmetic Act, 61, 65
Forbes, 193
Foreign competition, 507–508
Foreign exchange, 492
Foreign licensing, 491
Foreign manufacturing, 491
Foreign trade. *See* Trade
Form utility, 258
FORTRAN, 176
Fortune, 193
Franchise operation, 40, 473–475
Franklin Mint Corporation, 186
Freight transportation, 327–329
Freihofer, Wayne, 211
Freihofer Baking Company, 211
Fringe benefits, 117
Functional departmentalization, 102
Functional organization, 109
Fur Products Labeling Act, 61
Fusion, energy from, 505
FYI, 382

Gallagher, James J., 101
Gallagher Associates, 101
Gallen, Hugh, 96
Gantt chart, 217
Gasket manufacturing, 202–203
General Cinema Corporation, 244
General Foods, 264
General partner, 31
Genetic engineering, 505
Geographic departmentalization, 102
Georgia-Pacific Corporation, 62
Gerrity, Tom, 131
Glossary, 525–533

Goals, 98, 120
Gompers, Samuel, 139–140, 154
Goodman, Barry, 30
Goods, 5
consumer, 259–260
industrial, 260–261
services and, 236, 237–238
Goodwin, Alexandre, 458
Government(s), 12–13
competition and, 16
foreign trade and, 485–487
as source of information, 192
trends in, 509–511
Government affairs specialists, 520
Government regulation, 60–62, 486
Grapevine, 112
Graphs, 196–197
Great Northwestern Greeting Seed Co., 2
Green, George, 186
Greeting card business, 2, 478
Gregg, Hugh, 96
Grievance, 150
Grievance procedure, 150–151
Gross profit, 410
Guilderson, Paul, 96

Hard copy, 172
Hardware, 168
Hawthorne effect, 123
Hawthorne studies, 121, 123
Health insurance, 441–442
Hierarchy of needs, 123–124
Home appliance manufacturing, 230–231
Hotel managers, 251
Housing, sale of, 8–9
Human capital, 241
Human resources, 118–132
communication and, 129–132
management and, 119
motivation and, 119–129
Human resources specialist, 520
Human skills, 91

Ice resurfacers, 20
Image, 284
Importers, 498
Importing, 483, 484, 496
Import quota, 486
Income, consumer, 7
Income statement, 409–411, 416, 428
Indenture, 368–369
Index Systems, Inc., 131, 132
Individual Retirement Account (IRA), 358–359
Industrial goods, 260–261
Industrial unions, 139, 140
Informal organization, 111–112
Information, 190–194
Information technology, 505, 518, 520
Injunction, 52, 149–150
Input devices, 169–174
Insurance, 433
automobile, 441
bonding, 440
casualty, 438
credit, 441
health, 441–442

key person, 440
law of large numbers and, 434–436
liability, 439–440
life, 442–447
marine, 440
surety bond, 440
title, 440
Insurance companies, 349, 350, 447–448
Insured, 443
Intangible assets, 411
Interest, 19
Internal data, 191–192
International Brotherhood of Teamsters, 140, 154–155
International cartel, 487
International managers, 498
International trade. *See* Trade
Interstate Commerce Act, 60
Interstate Commerce Commission (ICC), 60, 244
Inventory, 219
Inventory control, 219
Inventory turnover, 422, 423
Investment, 384, 389–390
See also Securities
Investment banks, 351
Investment Company Act, 388
Investors, as producers, 9
Isenberg, Barbara, 279
Ishihara, Takashi, 485

Jacob, Jerry R., 221
Jeep safety, 46
Job enrichment, 128
Job hunting, 520–523
Job interviews, 522–523
Jobs:
in the future, 519–520
in international trade, 498
Job shop, 224
Johns-Manville Corporation, 62
Joint venture, 491–492
Jones & Laughlin Company, 208
Juvenile equipment, 458

Katz, Harold, 30
Keyboards, 172
Key person insurance, 440
Knights of Labor, 139
Kone, Jim, 40
Kooker, Jack, 496

Labor, 17
specialization of, 212–214
Labor-intensive economy, 483
Labor legislation, 142–143
Labor-Management Relations Act, 143
Labor unions, 138
collective bargaining by, 147–150
contract of, 146–147
history of, 139–142
issues facing, 152–155
membership in, 153
organizing of, 144–146
political power of, 154
security of, 145–146
settlement of conflicts with management, 150–152
Ladd, Dwight, 96

Laissez-faire leaders, 83
Land, 17
Landrum-Griffin Act, 143
Latin American Integration Association (LAIA), 488
Law, 48
agency, 53
bankruptcy, 56–57
consumer protection, 61–62
property, 54–56
sources of, 48–49
of tort, 54
Law firm, selection of, 51
Law of large numbers, 434–436
Leadership, 82
Leadership styles, 82–83
Lecture fees, 235
Legal system, 49–50
Levine, H. Eugene, 240
Levy, Paul, 279
Lewis, John L., 140
Liability, 362, 412
current, 412
limited, 34
long-term, 412
unlimited, 31
Liability insurance, 439–440
Life insurance, 442
comparison of types of, 445–446
endowment, 444–445
term, 443, 445, 446
terminology of, 443
universal, 444
whole, 444, 445, 446–447
Life insurance companies, 349, 350
Limited liability, 34
Limited partner, 32
Limited pay whole life insurance, 444
Limit order, 401
Lincoln Electric Company, 116
Lincoln Logs, Ltd., 8–9
Line-and-staff organization, 107–108
Line chart, 196
Line of credit, 367
Line organization, 106
Line printers, 172–173
Liquidation proceeding, 57
Liquidity, 419–420
Listening skills, 132
Loans, 360, 365–366, 367
Loan value, 443
Lockout, 149
Long-term financing, 367
bonds, 368–372
sources of, 368
stocks, 372–376
Long-term liabilities, 412
Loss, 5

McDonald's, 237
McGregor, Douglas, 124
Machine language, 175
MacNeil, Manford R., 136
Magazine advertising, 300
Magnetic tape, 171
Magnuson-Moss Warranty Act, 61
Mail, electronic, 510
Mailgrams, 382

Index

Maloney Act, 388
Management, 76
  careers in, 160–163
  levels of, 85–87
  personal traits needed in, 92
Management by objectives (MBO), 127
Management functions, 77
  controlling, 77, 83
  directing, 77, 82
  organizing, 77, 79, 82
  planning, 77, 78–81
Management information systems (MIS), 188
  computers and, 197–199
  need for, 189–190
  sources of information in, 191–194
  statistics in, 194–196
Management trainees, 160
Managerial skills, 91–92
Managers:
  benefits, 160–161
  business, 251
  complaints about information processes by, 190
  employees and, 119
  export, 498
  hotel and motel, 251
  international, 498
  as problem solvers and decision makers, 87–90
  as producers, 9
  questions asked by, 191
Manross, D. Neal, 116
Manufacturer's representatives, 249
Manufacturing, 210
  characteristics of, 210–214
  coordination of operations in, 217–219
  inventory and, 219
  management of, 215–217
  materials purchasing in, 224–226
  processes in, 214–215
  quality control in, 220, 221
  trends in, 226–227
Manufacturing plants, 220–224, 471
Margin, buying on, 401
Margin calls, 401
Marine insurance, 440
Market, 259
  products and, 259–261
  target, 261–262
Marketing, 256
  packaging and, 280
  pricing and, 280–286
  product and, 274–280
  utility and, 257–259
Marketing concept, 256–257
Marketing manager, 335
Marketing mix, 262
Marketing objectives, 280–281
Marketing research, 263–268
Marketing researcher, 336–337
Marketing strategy, 275, 277
Market order, 400–401
Marketplace, 13
Market segment, 261
Market skimming, 280–281
Markup, 281–282

Mars Company, 298
Marshall, John, 33
Maslow, Abraham H., 123
Mass production, 211–212, 214
Materials purchasing, 224–226
Mathewson, Barbara, 366
Mayo, Elton, 121, 123
Mean, 194–195, 196
Meany, George, 140
Mechanization, 210
Media, advertising, 298–306
Median, 195–196
Mediation, 151–152
Memory, 169
Men's clothing business, 95
Meyer, Ira, 237
Meyer, Stuart L., 26
Meywes, Henry, 116
Microprocessors, 181
Middleman, 316
Middle management, 86, 162–163
Midwest Stock Exchange, 386
Miller Brewer Company, 271
Minicomputers, 180
Minority Enterprise Small Business Investment Corporations (MESBICs), 472–473
Mixon, Jack, 96
Mode, 196
Modified capitalism, 21, 22
Monetary exchange controls, 486
Money, 342–343
Money market funds, 351–353
Money supply, 343
Monopolistic competition, 15, 16
Monopoly, 16
Moody's Investors Service Inc., 371, 372
Moody's Reports, 193
Moonlighting entrepreneurs, 26
Morale, 126
Mortality tables, 434–435
Mortgage bonds, 369, 370
Motel managers, 251
Motivation, 119–120, 127–128
Motivation theory:
  classical, 121
  Hawthorne studies, 121, 123
  Maslow's hierarchy of needs, 123–124
  Theory X and Theory Y, 124–125
  Theory Z, 126
Movie industry, 244
Multinational corporations (MNCs), 489–490
Multilateral trade agreements, 487
Mutual insurance companies, 447
Mutual savings banks, 350, 354–355

National Academy of Sciences–National Research Council (NAS–NRC), 65
National Association of Manufacturers (NAM), 193
National Association of Securities Dealers (NASD), 387
National Association of Securities Dealers Automated Quotations (NASDAQ) index, 394

National Labor Relations Act, 142–143
National Labor Relations Board, 142, 144
National Traffic and Motor Vehicle Safety Act, 61
Natural resources, 17
Needs, 119
  hierarchy of, 123–124
Negotiable order of withdrawal (NOW) accounts, 354–355
Neodata Services, 186
Net income, 409, 410–411, 417–419
New Hampshire, business in, 96
Newspaper advertising, 300
Newspapers, 518
New Yorker, The, 186
New York Stock Exchange (NYSE), 385, 386, 400
Nigro, Charles, 496
Nissan Motor Co., Ltd., 485
Nonprice competition, 286
Nonprofit and government services, 234
Norris-LaGuardia Act, 150
North American Bear Company, Inc., 279
North Central Tire Company, 289
NOW accounts, 354–355
Nuclear fusion, 505
NutriSystem, 30

Oakland A's baseball team, 379–380
Occupational Safety and Health Administration (OSHA), 463
Odd lot, 395
Offer, 401
Office electronics, 88
Oil consumption, 488
Oligopolistic competition, 16
Open shop, 146
Optical character reader (OCR), 170–171
Organization, 98
  committee, 109
  functional, 109
  informal, 111–112
  line, 106
  line-and-staff, 107–108
Organizational elements, 99–100
Organizational strategy, 110–111
Organization chart, 100–101
Organization of Petroleum Exporting Countries (OPEC), 487
Organizing, 77, 79, 82
  nature of, 98
  union, 144
Ouichi, William, 126
Output devices, 170–174
Over-the-counter (OTC) market, 386–387, 396
Owners' equity, 412

Pacific Coast Stock Exchange, 386
Packaging, 280
Paid-up policy, 443
Participating preferred stock, 376
Partnership, 31–33, 38
Par value, 372
PASCAL, 176

Penetration pricing, 280
Pens, 262
Personal property, 54
Personal selling, 306–309
Personnel managers, 161
PERT, 217–219
Philadelphia-Baltimore-Washington Stock Exchange, 386
Physiological needs, 123
Picket, 148
Pie chart, 25, 196
Pipelines, 328
Place utility, 258
Planning, 77, 78–81
Plants. See Manufacturing plants
Point-of-sale (POS) computer terminals, 197
Population characteristics, 508–509
Porreco, Lou, 485
Portfolio, 389
Possession utility, 258
Power, 103
Power of attorney, 53
Preemptive rights, 374
Preferred stock, 375–376
Premium, 443
Premium bond, 397
Price-earnings (P-E) ratio, 395
Price lining, 284
Prices, 7, 13
Pricing, 280–286
  breakeven analysis and, 282–283
  company image and, 284
  discounts in, 285–286
  flexible, 285
  with the market, 281
  markup and, 281–282
  policies on, 284
  psychological, 284–285
  restrictions on, 283–284
Primary data, 194
Prime interest rate, 366
Printers, 172–173
Pirnt media, 298, 300, 301, 302
Private brands, 278–280
Private carrier, 326
Problem, 87
Problem definition, 265
Problem solving, 87, 89–90
Process departmentalization, 102
Proctor & Gamble, 254
Producers, 7–9, 11
Producer services, 234
Product, 274–280
Product departmentalization, 102
Production, factors of, 17–19
  See also Manufacturing
Production automation, 197
Production planning, 215
Product liability, 54, 430
Product life cycle, 274–276, 281
Product mix, 274
Product proliferation, 272
Professional Air Traffic Controllers Union (PATCO), 142
Profit, 5, 19
Profitability, measures of, 415–416
Program, 175
Programming languages, 175–176
Project Evaluation and Review Technique (PERT), 217–219

Index

Promissory note, 366
Promotion, 292–294
  See also Advertising; Selling
Promotional discount, 286
Promotional mix, 292
Property, 54
Property law, 54–56
Prospectus, 387
Protective tariff, 486
Psychological pricing, 284–285
Public Health Cigarette Smoking Act, 61
Publicity, 306
Publishing, 333, 518
Pudding Pops, 264
Punched cards, 170
Punched paper tape, 170
Purchasing, 224–226
Pure competition, 15, 16
Pure risk, 432

Qualified endorsement, 56
Quality, 7
Quality circles, 110
Quality control, 220, 221, 243, 520
Quantity discount, 286
Quick ratio, 420

Radio advertising, 301
Radio Shack, 181
Railroads, 327–328
Ratio analysis, 415–424
Real Estate Settlement Procedures Act, 61
Real property, 54
Recission, 52
Records, computerized, 197
Refunding, 371
Registers, 169
Rent, 17
Rent-A-Mom, 40
Rent-A-Wreck, 74
Research design, 265–266
Reserve requirements, 344–346
Responsibility, 103
Restrictive endorsement, 55
Resumes, 521–522
Retailers, 317, 322–324, 471
Retailing, computers in, 197
Retail store managers, 161
Revenues, 362, 409, 410
Revenue tariff, 486
Revolving credit agreement, 367
Richey, Ed, 30
Risk, 432–436, 438–442
Risk management, 432–433, 437
Roach, John, 181
Robinson-Patman Act, 60, 283, 285
Robot technology, 216, 502
Romac Industries, Inc., 136
Ross, Percy, 470
Round lot, 395
Routing, 215

Safety needs, 123
Sales & Marketing Management, 193
Sales careers, 334–337
Sales promotion, 309
Satisfaction, consumer, 7
Savings and loan associations, 349–350, 354
Savings banks, 349–350, 354–355

Scheduling, 216–217
Schwartz, David, 74
Scientific Machines Corporation (SCM), 240
Secondary data, 194
Secret partner, 32
Secured loan, 367
Securities:
  investment in, 388–390
  orders for, 398–402
  price quotations on, 392–397
  prices of, 391
  speculation in, 391
  underwriting of, 391, 392
Securities Act, 387
Securities and Exchange Commission (SEC), 193, 244–245, 387–388
Securities Exchange Act, 387–388
Securities exchanges, 384–388
Securities market, 384
Seed company, 312
Self-actualization needs, 124
Self-service retailers, 324
Selling, personal, 306–309
Selling short, 402
Service Employees Union, 154
Service industries, 233–245
  development of, 239–243
  improvements of, 243
  regulation of, 244–245
Service jobs, 250
Services, 5, 234
  characteristics of, 235–237
  export of, 242–243
  goods and, 236, 237–238
  rising price of, 241
Sherman Antitrust Act, 60, 283
Ships, 328
Shop-at-home service, 314
Shopping goods, 260
Shopping malls, 324
Short-term finance, 363–367
Silent partner, 32
Sinking fund, 370
Skinner, Wickham, 69
Slowdown, 148
Small business, 460
  careers in, 497–498
  financing of, 462–463, 472–473
  franchising of, 473–475
  location of, 471–472
  nature of, 460–462
  personnel in, 464–465
  roles of, 461–462
  special problems of, 462–465
  startup of, 469–471
Small Business Administration (SBA), 473
Small Business Investment Corporations (SBICs), 472
Small claims court, 53
Smith, Richard A., 244
Socialism, 21, 22
Social needs, 123
Social utility, 258–259
Software, 168, 175
Solar power, 504
Sole proprietorship, 29, 31, 38
Sources and uses of funds statement, 413–415
Soviet Union, standard of living in, 24–25

Span of control, 104
Special endorsement, 56
Specialization, 483
Specialization of labor, 212–214
Specialty goods, 260
Speculative risk, 432
Speculators, 391
Sporting-goods store, 99–100
Staff departments, 107–108
Standard & Poor's, 371, 372
Standard & Poor's Index of 500 Stocks, 392, 394
Standardization, 212, 235
Standards of living, 24–25
Star Market, 277
Statement of changes in financial position, 413–415
Statistic, 194
Statistics, 194–196
Statutory law, 48–49
Steinmetz, Cynthia, 478
Stockbrokers, 398–399, 453
Stock dividends, 374
Stock exchanges, 384
  American, 386
  characteristics of, 385
  New York, 385
  over-the-counter market, 386–387
Stockholders, 33
Stock quotations, 392–396
Stocks, 372
  common, 372–374
  preferred, 375–376
  prices of, 391
  See also Securities
Stock ticker tape, 397–398, 399
Strike, 147–148
Strikebreakers, 142
Strollers, 458
Student labor, 122
Subchapter S corporations, 37
Sullair Corporation, 116
Supermarkets, 197, 277
Supervisory management, 86–87
Supply, 13
Surety bond, 440
Surveys, 265–266
Swain, Robert, 101
Swanson, David, 116
Synthetic process, 215
Systems analyst, 204

Tables, 196–197
Taft-Hartley Act, 143
Tamposi, Sam, 96
Tandy, Charles, 181
Tandy Corporation, 181
Target market, 261–262
Tariffs, 486
Taylor, Frederick W., 121
Teamsters, 140, 154–155
Technical skills, 91
Technological developments, 504–507
Teletype printers, 173
Television advertising, 290, 300–301, 303
Telex system, 382
Term life insurance, 443, 445, 446
Theory of comparative advantage, 483

Theory X, 125
Theory Y, 125
Theory Z, 126
Third-party liability insurance, 439
Third Wave, 514–515
Thomas, R. David, 474
Thompson, Debbie, 237
Ticker tape, 397–398, 399
Time sharing, 179–180
Time utility, 258
Tires, automobile, 289, 506
Title, 54
Title insurance, 440
Toffler, Alvin, 514
Tokyo Stock Exchange, 386
Top management, 85
Tort, 54
Trade, international:
  balance of payments and, 484
  balance of trade and, 484
  careers in, 498
  foreign exchange and, 492
  government and, 485–487
  importance of, 482–483
  other forms of, 490–492
  trends in, 487–490
Trade credit, 365
Trade discount, 285
Trademark, 277
Transponders, 382
Transportation, and distribution, 325–330
Transportation companies, largest, 326
Treasury bills, 363–364
Treasury notes, 344
Trial courts, 50
Trial purchase, 292–293
Trucks, 328
Trust Indenture Act, 369, 388
Truth in Lending Laws, 61

Umbroller, 458
Undercapitalization, 462–463
Underwriting, 391, 392
Uniform Commercial Code (UCC), 49, 55, 62
Uniform Consumer Credit Code, 62
Unions. *See* Labor unions
Union shop, 146
United Auto Workers (UAW), 149, 159
United States:
  business in, 4
  largest industrial corporations in, 35
  robot technology in, 216
  standard of living in, 24–25
Unity of command, 106
Universal life insurance, 444
Universal Product Code (UPC), 171, 197
Unlimited liability, 31
Unsecured loan, 365–366
U.S. News & World Report, 193
U.S. Supreme Court, 50
U.S. Treasury bills, 363–364
U.S. Treasury notes, 344
Utility, 257–259

Vanstone, Steven, 122
Venture capital, 384

Venture capitalist, 472
Vertical analysis, 415–416
Vesce, Thomas, 8
Video discs, 304
Video display terminal (VDT), 173
Videotex advertising, 304
Voice recognition, 173–174

Wages, 17
Wagner Act, 142–143
Wall Street Journal, 193, 392
Walsh, James, 506

Wang, An, 88
Wang Laboratories, 88
Warner-Lambert Company, 79–81
Watson, Dr. Jay Ray, 519
Wendy's, 474
Western Union, 382
Wheeler-Lea Act, 60
Whiston, William, 26
Whole life insurance, 444, 445, 446–447
Wholesalers, 318–321, 471
Wholesome Meat Act, 62

Wholesome Poultry Products Act, 62
Willis, George E., 116
Women:
 business careers of, 69–71
 in service industries, 242
 unionization of, 154
Wool Products Labeling Act, 62
Word processors, 180
Workers:
 future role of, 512–513
 as producers, 7, 9

See also Employees; Labor
Workers' compensation, 439
Working capital, 413–414
Working Women, 154

Yellow-dog contracts, 142
Yellow Pages, 301
Yield, 389

Zamboni, Frank, 20
Zamboni Ice Resurfacing Machine, 20